MW00604694

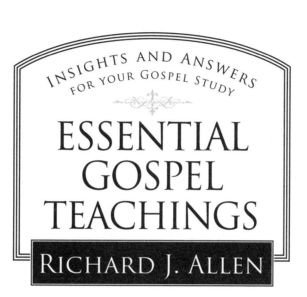

INSIGHTS AND ANSWERS
FOR YOUR GOSPEL STUDY

ESSENTIAL
GOSPEL
TEACHINGS

RICHARD J. ALLEN

To Bob & Daryl

We send best wishes to you
during this, your birthday season
of the year. We think of you
often and have you and your
family in our prayers. May the
Lord bless you always.

Love,

Richard & Carol Lynn
and Nathan

INSIGHTS AND ANSWERS
FOR YOUR GOSPEL STUDY

ESSENTIAL GOSPEL TEACHINGS

RICHARD J. ALLEN

Covenant Communications, Inc.

Cover image *These Twelve Jesus Sent Forth* © Walter Rane. For more information on art prints by Walter Rane, go to www.walterrane.com.

Cover and book design © 2009 by Covenant Communications, Inc.

Published by Covenant Communications, Inc.
American Fork, Utah

Copyright © 2009 by Richard J. Allen

All rights reserved. No part of this work may be reproduced by any means without the express written permission of Covenant Communications, Inc., P.O. Box 416, American Fork, UT 84003. This work is not an official publication of The Church of Jesus Christ of Latter-day Saints. The views expressed within this work are the sole responsibility of the author and do not necessarily reflect the position of The Church of Jesus Christ of Latter-day Saints, Covenant Communications, Inc., or any other entity.

Printed in United States of America
First Printing: November 2009

16 15 14 13 12 11 10 09   10 9 8 7 6 5 4 3 2 1

ISBN 978-1-59811-941-1

TABLE OF CONTENTS

PREFACE

And may God enable us to perform our vows and covenants with each other, in all fidelity and righteousness before Him, that our influence may be felt among the nations of the earth, in mighty power, even to . . . spread the light and truth of the everlasting Gospel from the rivers to the ends of the earth. —Joseph Smith (*HC* 2:375)

It is the love of our Father in Heaven that makes it possible for His children, sanctified through faith and obedience and ennobled as "joint-heirs with Christ" (Rom. 8:17), to come home again. It is through the "merits, and mercy, and grace of the Holy Messiah, who layeth down his life according to the flesh, and taketh it again by the power of the Spirit," that the sons and daughters of God have the hope and assurance of completing the mortal journey with valor and proving themselves worthy to inherit eternal life—"which gift is the greatest of all the gifts of God" (D&C 14:7). The roadmap for the journey is the fulness of the gospel of Jesus Christ, comprising the saving principles of truth preserved in the scriptures and spoken by the living prophets. The Liahona for the journey is the guidance of the Holy Spirit. Nephi expressed timeless wisdom when he counseled, concerning both the word and the Spirit: "feast upon the words of Christ; for behold, the words of Christ will tell you

all things what ye should do. . . . For behold, again I say unto you that if ye will enter in by the way, and receive the Holy Ghost, it will show unto you all things what ye should do" (2 Ne. 32:3, 5).

This book provides commentaries and insights on the fundamental principles of the gospel. It is designed as an aid in the study of the gospel—for the individual, for the family, in group discussions, and for talks and presentations. Each chapter focuses on one of the key themes of gospel living, with a series of sections presenting fundamental truths associated with the theme in such a way as to promote thought and encourage action.

Each chapter includes the following sections:

- "Opening the Window of Wisdom," outlining the doctrines and principles involved.
- "Inspired by Latter-Day Prophets," presenting a variety of statements by prophets of the Restoration, together with follow-up thoughts, interpretations, and suggested questions for discussion.
- "Truths to Liken," providing a number of scriptural passages relating to the theme. The scriptures are presented in the SOUL mode of instruction and enlightenment. SOUL is an acronym for Speaker (the person who is expressing the words in the scripture), Occasion

(the event or circumstance in which the words are spoken), Underlying doctrine (the principles being taught), and Likening (how the scripture can be applied in one's life). It is hoped that this method will help bring the scriptures to life and encourage productive pondering and discussion.

- "Rejoicing and Reasoning Together," asking a series of questions relating to the theme, with suggested answers and further ideas for discussion and action.
- "Real-life Stories for Heart and Mind," presenting several illustrations of an inspiring nature to encourage further discussion and action.
- "Pondering Prayerfully," listing additional scriptures to consider and suggested hymns that might be helpful in contributing to a spirit of understanding and gratitude about the theme being considered.
- "Remember and Be Sure," providing some concluding thoughts on the theme.

The material in this volume comes from a lifetime of prayerful thought and study on the basic principles of the gospel. Much of the material is original to this book; some of it has been adapted from books the author has written with coauthor Ed J. Pinegar over the past decade. These books, all published by Covenant Communications, include *Latter-Day Commentary on the Old Testament* (2001), *Teachings and Commentaries on the Book of Mormon* (2003), *Teachings and Commentaries on the Doctrine & Covenants* (2004, with Karl Ricks Anderson), *Teachings and Commentaries on the Old Testament* (2005), *Your Patriarchal Blessing* (2005), *Living by the Word: Becoming Disciples of Christ* (2005), *Teachings and Commentaries on the New Testament* (2006), *Look to the Temple: Finding Joy in Your Temple Worship* (2007), *Book of Mormon Who's Who* (2007), *Commentaries and Insights on the Book of Mormon*, Vol. 1 (2007), *Commentaries and Insights on the Book of Mormon*, Vol. 2 (2008), *Doctrine and Covenants Who's Who* (2008), and *Old Testament Who's Who* (2009). In addition, *You, Your Family, and the Scriptures* by Ed J. Pinegar (Salt Lake City: Deseret Book Company, 1975) provided much inspiration. The order of the material presented in this book was inspired by the classic manual *Gospel Principles* published by The Church of Jesus Christ of Latter-day Saints in successive editions (1978ff), including the most recent revised edition (2009).

Thanks to Covenant Communications for the commission to write this book, and especially to Barry Evans and Kathryn Jenkins for their guidance and encouragement. I wish also to express much thanks to my loving and lovely wife, Carol Lynn, for her support and inspiration over the years, and especially over the summer of 2009, which was dedicated completely to the accomplishment of this commission. It is hoped that the material provided in *Gospel Essentials* will be useful in promoting faith, strengthening testimonies, and encouraging "a godly walk and conversation" (D&C 20:69)—that way of life the Lord has asked us all to cultivate and practice as we strive to complete our mortal journey with honor and look forward in faith to returning home again.

Richard J. Allen

It is one thing to see the kingdom of God, and another thing to enter into it. We must have a change of heart to see the kingdom of God, and subscribe the articles of adoption to enter therein. —Joseph Smith (*HC* 6:58)

CHAPTER 1
Our Father in Heaven

I am inclined to acknowledge the hand of God in all things. If I see a man inspired with intelligence, with extraordinary ability and wisdom, I say to myself he is indebted to God for that wisdom and ability; and that, without the providence or interposition of the Almighty, he would not have been what he is. He is indebted to the Lord Almighty for his intelligence, and for all that he has; for the earth is the Lord's and the fulness thereof. God originated and designed all things, and all are his children. We are born into the world as his offspring; endowed with the same attributes. The children of men have sprung from the Almighty, whether the world is willing to acknowledge it or not. He is the Father of our spirits. He is the originator of our earthly tabernacles. We live and move and have our being in God our Heavenly Father. And having sprung from him with our talents, our ability, our wisdom, we should at least be willing to acknowledge his hand in all the prosperity that may attend us in life, and give to him the honor and glory of all we accomplish in the flesh. —Joseph F. Smith (*Gospel Doctrine: Selections from the Sermons and Writings of Joseph F. Smith,* 62)

Opening the Window of Wisdom

Our Heavenly Father loves us. We are His children. He is all-powerful (*omnipotent*—see Ether 3:4). He is all-knowing (*omniscient*—see 2 Ne. 9:20). He is in and through all things (*omnipresent*—see D&C 88:41). The Doctrine and Covenants teaches us: "By these things we know that there is a God in heaven, who is infinite and eternal, from everlasting to everlasting the same unchangeable God, the framer of heaven and earth, and all things which are in them" (D&C 20:17). Heavenly Father is not only unchangeable in His role and dealings with His children, He loves all alike, for He is no respecter of persons (see Moro. 8:18; D&C 38:16). His work and His glory consist of bringing to pass the immortality and eternal life of all of His children (see Moses 1:39). All of us can ask Heavenly Father for blessings and He will give according to our needs and faith, for He seeks to help us return to His presence.

Having a relationship with God is what life is all about. "And this is life eternal, that they might know thee the only true God, and Jesus Christ, whom thou hast sent" (John 17:3). When we know our Heavenly Father and our Savior, we will be humble because we will realize that we are the children of God and that we are totally dependent on Him for all things. Because we love our Heavenly Father, we will seek His will and will be forever grateful for all things.

The love of the Father is evident: "For God so loved the world, that he gave his only begotten Son, that whosoever believeth in him should not perish, but have everlasting life" (John 3:16). Our hearts should overflow with love for Him in return, something we demonstrate by keeping the commandments (see John 14:15), by doing good unto others (see Matt. 25:40), and through reverently worshipping Heavenly Father in the name of His Beloved Son, Jesus Christ. Our Heavenly Father and His Son have great joy over the soul who repents (see D&C 18:13). There is likewise great joy among our earthly fathers when we are obedient and committed to living the gospel: "I have no greater joy than to hear that my children walk in truth" (3 John 1:4).

Love is the motive of every righteous act. The commandment is clear: "A new commandment I give unto you, That ye love one another; as I have loved you, that ye also love one another. By this shall all men know that ye are my disciples, if ye have love one to another" (John 13:34–35). As we contemplate all the commandments and the counsel of the prophets concerning our Father in Heaven, we see that these words are encapsulated in the two great commandments: "Master, which is the great commandment in the law? Jesus said unto him, Thou shalt love the Lord thy God with all thy heart, and with all thy soul, and with all thy mind. This is the first and great commandment. And the second is like unto it, Thou shalt love thy neighbour as thyself. On these two commandments hang all the law and the prophets" (Matt. 22:36–40).

Inspired by Latter-Day Prophets

Brigham Young: He is our Heavenly Father; He is also our God and the Maker and upholder of all things in heaven and on earth. He sends forth His counsels and extends His providences to all living. He is the Supreme Controller of the universe (*Journal of Discourses* 11:41).

How do these words of a prophet dispel isolation and give you the assurance that you are not alone, but in the hands and heart of a Heavenly Father, who cares for you with infinite concern?

Wilford Woodruff: We know that we are created in the image of God, both male and female; and whoever goes back into the presence of God our Eternal Father will find that He is a noble man, a noble God, tabernacled in a form similar to ours, for we are created after His own image (*JD* 18:33).

Our Heavenly Father is a glorified individual Being—not an abstract essence, not a universal idea, not a disembodied concept. Your destiny is to return to Him someday to confirm what you already know in your heart: that He is your very Father in Heaven. How does this objective give you courage and hope for the future?

Lorenzo Snow: There is something grand in the consideration of the fact that the Lord loves us with a most ardent love. The love that a woman exercises toward her offspring cannot equal the love that God exercises toward us. He never leaves us. He is always before us, and upon our right hand and our left hand. Continually He watches over us (*CR*, October 1898, 2).

A mother's love for her child is magnificent. How does it make you feel to know that your Father in Heaven loves you individually with an even greater love than this? How does this knowledge increase your motivation to improve your life?

Ezra Taft Benson: God loves us. He is watching us. He wants us to succeed. We will know someday that He has not left one thing undone for the eternal welfare of each of us. If we only knew it, heavenly hosts are pulling for us—friends in heaven that we cannot now remember who yearn for our victory (*Ezra Taft Benson Remembers the Joy of Christmas*, 12).

Our Heavenly Father is at the forefront of a vast heavenly team committed to your success in every way. Knowing this, how do your plans for today—this very hour—receive added strength and confidence?

Truths to Liken

John 3:16—"For God so loved the world, that he gave his only begotten Son, that whosoever believeth in him should not perish, but have everlasting life."

- The Pharisee Nicodemus was secretly visiting the Savior at night. During these visits, the Savior taught Nicodemus plain and simple truths about the gospel of Atonement: Our Heavenly Father loves us so much that He was willing to sacrifice His Son for our eternal welfare.

- How does this help you discover a feeling of gratitude that reinforces your love for Heavenly Father (see Matt. 22:36–40) and enhances your overwhelming desire to keep His commandments (see John14:15)?

John 15:26–27—"But when the Comforter is come, whom I will send unto you from the Father, even the Spirit of truth, which proceedeth from the Father, he shall testify of me: And ye also shall bear witness, because ye have been with me from the beginning."

- On the eve of His Crucifixion, Jesus taught His disciples about a grand gift they would soon receive from the Father.
- The Holy Ghost proceeds from the Father through the agency of the Son. How does the Holy Ghost bless your own life as a witness of the reality of the Father and the Son?

1 Ne. 11:25—"And it came to pass that I beheld that the rod of iron, which my father had seen, was the word of God, which led to the fountain of living waters, or to the tree of life; which waters are a representation of the love of God; and I also beheld that the tree of life was a representation of the love of God."

- Nephi was shown in vision what his father Lehi had beheld concerning the iron rod and the tree of life.
- Heavenly Father loves us and seeks only that we might come and partake of that love as we hold to the iron rod, the word of God. That love is expressed through His grace and mercy in giving His Only Begotten Son for our eternal salvation (see John 3:16). The love of God is therefore an active element of our existence. Can you share some experiences in your own life where you have tasted of the living waters and have

partaken of the fruit of the tree of life?

Alma 26:35—"Now have we not reason to rejoice? Yea, I say unto you, there never were men that had so great reason to rejoice as we, since the world began; yea, and my joy is carried away, even unto boasting in my God; for he has all power, all wisdom, and all understanding; he comprehendeth all things, and he is a merciful Being, even unto salvation, to those who will repent and believe on his name."

- Ammon was rejoicing with his brethren following their successful fourteen-year mission among the Lamanites.
- Following the example of Ammon, should we not also rejoice in our Heavenly Father? When we have these feelings of gratitude and rejoicing, our life will be different. We will recognize and remember the goodness of God in all things—and that feeling will move us to such thanksgiving that we will want to be good and do good. Our lives will be centered in the gospel of Jesus Christ and the magnificent plan of happiness. Try reading Alma 26:35 once again, this time aloud, inserting your entire being into the words as if you were the one rejoicing. You might also want to read the verse to a loved one in this way as a personal witness of your joy in knowing of God's love and mercy.

3 Ne. 11:35–38—"Verily, verily, I say unto you, that this is my doctrine, and I bear record of it from the Father; and whoso believeth in me believeth in the Father also; and unto him will the Father bear record of me, for he will visit him with fire and with the Holy Ghost. And thus will the Father bear record of me, and the Holy Ghost will bear record unto him of the Father and me; for the Father, and I, and the Holy Ghost are one. And again I say unto you, ye must repent, and become as a little child, and be baptized in my name, or ye can in nowise receive these things. And again I say unto you, ye must repent, and be baptized in my name, and become as a little child, or ye can in nowise inherit the kingdom of God."

- These words were used by the resurrected Lord to teach His disciples in the New World the principles of His doctrine.

- Just as a little child knows his or her father, even so should we come to know our Father in Heaven through the witness of the Holy Ghost. The members of the Godhead witness of Themselves because They are one in purpose and cause. How has the witness of the reality of the Godhead come into your own life? How have you been able to testify to others of the reality of the Father, Son, and Holy Ghost?

Rejoicing and Reasoning Together

How Do the Scriptures Confirm the Individuality of the Father and the Son?

On several occasions in recorded history, the Father made His presence known—usually as a confirming witness to the mission of the Savior. At the baptism of the Savior, the Holy Ghost was manifest in the form of a dove, and the Father's voice was heard from heaven, saying, "This is my beloved Son, in whom I am well pleased" (Matt. 3:17; compare D&C 93:15–16). On the Mount of Transfiguration, where Elias and Moses appeared to Peter, James, and John in the presence of the Savior, the same voice reverberated over the scene: "behold, a bright cloud overshadowed them: and behold a voice out of the cloud, which said, This is my beloved Son, in whom I am well pleased; hear ye him" (Matt. 17:5; compare Mark 9:7; Luke 9:35; 2 Pet. 1:17). At the martyrdom of Stephen, we learn: "But he, being full of the Holy Ghost, looked up stedfastly into heaven, and saw the glory of God, and Jesus standing on the right hand of God, And said, Behold, I see the heavens opened, and the Son of man standing on the right hand of God" (Acts 7:55–56). As the risen Lord was about to appear before the assembled faithful at Bountiful in ancient America, the voice of the Father proclaimed the words of introduction: "Behold my Beloved Son, in whom I am well pleased, in whom I have glorified my name—hear ye him" (3 Ne. 11:7; see also 2 Ne. 31:11, 14–15, where the voice of both the Father and the Son were recorded and witnessed by Nephi).

In our day, the boy Joseph Smith learned first-hand the individuality of the Father and the Son, as revealed in the First Vision: "When the light rested upon me I saw two Personages, whose brightness and glory defy all description, standing above me in the air. One of them spake unto me, calling me by name and said, pointing to the other—*This is My Beloved Son. Hear Him!*" (JS–History 1:17). Later, during the vision of the degrees of glory given at Hiram, Ohio, on February 16, 1832, Joseph Smith and Sydney Rigdon were privileged to behold both the Father and the Son:

> And now, after the many testimonies which have been given of him, this is the testimony, last of all [meaning *most recently*], which we give of him: That he lives!
>
> For we saw him, even on the right hand of God; and we heard the voice bearing record that he is the Only Begotten of the Father—
>
> That by him, and through him, and of him, the worlds are and were created, and the inhabitants thereof are begotten sons and daughters unto God. (D&C 76:22–24)

In all of these instances, the Father is presented for what He is: an individual Being of infinite glory who is the supreme God for us all. In all of these instances, as well, the divine commission of the Son is authenticated and validated. We pray to and worship the Father, always in the name of the Son.

We each need to remember with gratitude the testimony of the Father about the Son and, in turn, testify of the goodness of God and the truth of the gospel "at all times, and in all things, and in all places" (Mosiah 18:9). What opportunities do you have to spread joy and inspiration to your loved ones and friends?

How Can We Come to Know God, Our Heavenly Father?

Our Father in Heaven—as presented in holy writ and confirmed to the devout and faithful through the Holy Ghost—is the Supreme Lord and God of all Creation, the Eternal Source of light and truth, the benevolent and ever-loving Father of our spirits (see Heb. 12:9; 1 Jn. 4:7–8), the Author of the glorious gospel plan of happiness (see Abr. 3:23–27), the Exemplar of the pattern for all holiness and perfection, the merciful Grantor of agency unto His children, and the Benefactor of all mankind through the gift of His Only Begotten Son, whose atoning sacrifice empowers the process for achieving immortality and exaltation. It is to our Father in Heaven that we pray, as directed by Jesus Christ Himself (see Matt. 6:9).

Our Father in Heaven has given Jesus Christ the sacred commission to be His Agent in governing and directing the unfolding of the divine gospel plan for the benefit of all humankind. It is through the Son that we come to know the Father, as confirmed by the witness of the Holy Spirit. The Savior declared during His intercessory prayer: "And this is life eternal, that they might know thee the only true God, and Jesus Christ, whom thou hast sent" (John 17:3). Later, the resurrected Savior admonished the Saints in ancient America: "Therefore I would that ye should be perfect even as I, or your Father who is in heaven is perfect" (3 Ne. 12:48; compare Matt. 5:48). In the latter days He has assured the Saints concerning the harmony and oneness of the Godhead: "Which Father, Son, and Holy Ghost are one God, infinite and eternal, without end. Amen" (D&C 20:28).

We pray to the Father in the name of the Son, just as the Son continually prayed to the Father for guidance and counsel. Through the Son we come to know the Father, for the two are alike in all respects. There is a cycle of fatherly knowledge in our mortal experience. You come to know your own mortal father and admire certain good qualities exhibited in his life. Though he is not perfect, he nevertheless reflects the ongoing process of being "perfected in him [Jesus Christ]" (Moro. 10:32). Similarly, you come to admire your "fathers"—your progenitors over time who exemplified courage and devotion to the cause of righteousness. In all of this, you become better trained to see in Jesus Christ the elements of fatherhood in the transcendent meaning of the word. It is ordained of the Father that we come to know Him through His Son. How does this process of seeing through the "lens of fatherhood" work in your own life?

How Are We to Understand the Word *God* or *Lord* as Used in the Scriptures?

The sacred unity of purpose reflected among the three members of the Godhead makes the terms *God* and *Lord* often interchangeable in the scriptures in regard to the Father and the Son. But there are distinctions among the individual Beings of the Godhead. Through the Prophet Joseph Smith

was revealed this truth: "The Father has a body of flesh and bones as tangible as man's; the Son also; but the Holy Ghost has not a body of flesh and bones, but is a personage of Spirit. Were it not so, the Holy Ghost could not dwell in us" (D&C 130:22). Moreover, as Joseph Smith also confirmed, the Father has preeminence: "Everlasting covenant was made between three personages before the organization of this earth, and relates to their dispensation of things to men on the earth; these personages, according to Abraham's record, are called God the first, the Creator; God the second, the Redeemer; and God the third, the witness or Testator" (*Teachings of the Prophet Joseph Smith*, 190). Paul declared: "But to us there is but one God, the Father, of whom *are* all things, and we in him; and one Lord Jesus Christ, by whom are all things, and we by him" (1 Cor. 8:6).

Because Jesus Christ is the divine Agent within the expanse of the Father's eternal dominion and infinite design, it is for the most part Jesus Christ who is the One revealed in the scriptures. Thus Jehovah (Jesus Christ) is the Word presented as God in the Old Testament. When the Decalogue was revealed from Sinai, the voice was that of Jehovah, the Mediator of the Father:

AND God spake all these words, saying,
I am the LORD thy God, which have brought thee out of the land of Egypt, out of the house of bondage.
Thou shalt have no other gods before me.
Thou shalt not make unto thee any graven image, or any likeness of any thing that is in heaven above, or that is in the earth beneath, or that *is* in the water under the earth. (Ex. 20:1–4)

By the process of what is called *divine investiture*, Jehovah speaks for the Father and as the Father. To Moses, Jehovah declared (as if officiating in the office of the Father): "I am the Beginning and the End, the Almighty God; by mine Only Begotten I created these things; yea, in the beginning I created the heaven, and the earth upon which thou standest" (Moses 2:1). He expressed the heavenly mission as follows: "For behold, this is my work and my glory—to bring to pass the immortality and eternal life of man" (Moses 1:39). Within this context, Jehovah (Jesus Christ) is indeed the Father of the faithful in the sense that they are adopted into His fold and become His seed through obedience to the gospel plan: "Though he were a Son, yet learned he obedience by the things which he suffered; And being made perfect, he became the author of eternal salvation unto all them that obey him" (Heb. 5:8–9; compare the words of Abinadi concerning the "seed" of the Lord as expounded by Isaiah in Mosiah 15:1–5, 10–11).

Modern revelation sheds further light on the stature and supremacy of our Father in Heaven and His role in establishing Jesus as His Mediator. *Father,* referring to Heavenly Father, occurs frequently in the text of the Doctrine and Covenants, including four occurrences of the term *God the Father* (D&C 21:1; 88:19; 107:19; 138:14). The word *God* itself (which can have reference to the Father or the Son or both, depending on the usage) occurs more than five hundred times. Among the most memorable references to our Father in Heaven in the Doctrine and Covenants are these: "For ye know that there is no unrighteousness in them [the revelations], and that which is righteous cometh down from above, from the Father of lights" (D&C 67:9). Additionally, concerning the oath and covenant of the priesthood, there is this well-known passage:

> And also all they who receive this priesthood receive me, saith the Lord;
>
> For he that receiveth my servants receiveth me;
>
> And he that receiveth me receiveth my Father;
>
> And he that receiveth my Father receiveth my Father's kingdom; therefore all that my Father hath shall be given unto him.
>
> And this is according to the oath and covenant which belongeth to the priesthood.
>
> Therefore, all those who receive the priesthood, receive this oath and covenant of my Father, which he cannot break, neither can it be moved. (D&C 84:35–40)

Furthermore, the following passage illustrates with clarity the inseparable relationship between the Father and the Son:

> VERILY, thus saith the Lord: It shall come to pass that every soul who forsaketh his sins and cometh unto me, and calleth on my name, and obeyeth my voice, and keepeth my commandments, shall see my face and know that I am;
>
> And that I am the true light that lighteth every man that cometh into the world;
>
> And that I am in the Father, and the Father in me, and the Father and I are one—
>
> The Father because he gave me of his fulness, and the Son because I was in the world and made flesh my tabernacle, and dwelt among the sons of men.
>
> I was in the world and received of my Father, and the works of him were plainly manifest. (D&C 93:1–5; compare John 17:22; 1 Jn. 5:7; Mosiah 15:4; 3 Ne. 11:27, 36; 20:35; 28:10; Morm. 7:7)

Heavenly Father is the one to whom we pray in the name of the Son (see D&C 20:77, 79, which provides the example of the sacramental prayers). He is the benevolent and ever-loving Father of our spirits. He is the source of truth and light, the pattern for all holiness and perfection.

> *As you read and ponder the scriptures, you can envision the Father, Son, and Holy Ghost as inseparably unified in the cause of bringing to pass the immortality and eternal life of man (see Moses 1:39). You can see Jesus as the Agent of the Father in teaching universal principles of truth and righteousness. You can see the Father as the Giver of all light and wisdom, the Grand Creator through the actions of the Son. You can see yourself as a child of God, with potential to become perfected through Christ according to the grace of heaven and your own devotion and valor.*

In What Ways Can We Show Our Gratitude to Heavenly Father for His Love and Kindness?

The Savior taught: "Man shall not live by bread alone, but by every word that proceedeth out of the mouth of God" (Matt. 4:4; compare Luke 4:4; Deut. 8:3; D&C 84:44). From the scriptures we can learn more about those aspects of Deity that should call forth our gratitude, praise, and rejoicing. Among the most frequently cited qualities of Heavenly Father declared in the scriptures are His mercy, mighty works, goodness, just judgments, righteousness, glory, greatness, creative majesty, answers to prayers, sense of eternal joy, power, holiness, lovingkindness, and grace. Thinking deeply about these and similar qualities can enlighten our minds and remind us of ways to exhibit our own love for Heavenly Father. Here are just three of the ways we can respond with devotion and valor:

- **Mercy**: How do I feel about the mercy of God toward me as an individual and toward the members of my family? Why is His mercy so indispensable for our happiness? Among mortals, no one but the Savior exhibited perfect compliance with the law; hence none of us is justified before God on the basis of our actions as imperfect beings (see 2 Ne. 2:5). It is only through the mercy of God and the redeeming mission of His Only Begotten Son that we have hope of transcending our imperfections through the plan of redemption based on faith, repentance, baptism, and the gift of the Holy Ghost. *How grateful we should be for the mercy of God that allows us to follow the strait and narrow pathway leading back into His presence.*

- **Mighty works**: We justly celebrate the epic deeds of God in rejuvenating life on earth through Noah and the ark, in liberating the Israelites from Egyptian bondage through the leadership of Moses, in transporting chosen families thousands of miles across the world to safety in ancient America, and in bringing about the Restoration of the gospel through the Prophet Joseph Smith. But do we also remember the mighty works of God in our own lives and family circles—the touch of God on our marriages and family relationships to guide and direct, bless and magnify, preserve and edify? *Take time to detect and discern the mark of the divine in what happens in your own family, for there are deeds rendered there by God every bit as miraculous as the work He did with Noah, Moses, Lehi, or Joseph Smith. God's work is to bring about your immortality and eternal life and that of all your family members. Such is the miracle of His blessing on you.*

- **Goodness**: Jesus said to the wealthy inquirer, "Why callest thou me good? there is none good but one, that is, God" (Mark 10:18; compare Matt. 19:17; Luke 18:19). In our Heavenly Father we have the perfection of goodness. Our certainty of His supreme goodness is the source of our faith in Him. We should speak with authentic thanksgiving concerning the goodness of God in our expressions of gratitude and praise, in our prayers, and in our lessons for our family—for that goodness is the model for our quest to attain perfection through the example and pattern set by the Savior. *As you thank the Father and the Son for Their goodness, you can strive with all your heart, might, mind, and strength to live worthy of Their matchless blessings.*

What Is Our Work in the Father's Grand Design for Eternal Life and Exaltation?

God's entire mission is centered on our well-being and on the well-being of all His children; knowing this should fill us all with gratitude and love for Him. Each of us has an important role to play in the grand plan of heaven. Each one of us can help God complete His work in bringing to pass the immortality and eternal life of His sons and daughters. That is our task and mission in life. What God said to Moses—"And I have a work for thee" (Moses 1:6)—He says to each one of us. He loves us. He wants us to return home to His presence to live forever.

We, like Moses, have a work to do. To Hyrum Smith the Lord declared: "Behold, this is your work, to keep my commandments, yea, with all your might, mind and strength" (D&C 11:20). This applies to us as well, for we are to be righteous disciples of Jesus Christ. We stand as witnesses. We are here to build up the kingdom of God. Our work is our Heavenly Father's work: the immortality and eternal life of our brothers and sisters. Why? Because we, like Heavenly Father, love our brothers and sisters. Love truly is the motive of the plan of happiness, which through the Atonement makes possible our eternal life if we repent and keep the commandments.

We can choose to follow the Lord's plan as outlined in the scriptures. All the prophets have written the word of the Lord as it has been given to them, and in our day the Prophet Joseph received additional scriptures—including the Book of Mormon—that restored again the written word of the gospel of Jesus Christ in its fulness. Without the written word we would wander off in strange paths and have no Liahona to guide our lives (see Alma 37:38–47). But by committing to daily scripture study and aligning our walk with the principles of truth, we can, like Moses, find on our "mount" of transcendence the faith, strength, and courage to participate with Heavenly Father and His Son in the quest to save and exalt the faithful and true. How can you improve your patterns of scripture study and application? How can you complete your life duties with valor and joy?

How Can We Relate in Our "Nothingness" to the Infinite Majesty of Our Father in Heaven?

When we pray to God, we are addressing a Being of infinite perfection and glory. How are we to feel in those circumstances? King Benjamin reminded the Saints of his day of their continual indebtedness to God, that in their "nothingness" (Mosiah 4:5) they needed to strive penitently for a mighty change of heart to become more like Him (see Mosiah 4:11; 5:2). Nephi also taught the key for gaining confidence before the majesty of our Heavenly Father: "For we labor diligently to write, to persuade our children, and also our brethren, to believe in Christ, and to be reconciled to God; for we know that it is by grace that we are saved, after all we can do" (2 Ne. 25:23). Lehi taught his sons an unforgettable lesson, that "by the law no flesh is justified" (2 Ne. 2:5)—meaning that no one, on his or her own, can measure up in perfect obedience to the laws of God. It takes something more—it takes "the merits, and mercy, and grace of the Holy Messiah" (2 Ne. 2:8). It takes the grace of God to make up the difference on behalf of those who humble themselves and achieve, through faith and repentance, the mighty change of heart that will bring them under the canopy of grace (see Alma 5:13).

To Moroni, rendered meek because of the monumental task given him, the Lord declared: "I give unto men weakness that they may be humble; and my grace is sufficient for all men that humble themselves before me; for if they humble themselves before me, and have faith in me, then will I make weak things become strong unto them" (Ether 12:27).

The grace of God is manifested by His great love, mercy, and kindness to His children. From the Creation to the Atonement, Resurrection, and on to eternal life, His grace is evident. It is the grace of God that makes up for all our weaknesses and fulfills the law of justice and mercy—and this "after all we can do" (2 Ne. 25:23). We become justified and sanctified through His grace (see D&C 20:30–32). Thus we become indebted to our Heavenly Father and our Savior for all things. Their grace is sufficient for all those who love Them and keep Their commandments.

What does the phrase "after all we can do" (2 Ne. 25:23) mean to you? Jot down a few thoughts on this matter, and then consider the following words of counsel from President Ezra Taft Benson:

> What is meant by "after all we can do"? "After all we can do" includes extending our best effort. "After all we can do" includes living His commandments. "After all we can do" includes loving our fellowmen and praying for those who regard us as their adversary. "After all we can do" means clothing the naked, feeding the hungry, visiting the sick and giving "succor [to] those who stand in need of [our] succor" (Mosiah 4:15)—remembering that what we do unto one of the least of God's children, we do unto Him (see Matt. 25:34–40; D&C 42:38). "After all we can do" means leading chaste, clean, pure lives, being scrupulously honest in all our dealings and treating others the way we would want to be treated. —Ezra Taft Benson (*The Teachings of Ezra Taft Benson,* 354)

Real-life Stories for Heart and Mind

"**W**ho Are You?" A young man excitedly shared with his father the news that a very special person had moved into their ward, someone with a very famous father. "Who are *you?*" asked the father in a kindly way. "Well, I'm your son." Then in response to the father's smiling silence, the young man said, "Oh, yes. I'm Heavenly Father's son!"

How can you help your children and other loved ones feel the satisfaction of being a son or daughter of God?

Royalty in Disguise. The family was not wealthy by worldly standards; they lived in a small home and wore modest clothing. But in the temple, they looked resplendent clothed in white and bearing a heavenly countenance. Such a family is royalty in disguise. In the house of the Lord they set aside the homely and simple everyday clothing of their poverty for the robes of spiritual abundance. They appeared as what they were all along—sons and daughters of God endowed with the capacity to be royal servants of the Almighty. Truly humility is the heavenly virtue.

Do you know anyone like the family described above? In what ways are you like that yourself, knowing that all of us are "poor" in the presence of God? Despite that, you enjoy the grand potential to become more like the Father and the Son through obedience and righteous living.

A Father's Blessing. On the eve of his temple marriage, a young man approached his father and asked for a father's blessing. Gladly responding, the father first prepared himself through fasting and prayer and then pronounced an inspiring blessing upon the head of his son. Included were the words: "And now my beloved son, as you journey forth into the uncertain world, reach up your hands to the lap of God. And if you will do this, He will lead you, He will guide you, save and exalt you in the eternal worlds."

What do you think it might have meant to the son when he heard the words "reach up your hands to the lap of God"? What blessings were attached in this case to the action of being humble and showing reverence to Heavenly Father? How can you teach your own children, guardians, and/or loved ones to "reach up your hands to the lap of God"?

"I've a Mother There." There is a memorable passage included in the inspiring hymn, "O My Father," written by Eliza R. Snow: "In the heav'ns are parents single? / No, the thought makes reason stare! Truth is reason; truth eternal / Tells me I've a mother there" (*Hymns*, 292). Joseph Fielding Smith stated: "If we had a Father, which we did, for all of these records speak of him, then does not good common sense tell us that we must have had a mother there also?" (*Answers to Gospel Questions*, 3:142).

We can be grateful for the reasonable conclusion that we have a Mother in Heaven in addition to a Father in Heaven. How would it be to think forward to the time when you will return to the presence of your Heavenly Father and be introduced also to your Heavenly Mother? Knowing what we do of mortal motherhood, imagine the glory of an eternal Mother in Heaven and the love She must radiate.

Pondering Prayerfully

Additional scriptures to consider and ponder:
- Eph. 2:8–10
- 2 Ne. 9:20
- 2 Ne. 10:24
- D&C 20:30–34
- D&C 88:41

In addition to "O My Father" (*Hymns*, 292) and "While of These Emblems We Partake" (*Hymns*, 174), the following hymns might help contribute to a spirit of worshipful reverence for our Father in Heaven:
- "God Loved Us, So He Sent His Son" (*Hymns*, 187)
- "How Gentle God's Commands" (*Hymns*, 125)
- "I Am a Child of God" (*Hymns*, 301)
- "O God, the Eternal Father" (*Hymns*, 175)

Remember and Be Sure

The enduring principle to remember is that Heavenly Father loved the world so much "that he gave his only begotten Son, that whosoever believeth in him should not perish, but have everlasting life" (John 3:16). Every time we sing the song "While of These Emblems We Partake" (*Hymns*, 174) and renew our covenants through the sacrament, we are reminded of the infinite love of our Father in Heaven and His Son, Jesus Christ. How the Father must have suffered over the agony of His Only Begotten in Gethsemane and at Golgotha. Every parent or guardian of youth understands the pain and anguish that accompanies the suffering of a child. And yet, that heavenly pain of the atoning sacrifice was transformed into eternal joy for a Father and a Son whose only purpose is to bring about the immortality of all mankind and the eternal life of all the faithful and pure.

We cannot say enough about the greatness and goodness of our Heavenly Father. His work, through the Son, is to help us return to His presence and enjoy a state of never-ending happiness. As we seek to know and love Him more fully, we will find a joy in life that is truly consuming. Life will take a different course as we realize with greater understanding why we came to earth and what Heavenly Father has in store for His faithful children: to give them all that He has, including eternal lives: "This is eternal lives—to know the only wise and true God, and Jesus Christ, whom he hath sent" (D&C 132:24).

To realize that we carry within us the genuine potential to become like our Father in Heaven is enough for us—with His divine blessing and grace—to begin the journey upward and out of the weaknesses and constraints of our mortal existence. It is enough to move us toward a higher state of being where we are worthy to return again to our heavenly home. God loves us. He knows all things. He acts for our eternal happiness. It is our choice to embrace the truths of the gospel as we rise valiant and obedient to achieve our potential of spiritual liberty according to the grand plan of heaven.

CHAPTER 2
Our Nature as Spirit Children in the Family of God

We believe that we are the offspring of our Father in Heaven, and that we possess in our spiritual organizations the same capabilities, powers, and faculties that our Father possesses—although in an infantile state.
—Lorenzo Snow (JD 14:300)

Opening the Window of Wisdom

"Where have we come from?" is a question that resonates in every heart. The gospel of Jesus Christ answers that question in a way that gives us understanding of the eternal relationship we have with our Heavenly Father and fills our lives with the grateful knowledge that we are the offspring of Deity—and that our home was in His premortal mansions. With insight into such roots, we are more apt to obey God's commandments so we can return to His presence one day. We are taught in modern-day scriptures about the Supreme Being: "That by him, and through him, and of him, the worlds are and were created, and the inhabitants thereof are begotten sons and daughters unto God" (D&C 76:24). Moreover, we learn that "Man was also in the beginning with God. Intelligence, or the light of truth, was not created or made, neither indeed can be" (D&C 93:29).

The fact that we were with God in a premortal realm before we came to earth extends our vision of the drama of man's existence and development. We see that our life is centered in a divine eternal plan laid down before the foundations of the world. We participated in that plan with full awareness of our role in coming to earth to experience mortality, build up the kingdom of God, and set the stage to return with our loved ones to our Father in Heaven. Through the principle of foreordination we obtained the promise for glorious opportunities and blessings in mortality and beyond, predicated on our valiant devotion to the cause of helping the Lord in bringing to pass the immortality and eternal life of man (see Moses 1:39).

Through the mercy of our Father in Heaven, we have been given a clear picture of our nature as spirit children in the family of God. Prophets have given us a better understanding of where we came from, why we are here, and our destiny in the coming postmortal phase of existence. As students of the scriptures, we are permitted to go with Abraham into the circle of the Lord, where resplendent truth is unfolded to our senses. With Moses we walk up into the mount to learn first-hand the saving principles of the gospel as taught by the Master Himself. With the prophets of the Restoration we gain splendid insights into the all-encompassing panorama of our pathway through existence—including premortal, mortal, and post-mortal experience. As we study, we have a vicarious involvement in the reality of what Abraham,

Moses, and Joseph Smith experienced in person; then the Spirit confirms the truth of these principles in a real and enduring way.

By studying the scriptures faithfully and prayerfully, we receive the comforting assurance that we, too, were once in the halls of glory with our Father in Heaven and His Son, where "the first lessons in the world of spirits" (D&C 138:56) were taught to prepare us for our sojourn on earth. It was there that we first learned how to see with godly vision, how to magnify our divinely endowed intelligence, how to prepare for the future mortal tasks assigned us there, how to honor and cherish the earth that had been prepared specifically as our temporal (and eventually spiritual) home, how to strengthen ourselves in anticipation of our probationary earth life, how to follow the will of the Father and the Son in all respects and at all times, and how to cultivate humility and meekness as an antidote to pride.

The memory of those early lessons in the premortal sphere has been graciously masked so that we can learn in mortality—line upon line, precept upon precept (see Isa. 28:10–13; 2 Ne. 28:30; D&C 98:12)—how to be faithful agents in making the correct choices in life. Through the promptings of the Spirit, we can look forward to the blessings that follow covenant promises, and we can see with our inner eye the time when we can return once again to the presence of the Maker, from whom all blessings flow.

Inspired by Latter-Day Prophets

Joseph Smith: Every man who has a calling to minister to the inhabitants of the world was ordained to that very purpose in the Grand Council of heaven before this world was. I suppose that I was ordained to this very office in that Grand Council (*HC* 6:364).

As you render service in your family and the kingdom of God, which experiences seem to confirm that you are doing the work you were intended to do? How might your patriarchal blessing or other priesthood blessings suggest ways for you to fulfill roles that might have been appointed unto you in the premortal realm?

Joseph Fielding Smith: Man is the child of God, formed in the divine image and endowed with divine attributes, and even as the infant son of an earthly father and mother is capable in due time

of becoming a man, so the undeveloped offspring of celestial parentage is capable, by experience through ages and aeons, of evolving into a God (*Improvement Era*, Nov. 1909, 75–81).

Within your being is the seed of godliness—the potential to become like your Father in Heaven and His Only Begotten Son. How does this understanding lift you above any self-doubt or lack of confidence as you face the challenges of this day and all those that follow?

Spencer W. Kimball: Remember, in the world before we came here, faithful women were given certain assignments while faithful men were foreordained to certain priesthood tasks. While we do not now remember the particulars, this does not alter the glorious reality of what we once agreed to. We are accountable for those things which long ago were expected of us just as are those whom we sustain as prophets and apostles (*My Beloved Sisters,* 37).

All mortals belong to the select group that supported the Father's plan of happiness presented in the premortal realm. You are one of those choice beings who sided with the cause of righteousness prior to coming to earth as a child of God. How does knowing this truth infuse hope, gratitude, and a sense of accountability in your everyday behavior? How can you help your loved ones confirm their noble heritage as children of our Heavenly Father?

Ezra Taft Benson: You are choice sons and daughters of God—precious souls sent to this earth at this special time for a special reason. God loves you, each and every one of His children, and His desire and purpose and glory is to have you return to Him pure and undefiled, having proven yourselves worthy of an eternity in His presence (*The Teachings of Ezra Taft Benson,* 560).

Why do you think you were reserved to come to earth in this, the dispensation of the fulness of times? What special privileges and obligations does that suggest for you during the final period of time before the Second Coming? How has your life been blessed by having access to such a monumental archive of scriptures from all dispensations of time?

Truths to Liken

Acts 17:28–29—"For in him we live, and move, and have our being; as certain also of your own poets have said, For we are also his offspring. Forasmuch then as we are the offspring of God, we ought not to think that the Godhead is like unto gold, or silver, or stone, graven by art and man's device."

- Paul was expounding the truth of man's divine heritage before a group of philosophers and thinkers on Mars Hill in Athens.
- Knowing that we are the literal children of Heavenly Father should instill within us a feeling of great worth. We were created in the image of God. We have the capacity to become like Him. We are His children. When we truly believe this, we will not only feel differently about ourselves, but we will act differently—we will try to act like and be like the Lord. What role does this insight play as a source of continuing inspiration to stand firm against the immorality of our age and to stand solidly in tune with your covenant obligations?

D&C 84:38—"And he that receiveth my Father receiveth my Father's kingdom; therefore all that my Father hath shall be given unto him."

- The Lord Jesus Christ was explaining the solemn obligations that come with accepting the oath and covenant of the priesthood—and the grand blessings that await those who honor their priesthood callings as foreordained in the premortal realm, implemented in mortality, and continued beyond the veil.
- The blessings of keeping the oath and covenant of the priesthood should teach us something immensely important. We are so valuable to our Heavenly Father that He wants to bless us with everything He has. He wants us to have a life like His life—that is, eternal life. Indeed, His very work and glory is to bring about our immortality and eternal life. He loves us. We are His children—most valued above all other things.

D&C 93:21–23—"And now, verily I say unto you, I was in the beginning with the Father, and am the Firstborn; And all those who are begotten through me are partakers of the glory of the same, and are the church of the Firstborn. Ye were also in the beginning with the Father; that which is Spirit, even the Spirit of truth."

- Through the Prophet Joseph Smith, the Savior explained our station and stature as members of the family of God. Many—if not most—feel we had some relationship with the Creator. But it is only through the restored gospel that we have a clear vision of our spiritual roots, which reach back to the presence of the Father and the Son.
- To know this part of our history is to inspire us with a greater desire to please God. After all, we pleased Him enough in the premortal world for us to come to earth. As you ponder this truth, how can you cultivate a stronger commitment to be more like Him so that you can one day return and report with confidence and joy?

D&C 138:55–56—"I observed that they were also among the noble and great ones who were chosen in the beginning to be rulers in the Church of God. Even before they were born, they, with many others, received their first lessons in the world of spirits and were prepared to come forth in the due time of the Lord to labor in his vineyard for the salvation of the souls of men."

- In President Joseph F. Smith's magnificent vision of the spirit realm, received in October 1918, he was granted an understanding of how God's spirit children were chosen and trained for their mortal missions before coming to the earth.
- In our premortal experience, we made covenants to come forward in these latter days for the salvation of mankind. We were blessed according to our righteousness and received assignments to carry out here in mortality. As you think of yourself being among the "many others" instructed in the

premortal assemblies of preparation for mortality, what sense of destiny comes to your mind? How does this knowledge strengthen your commitment to do all in your power to bless the lives of your loved ones and help build the kingdom of God?

Abr. 3:22–23—"Now the Lord had shown unto me, Abraham, the intelligences that were organized before the world was; and among all these there were many of the noble and great ones; And God saw these souls that they were good, and he stood in the midst of them, and he said: These I will make my rulers; for he stood among those that were spirits, and he saw that they were good; and he said unto me: Abraham, thou art one of them; thou wast chosen before thou wast born."

- The Lord taught Abraham about the eternal nature of the spirit family of God and the coming forth of chosen individuals to fulfill foreordained missions. Due to his righteousness, Abraham, like so many others, was called to his position before he came to earth. All of us, individually, were called at that time to be faithful servants to the Most High forever—especially during our mortal experience, when our choices would determine our eternal destiny.
- In general, we do not know what specific offices and callings might have been bestowed on us as individuals in the premortal realm. But we do know that we were faithful in the premortal sphere—otherwise we would not be here. How does this knowledge inspire in you a desire to continue your service with devotion?

Rejoicing and Reasoning Together

What Agenda for Life Do We Derive Through Our Divine Parentage?

God is endless and infinite in His wisdom and His works. He is our Father in Heaven. We can come to understand the character and attributes of God through study, prayer, and by the witness of the Holy Ghost. We need to know about His goodness and power so we may act with faith, show love, and be obedient. We are His children, and He knows us personally. We have a personal relationship with God, who said, "Behold, I am the Lord God Almighty, and Endless is my name . . . all things are present with me, for I know them all" (Moses 1:3, 6).

In the premortal realm, God chose many noble leaders to guide His work on the earth. Each of us was chosen to fulfill an important calling of service and love. As children of God, we stand in awe of the knowledge that this earth was created specifically as a mortal home for us. This truth fills us with humble gratitude to our Father in Heaven for His eternal love. The purpose for our earthly existence is to prove ourselves worthy, through our own free agency and obedience to the laws of heaven, to return to our Heavenly Father.

As children of our Heavenly Father (see Rom. 8:16), each of us is truly a divine being with the obligation to prove ourselves worthy of returning to His presence (see Abr. 3:25). We have the potential to become perfect like our Heavenly Father and our Savior Jesus Christ and to receive of Their fullness (see 3 Ne. 12:48; D&C 84:38). This knowledge fills our souls with faith, hope, and charity. Knowing that Heavenly Father loves us, we have hope of life eternal, which God promised before the world began (Titus 1:2). We exercise our faith in Heavenly Father and our Savior as we come to know of Their character and attributes (see *Lectures on Faith* 1, 2). As we come to understand our relationship to God, we are moved to action, recognizing our capacity and our potential. We have a divine destiny—for we are the children of God.

From these insights we begin to develop themes for our lives. One of the most sublime and reassuring aspects of revealed truth is the knowledge that our spiritual roots reach back into the premortal halls of glory, where we were personally schooled in the principles of righteousness by our Father in Heaven and His Son, just as were the prophets in all dispensations of time (see D&C 138:55–56). Based on that noble curriculum, we understand that whatever the Lord conceives, He inevitably brings into existence. Therefore, as children of God, we learn to envision only that which is noble, godly, and righteous.

As you think about the premortal realm and your long–forgotten experiences there, how do these latter-day insights about the Father's plan of happiness help you adjust your own personal agenda for living?

How Does the Principle of Foreordination Figure into Our Lives as Spirit Children of God?

In the premortal realm, each of us was present when God chose many noble leaders to guide His work on the earth: "And God saw these souls that they were good, and he stood in the midst of them . . . " (Abr. 3:23). We knew Abraham at that time, for he was one of the noble and great premortal spirits who was called to lead a dispensation of time. His posterity would be blessed forever through his lineage.

What did Abraham and others do premortally to be foreordained? ". . . being called and prepared from the foundation of the world according to the foreknowledge of God, on account of their exceeding faith and good works; in the first place being left to choose good or evil; therefore they having chosen good, and exercising exceedingly great faith, are called with a holy calling, yea, with that holy calling which was prepared with, and according to, a preparatory redemption for such" (Alma 13:3). Everything is predicated on obedience. Blessings and opportunities come to those who choose to follow the Lord. We were prepared during the premortal phase of our existence for our mortal experience today, as we learn from latter-day revelation.

Foreordination was and is part of the plan of salvation; it is based on the foreknowledge of God and the righteousness of individuals in premortal life. In premortal life many were foreordained (appointed and assigned) to future assignments prior to their coming to earth. Those foreordained had exhibited exceeding faith and good works.

Everyone who experiences mortality has the capacity to receive the blessings of exaltation according to his or her obedience to the laws and commandments of God. A calling does not exalt; only individual righteousness and the grace of God can lift one to a state of exaltation and eternal life.

Foreordination does not override the agency of man—we are free to choose good or evil. We had agency premortally, and we have it now. Those who chose righteousness and who had great faith were called to holy callings. We came here endowed with blessings and opportunities from our premortal life, but agency is the overriding principle (see 2 Ne. 2:27).

Our mortal sojourn is brief when viewed in God's overall design for His children. Even though your time on earth is but a few hours in the reckoning of God's sense of time (see Abr. 3:4), your personal blueprint for salvation and exaltation is as wide and all-encompassing as the eternities. Your actions today—this very hour—relate to the callings and commitments you accepted in the premortal realm. How does this knowledge enhance your desire to prepare yourself to meet your Maker someday and hear Him say the words, "Well done, thou good and faithful servant" (Matt. 25:21, 23)?

How Do the Roots of Humility Stem from the Premortal Realm?

Humility is a heavenly virtue that we learned in the premortal realm. We are dependent on the Lord for strength. Without God, man is nothing. With God, we have the promise of unending blessings. After Moses first met with God on the mount, he was for a time left alone, and he collapsed in his mortal weakness. "Now, for this cause," said Moses, a former regal prince in Egypt, "I know that man is nothing, which thing I had never supposed" (Moses 1:10). In the tutelage of the Creator, he learned the truth about mankind—that enduring strength comes only through God, and that man is totally dependent on divine power for his vitality and his very being. This knowledge gave Moses—who "was very meek, above all the men which were upon the face of the earth" (Num. 12:3)—a deep understanding of the virtue of humility.

Without humility there is no growth. Humility is the beginning virtue of exaltation (see Matt. 23:12). Humility is that quality that brings into our hearts a love of our fellowmen and a feeling of connectedness to all mankind. Humility causes us to relate to God in prayerful gratitude and love because we realize that we are His children, and we acknowledge our dependence on Him. Moses learned on the mount—as we must learn—that we need an enduring attitude of humility if we are to succeed in helping to build up the kingdom of God (see D&C 12:8).

In the premortal realm we learned a transcendent lesson in humility:

And there stood one among them that was like unto God, and he said unto those who were with him: We will go down, for there is space there, and we will take of these materials, and we will make an earth whereon these may dwell;

And we will prove them herewith, to see if they will do all things whatsoever the Lord their God shall command them;

And they who keep their first estate shall be added upon; and they who keep not their first estate shall not have glory in the same kingdom with those who keep their first estate; and they who keep their second estate shall have glory added upon their heads for ever and ever.

And the Lord said: Whom shall I send? And one answered like unto the Son of Man: Here am I, send me. And another answered and said: Here am I, send me. And the Lord said: I will send the first.

And the second was angry, and kept not his first estate; and, at that day, many followed after him. (Abr. 3:24–28)

We watched on that occasion as our Elder Brother, Jesus Christ, accepted in humility the calling to become our Redeemer and Savior. We saw Lucifer rebel in pride and anger against the Father's plan for our salvation and exaltation. The effect of that opposition—light over darkness, humility over rebellion—continues to this very day and hour and will continue until the advent of the millennial reign. "And there was war in heaven: Michael and his angels fought against the dragon; and the dragon fought and his angels, And prevailed not; neither was their place found any more in heaven" (Rev. 12:7–8). Today, like every day, we fight the war against evil—such a struggle is part of life. Through the strength of the Father and the Son, whom we knew personally in the premortal sphere, we can prevail.

> *You are at war every day against the forces of Satan and his minions—a war to protect your loved ones from the assault of evil pervasive in our modern society. How are you doing in that war? Is the armor of God upon you (see Eph. 6:13–18; D&C 27:15–18)? Is the spirit and aura of humility resting*

upon you and your family in these times of adversity and challenge? Are you able to say now, as we all did in emulating the majesty and humility of the Savior in the premortal realm: "Here I am, send me" (Abr. 3:27)?

What Did the Prophet Joseph Smith Mean When He Said, "Seek the Face of the Lord Always"?

In a revelation given through the Prophet Joseph Smith at Kirtland, Ohio, on December 16, 1833, this counsel was extended to the suffering Saints in Missouri: "And seek the face of the Lord always, that in patience ye may possess your souls, and ye shall have eternal life" (D&C 101:38). The Prophet Joseph was the epitome of one who sought the face of the Lord with untiring devotion. That quest began in the premortal existence, as the Prophet himself stated, when he was called as the Prophet of the Restoration: "It is the testimony that I want that I am God's servant, and this people His people. The ancient prophets declared that in the last days the God of heaven should set up a kingdom which should never be destroyed. . . . God will always protect me until my mission is fulfilled. I calculate to be one of the instruments of setting up the kingdom of Daniel by the word of the Lord, and I intend to lay a foundation that will revolutionize the whole world" (*Teachings of the Prophet Joseph Smith*, 365).

The Prophet's exemplary quest to "seek the face of the Lord always" is recorded in unforgettable episodes in the pages of the Doctrine and Covenants. The visions opened up to the Prophet of the Restoration are ample evidence that the worthy and anointed can indeed seek and find the face of the Lord—whose qualities and mission are reflected in exquisite detail throughout this sacred volume of modern scripture.

How does this relate to us in these latter days? From the word of the Lord in the scriptures and the messages of His prophets, we know that we have already seen the face of the Lord—even the face of the Father and the Son. They know us personally; we know them personally, having communed with them in the premortal sphere. Our calling is to live in such a way that we are worthy to return to Their presence and see Their faces once again in Their eternal glory. That exercise takes patience, endurance, faith, and obedience. The Savior told His disciples in Jerusalem: "In your patience possess ye your souls" (Luke 21:19).

The patience and humility we began to cultivate in the premortal spirit realm will help us achieve our goal to return to the presence of the Father and the Son one day. Imagine what it will be like to see Them once again. The Apostle John set the stage: "BEHOLD, what manner of love the Father hath bestowed upon us, that we should be called the sons of God: therefore the world knoweth us not, because it knew him not. Beloved, now are we the sons of God, and it doth not yet appear what we shall be: but we know that, when he shall appear, we shall be like him; for we shall see him as he is. And every man that hath this hope in him purifieth himself, even as he is pure" (1 Jn. 3:1–3). How does this passage help you imagine the wonder of once again seeing the face of the Lord?

Real-life Stories for Heart and Mind

The Precious Student. As grandparents looked at their newborn granddaughter in her mother's arms, they realized what a precious and beautiful soul she was. Just that day the grandfather had been pondering one of his favorite scriptures concerning the transition of God's children from the premortal realm to earth life: "Even before they were born, they, with many others, received their first lessons in the world of spirits and were prepared to come forth in the due time of the Lord to labor in his vineyard for the salvation of the souls of men" (D&C 138:56). As her grandfather gazed at her, he wondered, *What wisdom has she already learned? And what memories will come back through the scriptures and the inspired teachings of her parents?* Here was a miracle unfolding. Here was a child of God coming to earth in majesty and glory. The gospel plan of Heavenly Father was at work again. What a wonderful and stimulating experience awaited this newest grandchild—this precious student—to be able to relearn in life through the Spirit what the Father and the Son had already taught her in her previous home on high.

Hold a young baby in your arms and look into his or her eyes. What lessons do you learn to lift and inspire you?

Pure Intelligence. A woman often recalled vivid childhood memories of her father sitting in his easy chair, reading and pondering the scriptures. This image of her father faithfully opening up channels of pure intelligence through the word of God was an enduring source of inspiration and comfort to her. She remembered fondly the frequent times when he noticed her there and called her to his side to read a passage to her—most often from the Book of Mormon—and to share his feelings, often with a tear in his eye. This made a lasting and wholesome impression on his daughter—one that inspired her throughout her entire lifetime.

In the premortal realm we were all introduced to the principle of pure intelligence. Now we are actively trying to increase our pure intelligence and bring into our lives more fully the principles of eternal salvation. Learning is universal and unending. We learn and grow in all phases of our existence—premortally, in mortality, and in the worlds to come. At the center of this process of learning and growing is that we come to know and receive all the knowledge and blessings of God (see D&C 84:38). As you confirm these truths in your own life and work to bring light and truth into the lives of your loved ones, how have you set an example similar to the one set by the father in the above story? In what ways are you teaching by example the principle of seeking after pure intelligence?

Words of the Patriarch. Half a century and multiple careers later, a high priest looked back with increased gratitude at the words of inspiration included in his patriarchal blessing. There in plain language was the prophetic utterance that identified the very activity that would eventually bring him maximum joy in helping to build the kingdom of God.

What blessings might have been given to you in the premortal realm to inspire parts of your patriarchal blessing? Your patriarchal blessing can help you understand and appreciate some of the gifts and promises you were endowed with before you came to earth—as well as those you might receive in the future. What timeless counsel and inspiration have you discovered as you have pondered and prayed about your patriarchal blessing over the years? Your Heavenly Father has grand blessings in store for you if you are true and faithful. Like Abraham and other noble leaders in the premortal realm, you receive blessings according to your "exceeding faith and good works" (Alma 13:3).

Pondering Prayerfully

Additional scriptures to consider and ponder:
- Prov. 29:18
- Jeremiah 1:5
- Rom. 8:16
- Alma 7:23
- 3 Ne. 27:27
- D&C 93:36

The following hymns might increase understanding about our premortal life and future destiny:
- "How Great the Wisdom and the Love" (*Hymns,* 195)
- "If You Could Hie to Kolob" (*Hymns,* 284)
- "Thy Will, O Lord, Be Done" (*Hymns,* 188)

Remember and Be Sure

Our mission on the earth started in the premortal realm, where we were called to service based on the principle of foreordination, as anchored in our faith and valor. We knew before we started our mortal journey that the righteous would be persecuted for the sake of all truth and victory. We were schooled in premortal classrooms to recognize both the agony of guilt and the ecstasy of deliverance—because we were taught there the first principles and ordinances of the gospel of Jesus Christ. We were present "when the morning stars sang together, and all the sons of God shouted for joy" (Job 38:7) over the great plan of salvation. We knew before the foundations of the earth were laid that God's word would always be fulfilled, then as now, and we rejoiced in the coming opportunity to complete our mortal probation with dignity, loyalty, and virtue—no matter what adversity might come into our lives or what sacrifice we might be called on to make. Knowing this, we can go forward with courage to honor our covenant promises, increase our pure intelligence, and look forward to the blessings of joy and glory that await the faithful in the courts of the Almighty.

We are the children of Heavenly Father. He loves us and seeks our happiness and eternal life. He has a purpose for us here on earth. We cannot be casual in regard to our assignments, for they are part of a grand design for the immortality and eternal life of man (see Moses 1:39). As children of God, we are humble seekers of light, truth, and happiness. This is the time to remember the counsel from on high to "seek the face of the Lord always, that in patience ye may possess your souls, and ye shall have eternal life" (D&C 101:38).

CHAPTER 3
Jesus Christ: His Commission and Stewardship

We need to arise and shine and to get the vision of this great work and to incorporate it into our lives and homes and our families. If we do so the Lord will bless us because He loves us. We are His people. We have accepted His gospel. You have taken upon yourselves sacred covenants and He wants to bless you. He wants to pour out His blessings, the blessings of heaven, upon you and your families.
—Ezra Taft Benson (*The Teachings of Ezra Taft Benson*, 526)

Opening the Window of Wisdom

Jesus Christ was the firstborn premortally and the Only Begotten of God the Father in the flesh. He was the Creator of earth and all things under the direction of the Father. He performed the infinite and eternal Atonement through which all mankind could be saved and exalted. Everything of eternal worth centers in Jesus Christ: the gospel, the priesthood, the Church, and the plan of happiness. It is imperative to come to know Jesus Christ—for "this is life eternal" (see John 17:3).

The love of our Father in Heaven and His Son is manifest in all things. John bears witness of this truth in his epistles: "In this was manifested the love of God toward us, because that God sent his only begotten Son into the world, that we might live through him. Herein is love, not that we loved

God, but that he loved us, and sent his Son to be the propitiation for our sins" (1 Jn. 4:9–10; compare 1 Jn. 2:1–3).

The Son is the "Holy One of Israel, thy Saviour: . . . and beside me there is no saviour" (Isa. 43:3, 11; compare Isa. 47:4; 54:5; 2 Ne. 25:29). He is the "I AM" of the Old Testament (Ex. 3:14) and the "only name which shall be given under heaven, whereby salvation shall come unto the children of men" (Moses 6:52). The overarching reach of His divine influence in our lives traces a pattern of infinite grace and love. From Jehovah (the "Unchangeable One" and firstborn), to Messiah or Christ ("Anointed"), to Creator, to Emmanuel ("God Among Us"), to Jesus ("Jehovah is Help" or Savior), and finally to King, we can trace the agenda by which He sustains and perfects His immortal role as our Master and Redeemer. In the final analysis, we perceive in His divine stewardship many titles and offices, but only one Lord; many qualities, but only one unified manifestation of divine love; many influences and interactions with mankind, but only one cause: "to bring to pass the immortality and eternal life of man" (Moses 1:39).

In His omniscience and infinite wisdom, the Lord Jesus Christ saw from the beginning the pathway we would have to follow if we were to bear His image—a pathway marked by crucial points of passage. Following the Creation itself came the Fall of mankind, anticipated by our Father in Heaven as a necessary part of the journey. The grand counterbalance to the Fall was the Atonement of Jesus Christ, proclaimed from before the foundations of the earth, through which mankind could once again be reconciled with God by faith and obedience and return to His presence. Then came the indispensable experience of mortality through which Adam's posterity would receive mortal tabernacles and be granted a probationary opportunity. Even though the man and the woman were separated from their Maker for a time, they still had a growing awareness of the joy inherent in the plan of salvation, began to understand the purposes for life, and had joy in their posterity.

A central part of the mortal experience is the opportunity to exercise freedom of choice—to choose to love God and obey His will, or to love Satan and become entrapped in worldly enticements and sin (see 2 Ne. 2:27–29). This ability to choose is God-given and is a key part of the plan. All mortals are under strict command to teach their children the gospel plan, including the principles and ordinances of saving power. Those who choose the correct path, raising their families in light and truth, will be delivered from spiritual death through the power of the Atonement of Jesus Christ. The Resurrection will liberate everyone from temporal death, but the glory of exaltation and eternal lives is reserved for those who are reborn through the Atonement as sons and daughters of God and joint-heirs with Christ of everlasting joy (see Rom. 8:17).

Inspired by Latter-Day Prophets

Joseph F. Smith: The Gospel of Jesus Christ is the power of God unto salvation, and it is absolutely necessary for every man and woman in the Church of Christ to work righteousness, to observe the laws of God, and keep the commandments that he has given, in order that they may avail themselves of the power of God unto salvation in this life (*CR*, Oct. 1907, 2).

There is infinite power within our grasp. In a world where the competition for power is acute, to the point of obsession, we can have something of far greater glory and majesty than worldly station and supremacy: we can have the power of salvation through the blessing and grace of the Atonement of Jesus Christ. In what ways is the power of God working within your soul

and your family circle? How can you open up greater channels of light and power through your actions and choices?

Spencer W. Kimball: Men may know Christ. The ultimate and greatest of all knowledge, then, is to know God and his program for our exaltation. We may know him by sight, by sound, by feeling. While relatively few ever do really know him, everyone may know him, not only prophets—ancient and modern—but, as he said: "Every soul who forsaketh his sins and cometh unto me, and calleth on my name, and obeyeth my voice, and keepeth my commandments, shall see my face and know that I am." (D & C 93:1.) (*The Teachings of Spencer W. Kimball*, 7).

How can you come to know Christ better? How can you teach your loved ones to know Christ better and to avail themselves of greater joy and happiness?

Ezra Taft Benson: Without Christ there would be no Easter. Without Christ there can be no fulness of joy. In our premortal state, we shouted for joy as the plan of salvation was unfolded to our view. (See Job 38:7.) ("Joy in Christ," *Ensign*, Mar. 1986, 3).

Imagine your life without the influence of the Savior. What would you give up in terms of light and comfort, hope and foundation? Knowing that the Savior's influence is in fact pervasive in your life, ponder the things He gives you, the indescribable blessings His grace and love provide for you and for your family.

Howard W. Hunter: I witness that Jesus is the Christ, the Savior of the world. If only we could catch the vision and conform our lives to his teachings, we would find that joy which has been promised to us ("He Invites Us to Follow Him," *Ensign*, Sept. 1994, 2).

In what ways can you better "catch the vision" of the Savior's love and influence in your life? How might you be able to receive a greater measure of joy in your life? What corners of your existence could use additional light and happiness?

Truths to Liken

2 Ne. 25:26—"And we talk of Christ, we rejoice in Christ, we preach of Christ, we prophesy of Christ, and we write according to our prophecies, that our children may know to what source they may look for a remission of their sins."

- Nephi included these stirring and famous words among his concluding sermons and writings for his posterity.
- Note the sequence Nephi describes for how to focus on the Savior: talking (daily conversation), rejoicing (attitudes and feelings of joy and gratitude), preaching (spreading the good news about the Savior), prophesying (bearing inspired witness about the blessings of living the gospel), and writing (recording these grand insights for the coming generations). How are you doing with each of these as a blessing for your loved ones?

Ether 3:4—"And I know, O Lord, that thou hast all power, and can do whatsoever thou wilt for the benefit of man; therefore touch these stones, O Lord, with thy finger, and prepare them that they may shine forth in darkness; and they shall shine forth unto us in the vessels which we have prepared, that we may have light while we shall cross the sea."

- The brother of Jared had faith and confidence that the Lord would endow him with light to illuminate the journey ahead.
- When we know and appreciate the power and goodness of God, our faith in Him increases. The power and goodness of the Lord can preserve us in our journey. Think of yourself as the "stone" in this scripture. How can you better prepare yourself so that the touch of the Savior will illuminate your life to a greater degree? How are you, in turn, a light for your loved ones?

D&C 29:1–2—"Listen to the voice of Jesus Christ, your Redeemer, the Great I AM, whose arm of mercy hath atoned for your sins; Who will gather his people even as a hen gathereth her chickens under her wings, even as many as will hearken to my voice

and humble themselves before me, and call upon me in mighty prayer."

- The Savior gave this counsel through the Prophet Joseph Smith to a small gathering of elders at Fayette, New York, in September 1830.
- We can have immense hope through the Savior, who has opened the way for the faithful and obedient to follow Him home as they subdue the natural man and become His sons and daughters. In the words above, the Savior gave a covenant promise: those who humbly hearken to His voice in mighty prayer will be gathered unto the fold in the spirit of forgiveness. How would you define and describe "mighty prayer"? How is it operative in your life?

D&C 35:4–5—"Listen to him who is the advocate with the Father, who is pleading your cause before him—Saying: Father, behold the sufferings and death of him who did no sin, in whom thou wast well pleased; behold the blood of thy Son which was shed, the blood of him whom thou gavest that thyself might be glorified; Wherefore, Father, spare these my brethren that believe on my name, that they may come unto me and have everlasting life."

- These words were given through the Prophet Joseph Smith at Kirtland, Ohio, on March 7, 1831, as a warning to the Saints to disregard false teachers and focus on the central message of the Redeemer.
- What do the words *pleading your cause before Him* mean to you? What cause do you and your loved ones have that requires "pleading" by the Advocate before the Father? What do the words *spare these my brethren* mean to you? In what ways do you and your loved ones need "sparing"? How can you better qualify for the "pleadings" of the Savior?

D&C 50:44—"Wherefore, I am in your midst, and I am the good shepherd, and the stone of Israel. He that buildeth upon this rock shall never fall."

- These words were given through the Prophet Joseph Smith at Kirtland, Ohio, in May 1831 as part of a remarkable revelation on how the Saints can learn of the gospel through the Comforter and thus be edified and filled with light.

- The only security in this life—the only sure foundation upon which we can build and the only fail-safe strategy for happiness—is to follow the Redeemer. We depend on our Savior to plead for us that we might gain eternal life. During these times of turmoil and dislocation in the world, how can you build your life in fuller measure on the rock of the Redeemer?

Moses 5:58—"And thus the Gospel began to be preached, from the beginning, being declared by holy angels sent forth from the presence of God, and by his own voice, and by the gift of the Holy Ghost."

- From the record of Moses we learn how the Lord arranged to have His gospel taught from the beginning of time. That process continues to this very day and hour (see Matt. 24:14; Mark 16:15; Morm. 9:22; D&C 18:28).
- Who does the teaching? Holy angels, the voice of the Lord Himself, and the Holy Ghost. Where does that leave you? In what sense are *you* also a "holy angel" who brings the voice of the Lord into the lives of the honest at heart by introducing them to the scriptures and teaching them how to pray for the inspiration of the Holy Ghost?

Rejoicing and Reasoning Together

How Can We Come to Love the Lord More by Better Understanding His Mission?

Jehovah—In the King James Version of the Old Testament, the word *LORD* (with each letter capitalized) signifies that the original text contained the name *Jehovah*, which means "Unchangeable One" (see for example Ex. 6:2–3; Ps. 83:18; Isa. 12:2; 26:4; 2 Ne. 22:2; Moro. 10:34; D&C 109:34, 42, 56, 68; 110:3; 128:9; Abr. 1:16; 2:8). Out of respect for Deity, Jewish readers did not speak aloud the name *Jehovah* (or any of its variations), but substituted instead a Hebrew word such as *Adonai*, meaning "Lord." The name *Jehovah* signifies everlasting,

endless, and eternal God, a reflection of the supernal constancy of Deity. This everlasting state of being is confirmed in latter-day scripture: "Listen to the voice of the Lord your God, even Alpha and Omega, the beginning and the end, whose course is one eternal round, the same today as yesterday, and forever" (D&C 35:1; compare 2 Ne. 2:4; 27:23; 29:9; Alma 31:17; Morm. 9:9; Moro. 10:19; D&C 20:12; Heb. 13:8). It was under the auspices of this transcendent function of the everlasting and unchanging God—the Eternal I Am—that Jehovah conversed with Moses on the mount:

> And Moses said unto God, Behold, when I come unto the children of Israel, and shall say unto them, The God of your fathers hath sent me unto you; and they shall say to me, What is his name? what shall I say unto them?
>
> And God said unto Moses, I AM THAT I AM: and he said, Thus shalt thou say unto the children of Israel, I AM hath sent me unto you.
>
> And God said moreover unto Moses, Thus shalt thou say unto the children of Israel, The LORD God of your fathers, the God of Abraham, the God of Isaac, and the God of Jacob, hath sent me unto you: this is my name for ever, and this is my memorial unto all generations. (Ex. 3:13–15)

The nature of Jehovah as an eternal, unchanging, and everlasting Being derives from His relationship to, and grounding in, the Father. Jehovah is in very deed the Son of God, even the firstborn: "I will declare the decree: the LORD hath said unto me, Thou art my Son; this day have I begotten thee" (Ps. 2:7). Furthermore: "Also I will make him my firstborn, higher than the kings of the earth. My mercy will I keep for him for evermore, and my covenant shall stand fast with him. His seed also will I make to endure for ever, and his throne as the days of heaven" (Ps. 89:27–29). Isaiah confirmed the same truth: "Who hath wrought and done it, calling the generations from the beginning? I the LORD, the first, and with the last; I am he" (Isa. 41:4). In the New Testament, Book of Mormon, and the Doctrine and Covenants, the Savior's defining position as the First as well as the Last is embodied in the appellation *Alpha and Omega* (see Rev. 1:8, 11; 3 Ne. 9:18; D&C 19:1; 81:7;

132:66). Not only is Jehovah endless and eternal, but He also serves everlastingly as a member of the Godhead under the direction of the Father and in conjunction with the Holy Ghost.

The qualities of the Son—the "Unchangeable One"—that radiate from His magnificent position of grace and truth include divinity, everlasting nature, and godliness. These are the same qualities to which all of us are to aspire through obedience to His gospel plan of exaltation and by enduring in faith and honor to the end. What a glorious blessing it is to have a resplendent and perfected personage—even Jehovah—as our spiritual model and eternal guide: "Therefore, what manner of men ought ye to be? Verily I say unto you, even as I am" (3 Ne. 27:27). In this unstable world, how does it make you feel to remember each day that Jehovah is unchanging, that the principles of the gospel are permanent, and that the promise of eternal life for the faithful is absolute?

Messiah/Christ—*Messiah* is an Aramaic word meaning "the Anointed." Aramaic belongs to the Semitic language group (which also includes Hebrew and Arabic) and became the official language of the Assyrian and later the Babylonian and Persian empires. For centuries, Aramaic was the dominant language in Jewish worship and daily life; it was the language Jesus spoke.

The Greek equivalent of Messiah was "Christ." The word *Christ* does not appear in the King James Version of the Old Testament, but it does appear in four verses of the book of Moses in the Pearl of Great Price (see Moses 6:52, 57; 7:50; 8:24). The title *Messiah* appears only twice in the Old Testament (see Dan. 9:25, 26) and only once in the Pearl of Great Price (see Moses 7:53).

The important thing about the terms *Messiah* and *Christ* is their underlying meaning, "the Anointed"—signifying that Jesus was divinely commissioned of the Father to carry out the work of redemption and atonement on behalf of all mankind. He was foreordained to His mission: "And the Lord said: Whom shall I send? And one answered like unto the Son of Man: Here am I, send me. And another answered and said: Here am I, send me. And the Lord said: I will send the first" (Abr. 3:27; compare Gen. 3:14–15; Job

19:25; 38:1–7; Isa. 25:8–9). Jesus—as the *Messiah* and the *Christ*—is the authorized and empowered agent of the Father, and His express calling is to carry out the divine mission of saving and exalting mankind. Isaiah expresses this divine mission of the "Anointed One" in the following terms:

The Spirit of the Lord GOD is upon me; because the LORD hath anointed me to preach good tidings unto the meek; he hath sent me to bind up the brokenhearted, to proclaim liberty to the captives, and the opening of the prison to them that are bound;

To proclaim the acceptable year of the LORD, and the day of vengeance of our God; to comfort all that mourn;

To appoint unto them that mourn in Zion, to give unto them beauty for ashes, the oil of joy for mourning, the garment of praise for the spirit of heaviness; that they might be called trees of righteousness, the planting of the LORD, that he might be glorified. (Isa. 61:1–3)

The Old Testament confirms the divine authority of Jesus in a variety of additional passages, including this memorable one from Isaiah: "For unto us a child is born, unto us a son is given: and the government shall be upon his shoulder: and his name shall be called Wonderful, Counsellor, The mighty God, The everlasting Father, The Prince of Peace. Of the increase of his government and peace there shall be no end, upon the throne of David, and upon his kingdom, to order it, and to establish it with judgment and with justice from henceforth even for ever" (Isa. 9:6–7).

The office, function, and blessings of the "Anointed One" figure prominently in sacred revelation through the ages. It is from Jehovah, acting as the Agent of the Father, that salvation and redemption flow to those who believe and honor the covenants of the Lord. We are to follow in the footsteps of the Son of God. In what ways are you also "anointed" to rise in majesty as a son or daughter of God and perform indispensable works for the blessing of loved ones and the building up of the Church and kingdom of God?

Creator—The Unchangeable and Anointed One served as the principal divine Agent in laying the foundation of the world through the Creation itself. When God directed that the Creation should proceed (see Gen. 1–2; Moses 2–3; Deut. 4:32), it was through the Word of God (Jehovah, Messiah, Christ) that this divine process was initiated and completed: "By the word of the LORD were the heavens made; and all the host of them by the breath of his mouth" (Ps. 33:6).

Thus the Word of God was Creation itself, as John the Apostle explained: "In the beginning was the Word, and the Word was with God, and the Word was God. The same was in the beginning with God. All things were made by him; and without him was not any thing made that was made. In him was life; and the life was the light of men. And the light shineth in darkness; and the darkness comprehended it not" (John 1:1–5).

What greater symbolic representation could there be of the office and function of the Creator and Life-giver than the image of being the "light of the world" (John 8:12)? "And God said, Let there be light: and there was light. And God saw the light, that it was good: and God divided the light from the darkness" (Gen. 1:3–4; see also Moses 2:3–4). In keeping with the essence of this divine capacity, the Psalmist celebrated the Word of God as follows: "The LORD is my light and my salvation; whom shall I fear? the LORD is the strength of my life; of whom shall I be afraid?" (Ps. 27:1).

The Doctrine and Covenants speaks of the light that "proceedeth forth from the presence of God to fill the immensity of space—The light which is in all things, which giveth life to all things, which is the law by which all things are governed, even the power of God who sitteth upon his throne, who is in the bosom of eternity, who is in the midst of all things" (D&C 88:12–13). The divine Agent for that light is Jesus Christ:

> For the word of the Lord is truth, and whatsoever is truth is light, and whatsoever is light is Spirit, even the Spirit of Jesus Christ.
>
> And the Spirit giveth light to every man that cometh into the world; and the Spirit enlighteneth every man through the world, that hearkeneth to the voice of the Spirit.
>
> And every one that hearkeneth to the voice of the Spirit cometh unto God, even the Father.

> And the Father teacheth him of the covenant which he has renewed and confirmed upon you, which is confirmed upon you for your sakes, and not for your sakes only, but for the sake of the whole world. (D&C 84:45–48)

The predominant quality of Jesus Christ as Creator is one who completes, or one who—through faith, obedience, power, and divine light—generates and sustains life unto salvation. What an extraordinary Being to generate all the conditions and processes by which we can enjoy mortal life and look forward with hope to the time when we will inherit immortality and eternal life in the mansions of the Father and the Son. In that joyous hour, the faithful will meet once again the very Creator of our being, look upon His face with rapture, and speak His name in love: "And he shall be called Jesus Christ, the Son of God, the Father of heaven and earth, the Creator of all things from the beginning" (Mosiah 3:8; see also Moses 6:63; 7:56; Abr. 4:20).

> *As Creator, Jehovah embodies specific qualities, including being life-giving, creative, productive, and loyal. These are among the very qualities that define discipleship for the faithful who follow in the footsteps of the Savior by emulating His example. Should you not also seek to sustain and nurture life, be creative and productive in wholesome and uplifting ways, and display loyalty and obedience to God in all your dealings? He is named as the Gatekeeper of the eternal realm (see 2 Ne. 9:41), being also the Gatekeeper of life itself. Should you not also strive to be the faithful "gatekeeper" of your own stewardship—your home, family, and callings in the Church? Being a gatekeeper takes creativity and productivity, but we can do all things in the strength of the Lord (see Alma 20:4).*

Emmanuel (Immanuel)—One of the greatest of all the miracles of the gospel is the fact that the great Jehovah came among mortals to bring to pass salvation and redemption for all mankind. In this capacity, His office and title are known as *Emmanuel* (also rendered *Immanuel*)—that is, "God Among Us." As the Only Begotten of the Father, He accepted

His mortal mission to serve as the Messenger of the Covenant and experienced birth, grew to manhood, completed His ministry as the Good Shepherd, and suffered betrayal and death as the "author of eternal salvation" (Heb. 5:8–9).

Enoch saw in vision the entry of the Lord into mortality: "And behold, Enoch saw the day of the coming of the Son of Man, even in the flesh; and his soul rejoiced, saying: The Righteous is lifted up, and the Lamb is slain from the foundation of the world; and through faith I am in the bosom of the Father, and behold, Zion is with me" (Moses 7:47). This theme of the condescension of Christ as the Good Shepherd is most memorably expressed in the twenty-third Psalm—"The LORD is my shepherd; I shall not want" (Ps. 23:1)—but is also encapsulated in several other prophetic passages of great beauty and tenderness (see for example Ps. 80:2–3; 95:7; Ezek. 34:11–19; Zech. 13:7).

By nature of His divine calling and commission, the Good Shepherd is humble, patient, nurturing, and personal (focused on the needs of the individual in lovingkindness), exhibiting the characteristics of the longsuffering, noble counselor. Are these not the very qualities that followers of Christ should emulate if they are to fulfill the measure of their spiritual potential? How can you honor in all diligence the commandment to follow the Good Shepherd in humility and patience, cultivating with Him personally an enduring and liberating relationship of a child to a loving parent—even the Father of our eternal salvation? How can you better emulate the role of "God among us" by "being there" in love and charity for your own family members, loved ones, neighbors, and those who need your help?

Jesus—The name *Jesus* is the Greek form of the name *Joshua* or *Jeshua*, meaning "God IS Help" (or "Jehovah IS Help")—in other words, "Savior." The name implies the sacred office of Redeemer, Lamb of God, Bread of Life—the One who brings about the Atonement through the sacrificial crucifixion, the One who ushers in the process of the resurrection, the One who is in all respects the Life of the World. In this capacity as Savior, the Son of God is the means for rescuing all mankind from the effects of temporal death. He also enables the faithful and

obedient to escape the clutches of spiritual death if they obey the principles and ordinances of the gospel. Isaiah stated: "Yet it pleased the LORD to bruise him; he hath put him to grief: when thou shalt make his soul an offering for sin, he shall see his seed, he shall prolong his days, and the pleasure of the LORD shall prosper in his hand" (Isa. 53:10).

The concept of Jesus as the Lamb of God was made a regular part of the worship of ancient Israel through the ritual sacrifice of a lamb "without blemish" (Ex. 12:5, 13–14; Isa. 53:7, 10). The rejoicing over the triumph of the Redeemer of mankind as the Lamb of God is likewise found throughout the scriptures (see for example Ex. 15:2; 1 Sam. 2:6; Job 19:26–27; Ps. 16:9–10; Isa. 25:8; Hosea 13:14).

In all of this we see that Jesus as Savior, the Atoning One, is the singularly most powerful example of the qualities that belong to "Saviorhood": loving, obedient, redeeming, perfect, spotless. He is so loving that He verily weeps when we fall short of our potential (see Moses 7:40). At the same time, He rejoices when we repent and follow in His footsteps: "And how great is his joy in the soul that repenteth!" (D&C 18:13). Should we not all strive to cultivate within ourselves these same qualities? In what ways are you also a representative of the qualities of the Savior—loving, obedient, redeeming, striving to be "perfect in Christ" (Moro. 10:32)?

King—Jehovah was anointed in the premortal realm to lay the foundation of the world through the Creation and to serve as the Author of eternal salvation by coming to live among mortals, becoming the Savior to all the world. In the final chapter of the history of this world, Jesus Christ will return in glory as King, Judge, Lawgiver, Mediator, Advocate, and Prince of Peace to usher in the millennial reign and take His place as the covenant Father of all the righteous and redeemed. Job declared: "For I know that my redeemer liveth, and that he shall stand at the latter day upon the earth" (Job 19:25). There are many references to the coming role of Jesus as triumphant King, Ruler, and Judge.

We know from the scriptures that the Great Jehovah will consummate the final judgment and disposition of mankind by being just, merciful, righteous, full of grace, holy, and glorious. These are the qualities of His royal office. Alma provides perhaps the most compelling summary of the Savior's qualities in the plan of salvation: "And thus he shall bring salvation to all those who shall believe on his name; this being the intent of this last sacrifice, to bring about the bowels of mercy, which overpowereth justice, and bringeth about means unto men that they may have faith unto repentance. And thus mercy can satisfy the demands of justice, and encircles them in the arms of safety, while he that exercises no faith unto repentance is exposed to the whole law of the demands of justice; therefore only unto him that has faith unto repentance is brought about the great and eternal plan of redemption" (Alma 34:15–16).

All followers of Christ should emulate His example by aspiring to the same qualities He displays in perfected form—being just, merciful, righteous, full of grace, holy, and glorious. Surely our joy and peace in this world and the world to come will depend on the degree to which we can cultivate these qualities within our character, together with all others that pertain to the mission of the Lord as our eternal Exemplar. Consider how well you have incorporated these qualities, and how you might improve with the help of the Lord and the inspiration of the Holy Ghost.

How Is Our Understanding of Jesus Christ Enhanced through the Study of the Book of Mormon?

The central figure of the Book of Mormon is Jesus Christ—whose mission of the infinite Atonement leads to the immortality and eternal life of man. In the 6,607 verses of the Book of Mormon there are 3,925 references to our Savior, using more than one hundred different titles and descriptions. Everything in the Book of Mormon reflects the pervasive presence of the Lamb of God and His transcending love and mercy for all of God's children—from the title page to the final exhortation of Moroni: "Yea, come unto Christ, and be perfected in him, and deny yourselves of all ungodliness; and if ye shall deny yourselves of all ungodliness, and love God with all your might, mind and strength, then is his grace sufficient for you, that by his grace ye may be

perfect in Christ; and if by the grace of God ye are perfect in Christ, ye can in nowise deny the power of God" (Moro. 10:32).

The Book of Mormon is truly "Another Testament of Jesus Christ"—a sacred witness that He lives and acts for the "immortality and eternal life of man" (Moses 1:39). Within its pages He is identified variously as the "Holy One of Israel" (2 Ne. 25:29), "the rock" (Hel. 5:12), the "Well Beloved" (Hel. 5:47), "the God of the land" (Ether 2:12), "the God of the whole earth" (3 Ne. 11:14), and various other appellations.

Prophetic utterances about the divine nature of His Being and His redeeming mission abound. He was seen by many prophets—including Nephi and Jacob (see 2 Ne. 11:2–3), the brother of Jared (see Ether 3:13), and Moroni (see Ether 12:39). In His resurrected state, He was seen by thousands in the area of Bountiful (see 3 Ne.). He defined plainly the nature of His gospel as the divine plan of deliverance and exaltation, based on faith, repentance, baptism, receiving the gift of the Holy Ghost, and enduring to the end (see 3 Ne. 11:32–41; 27:13–27). He established His Church among the people and authorized His chosen servants to administer the saving teachings and ordinances of the gospel to lift and edify all those who came unto Him with a broken heart and contrite spirit (see 3 Ne. 12:19).

The most compelling and magnificent section of the Book of Mormon is the account of the visit of Jesus Christ to His "other sheep" (3 Ne. 15:21) on the American continent following His Crucifixion and Resurrection. From His visit we gain priceless lessons on how to use charity in our own missions in mortality. We marvel at the comprehensive pattern He followed: bearing testimony to truth (see 3 Ne. 9:15), teaching the fundamentals of the gospel (see 3 Ne. 11:31–41), bestowing enduring gifts on the people (see 3 Ne. 17:11–25), bringing a life-changing influence among the people (see 3 Ne. 12:47–48), teaching us our true identity as sons and daughters of God (see 3 Ne. 9:17), teaching us how to gain a fulness of truth (see 3 Ne. 17:3), teaching us how to participate in the ultimate fulfilling of the Father's covenant with the house of Israel (see 3 Ne. 16:4–5), and teaching us how to endure to the end (see 3 Ne. 12:1).

What a magnificent blueprint for service to others within the framework of the eternal plan of salvation! Studying the Savior's visit to ancient America brings us joy, for it gives us a checklist to follow in fulfilling our own assigned missions in the kingdom of God. We rejoice in bearing testimony. We find happiness in dispensing gifts of an enduring and spiritual nature. We are edified in helping one another to be better people by taking on a divine nature and following in the footsteps of the Savior. We renew our identity as sons and daughters of God and take courage in our divine potential to become heirs of eternal glory through obedience and righteousness. We remind one another of the importance of pondering and praying. We mutually strengthen commitments to honor our covenants. We are grateful for the opportunity to reinforce the principle of enduring to the end. All of this follows the example and teachings of the Savior as unfolded in the pages of the Book of Mormon.

The record of the Savior's visit to America is the heart and soul of the Book of Mormon and one of the most profound statements of spiritual truth available to mankind. The way in which the Savior conducted His visit established for all time a pattern of interaction with others, based on mercy and love—one that we, too, can emulate in our missions as parents, teachers, and leaders in Zion. By striving to use the Savior's model of the visit, we, too, can have a positive and uplifting influence on those around us whom we are called to serve. What a grand legacy to enjoy and pass on to coming generations! The ultimate question for you is this: How are you following the agenda of the Savior's visit in order to make your own presence edifying, enriching, and inspiring?

How Is Our Understanding of Jesus Christ Enhanced through the Study of the Doctrine and Covenants?

The presentation of the person and mission of our Lord Jesus Christ in the Doctrine and Covenants—much of it given directly in His own words—is nothing short of miraculous, proving to the world "that the holy scriptures are true, and that God does inspire men and call them to his holy work in this age and generation, as well as in generations of old; Thereby showing that he is

the same God yesterday, today, and forever" (D&C 20:11–12). The Doctrine and Covenants is thus a testament of the Only Begotten Son in communicating to mortals once again the will of the Father in the form of the Restoration of the fulness of the gospel, with all the priesthood keys, powers, and covenants necessary for the faithful and obedient to return one day to the presence of the Father and the Son.

The Doctrine and Covenants provides a rich and abundant source of saving truths concerning the Lord Jesus Christ, His divine qualities, His sacred mission, and His design and purpose in bringing forth the Restoration in the latter days. It testifies of Him as the Son of God—the Only Begotten of the Father, with whom He is one. It shows that His purpose in bringing about the Restoration in the latter days is to enable the obedient to become sons and daughters of God, to receive the riches of eternity, and to have the blessings of salvation and exaltation.

It was the Prophet Joseph Smith whom the Savior called as His ordained and elect agent in the unfolding of the Restoration. In all of this, Joseph Smith was not the author of the Doctrine and Covenants, but rather the conveyor of the truths of the Almighty. As the Lord reminded Sidney Rigdon, then serving as a scribe for Joseph, "the scriptures shall be given, even as they are in *mine own* bosom, to the salvation of mine own elect" (D&C 35:20; emphasis added). The Lord is thus the Author of the Doctrine and Covenants, according to the will of the Father, with Joseph Smith the spokesperson for Jesus Christ in the dispensation of the fulness of times.

Jesus Christ identifies Himself with clarity and precision through the Prophet Joseph Smith, so that all with ears to hear and eyes to see might come to understand the magnificent blessings shared directly from the Creator and Redeemer as the essence of the Restoration. The words of the Savior in the various sections establish the divine framework for latter-day communication from heaven. The Savior presents Himself in the specific dimensions of His nature and His mission. His presence in the pages of this sacred scripture is pervasive. Here is just one example of the sublime language He uses to introduce Himself to the listening world:

> I AM Alpha and Omega, Christ the Lord; yea, even I am he, the beginning and

the end, the Redeemer of the world.

I, having accomplished and finished the will of him whose I am, even the Father, concerning me—having done this that I might subdue all things unto myself—

Retaining all power, even to the destroying of Satan and his works at the end of the world, and the last great day of judgment, which I shall pass upon the inhabitants thereof, judging every man according to his works and the deeds which he hath done.

And surely every man must repent or suffer, for I, God, am endless. . . .

Learn of me, and listen to my words; walk in the meekness of my Spirit, and you shall have peace in me.

I am Jesus Christ; I came by the will of the Father, and I do his will. (D&C 19:1–4, 23–24)

Of all the standard works, the Doctrine and Covenants gives the most all-encompassing counsel of the Lord, presented in His own words. The book is in effect a direct script of the word of the Lord spoken to the Saints of the latter days. Here is the fundamental question: Have you personally heard the voice of the Lord? This is not such a surprising question, in light of the following: "And I, Jesus Christ, your Lord and your God, have spoken it. These words are not of men nor of man, but of me; wherefore, you shall testify they are of me and not of man; For it is my voice which speaketh them unto you; for they are given by my Spirit unto you, and by my power you can read them one to another; and save it were by my power you could not have them; Wherefore, you can testify that you have heard my voice, and know my words" (D&C 18:33–36).

How Did the Savior Describe the Gospel Plan?

The gospel, or the "good news," is best defined in the Savior's own words: "Behold I have given unto you my gospel, and this is the gospel which I have given unto you—that I came into the world to do the will of my Father, because my Father sent me. And my Father sent me that I might be lifted up upon the cross; and after that I had been lifted up upon the cross, that I might draw all men

unto me, that as I have been lifted up by men even so should men be lifted up by the Father, to stand before me, to be judged of their works, whether they be good or whether they be evil—And for this cause have I been lifted up; therefore, according to the power of the Father I will draw all men unto me, that they may be judged according to their works" (3 Ne. 27:13–15).

The gospel is the foundation of the Church. The doctrine of Christ—encompassing all of the principles and ordinances of the gospel (see 3 Ne. 11:31–41)—is what we accept and apply in order to make the Atonement and the plan of happiness active in our lives. The plan of happiness is known by a variety of titles: plan of redemption, plan of salvation, plan of exaltation, and so forth. What is implied by all of these terms is the all-encompassing plan of our Heavenly Father that Jesus Christ supported in our premortal state—and which we accepted as spirit children of the Father. Our Savior Jesus Christ is the center and pivotal point in the plan as the Creator, Redeemer, and Savior of the world through His infinite Atonement and His glorious Resurrection. If we are obedient to the laws and ordinances of the gospel and kingdom of God, we can partake of the blessings of eternal life, "which gift is the greatest of all the gifts of God" (D&C 14:7).

The Lord provided means to guide the Israelites in their journey out of Egypt and toward the Promised Land: "And the Lord went before them by day; in a pillar of a cloud, to lead them the way; and by night in a pillar of fire, to give them light to go by day and night" (Ex. 13:21). Similarly, He provides for us the light of the gospel and the voice of prophecy so that we might find our way safely back into His presence. His blessings to us today lead us from one milestone to the next in our journey toward spiritual liberation. We have the scriptures, including the Book of Mormon; we have the voice of living prophets to shed light on our condition and provide saving truths; we have the priesthood to provide authorized ordinances of salvation; we have the sealing ordinances of the temple; we have the Holy Spirit to illuminate our souls. Our blessings are overwhelming. Who are the pillars of light in the family? They are the parents of Zion who raise their children in light and truth and remind them always of the goodness of God in the past, the covenants of the present, and the hope of the future through the Atonement of Jesus Christ. How are you a "pillar of light" for your loved ones and neighbors?

How Is Jesus Both Father and Son?

The prophet Abinadi in the Book of Mormon explained the dual titles for the Savior: "The Father, because he was conceived by the power of God; and the Son, because of the flesh; thus becoming the Father and Son—And they are one God, yea, the very Eternal Father of heaven and of earth" (Mosiah 15:3–4). Later, in explaining Isaiah's question about the seed (or "generation") of Christ (see Isa. 53:8), Abinadi identified who that seed should be:

> And now I say unto you, who shall declare his generation? Behold, I say unto you, that when his soul has been made an offering for sin he shall see his seed. And now what say ye? And who shall be his seed?
>
> Behold I say unto you, that whosoever has heard the words of the prophets, yea, all the holy prophets who have prophesied concerning the coming of the Lord—I say unto you, that all those who have hearkened unto their words, and believed that the Lord would redeem his people, and have looked forward to that day for a remission of their sins, I say unto you, that these are his seed, or they are the heirs of the kingdom of God. (Mosiah 15:10–11)

If the Savior should receive "seed" consisting of those who come into His fold and follow the gospel plan, then He is, indeed, the Father by the power of heavenly adoption: "And being made perfect, he became the author of eternal salvation unto all them that obey him" (Heb. 5:9). Jesus put it this way: "the Father and I are one—The Father because he gave me of his fulness, and the Son because I was in the world and made flesh my tabernacle, and dwelt among the sons of men" (D&C 93:3–4). President Joseph Fielding Smith explained:

> Jesus Christ is our Father because he gave us life—eternal life—through his sacrifice. He is the Father because of his everlasting and presiding power—the fulness which he holds as one of the Godhead. He

never did say that he and his Father are the same personage, but always that his Father is greater than he. (See John 14:28, and 1 Cor. 15:27–28.) (Joseph Fielding Smith, *Church History and Modern Revelation*, 2:160)

We often speak of Jesus Christ as our Elder Brother, He being the Son of God, just as we are the children of God. From what perspective can you also say that Jesus is your Father?

Real-life Stories for Heart and Mind

A Solemn Reminder. It was an unusual invitation. The leaders of some two dozen Utah stakes were asked to meet on a particular day at the Manti Utah Temple for a solemn assembly with the First Presidency and other General Authorities. There was much conjecture among those invited concerning the nature and purpose of the meeting. What new policy or doctrinal innovation would require such a solemn gathering? The assembly room of the temple was packed with hundreds of priesthood leaders, all of whom were honored to have the sacrament blessed and passed to them by members of the Quorum of the Twelve and other General Authorities. Then there was rapt silence as the prophet arose, a tall and stately figure of leadership with his silver hair and white suit, and announced the reason he had called the meeting—simply to confirm that Jesus is the Christ, that He lives, and that He is at the head of this work. It was a powerful reminder from President David O. McKay about what is of primary and preeminent importance in this world—the Atonement of Jesus Christ and the reality of His life and mission. All were edified to be thus filled with the word of inspiration. All rejoiced in the compassion of a just Father in Heaven and His Son to have opened the way for the faithful and valiant to return one day to Their holy presence. No one in attendance will ever forget the witness of the Spirit that day that the Savior lives, that His prophet speaks for Him, and that life is indeed full of joy and hope.

The agenda of every meeting of the Church is to strengthen our testimonies of the Savior and His atoning sacrifice. The doctrine is not new; it originated in the halls of glory in the premortal realm and continues to give light and purpose to our lives in mortality and beyond. How can you contribute in your own way to confirm these truths for your own loved ones and those you serve?

Simple Truth. A member of the Church was pleased to accompany her friend to the stand where Ezra Taft Benson, then president of the Quorum of the Twelve, was receiving visitors. He had just spoken to a special gathering of Saints in the area, and the sister wanted her friend to meet him. This young woman had just that day—in the same stake center—been baptized a member of the Church, after many months of learning and being fellowshipped by her friend.

The two stood in line waiting for their turn to meet Elder Benson. When they finally reached the place where the Apostle was standing, the sister greeted him, and then introduced her friend as a new convert. He held the friend's hand and looked her straight in the eye. With a spirit of great kindness, but also soberness and firmness, he said to her, "The gospel is true. If you live it, you will be happy. If you don't, you won't." What a rare blessing for a new convert to hear a personal witness from an Apostle of the Lord and receive such direct and penetrating counsel.

There is no more succinct way to express the essence of the gospel of Jesus Christ than this: "If you live it, you will be happy. If you don't, you won't." In those plain words is a simple truth about agency and the power of the gospel. How can you share this kind of message with your family as well as with others seeking the truth?

How Do You Know the Savior Loves You? One day a husband asked his wife the question, "How do you know the Savior loves you?" She responded without hesitation: "Because there is so much love in the world imparted by God's children one to another."

We are "children of the prophets" and "children of the covenant," to use the Lord's expressions (see 3 Ne. 20:25–26). As such, we partake of the divine nature through obedience and humility, and thus have the innate potential of showing love to others. This love, displayed for all with eyes to see and hearts to feel, is evidence of the love of the Savior for us. It cannot be denied, for we are His children. Look around. See charity

being shown on all sides by good people, and know that this is a witness that the Savior loves you, just as He loves us all.

Pondering Prayerfully

Additional scriptures to consider and ponder:
- 3 Ne. 18:24
- D&C 45:3–5
- D&C 76:40–42

The following hymns bring to mind the mission of our Savior and Redeemer:
- "Abide with Me!" (*Hymns*, 166)
- "How Great the Wisdom and the Love" (*Hymns*, 195)
- "I Need Thee Every Hour" (*Hymns*, 98)
- "Jesus, the Very Thought of Thee" (*Hymns*, 141)
- "Rock of Ages" (*Hymns*, 111)
- "The Lord Is My Light" (*Hymns*, 89)

Remember and Be Sure

Heavenly Father's plan of happiness—centered in His Beloved Son, our Savior Jesus Christ—constitutes His work and His glory. This divine and eternal plan embraces man's existence and His eternal destiny. Let us make it our lifetime study and our enduring manner of living to conform to the plan of happiness—for obedience to this plan will bring us eternal life, a state of never-ending joy and happiness (see Mosiah 2:41). Through scripture study, prayer, worship, temple attendance, and righteousness we will come to know and understand the beauty and the power of the plan of happiness in our lives.

The fullness of the gospel was restored in these the latter days. The gospel of Jesus Christ is the foundation of the Church and kingdom of God. The Atonement of Jesus Christ is the core of the gospel. All things in the plan of salvation are centered in Jesus Christ. This is why "we talk of Christ, we rejoice in Christ, we preach of Christ, we prophesy of Christ, and we write according to our prophecies, that our children may know to what source they may look for a remission of their sins" (2 Ne. 25:26). We live the gospel as we practice its first four principles and ordinances: faith (in Jesus Christ), repentance (through Jesus Christ), baptism (by means of which we take upon ourselves the name of Jesus Christ), and the gift of the Holy Ghost from the Father (because of the atoning sacrifice of Jesus Christ)—plus enduring to the end. It is our duty to live the gospel and take it unto all the world.

The Lord has never left us alone, but has been constant in providing us direction through His light, His word (the gospel of Jesus Christ), and the Holy Spirit. On a personal basis, our Savior has been more explicit: "And whoso receiveth you, there I will be also, for I will go before your face. I will be on your right hand and on your left, and my Spirit shall be in your hearts, and mine angels round about you, to bear you up" (D&C 84:88). He not only goes before us, He pays for our sins, nurtures us, and comforts us in all things (see Alma 7:11–12). If we but look, we can clearly see His light. He is the life and light of the world (see D&C 6:21; 10:70). And when we have our eye single to the glory of our Father, our whole body will be filled with light, and we will be able to comprehend all things (see D&C 88:67). Truly the light of the Lord and the truths of the gospel plan can and will direct us in our lives.

CHAPTER 4
Agency as a Divine Gift: Consequences of Choice

There is the principle of God in every individual. It is designed that man should act as God, and not be constrained and controlled in everything, but have an independency, an agency and the power to spread abroad and act according to the principle of godliness that is in him, act according to the power and intelligence and enlightenment of God, that he possesses, and not that he should be watched continually, and be controlled, and act as a slave in these matters. —Lorenzo Snow (*JD* 20:367)

Opening the Window of Wisdom

In the premortal realm, Heavenly Father decreed that His children would be blessed with the gift of agency—the right to choose for themselves how to act. Only by learning to use agency in wise and spiritual ways, consistent with eternal principles of righteousness, would they become like their Maker. That right continues here on earth, for the Lord taught Adam and Eve to obey His commandments, but always in the context of agency: "nevertheless, thou mayest choose for thyself, for it is given unto thee" (Moses 3:17). Lehi taught his children the same principle—that they could choose liberty and eternal life or captivity and death:

Wherefore, men are free according to the flesh; and all things are given them which are expedient unto man. And they are free to choose liberty and eternal life, through the great Mediator of all men, or to choose captivity and death, according to the captivity and power of the devil; for he seeketh that all men might be miserable like unto himself. (2 Ne. 2:27)

The greatest example of obedience in the context of agency is the Savior, who, in perfect and humble submission to the will of the Father, offered Himself as Redeemer. To follow the Lord valiantly, we too can submit humbly to God's will throughout our mortal probation, just as we chose to do in the premortal realm. Our governing principle is this: "What would Jesus do?"

Agency is a free gift. The right to choose is an eternal truth that is necessary for our growth. We are a result of the use of our agency. Our choices and decisions determine the consequences of our actions—whether blessings and joy or pain and suffering. Agency can operate because there is opposition in all things, we have knowledge of good and evil, God has given laws and commandments, and we have freedom to choose. Recognizing these elements of agency gives us perspective to choose righteousness, for it magnifies our spiritual strength in the face of opposition and it leads to happiness and eternal life. This free gift is moral agency, which connotes responsibility and accountability in regard to our choices.

Agency was at the heart of the conflict that took place before this life. Satan sought to destroy our will by insisting that his way would save all—there would be forced obedience, and no free will. Satan demanded of the Father: "Behold, here am I, send me, I will be thy son, and I will redeem all mankind, that one soul shall not be lost, and surely I will do it; wherefore give me thine honor" (Moses 4:1). Instead, the Father chose Jesus to carry out His plan: "But, behold, my Beloved Son, which was my Beloved and Chosen from the beginning, said unto me—Father, thy will be done, and the glory be thine forever" (Moses 4:2). Thus Satan was cast out and consigned to darkness and eventual oblivion.

Now Satan and his minions use subtle tactics to thwart the wise use of agency, telling us that our choices don't really matter—sin a little, and you will still be saved. The truth is: we are what we choose to be. Our Savior Jesus Christ has already done His part and continues to bless us. It is now truly up to us. All good comes from the Godhead, with the Holy Ghost guiding us through personal revelation and comfort (see 2 Ne. 32:5). We show our love by doing the will of our Father—even as the Lord Jesus Christ. Our life is determined not by an accident and chance, but by choice.

Inspired by Latter-Day Prophets

Brigham Young: All rational beings have an agency of their own; and according to their own choice they will be saved or damned. . . . [God] has placed life and death before his children, and it is for them to choose. If they choose life, they receive the blessing of life; if they choose death, they must abide the penalty. This is a law which has always existed from all eternity, and will continue to exist throughout all the eternities to come (*Discourses of Brigham Young*, 62).

We have the right to make moral choices—but not the right to determine consequences. How can you teach this principle to your loved ones in a day and age of relative morality—where unwise role models preach that you can get away with anything?

Joseph F. Smith: If there is one principle of the gospel of Jesus Christ that goes directly to the very foundation of justice and righteousness, it is that great and glorious and God-like principle that every man will have to render an account for that which he does, and every man will be rewarded for his works, whether they be good or evil (*Improvement Era*, Vol. 21, p. 104).

Accountability is an eternal principle that impacts every moment of our lives, for blessings are given or withheld based on our ongoing decisions. When you pray with your family and ask for the Lord's blessings, how can you include references to accountability and the need for strength and guidance to do the Lord's will?

Joseph Fielding Smith: If our Eternal Father refused to permit evil to exist in the world, he would destroy one of the greatest gifts ever given to man—the gift of free agency. Take this great gift away and there could be no rewards or punishments; no exaltation and no condemnation. The result would be chaos, confusion. This is indeed the very plan that Lucifer presented in the great council in heaven. It is absolutely necessary to permit evil as well as it is necessary to reward good. Without the great gift of free agency, heaven would be destroyed and hell and Satan would gain the victory. There is a divine law that will bring rewards and punishment (*Answers to Gospel Questions*, 3:125).

During oppression and adversity, we often question how God could allow evils and tribulations to abound. Think of the challenges you and your family may currently be facing, and find ways to thank Heavenly Father for the opportunity granted to His children to choose their response by honoring His will in faith and devotion.

Spencer W. Kimball: If all the sick for whom we pray were healed, if all the righteous were protected and the wicked destroyed, the whole program of the Father would be annulled and the basic principle of the gospel, free agency, would be ended. No man would have to live by faith. If joy and peace and rewards were instantaneously given the doer of good, there could be no evil—all would do good but not because of the rightness of doing good. There would be no test of strength, no development of character, no growth of powers, no free agency, only satanic controls (*Faith Precedes the Miracle*, 97).

Growth comes with patience and faith. Strength comes through courage in the face of adversity. We expand our spiritual horizons by choosing to do so—no matter what the circumstances of mortality. How have you been strengthened by your experiences in life?

Truths to Liken

Josh. 24:14–15—"Now therefore fear the LORD, and serve him in sincerity and in truth: and put away the gods which your fathers served on the other side of the flood, and in Egypt; and serve ye the LORD. And if it seem evil unto you to serve the LORD, choose you this day whom ye will serve; whether the gods which your fathers served that were on the other side of the flood, or the gods of the Amorites, in whose land ye dwell: but as for me and my house, we will serve the LORD."

- After Joshua led the Israelites into the Promised Land following their long sojourn in the wilderness, he confirmed for them the principle of agency, counseling them to serve the Lord according to his example.
- In your decision-making and family councils, how can you use Joshua's example to reinforce the wise use of agency with full energy of soul?

2 Ne. 2:15–16—"And to bring about his eternal purposes in the end of man, after he had created our first parents, and the beasts of the field and the fowls of the air, and in fine, all things which are created, it must needs be that there was an opposition; even the forbidden fruit in opposition to the tree of life; the one being sweet and the other bitter. Wherefore, the Lord God gave unto man that he should act for himself. Wherefore, man could not act for himself save it should be that he was enticed by the one or the other."

- Lehi taught Jacob the doctrine of agency, which requires opposition as the catalyst to making wise decisions.

- Without opposition, trials, and temptation, we would be unable to exercise our agency and progress toward eternal life. How does this help you to gain perspective on the challenges, tribulations, and temptations that occur in your life from time to time? How can you follow the example of Lehi in teaching your own loved ones the principle of using agency wisely?

Alma 34:32–33—"For behold, this life is the time for men to prepare to meet God; yea, behold the day of this life is the day for men to perform their labors. And now, as I said unto you before, as ye have had so many witnesses, therefore, I beseech of you that ye do not procrastinate the day of your repentance until the end; for after this day of life, which is given us to prepare for eternity, behold, if we do not improve our time while in this life, then cometh the night of darkness wherein there can be no labor performed."

- Amulek, Alma's missionary companion, taught the Zoramites about the plan of salvation, encouraging them to take decisive action to mend their ways and come into the fold of Christ.
- We never know when our time will come to return home to our Heavenly Father. *This* is the time and place to repent. Our earthly probation is limited and determined by our Father, and if we procrastinate our repentance and seek instead earthly pleasures and worldly pursuits, we make our destruction sure (see Hel. 13:38). If you or your family members have procrastinated or delayed wise decisions and actions, how can you follow the counsel of Amulek by moving forward with full heart and courage to do better?

D&C 101:78—"That every man may act in doctrine and principle pertaining to futurity, according to the moral agency which I have given unto him, that every man may be accountable for his own sins in the day of judgment."

- These are the words of the Lord given through the Prophet Joseph Smith at

Kirtland, Ohio, December 16, 1833, at a time when the Saints in Missouri were suffering great persecutions.

- Moral agency dictates that we are accountable for our actions. We will be judged by our actions by Christ, who is our judge and the Keeper of the Gate (see 2 Ne. 9:41). We should have a great desire to keep His commandments, knowing that we must look into His face and knowing that He paid the price for our sins. With this knowledge, how can you teach the principle of accountability with greater effectiveness in your family and Church assignments?

Moses 4:3—"Wherefore, because that Satan rebelled against me, and sought to destroy the agency of man, which I, the Lord God, had given him, and also, that I should give unto him mine own power; by the power of mine Only Begotten, I caused that he should be cast down."

- The Lord taught Moses about the first great rebellion in the premortal realm; these words explain why Satan was cast out.
- In the strength of the Lord we can learn to make wise decisions so we will not be cast out like the satanic hosts. We can learn to detect and avoid the devious ways of Satan (see 2 Ne. 28:7–9; Alma 12:4; 3 Ne. 2:2; Moses 4:4), protecting our moral agency and preserving a righteous way of life. How can you help your loved ones detect and avoid harmful influences?

Rejoicing and Reasoning Together

What Compass Does the Lord Provide to Every Soul as a Resource for Agency?

The prophet Moroni gave us this inspired counsel from his father, Mormon, which teaches us how to be a child of Christ:

For behold, the Spirit of Christ is given to every man, that he may know good from evil; wherefore, I show unto you the way to judge; for every thing which inviteth to do good, and to persuade to believe in Christ, is sent forth by the power and gift of Christ;

wherefore ye may know with a perfect knowledge it is of God.

But whatsoever thing persuadeth men to do evil, and believe not in Christ, and deny him, and serve not God, then ye may know with a perfect knowledge it is of the devil; for after this manner doth the devil work, for he persuadeth no man to do good, no, not one; neither do his angels; neither do they who subject themselves unto him.

And now, my brethren, seeing that ye know the light by which ye may judge, which light is the light of Christ, see that ye do not judge wrongfully; for with that same judgment which ye judge ye shall also be judged.

Wherefore, I beseech of you, brethren, that ye should search diligently in the light of Christ that ye may know good from evil; and if ye will lay hold upon every good thing, and condemn it not, ye certainly will be a child of Christ. (Moro. 7:16–19; compare D&C 84:45–47)

These remarkable words define with precision what we refer to as our *conscience*. President David O. McKay stated: "The first condition of happiness is a clear conscience. No man who does wrong or who is unvirtuous will be happy. No unvirtuous woman can ever be happy unless . . . she fully repents. Uprightness of character, honesty in dealing with your fellowmen, honor bright, your word as good as your bond, then when your head touches your pillow at night, and you contemplate your actions during the day, you sleep with a good conscience" (*Gospel Ideals: Selections from the Discourses of David O. McKay*, 498). President Spencer W. Kimball advised: "Conscience stirs up a desire to repent. How wonderful that God should endow us with this sensitive yet strong guide we call a conscience! Someone has aptly remarked that 'conscience is a celestial spark which God has put into every man for the purpose of saving his soul'" (*The Teachings of Spencer W. Kimball*, 86).

Conscience is the light of Christ, a moral sense that helps us determine right from wrong and then influences us to do that which is morally right. We all have that voice within, but sometimes there is so much noise in our lives that we can't hear its counsel. Alternately, when we listen intently to the voice of our conscience and follow it, we are guided into pathways that bring us closer to our Father in Heaven and His Beloved Son.

What can we do to become more sensitive to our conscience and then to obey it? Everyone is born with a conscience, because everyone has the light of Christ. We know right from wrong. The only question is how we will use our agency. Our duty is to search our conscience and then have the courage to obey it, overcoming the temptations of the devil. What have you taught your children about the principle of following one's conscience? How can you strengthen your own response to your conscience? Here is a checklist you might find helpful: meditate and ponder frequently; pray always; search the scriptures; urge your mind and heart to listen; walk or exercise regularly; rise early; tap your creative powers; keep a journal; seek wisdom from others; leverage rewards through small, courageous acts; honor first impressions; take extra care in decision-making; practice self-control and discipline; be more loving; savor the peace of conscience.

How Can We Enhance the Power of Our Compass of Conscience?

As we learn to use our conscience effectively, we grow in spiritual strength and stamina. The Lord has reserved a miraculous blessing for those who yearn for higher inspiration and revelation—the whispering of the Holy Ghost and its magnificent gift of baptism of fire. The Holy Ghost enhances our conscience, giving us greater power to choose righteousness (see Rom. 9:1). Nephi taught: "For behold, again I say unto you that if ye will enter in by the way, and receive the Holy Ghost, it will show unto you all things what ye should do" (2 Ne. 32:5). As we search the scriptures, the word of God will nourish our spirit, and the Word of God—even the Savior—will illuminate our pathway, leading back to the presence of our Heavenly Father and His Son.

How has the Holy Ghost been a guide in your life and the lives of your loved ones? How can you enhance the influence of the Holy Ghost in your family circle? The following checklist may provide some helpful examples of how best to understand and apply the principles and doctrines that are necessary for agency to operate under the guidance of the Holy Spirit: see opposition as the key to growth; cultivate an attitude of hope and persistence in the face of opposition; control your environment by placing yourself where the Holy Ghost can feel welcome; follow the Spirit; cultivate a clear understanding of the outcomes of your actions; study the word of God; seek to become grounded in the doctrines of Christ; view the commandments as instruments of liberty; understand the connection between the commandments and happiness; view love as the bridge to obedience; seek the strength of the Spirit; remember to do as Jesus would do; set high standards well ahead of time; pray and fast; remember that ordinances empower us; seek priesthood blessings; ponder on your patriarchal blessing; be obedient in all things.

How Do Agency and Accountability Go Hand in Hand?

We are accountable for all the knowledge and blessings we receive from our Heavenly Father; in addition, we are accountable for our thoughts and desires and actions, beginning at the age of accountability (see D&C 29:47). The gift of moral agency requires this responsibility of all mankind. Blessings or consequences follow—a central part of the plan of salvation. The Articles of Faith confirm this doctrine: "We believe that men will be punished for their own sins, and not for Adam's transgression" (A of F 2). Alma defined the scope of accountability: "For our words will condemn us, yea, all our works will condemn us; we shall not be found spotless; and our thoughts will also condemn us; and in this awful state we shall not dare to look up to our God; and we would fain be glad if we could command the rocks and the mountains to fall upon us to hide us from his presence" (Alma 12:14).

Accountability is a basic tenet of the gospel of Jesus Christ: "for it is required of the Lord, at the hand of every steward, to render an account of his stewardship, both in time and in eternity" (D&C 72:3). Our every deed and action, including our use of time—even our very thoughts—belong to our personal history and will ultimately have to be accounted for. Yet these things unfold as a process, for it takes time to improve and become more responsible and accountable. Every blessing with which the Lord blesses us is part of His eternal investment in our well-being and must inevitably show up in the balance sheet of our life.

Our agency is a God-given gift, without which salvation would not be possible. Because of that gift, and the knowledge and understanding we acquire, we can look forward to a harvest of rich and empowering blessings based on valiant and righteous choices—or a reward of punishment and woe based on unrepentant disobedience. It is up to us.

How can each of us learn to make wise choices within the framework of eternal accountability? You may have your own checklist of helpful answers. Here is a sample checklist to consider: pray regularly; prepare your mind; each time you make a decision, ponder the consequences; choose your governing values in life; keep a journal; study the word of God; remember who you are; listen to the Spirit within; establish an environment for proper decision-making; choose that which edifies; surround yourself with positive reminders; fill leisure hours with uplifting influences; use the sacrament time each week to refresh your commitment to obedience; bear your testimony regularly; make your temple recommend interview and other important interviews a governing rehearsal for life; go to the temple often to experience the process of accounting to our Father in Heaven for all we do; work with others effectively; account to your loved ones for your behavior by expressing your witness of the peace and solace that come from obedience; have the courage to say you are sorry for any missteps and that you are committed to doing better; teach accountability to your children through family counsels and family home evening; praise others for their good work; help others to understand accountability.

What Is the Secret of Gaining Wisdom?

Wisdom is the ability to make wise choices based on truth that is based on the principles of the gospel of Jesus Christ, the foundation for making wise decisions and good choices. We recognize that those who make good choices are enlightened by the light of Christ and inspired by the Holy Ghost. We can and will be wise as we live worthy of the

Holy Ghost, since the Holy Ghost testifies of all truth (see Moro. 10:5) and shows all things we should do (see 2 Ne. 32:5).

Living by the Spirit, then, makes one wise. The Savior taught: "Therefore whosoever heareth these sayings of mine, and doeth them, I will liken him unto a wise man, which built his house upon a rock" (Matt. 7:24). Hearing and knowing is one thing, but wisdom requires action—doing things according to correct principles. We are not just to be hearers of the word, but should be wise "doers of the word" (James 1:22). By so doing, we build upon our Savior Jesus Christ and we will not fall (see Hel. 5:12).

The Prophet Joseph Smith was touched by these words of James: "If any of you lack wisdom, let him ask of God, that giveth to all men liberally, and upbraideth not; and it shall be given him" (James 1:5). By asking, the young Joseph became wise beyond his ability to grasp—for the Father and the Son appeared to him in the grove of trees and placed him at the center of the Restoration of the fulness of the gospel and the kingdom of God. If we want to learn the things of God, we must ask. Asking is a principle with a promise: God will answer our prayers just like He did those of Adam, Enoch, Noah, Abraham, Moses, Joseph, and His Son Jesus Christ.

Do you consider yourself wise? If you want more wisdom, what plan of action will you put into place? Surely you can be a wiser person by gaining knowledge based on truth and exercising your judgment based on sound principles. You have the power to make good decisions. When you follow the light of Christ and the Holy Spirit, you will gain wisdom as you are directed by the Spirit.

Real-life Stories for Heart and Mind

When You Do His Will. A young and enthusiastic father and husband sat in the bishop's office. It was his first time at the meetinghouse since his family had joined the Church, and he was seeking counsel about a principle of the gospel new to him—tithing. "Bishop," he said, "I believe in tithing, but our family budget is so tight that if I paid my tithing right now, there would not be enough left over for food." In response, the bishop opened the scriptures and reviewed with him the wonderful promise in Malachi where the

Lord invites us to "prove him" with respect to this principle, and determine "if I will not open you the windows of heaven, and pour you out a blessing, that there shall not be room enough to receive it" (Mal. 3:10). The bishop looked him in the eye and asked, "Do you have the faith to do the Lord's will?" The young father swallowed hard and then replied, in all sincerity, that he would go and do what the Lord commanded. The bishop then promised him that the Lord would bless him for it. The young father smiled, shook hands with the bishop, and left the office.

The following Sunday he came back for another conversation, even more enthusiastic than the previous week. "You will not believe what happened this past week," he said. "The principal of the school where I teach physical education came to me and gave me a raise—equal exactly to the tithing I paid the Lord!" That young father went on to grow in the gospel grace upon grace, line upon line, until not too many years later he became the bishop of that same ward. The Lord blesses those who do His will. "I, the Lord, am bound when ye do what I say; but when ye do not what I say, ye have no promise" (D&C 82:10).

Does the Lord always repay tithing contributions in kind—or are there occasions where doors are opened and opportunities identified so that the faithful steward can take care of temporal obligations using wise and productive choices? How have you been blessed in your life for having used your agency to keep the commandments of the Lord?

Don't Do It! A young man had been taught by his widowed mother to live by high principles, including never taking anything harmful into his body. He had promised her and his Heavenly Father that he would never do anything to hurt her or bring shame to her, and it was a promise that was sealed in his mind and heart. When he was in high school, his football team won an important game, and he and the other players were gathered at a friend's house to celebrate. One of the guests challenged everyone to take a sip from a bottle of sherry cooking wine that he had discovered in the kitchen. As the players started to take their sips, something in the heart and mind of the widow's son said, "Don't do it." Filled with boldness, he told them, "Don't do it." They responded that one little drink wouldn't hurt. He told them no, and that if they insisted on taking the drinks, he would leave the party. "Go ahead," they chided. "We don't like babies anyway." The young man left, disappointed in their standards and lack of concern for a supposed friend. As he walked home, a good feeling came over him. He had listened to his conscience, and it had saved him from disappointing his mother. The memory lingered on—choose the right and let the consequences follow. Obeying his conscience brought peace to his soul.

Which of your experiences have confirmed to your heart and mind that following the promptings of your conscience will bring great blessings?

The Title of Liberty. One of the inspiring stories in the Book of Mormon relates how Captain Moroni, leader of the Nephite forces, galvanized his nation into taking up the cause of liberty in the face of dire threats from evil power-seekers: "And it came to pass that he rent his coat; and he took a piece thereof, and wrote upon it—In memory of our God, our religion, and freedom, and our peace, our wives, and our children—and he fastened it upon the end of a pole. And he fastened on his head-plate, and his breastplate, and his shields, and girded on his armor about his loins; and he took the pole, which had on the end thereof his rent coat, (and he called it the title of liberty) and he bowed himself to the earth, and he prayed mightily unto his God for the blessings of liberty to rest upon his brethren, so long as there should a band of Christians remain to possess the land" (Alma 46:12–13). Because of Moroni's courage and leadership, the Nephites prevailed over their enemies: "And those who were faithful in keeping the commandments of the Lord were delivered at all times, whilst thousands of their wicked brethren have been consigned to bondage, or to perish by the sword, or to dwindle in unbelief, and mingle with the Lamanites. But behold there never was a happier time among the people of Nephi, since the days of Nephi, than in the days of Moroni" (Alma 50:22–23).

In what ways can you emulate Captain Moroni in your own stewardship with family and Church members by raising or applying a "title of liberty" of your own that will help people make important choices in support of the Lord's cause?

Pondering Prayerfully

Additional scriptures to consider and ponder:
- Rom. 9:1
- James 1:22
- 2 Ne. 9:41
- Hel. 5:12
- Hel. 13:38
- D&C 6:7
- D&C 136:31–33

The following hymns help us understand agency and wise choices:
- "Choose the Right" (*Hymns,* 239)
- "Do What Is Right" (*Hymns,* 237)
- "I'll Go Where You Want Me to Go" (*Hymns,* 270)
- "Teach Me to Walk in the Light" (*Hymns,* 304)

Remember and Be Sure

Of all of our blessings, the freedom to choose and act is one of the most cherished. Heavenly Father ordained it so because He loves us and seeks only our eternal life and happiness. Our choices can bring us eternal joy and glory through the Atonement of the Lord Jesus Christ.

We can use our agency wisely by responding to the light of Christ (see Moro. 7:15–17) and living by the Spirit (see 2 Ne. 32:5). We can act with moral courage to uphold the principles of the gospel and raise our own "Title of Liberty" to motivate others to join with us in building the kingdom of God and enhancing spiritual liberation.

Each of us has the power to make good decisions. As the Lord declared: "Verily I say, men should be anxiously engaged in a good cause, and do many things of their own free will, and bring to pass much righteousness; For the power is in them, wherein they are agents unto themselves. And inasmuch as men do good they shall in nowise lose their reward" (D&C 58:27–28). We have the promise of great joy in *choosing the right,* yet also the warning of potentially great sorrow in *not choosing the right.* This includes passively failing to act when action on principle is called for.

The use of agency can unleash the exalting power of the Atonement or suspend these heavenly blessings when we make poor choices and then fail to repent. We become what we are through our choices. Every choice has its consequences. In the strength of the Lord we can make an inviolable commitment to meet the challenges of life head-on with courage and in keeping with covenant principles of righteousness. That is the pathway of wisdom and glory.

CHAPTER 5
The Creative Process

The Lord never created this world at random; he has never done any of His work at random. The earth was created for certain purposes; and one of these purposes was its final redemption, and the establishment of his government and kingdom upon it in the latter days, to prepare it for the reign of the Lord Jesus Christ.
—Wilford Woodruff (*JD* 15:8)

Opening the Window of Wisdom

At the end of the six-day creative process, the Creator proclaimed, "And, behold, all things which I had made were very good" (Moses 2:31). The Agent of the Creation under the direction of the Father was Jesus Christ: "And there stood one among them that was like unto God, and he said unto those who were with him; We will go down, for there is space there, and we will take of these materials, and we will make an earth whereon these may dwell" (Abr. 3:24). Looking at the Creation from the Lord's perspective, we can see the grand scope and the divine goodness of the plan of life, and can appreciate our world as a manifestation of the power and glory of God at work.

The Creation provided an environment where agency could prevail. From the very beginning, it was God's purpose to give us the right to choose, based on His law and in accordance with the consequences thereof. This earth is therefore a probationary state: "And we will prove them herewith, to see if they will do all things whatsoever the Lord their God shall command them" (Abr. 3:25). Because we know our divine parentage, we can humbly set our course as a quest to become perfect, even as our Father and His Son are perfect (see Matt. 5:48; 3 Ne. 12:48). The Creation bears the indelible signature of the Creators—the Father of all goodness and His Son, Jesus Christ, who has charge of the heavenly light of life. The Creation is perfect; the plan behind it is perfect; and the majestic ebb and flow of life attest to the perfection of it all.

Inspired by Latter-Day Prophets

James E. Talmage: Every created thing has been made for a purpose; and everything that fills the measure of its creation is to be advanced in the scale of progression, be it an atom or a world . . . or man—the direct and literal offspring of Deity (*Jesus the Christ*, 299).

It is natural to think of the Creation as something "out there"—the earth in all its splendor. But the Creation is also you—and all other mortals as children of our Father in Heaven. In fact, from your perspective, the Creation is essentially you, and therefore is something "in here," something present to your innate senses and perceptions. How can you fill the measure of your creation? What is that measure? What is the index that will confirm the success of your creation, your being, your destiny?

Mark E. Petersen: The special creation of this earth was a vital part of the plan of salvation. It had a particular purpose. It was no afterthought. Neither was it an accident of any proportion, nor a spontaneous development of any kind. It was the result of deliberate, advance planning and purposeful creation. The Divine Architect devised it. The Almighty Creator made it and assigned to it a particular mission ("Creator and Savior," *Ensign*, May 1983, 63).

The Creation is a core aspect of our testimony of Deity, for as Alma said to the rebel Korihor, the earth is a witness of the reality of God: "even the earth, and all things that are upon the face of it, yea, and its motion, yea, and also all the planets which move in their regular form do witness that there is a Supreme Creator" (Alma 30:44). How can you use your influence in this godless world to confirm the truth that the earth itself is no accident, but a majestic testimony of the divine purposes of God to bring about our joy and happiness, now and in the eternities?

Ezra Taft Benson: Jesus Christ was and is the *Lord God Omnipotent.* (See Book of Mormon, Mosiah 3:5.) He was chosen before He was born. He was the all-powerful Creator of the heavens and the earth. He is the source of life and light to all things. His word is the law by which all things are governed in the universe. All things created and made by Him are subject to His infinite power (*Come unto Christ*, 128).

The great Elohim delegated the governing office for the unfolding design of the plan of salvation and exaltation to His Only Begotten Son. That is why we are commanded to do all things in the name of the Son, for He is the Creator, the Redeemer, the "author of eternal salvation" (Heb. 5:9), and "the light and the life of the world" (3 Ne. 9:18). How can you help your family and loved ones look upon the Savior as this light of power and perfection?

Truths to Liken

John 1:1–4—"IN the beginning was the Word, and the Word was with God, and the Word was God. The same was in the beginning with God. All things were made by him; and without him was not any thing made that was made. In him was life; and the life was the light of men."

- At the beginning of John's gospel, he laid down the framework for all creative enterprise in the universe, teaching us that it comes exclusively through the power and light of the Word of God, Jesus Christ.
- In general, the world considers Jesus to have been a great teacher and thinker. But He is infinitely more than that: He is the Creator of all things under the Father, and the Source of life and light for all mankind. What are some ways you might bear witness of the majesty and divinity of the Savior so that more people will come to know Him for who He is—the only name under heaven whereby eternal life can be received (see 2 Ne. 31:21; Moses 6:52)?

Col. 1:12–13, 16–17—"Giving thanks unto the Father . . . Who hath . . . translated us into the kingdom of his dear Son. . . . For by him were all things created, that are in heaven, and that are in earth, visible and invisible, whether they be thrones, or dominions, or principalities, or powers: all things were created by him, and for him: And he is before all things, and by him all things consist."

- Paul taught the Colossians about the role of Jesus as Creator and Redeemer.
- Gratitude for the mission and work of the Savior is essential if faith is to unfold and spiritual growth is to take place. How can you cultivate more gratitude for the Savior in your family circle and among your network of friends?

Rev. 4:11—"Thou art worthy, O Lord, to receive glory and honour and power: for thou hast created all things, and for thy pleasure they are and were created."

- The Apostle John was shown a vision of the celestialized world, a place and time in which all things worship the Almighty.
- The "pleasure" of the Lord consists of His joy and glory in bringing to pass the immortality and eternal life of the children of God (see Moses 1:39). What is the nature of your "pleasure" (joy, satisfaction) as you participate in building up the kingdom of God?

2 Ne. 2:14–15—"There is a God, and he hath created all things, both the heavens and the earth, and all things that in them are, both things to act and things to be acted upon. And to bring about his eternal purposes in the end of man."

- Lehi taught his sons about the purpose of the Creation and the grand plan of happiness for mankind.
- Lehi continually testified to his children about the reality of God and the plan of redemption, something we can greatly admire. How would you describe your own program for instructing your children and those for whom you have a responsibility as teacher and mentor?

Moses 1:33—"And worlds without number have I created . . . and by the Son I created them, which is mine Only Begotten."

- Moses learned on the mount that the Savior is the steward of all life, under the Father, being both Creator and Redeemer, the beginning and the end.
- The scope of the Creation extends beyond just this earth, for the Creator has organized worlds without number (see D&C 76:2; 93:10). The mind of man cannot conceive the endless scope of the Creation and the infinite power and grace of both the Father and the Son in caring for all of God's children. But during this very hour, you can focus on doing the work of the Lord to bless the lives of those within your own stewardship.

D&C 88:17–20—"And the redemption of the soul is through him that quickeneth all things, in whose bosom it is decreed that the poor and the meek of the earth shall inherit it. Therefore, it must needs be sanctified from all unrighteousness, that it may be prepared for the celestial glory; For after it hath filled the measure of its creation, it shall be crowned with glory, even with the presence of God the Father; That bodies who are of the celestial kingdom may possess it forever and ever; for, for this intent was it made and created, and for this intent are they sanctified."

- This was part of a revelation given through the Prophet Joseph Smith at Kirtland, Ohio, in December 1832 and January 1833. The revelation was subsequently designated as the "'olive leaf' . . . plucked from the Tree of Paradise, the Lord's message of peace to us" (*HC* 1:302–312).
- The creative process is still underway, for the earth has not yet completed the final phase of its creation, when it will be celestialized as the home for those who have attained celestial glory. Meanwhile, you might ask yourself: *What do I still need to do to "celestialize" my own home—to carry on the process of making it a more peaceful haven for the Spirit of the Lord as my loved ones and I prepare for the day when the Savior will return and the millennial reign will begin?*

Rejoicing and Reasoning Together

What Is Meant by the Spiritual Creation?

Concerning the Creation, the Lord told Moses:

> For I, the Lord God, created all things, of which I have spoken, spiritually, before they were naturally upon the face of the earth. For I, the Lord God, had not caused it to rain upon the face of the earth. And I, the Lord God, had created all the children of men; and not yet a man to till the ground; for in heaven created I them; and there was not yet flesh upon the earth, neither in the water, neither in the air; . . .
>
> And I, the Lord God, formed man from the dust of the ground, and breathed into his nostrils the breath of life; and man became a living soul, the first flesh upon

the earth, the first man also; nevertheless, all things were before created; but spiritually were they created and made according to my word. (Moses 3:5, 7)

We know that we were first created as literal spirit children of God before we received mortal tabernacles. We also know that God conceives all things before they become reality: "Now, if there be two things, one above the other, and the moon be above the earth, then it may be that a planet or a star may exist above it; and there is nothing that the Lord thy God shall take in his heart to do but what he will do it" (Abr. 3:17). It seems, then, that the spiritual creation has two aspects: one of setting forth the spiritual blueprint by which all things are to emerge, and the other comprising the literal creation of the spirit of real beings—beings that will in due time receive a mortal frame of existence in keeping with the grand design of God.

Though we do not understand all things concerning the Creation, we can ask our Heavenly Father to help us cultivate our own creative powers in order to become better servants in the kingdom of Heaven. Considering the magnificent statement that "there is nothing that the Lord thy God shall take in his heart to do but what he will do it" (Abr. 3:17), how can you strengthen your resolve to make your inner thoughts and desires align more closely with those of the Father and the Son? How can you become more productive in the cause of Zion by cultivating such thoughts and desires? What God thinks happens. That is a grand operating principle to emulate in your own life.

What Lessons Concerning Stewardship Can We Learn from the Creation?

Heavenly Father delegated the Creation, part of the plan of happiness, to His Only Begotten Son, assisted by other noble spirits—including Michael, to be known later as Adam (see D&C 27:11). This doctrine of stewardship is vital for the growth and development of the children of God. Heavenly Father loves us so much that He allows us to act for Him in His great work. In all stewardship service, the servant is responsible and accountable to the Master or priesthood leader. Here on earth we are constantly giving an accounting to our leaders for our well-being and the status of our assignments—both in the family as well as in the body of the Church.

As children of God, we stand in awe of the knowledge that this earth was created specifically as a mortal home for us. This truth should fill us with humble gratitude to our Father in Heaven for His eternal love. When we take the time to savor the grandeur of the Creation and return thanks to our Heavenly Father for the beauties of this world that He has prepared for us, we can ask ourselves, "What is our responsibility toward the Creation?" As Adam and Eve were given "dominion" over the earth (see Gen. 1:26; Moses 2:26, 28; Abr. 4:26, 28), we see that taking care of this earth is truly our responsibility and privilege. What can we do as faithful stewards to ensure that the natural resources around us are used wisely and with the spirit of thanksgiving?

Should we not take time to teach our children and others to express gratitude to God for these blessings and raise our voices in praise and rejoicing for this world of beauty? Knowing that heaven is the throne of God, should we not also honor the earth as His footstool (see Isa. 66:1; Acts 7:49; Abr. 2:7)?

Every individual has a stewardship in the kingdom of God (see D&C 104:11). Every individual is endowed with gifts, talents, light, and energy that enable him or her to perform creative deeds for the cause of Zion. You do not "create" the earth after the pattern of the Savior, but you do "create" a segment of the earth in the form of your stewardship in Zion—your home, your garden, your family circle, your area of service in the Church, your vineyard of good deeds on behalf of others, your temple and family history contributions, and much more. How can you enhance your "creativity" in the name of Jesus Christ and thereby be a valiant steward in His army? How can you teach the principles of creative stewardship to your loved ones and other "fellowcitizens with the saints, and of the household of God" (Eph. 2:19)? Following is a set of guidelines that may be helpful in answering such questions:

• Do you realize the goodness and mercy of God in creating this earth for you—a

place to dwell and prove yourself worthy to return to His presence (see Abr. 3:25)?

- Do you recognize His hand in all things?
- Do you drink in the beauty of the earth—the majesty of the mountains, the charm and delicacy of the flowers, the animals in all their varieties, the breathtaking fascination of the sky, the waters in all their expressions from the early morning dew to the grand and glorious waterfalls?
- Do you "dress" this garden and "keep it" (Gen. 2:15; Moses 3:15; Abr. 5:11)?
- Do you take good care of the earth and show enduring respect for its divine Creator?
- Are you kind and gentle to animals?
- As you become aware of all the glorious blessings given you through the Creation, do you feel closer to your Heavenly Father?
- Do you show gratitude and love for Heavenly Father by keeping the commandments, living the gospel, and enduring to the end?
- If you do these things, then the eternal purposes of your Heavenly Father and your Savior will not be in vain, but will bear fruit—the perfection of the sons and daughters of God.

Is Jesus Christ the Savior of Other Worlds?

The Doctrine and Covenants gives a clear answer to this question: "HEAR, O ye heavens, and give ear, O earth, and rejoice ye inhabitants thereof, for the Lord is God, and beside him there is no Savior" (D&C 76:1). We learn, furthermore, "that by him, and through him, and of him, the worlds are and were created, and the inhabitants thereof are begotten sons and daughters unto God" (D&C 76:24). The saving and redeeming influence of Jesus Christ extends to all the worlds He has created. In his poem "A Vision," the Prophet Joseph Smith recaptured the essence of this principle in even more specific language:

> By him, of him, and through him, the worlds were all made,
> Even all that career in the heavens so broad,
> Whose inhabitants, too, from the first to the last,

Are sav'd by the very same Saviour of ours;
And, of course, are begotten God's daughters and sons,
By the very same truths, and the very same pow'rs. (*Times and Seasons*, 4:83)

Thus in all the expanse of the universe of multiple worlds—"And worlds without number have I created" (Moses 1:33)—Jesus Christ is both Creator as well as Savior.

We are awed at the majesty of the Savior's grace and power as the Savior of the world, but the thought of Him being the Savior of worlds without number gives us even greater reason for reverence and worshipful admiration. How can you, as one of the sons or daughters of God, convey to your loved ones in greater measure the splendor and dignity of Jesus Christ as the Redeemer of all? How grateful we should be that the Father and the Son have allowed us to peek through the window of the Creation and gain even an inkling of the vast, endless reach of the power and glory of the Godhead. How humbled we should be to know that we have been created "in the image of God" (Gen. 1:27; see also Moses 2:26), with the potential to become even as He is.

Why Is Our Knowledge of the Details of the Creation So Limited?

Moses and Abraham were granted visionary insight into the creative process, as recorded in the history of the Creation of heaven and earth. We learn from the Hebrew that the word *create* refers to "organize" (see Abr. 4:27, 31). Matter has always existed. The earth and firmament were organized in six periods of time from matter that already existed. The Creation was concluded in the crowning moment when Adam and Eve were placed here upon the earth. We don't yet know the details of how the Creation happened. We are finite mortals, and as such we wouldn't be able to comprehend such encompassing truth: "For my thoughts are not your thoughts, neither are your ways my ways, saith the LORD. For as the heavens are higher than the earth, so are my ways higher than your ways, and my thoughts than your thoughts" (Isa. 55:8–9). However, the time will come, if we are true and faithful, when all things will be made known to those who honor the oath and covenant of the priesthood (see D&C 84:38; 121:26–32). For now, it is enough to know that the earth in all its splendor and beauty has a singular purpose—to be a place for Heavenly Father's children to live, receive mortal bodies, be tested, and receive all requisite preparations to reside in the celestial kingdom if found worthy. This earth was made for us.

> *We can learn of "languages, tongues, and people" (D&C 90:15). We can study geology, geography, physics, astronomy, history, and other disciplines to learn "of things both in heaven and in the earth, and under the earth; things which have been, things which are, things which must shortly come to pass; things which are at home, things which are abroad; the wars and the perplexities of the nations, and the judgments which are on the land; and a knowledge also of countries and of kingdoms—" (D&C 88:79). What we need to learn is that which will help us "be prepared in all things when I shall send you again to magnify the calling whereunto I have called you, and the mission with which I have commissioned you" (D&C 88:80). What can you study and learn that will help you prepare more fully for your stewardship in the Church? What can you do to help your loved ones become more fully instructed in those things that are requisite for their service in the kingdom of heaven?*

Real-life Stories for Heart and Mind

The Dandelion. The next time you have a chance, pick up and examine closely a dandelion. It is a homely plant, loathed by those who tend lawns and landscapes. But the Savior created it. There is a bit of glory captured in its simple golden crown. There is something of the flight of majesty in its delicate airborne seedlings. In its own simple way, it testifies plainly and clearly about the Creation and about the abundance of life. It is nothing like the orchid or the rose. But He created it, nevertheless. And it speaks a quiet lesson. We may not value its encroaching presence in our garden, but its aliveness, in and of itself, is a thing of no little beauty to those who can perceive the invisible hand at work in His world. It is, in its own unpretentious way, a tender

reminder that "without him was not anything made that was made" (John 1:3), and that all aspects of the Creation are a witness of God at work.

Perhaps we too, in our own spiritual infancy, in our own nothingness before the perfection of God, seem as dandelions from the higher perspective. Perhaps we too have a little of the crown of glory upon our heads. He created us. And as potential sons and daughters of God, we have within us the potential of flight, of transcendence to a higher level of spirituality where we will ultimately see ourselves truly to be in His own image.

> *Learn to enjoy the simple wonders of the Creation. Teach your loved ones to do the same.*

Water from the Sun. East of Lake Louise in Banff National Park lies Yoho National Park, just over the boundary between Alberta and British Columbia. One of the most spectacular sights in Yoho is Takakkaw Falls, where a free-flowing stream of water plunges some thousand feet over a cliff and into a beautiful Rocky Mountain canyon. The word *Takakkaw* is thought to derive from a Cree word meaning "magnificent." According to legend, the one who first viewed this extraordinary waterfall saw it against a brilliant sky and had the impression that the river was flowing directly out of the sun—and so called it "water from sun."

John Taylor once used the image of a stream and its fountain to explain the essential nature of the infinite Atonement as central to the plan of salvation. "Why did it need an infinite atonement? For the simple reason that a stream can never rise higher than its fountain; . . . A man, as a man, could arrive at all the dignity that a man was capable of obtaining or receiving; but it needed a God to raise him to the dignity of a God" (*The Mediation and Atonement*, 145). The water to which President Taylor referred was "water from the Son," the Son of God—the Creator, Redeemer, and "fountain of living waters" (Jer. 2:13; 17:13). It was He who was the source of the eternal water that would quench forever the thirst for spiritual vitality: "But whosoever drinketh of the water that I shall give him shall never thirst; but the water that I shall give him shall be in him a well of water springing up into everlasting life" (John 4:14).

> *The roadway leading to the fountain of living waters ("water from the Son") is marked by*

many challenges and tribulations. Full access to the breathtaking view afforded by the plan of salvation can be gained only through faith, humility, and obedience to the laws of the journey. One needs to hold constantly to the iron rod that Lehi saw in his dream (see 1 Ne. 8:19–20, 24, 30; 11:25). On the journey toward the living waters (see 1 Ne. 11:25) and the tree of life, our vision needs to be clear and open, "with an eye single to the glory of God" (D&C 4:5). In this manner, the journey becomes joyful—regardless of the barriers and switchbacks of life—and the outcome is worth it, for the reward that awaits the faithful traveler is to experience the satisfaction of the yearning for salvation, the ultimate attainment of the source of the stream—the Son of God, the Redeemer, the Holy One of Israel. It is not water from the sun that truly matters—but water from the Son. What can you do to improve your course of action as you travel the pathway leading to water from the Son? What can you do to help your loved ones reach the thirst-quenching water from the Son and thereby fill the measure of their creation and find their way back home again to the presence of the Father and the Son?

Pondering Prayerfully

Additional scriptures to consider and ponder:
- Matt. 5:5
- D&C 88:14–20
- D&C 88:45–47

The following hymns might help you feel gratitude about the Creation:
- "All Creatures of Our God and King" (*Hymns*, 62)
- "For the Beauty of the Earth" (*Hymns*, 92)
- "God Is Love" (*Hymns*, 87)

Remember and Be Sure

We are literally the spiritual children of God, the Eternal Father. Our first parents in mortality were Adam and Eve. They were created in the image and likeness of our Heavenly Father and our Savior Jesus Christ. Knowing this, we also know that each of us as a divine child of God has the potential for limitless growth, the capacity to be even as our Heavenly Parents. This understand-ing changes not only our perspective on life but also our thought process. It tells us where we came from, why we are here, and where we are going. It is imperative as parents that we teach this knowledge to our children so that they can appreciate the very image they carry within them and upon them.

The purpose for our earthly existence is to prove ourselves worthy, through our own free agency and obedience to the laws of heaven, to return to our Heavenly Father. Abraham learned from the Lord that we came here to be tested and to prove ourselves worthy to return to our Heavenly Father's presence. The test is primarily one of obedience. Will we do what the Lord commands us to do? The test is hard, but we agreed to it in the premortal realm, and shouted for joy to learn of it and endorse it (see Job 38:7).

In this test we will have opposition in all things, be tempted by the devil, and need to be willing to submit to whatever the Father inflicts on us. Sometimes it appears to be unfair. Some will have to endure extremely difficult circumstances. While some seem to have less difficult tasks, the challenge is still great. Heavenly Father knows best, and He and our Savior will judge us perfectly. It is simply our duty and joy to obey His word and keep His commandments, thus enjoying the blessings of the Holy Spirit.

We see that mankind was not created as just another aspect of the living panoply of fauna and flora unfolding upon the earth, but rather this earth was created, in fact, specifically for mankind, for the progress and development of the sons and daughters of God sent here willingly to emulate the model of righteous living exemplified in the life of the Savior, even Jesus Christ. "And it pleaseth God that he hath given all these things unto man; for unto this end were they made to be used" (D&C 59:20). Through the visions given to Abraham, Moses, and the other grand prophetic figures of the human family, we catch a glimpse of the magnificent plan held in store for this earth, which in the due time of the Lord will be celestialized as the everlasting dwelling place for the meek, the humble, and the faithful. Our gratitude for this earth expands as we understand and appreciate its glory and the purpose for which it was created, a gratitude that brings us closer to our Savior and our Heavenly Father and causes us to express our love in serving others and by keeping the commandments.

When the Lord looked upon the outcomes of the Creation, He proclaimed its goodness (see Moses 2:31), thus establishing the pattern for our own view. We too can look upon the divine creative process as transcendently "good." It is good because it bears the unmistakable signature of Deity, the Father of all goodness. It is good because the Savior is the Creator. It is good because men and women are created in the image of God—and being the product of goodness, they belong together in the Lord as companions and parents to their children. It is good because it is based on the dignifying principle of free agency, by which principle we can choose the way of immortality and eternal life through the Atonement of Christ. And it is good because it leads ultimately to the Lord's rest. Just as the Sabbath was divinely instituted to be the crowning glory of the creation and a day of rest, in just the same way we are striving to return, once again, through obedience and the grace of God, into His eternal rest—"which rest is the fulness of his glory" (D&C 84:24)—to dwell in joy with our families forever and ever.

CHAPTER 6
The Fall of Mankind

I believe in the fall of man, as recorded in the Bible; I believe that God foreknew everything, but did not foreordain everything; I deny that foreordain and foreknow is the same thing. He foreordained the fall of man; but all merciful as He is, He foreordained at the same time, a plan of redemption for all mankind. —Joseph Smith (*HC* 4:78)

Opening the Window of Wisdom

The Lord anticipated the Fall of mankind as a necessary part of man's journey toward immortality and eternal life: "And I, the Lord God, said unto mine Only Begotten: Behold, the man is become as one of us to know good and evil" (Moses 4:28). Prior to the Fall, Adam and Eve were in a state of innocence. They were in the presence of God, but they did not know good from evil and were not subject to death (see 2 Ne. 2:22–26). They were commanded to multiply and replenish the earth. They were also commanded not to partake of the forbidden fruit—yet they had the power to choose (see Moses 3:15–17).

Eve was beguiled by Satan and partook of the forbidden fruit (see Moses 4:7–13). Knowing consequently good from evil, she realized she would be cast out from the Garden of Eden and, being separated from Adam, would be unable to have children (see Moses 5:11). Now aware of this state of affairs, Adam chose and knowingly partook of the fruit: "Adam fell that men might be; and men are, that they might have joy" (2 Ne. 2:25). As a result, Adam and Eve were sent forth on their mortal journey (see Moses 4:23–25, 28–31).

The results of the Fall proved to be a blessing for all mankind. Because of the Fall, we now have a chance to grow and be tested and to prove ourselves worthy of returning to our Father's presence. Other outcomes of the Fall included these:

- Beginning with Adam and Eve, the spirit children of God the Father are provided mortal tabernacles (see Moses 5:10–11).
- All mankind will experience physical and spiritual death (see 2 Ne. 9:6).
- Opposition is necessary for our growth—including trials and tribulations in all things (see 2 Ne. 2:11).
- All mortals have the capacity to choose good or evil and receive the blessings or consequences (see 2 Ne. 2:27).
- The plan of redemption brings joy and eternal life if we follow it and obey (see Moses 5:10–11).
- Satan cannot frustrate God's plan, "for he knew not the mind of God, wherefore he sought to destroy the world" (Moses 4:6; see also D&C 3:1–3).

The mortal experience brought about by the Fall opens the gateway to salvation, exaltation, and eternal life through the Atonement of Jesus Christ. Though each of us faces many trials and tribulations along the path, the light of Christ illuminates our way toward peace, glory, and eternal joy. In the strength of the Lord we will prevail. The designs of the Almighty will be accomplished.

Inspired by Latter-Day Prophets

David O. McKay: There are those who have met disaster, which almost seems defeat, who have become somewhat soured in their natures, but if they stop to think, even the adversity which has come to them may prove a means of spiritual uplift. Adversity itself may lead toward and not away from God and spiritual enlightenment; and privation may prove a source of strength if we can but keep a sweetness of mind and spirit *(CR, October 1936, 103).*

> *The Fall of Adam and Eve, resulting in their separation from God and their embarking on the pathway of mortality, might seem to be the utmost in adversity; in truth, though, the Fall was the gateway to eternal joy through the righteous use of agency and the saving principles of the Atonement. How can you change your perception of the mortal tribulations you have experienced in your lifetime by seeing them as welcome gateways to supreme joy and happiness?*

Joseph Fielding Smith: The fall of Adam and Eve was foreknown, and preparation for this restoration had been made long before they had been placed on this earth. In the grand council held in heaven, Jesus Christ voluntarily accepted the mission of Redeemer, to come in the due time of the Father and make the sacrifice that would bring to pass this restoration through the shedding of his blood" *(Answers to Gospel Questions, 1:181).*

> *The plan of happiness involves divine design and heavenly certainty; there is no chance involved. The Father and Son know exactly how to optimize conditions for our temporal and spiritual progress. It is our responsibility to follow the gospel plan and harvest the rewards of obedience and righteousness. You*

> *may occasionally encounter those who feel they are caught up in the confusion of uncertainty and who suffer from a sense of victimization in a world they see as godless. How can you best persuade them that they can know of the precious and perfect design of God's plan by praying for guidance and assurance from the Holy Spirit?*

Joseph Fielding Smith: Mortal life is preparatory to eternal life. The "fall" of Adam and Eve was not a sin but an essential act upon which mortality depends. Mortality is a condition essential to exaltation, and men came into this world to be tried and tested preparatory to an exaltation in the kingdom of God or banishment from his presence, according to the individual deeds in mortality. Therefore mortality has been spoken of as a "probationary" state, for it is here the soul is tested and tried preparatory for a place in the eternity which is to come *(Answers to Gospel Questions, 5:15).*

> *We are here to prove ourselves worthy of the Father's choicest blessings. How can you impart to your loved ones a picture of the future celestial home so compelling and desirable that they will do all in their power to make themselves worthy to go there? (For inspiration, read the views of our celestial home given in Sections 76 and 137 of the Doctrine and Covenants.)*

Bruce R. McConkie: Thus, Creation is father to the Fall; and by the Fall came mortality and death; and by Christ came immortality and eternal life. If there had been no fall of Adam, by which cometh death, there could have been no atonement of Christ, by which cometh life *(A New Witness for the Articles of Faith, xvi).*

> *The three-fold interrelated reality of the Creation, the Fall, and the Atonement constitutes the crux of the plan of salvation. How does this set of three events provide a framework for viewing our destiny with clarity, establishing a personal plan for doing the will of the Father, and proving ourselves worthy of His choicest blessing?*

Truths to Liken

JST, Matt. 6:14—"And suffer us not to be led into temptation, but deliver us from evil."

- The Savior used these words in the Sermon on the Mount when teaching the people how to pray to the Father; in the King James Version, the words are, "And lead us not into temptation" (Matt. 6:13). The Prophet Joseph Smith made the correction showing that the Lord would never "lead" us to be tempted (see James 1:13), but rather "allows" us to be tempted as we exercise our agency.
- During mortality we are exposed to an endless stream of temptations that test our loyalty to covenant principles. How are you managing your daily life so you avoid environments where the Spirit would not prosper and where temptation would have greater sway over your thoughts and actions? How are you guiding your loved ones to "stand in holy places" (D&C 45:32) and avoid temptation?

James 1:12—"Blessed is the man that endureth temptation: for when he is tried, he shall receive the crown of life, which the Lord hath promised to them that love him."

- James began his general epistle by encouraging people to pray for guidance and the strength to resist temptation.
- Those who repel the tempter and endure all things well here upon the earth will be exalted with a crown of glory. How are you able to encourage your loved ones to keep in mind the rewards of being faithful? The superficial pleasures of life are eclipsed by the eternal joys that await those who pass the tests of life with honor.

Alma 12:24—"And we see that death comes upon mankind, yea, the death which has been spoken of by Amulek, which is the temporal death; nevertheless there was a space granted unto man in which he might repent; therefore this life became a probationary state; a time to prepare to meet God; a time to prepare for that endless state which has been spoken of by us, which is after the resurrection of the dead."

- Alma and his companion Amulek were trying to get the wayward people of Ammonihah to reform their ways and come into the fold of the Savior. Their message: Life here on earth is a temporary proving ground for our eternal destiny. It is a trial period for us to prove we are worthy to return to the presence of God. We should not procrastinate the day of our repentance, or we might lose the blessings of eternal life (see also Alma 34:33–35).
- How do you feel about "now"—the present moment? Later in his sermon, Alma said, "Now is the time to repent, for the day of salvation draweth nigh" (Alma 13:21).

Morm. 9:28—"Be wise in the days of your probation; strip yourselves of all uncleanness; ask not, that ye may consume it on your lusts, but ask with a firmness unshaken, that ye will yield to no temptation, but that ye will serve the true and living God."

- Moroni, son of Mormon, wrote these words to people in the generations to come, inviting them to repent and come unto the Lord.
- Being wise throughout mortality brings unspeakable blessings, now and in times that lie ahead. How are you applying this kind of wisdom in your daily life? How are you helping your family and friends to do the same?

Abr. 3:26—"They who keep their second estate shall have glory added upon their heads for ever and ever."

- Through the Urim and Thummim, Abraham was able to talk "with the Lord, face to face, as one man talketh with another" (Abr. 3:11); through that experience, he learned firsthand of the great plan of redemption. The premortal realm was the "first estate" in which the spirit children of God could exercise their agency in support of God's plan of salvation, following the example of the Son of God. As a result, they were able to enter mortality (the "second estate") and learn through their own experience how to choose good over evil.

- All of mankind in mortality kept their "first estate." This is an achievement of grand importance. Now our challenge is to keep the "second estate" with full loyalty to the Almighty. What are your thoughts about the key desires, thoughts, and actions that make this possible?

Rejoicing and Reasoning Together

What Is the True Nature of Mother Eve?

The meaning of the name *Eve* is "mother of all living" (Gen. 3:20; Moses 4:26). Eve, the first woman of humankind and divine "help meet" alongside Adam (see Gen. 2:18; Abr. 5:14, 21), is mentioned by name fairly often in the scriptures. From the latter-day vision of President Joseph F. Smith concerning the work of salvation in the spirit world, we have the most satisfying one-word attribute used to summarize the character and person of Eve: "glorious."

> Among the great and mighty ones who were assembled in this vast congregation of the righteous were Father Adam, the Ancient of Days and father of all,
>
> And our glorious Mother Eve, with many of her faithful daughters who had lived through the ages and worshiped the true and living God. (D&C 138:38–39)

Reading this scripture gives us insight into characteristics of Eve that justify using the word *glorious* to describe her. Eve was:

- **A child of God**—Like Adam, Eve was created in the image of the Almighty: "In the image of his own body, male and female, created he them, and blessed them, and called their name Adam, in the day when they were created and

became living souls in the land upon the footstool of God" (Moses 6:9).

- **An eternal mother**—Eve is the only child of God who has the eternal role of the "mother of all living."
- **Wisely discerning**—Eve had the capacity to weigh choices and act in ways that supported the ultimate design of God for His children. When she was "beguiled" by Satan to partake of the forbidden fruit, she realized that the consequences of transgressing would be in the best interests of her children—she being "the mother of all living"—for they could not "live" in the eternal sense unless the plan of happiness were enacted. She therefore used her God-given agency in wisdom—for the Lord had extended that privilege, even though it had explicit consequences: "But of the tree of the knowledge of good and evil, thou shalt not eat of it, nevertheless, thou mayest choose for thyself, for it is given unto thee; but, remember that I forbid it, for in the day thou eatest thereof thou shalt surely die" (Moses 3:17). In careful consideration of what was at stake, Eve made the conscious decision to partake of the fruit (see Moses 4:6–13). As she later described her position with respect to this decision—having learned of the great plan of salvation from the Lord— Eve articulated her profound insight in the form of a glorious pronouncement: "And Eve, his wife, heard all these things and was glad, saying: Were it not for our transgression we never should have had seed, and never should have known good and evil, and the joy of our redemption, and the eternal life which God giveth unto all the obedient" (Moses 5:11).
- **Willing to sacrifice**—Through her conscious transgression, Eve took upon herself the agony and suffering involved in bringing forth offspring: "Unto the woman he [the Lord] said, I will greatly multiply thy sorrow and thy conception; in sorrow thou shalt bring forth children" (Gen. 3:16; compare Moses 4:22).

- **Industrious**—When the Lord expelled Adam and Eve from the Garden of Eden to till the earth, the couple initiated a partnership of productivity: "AND it came to pass that after I, the Lord God, had driven them out, that Adam began to till the earth, and to have dominion over all the beasts of the field, and to eat his bread by the sweat of his brow, as I the Lord had commanded him. And Eve, also, his wife, did labor with him" (Moses 5:1). Thus Eve was a laboring soul, just like her husband. They both worked toward the success of their commission as "our first parents" (1 Ne. 5:11).

- **Prayerful**—Eve joined with her husband in fervent prayer, which allowed them to receive further light and knowledge concerning God's love and compassion for them and the majesty of the plan of salvation and redemption (see Moses 5:4–10).

- **Receptive and obedient**: "And Adam and Eve blessed the name of God, and they made all things known unto their sons and their daughters.... And Adam and Eve, his wife, ceased not to call upon God" (Moses 5:12, 16).

- **Compassionate and concerned**—When her son Cain descended into the abyss of sin, Eve joined with her husband in the deepest sorrow: "And Adam and his wife mourned before the Lord, because of Cain and his brethren" (Moses 5:27).

- **A great educator**—According to the record, Adam and Eve encouraged their children to keep a record of their experiences in mortality and thus to remember the covenants and promises and blessings of the Lord:

  And a book of remembrance was kept, in the which was recorded, in the language of Adam, for it was given unto as many as called upon God [including Adam and Eve and all of their faithful children] to write by the spirit of inspiration;

  And by them their children were taught to read and write, having a language which was pure and undefiled. (Moses 6:5–6)

Indeed, "our glorious Mother Eve" (D&C 138:39) was a child of God and the epitome of eternal motherhood—wisely discerning, willing to sacrifice, industrious, prayerful, receptive and obedient, compassionate and concerned for her children, and a great educator. Such a "glorious" and noble personality is an abiding example for her posterity through all generations of time.

If you are a woman, you can glory in your noble heritage and strive to emulate Eve's example in all that you do. If you are a man, you can honor and pay tribute to the "Eves" in your life and strive to praise and encourage them to continue the grand tradition of the "mother of all living."

What Is the True Nature of Adam?

From scripture we know that Adam (meaning "man" or "many") was the first man: "And worlds without number have I created; and I also created them for mine own purpose; and by the Son I created them, which is mine Only Begotten. And the first man of all men have I called Adam, which is many" (Moses 1:33–34). Abraham referred to Adam as "first father" (Abr. 1:3; compare D&C 107:40–53), meaning the head of the descending lineage of priesthood authority in the succession of dispensations on the earth. Modern revelation speaks of "Michael, or Adam, the father of all, the prince of all, the ancient of days" (D&C 27:11). The last of these titles, "ancient of days," is expounded by Daniel in various passages associated with the final period of the world (see Dan. 7:9, 13, 22; compare D&C 116:1; 138:38).

In latter-day revelation, Adam is also identified with the title *archangel:* "Michael, the prince, the archangel" (D&C 107:54). The name *Michael* in Hebrew means "one who is like God." Indeed, "Michael, mine archangel" (D&C 29:26) will have the assignment to accomplish the final defeat of Satan and his hosts at the end of the millennial period (see D&C 88:112–115)—just as he defeated Satan and his followers in the premortal realm (see Rev. 12:7–8).

On the occasion of the assembly at Adam-ondi-Ahman—where three years prior to his death,

Adam gave his final blessing to his posterity—the Lord appeared and said to Adam: "I have set thee to be at the head; a multitude of nations shall come of thee, and thou art a prince over them forever" (D&C 107:55). The title of *prince* in this context opens the view to the extraordinary authority and responsibility conferred upon Adam (or Michael) in terms of the plan of salvation: "Who hath appointed Michael your prince, and established his feet, and set him upon high, and given unto him the keys of salvation under the counsel and direction of the Holy One, who is without beginning of days or end of life" (D&C 78:16).

Thus Adam—Michael, first father, father of all, prince of all, ancient of days, archangel, head of a multitude of nations—is a figure of great importance in the work and glory of God, beginning in the premortal realm, continuing throughout mortality, and extending into the eternities. Daniel was given a vision of the future gathering involving Adam, the ancient of days, in his capacity as one holding the keys of salvation, being commissioned to meet the "Son of man" upon His return (see Dan. 7:9, 13–14). This consummating assembly is also spoken of in the Doctrine and Covenants (see D&C 27:5–13; 120) and marks the defining moment in time when Adam will receive from those holding priesthood stewardships and keys an accounting of these keys before conveying them back to Jesus Christ, the millennial King (see *Teachings of the Prophet Joseph Smith*, 158).

Adam has a pervasive presence throughout the scriptures, providing a remarkable account of this exemplary leader in the program of Heavenly Father and His Son, Jesus Christ. Some of the milestones in this history are the following:

- The actual creation of Adam and Eve in the image of God: "So God created man in his own image, in the image of God created he him; male and female created he them" (Gen. 1:27; compare Abr. 4:26–27)
- The marriage of Adam and Eve in the sacred precincts of the Garden of Eden (representative of celestial marriage in the house of the Lord)
- The Fall (see Moses 3:17; 4:8–9; 4:12–13, 29–31; 5:9–11; Gen. 3:23)
- The foundation of the family, with Adam and Eve having children and their children begetting children (see Moses 5:2–3; Gen. 4:1)
- Establishment of the true order of worship, the prescribed sacrificial offerings being "a similitude of the sacrifice of the Only Begotten of the Father, which is full of grace and truth. Wherefore, thou shalt do all that thou doest in the name of the Son, and thou shalt repent and call upon God in the name of the Son forevermore" (Moses 5:7–8)
- Institution of the ordinances of salvation (see Moses 5:9–11) and the teaching of the gospel of Jesus Christ (see Moses 5:58–59; D&C 29:42–44; compare 2 Ne. 2:25–27; Mosiah 5:2–3; Alma 5:13–14; Morm. 9:11–14)
- Keeping of a book of remembrance about his family (see Moses 6:5–6, 8–9)
- Giving of a final blessing to his posterity at a solemn gathering at Adam–ondi–Ahman (see D&C 107:53–56)
- The death of Adam at age 930 (see Moses 6:12)
- Participation of Adam, with many other angelic ministrants, in the Restoration of the gospel in our day (see D&C 128:21)

Through the wise agency of Adam and Eve, mankind experienced the Fall. Subsequently, through the wise choices of Adam and Eve, their posterity came to know the gospel of Jesus Christ. By our own choice, we can honor their example and follow in the pathway of righteousness.

> *If you are a man, you can have great satisfaction in your noble heritage and strive to emulate Adam's example in all you do. If you are a woman, you can honor and pay tribute to the "Adams" in your life, praising and encouraging them to continue the grand tradition of "the father of all, the prince of all, the ancient of days" (D&C 27:11).*

What Is the Key to Passing the Tests of Time During Mortality?

One of the most remarkable passages in the record of Moses is the account of how the gospel message was first unfolded to Adam and Eve following their expulsion from the Garden of Eden:

And Adam and Eve, his wife, called upon the name of the Lord, and they heard the voice of the Lord from the way toward the Garden of Eden, speaking unto them, and they saw him not; for they were shut out from his presence.

And he gave unto them commandments, that they should worship the Lord their God, and should offer the firstlings of their flocks, for an offering unto the Lord. And Adam was obedient unto the commandments of the Lord.

And after many days an angel of the Lord appeared unto Adam, saying: Why dost thou offer sacrifices unto the Lord? And Adam said unto him: I know not, save the Lord commanded me.

And then the angel spake, saying: This thing is a similitude of the sacrifice of the Only Begotten of the Father, which is full of grace and truth.

Wherefore, thou shalt do all that thou doest in the name of the Son, and thou shalt repent and call upon God in the name of the Son forevermore.

And in that day the Holy Ghost fell upon Adam, which beareth record of the Father and the Son, saying: I am the Only Begotten of the Father from the beginning, henceforth and forever, that as thou hast fallen thou mayest be redeemed, and all mankind, even as many as will.

And in that day Adam blessed God and was filled, and began to prophesy concerning all the families of the earth, saying: Blessed be the name of God, for because of my transgression my eyes are opened, and in this life I shall have joy, and again in the flesh I shall see God. (Moses 5:4–10)

In this account lies the key for passing the tests of time with valor and obedience: to sacrifice (meaning for us "a broken heart and a contrite spirit"—see 3 Ne. 9:20), repent, call upon God in the name of the Son forevermore, and thus be able to receive the testimony of the Holy Ghost as a witness that the Fall has been overcome through the power of the Atonement. In all, we need to give thanks to God.

At first, Adam did not understand the purpose of the sacrifices he was commanded to make, but he performed them anyway. Only later did he learn that these sacrifices were in similitude of the Only Begotten Son and His atoning sacrifice. This provides a powerful lesson: Obey and then learn, not the other way around. The question is: How can you cultivate humility (rather than pride), love (rather than selfishness), charity (rather than greed), spiritual purity (rather than sensuality), respect for others (rather than envy or jealousy), initiative (rather than apathy), knowledge of the truth (rather than ignorance), desire for the word of God (rather than the precepts of the world), fear of God (rather than fear of man), peace (rather than anger), prayerfulness (rather than self-containment), genuine goodness (rather than hypocrisy), faith (rather than unbelief), soft-heartedness (rather than hard-heartedness), a listening ear (rather than isolation from the Spirit of God), and a character reflecting the divine nature (rather than that of the natural man or woman)? The answer: Live the gospel of Jesus Christ and become like Him.

Real-life Stories for Heart and Mind

Inspired Dignity. In one of the mission homes of the Church, the mission staff often heard a knock at the door from a needy passerby requesting a hand-out. The mission president always received a needy person with kindness and forbearance, but always with the same invitation: "We have some yard work that needs to be done, and if you would like to help us, we will gladly have you join us for a warm meal." Mysteriously, this proposal seemed to instantly dissipate hunger, and virtually all of these people vanished—except for one. The pleasant-looking middle-aged man and his young son enthusiastically worked for hours in the yard, after which they joined the mission staff for dinner. This man felt that he was being treated with dignity to be given the opportunity of productive work, and he was prompted by the Spirit to find out what sort of people these were. He subsequently took the missionary discussions and, with his son, joined the Church. The whisperings of the Spirit—to both the mission president as well as the needy travelers—resulted in a mighty harvest of the "bread of life" (John 6:35).

Whenever you need a "handout" of spiritual sustenance, you can knock on the door and receive the blessings of heaven: "Ask, and it shall be given you; seek, and ye shall find; knock, and it shall be opened unto you" (Matt. 7:7; 3 Ne. 14:7).

Pondering Prayerfully

Additional scriptures to consider and ponder:
- Matt. 5:5
- 2 Ne. 2:11, 12, 15
- Jacob 4:10
- Alma 42:4, 13
- D&C 29:43
- D&C 62:1
- A of F 2

The following hymns help us understand the Fall and the experience of mortality:
- "Let Us All Press On" (*Hymns,* 243)
- "More Holiness Give Me" (*Hymns,* 131)

Remember and Be Sure

"What is the purpose of life?" is a question that escapes no mortal. All yearn to understand why we find ourselves where we are in the circumstances of life and mortality. Through the gospel of Jesus Christ we learn that this life is but the middle act of a greater drama that began in the premortal realm and will transition to a successive phase that holds out the promise of enduring glory and joy. Even though mortality is brief, its implications are awesome and eternal; indeed, our destiny is determined by our thoughts, desires, and actions while here.

We have come here to receive a body and pass through a probationary state in which our agency allows us to demonstrate allegiance to our Father in Heaven and obedience to His laws and commandments. This life is but a brief hour or two as measured by the clock of eternity—but what stakes there are for us in this mortal time! Let us be ever alert and watchful that we move forward with the "godly walk and conversation" (D&C 20:69) required of the Saints of God.

The Fall of Adam was and is essential for our eternal progression. It has provided for us the opportunity to prove ourselves worthy to return to the presence of our Heavenly Father and His Only Begotten Son. Mortality is truly the time for us to prepare to go back to our heavenly home. It should not be a time when we are obsessed with acquiring the wealth of the world, fame and fortune, position or status, or the honors of men. The scriptures teach us simple truths about mortality: As families we are to work, have children, call upon God, keep His commandments, remember the Savior's atoning sacrifice by applying it to our lives, and teach these things to our loved ones and all who seek the truth. When we keep the commandments and submit to the will of our Heavenly Father, we will enjoy the extraordinary blessing of having His Spirit always with us (see D&C 20:77, 79). Through obedience in heeding the promptings of the Spirit and honoring the covenant principles, we will be "favored of the Lord" (1 Ne. 1:1; 3:6; Mosiah 10:13; Alma 48:20; Ether 1:34) and welcomed home in due time to enjoy everlasting glory and eternal life.

CHAPTER 7
The Holy Ghost: Third Member of the Godhead

Only those who conform to the first ordinances of the Gospel are connected officially with the powers of the Holy Ghost in such a way as to secure added help. A distinct and real power comes to the individual who receives the Holy Ghost. It is as if he had been given a key to a vast and wonderful building which he may enter at his pleasure. However, if the key be unused, the gift is of no value.
—John A. Widtsoe (*A Rational Theology,* 96–97)

Opening the Window of Wisdom

The Holy Ghost is the third member of the Godhead—the one "which beareth record of the Father and of the Son; Which Father, Son, and Holy Ghost are one God, infinite and eternal, without end" (D&C 20:27–28; see also D&C 1:39; 42:17). Unlike the Father and the Son, who have glorified bodies of flesh and bones, "the Holy Ghost has not a body of flesh and bones, but is a personage of Spirit. Were it not so, the Holy Ghost could not dwell in us" (D&C 130:22).

The Holy Ghost is involved at every stage of the unfolding of the Father's plan of salvation. He is intimately connected with the instruction and enlightenment of the children of God through the ages—beginning with Adam, who, in his later years, "stood up in the midst of the congregation;

and, notwithstanding he was bowed down with age, being full of the Holy Ghost, predicted whatsoever should befall his posterity unto the latest generation" (D&C 107:56). When the Savior was baptized, "the heavens were opened, and the Holy Ghost descended upon him in the form of a dove, and sat upon him, and there came a voice out of heaven saying: This is my beloved Son" (D&C 93:15).

The influence and power of the Holy Ghost has been felt throughout the ages. He performs a wide range of sacred functions, including administering the many gifts of the Spirit (see D&C 46:10–33; 1 Cor. 12:3–11). He is the Spirit of Truth (see John 14:17; 15:26; 16:13) and the Holy Spirit of Promise (see Eph. 1:13; D&C 76:53). He comforts, testifies, sanctifies, and acts as the constant companion of those who have received the gift of the Holy Ghost and live worthy of it.

The Holy Ghost is the greatest gift we receive from our Heavenly Father to help us in our sojourn here on earth, because he will show us all things to do (see 2 Ne. 32:5). To live worthy of this blessing, we are to repent and be baptized, receive the Holy Ghost by the laying on of hands, and then keep the commandments (see D&C 20:77, 79). The Holy Ghost is the administering agent for the light of Christ, by which light—the light of revelation—we can come to know the Father and the Son and learn to comprehend all things (see D&C 88:67).

The knowledge of God is the knowledge that saves. We cannot live without it, because we would otherwise be left to ourselves. "Where there is no vision, the people perish" (Prov. 29:18). The goodness of God is continually before us as we receive direction for our lives through the Spirit. Our challenge is: do we follow the Spirit, the living prophets, the messages of angels, and the voice of the Lord? When we do, we will be free, for we will live by the light of the Lord.

The blessings we receive through the Holy Ghost are sublime. When we enjoy the companionship and blessings of the Holy Ghost, we will have peace, being comforted in all things and inspired to do good. We become self-mastered in the sense that our lives are Spirit-directed rather than carnally minded. We begin the process of sanctification as we yield to the enticings of the Holy Spirit (see Mosiah 3:19). We seek the will of Heavenly Father. We yield our hearts to the Lord. We have an eye single to His glory and feel motivated to bless and serve our fellowman.

The Holy Ghost gives direction to our lives. We should continually seek the promptings of the Spirit: "And now, verily, verily, I say unto thee, put your trust in that Spirit which leadeth to do good—yea, to do justly, to walk humbly, to judge righteously; and this is my Spirit" (D&C 11:12).

Inspired by Latter-Day Prophets

Joseph Smith: The spirit of revelation is in connection with these blessings [the visions opened up to the prophets of God over the ages]. A person may profit by noticing the first intimation of the spirit of revelation; for instance, when you feel pure intelligence flowing into you, it may give you sudden strokes of ideas, so that by noticing it, you may find it fulfilled the same day or soon. . . . by learning the Spirit of God and understanding it, you may grow into the principle of revelation, until you become perfect in Christ Jesus (*HC* 3:381).

Can you recall moments where you had a sense of "pure intelligence" flowing into your heart and mind? As you have heeded such promptings, how has your life been changed for the better?

Lorenzo Snow: It is your privilege, every one of you, to have enough of the spirit of revelation to know exactly what is proper for you to do. It is your privilege to know when men speak by the spirit of God and whether the counsel they give is proper or not (*The Teachings of Lorenzo Snow*, 114).

Receiving and living by the Spirit is a choice, based on desire and humility. What experiences have you or members of your family enjoyed that confirm this truth?

David O. McKay: If you have lived true to the promptings of the Holy Spirit, and continue to do so, happiness will fill your soul. If you vary from it, and become conscious that you have fallen short of what you know is right, you are going to be unhappy even though you have the wealth of the world (*Man May Know for Himself: Teachings of President David O. McKay*, 114).

Happiness flows into our lives through the Spirit, and the Spirit operates in our lives according to our faithfulness. As you consider the measure of happiness you have felt in your life, how can you link this happy condition with the blessings of the Spirit?

Bruce R. McConkie: That wisdom which leads to salvation comes from God by revelation. Every person on earth, in or out of the Church, can gain wisdom from the Lord, who is the source and font of all truth and righteousness. Those outside the Church who diligently seek will be led to the gospel of salvation where perfect wisdom resides; those in the Church, when they seek righteousness with all their hearts, will be led along the path of truth and revelation until they know all things and have all wisdom (*Doctrinal New Testament Commentary*, 3:246).

Heavenly Father loves all mankind. He wants the blessings of the Atonement through His Son to be available to all. The Spirit can prompt everyone to seek the fulness of the gospel; within the fold of Christ, the Spirit continues to give guidance until all things are known. How have you detected the workings of the Spirit among your friends who are not members of the Church? How have you been able to assist them to learn more about the gospel and discover how the Spirit can become a constant part of their lives?

Truths to Liken

Matt. 16:16–17—"And Simon Peter answered and said, Thou art the Christ, the Son of the living God. And Jesus answered and said unto him, Blessed art thou, Simon Bar-jona: for flesh and blood hath not revealed it unto thee, but my Father which is in heaven."

- The Savior asked His disciples a searching question: "Whom do men say that I the Son of man am?" (Matt. 16:13). Peter gave a response that revealed his spiritual insight into the issue.
- We can come to know that Jesus is the Christ in the same way Peter did—by revelation. It is the only way. It is central to the gospel plan that we receive a witness by the power of the Holy Ghost that Jesus is the Christ. This comes as we study, pray, and live His doctrine, knowing that He was indeed sent from God the Father to be the Savior of the world (see John 7:17–18). What has been your experience in gaining truth in this manner?

John 14:26—"But the Comforter, which is the Holy Ghost, whom the Father will send in my name, he shall teach you all things, and bring all things to your remembrance, whatsoever I have said unto you."

- Jesus taught His disciples the mysteries of the kingdom, in particular the sacred commission of the Holy Ghost.
- The Spirit will console and encourage us in our times of need. The Spirit will lead us to do good, walk humbly, do justly, judge righteously—and will enlighten our souls (see D&C 11:12–13). We can have wonderful feelings through the Spirit: among them love, peace, joy, and faith (see Gal. 5:22–23).

1 Cor. 12:3—"Wherefore I give you to understand, that no man speaking by the Spirit of God calleth Jesus accursed: and that no man can say that Jesus is the Lord, but by the Holy Ghost."

- Paul taught the Corinthians a central doctrine of the gospel—that revelation through the Holy Ghost is essential to salvation.
- The Revelator is the Holy Ghost. He will witness to us of the divinity of Jesus Christ. What has been your experience in having your testimony confirmed through the influence of the Holy Ghost? How can you teach your loved ones concerning the sweetness and peace that come from this kind of revealed knowledge?

Alma 5:46—"Behold, I say unto you they are made known unto me by the Holy Spirit of God. Behold, I have fasted and prayed many days that I might know these things of myself. And now I do know of myself that they are true; for the Lord God hath made them manifest unto me by his Holy Spirit; and this is the spirit of revelation which is in me."

- Alma had stepped down from his office as chief judge over the Nephites in order to preach the word of God throughout the land. As he did, he confirmed for the people how he had obtained his testimony of the gospel—that the blessings of the Spirit come only through much fasting and prayer.
- We have the opportunity, along with the prophets, to know the things of God (see D&C 42:61; 76:7). There is a price to pay; we are to do our part: study the word of God, fast and pray, exercise our faith, and ask for that which is righteous (see Alma 17:2–3). How can you encourage your loved ones and those whom you serve in the Church to strengthen their witness of the truths of the gospel through fasting and prayer?

Moro. 10:5—"And by the power of the Holy Ghost ye may know the truth of all things."

- Moroni, the final curator of the records from which the Book of Mormon was translated, gave powerful counsel to us, his future readership, about how to conduct our lives by the Spirit.
- The Spirit will witness the truth of all things to us and will answer our prayers

(see D&C 6:23; 9:8–9). We are not left alone to depend on our own devices. The Lord opens up to us a miraculous way to know how to proceed toward joy and exaltation. Many do not realize that this miracle is at hand. How can you assist others to open the doorway to spiritual revelation, that they might have comfort and assurance of how to proceed with their lives?

D&C 9:7–9—"Behold, you have not understood; you have supposed that I would give it unto you, when you took no thought save it was to ask me. But, behold, I say unto you, that you must study it out in your mind; then you must ask me if it be right, and if it is right I will cause that your bosom shall burn within you; therefore, you shall feel that it is right. But if it be not right you shall have no such feelings, but you shall have a stupor of thought that shall cause you to forget the thing which is wrong; therefore, you cannot write that which is sacred save it be given you from me."

- In one of the most remarkable passages in all of the scriptures concerning the operation of the Holy Ghost, the Lord counseled Oliver Cowdery about the process of receiving revelation.
- Receiving the blessings of the Spirit depends on a spiritual partnership: we study an issue in our minds carefully and contemplate the possible solutions, and then we ask the Lord in prayer for confirmation and guidance through the Spirit. He will answer our prayers. In your own life, as you have followed this counsel, how have the answers from the Lord come to you?

Rejoicing and Reasoning Together

How Is the Holy Ghost Described in the Old Testament?

The term *Holy Ghost* does not occur in the King James Version of the Old Testament. However, the office and function of the Holy Ghost are pervasively represented through the use of terms such as *the spirit, my spirit, spirit of God,* and similar expressions. In the first verse of the Old Testament we learn, "In the beginning God created the heaven and the earth" (Gen. 1:1); then, in the second verse, we learn that the dynamic spirit of generation was at work in that process: "And the Spirit of God moved upon the face of the waters" (Gen. 1:2)—an anticipation of the words of Job: "By his spirit he hath garnished the heavens" (Job 26:13). From the Creation forward, the Holy Spirit, as God's agent of light and truth, is found at work through all the generations of time portrayed in the Old Testament, guiding, illuminating, warning, counseling, confirming, and blessing the lives of God's children—both prophet-leaders as well as inspired people in the kingdom.

Although the Old Testament does not use the term *Holy Ghost,* latter-day additions to the scriptures make clear that this term was indeed part of spiritual worship and rejuvenation in ancient times—including the gift of the Holy Ghost. The Book of Moses contains ten references to the Holy Ghost, beginning with the experience of Moses on the mount when he was filled with the Holy Ghost after he had rejected the enticements of Satan (see Moses 1:24–25). From the record of Moses we know by what means the Holy Ghost came into the life of Adam and Eve and their offspring (see Moses 5:6–9, 14, 58; compare Moses 6:58–60, 64–68). Enoch was also intimately familiar with the workings of the Holy Ghost (see Moses 7:11, 27; 8:24).

The New Testament is filled with references to the operation of the Holy Ghost. The Book of Mormon likewise unfolds with clarity the blessings that come through the Spirit.

Moreover, the text of the Doctrine and Covenants includes 220 references to the Holy Ghost (including many related terms, such as *Spirit, my Spirit, Comforter, Holy Spirit, Spirit of truth, his Spirit, Spirit of God, Spirit of the Lord, Spirit of Christ, and thy Spirit*). In general, the Doctrine and Covenants outlines seven broad categories of the work of the Holy Ghost: (1) as the agent of the power and voice of the Word, Jesus Christ; (2) as the confirming central figure involved with the ordinances of salvation—baptism by water and by fire; (3) as the spiritual guide for the gathering of the Saints through missionary work; (4) as the key to personal revelation; (5) as the inspirational force to guide the organizational work of the Church and kingdom of God; (6) as the ongoing source of peace and comfort for the Saints as they endure to the end; and (7) as the Holy Spirit of Promise who places the seal of divine approval on the ordinances leading to eternal life and exaltation for the faithful and obedient. The Doctrine and Covenants is an extraordinary archive of doctrines and explanations concerning the operation and ministry of the Holy Ghost—perhaps the most revealing and complete of all the standard works.

We are blessed through modern revelation to have the fulness of the gospel of Jesus Christ, which provides important truths and enlightenment about the operation of the Holy Ghost. What are some of your favorite scriptural references concerning the third member of the Godhead?

Have You Ever Heard the Voice of the Lord?

The Holy Ghost is the agent for the voice of Jesus Christ. And it is Jesus Christ who renews the sacred covenants and promises of old on behalf of mankind in this, the last dispensation of time: "Wherefore, I say unto you that I have sent unto you mine everlasting covenant, even that which was from the beginning" (D&C 49:9). In doing so, He acts through the Spirit to impart the saving truths of heaven: "VERILY, verily, I say unto you, I who speak even by the voice of my Spirit, even Alpha and Omega, your Lord and your God—" (D&C 75:1; compare D&C 29:30). The Lord speaks to the world once again through His chosen prophet, who receives the word through the Comforter: "For, behold, I will bless all those who labor in my vineyard with a mighty blessing, and they shall believe on his [the prophet's] words, which are given him through me by the Comforter, which manifesteth that Jesus was crucified by sinful men for the sins of the world, yea, for the remission of sins unto the contrite heart" (D&C 21:9; see also D&C 90:14).

When the Lord speaks, the Spirit confirms: "I, the Lord, have spoken it, and the Spirit beareth record" (D&C 59:24). It is a celestial partnership of redemption and spiritual communion involving two members of the Godhead, acting by the will of the Father:

> These words are not of men nor of man, but of me [Jesus Christ]; wherefore, you shall testify they are of me and not of man;

> For it is my voice which speaketh them unto you; for they are given by my Spirit unto you, and by my power you can read them one to another; and save it were by my power you could not have them;

> Wherefore, you can testify that you have heard my voice, and know my words. . . .

> Behold, I, Jesus Christ, your Lord and your God, and your Redeemer, by the power of my Spirit have spoken it. Amen. (D&C 18:34–36, 47)

Based on this last scriptural reference, it is legitimate to ask the question: Have you ever heard the voice of the Lord? The power of the Spirit brings to life the word of the Lord as revealed in the scriptures through the prophets of God. When you read the scriptures in your family circle and as part of your lesson time, and do so with the blessings of the Holy Ghost, then you can "testify that you have heard my voice" (D&C 18:36). It is a miracle of no small measure made possible by the Holy Ghost as the agent for the voice and word of the Lord!

What Is the Role of the Holy Ghost in the Process of Rebirth?

The Holy Ghost plays a central function in the ordinances of the priesthood. The gospel of eternal salvation originates with, and emanates from, the Father; it is empowered and administered by the Son; and it is sustained and confirmed as a pathway to sanctification by the Holy Ghost. All three are invested in this mission, as the Lord said, speaking for the Godhead: "For behold, this is my work and my glory—to bring to pass the immortality and eternal life of man" (Moses 1:39). The process is as follows: "And this is my gospel—repentance and baptism by water, and then cometh the baptism of fire and the Holy Ghost, even the Comforter, which showeth all things, and teacheth the peaceable things of the kingdom" (D&C 39:6). Parents are under obligation to teach these important truths to their children and prepare them for baptism by water and by fire by age eight (see D&C 68:25).

The Holy Ghost serves a pivotal role in the process of applying gospel principles. Like the Father and the Son, He is invoked in the baptismal prayer (see D&C 20:73) and in the confirmation prayer, where the gift of the Holy Ghost is bestowed (see D&C 20:41; see also D&C 5:16; 20:37). The Holy Ghost may visit an individual, but not tarry (see D&C 130:23). It is the *gift* of the Holy Ghost that enables an individual who faithfully endures to the end to have the constant companionship of this member of the Godhead (see D&C 121:46). The sacramental prayers remind us that we need to renew our covenants perpetually and strengthen our commitment to keep the commandments so that we may always have the Lord's Spirit to be with us (see D&C 20:77, 79). So important is this doctrine that the Holy Ghost is also referenced in the work of the ministry in the spirit realm (see D&C 138:33).

How would you define the term rebirth *as it relates to the ordinances of salvation? Why is the Holy Ghost an essential figure in the performance and efficacy of priesthood ordinances?*

How Can Members of the Church Prophesy?

The Holy Ghost is the spiritual guide for the gathering of the Saints through missionary work. Consider the imperative role of the Holy Ghost in the process of gathering the elect from among the peoples of the earth through the ministry of those called as missionaries. The Spirit tells them where to go in their ministry (see D&C 31:11; 75:26–27; 79:2), what to say (see D&C 28:1, 4; 36:2; 42:6; 43:15; 50:14, 17; 52:9; 68:3; 97:1), and what to do (see D&C 46:7). So important is the companionship of the Holy Ghost in this work that missionaries simply cannot succeed on their own: "And the Spirit shall be given unto you by the prayer of faith; and if ye receive not the Spirit ye shall not teach" (D&C 42:14; see also 68:1; 71:1; 109:38). On the other hand, when the Spirit directs the teaching, then the agents of the Lord will know immediately what to say: "For it shall be given you in the very hour, yea, in the very moment, what ye shall say" (D&C 100:6).

Teaching by the Spirit constitutes prophecy: "Wherefore, lift up your voice and spare not, for the Lord God hath spoken; therefore prophesy, and it shall be given by the power of the Holy Ghost" (D&C 34:10; compare Alma 17:2–3; D&C 52:9; 95:4; 112:21–22). Remarkably, those who preach with the Spirit deliver the words of scripture:

And whatsoever they shall speak when moved upon by the Holy Ghost shall be scripture, shall be the will of the Lord, shall be the mind of the Lord, shall be the word of the Lord, shall be the voice of the Lord, and the power of God unto salvation.

Behold, this is the promise of the Lord unto you, O ye my servants. (D&C 68:4–5)

Equally remarkably, those who hear such words with open minds and hearts will receive confirmation through the Spirit that the words are true: "And I give unto you this promise, that inasmuch as ye do this the Holy Ghost shall be shed forth in bearing record unto all things whatsoever ye shall say" (D&C 100:8). The Holy Ghost will join the missionary companionship, along with the Lord Jesus Christ and His angels, as this famous passage from the Doctrine and Covenants confirms: "And whoso receiveth you, there I will be also, for I will go before your face. I will be on your right hand and on your left, and my Spirit shall be in your hearts, and mine angels round about you, to bear you up" (D&C 84:88). Through the gift of the Spirit, gospel learners around the world can hear the message of salvation in their own language (see D&C 90:11).

Is it a daunting thing to be called on to prophesy? As you study the scriptures above, how can you see your way clear to prophesy in this way in order to advance the growth of the kingdom of God on the earth?

What Is the Key for Receiving Personal Revelation?

The Lord gave Hyrum Smith a sacred promise: "Verily, verily, I say unto you, I will impart unto you of my Spirit, which shall enlighten your mind, which shall fill your soul with joy" (D&C 11:13). This blessing of enlightenment, given through the visitation of the Holy Ghost, is extended to all who will prayerfully seek it: "God shall give unto you knowledge by his Holy Spirit, yea, by the unspeakable gift of the Holy Ghost, that has not been revealed since the world was until now" (D&C 121:26).

The Lord shares that portion of knowledge and truth that is "expedient" for the individual to know concerning his or her salvation: "Ask the Father in my name, in faith believing that you shall receive, and you shall have the Holy Ghost, which manifesteth all things which are expedient unto the children of men" (D&C 18:18). The Saints are to call "on the name of the Lord for the Comforter, which shall teach them all things that are expedient for them" (D&C 75:10). Thus the sacred experience of receiving personal revelation is a universal opportunity: "And it shall come to pass that he that asketh in Spirit shall receive in Spirit" (D&C 46:28). All can pray for this blessing, for the Savior refers to "my Spirit, even the Comforter, which shall manifest . . . the truth of all things" (D&C 124:97).

Oliver Cowdery was taught to study things out in his mind before asking the Lord about a particular action, and then he could look forward to promptings from the Spirit that would guide the next steps (see D&C 9:7–9). The power of the Holy Ghost to impart eternal truth and divine knowledge to the pure in heart is central to all spiritual progression and unique in its ability to reveal "the works of the Lord, and the mysteries of his kingdom" (D&C 76:114). All Saints can seek and receive revelation pertaining to their own circumstances and commissions in the kingdom, provided they come before the Lord (as Hyrum was instructed) by putting their trust "in that Spirit which leadeth to do good—yea, to do justly, to walk humbly, to judge righteously; and this is my Spirit" (D&C 11:12). The revelations of God will then flow into the lives of the faithful "by the gift and power of the Holy Ghost, the voice of God, or the ministering of angels" (D&C 20:35).

When you write down a record of your inspired thoughts and experiences, you are preserving for your posterity your own form of personal revelation on behalf of yourself, your family, and your loved ones. How do you feel about the personal record you are preparing and its relationship to the promptings of the Holy Ghost?

What Is the Role of the Holy Ghost in Organizing the Affairs and Progress of the Church?

The chosen prophet of God is "inspired of the Holy Ghost to lay the foundation [of the Church], and to build it up unto the most holy faith" (D&C 21:2). At the same time, priesthood holders are blessed by the Spirit to rise to their potential according to the oath and covenant of the priesthood: "For whoso is faithful unto the obtaining these two priesthoods of which I have spoken, and the magnifying their calling, are sanctified by the Spirit unto the renewing of their bodies. They become the sons of Moses and of Aaron and the seed of Abraham, and the church and kingdom, and the elect of God" (D&C 84:33–34).

Each worthy brother called to the priesthood is to be "ordained by the power of the Holy Ghost, which is in the one who ordains him" (D&C 20:60). Furthermore, the leader of the Church and kingdom is "enabled to discern by the Spirit" (D&C 63:41) how to organize the Saints of Zion (see also D&C 72:24). Meetings are to be conducted as directed by the Holy Ghost: "But notwithstanding those things which are written, it always has been given to the elders of my church from the beginning, and ever shall be, to conduct all meetings as they are directed and guided by the Holy Spirit" (D&C 46:2; compare also D&C 20:45; 44:2).

In addition, special gifts are imparted to the sons and daughters of God through the blessing of the Spirit to help nurture and advance the cause of Zion (see D&C 46:8–26). The influence of the Spirit enables a servant of God to "expound scriptures, and to exhort the church, according as it shall be given thee by my Spirit" (D&C 25:7; 121:43). Those who are in tune with the Spirit are to strengthen others (see D&C 84:106) and to "reason together, that ye may understand" (D&C 50:10). In truth, "the power of my Spirit quickeneth all things" (D&C 33:16) and forms an integral part of the armor of God (see D&C 27:18). Clearly the Holy Ghost exerts an all-encompassing and magnificent influence for good on the Lord's Church.

In your Church callings and assignments, how have you experienced the guidance of the Spirit in fostering unity, understanding, and enlightenment?

What Is the Source of Peace in Our Lives?

The Holy Ghost is our ongoing source of peace and comfort as we endure to the end. One of the tender and memorable passages from the Doctrine and Covenants reads: "Learn of me, and listen to my words;

walk in the meekness of my Spirit, and you shall have peace in me" (D&C 19:23). The Holy Ghost brings peace into the lives of those who are humble and obedient, with a promise that "you shall receive my Spirit, the Holy Ghost, even the Comforter, which shall teach you the peaceable things of the kingdom" (D&C 36:2; compare D&C 112:22). Such blessings flow into the lives of the prayerful: "Pray always, and I will pour out my Spirit upon you, and great shall be your blessing—yea, even more than if you should obtain treasures of earth and corruptibleness to the extent thereof" (D&C 19:38). Direction and guidance "shall be signalized unto you by the peace and power of my Spirit, that shall flow unto you" (D&C 111:8). Those who endure to the end in obedience are assured that the "Holy Ghost shall be thy constant companion, and thy scepter an unchanging scepter of righteousness and truth; and thy dominion shall be an everlasting dominion, and without compulsory means it shall flow unto thee forever and ever" (D&C 121:46).

How grateful we should be for the divine influence of the Holy Ghost: "And ye must give thanks unto God in the Spirit for whatsoever blessing ye are blessed with. And ye must practise virtue and holiness before me continually. Even so. Amen" (D&C 46:32–33). Consider your own thoughts about the following comforting premise: When the Holy Ghost brings peace into your home, your home will indeed become (as in the case of the house of the Lord or the School of the Prophets) "a sanctuary, a tabernacle of the Holy Spirit to your edification" (D&C 88:137). In what ways is your home like that? Moroni provides this thought on the subject: "And the remission of sins bringeth meekness, and lowliness of heart; and because of meekness and lowliness of heart cometh the visitation of the Holy Ghost, which Comforter filleth with hope and perfect love, which love endureth by diligence unto prayer, until the end shall come, when all the saints shall dwell with God" (Moro. 8:26).

What Is Meant by "the Holy Spirit of Promise"?

The Doctrine and Covenants makes clear that all ordinances and covenants entered into by those striving for perfection are to be sealed—that is, ratified and confirmed—by the Holy Ghost in order to be efficacious beyond the mortal sphere. The Holy Ghost acting in this capacity is referred to as *the Holy Spirit of Promise* (see D&C 132:7, 18–19, 26). Those who keep the commandments of faith, repentance, baptism, and receiving the gift of the Holy Ghost by the laying on of hands by one in authority are then in a position to receive the ratifying blessing from the Holy Ghost that ensures that their obedience is recognized in heaven as well as on earth. These are they "who overcome by faith, and are sealed by the Holy Spirit of promise, which the Father sheds forth upon all those who are just and true. They are they who are the church of the Firstborn. They are they into whose hands the Father has given all things" (D&C 76:53–55; see also D&C 50:27–28; 67:11; 88:3–7; 124:124). The highest level of blessing granted through the Holy Spirit of Promise would be to have one's calling and election made sure through the "more sure word of prophecy" (2 Pet. 1:19), defined as follows: "The more sure word of prophecy means a man's knowing that he is sealed up unto eternal life, by revelation and the spirit of prophecy, through the power of the Holy Priesthood" (D&C 131:5).

So important is the role of the Holy Ghost in this eternal process that the only sin that makes one subject to the second death—separation from God—is to commit blasphemy against the Holy Ghost: "Having denied the Holy Spirit after having received it, and having denied the Only Begotten Son of the Father, having crucified him unto themselves and put him to an open shame" (D&C 76:35; see also D&C 132:27). By way of contrast is the grand and glorious fulfillment of one's celestial destiny through honor and obedience, according to the views reflected in the Prophet Joseph Smith's inspired prayer of dedication for the Kirtland Temple: "And that they may grow up in thee, and receive a fulness of the Holy Ghost, and be organized according to thy laws, and be prepared to obtain every needful thing" (D&C 109:15).

What are your thoughts about the sacred role of the Holy Ghost in ratifying and confirming all priesthood ordinances, including temple ordinances, for yourself and your loved ones? In this world of shadows and tribulations, think of what joy it brings to know that the Holy Spirit of Promise is at work among the faithful.

Real-life Stories for Heart and Mind

The Fifth Standard Work. As part of his personal history, one brother in the Church has a diary that he calls "The Fifth Standard Work"—the record of how the Lord has touched his life in personal, spiritual ways. He thinks of it as a private extension of the four canonized standard works: the Bible, the Book of Mormon, the Doctrine and Covenants, and the Pearl of Great Price. In this diary, which is a simple three-ring binder, he keeps copies of sacred personal blessings that form the milestones of his life, including father's blessings, his patriarchal blessing, and thoughts expressed by others during the process of settings apart or special interviews. Here too are preserved special inspirational thoughts received from time to time through the blessing of the Holy Spirit.

Everyone has a "fifth standard work"—either preserved in the heart as special memories or written down as a legacy for one's posterity. What special things do you have in your "fifth standard work"? Which of these do you share with your loved ones and others from time to time?

Sprouting Seeds. A young man had returned from his mission experience somewhat discouraged. He had distributed many copies of the Book of Mormon and had borne testimony of its truth to many individuals—but with few results. What he did not know at the time was that one of those who received a copy of the Book of Mormon from him had shared it with his brother, who subsequently studied it carefully and prayerfully for two years before following the promptings of the Spirit to join the Church. The brother's name was Young—Brigham Young. He gave his copy of the Book of Mormon to his sister, Fanny Young Murray, mother-in-law of Heber C. Kimball—who, along with his family, also became converted because of it. The young missionary who had provided that initial copy to Phineas, Brigham's brother, was Samuel Harrison Smith, younger brother to Joseph Smith. Samuel had also given a copy to Reverend John P. Greene, husband of Phineas's sister, Rhoda. Both were subsequently converted. Samuel later learned with joy that the sprouting seeds of the Spirit work wonders in the lives of the honest at heart.

What experiences in your life confirm that the "sprouting seeds" of testimony are constantly at work?

Pondering Prayerfully

Additional scriptures to consider and ponder:
- Matt. 5:5
- John 7:17
- John 14:26
- 1 Cor. 2:10
- Gal. 5:22
- Alma 17:33

The following hymns contribute to an understanding about the Holy Ghost:
- "The Spirit of God" (*Hymns,* 2)
- "Let the Holy Spirit Guide" (*Hymns,* 143)

Remember and Be Sure

The Holy Ghost is the source of great blessings in our lives. We simply could not accomplish our goals in the kingdom of God without its influence; the kingdom unfolds under inspiration from the Holy Ghost. We could not help carry out the mission of the Church without the Holy Ghost and its incredible gifts of inspiration and power.

In all things the Spirit is the key to understanding and living the gospel of Jesus Christ. The Spirit will indeed show us all things to do. Our duty is to live worthy of the companionship of the Spirit so that we can serve the Lord and build up the kingdom of God on earth.

CHAPTER 8
Prayer

The best way to obtain truth and wisdom is not to ask it from books, but to go to God in prayer, and obtain divine teaching.
—Joseph Smith (*HC* 4:425)

Opening the Window of Wisdom

We receive light and truth from the Spirit through the power of prayer. Prayer has many dimensions: it is the intimate communication with God, the channel for inspiration, the most direct means for expressing gratitude, the posture and essence of humility, the witness of a broken heart, the voice of a contrite spirit, and the start and the finish of the quest for forgiveness. All of these things and many more characterize the nobility and the sacredness of praying to our Heavenly Father. As such, the Lord taught and demonstrated the substance and manner of prayer on every occasion where He ministered to the people.

Prayer is the soul of gospel living: "Behold, verily, verily, I say unto you, ye must watch and pray always lest ye enter into temptation; for Satan desireth to have you, that he may sift you as wheat" (3 Ne. 18:18). And further: "Pray in your families unto the Father, always in my name, that your wives and your children may be blessed" (3 Ne. 18:21). In all things, the Savior gave the example: "And as I have prayed among you even so shall ye pray in my church, among my people who do repent and are baptized in my name. Behold I am the light; I have set an example for you" (3 Ne. 18:16).

We are assured that our prayers are recognized in heaven: "Behold, this is pleasing unto your Lord, and the angels rejoice over you; the alms of your prayers have come up into the ears of the Lord of Sabaoth, and are recorded in the book of the names of the sanctified, even them of the celestial world" (D&C 88:2; compare D&C 62:3). What a glorious miracle that the very words we express in prayers to God are registered on the pages of divine administration for our benefit and well-being. We need to express in our prayers our humble gratitude that we are indeed heard, and that our words of thanksgiving evidence our appreciation to God for the blessings He imparts.

We are promised that our prayers will be answered if we ask for that which is expedient, appealing to God in faith, nothing doubting: "Whatsoever ye ask the Father in my name it shall be given unto you, that is expedient for you" (D&C 88:64). We can use every teaching opportunity—in our family, the Church, and the community—to bear witness that prayers are heard and that this choice blessing should evoke our deep gratitude for the privilege of speaking directly to our Father in Heaven at any time, and on any occasion, in humility and faith.

Inspired by Latter-Day Prophets

Brigham Young: Above all things, seek closely to the Lord. Pray for His Holy Spirit to guide your steps and to deliver you from every snare (*Letters of Brigham Young to His Sons,* 168).

> *During the course of life we encounter many snares. If we are wise, we will stay close to the Lord and pray for His Spirit to guide us through the thickets of mortality. What snares have you encountered in your experience, and how did prayer help you to escape the grasp of temptation and the snags of unwise influences?*

Spencer W. Kimball: For this is the ultimate object of all prayer, to bring men closer to God, to give them a new birth, to make them heirs of his kingdom (*Faith Precedes the Miracle,* 211).

> *Do you think of prayer as a way to be "reborn"? What are your thoughts concerning the role of prayer in the process of becoming worthy to inherit the kingdom of heaven?*

Ezra Taft Benson: Prayer will bring solace and comfort. It has healed sickness, comforted those distressed, and has continued the faithful in paths of righteousness. The value of a man is evidenced in part by the dust on his knees (*The Teachings of Ezra Taft Benson,* 422).

> *What can you say to your loved ones about the "dust on your knees"? How can this help them follow the example of the Savior in supplicating the Father for the power of deliverance?*

Howard W. Hunter: The development of spiritual capacity does not come without effort. We must take time to prepare our minds for spiritual things. . . . There must be desire, effort, and personal preparation. This requires, of course, as you already know, fasting, prayer, searching the scriptures, experience, meditation, and a hungering and thirsting after the righteous life (*The Teachings of Howard W. Hunter,* 36).

> *If done authentically, prayer takes effort. Prayer is part of a wider process of self-development in the quest for self-perfection. What have you learned in your lifetime concerning the role that prayer plays in becoming more like the Savior?*

Truths to Liken

James 1:5–6—"If any of you lack wisdom, let him ask of God, that giveth to all men liberally, and upbraideth not; and it shall be given him. But let him ask in faith, nothing wavering. For he that wavereth is like a wave of the sea driven with the wind and tossed."

- James gave wise counsel to those who seek the truth. This classic scripture about prayer was the one that energized the young Joseph Smith to inquire of the Lord in his quest for truth. Heavenly Father will give freely to His children as they ask, with no condemnation or scolding. He *wants* us to ask. We can pray in humility, with real intent, having faith, truly revealing our innermost thoughts, and knowing that He loves us and will help us.
- What wisdom do you currently lack about how to bless your loved ones? In what areas do you need divine attention and assistance? How can you best approach your merciful Father in Heaven for guidance?

Enos 1:4–5—"And my soul hungered; and I kneeled down before my Maker, and I cried unto him in mighty prayer and supplication for mine own soul; and all the day long did I cry unto him; yea, and when the night came I did still raise my voice high that it reached the heavens. And there came a voice unto me, saying: Enos, thy sins are forgiven thee, and thou shalt be blessed."

- Enos, son of Jacob, poured out his soul while alone in the wilderness, yearning for comfort and forgiveness, wanting the peaceful knowledge that he was accepted of the Lord.
- How can prayer be the gateway to peace and comfort for you as well as for members of your family circle? How can you effectively teach others that prayer will bring peace and comfort?

Alma 13:28—"Humble yourselves before the Lord, and call on his holy name, and watch and pray continually, that ye may not be tempted above that which ye can bear, and thus be led by the Holy Spirit, becoming humble, meek, submissive, patient, full of love and all long-suffering."

- Alma was preaching repentance to the wayward leaders in the city of Ammonihah—including the lawyer Zeezrom—and teaching them that prayer is the way to gain the guidance of the Spirit.
- Every temptation has a threshold, and above that threshold, it becomes very difficult to maintain resistance to the temptation. In what way can prayer protect you from crossing that threshold? How can you help those you love use prayer in this way?

Alma 17:3—"But this is not all; they had given themselves to much prayer, and fasting; therefore they had the spirit of prophecy, and the spirit of revelation, and when they taught, they taught with power and authority of God."

- While on his journeys to preach the word of God among the people, Alma came upon his friends, the sons of Mosiah, who were returning from their fourteen-year mission among the Lamanites. The sons of Mosiah provide a great example of how prayer leads to great spiritual blessings.
- You have probably known people who stand out as examples of those who reflect the spirit of prophecy and speak with the power and authority of God. You can know of a surety that prayer and fasting are a central part of their lives. How can you help members of your extended family circle who are preparing for missions understand this great lesson from the Book of Mormon?

Moro. 10:4–5—"And when ye shall receive these things, I would exhort you that ye would ask God, the Eternal Father, in the name of Christ, if these things are not true; and if ye shall ask with a sincere heart, with real intent, having faith in Christ, he will manifest the truth of it unto you, by the power of the Holy Ghost. And by the power of the Holy Ghost ye may know the truth of all things."

- At the conclusion of the Book of Mormon, the prophet Moroni spoke to the future readers of the book, counseling them on how to know that it is true through sincere prayer and the blessings of the Spirit.
- What is your own testimony of the principle that we should pray with real intent, exercising our deepest faith in the Lord Jesus Christ, in whose name we pray?

D&C 112:10—"Be thou humble; and the Lord thy God shall lead thee by the hand, and give thee answer to thy prayers."

- These are the words of the Lord given through Joseph Smith on July 23, 1837, at Kirtland, Ohio, to Thomas B. Marsh, who at the time was president of the Quorum of the Twelve Apostles.
- Effective prayer requires humility. Humble prayer invites the Lord to take you by the hand and lead you at a time of need. What are your thoughts about this comforting promise?

Rejoicing and Reasoning Together

What Specific Counsel Did the Savior Give on How to Pray?

When the Savior taught the people the pattern for prayer, He said, "Thy will be done in earth, as it is in heaven" (Matt. 6:10). The fundamental framework for all prayer is deference to the will of the Father. In the Lord's Prayer and in Gethsemane the ever-submissive Savior always sought to fulfill the will of His Father in Heaven. Such submissiveness is the ultimate test of our humility, for it demonstrates whether we have learned to become easily entreated and willing to submit to all things that the Father sees fit to bring into our lives in order for us to grow and become like Him (see Mosiah 3:19). Furthermore, the Savior emphasized that prayer is to be conducted in a reverential and sincere manner—not for the purpose of attracting praise from others or putting on a display that includes "vain repetitions" (Matt. 6:6). The purpose is not so much to tell the Father what you need—"for your Father knoweth what things ye have need of, before ye ask him" (Matt. 6:8)—but rather to bring before the Father your needs in faith and humility, seeking to follow His will in all things. A further test of humility is that the person praying has a forgiving spirit: "And forgive our debts, as we forgive our debtors" (Matt. 6:12).

Also associated with sincere prayer is the practice of fasting, which the Lord admonishes the people to carry out in a genuine manner as part of one's worship before the Father, instead of for recognition and display (see Matt. 6:16). In another setting, the Lord taught the importance of praying aloud as well as privately and silently: "And again, I command thee that thou shalt pray vocally as well as in thy heart; yea, before the world as well as in secret, in public as well as in private" (D&C 19:28).

Furthermore, the Savior emphasized that prayer to the Father is always done in the name of the Son:

> Behold, verily, verily, I say unto you, ye must watch and pray always lest ye enter into temptation; for Satan desireth to have you, that he may sift you as wheat.
>
> Therefore ye must always pray unto the Father in my name;
>
> And whatsoever ye shall ask the Father in my name, which is right, believing that ye shall receive, behold it shall be given unto you.
>
> Pray in your families unto the Father, always in my name, that your wives and your children may be blessed. (3 Ne. 18:18–21)

Why do we pray in the name of the Son? Because, as He said, "I am the way, the truth, and the life: no man cometh unto the Father but by me" (John 14:6).

All of this counsel from the Savior on prayer belongs to His doctrine of serving God in such a way as to lay up for oneself eternal treasures in heaven, rather than putting one's trust in earthly treasures that expire: "For where your treasure is, there will be your heart also" (Matt. 6:21). When we remember to pray in this way—yielding to the will of the Father, being reverential and sincere, faithful and humble, forgiving as we ask for forgiveness, in the spirit of genuine fasting, vocally as well as in secret, always doing so in the name of the Son—then a miracle occurs: we generate in the

bosom of the Savior feelings of joy, such that He can say to us, as He said to the Saints at Bountiful: "Blessed are ye because of your faith. And now behold, my joy is full" (3 Ne. 17:20).

What feelings arise in your heart to think that your prayers are bringing joy to the Savior? How can this thought bless the lives of your loved ones as they pray?

How Do Pondering and Praying Go Together?

At one point in His visit with the Saints in Bountiful, the resurrected Lord perceived that they did not understand all of His words. "Therefore," He said unto them, "go ye unto your homes, and ponder upon the things which I have said, and ask of the Father, in my name, that ye may understand, and prepare your minds for the morrow, and I come unto you again" (3 Ne. 17:3).

When we ponder, meditate, and participate in mighty prayer, we truly exercise our faith. We are hungering and thirsting after righteousness. We want to know. We seek to understand. We want to be good. Our minds become attuned to things spiritual.

Nephi wanted to know and understand the things his father, Lehi, had seen concerning the tree of life: "For it came to pass after I had desired to know the things that my father had seen, and believing that the Lord was able to make them known unto me, as I sat pondering in mine heart I was caught away in the Spirit of the Lord, yea, into an exceedingly high mountain, which I never had before seen, and upon which I never had before set my foot" (1 Ne. 11:1). As a result, Nephi was granted a series of magnificent visions in which the things of the Lord were made manifest to him (see 1 Ne. 11–14). It all began with desire and pondering in his heart.

Many generations later Nephi's namesake—the son of Helaman—was "pondering" in his heart one day on the things of the Lord (see Hel. 10:2–4). In response, the Lord spoke to him and granted him a mighty blessing of the sealing keys and the power to stir the people up to repentance.

President Joseph F. Smith recorded the following: "On the third of October, in the year nineteen hundred and eighteen, I sat in my room pondering over the scriptures; And reflecting upon the great atoning sacrifice that was made by the

Son of God, for the redemption of the world; And the great and wonderful love made manifest by the Father and the Son in the coming of the Redeemer into the world; That through his atonement, and by obedience to the principles of the gospel, mankind might be saved. While I was thus engaged, my mind reverted to the writings of the Apostle Peter" (D&C 138:1–5). He, like the Nephis of old, was pondering. He was meditating over the scriptures—in particular, scriptures about the Atonement. He thought of the Apostle Peter's epistles and Christ's dealings with those in spirit prison (see 1 Pet. 3:18–20; 4:6). Having done this, he records, "As I pondered over these things which are written, the eyes of my understanding were opened, and the Spirit of the Lord rested upon me, and I saw the hosts of the dead, both small and great" (D&C 138:11). He then received Section 138 of the Doctrine and Covenants.

We too can receive revelation according to our eternal roles and our stewardships here on earth. When we invest valid effort through meditating, pondering, and mighty prayer, the windows of heaven can be opened according to our faith. The Prophet Joseph Smith explains how we can receive revelation in this way: "The Spirit of revelation is in connection with these blessings [in other words, the manifestation of the truths of the gospel to the prophets of God]. A person may profit by noticing the first intimation of the spirit of revelation; for instance, when you feel pure intelligence flowing into you, it may give you sudden strokes of ideas, so that by noticing it, you may find it fulfilled the same day or soon; (i.e.) those things that were presented unto your minds by the Spirit of God, will come to pass; and thus by learning the Spirit of God and understanding it, you may grow into the principle of revelation, until you become perfect in Christ Jesus" (*Teachings of the Prophet Joseph Smith*, 151).

Grand spiritual blessings flow to those whose hearts and minds are open, who search diligently, and who are sincerely prayerful in their quest to know the truth and become worthy and obedient children of God. After the Savior had counseled the people to go to their homes and ponder and pray for understanding (see 3 Ne. 17:3), He noticed their tears and discerned their yearning for Him to tarry (see 3 Ne. 17:5–6). Could it be that they had started already to ponder and pray in their hearts? In compassion, He then blessed their sick and afflicted and showed them in a miraculous way how He could pray to the Father on their behalf. He then arranged for angels to minister to their children and instituted the sacrament of the Lord's supper. It's obvious from this experience that pondering and praying results in extraordinary blessings and revelations based on humility and faith. What then happened is instructive: "And now it came to pass that when Jesus had ascended into heaven, the multitude did disperse, and every man did take his wife and his children and did return to his own home" (3 Ne. 19:1). Imagine the quality of pondering and praying that must have then occurred in these homes!

What experiences have you had as you have blended pondering and praying? How does this combination help prepare for the outpouring of blessings on you and your circle of loved ones, for the blessing of the sick in your family, for a greater understanding of God's purposes in your life, and for a deeper and more abiding appreciation of the sacrament and the other ordinances of the gospel?

Real-life Stories for Heart and Mind

Pondering and Meditating with Power. When the Prophet Joseph and his colleagues languished in the squalor of Liberty Jail from late autumn 1838 until the spring of 1839, they had a great deal of time to ponder on the trying conditions being experienced by the Saints and on the progress and challenges of the rising kingdom of God. In that contemptible place of confinement, the Prophet might have focused his attention completely on his dismal conditions and on the depressing and painful separation from his family. Instead, he became aware of the light within and the promptings of the Holy Spirit. Through the blessings of heaven, he was able to rise on the wings of inspiration and formulate truth unmatched in its dignity and nobility. On March 20, 1839, he put these thoughts to paper in a doctrinal epistle to the Church, in two segments totaling twenty-nine manuscript pages. He sent the epistle first to his beloved wife, with instructions that she read it and then send it to his parents, who were then to send it to the Church as a whole. Excerpts of this manuscript provided the substance for Sections 121, 122, and 123 of the Doctrine and Covenants—a magnificent harvest of spiritual meditation and pondering on the part of a prophet of God from within the confines of his prison.

Not all of what Joseph wrote has been canonized in the Doctrine and Covenants, though all of it is valuable for instruction and counsel. One segment in particular—occurring in the manuscript between what is now verses 25 and 26 of Section 121—sheds divine light on the correct process of meditation and pondering, as compared with a worldly and shallow kind of thinking. Here is what the Prophet taught on that occasion from within the walls of Liberty Jail:

A fanciful and flowery and heated imagination be aware of, because the things of God are of deep import and time and experience and careful and ponderous and solemn thoughts can only find them out. Thy mind, O Man, if thou wilt lead a soul unto salvation must reach as high as the utmost heavens, and search into and contemplate the lowest consideration of the darkest abyss, and expand upon the broad consideration of External Expanse. He must commune with God. How much more dignified and noble are the thoughts of God than the vain imaginations of the human heart. None but fools will trifle with the souls of men. How vain and trifling have been our spirits, our conferences, our councils, our meetings, our private as well as public conversations—too low, too mean, too vulgar, too condescending for the dignified characters of the called and chosen of God, according to the purposes of His will from before the foundation of the world, to hold the keys of the mysteries of those things that have been kept hid from the foundation until now, of which some have tasted a little and which many of them are to be poured down from heaven upon the heads of babes, yea, the weak and obscure and despisable ones of this earth. Therefore, we beseech of you brethren that you bear with those who do not feel themselves more worthy than yourselves, while we exhort one another to a reaffirmation, with one and all, both old and young, teachers and taught, both high and low, rich and poor, bond and free, male and female. Let honesty and sobriety,

and candor and solemnity, and virtue, and pureness, and meekness, and simplicity, crown our heads in every place, and, in fine, become as little children, without malice, guile, or hypocrisy: and now brethren, after your tribulations, if you do these things, and exercise fervent prayer, and faith in the sight of God, always he shall give unto you knowledge. (*The Personal Writings of Joseph Smith*, 396–397; spelling and punctuation modernized)

These thoughts are profound in suggesting how we should approach the task of pondering and meditating prayerfully on the mysteries of the kingdom—always with purity, solemnity, meekness, childlike faith, and prayerful humility. As you ponder on the words of the Prophet, what comes to your mind on how you might improve the quality of your pondering and praying, and how you might teach your loved ones to do the same as they seek the blessings of their Father in Heaven?

A Great Calm. The storm had come up suddenly. The waves on the main channel of the lake were surging, causing the boat to pitch and roll threateningly as the passengers made their way past towering cliffs toward the marina. Then without warning the engine started to sputter. If the engine lost power, there was no way to prevent the boaters from drifting against the cliffs, where the waves were crashing like demons in the tempest. The father ordered his family members to make sure their life preservers were securely fastened and to go into the lower cabin; he then frantically fought to keep the engine going as long as possible. The safety of the marina was still miles away. It was late afternoon and the darkness of the storm was closing in around them. Could they make it?

As the father leaned over the controls, fighting to see through the rain-spattered windshield, he heard a little voice calling him from the stairwell of the cuddy. "Dad," said the little voice. The father looked down from the captain's chair and saw his seven-year-old son peering up at him through the darkness. The boy was smiling—smiling at a time of such ominous danger. "Don't worry, Dad," he said. "We're going to make it. I prayed to Heavenly Father." The father was suddenly enveloped in a spirit of comfort and reassurance. The faith of a child had prevailed. They were going to make it. And they did. Since then, the words of the Savior have echoed in that father's mind repeatedly as he pondered this experience: "Peace, be still," the Savior said. From the record we know what happened next: "And the wind ceased, and there was a great calm" (Mark 4:39).

Have you or others in your circle of family and friends experienced times of ominous threats and challenges? How has prayer served to bring about a calming influence in those situations?

The Lost Needle. One day the oldest daughter in the family, a six-year-old, wanted to use a needle and thread to do some sewing with her friend. The mother had suggested that if they played with a needle and thread they would have to be careful because the youngest sister was playing in the same room and was just learning to crawl. The six-year-old continued to plead, so finally the mother relented and warned them to be very careful, because it would be very dangerous for the baby to swallow the needle. The two girls were excited and began to sew.

As fate would have it, within a minute the tiny needle was lost. The six-year-old was panicked, but her parents had always prayed together with their children, encouraging them to ask Heavenly Father for all things in gratitude. She quickly went to her bedroom and pleaded with the Lord, "Please help me find the needle." Hurrying back to the sewing area, she and her friend began to search. Her prayer was answered—through another, as the Lord often does. The friend exclaimed, "I've found it! I've found it!" The needle and thread were returned to her mother, and the six-year-old went directly to her bedroom to offer a prayer of gratitude.

What experiences can you think of where you as a child, or other children you know, might have learned the value of prayer in a practical way?

Pondering Prayerfully

Additional scriptures to consider and ponder:
- 1 Sam. 1:27–28
- Ps. 119:15
- Prov. 4:26

- Isa. 65:24
- 1 Thes. 5:17
- 1 Tim. 4:15
- 2 Ne. 32:9
- Jacob 3:1
- Alma 34:27
- Ether 2:14
- D&C 10:5–6
- D&C 76:19

The following hymns inspire gratitude for prayer:
- "Did You Think to Pray?" (*Hymns,* 140)
- "Prayer Is the Soul's Sincere Desire" (*Hymns,* 145)
- "Secret Prayer" (*Hymns,* 144)
- "Sweet Hour of Prayer" (*Hymns,* 142)

Remember and Be Sure

The Lord hears and answers prayers from all who are sincere at heart, and we are commanded to call upon God through prayer. The Savior taught: "Ask, and it shall be given unto you; seek, and ye shall find; knock, and it shall be opened unto you" (3 Ne. 14:7; compare Matt. 7:7). When we pray our lives are enriched. We will have greater power to do good. We are blessed with truth. Life is more meaningful, fulfilling, and enjoyable. Life is sweeter.

The blessings of prayer truly empower us to do all things. We can preach and teach with the power and authority of God (see Alma 17:3), seek forgiveness of sins (see Enos 1:4), gain knowledge of the truth (see Alma 5:46), help people who don't know God (see Alma 6:6), bless others through our righteous prayers (see Mosiah 27:14; Alma 10:23), counsel with the Lord and receive direction in our lives (see Alma 37:37), become stronger in our humility and firmer in our faith (see Hel. 3:35), and receive the blessings of charity when praying with all the energy of our heart (see Moro. 7:48). In all things we will be blessed as we call upon God.

There may be times when we don't receive the answers we anticipate or would like to hear. We sometimes don't receive the immediate or long-lasting relief that we seek. Patience and longsuffering are part of the growth process for our earthly existence. Recognizing this is a key part of prayer, because we can realize that we are always receiving blessings from God—though we may not always have the discernment to see them. When we come to this knowledge, we will never turn from God. There will be suffering; sometimes there may be many atrocities perpetrated (through man's wickedness). There could be many things that are simply hard to understand—even to the point where we say, "O God, where art thou?" (D&C 121:1). Let us be assured that He is always there.

The comforting blessings of peace come from God to His children. He will never forsake us, but it is up to us to initiate prayer—*we are to ask*. We are to pray often and regularly, with real intent, having faith, willing to accept the Lord's will, and above all willing to do our part in bringing about the righteous desires of our heart. The old saying applies: Pray as if everything depends on the Lord, and then work as if everything depends on you. Faith is exercised not just in belief, but also by works—and then through the grace and power of God, "after all we can do" (2 Ne. 25:23).

CHAPTER 9
Prophets Throughout the Dispensations

Never again will the sun go down; never again will all men prove totally unworthy of communication with their Maker; never again will God be totally hidden from his children on earth. Revelation is here to remain. Prophets will follow each other in a never-ending succession, and the secrets of the Lord will be revealed without measure.
—Spencer W. Kimball (*The Teachings of Spencer W. Kimball*, 433)

Opening the Window of Wisdom

Because Heavenly Father loves His children, He provides the means for blessing them with eternal truth—confirmed by His Spirit, unfolded through the channel of prayer, and renewed by prophets in every dispensation chosen to guide and warn them. The words of the prophets, preserved and conveyed in the holy scriptures, open the gateway for God's sons and daughters to enter the fold of the Savior and participate in the plan of salvation and exaltation.

The most potent force for instilling faith and turning hearts to righteousness is the word of God as presented by His inspired prophets. As Paul confirmed: "So then faith cometh by hearing, and hearing by the word of God" (Rom. 10:17). Alma used his prophetic office as a weapon of love: "And now,

as the preaching of the word had a great tendency to lead the people to do that which was just—yea, it had had more powerful effect upon the minds of the people than the sword, or anything else, which had happened unto them—therefore Alma thought it was expedient that they should try the virtue of the word of God" (Alma 31:5). In ancient times, God's servant Amos expressed the essence of the prophetic office in memorable terms: "Surely the Lord GOD will do nothing, but he revealeth his secret unto his servants the prophets" (Amos 3:7).

The pattern for revealing the secret of saving truth has always been the same from the beginning of time. God, angels, or living prophets, seers, and revelators—moved upon by the power of the Holy Ghost—have brought us the word of God, even the gospel of Jesus Christ. Adam and Eve, our first parents, were given the message in all its power and simplicity: "And thus the gospel began to be preached, from the beginning, being declared by holy angels sent forth from the presence of God, and by his own voice, and by the gift of the Holy Ghost" (Moses 5:58). From that time forth, prophets from Enoch and Abraham to Moses and beyond continued the pattern of service, providing mankind the means for enjoying the saving principles and ordinances of the gospel so they could return home one day to the presence of the Father and the Son.

The grand secret of God is the gospel itself—

the good news and plan of action, including divinely empowered and authorized keys and ordinances leading to the immortality and eternal life of man. This plan is designed for the blessing of the Saints as fellow citizens in the household of God, who are "built upon the foundation of the apostles and prophets, Jesus Christ himself being the chief corner stone; In whom all the building fitly framed together groweth unto an holy temple in the Lord: In whom ye also are builded together for an habitation of God through the Spirit" (Eph. 2:20–22). What a magnificent blessing it is to have in our midst a living prophet who conveys the stabilizing, inspiring, edifying, and vitalizing word of God to guide and direct us in these latter days.

Inspired by Latter-Day Prophets

John Taylor: Some years ago, in Nauvoo, a gentleman in my hearing, a member of the Legislature, asked Joseph Smith how it was that he was enabled to govern so many people, and to preserve such perfect order; remarking at the same time that it was impossible for them to do it anywhere else. Mr. Smith remarked that it was very easy to do that. "How?" responded the gentleman; "to us it is very difficult." Mr. Smith replied, "I teach them correct principles, and they govern themselves" ("The Organization of the Church," *Millennial Star,* Nov. 15, 1851, 339).

The office of the prophet is to teach eternal principles of salvation and exaltation. When these principles come alive in the hearts of the people, they know how to govern themselves. Very often people in the world reject the idea of a living prophet, regarding a prophet more as a dictator. How can you correct such opinions by adapting the approach used by the Prophet Joseph Smith, which combines revelations from God through a prophet with moral agency on the part of the people acting for good?

Wilford Woodruff: There never was a dispensation on the earth when prophets and apostles, the inspiration, revelation and power of God, the Holy Priesthood and the keys of the kingdom were needed more than they are in this generation . . . and there certainly never has been a generation of people on the earth that has had a greater work to perform than the inhabitants of the earth in the latter days (*JD* 15:8).

In this age of philosophical rumblings and the collapse of family values, how can you share with family and friends the hope and promise of modern-day revelation as the divinely appointed balance to offset the work of moral destruction taking place in modern society?

John A. Widtsoe: The most important prophet in any age is the living prophet. The prophets who have gone before have left to us their precious teachings which will be used for the instruction and comfort of mankind. But, it is the living prophet who helps us by his teachings, example, and direction to meet and to solve the problems of today, our day. To follow the living prophet, the interpreter of the past, is the essence of wisdom (*Evidences and Reconciliations,* 352).

Eternal principles apply to any age and any generation—but they are applied and adapted through the counsel of the current prophet. What in the words of the prophets today applies specifically to our current problems and challenges? In turn, how can you help your family members use eternal principles and the counsel of the prophets to resolve the problems of this very day and hour?

Ezra Taft Benson: We declare that God has not left man to grope in darkness as to His mind and will. By succession and ordination, there stands on earth today a prophet of God, whom we sustain and revere as president of the Church—prophet, seer, and revelator—the same as Moses of ancient days (*Come unto Christ,* 78).

Christians today generally believe in ancient prophets such as Moses, but not in a living prophet of today. Why do you think this concept is so difficult for Christian churches and sects to embrace in this day, when we so desperately need a prophet?

Truths to Liken

Gen. 45:7—"And God sent me before you to preserve you a posterity in the earth, and to save your lives by a great deliverance."

- These are the words of Joseph of Egypt to his brothers, who were shocked to learn that the governor confining them in the halls of authority in a strange land was the brother they had sold into slavery. Joseph's vision of the heavenly workings in the affairs of mankind allowed him to overlook the petty intrigues of his brethren and forgive them in the spirit of love. He was the forgiver, the guide, the mentor, the man of grace, the uniter, the family man—the prototype of the Savior Himself. Joseph had the miraculous power to see the good in all that transpired and to become a partner with God in bringing about divine purposes.
- How does the life of Joseph reflect the lives of all the prophets of God who yearn for the well-being of our families and strive to open the gates of eternal deliverance for each of us?

Matt. 10:40—"He that receiveth you receiveth me, and he that receiveth me receiveth him that sent me."

- The Savior was giving instruction to His Apostles concerning their mission among the people.
- How is accepting and following the prophets of God the same thing as following the Father and the Son?

1 Ne. 22:30–31—"Wherefore, my brethren, I would that ye should consider that the things which have been written upon the plates of brass are true; and they testify that a man must be obedient to the commandments of God. Wherefore, ye need not suppose that I and my father are the only ones that have testified, and also taught them. Wherefore, if ye shall be obedient to the commandments, and endure to the end, ye shall be saved at the last day. And thus it is. Amen."

- Nephi had just read his brethren excerpts from the brass plates of Laban, which contained the scriptures from generations past. He testified that the scriptures are true and conform to the words of the current prophets,

then invited his brethren to obey the commandments, endure to the end, and be saved.
- The written and spoken words of the prophets contain the plan of happiness. How do you blend the scriptures and the words of the living prophets with your own testimony as a force for good in the lives of your loved ones and those you serve in the Church?

3 Ne. 28:34–35—"And wo be unto him that will not hearken unto the words of Jesus, and also to them whom he hath chosen and sent among them; for whoso receiveth not the words of Jesus and the words of those whom he hath sent receiveth not him; and therefore he will not receive them at the last day; And it would be better for them if they had not been born. For do ye suppose that ye can get rid of the justice of an offended God, who hath been trampled under feet of men, that thereby salvation might come?"

- Mormon, having given a wondrous account of the visit of the resurrected Savior to the people at Bountiful, provided this solemn counsel to his readers to heed and obey the words of the Savior and His chosen servants.
- Following the words of the prophets of the Lord is a covenant obligation: to do so activates the promise of eternal life, and to fail to do so will result in the ultimate expulsion from the presence of God. How can you seek and obtain the Lord's help to encourage those who are "lukewarm" (see Rev. 3:16) to become actively engaged in the plan of happiness?

D&C 1:38—"What I the Lord have spoken, I have spoken, and I excuse not myself; and though the heavens and the earth pass away, my word shall not pass away, but shall all be fulfilled, whether by mine own voice or by the voice of my servants, it is the same."

- The Lord provided this powerful statement in the preface to the Doctrine and Covenants, given through the Prophet Joseph Smith at Hiram, Ohio,

November 1, 1831. This is the Lord's testimony that His chosen prophets speak for Him in all things.

- The words of the Lord and the words of His prophets stand on equal footing, with equal validity and equal consequences. What are your thoughts about the grand opportunity and vital need to heed and follow the living prophets?

D&C 43:2–3—"For behold, verily, verily, I say unto you, that ye have received a commandment for a law unto my church, through him whom I have appointed unto you to receive commandments and revelations from my hand. And this ye shall know assuredly—that there is none other appointed unto you to receive commandments and revelations until he be taken, if he abide in me."

- These are the words of the Lord given through the Prophet Joseph Smith at Kirtland, Ohio, in February 1831. Some who had made false claims that they were authorized to receive and provide revelations were causing commotion among the Saints.
- There is safety in giving strict heed to the authorized prophet of the Lord. What experiences have you had with those who profess to be the font of wisdom and knowledge, but who stand opposed to the teachings of the chosen prophets of God? How do you protect yourself and your loved ones from such people and their teachings?

Rejoicing and Reasoning Together

The Prophets Are Called to Speak and Counsel—The Saints Are Called to Heed and Follow. In What Way Is This a Formal Calling for the Saints?

The living prophet today is our "Moses," appointed to deliver us from the bondage of sin, the confinement of worldliness and pride, and the shackles of spiritual passivity: "And again, the duty of the President of the office of the High Priesthood is to preside over the whole church, and to be like unto Moses—Behold, here is wisdom; yea, to be a seer,

a revelator, a translator, and a prophet, having all the gifts of God which he bestows upon the head of the church" (D&C 107:91–92). The Lord has demonstrated great love in granting us the leadership and light of a living prophet to guide us across the often troubling and ever-challenging landscape of mortal experience and toward our beckoning heavenly home of peace and glory.

The Lord has made abundantly clear that our eyes need to be focused at all times and in all diligence on His appointed prophet as leader and director of the affairs of the kingdom: "Wherefore, meaning the church, thou shalt give heed unto all his words and commandments which he shall give unto you as he receiveth them, walking in all holiness before me; For his word ye shall receive, as if from mine own mouth, in all patience and faith. For by doing these things the gates of hell shall not prevail against you; yea, and the Lord God will disperse the powers of darkness from before you, and cause the heavens to shake for your good, and his name's glory" (D&C 21:4–6). We are to receive the counsel of the prophet as if it came from the Lord Himself (see D&C 1:38), for the prophet is endowed with indispensable gifts and powers of God in grand measure.

We are *all* called as servants of God, and we are *all* called to play a role in actualizing His divine purpose, which is "to bring to pass the immortality and eternal life of man" (Moses 1:39). In that sense, we ourselves participate in the fulfillment of God's word. Whenever we effect good in the world, whenever we bring ourselves into a state of becoming more obedient and more holy, whenever we bear witness through the Spirit, whenever we move forward along the pathway toward perfection, we are fulfilling the word of God, for He has promised that the faithful will participate with Him in building the kingdom.

The word of God is the bread of life that brings satisfaction to our hunger for spiritual fulfillment; it is the water of life that quenches our thirst for truth. God imparts His word through prophets and confirms the truth of their words through the inspiration of the Spirit. This simple process is profoundly important in the plan of salvation, for without the blessings of the continuing word of God, we could not have hope for a better world to come, nor faith in the power of the Atonement. When the prophets speak, it is the same as the Lord speaking. When we come to understand and appreciate this eternal truth, we will be more obedient to our prophets, both living and dead, and their words will be fulfilled.

Have you received a formal calling to follow the prophet? What might have been said in this regard during your confirmation as a member of the Church following baptism? What is said during the sacrament prayers that would constitute a reminder of your covenant promise to keep the commandments—which are surely expounded and confirmed by the living prophets?

Which of the Prophets Have Touched Your Life in a Special Way?

All of the chosen and ordained prophets of God convey the gospel message in truth and wisdom. All have profound influence on our lives. And yet, given the unique challenges and circumstances that each of us faces, particular counsel may make certain prophets particularly memorable for you. Below are brief portraits of just a few of the prophets over the ages. Perhaps you could use these as models for focusing on one or more of the prophets who have touched your life in some special way.

- **Abraham**—This paragon of obedience was willing to offer his own son as a sacrifice as commanded by the Lord. Abraham became the ensign for the Abrahamic covenant, still unfolding today, by which all the world could receive the blessings of the gospel and the priesthood of God (see Abr. 2:8–11).
- **Moses**—Moses was the great liberator—in keeping with the mission of all the prophets to guide the people to freedom through the redemptive power of the Atonement. Moses consoled the fearful hearts of the Israelites quaking on the shores of the Red Sea in the throes of the advancing hosts of Pharaoh: "And Moses said unto the people, Fear ye not, stand still, and see the salvation of the LORD, which he will shew to you to day: for the Egyptians whom ye have seen to day, ye shall see them again no more for ever. The LORD shall fight for you, and ye shall hold your peace" (Ex. 14:13–14).
- **Elijah**—In the monumental conflict between the forces of idolatry and the forces of truth, Elijah holds a special place of leadership. Having arranged for wicked king Ahab to assemble the prophets of Baal for a challenge to see for whom the Lord would display His miraculous power, Elijah articulates the issue with precision: "How long halt ye between two opinions? if the LORD be God, follow him: but if Baal, then follow him" (1 Kings 18:21). When the prophets of Baal failed in their attempt to call down fire upon their offering, Elijah called upon the Lord, who sent fire that utterly consumed the prophet's water-soaked altar and offering, invoking from the people this confession: "The LORD, he is the God; the LORD, he is the God" (1 Kings 18:39).
- **Isaiah**—The resurrected Lord declared that "great are the words of Isaiah, For surely he spake as touching all things concerning my people which are of the house of Israel" (3 Ne. 23:1–2). Isaiah had a consummate gift: within just a few verses, he was able to navigate the grand arches of time in great soaring visions of prophetic insight, crisscrossing the milestones of history from the foundations of the earth to the meridian of time and on to the millennial reign and back again, penetrating the human condition from the depths of Israel's wickedness to the highest levels of her righteous potential. Countless are the sayings of Isaiah that still resonate in our souls, such as this: "For unto us a child is born, unto us a son is given: and the government shall be upon his shoulder: and his name shall be called Wonderful, Counsellor, The mighty God, The everlasting Father, The Prince of Peace" (Isa. 9:6).
- **Paul**—When the Lord appeared to Paul to redirect his misguided ways, the penitent leader had the courage to say: "What shall I do, Lord?" (Acts 22:10). Paul became a consummate teacher and counselor, full of charity and imbued with the Spirit of the Lord, ever committed to speaking the truths of saving grace and obedience to

the Lord's commandments.

- **Nephi**—From the beginning of his service, Nephi was exemplary in following the pathway of obedience: "And it came to pass that I, Nephi, said unto my father [the living prophet]: I will go and do the things which the Lord hath commanded, for I know that the Lord giveth no commandments unto the children of men, save he shall prepare a way for them that they may accomplish the thing which he commandeth them" (1 Ne. 3:7). Nephi had the faith and purity to receive magnificent visions concerning the design of the Almighty to bless His children (see 1 Ne. 11–14). He also had the prophetic leadership to guide his people in the pathway of joy: "And it came to pass that we lived after the manner of happiness" (2 Ne. 5:27).

- **King Benjamin**—Here was a leader who continually taught of the goodness of God and our dependence on Him: "I say, if ye should serve him with all your whole souls yet ye would be unprofitable servants" (Mosiah 2:20–21). And furthermore: "And behold, I tell you these things that ye may learn wisdom; that ye may learn that when ye are in the service of your fellow beings ye are only in the service of your God" (Mosiah 2:17).

- **Joseph Smith**—In the words of John Taylor, present at the martyrdom of the Prophet: "Joseph Smith, the Prophet and Seer of the Lord, has done more, save Jesus only, for the salvation of men in this world, than any other man that ever lived in it. In the short space of twenty years, he has brought forth the Book of Mormon, which he translated by the gift and power of God, and has been the means of publishing it on two continents; has sent the fulness of the everlasting gospel, which it contained, to the four quarters of the earth; has brought forth the revelations and commandments which compose this book of Doctrine and Covenants, and many other wise documents and instructions for the benefit of the children

of men; gathered many thousands of the Latter-Day Saints, founded a great city, and left a fame and name that cannot be slain. He lived great, and he died great in the eyes of God and his people; and like most of the Lord's anointed in ancient times, has sealed his mission and his works with his own blood; and so has his brother Hyrum. In life they were not divided, and in death they were not separated!" (D&C 135:3).

These short portraits of some of the chosen prophets of God might help you ponder and study the various prophets of God who have had a special influence on your life. All the prophets are important, but some may have touched you in tender and special ways that to this day remain present. How can you enrich and supplement your personal history with your written testimony of how the prophets have blessed your life? How can you more often bear witness of these truths for all to hear?

Real-life Stories for Heart and Mind

The Great Divide. A few miles west of magnificent Lake Louise in Banff National Park, Alberta, Canada, there is a small stream that flows down the western slope of the mountain ridge and passes under the Trans Canada Highway, where it soon encounters an outcropping of rocks and divides into two tiny streamlets, each one barely a foot across. One of them flows northward into the Bow River and then eastward via major waterways into the Hudson Bay. The other flows southward into the Kicking Horse River, and from thence into the Columbia River and eventually into the Pacific Ocean. A droplet of water flowing down that stream would at the Great Divide face the prospect of going either toward the frozen expanse of the north or toward the more hospitable waters of the Pacific. One of the most compelling sights for tourists is the place near the large sign spanning the highway that identifies "The Great Divide." The visitors can walk down a path along the small stream and peer with fascination at the spot where it divides into two. On one occasion, a tour guide noticed a woman staring engrossed at the dividing stream for several minutes. "Why are you so interested in that stream?" he asked her. "Because," she said quietly, "that's life." And so it is. Life is a series of small daily choices that define our ultimate directions. Out of the small choices of today will flow the mighty downstream rivers of tomorrow. In life the small often defines the large; the seemingly insignificant frequently determines the big picture.

What do you see at your own Great Divide? What major questions prompt you in your mortal experience to consider the choices at hand? One example might be President David O. McKay's famous sentence: "No other success can compensate for failure in the home" (Family Home Evening Manual, 1968, iii). Following it is the equally celebrated sentence of President Harold B. Lee: "The most important work of the Lord's work you will ever do is within the walls of your own home" (The Teachings of Harold B. Lee, 280). And then there is the related warning sentence from the proclamation on the family: "Further, we warn that the disintegration of the family will bring upon individuals, communities, and nations the calamities foretold by ancient and modern prophets" (Ensign, Nov. 1995, 102). By writing such words of the prophets upon our hearts and abiding by the precepts upon which they are founded, we prepare ourselves with the correct and effective responses at the Great Divide, opening the doorway to admit into our lives the enlightenment that comes only through the Spirit of Truth.

Calm Leadership. In May 1842, a wo`uld-be assassin wounded former Missouri Governor Lilburn W. Boggs; local authorities and apostate John C. Bennett accused Joseph Smith of complicity in the crime. As a result, an attempt—the second such one—was made to extradite the Prophet to Missouri for a sham trial. Joseph fled into hiding on a Mississippi River island in order to elude his enemies and protect his life. Rumors begin to multiply in Nauvoo regarding possible attacks from the militia, mob violence, and writs; these rumors were so threatening that by the time some of the brethren (including Hyrum Smith) hastened to the Prophet to warn him of all sorts of real or imagined dangers, they had worked themselves into somewhat of a frenzy. Joseph calmly evaluated

the situation: "I discovered a degree of excitement and agitation manifested in those who brought the report, and I took occasion to gently reprove all present for letting report excite them, and advised them not to suffer themselves to be wrought upon by any report, but to maintain an even, undaunted mind. Each one began to gather courage, and all fears were soon subsided, and the greatest union and good feeling prevailed amongst all present. Various subjects were then conversed upon, and counsel given which was felt to be most seasonable and salutary" (*HC* 5:97–98).

Joseph Smith's example shows the wisdom of cultivating composure under stress, of carefully separating fact from fiction when making judgments, and, above all, of continually maintaining faith in the guidance of the Lord, who has counseled: "Wherefore, be of good cheer; and do not fear, for I the Lord am with you, and will stand by you" (D&C 68:6). In your various roles and functions, how can you remember to cultivate the kind of calm leadership that maintains a clear head and models a willingness to turn to the Lord and His prophets in humility and obedience? How can you teach your loved ones to apply calm leadership—such as displayed by the living prophets—in all that they do?

Pondering Prayerfully

Additional scriptures to consider and ponder:
- Ezek. 3:27
- Joel 2:28
- Matt. 22:40
- Luke 1:68–70
- Eph. 4:11–12
- Mosiah 8:16
- D&C 52:9
- D&C 58:18

The following hymns increase our gratitude for prophets:
- "Come, Listen to a Prophet's Voice" (*Hymns*, 21)
- "Praise to the Man" (*Hymns*, 27)
- "We Thank Thee, O God, for a Prophet" (*Hymns*, 19)

Remember and Be Sure

Prophets speak the words of eternal salvation and exaltation. By listening to the prophet's voice today and pondering the written word of the Lord preserved in the scriptures, we are promised the comforting blessing of peace: "Learn of me, and listen to my words; walk in the meekness of my spirit, and you shall have peace in me" (D&C 19:23). To the extent we make ourselves worthy of achieving that kind of spiritual peace, we are the living fulfillment of prophecy, for we will be enjoying the blessings of eternal life as promised through prophetic declarations since the beginning of the world. The counsel of Amos is as true today as it was when he first spoke it: "Seek the Lord, and ye shall live" (Amos 5:6). There are eternal blessings in store when we follow the prophets: "For he that receiveth my servants receiveth me; and he that receiveth me receiveth my Father; and he that receiveth my Father receiveth my Father's kingdom; therefore all that my Father hath shall be given unto him" (D&C 84:36–38).

We are blessed to have living prophets, seers, and revelators to guide the Church today. As we live "by every word that proceedeth forth from the mouth of God" (D&C 84:44), we show our love for Him and His servants. We are well advised to follow the counsel of the Lord's prophets daily by reading the scriptures faithfully and prayerfully, listening to the words of the living prophets as given through general conference and channeled through our local priesthood leaders, and taking the opportunity to raise our hands in sustaining God's servants in positions of authority. We can step forward to extinguish evil speaking of the Lord's anointed by setting a loving and supportive example. We can exercise faith in the Lord's hand as He places valiant prophets at the helm of His kingdom. For the last time in human history, the Lord has empowered prophets to guide His work to completion. The succession of such leaders in this last dispensation, from Joseph Smith unto the present time, will continue uninterrupted until the stone, "cut out of the mountain without hands" (Dan. 2:45), rolls forth to fill the whole earth with the glory and truth of the restored gospel of Jesus Christ.

CHAPTER 10
Scriptures: The Word of God

The Old and New Testaments, the Book of Mormon, and the book of Doctrine and Covenants . . . are like a lighthouse in the ocean or a finger-post which points out the road we should travel. Where do they point? To the fountain of light. . . . That is what these books are for. They are of God; they are valuable and necessary; by them we can establish the doctrine of Christ. —Brigham Young (*JD* 8:129)

Opening the Window of Wisdom

The word of God—given to His children by His own voice or by the voice of holy angels and chosen prophets—is compelling evidence of His unbounded love. His word, preserved in the scriptures and confirmed to the prayerful reader by the comforting whisperings of His Spirit, unfolds the majesty of the covenant promises leading to eternal joy and exaltation.

The scriptures provide a magnificent and unique environment for learning, introspection, building testimony, and strengthening gospel commitments. There is no aspect of the human experience—other than direct personal inspiration and revelation—that equals the blessings of being immersed in the word of the Lord given through His prophets. Just a single passage of scripture—such as "God is love" (1 John 4:8)—provides a universe of truth and

wisdom to explore. From such a beautiful and brief passage, and hundreds of others like it, we learn important vital themes that apply to our day-to-day experiences. The scriptures lift, elevate, edify, expand, encourage, fortify, and bless. Let us be ever grateful for the word of God.

It is wisdom in God that His word is preserved in written form to be handed down to His children, including all that is "expedient" for them to know (see 2 Ne. 3:19; 3 Ne. 26:9; D&C 75:10; 88:127). The reason is clear, as Alma explained to his son Helaman: "And now, it has hitherto been wisdom in God that these things should be preserved; for behold, they have enlarged the memory of this people, yea, and convinced many of the error of their ways, and brought them to the knowledge of their God unto the salvation of their souls" (Alma 37:8). It is ultimately from the written records that the people will be judged: "For I command all men, both in the east and in the west, and in the north, and in the south, and in the islands of the sea, that they shall write the words which I speak unto them; for out of the books which shall be written I will judge the world, every man according to their works, according to that which is written" (2 Ne. 29:11).

The word of God, planted in hearts of faith and minds of yearning, unfolds as a living entity, destined, as Alma said, to become "a tree springing up unto everlasting life" (Alma 32:41). If we will but desire to try the word of God in faith, we will find that it will enlarge and enlighten our souls, confirming its efficacy within us. If we will then nourish the word with continuing faith and hope, and with charitable obedience, it will bring us everlasting blessings.

The central objective of the scriptures is to provide a continuous flow of light that illuminates the pathway leading to Christ. By following the word of God, we can come unto Christ and partake of the blessings of the gospel: "And now, my beloved brethren, I would that ye should come unto Christ, who is the Holy One of Israel, and partake of his salvation, and the power of his redemption. Yea, come unto him, and offer your whole souls as an offering unto him, and continue in fasting and praying, and endure to the end; and as the Lord liveth ye will be saved" (Omni 1:26). By feasting upon the words of Christ—who is "the light, and the life, and the truth of the world" (Ether 4:12)—and following the promptings of the Spirit, we will know all that we are to do in our quest for joy and happiness (see 2 Ne. 32:3, 5).

The Restoration has enriched our treasure of scriptural truth concerning the eternal covenant between God and His children. Isaiah predicted a future era when light would burst forth and the word of God would rise from the dust to fill the world with truth: "Therefore, behold, I will proceed to do a marvellous work among this people, even a marvellous work and a wonder: for the wisdom of their wise men shall perish, and the understanding of their prudent men shall be hid" (Isa. 29:14). Jeremiah also foresaw this awakening: "Behold, the days come, saith the Lord, that I will make a new covenant with the house of Israel, and with the house of Judah: Not according to the covenant that I made with their fathers in the day that I took them by the hand to bring them out of the land of Egypt . . . . but this shall be the covenant that I will make with the house of Israel; After those days, saith the Lord, I will put my law in their inward parts, and write it in their hearts; and will be their God, and they shall be my people" (Jer. 31:31–33).

That day has come. The Book of Mormon has brought back the "the fulness of the gospel of Jesus Christ" (D&C 20:9). The Doctrine and Covenants has restored the foundation of priesthood precepts and principles for unfolding the kingdom of God on the earth. The Pearl of Great Price has confirmed the eternal pattern of how God relates to mankind—past, present, and future. This restored word of God, when written in the hearts of the Saints and infused in their thoughts, actions, and patterns of living, becomes the testament of salvation and the constitution of exaltation unto all who will yield to the will of the Father and the Son. From the word springs faith, and from faith courage, and from courage "a godly walk and conversation" (D&C 20:69) appropriate for those becoming sons and daughters of God.

When Jesus spoke with the Samarian woman at Jacob's well and received from her hands a drink of water, He said, "Whosoever drinketh of this water shall thirst again: But whosoever drinketh of the water that I shall give him shall never thirst; but the water that I shall give him shall be in him a well of water springing up into everlasting life" (John 4:13–14). This same Jesus who fulfilled His mission in the meridian of time was Lord and Savior from the beginning. By taking His word into our hearts and minds, we will satisfy our thirst for the truth by drinking of the eternal well of wisdom and grace awaiting those who enter into the fold of Christ and endure to the end. Search the scriptures, for in them you will come to know that Jesus is the Christ. The scriptures testify and witness that He is indeed the promised Messiah, the Savior and Redeemer of the World, and that through Him and through obedience to His word we can gain eternal life.

Inspired by Latter-Day Prophets

Joseph Smith: Take away the Book of Mormon and the revelations, and where is our religion? We have none (*HC* 2:52).

Our religion is founded upon the bedrock of revelation—which is the scriptural fountain that supplies all spiritual truth. Without this fountain, which has its source in God, there is no religion. What are your thoughts on this deep subject?

Brigham Young: Do you read the scriptures, my brethren and sisters, as though you were writing them a thousand, two thousand, or five thousand years ago? Do you read them as though you stood in the place of the men who wrote them? If you do not feel thus, it is your privilege to do so (*JD* 7:333).

The scriptures have a miraculous way of bridging time, carrying us backward millennia or forward into the eternities. The Lord told Moses on the mount: "And all things are present with me, for I know them all" (Moses 1:6). How do the scriptures make all things (whether of ancient date or future application) seem "present" to you? How do the scriptures bring eternal truth into the here and now for you to enjoy and apply?

Ezra Taft Benson: The word of God, as found in the scriptures, in the words of living prophets, and in personal revelation, has the power to fortify the Saints and arm them with the Spirit so they can resist evil, hold fast to the good and find joy in this life. . . . Let us not treat lightly the great things we have received from the hand of the Lord. His word is one of the most valuable gifts He has given us (*The Teachings of Ezra Taft Benson,* 44).

Inspiration, fortification against evil, finding joy, power to serve—these are the rewards that come from reading and following the word of God. What has been your experience harvesting such rewards from the scriptures? How have you been able to share this process with your loved ones and those you serve?

Truths to Liken

Luke 24:45—"Then opened he their understanding, that they might understand the scriptures."

- Shortly after His resurrection, the Lord encountered two men on the road to Emmaus. Without revealing His identity, He comforted them in their sadness over the loss of their crucified Master.
- The Savior has declared in the latter days: "The scriptures shall be given, even as they are in mine own bosom, to the salvation of mine own elect" (D&C 35:20). Who can better open our understanding to the scriptures than the Savior Himself, through the blessings of the Spirit? As you read and study the scriptures, think of yourself on the road to Emmaus, encountering

your Lord and Redeemer, who loves you and unfolds to you the meaning of His sacred word. How does this help you to understand the scriptures?

John 5:39—"Search the scriptures; for in them ye think ye have eternal life: and they are they which testify of me."

- Jesus was addressing Jewish leaders who had objected to Him healing a man on the Sabbath. He confirmed to them that they *thought* they had eternal life through the scriptures—but He made clear that they need to search the scriptures, for they had not the love of God in their hearts, having rejected the Son of God.
- The counsel of the Lord to us is to search the scriptures and *know* that we have eternal life, for the scriptures confirm the reality and mission of the Redeemer. How have the scriptures given you confidence in the mission of Jesus as Redeemer?

1 Ne. 19:23–24—"For I did liken all scriptures unto us, that it might be for our profit and learning. Wherefore I spake unto them, saying: Hear ye the words of the prophet, . . . and liken them unto yourselves, that ye may have hope as well as your brethren from whom ye have been broken off; for after this manner has the prophet written."

- Nephi had been expounding the words of the prophets—especially those of Isaiah—to his brothers in order to inspire them with hope.
- This famous passage brings to life the verb *liken,* for it explains how a prophet of God uses the scriptures in a practical way to give strength and hope for one's everyday life. As you take time to study and ponder the word of God each day, how have you received special blessings from your Father in Heaven?

2 Ne. 4:15—"For my soul delighteth in the scriptures, and my heart pondereth them, and writeth them for the learning and the profit of my children."

- Not long after the passing of his father, Lehi, Nephi was confronted by his older brothers, who were angry at him for having continually brought to their attention the counsel contained in the word of God. Nephi explained to his future readership what his purpose was in pondering, writing, and expounding the scriptures—not to give offense, but to bless family members in the spirit of love.

- Among God's greatest gifts to mankind is the gift of His scriptural word, granted as a loving endowment to build faith, secure obedience, and open the gateway to immortality and eternal life. The mission of the prophets is to preserve this scriptural word and convey it to God's children. When our hearts ponder the word of God, our love for God is increased as we recognize His goodness in our lives. What has been your experience in teaching the scriptures to others? How have you been able to project a spirit of love and understanding?

2 Ne. 32:3—"Angels speak by the power of the Holy Ghost; wherefore, they speak the words of Christ. Wherefore, I said unto you, feast upon the words of Christ; for behold, the words of Christ will tell you all things what ye should do."

- Toward the end of his compiled scriptural treasure, Nephi gives wise counsel and promise to his future readership concerning the words of Christ.

- As we feast on the scriptures with delight and joy, studying with real intent, the word of the Lord will truly tell us the things we need to do—not some, but *all* things to do pertaining to righteousness. This is truly a commandment with a promise. Like all of us, you are to make scripture study part of your daily plan. How has this promise been fulfilled in your personal life and in the lives of your family members?

Mosiah 1:5–7—"I say unto you, my sons, were it not for these things, which have been kept and preserved by the hand of God . . . even our fathers would have dwindled in unbelief. . . . O my sons, I would that ye should remember that these sayings are true, and also that these records are true . . . and we can know of their surety because we have them before our eyes. And now, my sons, I would that ye should remember to search them diligently, that ye may profit thereby; and I would that ye should keep the commandments of God, that ye may prosper in the land according to the promises which the Lord made unto our fathers."

- King Benjamin bore witness to his sons concerning the value of the scriptures and exhorted them to search the scriptures and keep the commandments.

- There are grand opportunities in life to bear testimony about the truth and power of the scriptures. What experiences have you had in doing this for others, and what have been the positive outcomes?

Moro. 10:3–5—"Behold, I would exhort you that when ye shall read these things, if it be wisdom in God that ye should read them, that ye would remember how merciful the Lord hath been unto the children of men, from the creation of Adam even down until the time that ye shall receive these things, and ponder it in your hearts. And when ye shall receive these things, I would exhort you that ye would ask God, the Eternal Father, in the name of Christ, if these things are not true; and if ye shall ask with a sincere heart, with real intent, having faith in Christ, he will manifest the truth of it unto you, by the power of the Holy Ghost. And by the power of the Holy Ghost ye may know the truth of all things."

- At the conclusion of his account in the Book of Mormon, Moroni reminds his future readership that we have the scriptures because of the mercy of God and can know of their truthfulness through the blessings of the Spirit.

- Moroni's promise is to all. We can all know the truth by the power of the Holy Ghost as we sincerely seek the knowledge of God through study, pondering the things we learn, and then asking with a sincere heart. What are your thoughts about this magnificent promise and the blessings associated with it?

D&C 43:34—"Hearken ye to these words. Behold, I am Jesus Christ, the Savior of the world. Treasure these things up in your hearts, and let the solemnities of eternity rest upon your minds."

- These are the words of the Lord given through the Prophet Joseph Smith at Kirtland, Ohio, in February 1831, at a time when the people wanted to know the true source of revelation.
- The true source of revelation is the word of the Lord given through His chosen and authorized servant, the living prophet of the day. What do you think is meant by the admonition to let "the solemnities of eternity rest upon your minds"?

D&C 84:43–46—"And I now give unto you a commandment to beware concerning yourselves, to give diligent heed to the words of eternal life. For you shall live by every word that proceedeth forth from the mouth of God. For the word of the Lord is truth, and whatsoever is truth is light, and whatsoever is light is Spirit, even the Spirit of Jesus Christ. And the Spirit giveth light to every man that cometh into the world; and the Spirit enlighteneth every man through the world, that hearkeneth to the voice of the Spirit."

- In this revelation on the priesthood—given through the Prophet Joseph Smith at Kirtland, Ohio, September 22 and 23, 1832—the Lord gives His witness and admonition about the scriptures.
- The scriptures are our compass for life (see Alma 37:37–47). Life can full of light and truth as we hold to the iron rod and stay on the straight and narrow path to partake of the precious fruit. How have the scriptures blessed your life and the lives of your loved ones over the years?

Rejoicing and Reasoning Together

With the Vast Scriptural Canon Now Available to Us, How Can We Master All of It?

Long ago the prophet Isaiah raised a question concerning the designs of God to spread saving truth: "Whom shall he teach knowledge? and whom shall he make to understand doctrine? . . . For precept must be upon precept, precept upon precept; line upon line, line upon line; here a little, and there a little" (Isa. 28:9–10). In our day the principle has been renewed: "For he will give unto the faithful line upon line, precept upon precept; and I will try you and prove you herewith" (D&C 98:12). The Lord makes clear that line upon line and precept upon precept is the mode and process of learning: the faithful receive more while those who say they have enough or reject the teachings find that the portion given will be taken away. Alma taught this doctrine to the doubting Zeezrom:

> It is given unto many to know the mysteries of God; nevertheless they are laid under a strict command that they shall not impart only according to the portion of his word which he doth grant unto the children of men, according to the heed and diligence which they give unto him.
>
> And therefore, he that will harden his heart, the same receiveth the lesser portion of the word; and he that will not harden his heart, to him is given the greater portion of the word, until it is given unto him to know the mysteries of God until he know them in full.
>
> And they that will harden their hearts, to them is given the lesser portion of the word until they know nothing concerning his mysteries. (Alma 12:9–11)

The faithful need not fear. They can learn line upon line, here a little and there a little, for the reward will be an expanding understanding of the glories of the gospel, one segment at a time. It is a continuum of learning, a process of spiritual development leading to increasingly more light. We can dwell on a principle until we understand it, pondering and repeating the scriptural passages until they are part of our bosom—much like the angel Moroni repeated his comprehensive message to the young Joseph Smith three times in the night of September 21 to 22, 1823, and then once again in the morning of the new day (see JS—H 1:45–46, 49). Divine repetitions of this kind illustrate how we learn the gospel—important precepts and principles are reviewed time and again in our meetings and conferences, for example. Repetition and emphasis are keys to learning and internalizing truth to the depths of our soul.

Genuine progress and growth take time. It is a process of becoming. The Lord in His infinite wisdom said, "I will give unto the children of men line upon line, precept upon precept, here a little and there a little; and blessed are those who hearken unto my precepts, and lend an ear unto my counsel, for they shall learn wisdom; for unto him that receiveth I will give more; and from them that shall say, We have enough, from them shall be taken away even that which they have" (2 Ne. 28:30). As we hearken (listen, learn, and do), we gain knowledge and wisdom. We act wisely on that which we have received, and then the Lord gives us more. We grow a step at a time. At times there can be life-changing moments, and then we act upon those with dedication and consistency. Each day can be a growing experience filled with hope, representing yet another forward advance, one step at a time.

As you spend time reading the scriptures and attending meetings each week, you notice a familiar voice calling you. The message is always the same: "Come, follow me" (Luke 18:22). The Good Master is known to the flock: "And when he putteth forth his own sheep, he goeth before them, and the sheep follow him: for they know his voice" (John 10:4). Gradually the harvest of the familiar grows in abundance and volume until it fills the soul and dispels all darkness. What has been your experience with this process of growing in knowledge and wisdom, one step at a time, here a little and there a little?

What Are Three Unique Blessings Available through the Book of Mormon?

First, through the Book of Mormon we have once again what the Lord has called "the fulness of the gospel of Jesus Christ to the Gentiles and to the Jews also" (D&C 20:9). According to the vision of Nephi, the word of God at the time of Christ went forth "from the Jews in purity unto the Gentiles, according to the truth which is in God" (1 Ne. 13:25). But after it had gone forth out the hands of the Twelve Apostles of Christ, it suffered changes by misdirected handlers who took away "many parts which are plain and most precious; and also many covenants of the Lord have they taken away" (1 Ne. 13:26), thus causing many to "stumble" (1 Ne. 13:29). Therefore, in mercy, the Lord arranged for a branch of Israel (the prophets of the Book of Mormon) to "write many things which I shall minister unto them, which shall be plain and precious; and after thy seed shall be destroyed, and dwindle in unbelief, and also the seed of thy brethren, behold, these things shall be hid up, to come forth unto the Gentiles, by the gift and power of the Lamb. And in them shall be written my gospel, saith the Lamb, and my rock and my salvation" (1 Ne. 13:35–36).

The "fulness of the gospel" as described by the Lord contains the fundamental principles of salvation through which the honest at heart can be admitted into the fold of Christ in full fellowship, prepared to go forward along the pathway leading to eternal life. The Book of Mormon is filled with the spirit and influence of the Savior and is, in effect, "Another Testament of Jesus Christ," as the subtitle confirms. President Ezra Taft Benson explains:

As far as preaching the gospel is concerned, the Book of Mormon contains the clearest, most concise, and complete explanation. There is no other record to compare with it. In what record do you get such a complete understanding of the nature of the Fall, the nature of physical and spiritual death, the doctrine of the Atonement, the doctrine of justice and mercy as it relates to the Atonement, and the principles and ordinances of the gospel? The Book of Mormon contains the most comprehensive account of these fundamental doctrines. (*The Teachings of Ezra Taft Benson*, 56)

How grateful we should be for the purity and consistency of the gospel essentials taught in the Book of Mormon. On Sunday, November 28, 1841, the Prophet Joseph Smith declared to members of the Quorum of the Twelve Apostles this now-famous statement: "I told the brethren that the Book of Mormon was the most correct of any book on earth, and the keystone of our religion, and a man would get nearer to God by abiding by its precepts, than by any other book" (HC 4:461). That was a covenant statement—one with a duty, a promise, and a reward. The duty is to abide by the precepts in the book; the promise is to get nearer to God; the reward, or outcome, depends on our faithfulness. How has your reading and "abiding" by the truths of the Book of Mormon—containing the fulness of the gospel—brought you nearer to the Savior and to your Father in Heaven?

Second, the Book of Mormon is the only work of scripture that was written of old principally for us in this, the dispensation of the fulness of times. Through the grace of God, an array of prophets from the distant past focused their discerning eye on our day and laid out a roadmap of truth aligned specifically with our modern needs as we attempt to answer the compelling questions of the latter days and find our way through the highways and byways of a largely godless society. Truly the Book of Mormon is a compass and a guide for the faithful in modern times. Moroni, the last of the ancient compilers, addressed his words directly and emphatically to latter-day readers: "Behold, I speak unto you as if ye were present, and yet ye are not. But behold, Jesus Christ hath shown you unto me, and I know your doing" (Morm. 8:35). Knowing that so many servants of God over the ages have been mindful of our challenges and anxiously engaged in providing the precise counsel for returning home should engender in us a continual feeling of gratitude for their sacrifices on our behalf.

The prophet Nephi—at the beginning of the process that generated the Book of Mormon—knew that he was writing for compatriots who would be living in a future day, just as did Moroni at the ultimate end of that process. His deepest motivation was to persuade others to believe in Christ and follow the gospel plan, for he knew that was the only way to achieve lasting happiness.

What a singularly uplifting experience it is for modern readers to peruse the pages of a sacred book whose compilers, acting under inspiration, were speaking directly to them. Moroni knew the conditions that would prevail at the time of the Restoration, of which the publication of the Book of Mormon was one of the earliest manifestations: "And no one need say they [the records] shall not come, for they surely shall, for the Lord hath spoken it; for out of the earth shall they come, by the hand of the Lord, and none can stay it; and it shall come in a day when it shall be said that miracles are done away; and it shall come even as if one should speak from the dead" (Morm. 8:26).

The Book of Mormon was written especially for our day. In that context, President Ezra Taft Benson gives us the following specific assignment: "Each of the major writers of the Book of Mormon testified that they wrote for future generations. . . . If they saw our day, and chose those things which would be of greatest worth to us, is not that how we should study the Book of Mormon? We should constantly ask ourselves, 'Why did the Lord inspire Mormon or Moroni or Alma to include that in their records? What lesson can I learn from that to help me live in this day and age?'" (The Teachings of Ezra Taft Benson, 58–59). As you ponder and study the Book of Mormon, what depicted themes, patterns of behavior, practices, and events seem to have a relationship to our day and age, and what counsel given in the Book of Mormon helps us avoid the pitfalls of waywardness and enjoy the guidance of the Lord?

Third, the Book of Mormon blesses our lives by completing a grand circle in which the word of God is brought together as part of the divine design of gathering. Since the initial printing of 5,000 copies of the Book of Mormon in March 1830, this monumental work has attained a circulation of well more than 100 million copies in multiple languages. It is by far the most compelling and effective missionary tool for spreading the gospel in the latter days.

The coming forth of the Book of Mormon as a central dimension of the Restoration was foretold by the Lord's messengers. Isaiah spoke of a voice that would "whisper out of the dust" and be part of "a marvellous work and a wonder" that would transcend the wisdom and understanding of the world's prudent (Isa. 29:4, 14). Ezekiel spoke of a record—the "stick of Joseph" (the Book of Mormon)—that would be paired with the "stick of Judah" (the Bible) in the latter days as one unified message of truth (Ezek. 37:15–17). Thus multiple testimonies of the truth of the gospel would be established and blended together through divine intervention, as John the Revelator proclaimed: "And I saw another angel fly in the midst of heaven, having the ever-lasting gospel to preach unto them that dwell on the earth, and to every nation, and kindred, and tongue, and people" (Rev. 14:6).

Bringing together the word of God in the latter days as a profound endowment of truth was also foreseen by Nephi: "And it shall come to pass that my people, which are of the house of Israel, shall be gathered home unto the lands of their possessions; and my word also shall be gathered in one. And I will show unto them that fight against my word and against my people, who are of the house of Israel, that I am God, and that I covenanted with Abraham that I would remember his seed forever" (2 Ne. 29:14).

The purpose of the Lord in bringing forth the Book of Mormon is stated plainly by Moroni on the title page: "Which is to show unto the remnant of the House of Israel what great things the Lord hath done for their fathers; and that they may know the covenants of the Lord, that they are not cast off forever— And also to the convincing of the Jew and Gentile that JESUS is the CHRIST, the ETERNAL GOD, manifesting himself unto all nations." The Book of Mormon provides great and inspiring stories from the past, great covenants for the present, and great hope for the future, all founded on the mission and Atonement of Jesus Christ. How can you deepen your understanding and appreciation of this monumental work and confirm why President Ezra Taft Benson called it "the keystone of our religion" (The Teachings of Ezra Taft Benson, 41)?

What Are Three Unique Blessings Available through the Doctrine and Covenants?

First of all, the Doctrine and Covenants is comprised, for the most part, of direct pronouncements of the Savior in His own sacred words, given as a warning to the world and as specific instructions for His Saints on their homeward journey. He declares: "These words are not of men nor of man, but of me; wherefore, you shall testify they are of me and not of man; For it is my voice which speaketh them unto you; for they are given by my Spirit unto you, and by my power you can read them one to another; and save it were by my power you could not have them; Wherefore, you can testify that you

have heard my voice, and know my words" (D&C 18:34–36).

Second, by hearing the voice of the Savior and obeying His commandments, we can participate in the unfolding of the kingdom of God and the operation of the Abrahamic covenant. The Doctrine and Covenants provides the constitution of priesthood administration in the dispensation of the fulness of times leading up to the Second Coming, including meticulous instructions concerning the offices of the priesthood and the ordinances of salvation (as examples, see Sections 20, 84, 88, 107, and 121).

Third, while the Book of Mormon restores the essentials of the gospel in its fulness as a means to enter into the fold of Christ, the Doctrine and Covenants gives the roadmap and compass for completing the journey all the way to the gateways of heaven, including the keys of consecration and temple covenants that prepare the faithful for an everlasting celestial glory (as examples, see Sections 76, 127, 128, and 132). The voice of the Lord, the constitution of His kingdom, and the roadmap for the final journey are provided in the pages of the Doctrine and Covenants. Just as the Book of Mormon is "Another Testament of Jesus Christ," we can say that the Doctrine and Covenants is a modern testament of Jesus Christ, or what President Ezra Taft Benson calls the "capstone" of our religion, being the manifestation and essence of continuing revelation (see *The Teachings of Ezra Taft Benson*, 41).

The Savior referred to His flock as "the children of the prophets" and the "children of the covenant" (3 Ne. 20:25–26). How does the Doctrine and Covenants help you to see yourself in this role and therefore perform according to the Lord's expectations, for "of him unto whom much is given much is required" (D&C 82:3)?

Real-life Stories for Heart and Mind

"**A Covert from Storm and from Rain.**" An institute instructor had just begun the course of study on the Book of Mormon with a group of choice young singles when the terror attack of September 11, 2001, took place. Like everyone in the nation, the students were shocked by the devastating upheaval wrought upon our way of life by evil forces. Could there be any security and peace after such a revolutionary shift in the status quo?

And then the class read together the words of Isaiah that Nephi included in his record: "And the Lord will create upon every dwelling-place of mount Zion, and upon her assemblies, a cloud and smoke by day and the shining of a flaming fire by night; for upon all the glory of Zion shall be a defence. And there shall be a tabernacle for a shadow in the day-time from the heat, and for a place of refuge, and a covert from storm and from rain" (2 Ne. 14:5–6; compare Isa. 4:5–6). Faithfully, the class continued to study the Book of Mormon together and find within its pages the hope and guidance needed for this day and age.

One of the students later wrote a letter expressing how the Book of Mormon, specifically that passage from Isaiah and Nephi, had been a blessing and a guide at a time of challenge: "When I consider 2 Nephi 14:5–6, I can't help but think of our nation's recent events. In a time when evil is so apparent and terror so present, I have asked myself where I might find refuge or safety. Right now I live far from the 'holy places' of my youth, namely with my family and dear friends. But even so far away, I can find refuge in many places, like Institute. After a hectic day at work, where my attention is distracted by so many busy, yet less important, things, I am glad to have Institute as a refuge, a place to associate with other Saints, to feel the Spirit, and to study the word of God. It has truly been a blessing, 'a covert from storm and from rain.'" This experience shows once again how the Book of Mormon is a spiritual haven of security for our day.

How have the scriptures provided for you and your loved ones a place of security where hope and reassurance come through the Spirit in times of great challenge and upheaval?

Something Happened Inside. A Book of Mormon instructor at BYU taught courses on the Book of Mormon every year and, despite all the repetition, still found things he'd never even seen before. So he gave students an extra-credit assignment to read 2 Nephi 9 or Enos each day for thirty days in a row before going to bed. A student once asked the instructor, "Why do we need to read it every day? I mean, I'll get it after just a night or two." "You just read it and see," the instructor answered.

Then one day as the instructor was walking to class, he found a young man waiting for him by the door. This student literally leapt on the instructor and gave him a hug, saying, "It's true, it's true!" The instructor replied, "I know it's true, Elder." "I understand what you mean now," he said. "I read Enos every day, and on the twenty-first day something happened inside. I wanted everybody to be converted. I'm thinking of checking out of school and going on my mission today." "Can't you just wait two more weeks until the semester ends?" the instructor asked with a twinkle in his eye. This young man had fallen in love with the Book of Mormon because he did what the prophet said—again and again and again—and then he applied it in his life.

Nephi said, "For my soul delighteth in the scriptures, and my heart pondereth them" (2 Ne. 4:15). How has a committed, repeated reading of the word of God given you refreshing joy? How have you been able to teach this lesson to your loved ones?

Pondering Prayerfully

Additional scriptures to consider and ponder:
- 1 Ne. 15:24
- 2 Ne. 33:4
- 3 Ne. 23:5
- D&C 1:37
- D&C 11:22
- D&C 42:12
- D&C 84:85

The following hymns inspire gratitude for the scriptures:
- "As I Search the Holy Scriptures" (*Hymns,* 277)
- "How Firm a Foundation" (*Hymns,* 85)
- "The Iron Rod" (*Hymns,* 274)

Remember and Be Sure

The purpose of the word of God is to persuade us to do good, to believe in Christ, and to endure to the end. There are not enough words to adequately express the magnificence of the word of God—its sanctity, its monumental importance in the eternal scheme of things, its profound value as a gift of our Father in Heaven to His children. When we yield our hearts to His word so that it takes root in us, we can live by its light and enjoy the blessings of heaven in all dimensions of our lives. This is our challenge, our opportunity, and our blessing.

Let us humbly pay the price of diligently feasting upon the word and thus receive the "power of God unto salvation" (D&C 68:4). Through the scriptures we can come to know our Heavenly Father and our Savior. When our hearts receive and accept the word, our lives are changed.

We need the spiritual nourishment that the word of God can give us. It is our beacon of hope along a mortal pathway all too frequently marked by challenges to our endurance and by trials of our faith. As Nephi stated: "Wherefore, ye must press forward with a steadfastness in Christ, having a perfect brightness of hope, and a love of God and of all men. Wherefore, if ye shall press forward, feasting upon the word of Christ, and endure to the end, behold, thus saith the Father: Ye shall have eternal life" (2 Ne. 31:20).

CHAPTER 11
Mortal Mission of Christ

When Jesus came, He came as a sacrifice not simply in the interest of Israel . . . but in the interest of the whole human family, that in Him all men might be blessed, that in Him all men might be saved; and His mission was to make provision by which the whole human family might receive the benefits of the everlasting Gospel . . . not alone those dwelling upon the earth, but those also in the spirit world. —Lorenzo Snow (*Deseret Weekly News*, 32:18)

Opening the Window of Wisdom

Of all the numberless worlds for which Jesus Christ served as Creator and Redeemer, ours is the only world where He chose to live in mortality to bring about His supreme and universal sacrifice that all might live. The most transcendent event in all of history was the coming of the Son of God to this earth to complete His mission of redemption. He was the Only Begotten Son of God in the flesh, born of the virgin Mary, commissioned to deliver the doctrines, laws, and ordinances concerning eternal life. He bestowed the power to act in the name of God, performed the infinite and eternal Atonement, and by the power of the Resurrection made it possible that through Him all mankind might return to the Father—if

they would but come unto the Lord and keep His commandments. When we come to understand and appreciate this sublime plan of exaltation made possible by the goodness of God the Father and the sacrifice of our Lord and Savior, we should rejoice in knowing that the Son of God did come to earth to carry out the will of the Father in an act of divine love and mercy. Jesus is the Son of God. He is "the light and life of the world" (D&C 10:70) and the "bread of life" (John 6:35, 48).

Prophets from the beginning of time foresaw the birth, life, and sacrifice of the Savior. Adam learned that his own sacrifices in obedience to the word of God were "a similitude of the sacrifice of the Only Begotten of the Father, which is full of grace and truth" (Moses 5:7). Isaiah, looking into the future, declared, "For unto us a child is born, unto us a son is given: and the government shall be upon his shoulder: and his name shall be called Wonderful, Counsellor, The mighty God, The everlasting Father, The Prince of Peace" (Isa. 9:7). Nephi saw in vision a virgin "bearing a child in her arms. And the angel said unto me: Behold the Lamb of God, yea, even the Son of the Eternal Father!" (1 Ne. 11:20–21). King Benjamin taught his people, "And he shall be called Jesus Christ, the Son of God, the Father of heaven and earth, the Creator of all things from the beginning; and his mother shall be called Mary" (Mosiah 3:8). Alma declared to the people at Gideon:

For behold, the time is not far distant that the Redeemer liveth and cometh among his people . . . .

And behold, he shall be born of Mary, at Jerusalem which is the land of our forefathers, she being a virgin, a precious and chosen vessel, who shall be overshadowed and conceive by the power of the Holy Ghost, and bring forth a son, yea, even the Son of God.

And he shall go forth, suffering pains and afflictions and temptations of every kind; and this that the word might be fulfilled which saith he will take upon him the pains and the sicknesses of his people.

And he will take upon him death, that he may loose the bands of death which bind his people; and he will take upon him their infirmities, that his bowels may be filled with mercy, according to the flesh, that he may know according to the flesh how to succor his people according to their infirmities. (Alma 7:7, 10–12)

Without exception, the prophets of God have focused their message on the mission and Atonement of the Savior. All scriptures testify and witness that Jesus was and is the promised Messiah, the anointed one, even the Savior and Redeemer of the world. Our testimonies of Christ will deepen as we come to realize and remember His goodness and our total dependence on Him in fulfilling the plan of our Heavenly Father. We are commanded to seek our Savior and come to know Him: "And this is life eternal, that they might know thee the only true God, and Jesus Christ, whom thou hast sent" (John 17:3). As our knowledge and testimony of Christ increase, we will seek to become like Him and take upon ourselves His divine nature (see 2 Pet. 1:3–12).

Inspired by Latter-Day Prophets

Heber J. Grant: We all know that no one ever lived upon the earth that exerted the same influence upon the destinies of the world as did our Lord and Savior Jesus Christ; and yet He was born in obscurity, cradled in a manger. He chose for His apostles poor, unlettered fishermen. More than nineteen hundred years have passed and gone since His crucifixion, and yet all over the world, in spite of all strife and chaos, there is still burning in the hearts of millions of people a testimony of the divinity of the work that He accomplished (*Improvement Era*, 43:713).

How does the Savior's meekness and acceptance of the role of Lamb of God strengthen your resolve to do as He has commanded? How can you best express before your family and other loved ones your conviction of the divinity of Jesus Christ?

Ezra Taft Benson: There is the ever-expectancy of death, but in reality there is no death—no permanent parting. The Resurrection is a reality (*The Teachings of Ezra Taft Benson*, 34).

The majesty of Christ's Resurrection three days following His Crucifixion is a marvel of singular importance, unprecedented in the history of mankind. His triumph over death made possible the immortality of all of God's children, for all will be resurrected according to His grace. How does the principle of the resurrection give you hope and comfort—especially in light of the fact that you have lost loved ones or have some in your circle of friendship who have chronic ailments or physical deficiencies that will be resolved in the world to come?

Bruce R. McConkie: Isaiah, David, Nephi, Nephi the son of Helaman, and Samuel the Lamanite . . . speak pointedly of the fact that God himself, having come into mortality, would die. . . . That this death should result from crucifixion was forerevealed by Isaiah, Nephi, Jacob the brother of Nephi, and Enoch, among others. . . . And the glorious resurrection of our Lord was spoken of on many occasions (*Mormon Doctrine*, 490).

The Son of God was chosen as the Lamb of Life from the foundation of the world. There is no mystery about His role in the Atonement or His triumph over the grave. All of the prophets of God have known about these things and have proclaimed through all generations of time the truth of the plan of salvation. All have identified Christ as the Redeemer. In the world such truths are often rejected or denied or ignored. What has been your experience testifying to the world of the divinity of Christ and the need to come unto Him for life and salvation?

Truths to Liken

John 8:28–32—"Then said Jesus unto them [the Pharisees], When ye have lifted up the Son of man, then shall ye know that I am he, and that I do nothing of myself; but as my Father hath taught me, I speak these things. And he that sent me is with me: the Father hath not left me alone; for I do always those things that please him. As he spake these words, many believed on him. Then said Jesus to those Jews which believed on him, If ye continue in my word, then are ye my disciples indeed; And ye shall know the truth, and the truth shall make you free."

- The Savior was explicit during His earthly ministry in bearing personal testimony of His true identity.
- Our moment of truth in the wake of such testimony is to seek the confirmation of the Spirit so that we might also stand as witnesses of the divinity of the Savior and His mission. Each time we express before others our heartfelt conviction of the truth of the gospel of Jesus Christ, we add a thread of strength and courage to the magnificent tapestry depicting the history of God's dealings with His children within the framework of the plan of salvation. What are your thoughts about how we can know the truth about the divine mission of the Savior and how this conviction can make us free?

John 14:6—"Jesus saith unto him, I am the way, the truth, and the life: no man cometh unto the Father, but by me."

- On the eve of His atoning sacrifice, Jesus taught His disciples about His divine commission. These words were the Savior's response when Thomas asked which way to go.
- The Savior Jesus Christ is the only way back to the presence of our Heavenly Father. Happiness and joy come through His infinite and eternal Atonement, the blessings of His gospel, the power of His priesthood with accompanying covenants and ordinances, and His teachings and doctrines. How would you respond if someone asked you the Thomas question: "What way should I go?"

John 18:37—"Pilate therefore said unto him, Art thou a king then? Jesus answered, Thou sayest that I am a king. To this end was I born, and for this cause came I into the world, that I should bear witness unto the truth. Every one that is of the truth heareth my voice."

- These were among the final words of the Savior during the proceedings against Him by the authorities. He bore solemn witness of His true identity. Never did He deny His mission, not even on the eve of His Crucifixion.
- The Savior's noble representation of the truth is a supreme example of His courage and His devotion to His commission from the Father. What opportunities have you had in your lifetime to stand firm in your testimony in the presence of disbelievers? What was the source of your courage and how did it make you feel to take a stand for the truth?

Acts 1:3—"To whom [the Apostles] also he shewed himself alive after his passion by many infallible proofs, being seen of them forty days, and speaking of the things pertaining to the kingdom of God."

- At the beginning of Acts—Luke's continuing saga of the life and ministry of the Savior and His disciples—we find confirmation that the resurrected Lord showed Himself to the Apostles and spent forty days with them, instructing them concerning heavenly things.
- It would have been a transcendent experience to spend forty days with the resurrected Son of God, learning more about the operation of the kingdom of God. The disciples in the New World had a similar experience for a period of

time. Where can you go to be instructed in the higher truths of the gospel of salvation and exaltation? How does the temple experience relate to such instruction?

Alma 34:15—"And thus he shall bring salvation to all those who shall believe on his name; this being the intent of this last sacrifice, to bring about the bowels of mercy, which overpowereth justice, and bringeth about means unto men that they may have faith unto repentance."

- Amulek, missionary companion to Alma, taught the Zoramites about the coming of the Savior and Redeemer.
- The mercy and grace of the Redeemer serve to satisfy the demands of justice in the case of those who repent and follow the gospel plan. What are your thoughts about the phrase *bringeth about means* as it relates to faith?

Hel. 14:15—"For behold, he surely must die that salvation may come; yea, it behooveth him and becometh expedient that he dieth, to bring to pass the resurrection of the dead, that thereby men may be brought into the presence of the Lord."

- In this passage, Samuel the Lamanite was preaching to the people of Zarahemla about the impending birth of the Savior and His mission of grace and power. Samuel's message fell largely on deaf ears, but many of the Saints in his day still lived with the hope of the coming of the Savior, His sacrifice, and His Resurrection to the newness of life.
- The glorious news, even the good news of the gospel of Jesus Christ, is what gives us hope—hope that the Lord and Savior died and that we might live again through the power of the resurrection. What are your thoughts about the Resurrection and its implication for future happiness?

3 Ne. 1:12–14—"And it came to pass that he cried mightily unto the Lord all that day; and behold, the voice of the Lord came unto him, saying: Lift up your head and be of good cheer; for behold, the time is at hand, and on this night shall the sign be given, and on the morrow come I into the world, to show unto the world that I will fulfil all that which I have caused to be spoken by the mouth of my holy prophets. Behold, I come unto my own, to fulfil all things which I have made known unto the children of men from the foundation of the world, and to do the will, both of the Father and of the Son—of the Father because of me, and of the Son because of my flesh. And behold, the time is at hand, and this night shall the sign be given."

- Nephi, son of Nephi and grandson of Helaman, had been laboring under great stress; the dissenters in the land had threatened to kill those who believed in the prophecy of Samuel the Lamanite that the signs of Christ's birth would be manifested five years hence. As these words were spoken by the Lord, the five-year time period was about to expire, and mass execution was looming.
- The voice of the Redeemer spoke peace and consolation to Nephi at the urgent hour. Often we have times of stress in our own lives. How has the voice of the Lord or that of His chosen servants brought comfort and hope when things seemed dark and hopeless? How can you teach your loved ones to listen for that voice and be of good cheer?

Rejoicing and Reasoning Together

What Can We Learn from the Example of Mary?

The mother of our Lord Jesus Christ was the paragon of virtue, obedience, and rectitude. Similarly, righteous mothers through all generations of time have set the standard for enduring sacrifice and love, fulfilling their eternal commission to bring into the world the sons and daughters of God. As such, they participate in the work and glory of God "to bring to pass the immortality and eternal life of man" (Moses 1:39) and merit our everlasting gratitude and honor.

Concerning the mortal Messiah, Alma prophesied: "And behold, he shall be born of Mary, at Jerusalem which is the land of our forefathers, she being a virgin, a precious and chosen vessel, who shall be overshadowed and conceive by the power of the Holy Ghost, and bring forth a son, yea, even the Son of God" (Alma 7:10). The moment in time when Mary learned that she would serve as the mother of Jesus is a sacred moment, for it announced and confirmed the impending fulfillment of the will of God to provide a Lamb of Life on behalf of His children. Through the family gateway that was to be provided by Mary and Joseph, the young Lord would enter into the realm of His mortal ministry and grow in wisdom and stature to the measure of the Redeemer, being blessed and empowered by a gracious Father in Heaven and nurtured by a loving mother chosen from before the foundations of the world for this very commission.

When Gabriel announced to Mary her endowed role as the mother of the Savior, she replied with simple humility: "Behold the handmaid of the Lord; be it unto me according to thy word" (Luke 1:38). Later, while visiting Elisabeth, she declared the celebrated words: "My soul doth magnify the Lord, And my spirit hath rejoiced in God my Saviour" (Luke 1:46–47). Not many births are announced like this by an angelic emissary, but many are announced through the promises and pronouncements of the patriarchs of the Church, who envision under inspiration the coming forth of the sons and daughters of God as blessings and gifts to mortal mothers and fathers—parents who aspire to fulfill the righteous purposes of our Father in Heaven.

We can scarcely imagine the joy of Mary in fulfilling the promise of the annunciation of Gabriel by bringing the Savior into the world—a healthy and radiant child whose mission was to ensure the vitality and well-being of all mankind. The angel who appeared in glory to the shepherds guarding their flocks on that occasion set the tone for the appropriate response: "Fear not: for, behold, I bring you good tidings of great joy, which shall be to all people. For unto you is born this day in the city of David a Saviour, which is Christ the Lord" (Luke 2:10–11).

Mary epitomizes virtue and motherly love. She is the only mortal mother to bring into the world the literal Son of God. Yet all mothers bring into the world children who were first created as spirit children of our Father in Heaven. What examples of motherly love and faithfulness do you think

about frequently in your life and represent to others as admirable models of goodness and kindness?

What Qualities and Patterns of Living Do You Admire Most in the Life of the Mortal Messiah?

Reflected in the life of the Savior are many exemplary qualities, including that of a grand organizer who established His Church and installed and empowered officers of various kinds for the good of the Saints. He was a worker of miracles and a loving and forgiving Master. He was our Advocate with the Father. Following are just a few examples to think about and consider:

He was a master teacher. The Savior frequently taught in engaging parables, wanting to add truth to the lives of those who willingly accepted His word while concealing truth from those who rejected it. Those who were His disciples understood the mysteries of the kingdom as reflected in the parables, while those who were antagonistic and not of the Spirit could not penetrate to the layer of wisdom lying below (see Matt. 13:10–13).

Parables are used to teach not only the doctrines of the gospel, but how to live each day—they teach a new way of thinking and behaving. They give us a true perspective of things as they really are. They show us the way to respond to situations that arise in life. They unfold the mysteries of the gospel in practical ways. When we learn to liken the parables to ourselves, these scriptures will become part of our lives. If we live by the Spirit and seek to understand by that same Spirit, the magnificent truths of the parables will be unfolded to us and the doctrine will distill upon our souls as the dews from heaven (see D&C 121:45)—and we will change for the better.

What are some of your favorite parables taught by the Savior? How do you use them in your life?

He wrought mighty miracles. As just one example, Jesus demonstrated on many occasions His power over the elements—including His miraculous walk on the sea: "But the ship was now in the midst of the sea, tossed with waves: for the wind was contrary. And in the fourth watch of the night Jesus went unto them, walking on the sea.

And when the disciples saw him walking on the sea, they were troubled, saying, It is a spirit; and they cried out for fear. But straightway Jesus spake unto them, saying, Be of good cheer; it is I; be not afraid" (Matt. 14:25–26).

As we exercise faith, we too can bring about miracles by serving as instruments in the hands of God. If we have faith to follow the Savior on the waters of life, we can accomplish many worthwhile things in blessing the lives of others. What sorts of "miracles" have you been able to accomplish as you have depended on the strength of the Lord?

He was and is the loving Shepherd. The Lord loves and cares for His children even as a shepherd truly cares for his flock. As a master teacher, the Savior understands how to transfer truth from His bosom, where the scriptures reside (see D&C 35:20), to the hearts and minds of believing listeners. Using the metaphor of the Good Shepherd—which echoed the anticipatory sayings of the prophets of old and resonated with His contemporary and future disciples—He illustrated His love for His sheep in words of unsurpassed persuasion and power:

The thief cometh not, but for to steal, and to kill, and to destroy: I am come that they might have life, and that they might have it more abundantly.

I am the good shepherd: the good shepherd giveth his life for the sheep.

But he that is an hireling, and not the shepherd, whose own the sheep are not, seeth the wolf coming, and leaveth the sheep, and fleeth: and the wolf catcheth them, and scattereth the sheep.

The hireling fleeth, because he is an hireling, and careth not for the sheep.

I am the good shepherd, and know my sheep, and am known of mine.

As the Father knoweth me, even so know I the Father: and I lay down my life for the sheep. (John 10:10–15)

Referring to His "other sheep" in ancient America (John 10:16), the Savior continued to expound His mission and role as Good Shepherd and Redeemer. The Jewish leaders took offense at His doctrine, but He bore solemn witness of His divine Sonship and declared: "My sheep hear my voice, and I know them, and they follow me" (John 10:27). Furthermore, He responded to charges of blasphemy—that He had testified that He was the Son of God—by appealing to the ancient scriptural declaration: "I have said, Ye are gods; and all of you are children of the most High" (Ps. 82:6). Why, therefore, should they take offense at Him for saying that He was the Son of God? After all, He was doing the works of His Father—and these works could be the pathway to their belief. But they believed Him not, and sought to take His life, so He departed from their midst and resorted to the place where John the Baptist had first baptized. Here many came to listen to Him and believed on Him, accepting Him as the Good Shepherd of the fold of God.

Jesus Christ is our foundation and the only way by which we can return to our Heavenly Father. He is the Good Shepherd. How can you use this image to help others, especially children and youth, to understand the love and mercy of the Savior?

He taught us how to pray. On the eve of His departure from mortality, the Savior announced the coming gift of the Holy Spirit—God's gift of comfort, light, confirmation, and divine remembrance for the faithful (see John 16). As He prepared for the hour of the Atonement—an event prophesied and foretold by all of God's prophets from the beginning of time—the Savior offered one of the greatest of all prayers ever sent up from the vales of the earth to the courts of heaven: the great intercessory prayer (see John 17). This sacred prayer memorialized the key to eternal life—knowing God and Jesus Christ (John 17:3) and then acting in faith and unity to follow the commandments in strict obedience to the will of the Father. We learn in that prayer the ultimate motivation of the Redeemer in completing His work: "And for their sakes I sanctify myself, that they also might be sanctified through the truth" (John 17:19).

How have you been able to sanctify yourself, using the pattern of the Savior, in order to help your loved ones "sanctify themselves through the truth"?

He was the Master of forgiveness and the Preserver of life. The accounts of the Savior's Crucifixion resonate with unforgettable views: the intense suffering of our Lord; His forgiving mercy toward the soldiers (see Luke 23:34); His consciousness of having to complete His divine mission alone (see Mark 15:34); and His tender concern for His mother (see John 19:27). When all was done, the Savior "bowed his head, and gave up the ghost" (John 19:30). The Atonement was complete, and the Redeemer had fulfilled the will of the Father: "Though he were a Son, yet learned he obedience by the things which he suffered; And being made perfect, he became the author of eternal salvation unto all them that obey him" (Heb. 5:8–9).

The culmination of the Atonement was the glorious Resurrection of the Lord Jesus Christ. Knowing of the power of the Resurrection gives us hope to carry on in life's deepest hours of trial, tribulation, and even death—for we will all live again. We can have hope to come forth in the morning of the first resurrection if we keep the covenants (see D&C 76:64–65).

Many in the Savior's day witnessed the reality of His Resurrection, and the confirming testimony in this dispensation echoes in our hearts from the Prophet Joseph and Sidney Rigdon: "And now, after the many testimonies which have been given of him, this is the testimony, last of all, which we give of him: That he lives! For we saw him, even on the right hand of God; and we heard the voice bearing record that he is the Only Begotten of the Father—That by him, and through him, and of him, the worlds are and were created, and the inhabitants thereof are begotten sons and daughters unto God" (D&C 76:22–24).

In what ways has the Savior's example of forgiveness and His commitment to save lives been the governing motivation for you in your family and Church callings?

Real-life Stories for Heart and Mind

"**Come, Follow Me.**" On one occasion some years ago, a high priest took his young son and several others on a fishing trip to a remote lake in the Canadian Rockies. They hiked over a towering summit and down into the lake area, otherwise accessible only by a narrow goat trail leading across and up a dangerous cliff at the end of a box canyon. Unfortunately, the inbound hike took much longer than expected, and they were faced with an unpleasant choice: they had to spend the night in the wilds without any overnight equipment, or they had to brave the treacherous trip down the cliff located a short distance beyond the edge of the lake. Just looking over the edge at the valley floor thousands of feet below was enough to instill terror in their hearts. What could they do? Just at the moment of their greatest dismay, they were surprised to hear laughter and whistling through the evergreen trees. Two men appeared from nowhere, carrying their fishing gear and wearing broad smiles. They must have sensed how forlorn the strangers were, for they joked and teased with their banter. Then one of them said, "We can take you down the cliff. Come, follow us. And don't look down." With that, the followers inched their way behind the leaders along the goat trail, in some parts only an inch or two wide, clutching the rock face above them for balance. After following the expert guides each step of the way for what seemed like an eternity, they finished the descent and moved gratefully into safer territory.

Since then, the rescued individuals have often thought of the words of those guides: "Come, follow us." They knew the trail. They knew the dangers. They had cultivated the techniques—and the attitude of success. And they knew how to lead the inexperienced to safety.

There are dangers lurking on the cliffs of life, as well. There is an abyss of spiritual emptiness that yawns upward to the lonely traveler. But then the words of the Savior echo in our hearts: "Come, follow me" (Luke 18:22), and we know that the Shepherd is near, guiding us into pathways of security and joy. "My sheep hear my voice," He said, "and I know them, and they follow me" (John 10:27). The word of the Lord is the iron rod across the cliffs of life—the anchor to the fearful heart. It is the comfort to the wary, and the balance to the unsteady.

How have the words "Come, follow me" echoed in your own life? How has the example of the Savior guided you through dangers and into the safety and security of the straight and narrow pathway leading to eternal life?

The Greater Honor—A Little Parable. Several years ago a member of the Church was sharing the gospel with one of his nonmember friends. The friend came to him one day with an anti-Mormon pamphlet that a colleague had given to him—ostensibly as a means of dissuading him from accepting the truths of the Restoration. The member read the pamphlet carefully and prepared for his friend a scripture-based response to correct the misconceptions and untruths it reflected. It saddened him to observe that yet another detractor was degrading the glory and dignity of the plan of salvation and attempting to deprive an honest seeker after truth of the happiness that comes from embracing the principles and ordinances of the gospel of Jesus Christ. He felt impressed to pen a little parable to convey to his friend his perspective on the situation:

> A certain man had a garden which he cultivated with care from sunrise to sunset. Every day this man gave thanks to God for the bounteous and delicious harvest, and for the sunshine, rain, and good seed that made it possible. With the fruit of the garden, he nourished his family, generously remembered his neighbors in need, and laid up the surplus against the winter season. However, a certain neighbor took offense at the garden, and noised about that the fruit thereof was of no worth. Then by night, he crept into the garden and trampled it underfoot, so that the owner had to start afresh. Which of these two now is of greater honor before God and His angels? What say ye?

The friend received this little parable with a smile and a twinkle in his eye. He understood the principle and continued with his study of the gospel—the pearl of great price—undeterred by the voices of hostility and dissent that so often ricochet off the solid defenses that protect the honest-at-heart. As the Savior said: "Again, the kingdom of heaven is like unto a merchant man, seeking goodly pearls: Who, when he had found one pearl of great price, went and sold all that he had, and bought it" (Matt. 13:45–46).

There are many ways to present the truths of the gospel—but the most effective way is to follow the promptings of the Spirit. What experiences have you had to confirm this principle?

Pondering Prayerfully

Additional scriptures to consider and ponder:
- 1 Ne. 15:15
- Mosiah 3:17–19
- Alma 5:38–40
- Alma 26:12

The following hymns help bring gratitude for the mortal ministry of the Savior:
- "Away in a Manger" (*Hymns,* 206)
- "Come, Follow Me" (*Hymns,* 116)
- "He Died! The Great Redeemer Died" (*Hymns,* 192)
- "Jesus, Once of Humble Birth" (*Hymns,* 196)

Remember and Be Sure

The Savior boldly and fearlessly declared to the people precisely who He was: the Son of God, the Redeemer of the world. He told the truth, and many were offended by His assertions because of the troubling implications for their comfort and the threats to their supposed authority. But in the face of such disbelief, the Savior continued with His practice of showing forth miracles and teaching by the power of God. He magnified the gift of a small boy by compounding five loaves and two fishes into a feast for five thousand. He walked on the stormy sea and calmed the elements. He presented Himself as the "bread of life" through which spiritual hunger could be satisfied forever. He opened the pathway for His followers to come unto Him in faith and righteousness.

If we will but follow Him and partake of the bread of life, we will become in His hands a miracle of transformation, a wonder of conversion, a marvel of edification. In all our amazement at His unsurpassed deeds and words, we can remember that the greatest miracle of all is the mighty change of heart that each of us can experience through obedience to the principles and ordinances that He has provided for our eternal blessing.

When we all take time to reflect upon our own lives, we can see our dependence on our Savior Jesus Christ. He is the way, the truth, the light, and the life of the world. He is the vine that gives us all the strength to carry on. He is the Shepherd that guards and guides us. Stop and think: He preserves our very lives and lends us breath from one moment to the next (see Mosiah 2:21). He supports us as we deflect temptations of every kind. He succors us in all our afflictions (see Alma 7:11–12). He atoned for our sins because He loved us (see 2 Ne. 26:24). He has set the perfect example for us (see 3 Ne. 27:27). He has given us the way back to the Father by showing us how to keep His commandments and endure to the end (see 2 Ne. 31:20). As we come to understand and appreciate these wonderful truths, we will truly seek our Savior and His ways in all that we do. Our motto would simply become, "Do as Jesus would do."

It is only in and through Christ that salvation can be received (see Mosiah 3:17). As we remember with reverence the birth of our Lord Jesus Christ and rejoice in His mission as the promised Messiah, we can show our gratitude by following His matchless example in all that we do, especially in preparing ourselves more fully to serve in building up His kingdom.

CHAPTER 12
The Savior's Atoning Sacrifice

Christ is real; he lives! His life is real. He is the Son of God. The Babe of Bethlehem, The One Perfect Gentleman who ever lived—the Ideal Man whose character was supreme; our Brother, Our Savior, The "Anointed One." God help us to believe in him with all our souls to make him real in our lives!
—David O. McKay (*Man May Know for Himself: Teachings of President David O. McKay,* 423)

Opening the Window of Wisdom

The Atonement is central to all aspects of the gospel, the pillar of God's design for "the immortality and eternal life of man" (Moses 1:39). Every member of the Church, even the very young, have these words on the tongue: "We believe that through the Atonement of Christ, all mankind may be saved, by obedience to the laws and ordinances of the Gospel" (A of F 3). Because the Son accommodated Himself fully to the will of the Father, the Atonement, in all of its glory, unfolded as a magnificent gift to mankind, empowering the Resurrection and giving the opportunity for the faithful and obedient to gain access once again to the presence of God.

Hope springs eternal through the triumph of the Redeemer over death: "And this is the gospel, the glad tidings, which the voice out of the heavens bore record unto us—That he came into the world, even Jesus, to be crucified for the world, and to bear the sins of the world, and to sanctify the world, and to cleanse it from all unrighteousness; That through him all might be saved whom the Father had put into his power and made by him" (D&C 76:40–42).

Understanding the Atonement of Christ and its relationship to our eternal existence is the greatest knowledge we can have in support of our quest to return to God, our Eternal Father. The Atonement is the vital core of the gospel of Jesus Christ. When we diligently apply its principles to our lives through the covenant process—through faith unto repentance, baptism, and receiving the gift of the Holy Ghost—we become liberated from the fallen state we are in through the "merits, and mercy, and grace of the Holy Messiah" (2 Ne. 2:8). We become free through Christ by obedience. It is by the grace of God that we are saved, "after all we can do" (2 Ne. 25:23).

Redemption from temporal and spiritual death comes through the Atonement of the Lord Jesus Christ (see 2 Ne. 2:6). There is no other way. Simple and profound, all-encompassing in its heavenly majesty, the gospel of Jesus Christ is the means to be lifted up and enter eternal rest. The Savior's witness about His atoning mission gives the pattern of action that is required of all who will gain eternal life and exaltation: "Now this is the commandment:

Repent, all ye ends of the earth, and come unto me and be baptized in my name, that ye may be sanctified by the reception of the Holy Ghost, that ye may stand spotless before me at the last day. Verily, verily, I say unto you, this is my gospel; and ye know the things that ye must do in my church; for the works which ye have seen me do that shall ye also do; for that which ye have seen me do even that shall ye do" (3 Ne. 27:20–21).

Inspired by Latter-Day Prophets

John Taylor: Through the great atonement, the expiratory sacrifice of the Son of God, it is made possible that man can be redeemed, restored, resurrected, and exalted to the elevated position designed for him in the creation as a Son of God. . . . The Savior thus becomes master of the situation—the debt is paid, the redemption made, the covenant fulfilled, justice satisfied, the will of God done, and all power is now given into the hands of the Son of God . . . the captain of our salvation, the apostle and high priest of our profession, the Lord and giver of life (*The Gospel Kingdom: Selections from the Writings and Discourses of John Taylor*, 114).

The Atonement and its universal influence was and is an act of power. No greater power can be unleashed and made available to mankind than that. In return, how can you increase the personal effort and power you invest in service and charity as a way of expressing gratitude for the consummate gift of the Atonement?

Howard W. Hunter: It is our firm belief that [the Atonement] is a reality, and nothing is more important in the entire divine plan of salvation than the atoning sacrifice of Jesus Christ. We believe that salvation comes because of the Atonement. In its absence the whole plan of creation would come to naught (*The Teachings of Howard W. Hunter*, 7).

How can you add your own testimony to such words as these and blend your conviction with that of a prophet? How can you use every opportunity—family home evening meetings, family councils, fast and testimony meeting, class discussions, conversations with those not of the Church, and so on—to testify of the truth of these things?

Bruce R. McConkie: Salvation comes by getting Christ into our hearts today, by being born again, by becoming new creatures of the Holy Ghost, by receiving personal revelation, by exercising the gifts of the Spirit, by having the power of God manifest in our lives (*CR*, October 1968, Afternoon Meeting, 135).

The Atonement calls forth decisive action on the part of those who enter the fold of Jesus Christ. As you consider your experiences in the kingdom of God, what actions on your part have increased your happiness and the happiness of your loved ones?

Truths to Liken

John 6:35—"And Jesus said unto them, I am the bread of life: he that cometh to me shall never hunger; and he that believeth on me shall never thirst."

- Jesus spoke to some of the people who participated in the miracle of the loaves and fishes the previous day. The Savior wanted them to understand that the true bread of life comes through the blessings of the gospel of redemption.
- This scripture makes it clear that the food of eternal life comes only through the Lord Jesus Christ. When we come unto Christ, He blesses us and strengthens us in all things. How does the sacrament remind you each week that the Savior is the "bread of life"? What does the word *life* mean in that expression?

Alma 34:9–10—"For it is expedient that an atonement should be made; for according to the great plan of the Eternal God there must be an atonement made, or else all mankind must unavoidably perish; yea, all are hardened; yea, all are fallen and are lost, and must perish except it be through the atonement which it is expedient should be made. For it is expedient that there should be a great and last sacrifice; yea, not a sacrifice of man, neither of beast, neither of any manner of fowl; for it shall not be a human sacrifice; but it must be an infinite and eternal sacrifice."

- Amulek was speaking to the assembled Zoramites, expressing to them his witness of the mission and mercy of Jesus Christ.

- The plan of salvation applies to all, for all are lost without an infinite Atonement. Only Deity has the power to lift all to a level where "the merits, and mercy, and grace of the Holy Messiah" (2 Ne. 2:8) can redeem them from their hardened and fallen state through faith, repentance, and obedience to the commandments of the gospel. If someone not of the Christian faith were to ask you why an infinite Atonement is necessary, how would you respond?

3 Ne. 27:13–15—"Behold I have given unto you my gospel, and this is the gospel which I have given unto you—that I came into the world to do the will of my Father, because my Father sent me. And my Father sent me that I might be lifted up upon the cross; and after that I had been lifted up upon the cross, that I might draw all men unto me, that as I have been lifted up by men even so should men be lifted up by the Father, to stand before me, to be judged of their works, whether they be good or whether they be evil—And for this cause have I been lifted up; therefore, according to the power of the Father I will draw all men unto me, that they may be judged according to their works."

- In this passage, Jesus had joined His recently installed disciples in the New World as they were traveling about, teaching His words and baptizing the people. He explained to them the essence of the gospel plan.
- The action of lifting reminds us of the Crucifixion, just as it also applies to the power of the gospel to draw people into the fold of Christ and lift them to a fulfillment of their spiritual potential. Being drawn to the Savior and lifted up defines the motion and direction of those coming under the divine influence of the Atonement. Our resurrection lies in the future, of course, but how have you experienced so far the "drawing and lifting" power of the Atonement?

D&C 18:11–13—"For, behold, the Lord your Redeemer suffered death in the flesh; wherefore he suffered the pain of all men, that all men might repent and come unto him. And he hath risen again from the dead, that he might bring all men unto him, on conditions of repentance. And how great is his joy in the soul that repenteth!"

- The Lord was speaking through the Prophet Joseph Smith at Fayette, New York, June 1829, to Oliver Cowdery and David Whitmer, teaching them how to render service in building up the kingdom of God.
- We learn that the Savior, having performed the infinite Atonement through His suffering and mercy, feels great joy when people respond to His invitation to repent and come into the fold. What are your thoughts about the joy you give the Savior through your own obedience to gospel principles?

D&C 88:14–17—"Now, verily I say unto you, that through the redemption which is made for you is brought to pass the resurrection from the dead. And the spirit and the body are the soul of man. And the resurrection from the dead is the redemption of the soul. And the redemption of the soul is through him that quickeneth all things, in whose bosom it is decreed that the poor and the meek of the earth shall inherit it."

- These words are part of the revelation given through the Prophet Joseph Smith at Kirtland, Ohio, December 27, 1832, designated by the prophet at the "olive leaf . . . plucked from the Tree of Paradise, the Lord's message of peace to us."
- This message of peace confirms the reality of the Resurrection—that the spirit and body of each mortal will be inseparably reunited in triumph over physical death, opening the way for each to receive "a fulness of joy" (D&C 93:34). What are your thoughts about the future experience of being resurrected, when the infirmities and weaknesses of the mortal frame will be a thing of the past?

Moses 6:59–60—"That by reason of transgression cometh the fall, which fall bringeth death, and inasmuch as ye were born into the world by water, and blood, and the spirit, which I have made, and so became of dust a living soul, even so ye must be born again into the kingdom of heaven, of water, and of the Spirit, and be cleansed by blood, even the blood of mine Only Begotten; that ye might be sanctified from all sin, and enjoy the words of eternal life in this world, and eternal life in the world to come, even immortal glory; For by the water ye keep the commandment; by the Spirit ye are justified, and by the blood ye are sanctified."

- Enoch taught the people the words of the Lord to Adam, confirming that the gospel plan and the power of the Atonement were known and felt from the beginning of time.

- The power of the Atonement brings about a rebirth for all who obey the principles of the gospel and receive the associated priesthood ordinances of salvation. The Father, the Son, and the Holy Ghost are all central to this process. What are your thoughts about the state of being "reborn" through the effects of the Atonement, and how can you perpetuate this state as an enduring blessing to you and your loved ones?

Rejoicing and Reasoning Together

What Was the Greatest Moment in the History of Mankind?

The suffering of the Savior on the cross at Golgotha was unspeakable and intense—yet it was during His travail in the Garden of Gethsemane, preceding the Crucifixion, that the moment of redeeming triumph was ultimately attained, as He later confirmed: "Nevertheless, glory be to the Father, and I partook and finished my preparations unto the children of men" (D&C 19:19).

That moment in the Garden of Gethsemane was at the center of the flow of all history, both human and divine. This was a moment in time unlike any other. It was a moment of both infinite agony and redeeming charity, both sorrow "unto death" (Matt. 26:38) and atonement unto life—the ultimate result of eternal design and heavenly will. What did this moment mean to humankind? It meant the victory of life over death; the hope of liberty over the reality of everlasting spiritual imprisonment; the possibility of eternal joy in the presence of God over the horror of a never-ending night of separation from one's heavenly roots and home. This was the moment when faith for all God's children was raised to a higher power—"this being the intent of this last sacrifice, to bring about the bowels of mercy, which overpowereth justice, and bringeth about means unto men that they may have faith unto repentance" (Alma 34:15). This moment in time was motivated by love, empowered by grace, sustained by courage, and accomplished by the inexorable will of God unto the saving of all mankind.

How raptly focused must have been the view of the legions of heaven on this moment in time as the curtains were drawn back. The Savior was about to do the will of the Father and bring under His feet all enemies of God's supernal plan of salvation, including death. Gethsemane was the scene of His triumph; Golgotha was the scene of His benediction: "And when Jesus had cried with a loud voice, he said, Father, into thy hands I commend my spirit: and having said thus, he gave up the ghost" (Luke 23:46). Following His Resurrection, He could declare: "And behold, I am the light and the life of the world; and I have drunk out of that bitter cup which the Father hath given me, and have glorified the Father in taking upon me the sins of the world, in the which I have suffered the will of the Father in all things from the beginning" (3 Ne. 11:11). The greatest moment of all time had been sanctified and memorialized as a blessing to all mankind.

Only one other moment in time approaches the importance of this one—and that is the moment in which each individual will decide, in faith and hope, to accept the Atonement of the Redeemer in all devotion and valor, taking upon himself or herself the name of Jesus Christ, thereafter to live in a state of humble and grateful compliance with all the commandments of God. Such a moment of commitment in the life of each individual honors and validates that moment of infinite reach when the Savior gave His all for our happiness and joy. What are your thoughts about this glorious theme? How is the Atonement the centerpiece of your life and the lives of your loved ones?

How Do We Repay Our Debt to the Savior for His Atoning Sacrifice?

It is our deepest obligation never to forget the love that the Lord Jesus Christ has shown for us. Nephi described His love with these words: "He doeth not anything save it be for the benefit of the world; for he loveth the world, even that he layeth down his own life that he may draw all men unto him. Wherefore, he commandeth none that they shall not partake of his salvation" (2 Ne. 26:24). When we recognize what He went through to be an offering for our sins, and when we try to understand and appreciate His infinite Atonement, our love for and devotion toward our Savior will increase.

From Gethsemane to Golgotha He suffered pain of body and of heart, false accusations, scourging, and then finally was hung on the cross and crucified. We should become like the people of King Benjamin when they came to understand that Jesus was the Christ and Redeemer of the world and their personal Savior. They expressed their feelings in this way: "And they all cried with one voice, saying: Yea, we believe all the words which thou hast spoken unto us; and also, we know of their surety and truth, because of the Spirit of the Lord Omnipotent, which has wrought a mighty change in us, or in our hearts, that we have no more disposition to do evil, but to do good continually" (Mosiah 5:2). Love and gratitude for our Savior and His sacrifice for us should move us to righteousness.

From choice passages in the Doctrine and Covenants and related scriptures, we gain a lucid understanding of the plan of salvation. The moment of truth that enlivens these passages with enduring meaning is the sacred act of the Atonement itself: "For behold, I, God, have suffered these things for all, that they might not suffer if they would repent; But if they would not repent they must suffer even as I" (D&C 19:16–17). Knowing that the Savior lifted the burden of suffering from our being fills our heart with gratitude. Knowing of His love and mercy gives us the desire to accept, in full faith and devotion, the atoning sacrifice of the Savior as the essence of our existence and the redeeming force to lift us to the pinnacle of our potential as sons and daughters of God.

How can you conduct your life in such a way as to demonstrate more fully your gratitude to the Savior for His love and atoning sacrifice? How can you help your family and loved ones share in your testimony of the reality of the Atonement and its central place in the design of the Almighty?

Real-life Stories for Heart and Mind

Balm of Gilead. In the well-known hymn, "Did You Think To Pray?" the final verse asks the searching questions, "When sore trials came upon you, did you think to pray? When your soul was full of sorrow, Balm of Gilead did you borrow, at the gates of day?" Several years ago a ward bishop was approached by a new convert to the Church, a young father, who took him aside after a meeting and, in hushed tones, asked him to explain the meaning of "Balm of Gilead." Smiling, the bishop explained that "Balm of Gilead" was simply a traditional natural remedy from the Holy Land that had healing effects and was widely used by the Israelites. As such, it is an image for the healing essence of the Atonement. The new convert seemed almost relieved at the simplicity of the principle, and went on his way with a smile on his face.

Since then the bishop has thought many times about the question concerning the Balm of Gilead, for it is another way of asking, "What is the mystery of the Atonement, that it should bring to mankind its miraculous healing influence?" When Joseph was betrayed by his jealous brothers, they sold him into the hands of itinerant Ishmaelite tradesmen who were en route from Gilead to Egypt with camels bearing "spicery and balm and myrrh" (Gen. 37:25). Gilead was a wooded highland region located to the east of Jordan, with many bushes that produced the resin used to make the healing gum or balm known throughout the area. Later, when it was time for Jacob to persuade the Egyptian viceroy—alias his own missing son Joseph—to provide food for his family in a time of dire famine, he thought to facilitate the bargain by sending his other sons back to Egypt with gifts of nuts, myrrh, and native balm (see Gen. 43:11). Because forgiveness was the governing nature of Joseph, he took compassion on his family in a time of need and readily forgave his brothers their trespass.

Similarly, because forgiveness is the essence of the divine nature, the Savior readily extends His lovingkindness to all mankind and rescues them from ultimate temporal and spiritual death.

Like the Balm of Gilead in the temporal sphere, the Balm of the Atonement is the healing power of salvation proclaimed from the foundation of the earth as the answer to the spiritual quest of mankind. Upon the administration of that kind of balm, there will be no remaining ailment, no enduring injury—for its renewing curative power is eternal, coming from the "Son of righteousness," with "healing in his wings" (3 Ne. 25:2).

How have you experienced the calming and healing influence of the "Balm of the Atonement" in your own life? How can you better extend to others encouragement to use this kind of Balm as the supreme nurturing and healing power in their own lives?

The Royal Adoption. During the process of adopting a child, a couple appeared before the court to answer a sobering question, with words to this effect: "Are you willing to take upon yourselves all responsibility for the welfare and well-being of this child, to nurture and care for the child under all circumstances just as if the child were your natural-born child?" As they answered yes to this question and completed the legally binding covenants relative to the adoption, they sensed that an extraordinary change in their status had occurred: the man became a father and the woman a mother to the adopted child—and the child became a child of the adoptive parents.

This is similar to the covenant relationship we have with the Savior through the Atonement. The doctrine of adoption into the kingdom of God was explained by King Benjamin as follows: "And now, because of the covenant which ye have made ye shall be called the children of Christ, his sons, and his daughters; for behold, this day he hath spiritually begotten you; for ye say that your hearts are changed through faith on his name; therefore, ye are born of him and have become his sons and his daughters" (Mosiah 5:7). The question might be: Who shall be able to identify Christ's children, His seed, since He was "cut off out of the land of the living"? (Mosiah 14:8). The answer to that question is given in a succinct formulation by Isaiah, quoted by Abinadi: "When thou shalt make his soul an offering for sin [in other words, when we accept the Atonement and keep the covenant commandments], he shall see his seed, he shall prolong his days, and the pleasure of the LORD shall prosper

in his hand" (Isa. 53:10). In effect, the Savior took upon Himself the responsibility to be our eternal Caregiver and to assure that we, as His adopted sons and daughters, enjoy everlasting vitality and nurture, being born again through a royal adoption into the family of Christ.

What are your thoughts on the theme that the Atonement is in truth a process of adoption? How is the sacrament prayer a reminder of this process: "that they are willing to take upon them the name of thy Son, and always remember him and keep his commandments which he has given them" (D&C 20:77)?

Pondering Prayerfully

Additional scriptures to consider and ponder:
* Ps. 8:4–5
* Ps. 82:6
* Ps. 118:22
* 2 Ne. 9:7
* 2 Ne. 9:21–22
* 2 Ne. 9:26
* Alma 11:43–44
* Alma 34:14
* Moro. 8:11–12
* D&C 50:44
* D&C 76:40–42

The following hymns help inspire gratitude for the Atonement:
* "Come unto Jesus" (*Hymns,* 117)
* "There Is a Green Hill Far Away" (*Hymns,* 194)

Remember and Be Sure

From the record of the scriptures and the confirmation of the Comforter, we know that the Savior suffered to take our sins and infirmities upon Himself and to bring about the universal Resurrection. The Atonement of Jesus Christ is our only hope for salvation, immortality, and eternal life. No individual can gain these blessings through perfect compliance with the laws and commandments of God, for no one other than the Savior who has ever lived upon the earth, or who will ever live upon the earth, is perfect. Therefore, there must of necessity be a way to make up the difference— a divine plan to bring about the Atonement and satisfy the demands of justice through an infinite sacrifice of mercy and compassion.

What do we need to do to merit the magnificent blessing of the Atonement? Our assignment for mortality is abundantly clear: "Behold, this is your work, to keep my commandments, yea, with all your might, mind and strength" (D&C 11:20). The roadmap to salvation is mercifully simple and straightforward, marked by the steps of faith in the Lord Jesus Christ, repentance made possible by His atoning sacrifice, baptism by immersion and taking upon us His name, receiving the gift of the Holy Ghost by the laying on of hands, and enduring to the end along the pathway to eternal life. The message is pure and undefiled: "Wherefore, redemption cometh in and through the Holy Messiah; for he is full of grace and truth. Behold, he offereth himself a sacrifice for sin, to answer the ends of the law, unto all those who have a broken heart and a contrite spirit; and unto none else can the ends of the law be answered" (2 Ne. 2:6–7). The outcome is certain: "And as many as repent and are baptized in my name, which is Jesus Christ, and endure to the end, the same shall be saved" (D&C 18:22.)

CHAPTER 13
Nature and Power of the Priesthood

Again, let me ask who, among all mortal men, really knows what this marvelous priesthood power actually is? Obviously it is power; its source, obviously, too, is God. Why not call it then for what it truly is—the power of God?
—Joseph F. Smith (as quoted by William J. Critchlow in *CR*, October 1963)

Opening the Window of Wisdom

The priesthood is the authority and power of God given to man on earth to act for the blessing and salvation of God's children. It is the power by which all things are done in the grand and eternal design of God. It is the divine agency and vital administering principle by means of which the Creation was accomplished and the plan of salvation made operational for achieving the "immortality and eternal life of man" (Moses 1:39).

The priesthood operates as the government of God and gives direction to the Church and kingdom of God on earth under the leadership of the Lord Jesus Christ through His holy prophets. The Holy Ghost inspires us to use the priesthood in righteousness. The power of the priesthood is faith. The underlying purpose of the priesthood is to bless people's lives.

The Doctrine and Covenants is the principal scripture in the latter days for understanding and applying the principles and policies embodied in the priesthood as it has been restored to the earth once again by divine intervention and blessing (see especially D&C 13, 20, 84, 107, 121). Few things could be deemed of greater worth to mankind, and few things should inspire more humble devotion and enduring commitment than the singular honor of holding and administering the priesthood of God for and in behalf of His sons and daughters.

Inspired by Latter-Day Prophets

Brigham Young: The Priesthood of the Son of God, which we have in our midst, is a perfect order and system of government, and this alone can deliver the human family from all the evils which now afflict its members, and insure them happiness and felicity hereafter (*Discourses of Brigham Young,* 130).

Of the many nations and governments in the world, some are more effective than others in preserving the liberty and inalienable rights of the people. The government of God, empowered and sustained by His holy priesthood, is destined to eternalize the liberty and happiness of God's children. How does it magnify your understanding of the operation of the priesthood to see it this way—as the fiber and strength of the perfect government of God?

Harold B. Lee: The strength of the Church is not in a large membership, but the real strength of this church lies in the power and authority of the holy priesthood which our Heavenly Father has given to us in this day. If we exercise properly that power and magnify our callings in the priesthood, we will see to it that the missionary work shall go forward, that the tithing shall be paid, that the welfare plan shall prosper, that our homes shall be safe, and that morality among the youth of Israel shall be safeguarded (*The Teachings of Harold B. Lee*, 487).

The meaning of power has come to be associated with mass, numbers, and overwhelming force arrayed on the stage of worldly affairs. But priesthood power is of a different caliber: it is the strength and authority of the Lord applied according to eternal principles for the blessing of all His children—one person at a time, one family at a time, one ward at a time, one stake at a time, one mission at time. In what ways have you experienced the power of the priesthood in your life as you have done your part in building up the kingdom of Heaven on earth?

Bruce R. McConkie: What, then, is the doctrine of the priesthood? . . . It is that we have power . . . to stand in the presence of God and be like him because we have gained his faith, his perfections, and his power, or in other words the fulness of his priesthood ("The Doctrine of the Priesthood," *Ensign*, May 1982, 32).

This statement about the doctrine of the priesthood opens up a panoramic vista concerning the nature and blessings of priesthood power. In what ways is your understanding about the priesthood magnified and expanded by studying and pondering this definition?

The First Presidency: Aware of the promises made by the prophets and presidents of the Church who have preceded us that at some time, in God's eternal plan, all of our brethren who are worthy may receive the priesthood, and witnessing the faithfulness of those from whom the priesthood has been withheld, we have pleaded long and earnestly in behalf of these, our faithful brethren, spending many hours in the Upper Room of the Temple supplicating the Lord for divine guidance.

He has heard our prayers, and by revelation has confirmed that the long-promised day has come when every faithful, worthy man in the Church may receive the holy priesthood, with power to exercise its divine authority, and enjoy with his loved ones every blessing that flows therefrom, including the blessings of the temple. Accordingly, all worthy male members of the Church may be ordained to the priesthood without regard for race or color." (D&C Official Declaration—2.)

This Official Declaration, which extends the reach of priesthood blessings to all worthy male members, is a primary example of modern-day, continuing revelation through God's living prophets. Where were you when you first heard of this glorious news? What was your reaction? What was your experience in sharing this revealed priesthood declaration with friends of a different race or color who were waiting for the good news?

Truths to Liken

D&C 13:1—"Upon you my fellow servants, in the name of Messiah I confer the Priesthood of Aaron, which holds the keys of the ministering of angels, and of the gospel of repentance, and of baptism by immersion for the remission of sins; and this shall never be taken again from the earth, until the sons of Levi do offer again an offering unto the Lord in righteousness."

- These are the words of the angelic messenger John the Baptist, sent to bestow upon Joseph Smith and Oliver Cowdery the Aaronic Priesthood along the banks of the Susquehanna River near Harmony, Pennsylvania, on May 15, 1829.
- The Lord has seen fit to restore the Aaronic Priesthood and bless the young men of the Church with callings in this, the lesser priesthood, as they prepare for the Melchizedek Priesthood (restored not much later under the hands of Peter James, and John), together with all of its accompanying opportunities to serve. All Aaronic Priesthood bearers should understand the mission of the Aaronic

Priesthood, become converted to the gospel, magnify their priesthood callings, give of themselves in service, prepare to receive the Melchizedek Priesthood and serve a mission, live worthy to receive the blessings of the temple, and prepare to become righteous husbands and fathers. What has been your experience in helping the young men of the Church magnify their callings in the Aaronic Priesthood? How have you seen the priesthood bless their lives?

D&C 84:19–22—"And this greater priesthood administereth the gospel and holdeth the key of the mysteries of the kingdom, even the key of the knowledge of God. Therefore, in the ordinances thereof, the power of godliness is manifest. And without the ordinances thereof, and the authority of the priesthood, the power of godliness is not manifest unto men in the flesh; For without this no man can see the face of God, even the Father, and live."

- These words were given by the Lord through the Prophet Joseph Smith at Kirtland, Ohio, on September 22 and 23, 1832.
- The Melchizedek Priesthood allows mankind the privilege of understanding the mysteries of God (in other words, the doctrines and truths that bring joy and eternal life—see D&C 42:61), receiving all the ordinances of salvation and exaltation and preparing to return to the presence of the Father and the Son. In this context, it's easy to see the goodness of God in allowing His children the privilege of exercising His power and authority here on earth. How do these verses of scripture inspire you with gratitude for the Melchizedek Priesthood and encourage you to live worthy at all times to participate in the blessings of this higher priesthood?

D&C 84:26–27—"And the lesser priesthood continued, which priesthood holdeth the key of the ministering of angels and the preparatory gospel; Which gospel is the gospel of repentance and of baptism, and the remission of sins, and the law

of carnal commandments, which the Lord in his wrath caused to continue with the house of Aaron among the children of Israel until John, whom God raised up, being filled with the Holy Ghost from his mother's womb."

- These words continue the Lord's revelation through the Prophet Joseph Smith at Kirtland, Ohio, on September 22 and 23, 1832.
- When the Israelites in the wilderness rejected the higher blessings of the priesthood under Moses, the Lord instituted the lesser priesthood as a "schoolmaster" to train them to receive greater light and knowledge (see Gal. 3:24–25). As you observe the Aaronic Priesthood youth serving in their assigned functions, how is your heart warmed and your understanding of the magnificence of the preparatory priesthood enhanced and expanded?

D&C 107:8—"The Melchizedek Priesthood holds the right of presidency, and has power and authority over all the offices in the church in all ages of the world, to administer in spiritual things."

- These are words from an important revelation on priesthood given through the Prophet Joseph Smith at Kirtland, Ohio, on March 28, 1835.
- The Lord's servants—the prophet and First Presidency, the Quorum of the Twelve Apostles, the Seventy, stake presidents, bishops, and Melchizedek quorum presidents—are given keys to administer the spiritual things of the kingdom within their stewardships. The prophet holds all the keys, and under his direction all things are done here on earth (see D&C 81:2). How would you explain the difference between the *authority* of the priesthood and the *keys* of the priesthood?

D&C 121:34–36—"Behold, there are many called, but few are chosen. And why are they not chosen? Because their hearts are set so much upon the things of this world, and aspire to the honors of men, that they do not learn this one lesson—

That the rights of the priesthood are inseparably connected with the powers of heaven, and that the powers of heaven cannot be controlled nor handled only upon the principles of righteousness."

- These words were written by the Prophet Joseph Smith from the confines of prison at Liberty, Missouri. The epistle was dated March 20, 1839, and was sent first to his wife, Emma, with instructions to forward it first to his parents and then to the Church in general.

- To exercise the priesthood we are to be worthy, inspired by the Holy Ghost, and committed to do the will of the Lord. The principle of power by which the priesthood operates is faith—faith in our God and in our Savior Jesus Christ. Faith is the foundation of all righteousness (see Joseph Smith, *Lectures on Faith*, 1:3). Priesthood and righteousness are inseparably connected, assuring that those who are "called" are also "chosen"—chosen to proceed forward in devotion along the pathway leading to exaltation. In this context, how would you explain the meaning of the expression, "there are many called, but few are chosen"?

Rejoicing and Reasoning Together

What Is Meant by the Oath and Covenant of the Priesthood?

The following passage from the Doctrine and Covenants contains the doctrine concerning the oath and covenant of the priesthood:

> For whoso is faithful unto the obtaining these two priesthoods of which I have spoken, and the magnifying their calling, are sanctified by the Spirit unto the renewing of their bodies.
>
> They become the sons of Moses and of Aaron and the seed of Abraham, and the church and kingdom, and the elect of God.
>
> And also all they who receive this priesthood receive me, saith the Lord;

> For he that receiveth my servants receiveth me;
>
> And he that receiveth me receiveth my Father;
>
> And he that receiveth my Father receiveth my Father's kingdom; therefore all that my Father hath shall be given unto him.
>
> And this is according to the oath and covenant which belongeth to the priesthood.
>
> Therefore, all those who receive the priesthood, receive this oath and covenant of my Father, which he cannot break, neither can it be moved.
>
> But whoso breaketh this covenant after he hath received it, and altogether turneth therefrom, shall not have forgiveness of sins in this world nor in the world to come. (D&C 84:33–41)

The oath and covenant of the priesthood carries with it eternal blessings for those who are faithful: becoming sanctified, having a renewal of the body, being the seed of Abraham and the elect of God, and receiving all that the Father has. It also provides severe punishments for those who turn away from this divine covenant after receiving it, for where "much is given much is required" (D&C 82:3; Luke 12:48). The promise that those honoring the covenant will be granted all that the Father has is extraordinary, confirming the truth that "he that hath eternal life is rich" (D&C 11:7). What are your thoughts about such a transcendent eternal blessing in contrast with the fleeting treasures of a worldly nature?

What Do We Know About the Great Priesthood Leader Melchizedek?

Melchizedek—meaning *king of righteousness,* from *melek* ("king") and *tsedek* ("righteous")—was the great high priest, prophet, and king of Salem (Jerusalem) who lived at the time of Abraham, around two thousand years before Christ. The Old Testament contains only two references to Melchizedek (see Gen. 14:18–20 and Ps. 110:4). The New Testament describes the exalted station of Jesus Christ as "called of God an high priest after the order of Melchisedec" (Heb. 5:10) and "made an high priest for ever after the order of Melchisedec" (Heb. 6:20).

Clearly Melchizedek was an extraordinary exemplar of righteousness and priesthood valor—but it is only in the context of latter-day scripture that we gain a fuller understanding of his mission. The story of Melchizedek is the story of peace, for it represents the transformation of a wayward society through the redemptive power of spiritual principles of faith, repentance, and committed righteousness.

When Melchizedek assumed the office of prophet/leader, Salem (later called Jerusalem) was under a veil of spiritual darkness and rebellion— "yea, they had all gone astray" (Alma 13:17). But Melchizedek was well-prepared for his mission: "Now Melchizedek was a man of faith, who wrought righteousness; and when a child he feared God, and stopped the mouths of lions, and quenched the violence of fire. And thus, having been approved of God, he was ordained an high priest after the order of the covenant which God made with Enoch" (JST, Gen. 14:26–27). What Melchizedek accomplished was nothing short of a miracle, for his influence on the people had the astounding effect of bringing them all back into the fold (see Alma 13:18–19.)

So great was Melchizedek's office and stature that he was also placed in charge of the abundance of the Lord's kingdom: "And he lifted up his voice, and he blessed Abram, being the high priest, and the keeper of the storehouse of God; Him whom God had appointed to receive tithes for the poor. Wherefore, Abram paid unto him tithes of all that he had, of all the riches which he possessed, which God had given him more than that which he had need" (JST, Gen. 14:37–39). Through the portrait of Melchizedek, augmented by modern revelation, we can understand much better the magnificence of the holy priesthood, its eternal nature, its relationship to the atoning mission of the Son of God, and the sacred role of covenants in our eternal progression. We also understand how we too can become the sons and daughters of God through the power of the priesthood and the blessings of the gospel. Melchizedek was honored to have the priesthood called after his own name:

> Why the first is called the Melchizedek Priesthood is because Melchizedek was such a great high priest.

> Before his day it was called *the Holy Priesthood, after the Order of the Son of God.*

> But out of respect or reverence to the name of the Supreme Being, to avoid the too frequent repetition of his name, they, the church, in ancient days, called that priesthood after Melchizedek, or the Melchizedek Priesthood. (D&C 107:2–4)

Melchizedek is the prototype of the person who promotes peace; in fact, he is a type of the Master Himself, the divine Prince of Peace. The depth of understanding concerning Melchizedek's role is magnified in his relationship to Abraham, as we learn again from the Prophet Joseph Smith's translation of the Bible: "And Melchizedek, king of Salem, brought forth bread and wine; and he break bread and blest it; and he blest the wine, he being the priest of the most high God, And he blessed him, and said, Blessed be Abram of the most high God, possessor of heaven and of earth; And blessed be the most high God, which hath delivered thine enemies into thine hand. And Abram gave him tithes of all" (JST, Gen. 14:17–20).

The same principle is confirmed in the Book of Mormon, where we learn from Alma the following: "Yea, humble yourselves even as the people in the days of Melchizedek, who was also a high priest after this same order which I have spoken, who also took upon him the high priesthood forever. And it was this same Melchizedek to whom Abraham paid tithes; yea, even our father Abraham paid tithes of one-tenth part of all he possessed. Now these ordinances were given after this manner, that thereby the people might look forward on the Son of God, it being a type of his order, or it being his order, and this that they might look forward to him for a remission of their sins, that they might enter into the rest of the Lord" (Alma 13:14–16).

What made Melchizedek so great? Why was he so honored to have the Lord's priesthood named after him? He "exercised mighty faith" (Alma 13:18), magnified his holy office in the priesthood, and preached repentance with miraculous effect in bringing people to the Lord. His people became a holy people like the people of Enoch, for that is what Melchizedek sought: "And his people wrought righteousness, and obtained heaven, and sought for the city of Enoch which God had before taken, separating it from the earth, having reserved it unto the latter days, or the end of the world; . . . And this Melchizedek, having thus established righteousness, was called the king of heaven by his people, or, in other words, the King of peace" (JST, Gen. 14:34, 36).

As we come to appreciate the great mission and ministry of Melchizedek, we can understand how our daily lives are affected for good by the contribution and example of that ancient prophet after whom the higher priesthood is named. Melchizedek helped to prepare Abraham for his mission, and through Abraham and his seed all nations of the earth will be blessed. Melchizedek was of the order of the priesthood that opened up the blessings of eternal life, as the Prophet Joseph Smith confirmed: "The King of Shiloam (Salem) had power and authority over that of Abraham, holding the key and the power of endless life" (Teachings of the Prophet Joseph Smith, 322). How have you confirmed in your own life that it is our glory and joy to bring to others the gospel of Jesus Christ so that they, like the people of Melchizedek, might enjoy peace through righteousness and the blessings of covenant principles and ordinances?

What Special Blessings Flow unto Us through the Priesthood of God?

The following three ideas help us understand the power, purpose, and blessings of the priesthood and how to be worthy to exercise it:

1. Worthiness to exercise the priesthood comes through living a righteous life.

- **Repentance**—The priesthood operates on the principle of righteousness (see D&C 121:36). We are to purify ourselves through repentance and sanctify ourselves by yielding our heart to God (see Hel. 3:35).
- **Following the will of the Lord**—We are to seek the Lord's will and not our own as we utilize His priesthood power.
- **Inspiration**—When we are pure and clean, we can receive direction from the Holy Ghost.

- **Preparation**—Let us make a commitment to be spiritually prepared to exercise our priesthood whenever we are called upon to do so.
- **Gratitude**—Let us give thanks continually for the privilege of having the priesthood on earth with all of its blessings.

2. Blessings of the priesthood flow from God.

- **The process of returning to the presence of God**—We can be brought back into the presence of God only by receiving and keeping the covenants and ordinances of the Melchizedek Priesthood. Let us make a commitment to keep the covenants we have made.
- **Worthiness**—Receiving the blessings of the priesthood is always predicated on our worthiness.
- **Sacred blessings**—Lives have been blessed in every possible situation by the power of the priesthood, from raising the dead to healing the sick, from giving comfort to giving direction to one's life. The responsibility lies with us to ask for the blessings of the priesthood, be worthy, and exercise our faith.
- **Patriarchal blessings**—Everyone of age should prepare for, and be worthy of, receiving a patriarchal blessing to give comfort, advice, and direction for his or her life.
- **Power of God**—Let us never forget that everything on earth comes from the blessings of the priesthood. It is the power of God on the earth.

3. The purpose of the priesthood has been taught by the prophets of every dispensation.

- **Direction for the kingdom of God**—In all dispensations of time, the priesthood has been on earth to direct the kingdom of God and bless Heavenly Father's children.
- **Sealing power**—The priesthood provides the sealing power, enabling families to endure forever, bringing about the gathering of Israel, and making it possible

that through us, all generations will be blessed (see D&C 110:11–13).

- **Covenant power**—The priesthood provides for the governing of the Church and all the priesthood covenants and ordinances that manifest the power of godliness (see D&C 84:21).
- **Opening the way to return home**— The priesthood is here to help Heavenly Father's children return to His presence.

Real-life Stories for Heart and Mind

Steps to the Master. Melchizedek Priesthood holders today can trace their priesthood authority in a sequence of short steps directly back to the Master. The reason is explained clearly in the fifth Article of Faith: "We believe that a man must be called of God, by prophecy, and by the laying on of hands by those who are in authority, to preach the gospel and administer in the ordinances thereof." The Savior called and ordained Peter, James, and John as a presidency over the higher priesthood in their day (see John 15:16). They were later sent to the Prophet Joseph Smith and Oliver Cowdery to restore the keys of the Melchizedek Priesthood and authorize once again the administration of the saving gifts and ordinances on earth (see D&C 27:12–13). The line of priesthood authority then went from Joseph Smith to the Three Witnesses (see *HC* 2:187–188), and from them to Brigham Young, who was ordained an Apostle on February 14, 1835, and who became the second president of the Church in December 1847.

Beginning with Brigham Young, Melchizedek Priesthood holders can trace their line of authority forward to their own ordination in just a few steps. In an uninterrupted sequence of ordinations, the line of authority extends directly back to Jesus Christ. What a solemn and profound feeling comes over one to know that he has the same fundamental priesthood authority that was held by Abraham, Melchizedek, Joseph Smith, and all holders of the higher priesthood who have enjoyed and do enjoy such blessings from the Almighty. Through obedience and righteousness, priesthood holders can render an indispensable service to their families and many others of God's children.

If you are a Melchizedek Priesthood holder, prepare or review your priesthood lineage and ponder the supreme honor of being connected directly to the Savior in your priesthood calling. Others can ask a Melchizedek Priesthood holder in the family to provide a copy of his priesthood lineage and express his testimony concerning it.

"All That My Father Hath." One father was motivated by a feeling of wanting to serve others—especially those who did not have much of the world's abundance. During the summer months, he occasionally invited a young man from one of several needy families to join him and his own son on a Saturday fishing expedition to a nearby mountain park. As it turned out, the highway to the park passed along the boundaries of a large cattle ranch that was at the time owned and operated by the Church as part of the welfare program.

On one of those trips, the father, speaking to his twelve-year-old guest, asked: "See that land over there?" "Yes," replied the boy, looking through the car window at what seemed like an endless expanse of rolling hills and green fields. "That's your land," said the father. There was a moment of profound silence as eyes grew large and questions began to rise up in a young soul. "My land?" asked the young lad, with a hint of excitement in his voice. "Yes," replied the father. "The Lord tells us that if a man lives faithful to his priesthood callings, that 'all that my Father hath shall be given unto him' (D&C 84:38). Since that ranch belongs to the Church, I guess it belongs to you as well. It's your land." There was more prolonged silence as a young lad—someone who had virtually nothing of the world's material goods—processed within his soul for the first time a sense of the vast wealth that spiritual dominions of the faithful encompass. He smiled, and a valuable lesson had been learned.

As you consider this true story, what opportunities might you have to help others (particularly the young) understand the grand blessings that await them if they are faithful to their callings and honor their covenants with devotion? The principle is clear: "But seek ye first the kingdom of God, and his righteousness; and all these things shall be added unto you" (Matt. 6:33; compare 3 Ne. 13:33).

Pondering Prayerfully

Additional scriptures to consider and ponder:
- D&C 27:12–13
- D&C 107:1–5
- D&C 107:18–19
- D&C 107:20
- D&C 128:20

The following hymns help inspire gratitude for the priesthood:
- "Brightly Beams Our Father's Mercy" (*Hymns,* 335—Men)
- "Come, All Ye Sons of God" (*Hymns,* 322—Men)
- "Come, Sing to the Lord" (*Hymns,* 10)
- "Ye Elders of Israel" (*Hymns,* 319—Men)

Remember and Be Sure

Through His Son Jesus Christ, Heavenly Father has given us the magnificent blessing to exercise His power and authority on earth for the blessing and salvation of mankind. In gratitude, we can reverence our Heavenly Father by honoring the priesthood and by keeping our covenants. If we do so, through charity and virtue, then magnificent benefits will flow to us and our families: "Then shall thy confidence wax strong in the presence of God; and the doctrine of the priesthood shall distil upon thy soul as the dews from heaven. The Holy Ghost shall be thy constant companion, and thy scepter an unchanging scepter of righteousness and truth; and thy dominion shall be an everlasting dominion, and without compulsory means it shall flow unto thee forever and ever" (D&C 121:45–46).

Through the Restoration of the gospel of Jesus Christ in the latter days, the powers, purposes, and blessings of the priesthood of God have again been made manifest in the world for the redemption and edification of God's children. Priesthood doctrines, keys, and administrative policies were revealed in an orderly process through the Prophet Joseph Smith and his colleagues as the kingdom of God was once again established in its glory and fulness. Ultimately all of the keys—including the sealing powers—were restored for the consummation of the "marvellous work and a wonder" (Isa. 29:14) foretold by prophets of old and confirmed by Apostles in the meridian of time (see Acts 3:19–21). The restoration of priesthood keys laid the foundation for preparing mankind—all those who would choose the paths of righteousness and obedience—for the Second Coming: "Therefore, the keys of this dispensation are committed into your hands; and by this ye may know that the great and dreadful day of the Lord is near, even at the doors" (D&C 110:16).

CHAPTER 14
Organized to Serve

Now, while we live and labor let us magnify our calling. Let no man be found recreant to his opportunities. Let us not turn our backs upon the blessings of the Lord, but day by day go faithfully on blessing our father's children.
—George Albert Smith (*The Teachings of George Albert Smith,* 95)

Opening the Window of Wisdom

In Section 88 of the Doctrine and Covenants, the Lord directed the priesthood leaders of the early Restoration to act decisively in carrying out their stewardships: "Organize yourselves; prepare every needful thing; and establish a house, even a house of prayer, a house of fasting, a house of faith, a house of learning, a house of glory, a house of order, a house of God" (D&C 109:8). The reference to *a house of God* is an image of broad sweep, embracing the interrelated elements of heaven's design: the homes of Zion, the quorums and congregations of the faithful, the temples soon to be constructed, and the kingdom of God itself. All of these, severally and together, might be thought of as comprising "the house of God"—the grand spiritual edifice constituting the work of the priesthood and the unfolding of its programs of service in support of the cause of salvation and exaltation. Paul referred to this divine organization as the "household of God":

Now therefore ye are no more strangers and foreigners, but fellowcitizens with the saints, and of the household of God;

And are built upon the foundation of the apostles and prophets, Jesus Christ himself being the chief corner stone;

In whom all the building fitly framed together groweth unto an holy temple in the Lord: In whom ye also are builded together for an habitation of God through the Spirit. (Eph. 2:19–22)

How is this household of God organized to serve and to accomplish the divinely appointed mission of the Church? It is organized according to the revealed pattern of leadership found in the scriptures (especially the Doctrine and Covenants) and confirmed and directed by the living prophet called of God to carry out His will. The priesthood is the governing force in the Church and kingdom of God. Each person in his or her own callings, acting under the direction of the priesthood, plays a vital leadership role in the kingdom of God. The obedient and faithful are sustained by the Lord and magnified in the eyes of others—parents in their families, teachers in their classes, bishops in their wards, stake presidents in their stakes, missionaries in the field, prophets in their callings—that all might be edified and prosper spiritually.

No matter what the office or calling—deacon, teacher, priest, elder, high priest, bishop, stake president, patriarch, seventy, Apostle, home teacher, Relief Society president, visiting teacher, or any of the other callings in the Church—the key is to act in the strength of the Lord and magnify those callings in devotion and love. Each calling or role, honorably fulfilled, ultimately blesses someone's life—so when we magnify our callings, we build up, enlarge, and strengthen the people we serve through that calling, thus helping to build the kingdom of God (see D&C 108:7). Magnifying our callings in this way is serving God (see Mosiah 2:17) and assisting in His work (see Moses 1:39).

Each role and calling is important within its stewardship. Everyone is needed. Everyone is important in his or her callings—for we all have need of each other (see 1 Cor. 12:14–27). As we diligently seek to magnify our eternal roles and callings, we take steps to qualify ourselves to return to the presence of our Heavenly Father.

Inspired by Latter-Day Prophets

Brigham Young: We all believe that the Lord will fight our battles; but how? Will he do it while we are unconcerned and make no effort whatever for our own safety when an enemy is upon us? If we make no efforts to guard our towns, our houses, our cities, our wives and children, will the Lord guard them for us? He will not; but if we pursue the opposite course and strive to help him to accomplish his designs, then will he fight our battles (*Discourses of Brigham Young*, 303).

Every calling in the Church is a call to arms, a call to deploy on the battlefield of the cause of Zion. Every calling proceeds "in the strength of the Lord" (Alma 20:4; 46:20), but it also requires initiative, devotion, the wise use of agency, and a high investment of time and effort in order to prepare and perform well. As you consider your assignments in the kingdom of God, how can you balance your efforts, depending on the Lord and His strength on the one hand, and on the power of your own commitment, courage, initiative, talents, and hard work on the other?

George Albert Smith: Do you believe that this is The Church of Jesus Christ of Latter-Day Saints?

Do you believe that Joseph Smith was a prophet of the Lord? Do you believe that the man who stands at the head represents our Heavenly Father? He may make mistakes. The Prophet Joseph made his. Moses, the greatest leader of ancient times, made his mistakes. But I want to say that as long as the Lord sustains his leaders we should sustain them (*CR*, October 1936, 76).

We are all enlisted as imperfect beings in the perfect cause of the Lord. We can all rise in humility and faith above our imperfections and have "weak things become strong" (Ether 12:27) through the grace of God. We can see others in this same light as we sustain them in their callings, knowing that they are striving to perform their labors honorably and to the best of their capability. What follow-through actions on your part are required by your sustaining vote?

Howard W. Hunter: The Lord never calls a man to any office in his Church but what he will by revelation help that man to magnify his calling (*The Teachings of Howard W. Hunter*, 215).

What has been your experience with inspiration and revelation as you have fulfilled your various Church callings? How can you teach your loved ones to seek and receive this kind of guidance in all they do to help build the kingdom of God?

Bruce R. McConkie: The keys of the priesthood are the right and power of presidency. They are the directing, controlling, and governing power. Those who hold them are empowered to direct the manner in which others use their priesthood. Every ministerial act performed by a priesthood holder must be done at the proper time and place and in the proper way. The power of directing these labors constitutes the keys of the priesthood. Every elder, for instance, has the power to baptize, but no elder can use this power unless he is authorized to do so by someone holding the keys (*A New Witness for the Articles of Faith*, 309).

The Lord governs His kingdom through the operation of the priesthood, with its keys of leadership bestowed on chosen individuals who direct and control the forward motion of the work of Zion. No one serves in isolation and independence; instead, everyone fits in as a contributing servant in the large blend of groups, quorums, auxiliaries, and family circles following the counsel of the living prophet. This perspective is unique in all the world, for it teaches the true essence of belonging to the household of God, being integrated into His designs according to the pattern of service He has established for our blessing and good. What are your thoughts on this grand system of leadership in the Church? How can you teach your loved ones the majesty and joy of being a part of such an organization?

Truths to Liken

Matt. 23:11—"But he that is greatest among you shall be your servant."

- Jesus was teaching the people and His disciples to follow a pathway diverging from the course of the hypocritical scribes and Pharisees who were obsessed with station and the honors of men.
- Leadership is all about service. The term *servant leader* is really the operant mode in leadership. One cannot lead or influence others unless he or she is perceived as one who serves and cares about those who are led. Think of the Church leaders whom you have come to admire in your lifetime. What qualities stand out to you in their service?

Mosiah 23:14—"And also trust no one to be your teacher nor your minister, except he be a man of God, walking in his ways and keeping his commandments."

- After liberating his people from bondage under wicked King Noah, Alma the Elder declined to be their king and cautioned them to follow only righteous priesthood leadership.
- Leadership requires an exemplary life; leaders need to be full of faith and teach the people the ways of the Lord (see Jarom 1:7). Righteousness engenders trust and preserves freedom. How does this principle relate to the Savior's

dictum, "Therefore, what manner of men ought ye to be? Verily I say unto you, even as I am" (3 Ne. 27:27)?

D&C 81:5—"Wherefore, be faithful; stand in the office which I have appointed unto you; succor the weak, lift up the hands which hang down, and strengthen the feeble knees."

- These words were included in a revelation given through the Prophet Joseph Smith at Hiram, Ohio, in March 1832, concerning the duties of a counselor in the First Presidency, which was about to be formally organized.
- In every office and calling it is the people served that count. You are needed in your role; every person is important in his or her calling in the Lord's kingdom on earth (see D&C 84:109–110). Whom do you know with "hands which hang down" or "feeble knees"? How can you best strengthen such people as part of the service of your calling—including your calling as a member of The Church of Jesus Christ of Latter-day Saints?

D&C 107:99–100—"Wherefore, now let every man learn his duty, and to act in the office in which he is appointed, in all diligence. He that is slothful shall not be counted worthy to stand, and he that learns not his duty and shows himself not approved shall not be counted worthy to stand. Even so. Amen."

- These are the closing words of the revelation on the priesthood that was given through the Prophet Joseph Smith at Kirtland, Ohio, on March 28, 1835.
- Leaders have the responsibility to learn their duty, for that is part of being accountable. But the word *let* in this scripture has further meaning, as President Harold B. Lee taught: "It becomes the responsibility of those of us who lead to *let*, to *permit*, to *give opportunity* for every man to learn his duty and to be prepared to act in his office and calling according to his appointment" (Harold B. Lee, *The Teachings of Harold B. Lee*, 512). In your several callings and responsibilities in the

family and in the Church, how successful have you been at "letting" others learn their duty through your encouragement and example, and by your honoring their agency to act accountably?

Rejoicing and Reasoning Together

What Does It Mean to "Magnify" Our Office and Calling?

Following the death of Nephi, his brothers Jacob and Joseph followed in his footsteps as priesthood leaders among the people. Jacob taught them in the temple by giving them words of repentance and righteousness, for he and Joseph took very seriously the charge to magnify their calling, as he explained in these words: "And we did magnify our office unto the Lord, taking upon us the responsibility, answering the sins of the people upon our own heads if we did not teach them the word of God with all diligence; wherefore, by laboring with our might their blood might not come upon our garments; otherwise their blood would come upon our garments, and we would not be found spotless at the last day" (Jacob 1:19).

To *magnify* as used in such scriptures means to make greater or more splendid. There are at least four kinds of magnifying evidenced in the gospel. First, there is the process of magnifying an office by accepting it with humility, gratitude, soberness, and devotion—as Jacob exemplified when he spoke of "taking upon us the responsibility, answering the sins of the people upon our own heads if we did not teach them the word of God with all diligence" (Jacob 1:19; see also Jacob 2:2). A similar usage is reflected in the revelation given to Joseph Smith: "Keep these sayings, for they are true and faithful; and thou shalt magnify thine office, and push many people to Zion with songs of everlasting joy upon their heads" (D&C 66:11). Perhaps the most celebrated usage of this kind is found in the oath and covenant of the priesthood: "For whoso is faithful unto the obtaining these two priesthoods of which I have spoken, and the magnifying their callings, are sanctified by the Spirit unto the renewing of their bodies" (D&C 84:33).

Second, the main purpose of gospel service is to bring glory to God—to magnify Him and His Son and cause others to do the same: "O magnify the Lord with me, and let us exalt his name together" (Ps. 34:3). Nephi declared: "Wherefore, my soul delighteth to prophesy concerning him, for I have seen his day, and my heart doth magnify his holy name" (2 Ne. 25:13). Perhaps the most famous of such instances was uttered by the mother of the Redeemer: "And Mary said, my soul doth magnify the Lord, And my spirit hath rejoiced in God my Saviour" (Luke 1:46–47).

Third, gospel service causes people themselves to be magnified or rendered more splendid in the spiritual sense. "And the Lord said unto Joshua, This day will I begin to magnify thee in the sight of all Israel, that they may know that, as I was with Moses, so I will be with thee" (Joshua 3:7).

Finally, to *magnify* one's office is to give those served such a pure view of gospel truths (magnified, enlarged, expanded, and broadened) that they cannot misunderstand the vital obligation and choice to come into the fold of Christ and obey His commandments. If the teaching is in that way, then the responsibility is on the listeners to take action in obedience, and the teacher has fulfilled his or her charge with devotion. When we magnify our calling, we labor with all our might, mind, and strength so that we can stand blameless before the Lord (see D&C 4:2).

These scriptures imply a continual process. We *magnify* the office to which we are called by filling it with faith and humility, thus *magnifying* the Lord and enlarging His holy name before the world—for which we are in turn personally *magnified* through His blessings to us, allowing us to *magnify* the gospel message for others so that the pathway to salvation and exaltation is illuminated with the light of Christ. This process of enlargement—this eternal circle of service—is a lifting force. As the four stages are completed, the cycle starts again at a higher level. Thus we see emerging a *magnificent spiral* that carries us ever upward as we contribute to, and are nurtured by, the process of magnification. What a blessing to have a part in such a program of enlargement as the kingdom of God expands and grows like the stone that was cut from the mountain without hands and rolls forth to fill the whole world (see Dan. 2:34–35).

There are, of course, circumstances where it might be difficult or impossible to respond to a calling. At such times the Lord, in His compassion, may judge the heart of those involved and confirm that they "cease not their diligence"—and thus "require that work no more" of them, but "accept of their offerings" (D&C 124:49).

Consider your own duties and assigned obligations. Which of these belong to the class of duties and obligations that no one else can perform? How are you magnifying your calling with respect to these?

How Can We Improve Our Leadership Skills and Become More Organized to Serve?

The following checklist may be helpful:

1. Learn our duty.

- Search the scriptures for direction (see 2 Ne. 32:3; Alma 37:37–47).
- Seek counsel from the Lord (see Jacob 4:10; James 1:5–6).
- Study the Church manuals (see D&C 88:118).
- Attend the temple with a prayer in our heart (see D&C 97:13–14).
- Seek direction from the prophet and from our other leaders (D&C 21:4–5; 38:23).
- Attend our training meetings (see D&C 43:8–10).
- Learn and do our duty so we are not slothful servants (see D&C 107:99–100).

2. Be directed by the Spirit.

- Be worthy of the Spirit with faith (see 1 Ne. 10:17), love and purity (see D&C 76:116), and obedience (see D&C 20:77, 79).
- The Spirit will show us all things to do (see 2 Ne. 32:5).
- The Spirit will give us at the very moment the things we need to say (see D&C 100:5–6).
- The Spirit will direct us even if we don't always know the things to do (see 1 Ne. 4:6).

3. Understand the needs of those we serve.

- Get acquainted with those we serve.
- Build relationships of trust so that we can understand them and have credibility with them.
- Number and name those we have a responsibility for and, according to their needs, nurture them with the word of God (see Moro. 6:4).

4. Pray for understanding and direction (see James 1:5–6).

- Pray for special help (see Mosiah 27:14).
- Pray to have success in blessing others (see Alma 31:34–35).

5. Diligently seek to serve and bless our fellowmen.

- Labor with all our might within our stewardship (see Moro. 9:6).
- Seek the one who struggles or who is lost (see D&C 81:5; Luke 15:6).
- Remember that when we are helping another person we are helping the Lord (see Matt. 25:40; Mosiah 2:17).
- Serve with all our heart so that we may stand blameless before the Lord (see D&C 4:2).

How Can We Serve More Faithfully as Home Teachers and Visiting Teachers?

We are a visiting Church. We visit with one another in family gatherings. We visit the sick and afflicted. We visit the homes of the Saints in fulfilling our home teaching and visiting teaching assignments.

Home teaching is the Lord's way of watching over His flock (see D&C 20:53–55, 59). It is a program organized through the priesthood, allowing us as disciples to show charity and love (see John 13:34–35), to strengthen and help others (see D&C 81:5; 108:7), and to nurture the Saints (see Moro. 6:4). Home teachers serve the people they visit, counseling with the head of the home to understand the family's needs and concerns. They pray for strength and wisdom as they represent the Lord and Church leaders in this most important assignment. Surely the home teacher, acting as an under-shepherd of the Lord, is the first line of defense for the flock.

Visiting teaching is similar to home teaching. The sisters emphasize caring relationships and strengthen each other as they both give and receive messages of the gospel of Jesus Christ. Visiting teachers support and comfort their sister members of the Relief Society. As visiting teachers and disciples of the Lord Jesus Christ, they show charity (see John 13:34–35), strengthen and help others (see D&C 81:5; 108:7), and nurture them in love (see Moro. 6:4). Visiting teachers pray for strength and wisdom as they represent the Lord and Church leaders in this most important assignment.

What is the model of the Christian visit? The visit of the resurrected Lord to the Saints of ancient America likely established the model and standard for home teachers, visiting teachers, priesthood and Relief Society leaders, missionaries, and families—all of whom use visits to strengthen the Church and enlarge the kingdom of God. Consider the following checklist prepared from a thorough review of the Savior's visit as reported in the Book of Mormon (all references are from 3 Nephi):

- **The Savior bore testimony**—"Behold, I am Jesus Christ the Son of God" (9:15).
- **The Savior taught only the fundamentals of the gospel**—See 11:31–41; 15:1; 17:20; 27:13–21.
- **The Savior brought enduring gifts to the people**—Peace, light, love, and life (17:21–25).
- **The Savior brought a life-changing influence**—"Old things are done away, and all things have become new. Therefore, I would that ye should be perfect even as I, or your Father who is in heaven is perfect" (12:47–48; 27:27).
- **The Savior taught us who we are**—"The sons of God" (9:17); "the children of your Father who is in heaven" (12:45); "the children of the prophets . . . the children of the covenant" (20:25).
- **The Savior taught us how to gain a fullness of understanding**—"Go ye unto your homes and ponder upon the things which I have said, and ask of the Father, in my name, that ye may understand, and prepare your minds for the morrow" (17:3).
- **The Savior taught us how to participate in the ultimate fulfilling of the Father's covenant with the house of Israel**—"And then will I gather them in from the four quarters of the earth; and then will I fulfil the covenant which the Father hath made unto all the people of the house of Israel" (16:5).
- **The Savior taught us how to endure to the end**—"give heed unto the words of these twelve" (12:1); the sacrament (see 18:1–14); "watch and pray always" (18:15); "pray in your families" (18:21); "meet together oft" (18:22); hold "up

your light that it may shine unto the world" (18:24); read the scriptures (see 23:1, 5, 8–14); pay tithing (see 24:10).

No visit could be as perfect as the visit of the Savior to His Saints, but we can strive to follow His pattern and improve day by day. How might this checklist be adapted for your use in fulfilling your various callings in the Church?

How Is the Power of Godliness Revealed through the Priesthood?

Several important sections of the Doctrine and Covenants contain key references to the priesthood—its offices and organization, its functions and duties, and its blessings for mankind (see especially Sections 20, 84, 88, 90, 102, 107, and 121). The restoration of the priesthood of God to the earth in 1829 (see D&C 13:1; 27:12–13) was a moment of grand historical importance, for it inaugurated the era of priesthood leadership in the dispensation of the fullness of times—never again to be interrupted or terminated—and opened up the gateway for countless millions to be blessed through the power of sacred ordinances and sealing powers. The Lord's work "to bring to pass the immortality and eternal life of man" (Moses 1:39) was made possible by this divine act of grace and love through which the power and authority to act in God's name on behalf of His children was once again bestowed on His servants of the latter days.

The priesthood of God blesses our lives on a daily basis through its operations and functions. Following the restoration of the priesthood in 1829, the Lord unfolded the priesthood organization and protocols line by line, precept by precept, here a little and there a little, as the Saints became capable of learning more and more about this extraordinary power and how to use it based on righteous principles. The Doctrine and Covenants contains the chronicle of this unfolding of priesthood quorums and offices, including:

- Apostles, elders, priests, teachers, deacons (see D&C 20:38–60)
- Bishop (see D&C 41:9–10)
- High priests (see heading to D&C 52)
- First Presidency (see D&C 81; 90)
- Patriarch (see D&C 124:91)

- High council (see D&C 102)
- Quorum of the Twelve Apostles (see D&C 107:23–24)
- Seventies (see D&C 107:25)
- First Quorum of the Seventy (see D&C 107:26, 93–97)

As the Church continues to grow, modern revelation through our living prophets has created additional Quorums of the Seventy, Area Authority Seventies, as well as many auxiliaries to the priesthood. These are all for the building up of the kingdom of God and the establishment of Zion. They all operate under the direction of the priesthood. They all have a similar purpose—to bless lives and help people come unto Christ.

What are your thoughts concerning the magnificent organization of the priesthood as a divine manifestation of God's love and mercy on behalf of His children?

Real-life Stories for Heart and Mind

Who Is in Charge? It is an overwhelming assignment to be called as a bishop—especially in a large, diverse ward with many complex challenges, and especially for a twenty-seven-year-old graduate student with a young family. But after sincere prayer, and with the support of a loving wife, the young man humbly accepted the calling, despite great feelings of inadequacy. It was an act of sheer faith. Following the sustaining vote that Sunday, the new bishop was shaking hands with a line of well-wishers outside the chapel when he was approached by one member known for his candid method of expression. This man was a merchant seaman who had seen many a dangerous campaign in his career. Looking directly into the eyes of the new leader, he said, in all seriousness, "I just cannot understand how they could put an ensign in charge of the ship." There was a moment of silence as the newly called bishop searched for a satisfying response. Then a light suddenly came on, and the Spirit whispered the words (which were dutifully announced): "*An ensign is not in charge of the ship. The Lord is in charge of the ship.*" The brother listened and paused, then nodded his approval, and subsequently became one of the most stalwart supporters in the ward. It is always good to sail on a ship where the Lord is in charge.

As you ponder the callings that have come to you in the past, that you currently hold, and that may come in the future, how does it give solace and peace of mind to know that the Lord is in charge, and that through His strength you can accomplish whatever is asked of you by giving your all in His service?

Overcoming the Tentacles of the World. Some years ago Elder Ezra Taft Benson, then president of the Quorum of the Twelve, contacted the presidency of one of the stakes in the eastern United States and commended them for the notable advancement of some 19 percent of the prospective elders in the stake during the previous year. Elder Benson asked the stake leaders to research the reasons for the success. After a thorough review of the situation, including many interviews, they identified two key strategies that proved to be the most overwhelmingly effective in reactivating almost 100 brethren that year: (1) the influence of faithful and interested home teachers (and in some cases Relief Society visiting teachers), and (2) getting the prospective elders to be involved in opportunities for serving in the quorum and ward. It is not surprising that home teaching and personal callings—whether in the ward choir, on a welfare project, teaching a class, or as a member of a home teaching team—were the decisive factors, since these are both divinely appointed functions (see D&C 20:42, 46, 51, 53–55; 107:99).

In most cases the tenacious tentacles of inactivity were overcome by the more tenacious outreach of love on the part of devoted leaders—bishops, quorum presidents, home teachers, and ward members. One of the questions asked during dozens of interviews with the reactivated brethren was this: "What was the most difficult thing you had to overcome in returning to activity?" The predominant answer was very revealing. The majority said the most inhibiting factor was the feeling they had to overcome that one had to be "perfect" to be welcomed at Church. It is a reminder that all of us need to open our minds and hearts to those around us who have a desire to become active but find that inertia or the tentacles of the world are holding them back. We don't need to be perfect to come to Church and participate in the fold of the Savior. We just need to believe that we can, in the circle of loving fellowship and through the strength of the Lord, "come unto Christ, and be perfected in him" (Moro. 10:32).

Do you know anyone in the shadows of inactivity who may have the wrong impression that they need to be "perfect" to come back to Church? How can you help these individuals feel comfortable among the Saints as they seek, with faith and patience, to become "perfect in Christ" (Moro. 10:33)?

Pondering Prayerfully

Additional scriptures to consider and ponder:
- Eph. 4:11–13
- 2 Tim. 1:7
- James 1:27
- D&C 20:53–55
- D&C 58:26–28
- D&C 107:27
- D&C 108:7
- D&C 123:17

The following hymns inspire gratitude about the process of organizing to serve:
- "Because I Have Been Given Much" (*Hymns,* 219)
- "Called to Serve" (*Hymns,* 249)
- "Put Your Shoulder to the Wheel" (*Hymns,* 252)
- "We Are All Enlisted" (*Hymns,* 250)

Remember and Be Sure

A glorious dawn illuminated the earth as the Restoration of the gospel and the priesthood endowed mankind once again with truth, power, and the means for rising toward their inborn potential to be like God and return to Him one day. With loving kindness and grace, the Lord taught His servants the principles upon which those called could also be the chosen: righteousness, persuasion, long-suffering, gentleness, meekness, love unfeigned, kindness, pure knowledge, avoiding hypocrisy and guile, ever following the Spirit, increased love, faithfulness, charity towards all men and to the household of faith, and inward-garnishing virtue (see D&C 121:34–45). The blessings of magnifying our callings under the direction of the priesthood in this way are made clear by the Lord: "Then shall thy confidence wax strong in the presence of God; and the doctrine of the priesthood shall distil upon thy soul as the dews from heaven. The Holy Ghost shall be thy constant companion, and thy scepter an unchanging scepter of righteousness and truth; and thy dominion shall be an everlasting dominion, and without compulsory means it shall flow unto thee forever and ever" (D&C 121:45–46).

Heavenly Father and our Savior have provided every needful thing for the eternal salvation for all mankind—because They love us. We have been given prophets, seers, and revelators; a perfectly organized Church with the priesthood of God directing the work on earth; continuous revelation for our enlightenment and guidance; temples in which to receive the ordinances and covenants of eternal life; and all things necessary for our well-being now and in the eternities.

Each member of the fold of Christ is needed. Each is loved. The Lord gives to His children the gift of agency, causes them to be taught correct principles, and then holds every individual accountable for his or her own actions. At the same time, the Lord holds the shepherds of Israel accountable—all who have stewardship over the flock at whatever level of responsibility—to teach the principles of righteousness valiantly in the spirit of light and truth, shirking no opportunity to bring the sheep unto Christ. Shepherds are called to guide the Saints in the pathway of righteousness, and to help restore any wayward and wandering souls to the fold. Great blessings flow when we receive our callings with gratitude and accept the responsibility to perform to our utmost ability while we are on the errand of the Lord.

CHAPTER 15
Our Priesthood Covenants

If there is anything calculated to interest the mind of the Saints, to awaken in them the finest sensibilities, and arouse them to enterprise and exertion, surely it is the great and precious promises made by our heavenly Father to the children of Abraham. —Joseph Smith (*HC* 4:128)

Opening the Window of Wisdom

The bonds between Heavenly Father and His children are always sealed and confirmed by covenants. Zion is a covenant society. Covenant promises made by the Saints in honor and faithfulness—when activated in the name of Christ through priesthood ordinances and perpetuated through obedience, integrity, and faithfulness—lead to supreme joy and happiness.

Eternal covenants are binding agreements between God and His children. God reveals covenants through His prophets. We, with our moral agency, have the opportunity to enter into these covenants on the basis of our worthiness. The covenants and ordinances of salvation and exaltation include baptism, the bestowal of the gift of the Holy Ghost, the oath and covenant of the Melchizedek Priesthood, and temple covenants and ordinances. These sacred covenants, along with other gospel ordinances such as the holy sacrament, provide the means whereby, through honor and obedience, we can receive the

blessings of exaltation from our Heavenly Father and be admitted one day into His presence as "joint-heirs" with Jesus Christ. Paul declared: "The Spirit itself beareth witness with our spirit, that we are the children of God: And if children, then heirs; heirs of God, and joint-heirs with Christ; if so be that we suffer with him, that we may be also glorified together" (Rom. 8:16–17).

Our sufferings unto glory (to use the context of Paul) come externally through our triumph over persecution and adversity, and internally through our covenant sacrifice of "a broken heart and contrite spirit" (2 Ne. 2:7). It is upon the heart, that our covenant agreement is symbolically written. Paul put it this way: "ye are manifestly declared to be the epistle of Christ ministered by us, written not with ink, but with the Spirit of the living God; not in tables of stone, but in fleshy tables of the heart" (2 Cor. 3:3). In reference to Jesus Christ—"the mediator of a better covenant, which was established upon better promises" (Heb. 8:6)—Paul reminds us that the Messiah, through His atoning sacrifice, instituted a new covenant with His people: "For this is the covenant that I will make with the house of Israel after those days, saith the Lord; I will put my laws into their mind, and write them in their hearts: and I will be to them a God, and they shall be to me a people" (Heb. 8:10; compare Jer. 31:33).

The resurrected Lord honored His Saints in ancient America by calling them "the children of the prophets" and "the children of the covenant" (3 Ne. 20:25–26). The Saints of today are the children of the covenant by virtue of their participating in the new and everlasting covenant restored in the latter days, embracing as it does all the ordinances of salvation and exaltation, including celestial marriage. The Saints of today are the children of the prophets by virtue of their participating in the Abrahamic covenant—the glorious commission by means of which the blessings of the gospel and the priesthood are made available to all the peoples of the earth (see Abr. 2:9–11). Covenant blessings endow the faithful Saints with the privilege of being able to "gather together, and stand in holy places" (D&C 101:22), including the homes of the faithful, the congregations of the righteous in the wards and stakes of Zion, and the sacred temples of God.

Our commitment and loyalty to the Savior are expressed by our honoring our covenants. Our stalwart devotion will cause us to remember at all times and in all places the teachings and values of the gospel of Jesus Christ. We will act with no hypocrisy and have no guile. We will have the desire to take upon us the divine nature of Christ. We will seek to act and do as the Savior would have us do: "Verily, verily, I say unto you, He that believeth on me, the works that I do shall he do also; and greater works than these shall he do; because I go unto my Father. And whatsoever ye shall ask in my name, that will I do, that the Father may be glorified in the Son" (John 14:12–13).

Through the Spirit we can know that keeping our sacred covenants is a matter of eternal life—*our* eternal life. Blessings are predicated upon our faithfulness to our covenants (see D&C 130:20–21) and flow into our lives through our diligence and valor. Covenants bear the seal of promise—our solemn promise to Heavenly Father to obey His commandments and His infallible promise to us to grant us eternal life.

Inspired by Latter-Day Prophets

Brigham Young: To the Latter-day Saints I say, live your religion, sanctify the Lord God in your hearts, live by every word that proceeds from the mouth of God, and we shall be prospered (*Discourses of Brigham Young,* 229).

Covenants give an express definition of actions required, together with a promised

blessing. How does Brigham Young define these? How can you honor your covenants with greater devotion? How can you help your loved ones understand the nature of priesthood covenants (requirements as well as blessings) and honor them more fully?

John Taylor: I would rather have God for my friend than all other influences and powers outside (*The Gospel Kingdom: Selections from the Writings and Discourses of John Taylor,* 343).

President Taylor expresses the essence of our covenant relationship with God—that we come to be His friend. How can you use this idea to explain the nature of covenants to others, especially young children and people who are not members of the Church?

Spencer W. Kimball: But for those Latter-day Saints who are valiant, who fulfill the requirements faithfully and fully, the promises are glorious beyond description: "Then shall they be gods, because they have no end; therefore shall they be from everlasting to everlasting, because they continue; then shall they be above all, because all things are subject unto them. Then shall they be gods, because they have all power, and the angels are subject unto them (D&C 132:20) (*The Miracle of Forgiveness,* ix).

The ultimate reward for honoring the new and everlasting covenant, including the covenant of celestial marriage, is expressed in the scripture cited by President Kimball. The outcome is breathtaking. What are your thoughts about the sublime promise made by the Lord for the everlasting destiny of the faithful?

Howard W. Hunter: This is a day for action. This is the time for decision, not tomorrow, not next week. This is the time to make our covenant with the Lord. Now is the time for those who have been noncommittal or who have had a halfhearted interest to come out boldly and declare belief in Christ and be willing to demonstrate faith by works (*The Teachings of Howard W. Hunter,* 46).

Covenants are action agreements that require faith leading to good works. How can you encourage others in charitable and loving ways to be about the Lord's business in honoring their covenants? How can you be an example to them?

Truths to Liken

Deut. 6:5–7—"And thou shalt love the Lord thy God with all thine heart, and with all thy soul, and with all thy might. And these words, which I command thee this day, shall be in thine heart. And thou shalt teach them diligently unto thy children, and shalt talk of them when thou sittest in thine house, and when thou walkest by the way, and when thou liest down, and when thou riseth up."

- In speaking with the people to remind them of their obligations under their covenant with God, Moses captured the essence of what the people had promised to do, for "The LORD made not this covenant with our fathers, but with us, even us, who are all of us here alive this day" (Deut. 5:3).
- How often are we to teach covenant truths to our children and those we love? How can you be assured that the covenant obligations "shall be in thine heart" as well as in their hearts of your loved ones?

Matt. 5:16 (also 3 Ne. 12:16)—"Let your light so shine before men, that they may see your good works, and glorify your Father which is in heaven."

- In the Sermon on the Mount, the Savior expressed in memorable terms the obligation of the Saints who follow in His footsteps.
- The privilege of entering into a covenant with God brings great responsibility, for light given must be shared. In what ways can you share more of the light of the gospel with others?

Mosiah 5:8–9—"And under this head ye are made free, and there is no other head whereby ye can be made free. There is no other name given whereby salvation cometh; therefore, I would that ye should take upon you the name of Christ, all you that have entered into the covenant with God that ye should be obedient unto the end of your lives. And it shall come to pass that whosoever doeth this shall be found at the right hand of God, for he shall know the name by which he is called; for he shall be called by the name of Christ."

- In his final discourse, the aging King Benjamin taught his people the connection between entering into a sacred covenant with God and achieving within their hearts the "mighty change" (Mosiah 5:2) characteristic of those who want only to do good.
- Receiving a new name, the name of Christ, is part of the gospel covenant process. How does obedience ensure that you can retain this sacred identity and thus be found worthy to remain in the fold of Christ forever?

Alma 5:14—"And now behold, I ask of you, my brethren of the church, have ye spiritually been born of God? Have ye received his image in your countenances? Have ye experienced this mighty change in your hearts?"

- Alma, having stepped down as chief judge, devoted all his time to preaching the gospel throughout the land in an effort to bring the people to a remembrance of their covenants. These words are from his discourse.
- How would you answer the questions posed by Alma in regard to your own "mighty change"?

Alma 53:20–21—"And they were all young men, and they were exceedingly valiant for courage, and also for strength and activity; but behold, this was not all—they were men who were true at all times in whatsoever thing they were entrusted. Yea, they were men of truth and soberness, for they had been taught to keep the commandments of God and to walk uprightly before him."

- Mormon was describing the two thousand stripling warriors—sons of Helaman—who had "entered into a covenant to fight for the liberty of the Nephites" (Alma 53:17)—much as we enter into a covenant to uphold the principles of spiritual liberty in the kingdom of God.

- How can you help inspire the youth of the Church into active participation in the campaign to honor their covenants and help others to be liberated spiritually through the power of the gospel? How can you, in your own way and manner of activity, take on the role of Helaman?

D&C 136:4—"And this shall be our covenant—that we will walk in all the ordinances of the Lord."

- The Lord gave these words through President Brigham Young at Winter Quarters, Omaha, near Council Bluffs, Iowa, on January 14, 1847, the eve of the exodus to the West.
- We are following in the footsteps of the pioneers, who honored their sacred covenants by doing all that the Lord required of them to establish His kingdom in the latter days. To "walk in all the ordinances of the Lord" implies action and committed performance. Think of your many daily tasks and duties: How can you place these in the context of covenant action, even though you may not be laboring across the plains with a handcart?

Rejoicing and Reasoning Together

What Is the Nature and Purpose of the Abrahamic Covenant?

Few aspects of the gospel have more profound impact on the mind and soul of the Latter-day Saints than the joy of participating in the mission of the Abrahamic covenant. Abraham (meaning *father of a multitude*), with whom the Lord established His ongoing and eternal covenant, was born more than two millennia before the coming of Christ. Abraham is among the most admired and celebrated of the Lord's chosen prophets. For many, the most memorable aspect of Abraham's life might well be his consummate obedience, demonstrated by his willingness to sacrifice his own son as the Lord had commanded (see Gen. 22). However, the aspect of Abraham's story that touches everyone in

the most direct way is his central role regarding the archetypal covenant that the Lord set up with him and his seed to bless the lives of all the sons and daughters of God throughout the world. As the Lord declared: "I will make of thee a great nation, and I will bless thee above measure, and make thy name great among all nations, and thou shalt be a blessing unto thy seed after thee, that in their hands they shall bear this ministry and Priesthood unto all nations" (Abr. 2:9).

The covenant made by the Lord with Abraham and his posterity continues to be at the center of the practices and operations of the restored Church as it reaches out in its ordained commission to cry repentance to the world and bring the world saving truths and ordinances. Through the Abrahamic covenant, the Lord promises and extends grand blessings predicated upon worthiness, obedience, and service. The blessings that begin in the mortal sphere extend to the world hereafter, including divinely appointed places of gathering and repose, the unfolding of an immense posterity, and the enjoyment of redeeming truths here and in the eternities. Our part of the covenant is obedience and righteous living and a willingness to be the spiritual servants of the world through faithful missionary service. The Latter-day Saints have a sense of being part of the "peculiar people" (as in Deut. 14:2) from the standpoint that they are chosen to be servants on the Lord's errand.

On April 3, 1836, as part of a magnificent sequence of heavenly manifestations in the newly completed Kirtland Temple, Joseph Smith and Oliver Cowdery witnessed and experienced a visit by Elias, who "committed the dispensation of the gospel of Abraham, saying that in us and our seed all generations after us should be blessed" (D&C 110:12). Thus the continuity of the Lord's ancient covenant program was ensured in the latter days.

The Lord delights in blessing His children. He gives them places of refuge in this world (lands and gathering places, such as the stakes of Zion). He gives them hope for eternal mansions on high. He makes them fruitful in their posterity and gives them the hope of eternal increase through the blessings of temple marriage. He provides the fulness of the everlasting gospel of Jesus Christ and the priesthood of God, with its ennobling and redeeming power to grant immortality and eternal life to the valiant who endure to the end. For all of these extraordinary blessings, He asks only that we walk in righteousness and obey his commandments—sharing our witness to the world to gather in the honest at heart—including the scattered remnants of Israel or the adopted sons and daughters of God no matter what their lineage or extraction might be. Are any people more blessed and more privileged? Could there be any mission more sacred or more important than to follow through with full commitment of heart, mind, and soul in our task of being servants of the Lord and building up the kingdom of God?

The Lord promised that those who honor their priesthood covenants should become "the seed of Abraham, and the church and kingdom, and the elect of God" (D&C 84:34). Those who become the "seed of Abraham" participate in the fulfillment of the covenant promise the Lord made to Abraham that he would become "a great nation" (Abr. 2:9). How can you more fully help those you serve in the Church feel inspired and motivated as "the seed of Abraham"—fulfilling their covenant obligations by spreading the gospel blessings to others?

How Are the Latter-day Saints a "Peculiar" People?

Why is it that Latter-day Saints, traveling to other places in the world and attending Church services in other wards or branches, immediately feel a sense of "belonging" and fellowship—regardless of the setting? Certainly much of the friendship and bonding derives from a common sense of mission to live the gospel and be a light to the world—precisely the design of duty and service inherent in the Abrahamic covenant. In Old Testament passages, the Lord often called His people "a peculiar people" (see Ex. 19:5, Deut. 14:2; 26:18, Ps. 135:4). In the New Testament, the Apostle Peter echoes this theme by saying, "But ye are a chosen generation, a royal priesthood, an holy nation, a peculiar people; that ye should shew forth the praises of him who hath called you out of darkness into his marvellous light" (1 Pet. 2:9).

But what does the word *peculiar* really mean? Does it mean eccentric and different, apart from the mainstream practice, as the world usually understands it? The German translation of the Bible comes closer to the true meaning. Martin Luther rendered the phrase "ye shall be a peculiar treasure"

(Ex. 19:5) as *so sollt ihr mein Eigentum sein*—"then you shall be my possession" (meaning "that which belongs to me"). Our English word *peculiar* is derived from a Latin source meaning "belonging to"—exactly the sense that the Lord was conveying. He "owns" us. He has "bought" us (1 Cor. 6:20). We "belong" to Him. We are His peculiar people commissioned to give service to the world.

That deep sense of belonging shines through among the faithful Saints when they gather together, even as strangers to one another. We "belong" to each other in the same sense precisely because "together" we belong to the Lord. Temple marriage as a blessing under the Abrahamic covenant imparts the same feeling of belonging and permanence to a union. That is why a husband in the covenant feels so deeply that he "belongs" to his wife, and that she "belongs" to him, and that their children "belong" to them. All of these things are evidence that the marvelous spirit of the Abrahamic covenant is at work throughout the world as the Saints strive to emulate the challenge given by the Lord to Abraham: "I am the almighty God; walk before me, and be thou perfect, And I will make my covenant between me and thee" (Gen. 17:1–2).

When you next hear or read comments about members of the Church being "peculiar," smile inwardly and say to yourself in gratitude, "Yes, I belong to God."

How Is "Remembering" Part of Our Covenant?

The Lord remembers Israel. He keeps His covenant promises. To help the Israelites of old remember His miraculous intervention on their behalf, He instituted the Passover, with detailed rules and observances that reminded the people of His blessings to them and pointed to the atoning sacrifice of the Son. Following the infinite sacrifice of the Savior, the sacrament was instituted as a lasting memorial to His atoning redemption and as a way to help us remember our covenant promises and renew our commitment to obey the Lord's commandments. In the sacrament prayer on the bread and on the water, the words *remembrance* and *remember* are both used as a token of this key doctrine. We are to teach our children to remember always the goodness of the Lord and the utter necessity of living His gospel principles.

Moroni counseled future readers of the Book of Mormon: "Behold, I would exhort you that when ye shall read these things, if it be wisdom in God that ye should read them, that ye would remember how merciful the Lord hath been unto the children of men, from the creation of Adam even down until the time that ye shall receive these things, and ponder it in your hearts" (Moro. 10:3; compare Mosiah 4:10–12). Our spiritual growth is enhanced when we recognize the goodness of God, for we are to "remember the worth of souls is great in the sight of God" (D&C 18:10). As we recognize and remember the goodness and tender mercies of God, we will begin to deepen our trust, our respect, and our love for God. We will begin to look to God and live. President Spencer W. Kimball stated, "When you look in the dictionary for the most important word, do you know what it is? . . . Remember is the word" ("Circles of Exaltation" [Address to religious educators, BYU, 28 June 1968], 8).

How do you teach yourself to be better at remembering? Remembering is a dynamic spiritual process of bringing key things to mind on a continual basis in order to cultivate "a godly walk and conversation" (D&C 20:69) in keeping with priesthood covenants. To remember is to align oneself with the will of God in order to become, on a daily basis, more and more like Him. Thoughts lead to action—so remembering in a faithful and obedient way leads to living in that same way. The scriptures and the prophets counsel us to remember the following: Heavenly Father, His Son Jesus Christ, the scriptures, the doctrines and commandments, the covenants, our neighbors in need, and ourselves. Of these, which do you need to better remember?

Real-life Stories for Heart and Mind

Friend of the Covenant. In the Church we hold the General Authorities in high esteem and rightly look to the Lord's prophets, seers, and revelators in the First Presidency and Quorum of the Twelve as the bastions of God's will and the pillars of godly leadership. But there is also a local "prophet" in our midst, sent to be a special kind of "friend of the covenant" to us—and that is our bishop. As presiding high priest and father of the ward, he uses his gift of prophecy and discernment to help us remember our covenants and be faithful and true. There are thousands of such "friends" in the world today, sent from the Lord to help us uphold our covenant promises. The bishop's message to us can be summarized in the words of the Lord: "Search diligently, pray always, and be believing, and all things shall work together for your good, if ye walk uprightly and remember the covenant wherewith ye have covenanted one with another" (D&C 90:24). No one need look any further than his or her bishop to find an example of the kind of friendship that is based on covenant principles of truth. Typically a bishop does not aspire to his calling, but responds willingly and to the best of his ability, often giving more time to his Church service than to his profession.

If you want an interesting exercise in counting your blessings, make a list of all the bishops in your life. If you are young, there may be only a few; if you are maturing in age, there may be a dozen or more. In any case, write down a quality that you remember about each one of them. One person doing this exercise recalled a bishop who never failed to phone each of his ward members (including young children) on their birthday to extend greetings and give an encouraging thought—thus exemplifying in a simple yet memorable way the quality of being sensitive and kind. Another bishop exemplified humility; because of a medical condition he had, he found it difficult to stay awake at times on the stand and would often ask the ward's forgiveness for his weakness, thus setting a tender example for his ward members on how they, too, could confess their weaknesses and overcome their difficulties. Assemble a list of qualities for all of your bishops in this way and see what aggregate portrait of a "friend of the covenant" will emerge. Will it display a person who is kind and humble, positive and truthful, charitable and faithful, gracious and prayerful, cheerful as well as firm and principled? When you are done, you will have the very portrait that you can wish for yourself in honoring and keeping your own covenants before the Lord. Thank heaven for our bishops—our covenant friends and the local "prophets" in our lives.

An Understanding Moment. There is no greater joy than to rejoice in the goodness and success of others (see Alma 29:14). A fruitful lineage in the spirit of the Abrahamic covenant, particularly one that is great in righteousness, is quintessential joy. John said: "I have no greater joy than to hear that my children walk in truth" (3 John 1:4). A father or mother pleased with a child's performance has a feeling of satisfaction. The feeling of observing a righteous decision or act by a child simply transcends all understanding. Parents literally live for this. One person, looking back from a position of senior years, said: "As a father and grandfather, I now understand my sweet angel mother. I would ask, 'Mom, what do you want for Christmas? What do you want for your birthday? What do you want for Mother's Day?' The answer was always the same: 'Oh, I have everything I need. Just be good—just be good.' Now I understand more fully the blessings of a righteous posterity. Now I understand Heavenly Father's purpose more fully—to help His children be fruitful and enjoy eternal increase, even immortality and eternal life."

Lift this story to the heavenly level. You can hear yourself praying to your Heavenly Father and asking, "What can I do, Father, to show my thanks unto thee for my covenant blessings?" And you hear the kindly words in response: "Just be good—just be good."

Pondering Prayerfully

Additional scriptures to consider and ponder:
- Prov. 23:7
- Jer. 31:33
- John 13:34–351
- 1 Ne. 22:11–12
- D&C 3:19–20
- D&C 41:5
- D&C 132:6–7
- D&C 136:2–4

The following hymns might help us understand and appreciate our covenants:
- "Families Can Be Together Forever" (*Hymns,* 300)
- "Lead Me into Life Eternal" (*Hymns,* 45)
- "Lord, Accept into Thy kingdom" (*Hymns,* 236)
- "True to the Faith" (*Hymns,* 254)

Remember and Be Sure

Keeping our sacred covenants is a matter of eternal life—yes, *our* eternal life. Blessings are predicated upon our faithfulness to our covenant commitments, and diligent obedience brings abundant blessings. We have faith that God will always keep His word and honor His promises. We can testify before our family members and others that they can trust in God, knowing that He acts without the slightest variance on the principles of truth and light: "For God doth not walk in crooked paths, neither doth he turn to the right hand nor to the left, neither doth he vary from that which he hath said, therefore his paths are straight, and his course is one eternal round" (D&C 3:2).

The covenants we make and keep bring us blessings now and into the eternities. The gospel of Jesus Christ, centered in the atoning sacrifice of our Savior, is the expression of the love of God, described by Lehi as the fruit of the tree of life, "whose fruit was desirable to make one happy" (1 Ne. 8:10). When we partake of the fruit of life we enjoy the grace of God through the Atonement of Jesus Christ. As we become as He is, through charity and personal righteousness (the oil in our lamps), we honor our covenants, and if we endure to the end, we will enjoy a state of never-ending happiness. The blessing of the gospel of Jesus Christ is the promise of eternal life.

Our covenants extend beyond the personal sphere to fill the expanse of the entire world. Every child needs to live up to the divine lineage of being a son or daughter of God, created in His image. In a special way, all those who participate in the Abrahamic covenant are at work being true to their birthright and calling as servants of the Lord, commissioned to be exemplars of obedience and righteousness in carrying the gospel to the world. In doing so, they also extend their covenant joy into the eternities, for they can look forward to the time when they will be admitted into the presence of the Father and the Son as the consummating glory of their covenants fulfilled.

CHAPTER 16
The Church in Earlier Times

Every member of the Church should so live that by study, reflection, faith and prayer, and association with his fellow members in study, he may understand the order of the Church and how it is governed. Then if we will be faithful to the principles of truth that have been given us for our guidance we will be sanctified and will act in all holiness before the Lord. —Joseph Fielding Smith (*Church History and Modern Revelation,* 1:174)

Opening the Window of Wisdom

Throughout the dispensations of time, the Lord has ordained and arranged for a divine organization to govern the unfolding of His kingdom as a way to bless and sanctify His people. The structure and organization of the Church, with its various offices and circles of leadership, did not evolve by chance, but was a prepared gift from heaven, given to optimize the process of making saving truths and ordinances available to the sons and daughters of God in their quest to return home once again. The celestial kingdom itself is organized on principles of glory and eternal light. The kingdom of God on earth is a type and likeness of what awaits the faithful in the coming world.

Adam and Eve had an organization to facilitate spreading the principles of the gospel. In a long patriarchal sequence of leadership, Adam's family was instructed and organized around the principles of eternal salvation. Toward the end of his earthly ministry, Adam convened his posterity of high priests in a sacred congregation to bless them and receive a blessing from the Lord in person (see D&C 107:53–56). Enoch presided over a Church of Zion that was taken up in righteousness and reserved for reuniting with the Church on earth at the time of the Second Coming (see Moses 7:21–23, 63). Noah presided over a dispensation where affairs were organized to help disseminate the light of the gospel (see Moses 8:19). During the days of Melchizedek and Abraham, an organizational structure enabled the blessings of the priesthood to be extended to the faithful.

The Lord taught Moses and his successors how to organize the Israelites for instruction and worship according to their circumstances and needs through the administration of priests of the Aaronic order. During the meridian of time, the Lord organized His Church and kingdom according to specific principles and stewardships:

> And he gave some, apostles; and some, prophets; and some, evangelists; and some, pastors and teachers;
>
> For the perfecting of the saints, for the work of the ministry, for the edifying of the body of Christ:

Till we all come in the unity of the faith, and of the knowledge of the Son of God, unto a perfect man, unto the measure of the stature of the fulness of Christ. (Eph. 4:11–13)

Among His Saints of the New World, the resurrected Lord organized and empowered His Church just as in the Old World. And in modern times, the Restoration has brought about the return of the keys, powers, offices, and service arrangements that existed in former times prior to the Great Apostasy: "We believe in the same organization that existed in the Primitive Church, namely, apostles, prophets, pastors, teachers, evangelists, and so forth" (A of F 6).

The kingdom of God on the earth is The Church of Jesus Christ of Latter-day Saints. We are today organized after the manner of the Church during the dispensation of our Savior Jesus Christ. God has ordained that prophets will regulate the affairs of His Church and kingdom according to eternal principles. We are all one in Christ. We are all needed to work together to bless and serve one another. We are dependent on one another—organized according to a relationship of mutual support and benefit and called on to practice unity and work together synergistically. We need each other, and the Lord needs us to build up His kingdom. Everything of God is done in order. The leaders who serve in the kingdom ensure that all things are done according to the established order of the Church.

Inspired by Latter-Day Prophets

Joseph F. Smith: Take away the organization of the Church and its power would cease. Every part of its organization is necessary and essential to its perfect existence. Disregard, ignore, or omit any part, and you start imperfection in the Church; and if we should continue in that way we would find ourselves like those of old, being led by error, superstition, ignorance, and by the cunning and craftiness of men. We would soon leave out here a little and there a little, here a line and there a precept, until we would become like the rest of the world, divided, disorganized, confused and without knowledge; without revelation or inspiration, and without Divine authority or power (*Gospel Doctrine: Selections from the Sermons and Writings of Joseph F. Smith*, 149).

What are your thoughts about the essential, perfect, and complete organization of the Church? How can you help others who may have a limited view of the function and role of the Church to see the full picture?

Joseph Fielding Smith: There is no reason in the world why each member of the Church should not have a thorough understanding of the principles of the gospel, of the order of the Church, and the government of the Church, so that none need be led astray by any wind of doctrine, or notion that prevails among the children of men, which may come to his attention (*Doctrines of Salvation*, 1:287).

Principles, order, and government—these constitute our learning agenda in being well instructed about the gospel and the Church. Of these, which do you feel most comfortable with? Which do you feel you need to learn more about?

Harold B. Lee: The Master's church was an orderly, organized body "built upon the foundation of the apostles and prophets, Jesus Christ himself being the chief corner stone." (Ephesians 2:20.) . . . The Lord told His apostles: "Ye have not chosen me, but I have chosen you, and ordained you, that ye should go and bring forth fruit. . . ." (John 15:16.) and to the chiefest of the apostles He gave the "keys" of the kingdom of God, or in other words, the keys of authority to the Church of Jesus Christ, that whatsoever would be bound in earth should be bound in heaven (*Stand Ye in Holy Places*, 315).

In the space of only three years the Savior put in place a dynamic, empowered, and orderly institution that bore the signature of divine perfection. It was complex yet unified, domestic in its outreach yet authorized directly by Deity, designed for the everyday yet governed by keys extending to heaven. As you compare this wonderful Church in the meridian of time to the various non-LDS churches of today, what are the main differences that have evolved in the two millennia since the original Church of Christ was founded?

Truths to Liken

Matt. 5:16—"Let your light so shine before men, that they may see your good works, and glorify your Father which is in heaven."

- The Savior included these words, along with the Beatitudes, in His instructions to His disciples in the Holy Land (see also 3 Ne. 12:16).
- The light of the gospel in each individual radiates warmth and confirmation to those who perceive it. The light of the gospel magnified in the congregations of the Saints, reflected collectively and outwardly from the Church, becomes an ensign of glory that beckons all to come into the fold of Christ. What aspects of the membership of the Church do you feel attract the most avid attention from honest seekers after the truth? How are you contributing to this outreach task?

Matt. 13:31–32—"Another parable put he forth unto them, saying, The kingdom of heaven is like to a grain of mustard seed, which a man took, and sowed in his field: Which indeed is the least of all seeds: but when it is grown, it is the greatest among herbs, and becometh a tree, so that the birds of the air come and lodge in the branches thereof."

- The Savior taught the multitude using a series of parables, including this one about the mustard seed. Concerning the meaning of this parable, Joseph Smith said: "Now we can discover plainly that this figure is given to represent the Church as it shall come forth in the last days. . . . Let us take the Book of Mormon, which a man took and hid in his field, securing it by his faith, to spring up in the last days, or in due time; let us behold it coming forth out of the ground, which is indeed accounted the least of all seeds, but behold it branching forth, yea, even towering, with lofty branches, and Godlike majesty, until it, like the mustard seed, becomes the greatest of all herbs. And it is truth, and it has sprouted and come forth out of the earth, and righteousness begins to look down from heaven, and God is sending down His powers, gifts and angels, to lodge in the branches thereof. . . . The kingdom of heaven is like unto a mustard seed. Behold, then is not this the kingdom of heaven that is raising its head in the last days in the majesty of its God, even the Church of the Latter-day Saints, like an impenetrable, immovable rock in the midst of the mighty deep, exposed to the storms and tempests of Satan, but has, thus far, remained steadfast" (*HC* 2:268).

- It is a grand privilege to labor on the rock of the Church (to use an additional metaphor of the Prophet Joseph), protected beneath the canopy of the branches of the "mustard tree" as it expands from a small seed to fulfill its appointed destiny. How can you help your loved ones and those you are called on to teach to understand and grasp the grand mission of the Church, founded by the Savior during His mortal ministry and restored again through the Prophet Joseph Smith in our day?

Alma 6:6—"Nevertheless the children of God were commanded that they should gather themselves together oft, and join in fasting and mighty prayer in behalf of the welfare of the souls of those who knew not God."

- After Alma stepped down as chief judge over the land, he devoted himself fully to preaching throughout the land and regulating the Church to ensure that it operated according to eternal principles.
- The united effort of the Church in Alma's day was to reach out to those outside the Church who were not familiar with gospel principles. Note that the strategy included fasting and praying together for the blessing of others. This practice is applicable today, reminding us to fast with a purpose on behalf of those less active and those "who are only kept from the truth because they know not where to find it" (D&C 123:12). What worthy purposes and goals do you attach to your fasting and praying? What purposes

do your ward and stake leaders ask that you associate with your fasting and praying from time to time? How can you help your loved ones fast and pray with purpose and the spirit of charity?

3 Ne. 12:46–48—"Therefore those things which were of old time, which were under the law, in me are all fulfilled. Old things are done away, and all things have become new. Therefore I would that ye should be perfect even as I, or your Father who is in heaven is perfect."

- The resurrected Lord taught His Saints in the New World that the Law of Moses had been fulfilled in Him. He brought a higher law and put it into practice, changing forever the age-old rites and traditions of the Mosaic code, the preparatory schoolmaster in eternal principles (see Gal. 3:24–25).
- How did the new practices of the Church established by Christ during His mortal ministry and shortly thereafter on the American continent constitute a higher law? What was the nature of the sacrifice that was now required (see 3 Ne. 9:20; 12:19; 27:27; Moro. 7:48; D&C 59:8)?

Rejoicing and Reasoning Together

What Were the Key Qualities and Features of the Savior's Original Church?

The Church was established on the foundation of revelation, Jesus Christ being the "chief corner stone" (Eph. 2:20). When the Savior asked His disciples who they thought He was, Peter declared:

Thou art the Christ, the Son of the living God.

And Jesus answered and said unto him, Blessed art thou, Simon Bar-jona: for flesh and blood hath not revealed it unto thee, but my Father which is in heaven.

And I say also unto thee, That thou art Peter, and upon this rock [i.e., the principle of revelation, by which Peter knew that Christ was the Son of God] I will build my church; and the gates of hell shall not prevail against it.

And I will give unto thee the keys of the kingdom of heaven: and whatsoever thou shalt bind on earth shall be bound in heaven: and whatsoever thou shalt loose on earth shall be loosed in heaven. (Matt. 16:16–19)

It was through the power of revelation and the communion with heavenly messengers that the sealing keys of the priesthood were granted soon thereafter to Peter, James, and John on the Mount of Transfiguration (see Matt. 17:1–13). Moreover, all who were called to positions in the Church established by Christ were called by the authority of God and empowered to act in the name of the Lord. A diverse yet integrated system of priesthood offices was set up: "And are built upon the foundation of the apostles and prophets, Jesus Christ himself being the chief corner stone; In whom all the building fitly framed together groweth unto an holy temple in the Lord: In whom ye also are builded together for an habitation of God through the Spirit" (Eph. 2:20–22; see also Eph. 4:11–14; Luke 10:1). Succession in the apostolic order was made operational as illustrated following the defection of Judas (see Acts 1:23–26).

Fundamental principles of the gospel were central to the teachings promoted through the Church, including faith (see Heb. 11); baptism for the living (see John 3:5) and the dead (see 1 Cor. 15:29); mercy extended to those who had departed mortality and were waiting for instructions in the spirit realm (see 1 Pet. 3:18–20; 4:6); the universal love of the Father for His children (see John 3:16); the power and efficacy of the Atonement; the reality of resurrection as a universal gift of grace to mankind (confirmed by the Resurrection of the Lord); and intimations concerning the various degrees of glory in the hereafter (see 1 Cor. 15:40; John 14:2). Gifts of the Spirit were active among the Saints (see 1 Cor. 12:4–11). The sacrament was instituted (see Matt. 26:26–28), missionary work was inaugurated (see Matt. 28:19–20), and great miracles were performed throughout the land. All of these features established in the original Church are familiar to the Latter-day Saints of today.

As you consider this brief depiction of the original Church, being as it was the exact prototype of the restored Church of today, how is your testimony of the love of God confirmed, in that He has extended to

His Saints of today the same blessings and opportunities granted unto His followers in the meridian of time? How does this insight help you to converse with investigators of the Church who are looking for the truth?

Why Did the Original Church Not Last?

The leaders of the original Church were aware that an apostasy was inevitable: "Let no man deceive you by any means: for that day [the Second Coming] shall not come, except there come a falling away first, and that man of sin be revealed, the son of perdition" (2 Thes. 2:3; see also 2 Pet. 2:1). Peter foresaw a day when there would be a restoration of all things established by Jesus Christ during His mortal mission (see Acts 3:19–21). As James E. Talmage stated: "The restored Church affirms that a general apostasy developed during and after the apostolic period, and that the primitive Church lost its power, authority, and graces as a divine institution, and degenerated into an earthly organization only. The significance and importance of the great apostasy, as a condition precedent to the re-establishment of the Church in modern times, is obvious. . . . The evidence of the decline and final extinction of the primitive Church among men is found in scriptural record, and in secular history" (*The Great Apostasy,* iii).

The occurrence of the Great Apostasy—promoted by influences from within the growing Church population as well as cultural, philosophical, and political movements of the early post-Christian era—was a tragic historical event. Lost were the apostolic offices of prophets, seers, and revelators; lost was priesthood authority; lost was continuing revelation and the purity of the fulness of gospel doctrine; lost was the essence and structure of the original Church of Jesus Christ. Still, preserved forever was the reality and power of the Atonement and the Resurrection. Preserved as well was the prophetic vision of a time to come when a restoration would bring back the wonder and power of the Church, including the fulness of the gospel of Jesus Christ in the latter days.

The Lord sees all from the divine perspective. He knows the patterns of human action—the good and the bad. He knows the trends of human endeavor—sometimes sublime and noble, sometimes misguided and destructive.

In love and mercy He forgives our weaknesses as we repent, and He oversees the design of the plan of happiness that will, eventually, bring salvation and exaltation to so many of the sons and daughters of God. In many of our lives there is a pattern of apostasy and rejuvenation, retreat and return. How are you dealing with this trend in your own extended family circle or in the circle of your acquaintances? How are you bringing light into areas of darkness, joy into areas of doubt and gloom?

How Can We Benefit from an Understanding of the Apostasy?

The apostasy and the Restoration are key interdependent themes in the process of gospel learning. *Apostasy* is the periodic and widespread falling away from covenant principles, such as occurred among the Saints following the earthly mission of the Savior and His apostolic leaders. Apostasy necessitates a restoration of divine truth to mankind through divine intervention. It might be useful to turn to astronomy for symbolic help in gaining a fuller understanding of the severe implications of the apostasy—and discover in the Restoration the antidote to such an alienated state of existence. As any student of astrophysics knows, heavenly bodies (including satellites) move in elliptical orbits, with the controlling center of gravity at one of the focal points—for example, the moon moves around the earth, and the earth moves around the sun. As the earth moves in its orbit, its distance from the sun varies; the furthest point from the sun is the *apogee,* and the closest point to the sun is the *perigee.* All orbiting bodies follow this same pattern.

The word *apogee* is related to the word *apostasy:* the prefix *apo* is common to both words. *Apo* (from the Greek) means "away from." In that sense, *apostasy* implies moving away from a set of principles or values, thus abandoning one's beliefs or "standing far away" from the truth.

The main symbolic parallel is evident. When we are on a course that takes us away from our center of gravity, we are moving toward the "apogee of existence," toward that point in our journey that represents the furthest distance away from home base. If our home base is a source of light and life (as the sun is to the earth), then an apostasy deprives us of that light and life and detaches us from vitality.

What is vitality in the gospel sense? The scriptures are replete with references to the Savior as being the source of light and life; one example: "Behold, I am Jesus Christ, the Son of God. I am the life and the light of the world" (D&C 11:28). Our charge is to stay close to the Savior, to be part of His plan of life and perfection—the plan of salvation.

When we choose to separate ourselves from the Savior and His light, we move into a state of apostasy. In Lehi's dream, there were many who became lost in the mists of darkness and could not, or would not, find their way to the tree of life. Lehi's experience was different: "And it came to pass that I did go forth and partake of the fruit thereof; and I beheld that it was most sweet, above all that I ever before tasted. Yea, and I beheld that the fruit thereof was white, to exceed all the whiteness that I had ever seen" (1 Ne. 8:11). Lehi and his faithful family members were at the closest point to the source of spiritual vitality and the love of God. By contrast, the wanderers on strange pathways were far away—and thus in spiritual darkness.

Where there has been an apostasy—or a falling away—there is a vacuum that can be redressed only through a restoration, or a coming back once again into a closeness with the Lord and His gospel. Such a restoration, on a grand scale, was launched through the First Vision experienced by the boy Joseph Smith in the spring of 1820. That magnificent event inaugurated a series of significant happenings that resulted in the reestablishment of the kingdom of God upon the earth once again as an enduring blessing to God's children—"unto the bringing of them out of darkness unto light—yea, out of hidden darkness and out of captivity unto freedom" (2 Ne. 3:5).

As we work in the Church and kingdom, we become aware of the constant need to remain vigilant in order to stay on a pathway that will bring us ever closer to our Father in Heaven and His Son Jesus Christ. In a sense, we occasionally find ourselves moving in orbits where we are at times closer to the Lord, and at other times—through our imperfect behavior, through our doubts and pride—further away. The process of sincere repentance can help us move back into a relationship of confidence and comfort close to the Lord (see D&C 121:45). Similarly, when our loved ones move away from the

light, we feel anguish and concern. When they move closer to the light, we rejoice and feel comfort. The spiritual orbit is the restored gospel of Jesus Christ, which brings us through grace and redeeming love toward the light: "And that which doth not edify is not of God, and is darkness. That which is of God is light; and he that receiveth light, and continueth in God, receiveth more light; and that light groweth brighter and brighter until the perfect day" (D&C 50:23–24). How can you help your loved ones understand more fully the opposing forces of apostasy and restoration and keep their "orbit" close to the Savior and His redeeming love and grace?

Real-life Stories for Heart and Mind

The Precious Fold. On one occasion, after reading about how the Savior had taught His Apostles of the Father's love for them, a father was thinking about his love for his own children. He wanted to share that love with them, and so long before sunrise he emailed each of them the following message:

Sometimes when I get an insight there is no one to share it with at that moment. Your mom is still asleep, having spent much time last evening pondering and planning on behalf of our children. So maybe I could share this thought with you in the wee hours of the morning. I have just been reviewing those passages from the New Testament concerning the calling of the Twelve Apostles by Jesus. He is teaching His Apostles how valuable they are, and says to them, "Are not two sparrows sold for a farthing? and one of them shall not fall on the ground without your Father. But the very hairs of your head are all numbered. Fear ye not therefore, ye are of more value than many sparrows" (Matt. 10:29–31). If the Father is aware of each sparrow ("not one of them is forgotten before God"—Luke 12:6), how much more is He aware of each of His sons and daughters in His eternal lovingkindness! So my thought is this: you are valuable before God, just as your siblings are valuable before Him, and just as our precious grandchildren are valuable before Him. He loves you and cares for you—just as we, your parents, do. You are part of His precious fold. Love, Dad.

Unbeknownst to that father, one of his daughters had just experienced a major setback at work and her spirit needed to be buoyed and hope engendered. The email reached her at just the right moment. As she reported to her parents the next day, she was able to transcend the challenge through much prayer and faith—and things worked out well.

If our Father in Heaven is aware of every sparrow that falls to the ground, how much more aware He is of His children, for whom He has infinite love and compassion—just as the Savior does. This lesson in leadership from the Savior should inspire each of us in the Church charged with the responsibility to mobilize workers in Zion with enthusiasm and conviction and every parent with the duty to draw children onward into the process of spiritual development. The first lesson in Church leadership is to let others know that you love them unconditionally, just as the Father and His Son do. What experiences in your life demonstrate the positive outcomes of using this principle?

The Business of Saving Souls. A new couple in a ward soon became aware of a controversy that was fomenting a good deal of discussion in hallway and classroom alike. It seemed that an evergreen tree near the front entrance had originally been planted somewhat too close to the building during the construction phase many years earlier. Now the mature tree was growing at a considerable angle to the wall, which was of concern to many. The ward seemed to be divided into factions—one of them wanting to remove the tree, another insisting on doing nothing, and a third voting to trim the tree aesthetically. The husband noted that priesthood meetings were often given over to debating the issue. Finally, the couple arrived at church one Sunday and found that the tree had completely disappeared. It seems that one resourceful brother, having had his fill of the bickering and murmuring, had come on Saturday and taken the tree out all by himself, cleaning up all the debris so no trace was

left. He showed up at the meetings that day with a peaceful and satisfied look on his face—and many, if not most, said a silent prayer of thanks in their hearts that someone had had the wisdom to banish the spirit of contention and arguing over matters of secondary importance. After that, it seemed much easier to get back to the business of saving souls.

The Lord declared, concerning the operation of His Church: "And there shall be no disputations among you, as there have hitherto been; . . . For verily, verily I say unto you, he that hath the spirit of contention is not of me" (3 Ne. 11:28–29). How can harmony, cheerfulness, and focusing on gospel essentials contribute to good fellowship in the kingdom of God?

Pondering Prayerfully

Additional scriptures to consider and ponder:
- Isa. 29:13–14
- Amos 8:11–12
- Matt. 24:11–13
- Acts 20:29–30
- 3 Ne. 15:9
- D&C 1:15–16
- D&C 4:1–2
- D&C 132:8

The following hymns might contribute to a spirit of understanding about the Church in earlier times:
- "A Poor Wayfaring Man of Grief" (*Hymns,* 29)
- "Lord, I Would Follow Thee" (*Hymns,* 220)

Remember and Be Sure

From the scriptures we learn that Jesus proclaimed His role as the promised Messiah and began to set up His kingdom on the earth. He called His apostles and prophets after spending the night on a mountain in prayer (see Luke 6:12). The Savior, ever following the will of the Father, sought Him in mighty prayer continually. Thus the Lord's Apostles were called by revelation—and it is the same today. We learn from the fifth Article of Faith the following: "We believe that a man must be called of God, by prophecy, and by the laying on of hands by those who are in authority, to preach the

Gospel and administer in the ordinances thereof." We show our respect and love for our Heavenly Father as we sustain His leaders with all our heart. Heavenly Father loves and respects us as we participate in the law of common consent (see D&C 20:63; 26:2; 28:13; 38:34; 104:21; 124:144)—the act through which we show our love and devotion to God by accepting and sustaining our leaders. We too are called of God in our various capacities of service in His kingdom. This doctrine of being called of God through revelation should bring joy to our souls, knowing as we do that Heavenly Father cares about each of us.

By sustaining those in authority over us we are in fact showing reverence to God. Similarly, we show our reverence and gratitude by accepting our own calls to serve faithfully and willingly. As President David O. McKay stated: "The body of the Church is composed of many members, yet all one body; and it is healthy, vigorous, strong, and influential when all the members of that body are working harmoniously together" (*Gospel Ideals: Selections from the Discourses of David O. McKay,* 176).

The Savior announced to His Apostles at the end of His post-resurrection ministry: "All power is given unto me in heaven and in earth" (Matt. 28:18), whereupon He gave to them the universal commission: "Go ye therefore, and teach all nations, baptizing them in the name of the Father, and of the Son, and of the Holy Ghost: Teaching them to observe all things whatsoever I have commanded you: and lo, I am with you alway, even unto the end of the world. Amen" (Matt. 28:19–20). This evangelical commission included the elements of going forth, teaching, baptizing, cultivating obedience, and—in accordance with the charge to Peter to "feed my sheep" (John 21:15–17)—serving the people with godlike charity. To do these things with power and authenticity, the Apostles needed two things: (1) the Savior to be with them continually (as He promised them), and (2) the endowment of the Holy Ghost.

The Savior was called to His atoning office from before the foundations of the world. He is the promised Messiah. In a similar way, let us have the courage to present ourselves with devotion as representatives of His Church and kingdom, and bear solemn witness that the gospel is true.

CHAPTER 17
The Restored Church of Today

The mission of the Church is glorious—to invite all of us to come unto Christ through proclaiming the gospel, perfecting our lives, and redeeming the dead. As we come unto Christ, we bless our own lives, those of our families, and our Father in Heaven's children, both living and dead. —Ezra Taft Benson *(The Teachings of Ezra Taft Benson, 179)*

Opening the Window of Wisdom

On April 6, 1830, an event of singular importance in the history of the world took place in a humble cabin in the small town of Fayette, New York (see D&C 20:1). On that occasion the Lord's Church was formally organized in this dispensation as a divine blessing for all who would come with broken hearts and contrite spirits and covenant to be His children by taking upon them His name and serving Him forever in righteousness. The Church is indeed the organized and authorized structure through which the Saints are to be perfected, the gospel preached unto all the world, and salvation administered and secured for all the hosts of Creation—both living and dead.

The founding of the Church took place a decade after the young Joseph Smith had experienced a transcendent event in a grove of trees near his parents' farm in Palmyra, New York. "Oh, how

lovely was the morning!" begins the beloved hymn recounting Joseph Smith's first uttered prayer in the shady grove that was to become sacred to generations of truth-seekers everywhere. What occurred that spring morning in 1820 ushered in the Restoration of the gospel in the dispensation of the fulness of times. It was no accident that Joseph saw the living God and His Son, Jesus Christ, on that occasion and received truth and light in abundance. It was no accident that he participated in that glorious opening event of the Restoration of the gospel of Jesus Christ. From the foundations of the world this moment had been planned and anticipated as an essential step in Heavenly Father's design: "That in the dispensation of the fulness of times he might gather together in one all things in Christ, both which are in heaven, and which are on earth; even in him" (Eph. 1:10). The First Vision ended generations of spiritual darkness fostered by the Great Apostasy—the general falling away from truth foreseen by prophets of old and foretold by the Savior and His Apostles. The First Vision confirmed that the Father and Son are individual persons of infinite glory, that They love us with a perfect love, and that They are the source of light and truth essential for our becoming worthy to return to our heavenly home some day.

The sequence of events inaugurated by the First Vision resulted in the complete restoration of the gospel of redemption and the reestablishment of the living Church and kingdom of God through the instrumentality of the Prophet Joseph Smith. The priesthood of God was restored in 1829 through the visitation of angelic ministrants, John the Baptist (see D&C 13) and Peter, James, and John (see D&C 27:12; 128:20). Power was given to the Prophet Joseph to translate the Book of Mormon:

> Which contains a record of a fallen people, and the fulness of the gospel of Jesus Christ to the Gentiles and to the Jews also;
>
> Which was given by inspiration, and is confirmed to others by the ministering of angels, and is declared unto the world by them—
>
> Proving to the world that the holy scriptures are true, and that God does inspire men and call them to his holy work in this age and generation, as well as in generations of old;
>
> Thereby showing that he is the same God yesterday, today, and forever. Amen. (D&C 20:9–12)

Following the publication of the Book of Mormon in March 1830 and the formal organization of the Church a month later, the principles and powers of the kingdom were revealed through the Prophet Joseph, line upon line and precept upon precept, until the all-encompassing design of the Almighty for the salvation and exaltation of His children was set in place. Thus the stone foreseen by Daniel as "cut out of the mountain without hands" (Dan. 2:45) could roll forth, under the direction of God, until it should fill the entire earth and "stand for ever" (Dan. 2:44; compare D&C 65:2).

The birth of the restored Church was a process of supreme joy, tempered by intense sacrifice and the need to overcome daunting challenges. The process of restoring the gospel unfolded systematically over the ensuing years under divine guidance until the Prophet's mission was complete and he had sealed his work and his testimony through his martyrdom on June 27, 1844. In the pages of the Doctrine and Covenants we see recounted the steps of the Restoration in all of its majesty. Through the Spirit of the Holy Ghost, the sincere student of truth can find confirmed the truth of the mighty work of God in these latter days, even that "marvellous work and a wonder" foreseen by a prophet of old (Isa. 29:14)

that opened the gates of salvation and eternal joy for God's children prior to the Second Coming. What Peter called the "times of refreshing" and "the times of restitution of all things" (Acts 3:19, 21) has unfolded in our day as the Restoration of the gospel of Jesus Christ and the organization of what the Lord designated as The Church of Jesus Christ of Latter-day Saints (see D&C 115:4).

John the Revelator, in the meridian of time, prophesied of the same divine intervention: "And I saw another angel fly in the midst of heaven, having the everlasting gospel to preach unto them that dwell on the earth, and to every nation, and kindred, and tongue, and people, Saying with a loud voice, Fear God, and give glory to him; for the hour of his judgment is come: and worship him that made heaven, and earth, and the sea, and the fountains of waters" (Rev. 14:6–7). How grateful we should be that the Lord has seen fit to allow us to be active participants and servants in the building up of His kingdom during the dispensation of the fulness of times.

Inspired by Latter-Day Prophets

John Taylor: We are here to co-operate with God in the salvation of the living, in the redemption of the dead, in the blessings of our ancestors, in the pouring out [of] blessings upon our children; we are here for the purpose of redeeming and generating the earth on which we live, and God has placed His authority and His counsels here upon the earth for that purpose, that men may learn to do the will of God on the earth as it is done in heaven. This is the object of our existence (*JD* 21:94).

> *With so many on earth languishing without purpose and floundering without the anchor of eternal principles, it is refreshing to hear a prophet of God tell us in direct but simple words that life has deep meaning, that a divine commission rests on our souls, and that we are in partnership with God to bring about His eternal design for the well-being and happiness of His children. What are your thoughts about the sublime stewardship we have? How can you help others on a continual basis to remember how precious they are, and how much our Father in Heaven and His Son love them and want them to have enduring joy through the gospel plan?*

George Albert Smith: The distinction between this great Church and that of all other churches from the beginning has been that we believe in divine revelation; we believe that our Father speaks to man today as He has done from the time of Adam. We believe and we know—which is more than mere belief—that our Father has set His hand in this world for the salvation of the children of men (*CR,* April 1917, 37).

Those not of the LDS faith might still rejoice in the revelations of the past and put their hope in following the word of God as preserved in scripture—but when they deny continuing revelation, they sail on a ship without a captain at the helm. Only continuing revelation through a living prophet can ensure that the journey is kept on course according to the will of God. What are some examples of how our living prophets in the recent past have counseled us to do certain things, follow specific patterns in our life, and apply eternal principles in ways that relate to modern-day challenges?

Ezra Taft Benson: This work is true. God the Father and his beloved Son did appear to Joseph Smith. This was the greatest event that has transpired in the world since the resurrection of the Master. This is our message and our warning to the world (*God, Family, Country: Our Three Great Loyalties,* 95).

Prophets counsel, expound, reveal, praise, and encourage—but they also warn and call to repentance. The Lord has counseled: "Behold, I sent you out to testify and warn the people, and it becometh every man who hath been warned to warn his neighbor" (D&C 88:81). In your opinion, in what form and tone should this warning be extended to our neighbors?

Bruce R. McConkie: The true Church is built upon the rock of his gospel, upon the rock of faith in the Lord Jesus Christ, upon the rock of personal revelation, which, coming by the power of the Holy Ghost, reveals that he is the Son of the living God, who was crucified for the sins of the world (*The Millennial Messiah,* 127).

Continuing revelation given to the living prophets brings essential light and truth into the world concerning the will of God. At the same time, personal revelation to each individual of faith brings the assurance, through the Spirit, that the gospel is true and of divine origin, and that Jesus Christ is our Savior. How has personal revelation been a strength to you and your loved ones as you have moved through mortality toward the tree of life (see 1 Ne. 8:10–28)?

Truths to Liken

James 1:5–7—"If any of you lack wisdom, let him ask of God, that giveth to all men liberally, and upbraideth not; and it shall be given him. But let him ask in faith, nothing wavering. For he that wavereth is like a wave of the sea driven with the wind and tossed. For let not that man think that he shall receive any thing of the Lord."

- It was this passage that prompted Joseph Smith to inquire of the Lord—resulting in the remarkable manifestation of the First Vision in the spring of 1820 (see JS–H 1:11–14).
- In keeping with the pattern demonstrated by the Prophet Joseph Smith, let us seek wisdom and understanding through daily scripture study and the devoted prayer of faith. How would you define the term *nothing wavering* as it relates to prayer? How would you describe the opposite state or condition?

D&C 4:1–2—"Now behold, a marvelous work is about to come forth among the children of men. Therefore, O ye that embark in the service of God, see that ye serve him with all your heart, might, mind and strength, that ye may stand blameless before God at the last day."

- This revelation was given through the Prophet Joseph Smith to his father, Joseph Smith, Sr., at Harmony, Pennsylvania, in February 1829. The work of the Restoration provides a grand opportunity for the servants of God to rise in majesty and devotion by giving their all for the building up of the Church and kingdom of God on the earth. Desire, charity, faith, virtue, and all other elements of the divine nature qualify and empower individuals to engage productively in the urgent work and thus bring salvation to their own souls and bless the lives of countless others.

- Truly Section 4 is a miniature beacon of spiritual light, unparalleled in its power to illuminate the entire landscape of righteous service in the most economical of terms. Every missionary—indeed, every laborer in the Church—should commit the words of this short revelation to memory and ponder them frequently as a standard of service in the Lord's kingdom. How does serving God "with all your heart, might, mind and strength" protect you from blame at the final judgment? In that same context, how does charitable service before God "cover the multitude of sins," as Peter declares (see 1 Pet. 4:8)?

D&C 21:4–6—"Wherefore, meaning the church, thou shalt give heed unto all his words and commandments which he shall give unto you as he receiveth them, walking in all holiness before me; For his word ye shall receive, as if from mine own mouth, in all patience and faith. For by doing these things the gates of hell shall not prevail against you; yea, and the Lord God will disperse the powers of darkness from before you, and cause the heavens to shake for your good, and his name's glory."

- These words were given through the Prophet Joseph Smith on Tuesday, April 6, 1830, in the home of Peter Whitmer, Sr., at Fayette, Seneca County, New York, when the Church was organized. The six individuals who acted as charter members for the organizing process were Joseph Smith, Oliver Cowdery, Hyrum Smith, David Whitmer, Samuel H. Smith, and Peter Whitmer, Jr.
- This is a covenant statement that applies to all, giving a commandment and a promise to those who obey. In patience and faith we are to accept the revelations from the living prophet as if

they were coming from the mouth of the Lord. How would you put into your own words the promises stated in this revelation? How have these promises been fulfilled in your own life and the lives of your loved ones?

D&C 38:27—"I say unto you, be one; and if ye are not one ye are not mine."

- This oft-cited statement is from Section 38 of the Doctrine and Covenants, given through the Prophet Joseph Smith on Sunday, January 2, 1831, at Fayette, Seneca County, New York, at a conference of the Church held at the home of Peter Whitmer, Sr. In this revelation the Lord commanded the people of His Church to practice holiness and cultivate harmony before Him, every man esteeming his brother as himself. If they are not one, they are not His. If they are prepared, they shall not fear (see D&C 38:30).
- We cannot look at unity and oneness in a casual or uncommitted manner. It is vital that we truly seek to obtain this oneness in our families. When we as family members agree on a value system, then unity of action begins. Agreed-upon values bring unity not only to the family, but to the Church and the community. What has been your experience as you have better tried to practice this principle?

D&C 46:2—"But notwithstanding those things which are written, it always has been given to the elders of my church from the beginning, and ever shall be, to conduct all meetings as they are directed and guided by the Holy Spirit."

- This instruction from the Lord was part of the revelation given by the Prophet Joseph Smith on March 8, 1831, at Kirtland, Ohio. During the restoration period, the Lord unfolded to His fledgling Church through the Prophet Joseph Smith the principles and practices that would bring about the emergence of the kingdom of God from obscurity into fullness, richness, and glory. This particular counsel from the Lord defines an absolute for the conducting of meetings: always follow the Spirit.

- Let us be worthy of the Spirit in order to conduct meetings in the family or in the Church according to the will of God. The Spirit will guide us according to the commandments and revelations of God (see D&C 20:45). The Spirit will also inspire us how to preach, exhort, pray, supplicate, or sing praises to our God (see Moro. 6:9).

D&C 65:2—"The keys of the kingdom of God are committed unto man on the earth, and from thence shall the gospel roll forth unto the ends of the earth, as the stone which is cut out of the mountain without hands shall roll forth, until it has filled the whole earth."

- This is an excerpt from a revelation given through the Prophet Joseph Smith in October 1831 at Hiram, Ohio. The Lord declares that the gospel will roll forth as the stone cut from the mountain without hands (see Dan. 2) until it fills the whole earth.
- The Church, though expanding fairly rapidly, is still relatively small in number. How does it touch your sense of hope and joy in the gospel to look forward to the time when the Church will fill "the whole earth"? According to the passage above, why is this destined to happen?

D&C 105:5–6—"And Zion cannot be built up unless it is by the principles of the law of the celestial kingdom; otherwise I cannot receive her unto myself. And my people must needs be chastened until they learn obedience, if it must needs be, by the things which they suffer."

- These words are from a revelation given through the Prophet Joseph Smith on June 22, 1834, on Fishing River, Clay County, Missouri.
- Obedience to the laws and principles of the celestial kingdom is the greatest lesson we learn by looking back on this period of intense persecution and tribulation in Church history. As we look forward, we can take into our lives the principles of covenant valor in planning—through faith and hope—for the eventual establishment of Zion on this the American continent (see A of F 10) and the redemption of the Lord's people. What role has chastening played in your own life and the life of those in your family circle? How is chastening a testimony of God's love (see D&C 95:1)?

Moses 7:18—"And the Lord called his people ZION, because they were of one heart and one mind, and dwelt in righteousness; and there was no poor among them."

- During the days of Enoch the Lord blessed His people with miracles of protection and caused them to flourish as "the City of Holiness, even ZION" (Moses 7:19).
- To be a Zion people we are to be unified and pure in heart (see D&C 97:21). This oneness and purity, as with the Nephites following the visit of the resurrected Lord, brings peace and righteousness. How does unity and purity bring peace and happiness to your own home?

Rejoicing and Reasoning Together

How Does Membership in the Restored Church Bring Blessings to Us that Are Available Nowhere Else?

Abundant blessings flow to members of the restored Church through covenant obedience to the commandments of our Father in Heaven. Any one of the following would be an extraordinary source of joy and edification—but all of them combined form an overwhelming and majestic endowment of eternal benefits that cannot be accessed in any other way than through The Church of Jesus Christ of Latter-day Saints:

- **Divine Approval**—You belong to a Church and kingdom established by the direct intervention of God, who has declared it to be "the only true and living church upon the face of the whole earth, with which I, the Lord, am well pleased, speaking unto the church collectively and not individually" (D&C 1:30).

- **Prophecy Fulfilled**—You are personally part of the fulfillment of ancient prophecy concerning the coming forth of the restored Church as a channel for blessing mankind in momentous ways: as "a marvellous work among this people, even a marvellous work and a wonder: for the wisdom of their wise men shall perish, and the understanding of their prudent men shall be hid" (Isa. 29:14); as the administrator of "a new covenant with the house of Israel, and with the house of Judah" in the latter days (Jer. 31:31); as the stone "cut out from the mountain without hands" that would roll forth and fill the whole earth (Dan. 2:45); as the "restitution of all things, which God hath spoken by the mouth of all his holy prophets since the world began" (Acts 3:21); and as the sublime latter-day design of the Lord envisioned by John the Revelator for preaching the gospel "to every nation, and kindred, and tongue, and people" (Rev. 14:6).

- **Continuing Revelation**—You are the direct beneficiary of continuing revelation from God unto His Church and kingdom through living prophets (see Amos 3:7; D&C 1:38), as well as direct revelation by the Holy Ghost to you as an individual to sustain your testimony and guide you in your personal and family service (see D&C 8:2).

- **Multiple Witnesses in the Canon**—You are a member of the only Church that has multiple witnesses of the truth of the gospel of Jesus Christ in interconnected standard works of scriptures: the Old Testament, the New Testament, the Book of Mormon, the Doctrine and Covenants, and the Pearl of Great Price. In addition, the Joseph Smith Translation of the Bible restores much light and truth lost from holy writ over the centuries.

- **Keys and Powers of the Priesthood**—You have the direct benefit of blessings that flow to you and your loved ones through the priesthood of God, restored in our day to ensure that all can participate in the ordinances of the gospel essential for salvation and exaltation, including baptism by water and fire and the glorious blessings of the temple. The majestic design of the Almighty—with a divinely appointed system of priesthood offices and stewardships for His Church ensuring participation by all—brings a dynamic, harmonious, living entity into our lives. Continuity of leadership at all levels, from wards and stakes throughout the Church to the quorums of prophets, seers, and revelators at the head, ensures an uninterrupted unfolding of gospel programs to perfect the Saints, redeem the dead, and extend missionary service to the four quarters of the earth.

- **Fulness of the Gospel of Jesus Christ**—You have the blessing of all truth restored concerning the plan of salvation to "bring to pass the immortality and eternal life of man" (Moses 1:39); all principles and precepts needed to guide you and your family home again to your Heavenly Father and His Son, Jesus Christ; all understanding of the premortal, mortal, and postmortal spheres of existence; and all requisite revelations that teach you through the Spirit about your true identity as a son or daughter of God, showing you how to take on the divine nature (see D&C 4; 2 Pet. 1:8–13) and become "perfect in Christ" (Moro. 10:33).

- **New and Everlasting Covenant**—You participate in the eternal covenant between God and His children that has existed from Adam onward through all dispensations of time, embracing all sacred contracts with Heavenly Father that you make through the blessings and ordinances of the priesthood (including eternal marriage) and continuing today under the outreach of the Abrahamic covenant to bring the blessings of the priesthood and the gospel of salvation and exaltation to all peoples of the world in preparation for the Second

Coming and the inauguration of the millennial reign (see Abr. 2:8–11).

- **Holy Places to Stand**—You belong to the family of God, with the privilege of having a stewardship to establish a home of Zion according to celestial principles, to enjoy the security and fellowship of the expanding array of the stakes of Zion, and to rejoice in the peace and exalting blessings of the temple: "Behold, it is my will, that all they who call on my name, and worship me according to mine everlasting gospel, should gather together, and stand in holy places; And prepare for the revelation which is to come, when the veil of the covering of my temple, in my tabernacle, which hideth the earth, shall be taken off, and all flesh shall see me together" (D&C 101:22–23; also D&C 124:36; 127; 128; 132).

- **Perfect Oneness**—In a world of confusion and turmoil, you have the blessing of belonging to a Church reflecting unity of purpose and harmony of fellowship, where the workings of the Spirit dispel differences, generate peace, and bring people together in the cause of building up the kingdom of God. The principle of common consent ensures the sustaining and support of appointed leaders (see D&C 26:2); meetings are directed by the Spirit (see D&C 46:2); music that is ordained of God sweetens the air and instills accord in the hearts of the people (see D&C 25); and members enjoy the confirming knowledge that they "are no more strangers and foreigners, but fellowcitizens with the saints, and of the household of God" (Eph. 2:19). Where in all the world is there an organization comprising so much diversity in cultural origins and backgrounds that consistently enjoys the spirit of unity and common purpose?

- **Liberty**—As a member of the Church, you enjoy the ultimate opportunity of being freed from the effects of sin through the gospel of Jesus Christ; freed from the isolation of loneliness by being part of an eternal family; freed from the bondage of ignorance by being lifted and edified through the knowledge of saving and exalting principles; freed from the burdens of temporal concerns through programs of spiritual providence and self-reliance based on the laws of consecration, tithes and offerings, and charitable support; and ultimately freed from the tyranny of worldly oppression through the dawning of the coming millennial reign of peace and glory. The Church is an institution of liberty, restored at a time when the Lord prepared the environment of the Gentile world for just such an event: "Therefore, it is not right that any man should be in bondage one to another. And for this purpose have I established the Constitution of this land, by the hands of wise men whom I raised up unto this very purpose, and redeemed the land by the shedding of blood" (D&C 101:79–80). Divine and everlasting liberty shall come for all those who through obedience and valor are blessed with the glory of the celestial kingdom:

> These are they who are come unto Mount Zion, and unto the city of the living God, the heavenly place, the holiest of all.
>
> These are they who have come to an innumerable company of angels, to the general assembly and church of Enoch, and of the Firstborn.
>
> These are they whose names are written in heaven, where God and Christ are the judge of all.
>
> These are they who are just men made perfect through Jesus the mediator of the new covenant, who wrought out this perfect atonement through the shedding of his own blood. (D&C 76:66–69)

As you consider this list of unique blessings that come to you and your family through the restored Church, in what ways can you more fully express your gratitude to Heavenly Father and His Son for such a rich endowment of spiritual wealth? How does the above list help explain what John Taylor meant when he said, following his witnessing of the martyrdom of the prophet by a ruthless mob on June 27, 1844: "Joseph Smith, the Prophet and Seer of the Lord, has done more, save Jesus only, for the salvation of men in this world, than any other man that ever lived in it" (D&C 135:3)? How can you help your family gain a fuller understanding of the extraordinary blessings available through the Church—and nowhere else? Even though there is much truth and goodness in other churches of the world, how can you share the restored truths of the gospel of Jesus Christ with others not of our faith, so that they, too, can find joy and eternal happiness through "the only true and living church upon the face of the whole earth" (D&C 1:30)?

Real-life Stories for Heart and Mind

"**That All May Be Profited.**" On one occasion a young man came to a member of the stake presidency in his stake to complain that various leaders in his ward were giving him sometimes conflicting advice when he asked them for help on a challenging marital situation. He felt that the Relief Society president had the most valuable counsel to give, and was troubled that the bishop hadn't come up with any better solutions himself. The member of stake presidency listened patiently to the young man and then assured him, first of all, that it was the individual's responsibility to consider prayerfully all options and then make the decision based on correct principles. He also assured the young husband that each one of his mentors would look at his situation with a different level of understanding, viewed from a unique set of personal experiences—and thus diversity of opinion is inevitable. But the main point was made in a follow-up letter to this young man a few days later:

A bishop is the common judge in Israel, which means that he must decide on matters of serious moral consequence and must issue temple recommends as well as monitor progress of priesthood brethren in relation to their advancement. The bishop is also the presiding high priest in the ward and is responsible for receiving and accounting for the funds contributed. The bishop is nearly always a loving and concerned man, is frequently a radiant and warm individual, and is typically an effective counselor. He is almost never the single and ultimate font of wisdom for all members of his ward in all matters and at all times. . . . It seems to me that the Lord intended His Church to be a community of mutual support and mutual trust. There is a natural tendency for us to look to the leaders for guidance and direction; surely this is proper. However, the Church—if I understand 1 Corinthians 12 and D&C 46 correctly—is a complete network of resources where even the humblest and least visible member is of value and worth. In fact, it might be from the most unlikely source that inspiration might flow to one in need (not just from the bishop or Relief Society president). The reason that not all have all gifts is, it seems to me, so that we might have a need to depend on one another, "that all may be profited thereby" (D&C 46:12).

Who are counselors in the Church and kingdom of God? Everyone! We all teach continually—through word and deed. It seems to be the design of the Almighty that we should depend on one another and benefit from mutual assurances and the sharing of our spiritual gifts and talents. It is not only from our bishops and other Church leaders that we receive valuable counsel, but also from the myriad "angels on earth" who comprise our circle of friends and "fellowcitizens with the Saints" (Eph. 2:19). How have you been able to serve, on occasion, as an "angel of earth" to give encouragement, praise, and counsel to someone in need?

"**By Small Means the Lord Can Bring About Great Things**" (1 Ne. 16:29). It was just a small garden house where the missionaries taught the gospel—really just a tool shed perhaps six feet by ten feet in size, with a narrow door and a few tiny windows. It was nestled in a beautiful hilly orchard located behind the home of the only member family in the city. Because the owner was also the proprietor of a small neighborhood grocery store, she was fearful that her business would suffer should it become known by her intolerant neighbors that she was hosting Church services in her home. Therefore, she suggested that the two missionaries assigned to the town use the garden house for meetings on Sundays, everyone coming up through the back of the property from different directions through the trees in order to escape detection. And that's what happened. The missionaries would teach the gospel in the tiny shed to a handful of investigators (typically two or three) who would crowd into this humble facility to learn true principles. During one of the meetings it rained so hard that the noise of the water on the roof made it difficult to present the lesson on the Spirit of the Holy Ghost. But the Spirit nevertheless touched hearts in that lowly setting. Testimonies were cultivated. Lives were changed.

It was all part of the forward motion of that stone cut from the mountain without hands (see Dan. 2:45). It was all part of the process by which the influence of restored truths was being felt once again—even in remote parts of the world. When the Prophet Joseph Smith conducted that historic meeting on April 6, 1830, at the Peter Whitmer farmhouse in Fayette, New York, at which the kingdom of God was once more organized on the earth, he very likely saw in his mind's eye the prophetic view of the destiny of that kingdom—and how a small stone rolling forth "became a great mountain, and filled the whole earth" (Dan. 2:35). The Great Architect knows the final design: "Wherefore, be not weary in well-doing, for ye are laying the foundation of a great work. And out of small things proceedeth that which is great" (D&C 64:33).

The Savior taught: "For where two or three are gathered together in my name, there am I in the midst of them" (Matt. 18:20). The Church is expanding quickly in worldwide growth. But, in effect, the size of the Church is no bigger than the size of one of its Zion families. It is the collection of Zion families that constitutes the Church and kingdom of God on the earth. How is your Zion family contributing to the light and joy of the Church? How can you ensure that the Spirit of the Lord is present with you and

your loved ones as you move forward as an eternal family?

Pondering Prayerfully

Additional scriptures to consider and ponder:
- Matt. 10:40
- Philip. 2:2
- 3 Ne. 27:7–8
- D&C 43:3
- D&C 43:8–10
- D&C 107:22
- D&C 107:30–31

The following hymns increase our gratitude for the restored Church:
- "An Angel from on High" (*Hymns*, 13)
- "High on the Mountain Top" (*Hymns*, 5)
- "Joseph Smith's First Prayer" (*Hymns*, 26)
- "Praise to the Man" (*Hymns*, 27)

Remember and Be Sure

In describing the kingdom of God on the earth, the Apostle Paul spoke of its members as being "built upon the foundation of the apostles and prophets, Jesus Christ himself being the chief corner stone; In whom all the building fitly framed together groweth unto a holy temple in the Lord" (Eph. 2:20–21). The stone that rolls forth to fill the world is the gospel kingdom of Jesus Christ, in its fulness a mighty temple unto God. In a special and unique way, the stone is the Savior Himself: "Therefore thus saith the Lord God, Behold, I lay in Zion for a foundation a stone, a tried stone, a precious corner stone, a sure foundation: he that believeth shall not make haste" (Isa. 28:16). Thus the foundation for the spiritual existence of the sons and daughters of God, for the salvation of all mankind and the exaltation of the faithful, is Jesus Christ. By doing our part to advance the cause of the "stone," we help build the kingdom of God and assist in the godly mission to fill the world with the peace, joy, and eternal blessings that only the gospel of Jesus Christ can bring.

CHAPTER 18
Faith

Faith centers in Christ. Let it be uppermost in your minds, now and at all times, that Jesus is the Christ, the Son of the living God, who came into the world to lay down his life that we might live. That is the truth and is fundamental. Upon that our faith is built. It cannot be destroyed. —Joseph Fielding Smith (*Doctrines of Salvation*, 2:302)

Opening the Window of Wisdom

The third Article of Faith states: "We believe that through the Atonement of Christ, all mankind may be saved, by obedience to the laws and ordinances of the Gospel." The Lord's plan for ensuring eternal happiness for His children through the power of the Atonement is profoundly simple and glorious, based on just four key steps enumerated in the fourth Article of Faith: "We believe that the first principles and ordinances of the Gospel are: first, Faith in the Lord Jesus Christ; second, Repentance; third, Baptism by immersion for the remission of sins; fourth, Laying on of hands for the gift of the Holy Ghost." The scriptures reveal, explain, confirm, and empower the vital and indispensable program for incorporating these principles and ordinances into our lives in order to merit, through obedience and the grace of God, the welcoming approval of heaven to return once again to the presence of the Father and the Son.

Faith is the first principle of the gospel of Jesus Christ and the governing principle in applying the Atonement to our lives. We learn that it is impossible to please God except through faith (see Heb. 11:6). Faith is essential to accomplish the will of God while we are on the earth, just as it is essential to gain eternal life in the world beyond this. Alma defined faith in these terms: "And now as I said concerning faith—faith is not to have a perfect knowledge of things; therefore if ye have faith ye hope for things which are not seen, which are true" (Alma 32:21). Paul confirmed this truth in his day: "NOW faith is the substance of things hoped for, the evidence of things not seen" (Heb. 11:1).

In the *Lectures on Faith*, the Prophet Joseph Smith identifies three degrees of faith, the first corresponding to the words of Alma and Paul—that faith is the substance of things hoped for (see *Lectures on Faith* 1:7–8). Then the Prophet Joseph extends the meaning further to a second degree, saying that "Faith is the moving cause of all action in temporal concerns" (*Lectures on Faith* 1:12). The third degree of faith declares it to be the principle and source of power (see *Lectures on Faith* 1:15). When all three degrees are applied, faith is exercised to its fullest—faith being not only hope and belief, but the moving cause of our actions (see James 2:18) and the power to do the will of the Lord (see

Heb. 11; Ether 12). The Prophet goes on to say: "Faith, then, is the first great governing principle which has power, dominion, and authority over all things; by it they exist, by it they are upheld, by it they are changed or by it they remain agreeable to the will of God" (*Lectures on Faith* 1:24).

Faith, as a principle of action and power, leads to repentance, acceptance of the sacred covenant of baptism, and the gift of the Holy Ghost. With faith we can endure to the end. Surely the just can live only by faith (see Rom. 1:17; Gal. 3:11)—and those who are just shall indeed be made perfect (see D&C 76:69). We increase our faith as we hear the word of God (see Rom. 10:17), as we fast and pray with all our hearts (see Hel. 3:35), and as we witness and emulate the exemplary lives of the prophets of God and His righteous children.

Faith precedes miracles (see Ether 12:16–18). In the gardens of spiritual living, sweet and priceless miracles spring up as a natural outgrowth of faith and godly power, sustained by the light of heavenly compassion and the warmth of heavenly love. Miracles are a blessing from God, and are wrought by the power of faith (see 2 Ne. 26:13). It is at the hands of the righteous that miracles take place. There can be no miracles performed save it be in the name of Jesus Christ (see 3 Ne. 8:1). Miracles happen every day as lives are changed through spiritual transformation (see John 3:5); they unfold through prayer and by the power and authority of the priesthood. If we have eyes to see and hearts to feel, we can and will see everyday miracles, for God is a God of miracles, being "the same yesterday, today, and forever, and in him there is no variableness neither shadow of changing" (Morm. 9:9.) He loves us now just as He loved the Saints of yesterday. He seeks to bless us—and He will and does bless us on a daily basis. Miracles never cease to occur in the household of faith. The ancient American prophet Mormon perceived the universal reality of continuing miracles, saying to the modern reader: "God has not ceased to be a God of miracles" (Morm. 9:15). Just as in former times, God blesses us with miracles as a natural product of our faith and devotion.

Perhaps the greatest miracle of all in the course of our daily life is the unfolding of faith as a living manifestation of our godly potential. If we will desire to try the word of God in faith, we will find that it will enlarge and enlighten our souls, confirming its efficacy within us; and then if we will nourish the word with continuing faith and hope, and with charitable obedience, it will bring us everlasting blessings. In the language of Alma's masterful discourse on faith as a seed, we are counseled:

> But if ye will nourish the word, yea, nourish the tree as it beginneth to grow, by your faith with great diligence, and with patience, looking forward to the fruit thereof, it shall take root; and behold it shall be a tree springing up unto everlasting life.
>
> And because of your diligence and your faith and your patience with the word in nourishing it, that it may take root in you, behold, by and by ye shall pluck the fruit, which is most precious, which is sweet above all that is sweet, and which is white above all that is white, yea, and pure above all that is pure; and ye shall feast upon this fruit even until ye are filled, that ye hunger not, neither shall ye thirst.
>
> Then, my brethren, ye shall reap the rewards of your faith, and your diligence, and patience, and long-suffering, waiting for the tree to bring forth fruit unto you. (Alma 32:41–43)

Inspired by Latter-Day Prophets

Joseph Fielding Smith: Faith is knowledge that transcends ordinary boundaries. The range of the physical eye is sharply limited, it reaches only a part of the material world; but the vision of faith perceives the mystery of the invisible world and its limits are ever expanding (*The Restoration of All Things*, 189–190).

> *How has "the vision of faith" opened your understanding of the mysteries of God—those wondrous truths of the gospel that save and exalt? How can you assist others—your family, your friends, those you teach—to use the power of faith to see deeper, wider, and higher than just the confines of our daily world?*

Spencer W. Kimball: Under the gospel's beneficent laws, everyone—rich or poor, learned or unlearned—is encouraged first to perceive with the eye of faith and then, through effort, to express that faith in a higher, nobler life (*The Teachings of Spencer W. Kimball*, 72).

How does one measure faith? Faith is measured by the noble works empowered by that faith. How strong is your faith? How can you teach your loved ones the wise counsel of James: "Yea, a man may say, Thou hast faith, and I have works: shew me thy faith without thy works, and I will shew thee my faith by my works" (James 2:18).

Howard W. Hunter: If what you say is the truth, and you say it purely and with honest conviction, those students will feel the spirit of the truth being taught them and will recognize that inspiration and revelation has come into their hearts. That is how we build faith. That is how we strengthen testimonies—with the power of the word of God taught in purity and with conviction (*The Teachings of Howard W. Hunter,* 185).

It is humbling yet inspiring to know that we have the power to help others increase their faith in God. How have the words of others helped you to increase your faith? How can you more fully use your testimony of the gospel to help others enlarge and strengthen their faith?

Bruce R. McConkie: Faith is thus born of scriptural study. Those who study, ponder, and pray about the scriptures, seeking to understand their deep and hidden meanings, receive from time to time great outpourings of light and knowledge from the Holy Spirit (*Sermons and Writings of Bruce R. McConkie,* 238).

Like a seed, faith is nurtured through the word of God and expands and unfolds as we are continually immersed in the scriptures. What passages of scripture have given you strength in the past and will continue to inspire you in the future to do as the Savior would have you do in faith, nothing wavering?

Truths to Liken

1 Sam. 17:45—"Thou comest to me with a sword, and with a spear, and with a shield: but I come to thee in the name of the Lord of hosts, the God of the armies of Israel, whom thou hast defied."

- As King Saul looked on, all the mighty men of Israel quaked at the Philistine hordes and shrank at the defiant strength of the giant, Goliath. But the anointed young David, stepping forward in the strength of the Lord, spoke the inspired words given above, then applied his honed skill to thwart the arrogant enemy. The story of David and Goliath is perhaps the supreme emblem in all of world literature of how the weak things of the earth can, through hope and faith, vanquish any enemy, even one of imposing power.

- When we go about the Lord's errand by relying on His power and by following His Spirit in faith, we are assured of ultimate victory, for the purposes of the Lord cannot be thwarted or compromised. How can you build faith and courage to step forward like David when challenges arise? How can you help others—especially young people—to do the same?

2 Kgs. 6:16–17—"And he answered, Fear not: for they that be with us are more than they that be with them. And Elisha prayed, and said, LORD, I pray thee, open his eyes, that he may see. And the LORD opened the eyes of the young man; and he saw: and, behold, the mountain was full of horses and chariots of fire round about Elisha."

- The prophet Elisha gave wise counsel to the Israelite kings on how to conduct their war with Syria. At this point, the Syrians came seeking to destroy him. When Elisha's servant viewed with fear the surrounding hordes of the enemy, Elisha prayed that the Lord might open the servant's eyes to see the amassed forces of heaven arrayed against the enemy. The servant indeed beheld, and was filled with hope and courage. Soon thereafter the Lord intervened to render the Syrian army powerless.

- Through the vision of faith we become aware of the forces for good that surround and bolster us in time of need. The Lord has promised His servants: "And whoso receiveth you, there I will be also, for I will go before your face. I will be on your right hand and on your left, and my Spirit shall be in your hearts, and mine angels round about you, to bear you up" (D&C 84:88). How do you feel about this promise? How has your faith given you confidence that you are not alone in the battle for the cause of good?

Luke 17:5—"And the apostles said unto the Lord, Increase our faith."

- This was the supplication of the disciples to Jesus as He counseled them to forgive others continually.
- If the disciples of the Lord needed an increase in faith, then how much more do we need faith in our lives! The Lord's next word of counsel to His disciples was to begin with the faith of a mustard seed, and then to behold miracles happening in their lives. If you were to approach the Lord in prayer and ask Him to increase your faith, what counsel do you believe He would give you in your circumstances?

Rom. 10:17—"So then faith cometh by hearing, and hearing by the word of God."

- Paul gave this wise advice to the Roman Saints in his day on how to open the source of faith in their lives.
- How do we increase our faith through the word of the Lord? By listening to the living prophets (see D&C 21:4–5), searching the holy scriptures (see 2 Ne. 32:3), seeking the promptings of the Holy Spirit (see 2 Ne. 32:5), and applying the power of prayer in our lives (see James 1:5–6). How can you help those you love to make the word of the Lord an active part of their lives and thus increase their faith?

Heb. 11:6—"But without faith it is impossible to please him: for he that cometh to God must believe that he is, and that he is a rewarder of them that diligently seek him."

- This sentence from Paul's superb treatise on faith captures the covenant power of the principle of faith: by acting in sincere faith, knowing that God lives and loves us, we receive the promised blessing of knowing that we are pleasing Him.
- As the children of God, our desire is to please Him and do His will. Recognizing this fact makes having and exercising faith in God and the Lord Jesus Christ paramount in our lives. What are your feelings about the connection between your faith and your confidence in having a pleasing relationship with God?

Ether 3:9—"And the Lord said unto him: Because of thy faith thou hast seen that I shall take upon me flesh and blood; and never has man come before me with such exceeding faith as thou hast; for were it not so ye could not have seen my finger."

- The brother of Jared had seen the finger of the Lord—and was soon blessed to behold the full person of the Lord in His spiritual essence.
- Faith sees through the veil covering the mysteries of God, allowing us to perceive the truths of heaven relating to our divine potential to become like the Lord. We too can know our God and our Savior. We can pray and put away our fears and jealousies and humble ourselves before God. The veil will be rent and in the Spirit we can see God (see D&C 67:10). If we continue faithful and gain true charity, we can become the sons and daughters of God so that when the Savior appears we will be like Him and see Him as He is (1 Jn. 3:2). How has faith enabled you to gain a greater understanding of the plan of salvation as a means to one day come into the presence of the Father and the Son and behold Their glory?

Ether 12:27—"And if men come unto me I will show unto them their weakness. I give unto men weakness that they may be humble; and my grace is sufficient for all men that humble themselves before me; for if they humble themselves before me, and have faith in me, then will I make weak things become strong unto them."

- Moroni, the last of the keepers of the Book of Mormon chronicle, was imbued with a compelling desire to impart the lessons of truth that the Lord wanted future generations to receive through the account of the Jaredite experience. But Moroni also had a keen sense of his inadequacy with the written word, and he agonized that future readers would mock his efforts (see Ether 12:24). At that point the Lord taught Moroni—and, by extension, all of us—a powerful and comforting lesson about the operation of faith and the eternal gift of grace that can make our weaknesses strong.
- Humility—our sincere feeling of dependency upon the Lord—is the empowering quality that lets us receive the influence of His power and grace in our lives. If we will acknowledge our weaknesses in humility and ask the Lord for blessings, having faith, He will impart grace sufficient to make our weaknesses strong so that we might fulfill our stewardships in life. What is your sense about your own perceived weaknesses? How can faith and humility render these weaknesses as strengths though the blessing of a loving and merciful God?

D&C 88:118—"And as all have not faith, seek ye diligently and teach one another words of wisdom; yea, seek ye out of the best books words of wisdom; seek learning, even by study and also by faith."

- These words are part of a revelation given through the Prophet Joseph Smith at Kirtland, Ohio, December 27, 1832, and designated by him as the "olive leaf . . . plucked from the Tree of Paradise, the Lord's message of peace to us" (D&C 88, section heading). There is peace in the Lord's counsel to increase our faith by searching the written records of wisdom. The action words are *seek, teach, learn, study,* and *exercise faith*—all to increase our faith.
- Even in our weakness the Lord will make us wise and increase our faith as we use the faith that we have. It is a blessed spiral: our faith increases as our faith increases our faith, on and on! What are your thoughts and experiences about teaching one another words of wisdom to increase faith?

Rejoicing and Reasoning Together

Some Say It Is by Grace through Faith That We Are Saved. Others Say It Is by Works. What Do You Think?

Paul declared in his epistle to the Ephesians: "For by grace are ye saved through faith; and that not of yourselves: it is the gift of God: Not of works, lest any man should boast" (Eph. 2:8–9). James declared:

> Even so faith, if it hath not works, is dead, being alone.
> Yea, a man may say, Thou hast faith, and I have works: shew me thy faith without thy works, and I will shew thee my faith by my works. . . .
> Ye see then how that by works a man is justified, and not by faith only. . . .
> For as the body without the spirit is dead, so faith without works is dead also. (James 2:17–18, 24, 26)

Is there a conflict between these two positions?

In the Book of Mormon, Nephi shows in a simple statement how these two positions can be reconciled and harmonized: "For we labor diligently to write, to persuade our children, and also our brethren, to believe in Christ, and to be reconciled to God; for we know that it is by grace that we are saved, after all we can do" (2 Ne. 25:23). Thus our faithful obedience and good works carry us some distance along the pathway of life—but it is the grace of God that carries us all the way to our destination, "after all we can do." What is meant by the words *after all we can do*? Lehi taught his sons with clarity that no mortal can claim perfect obedience to the laws of God: "And men are instructed sufficiently that they know good from evil. And the law is given unto men. And by the law no flesh is justified. . ." (2 Ne. 2:5). Thus the Lord makes up the difference for those exercising faith in His atoning power:

> Wherefore, redemption cometh in and through the Holy Messiah; for he is full of grace and truth.
>
> Behold, he offereth himself a sacrifice for sin, to answer the ends of the law, unto all those who have a broken heart and a contrite spirit; and unto none else can the ends of the law be answered.
>
> Wherefore, how great the importance to make these things known unto the inhabitants of the earth, that they may know that there is no flesh that can dwell in the presence of God, save it be through the merits, and mercy, and grace of the Holy Messiah, who layeth down his life according to the flesh, and taketh it again by the power of the Spirit, that he may bring to pass the resurrection of the dead, being the first that should rise. (2 Ne. 2:6–8)

If we combine the words of father and son, it is "through the merits, and mercy, and grace of the Holy Messiah" that we are saved, "after all we can do" by way of our faith, our broken hearts and contrite spirits, and our service to God and mankind.

There is no conflict in the doctrines of faith, grace, and works—only the perfect harmony of the eternities.

It is the position of some in the Christian world that they are "saved" by grace, almost independent of their actions based on faith and obedience. How would you help those of this mindset broaden their understanding of the synergy of personal faith, works of obedience, and the operation of divine grace?

What Personal Qualities Can Serve as Pillars to Strengthen Your Faith?

Consider the following qualities as they may relate to your own life and the lives of your family members as a way of strengthening and bolstering faith:

- **Desire**—To *desire* is to wish for something earnestly or to long for some wholesome outcome. Desire is often called the mother of change. It is the motivation from within. It is the incentive for sincere prayer (see 3 Ne. 14:7). Cultivating righteous desires is the nurturing influence for faith. Desire kindles faith to action: "Verily I say, men should be anxiously engaged in a good cause, and do many things of their own free will, and bring to pass much righteousness" (D&C 58:27).

- **Hope**—Our anticipation and expectation for things to be good or better in our lives is called *hope*. Our hope is based on the Lord Jesus Christ and on the plan of happiness and eternal life, which God promised to the faithful before the world began (see Titus 1:2). Hope provides one with a sense of confidence in looking forward in life in righteousness. Hope is the sister of faith; if hope creates a blueprint for action, then faith carries it out. A life without hope is empty, but a life filled with hope is a life filled with light and meaning. "Wherefore, ye must press forward with a steadfastness in Christ, having a perfect brightness of hope, and a love of God and of all men. Wherefore, if ye shall press forward, feasting upon the word of Christ, and endure to the end, behold, thus saith the Father: Ye shall have eternal life" (2 Ne. 31:20).

- **Cheerfulness**—Cheerfulness is one of the most uplifting and contagious attributes one can possess. It brightens both the giver and those who choose to receive it. It is the halo of hope and the banner of faith. It enlivens hopefulness and optimism for the day ahead and even enhances physiological and emotional health. You can learn to be cheerful. The Savior said, "Wherefore, be of good cheer, and do not fear, for I the Lord am with you, and will stand by you . . ." (D&C 68:6). The admonition to "be of good cheer" is repeated no fewer than thirteen times in the scriptures—almost becoming an "eleventh commandment."

- **Courage**—Courage is the power to act in difficult situations. Courage is faith in action. It can be an act of bravery in every sense of the word, whether in battle or in the personal trials of life. Courage is the attribute of character that often separates the winner from the defeated, success from failure, and happiness from misery. Courageous deeds are often acts of initiative on a grand scale, but there are millions of patient, quiet, and enduring acts of faithful courage going on in our homes, schools, and workplaces every day. Courage in honoring one's covenants before the Lord is the highest form of this sterling quality, because that kind of courage flows from an individual's deep reservoir of faith and honor. We can take to heart the counsel that Moses gave to his successor, Joshua: "Be strong and of a good courage, fear not, nor be afraid . . . for the Lord thy God, he it is that doth go with thee; he will not fail thee, nor forsake thee" (Deut. 31:6).

Sustained through desire, hope, cheerfulness, and courage, our faith strengthens our resolve to practice obedience and valor in honoring our covenants. Of these four qualities that support faith, which have been most characteristic of your faith in the Lord? Which do you need to call upon more fully in your forward motion?

Real-life Stories for Heart and Mind

The Faith of a Child. One father regularly visited with his children to see how things were going and see if he could help in some way. He talked with them about life, fun times, school, family things, and especially how they felt about Heavenly Father and their prayers—and of course if they had any problems or concerns. As each school year began, he gave each of them a blessing. When special problems or concerns arose, they would also ask for a blessing, especially if they were sick. One day, a little boy just starting kindergarten didn't feel very good. He asked, "Daddy, I need a prayer." He meant a blessing. He had watched the other children receive their blessings for school. That night his father gave him a blessing before bed. He slept through the night, and in the morn-

ing was up for scripture time with the family. One of his sisters remarked to him, "I thought you were sick." He replied, "Didn't you know Daddy gave me a blessing? I have to be well." Oh, the faith of a child. They believe!

As part of his wonderful discourse on faith, Alma said: "And now, he imparteth his word by angels unto men, yea, not only men but women also. Now this is not all; little children do have words given unto them many times, which confound the wise and the learned" (Alma 32:23). When have you experienced little children expressing their faith in moving and inspiring words?

The Words of the Mothers. A counselor in a stake presidency shared this experience concerning the women of his stake:

It was my honor a number of years ago to work with the young women of the Relief Society in a campus stake. In that capacity I was able to observe firsthand the extraordinary nobility of these young women who were, as mothers-in-training, preparing for a future of faithful service in God's kingdom. Their devotion to the cause of truth and charity was reflected in the glow of their countenance and the exemplary rectitude of their patterns of life.

I could almost see the scene unfold before me of how these future mothers in Zion would infuse the lives of their own sons and daughters with the same principles that took root in the souls of Helaman's stripling warriors and emerged as character qualities of profound influence: "And they were exceedingly valiant for courage; and also for strength and activity; but behold, this was not all—they were men who were true at all times in whatsoever thing they were entrusted. Yea, they were men of truth and soberness, for they had been taught to keep the commandments of God and to walk uprightly before him" (Alma 53:20–21). Furthermore, "they had been taught by their mothers, that if they did not doubt, God would deliver them. And they rehearsed unto me [Helaman] the words of their mothers, saying: We do not doubt our mothers knew it" (Alma 56:47–48).

Faith, trust, valor, soberness, obedience, firmness of heart, righteousness—these sterling qualities come to children in great measure through the teachings and example of their mothers. What a supernal commission attends the motherly mission in life, knowing as they do that "charity never faileth" (1 Cor. 13:8). What lessons did you learn from your mother and father, your grandmother and grandfather—or other caring adults concerned for your well-being and progress? How can you impart encouragement and truth to your own family members and others you might be called on to teach?

Pondering Prayerfully

Additional scriptures to consider and ponder:
- Prov. 10:28
- Jer. 17:7
- Luke 18:42
- 1 Ne. 16:28
- Mosiah 25:22
- Alma 5:14–15
- Alma 34:15
- Ether 12:3
- Ether 12:9
- Ether 12:12
- D&C 8:10
- D&C 21:4–5
- D&C 29:6

The following hymns remind of faith:
- "Be Still, My Soul" (*Hymns,* 124)
- "Faith of Our Fathers" (*Hymns,* 84)
- "Press Forward, Saints" (*Hymns,* 81)

Remember and Be Sure

Let's not strive to move all the mountains today; instead, let us have faith to follow the prophet. Let's not go about healing the entire world or raising the dead; instead, let's have faith enough to move ourselves to action by being a loving parent, a devoted and obedient child, a sensitive neighbor. Let's not exercise our faith to gain the whole world; instead, let's exercise faith for the building up of the kingdom of God through love and service to our fellow beings. Through small and simple things, great things come to pass—simply through the exercising of faith (D&C 64:33).

So let us commit. Let us search the scriptures. Let us fast and pray. Let us be full of humility and love so that we can teach our children and other loved ones to increase in their faith. Let us start today with some goals and a plan to increase in our faith that we might be an instrument in the hand of the Lord to bless our family and all mankind, remembering what Jesus said: "With God all things are possible" (Matt. 19:26).

Each person comes to earth with an immense storehouse of experiences and insights from the premortal realm, softly blanketed with a filter of forgetfulness by a merciful Father who wants us to learn line upon line, precept upon precept, how to rise on the wings of obedience and faith to a state where we can return home again. From time to time our inner eye allows us to catch a glimpse of the divine at work in our lives. Almost as an "unforgetting" we find ourselves on occasion comforted with the familiar and tender inklings of our long-standing personal relationship with our Father and His Son—and with a vision, though sometimes darkened and obscured by our mortal state, that the hand of the Lord is securely above us, and that we are encircled "in the robe of [His] righteousness" (2 Ne. 4:33). It is among the greatest gifts of God that He allows us from time to time to catch a glimpse of His "chariots of fire" circling above us with protecting power. This spiritual insight is the essence of faith: "the substance of things hoped for, the evidence of things not seen" (Heb. 11:1). And through faith, His children can facilitate this kind of inner vision by cultivating a desire for righteousness, by their humble willingness to abide by the simple and fundamental laws of the gospel, by giving selfless service based solely on love, and by accepting with grateful and contrite hearts the blessings of God to the obedient who are willing to look and behold His majesty at work on their behalf.

Let us remember that the foundation of righteousness is faith. We do all things by faith (see Moro. 7:33). Faith is the shield of protection from the fiery darts of the adversary (see Eph. 6:16). Faith is evidenced by our works (see James 2:18). By faith we receive the blessing of the gift of the Holy Ghost. Faith gives us strength (see Alma 2:30; 14:26), and it can accomplish all things. We obtain faith through fasting and prayer (see Hel. 3:35) and by searching and hearing the word of God (see Rom. 10:17). Again, in the words of the Prophet Joseph Smith: "Faith, then, is the first great governing principle which has power, dominion, and authority over all things; by it they exist, by it they are upheld, by it they are changed, or by it they remain, agreeable to the will of God" (*Lectures on Faith* 1:24).

CHAPTER 19
Becoming Clean: Repentance

The second principle of the gospel of salvation, is repentance. It is a sincere and godly sorrow for and a forsaking of sin, combined with full purpose of heart to keep God's commandments. —John Taylor (*The Mediation and the Atonement,* 182)

Opening the Window of Wisdom

From the foundation of the world in the premortal realm it was decreed that our mortal life would be a testing time: "And we will prove them herewith, to see if they will do all things whatsoever the Lord their God shall command them" (Abr. 3:25). A Savior was provided from the beginning to empower the plan of redemption so that the children of God could overcome their weaknesses and transgressions and rise to their divine potential.

The Atonement of Jesus Christ makes possible the miracle of repentance and forgiveness. Repentance is the process of becoming clean from sin. Through faith on Jesus Christ we can be forgiven and our guilt can be swept away (see Enos 1:6–8). Faith and repentance are preached continually throughout all the scriptures and by our living prophets today. Repentance is necessary to our salvation (see D&C 20:29). Repentance and baptism are the gateway into the kingdom of God and a prerequisite for entrance into the celestial

kingdom (see D&C 20:71). All have need to repent, for all have sinned (see 2 Ne. 2:5), and if we do not repent, we are consigned to suffer even as our Savior Jesus Christ suffered on behalf of all mankind (see D&C 19:15–19).

Salvation and forgiveness come solely through the redemptive mission of Jesus Christ. The message of the Savior, through His prophets, is that the faithful and obedient may come and freely partake of the eternal joys of the gospel, while the rebellious and impenitent will suffer the consequences of damnation—being cut off by their own choice from the presence of God and suspended in their quest for spiritual progression. The Lord makes no allowance for sin, but is compassionate and merciful to the repentant sinner (see D&C 1:31–32)—for we cannot be saved in our sins (see Alma 11:37).

Return from the burden of sin is what Paul termed *godly sorrow*: "For godly sorrow worketh repentance to salvation not to be repented of: but the sorrow of the world worketh death" (2 Cor. 7:10). Godly sorrow works by the Spirit. Our hearts are broken and our spirits are contrite. We recognize our offense against God and against those whom we have wronged. We confess and forsake and seek to restore that which was taken or lost. It is this godly sorrow for sin, with the resulting repentance and renewal of the spirit through the Atonement of Christ, that transforms individuals into liberated sons and daughters of God—those who find their "sufficiency" in God: "Not that we are sufficient of ourselves to think any thing as of ourselves; but our sufficiency is of God; Who also hath made us able ministers of the new testament; not of the letter, but of the spirit: for the letter killeth, but the spirit giveth life. . . . Now the Lord is that Spirit: and where the Spirit of the Lord is, there is liberty" (2 Cor. 3:5–6, 17).

The key to liberation through godly sorrow is to yield our hearts to the Spirit. King Benjamin taught us well concerning the natural man, one who is an enemy to God and who will not repent:

> For the natural man is an enemy to God, and has been from the fall of Adam, and will be, forever and ever, unless he yields to the enticings of the Holy Spirit, and putteth off the natural man and becometh a saint through the atonement of Christ the Lord, and becometh as a child, submissive, meek, humble, patient, full of love, willing to submit to all things which the Lord seeth fit to inflict upon him, even as a child doth submit to his father. (Mosiah 3:19)

We learn also in this verse that the only way to overcome the natural man—one who loves Satan more than God and who becomes carnal, sensual and devilish (see Moses 5:13)—is to yield to the enticings of the Holy Spirit and thus become a Saint. This is all made possible through the Atonement of Jesus Christ. We then become innocent, like a child, because our guilt is swept away through faith on Jesus Christ and by practicing the principle of repentance (see Enos 1:6–8). Note the words *submissive, meek, humble, patient,* and *full of love.* When we are in this state, we are willing to offer our sacrifice before the Lord, which is part of the process of repentance. And what is that sacrifice? "And ye shall offer for a sacrifice unto me a broken heart and a contrite spirit. And whoso cometh unto me with a broken heart and a contrite spirit, him will I baptize with fire and with the Holy Ghost" (3 Ne. 9:20). We must have godly sorrow in our lives so that we might become purified, justified, and sanctified through the Lord Jesus Christ—because we are willing to repent (see Moses 6:60).

Sometimes the Lord, in His love and mercy, chastens us in order to gather us from the shadows of sin and into the redeeming light of the gospel of happiness (see Heb. 12:6). He wants to help us stay on the straight and narrow path. He wants our remorse over sin to motivate us to repent. Sometimes He uses external means such as famine, pestilence, and other hardships to bring His people into a state of humility so that they can be taught and persuaded to change their ways (see Hel. 11:4–18; 12:3–6). Through chastening we can grow, provided we are easily entreated and recognize the chastening as leverage toward a "course correction" or "pruning," if you will, to keep us on the right course. The Lord's people "must needs be chastened until they learn obedience, if it must needs be, by the things which they suffer" (D&C 105:6). It is in the trials and tribulations that we are humbled and turn to the Lord so that He can nurture and succor us in all of our afflictions (see Alma 7:11–12).

Being forgiven through repentance requires forgiveness on our part. The capacity to forgive is one of the most divine attributes one can possess. It is a commandment of God (see Matt. 6:15). It is a quality that will bring peace to one's soul and allow others to find peace. True forgiveness is without a doubt the most difficult aspect of all human behavior to express. It is an expression of godliness. Early one morning the Savior came to the temple to teach. The scribes and Pharisees, who were plotting against Him, brought to Him a woman taken in adultery, and, referring to the provision in the Law of Moses requiring capital punishment for such an offense (see Lev. 20:10), asked the Lord how He would handle the matter. The Savior responded by stooping down to write something on the ground, and then spoke the riveting words: "He that is without sin among you, let him first cast a stone at her" (John 8:7). As He stooped down again to write something on the ground, the accusers departed one by one until the Savior and the woman were left alone. "When Jesus had lifted up himself, and saw none but the woman, he said unto her, Woman, where are those thine accusers? hath no man condemned thee? She said, No man, Lord. And Jesus said unto her, Neither do I condemn thee: go, and sin no more" (John 8:10–11). The lesson is unmistakable: God is the judge. We are to forgive others their trespasses if we are to be forgiven our own trespasses. That is the spirit and essence of the Lord's Prayer (see Matt. 6:9–13) and the Lord's commentary on it: "For if ye forgive men their trespasses, your heavenly Father will also forgive you: But if ye forgive not men their trespasses, neither will your Father forgive your trespasses" (Matt. 6:14–15).

Repentance is the second principle of the gospel of Jesus Christ, after faith. It calls for godly sorrow. It calls for humility in accepting the loving chastening of the Lord. It calls for us to cultivate a forgiving spirit. It calls for honoring our baptismal covenant in righteousness. The blessings are magnificent: joy, peace, comfort, an enhanced love for our Heavenly Father and His Son, greater capacity to receive light and truth, and the ability to bless the lives of others and show them the way of happiness. May God bless us all to repent and take upon ourselves the divine nature, for that is the only pathway leading to the celestial kingdom.

Inspired by Latter-Day Prophets

Joseph Smith: Meekly persuade and urge everyone to forgive one another all their trespasses, offenses and sins, that they may work out their own salvation with fear and trembling. . . . To every ordained member, and to all, we say, be merciful and you shall find mercy (*HC* 2:229–230).

"Bear and forbear one with another" is a striking motto for life and an ensign of the doctrine of repentance. We are fully dependent on the Savior for liberation from the burdens of sin. A sign that we are humbly submissive to His will and prepared to come before Him, penitent and committed to a better way of life, is for us to forgive others as He forgives us. What do you think is meant by the statement of the Prophet Joseph concerning the people "that they may work out their own salvation with fear and trembling"? (For more guidance, see Philip. 2:12; Alma 34:37; Morm. 9:27.)

Joseph F. Smith: When we commit sin, it is necessary that we repent of it and make restitution as far as lies in our power. When we cannot make restitution for the wrong we have done, then we must apply the grace and mercy of God to cleanse us from that iniquity (*Gospel Doctrine: Selections from the Sermons and Writings of Joseph F. Smith*, 98).

Our Father in Heaven offers us a transcendent gift, a gift that can do for us something that we cannot do for ourselves—cleanse us of the effects of sin as we repent and yield to the power and blessings of the Atonement of Jesus Christ. How does your gratitude toward Heavenly Father expand and unfold in pondering this choice gift of grace?

Harold B. Lee: In order for good to blossom it must be cultivated and exercised by constant practice, and to be truly righteous there is required a daily pruning of the evil growth of our characters by a daily repentance from sin (*The Teachings of Harold B. Lee*, 113).

When we experience the mighty change of heart that signifies true repentance, we have "no more disposition to do evil, but to do good continually" (Mosiah 5:2) and we have the Lord's "image in our countenances" (Alma 5:14). Such a desirable state is possible only when we repent daily and renew our covenant of obedience weekly through the sacrament. What are your thoughts about the span of time for repentance being each day of your life? When you focus daily on the need to repent, how is that an insurance policy to secure the eternal blessings you seek?

Spencer W. Kimball: He who will not forgive others breaks down the bridge over which he himself must travel (*The Miracle of Forgiveness*, 269).

As we forgive others and build bridges of fellowship toward them in the spirit of charity, we can have a vision of building a bridge to heaven where "our confidence [shall] wax strong in the presence of God" (D&C 121:45). What peace have you experienced as you have forgiven others?

Truths to Liken

Alma 34:33—"And now, as I said unto you before, as ye have had so many witnesses, therefore, I beseech of you that ye do not procrastinate the day of your repentance until the end; for after this day of life, which is given us to prepare for eternity, behold, if we do not improve our time while in this life, then cometh the night of darkness wherein there can be no labor performed."

- Amulek, missionary companion to Alma, taught the wayward Zoramites how they could receive the blessings of joy and redemption.
- The clock is ticking. We are to receive and accept the multiple witnesses of gospel truth (the scriptures, the word of the living prophets, the promptings of the Spirit) and, repenting of our sins, come unto Christ without delay. As you consider friends and associates who may need encouragement and kindly reminders, how do you proceed lovingly to help them find their way back into the fold?

D&C 1:31–32—"For I the Lord cannot look upon sin with the least degree of allowance; Nevertheless, he that repents and does the commandments of the Lord shall be forgiven."

- These words from the Lord's "Preface" to the Doctrine and Covenants—given through the Prophet Joseph Smith during a special priesthood conference held at Hiram, Ohio, on November 1, 1831—confirm the Lord's mercy and love in forgiving those who repent.
- The Lord cannot condone sin because the law of justice must be satisfied. But when people sincerely repent of their sins and come unto the Lord, the law of justice is satisfied through "the merits, and mercy, and grace of the Holy Messiah" (2 Ne. 2:8). If someone were to come to you despondent because of their shortcomings, how could you use this comforting principle to help them have hope and confidence?

D&C 18:10–14—"Remember the worth of souls is great in the sight of God; For, behold, the Lord your Redeemer suffered death in the flesh; wherefore he suffered the pain of all men, that all men might repent and come unto him. And he hath risen again from the dead, that he might bring all men unto him, on conditions of repentance. And how great is his joy in the soul that repenteth! Wherefore, you are called to cry repentance unto this people."

- These words were included in a revelation given to the Prophet Joseph Smith, Oliver Cowdery, and David Whitmer, at Fayette, New York, in June 1829.
- For all who would wish to bring the Savior joy, the easiest way is to repent and be an instrument for others to repent as well. Imagine having the ability to create joy for the Creator and to cause the angels of heaven to rejoice: "Behold, this is pleasing unto your Lord, and the angels rejoice over you; the alms of your prayers have come up into the ears of the Lord of Sabaoth, and are recorded in the book of the names of the sanctified, even them of the celestial world" (D&C 88:2). How satisfying to bring joy to the Savior and the hosts of heaven!

D&C 19:15–16—"Therefore I command you to repent—repent, lest I smite you by the rod of my mouth, and by my wrath, and by my anger, and your sufferings be sore—how sore you know not, how exquisite you know not, yea, how hard to bear you know not. For behold, I, God, have suffered these things for all, that they might not suffer if they would repent."

- These words were included in a revelation given to Martin Harris through Joseph Smith at Manchester, New York, in March 1830. The revelation provides in the Savior's own words the most complete description of the agony of the Atonement of any passage in scripture.
- When we understand and appreciate that Jesus is the Christ, who suffered and died for us that through repentance we might be forgiven and live again in the presence of the Father and the Son, we will change. This is the essence of the Atonement—the centerpiece of the plan of happiness: it draws all mankind to Christ through His atoning sacrifice. The Savior loves us and has suffered for us if we will but repent. If we choose not to repent, then justice requires that we suffer intensely for our sins—beyond our comprehension. To avoid that suffering and receive the power of the redemption into our lives, we can choose to repent

and be liberated by the love and mercy of the Father and the Son. What are your thoughts about the transcendent gift of the Atonement and its power to spare us the agony of suffering for our sins through repentance? How can you share your thoughts and testimony with others to help them find a fuller measure of joy in life?

D&C 58:42–43—"Behold, he who has repented of his sins, the same is forgiven, and I, the Lord, remember them no more. By this ye may know if a man repenteth of his sins—behold, he will confess them and forsake them."

- These words were included in a revelation given through the Prophet Joseph Smith in Zion (Jackson County, Missouri) on August 1, 1831, in response to the Saints' desire to learn the will of the Lord as they were gathering in a new environment.
- It is a remarkable principle that the Lord does not remember our sins when we have repented of them, confessed them, and forsaken them. The joy of knowing that the Lord will not remember our sins and that our guilt is swept away should be motive enough for us to repent and be clean of our sins. How important it is, therefore, that we forgive ourselves as well and look forward in confidence to a future of righteous covenant valor rather than dwelling on the sorrows of the past. How does it help you to know that a new foundation for building your future is established when the mistakes of the past are forgotten through the blessings of the gospel of Jesus Christ?

D&C 64:9–10—"Wherefore, I say unto you, that ye ought to forgive one another; for he that forgiveth not his brother his trespasses standeth condemned before the Lord; for there remaineth in him the greater sin. I, the Lord, will forgive whom I will forgive, but of you it is required to forgive all men."

- This counsel was included in a revelation given through the Prophet Joseph Smith

to the elders of the Church at Kirtland, Ohio, on September 11, 1831.

- Forgiveness is aligned with our righteousness to such an extent that we are condemned of the Lord and we have the greater sin if we fail to forgive others. How does this apply when we are sometimes victims? The Lord was the greatest victim of all, and yet He uttered, "Father, forgive them; for they know not what they do" (Luke 23:34). Surely having a forgiving heart is the attribute of godliness. When you hear people expressing blame for the deeds of others, how can you, in kindness and charity, encourage them to redirect their feelings toward the need to let God be the judge as we work to fill our own lives with humility and gratitude for the Savior's atoning sacrifice?

D&C 95:1–2—"Verily, thus saith the Lord unto you whom I love, and whom I love I also chasten that their sins may be forgiven, for with the chastisement I prepare a way for their deliverance in all things out of temptation, and I have loved you—Wherefore, ye must needs be chastened and stand rebuked before my face."

- These words were included in a revelation given through the Prophet Joseph Smith at Kirtland, Ohio, on June 1, 1833, at a time when the Saints had not moved forward with sufficient commitment to build the house of the Lord as commanded.
- All of us, as individuals, are to build a house unto the Lord, even a celestial home in which the principles of the gospel take root and flourish. When we have feelings of inadequacy concerning the quality of our stewardship, then we may be feeling the chastisement of a loving God who loves us and wants us to rise to our potential in righteous endeavor. What are your thoughts about the Lord's promise that chastisement always comes with a heavenly promise for "deliverance in all things out of temptation"? How does that instill hope and confidence to transcend

your missteps and failures through the strength of the Lord?

Rejoicing and Reasoning Together

From Exquisite Remorse to Exquisite Joy—How Does One Make the Transition?

The scriptures contain many stories about the transition from the crushing burden of sin to the enlivening and liberating joy of repentance and forgiveness through the blessings of the gospel of Jesus Christ. One of the most dramatic is the story of Alma, whose misguided career of destruction against the Church in Zarahemla during his younger years was terminated abruptly by an angel of God sent to block his rebellion against truth and light (see Mosiah 27:10–32). As he later described his ordeal to his son Helaman, he was on that occasion racked with guilt for three days and three nights—"even with the pains of a damned soul" (Alma 36:16). During that time of suffering, a transformation began to unfold within him:

> And it came to pass that as I was thus racked with torment, while I was harrowed up by the memory of my many sins, behold, I remembered also to have heard my father prophesy unto the people concerning the coming of one Jesus Christ, a Son of God, to atone for the sins of the world.
>
> Now, as my mind caught hold upon this thought, I cried within my heart: O Jesus, thou Son of God, have mercy on me, who am in the gall of bitterness, and am encircled about by the everlasting chains of death.
>
> And now, behold, when I thought this, I could remember my pains no more; yea, I was harrowed up by the memory of my sins no more. (Alma 36:17–19)

The transition in his state of being was remarkable in its polarity, darkness being immediately changed into light and anguish into joy: "And oh, what joy, and what marvelous light I did behold; yea, my soul was filled with joy as exceeding as was my pain! Yea, I say unto you, my son, that there could be nothing so exquisite and so bitter as were my pains. Yea, and again I say unto you, my son, that on the other hand, there can be nothing so exquisite and sweet

as was my joy" (Alma 36:20–21). From that time forth, Alma took steps to render his repentance complete by working tirelessly to confess his faults, rectify the damage he had done, and proclaim the truths of the gospel across the land (see Mosiah 27:32–37).

The process of repentance illustrated in the story of Alma, who became renowned as a teacher of faith and repentance among the people for the remainder of his life as prophet, is the same pattern we can all follow. Repentance is a divine gift empowered through the Atonement of Jesus Christ—but it must be done in the Lord's way, always including godly sorrow and the pain of contrite transformation and renewal. For every individual there is a daily, even hourly, reference point for the application of the doctrines of the plan of salvation. Central to that plan is ongoing repentance of a very real and active nature, the steps for which can be outlined as follows:

- **Recognize your sin**: Become aware of your transgression to the point that you realize you should repent.
- **Feel godly sorrow for sin**: This entails having a broken heart and contrite spirit as an offering you give to the Lord in the spirit of love and genuine repentance (see 2 Cor. 7:10; 3 Ne. 9:20).
- **Forsake the sin**: Turn altogether from it even to the point of having no desire to sin but to do good continually (see Mosiah 5:2; D&C 58:42–43).
- **Confess the sin**: Confess your sins to Heavenly Father and, when necessary, to the bishop (see D&C 64:7).
- **Make restitution for the sin**: Attempt to restore where possible that which was taken or destroyed. Often we cannot make full restitution due to the nature of the sin. In those cases, the power of the Atonement enables us to overcome our inadequacies through our Savior Jesus Christ (see Alma 7:11–12).
- **Make a commitment not to sin again**: Such a commitment—a covenant in the case of baptism and partaking of the sacrament—is a promise to be obedient to all the commandments and endure to the end in righteousness (see 2 Ne. 31:19–21).

- **Forgive others**: We must forgive everyone—especially those who might be involved in trespasses against us. "For if ye forgive men their trespasses, your heavenly Father will also forgive you" (Matt. 6:14).
- **Serve with valor**: Consecrate your life to helping build the kingdom of God, sharing the gospel with others, and seeking to take within yourself the divine nature of the Savior with diligence and steadfastness (see D&C 4; 2 Pet. 1:2–8).
- **Savor with gratitude the certainty of forgiveness**: We can have joy in the knowledge that we are indeed forgiven, as the people of King Benjamin experienced through the blessings of the Spirit (see Mosiah 4:3).

As you consider these steps for repentance, review your life and your standing before God. Remember the words of the resurrected Savior to the Saints in Bountiful: "And this is my doctrine, and it is the doctrine which the Father hath given unto me; and I bear record of the Father, and the Father beareth record of me, and the Holy Ghost beareth record of the Father and me; and I bear record that the Father commandeth all men, everywhere, to repent and believe in me" (3 Ne. 11:32). Repentance and obedience to all the Lord's commandments is the key to the transition from agony to joy—joy of a permanent and eternal nature.

What Is the Most Universal of Sins—and How Can We Avoid It?

Pride is at the crux of almost all sin. It is the sin that is most universal in nature, and most all are afflicted to one degree or another with pride. Pride is expressed in arrogance, haughtiness, self-love, vanity, and egotism. Pride creates enmity between God and man. We should all strive to avoid pride at all costs, and to repent of prideful sin should it occur in our lives.

Pride is directly opposed to the Christlike quality of humility. Pride was the downfall of the Jaredites and Nephites (see Moro. 8:27; D&C 38:39). Pride can be our downfall as well, if we are not vigilant and mindful of our covenants. It is not only an attitudinal problem; prideful thoughts are so powerful that they lead to sinful behavior—sins of both commission and omission. Pride brings with it other sins that are all too easily expressed, such as selfishness, greed, lust, jealousy, power-seeking, envy, and a whole host of trailing problems that will tempt us and lead us to sin. This is why the Lord continually counsels us against pride: "God resisteth the proud, but giveth grace unto the humble" (James 4:6).

In his classic sermon on pride given at general conference in April 1989, President Ezra Taft Benson stated: "Pride is the universal sin, the great vice" (Ezra Taft Benson, "Beware of Pride," *Ensign*, May 1989, 4). He explained: "Most of us think of pride as self-centeredness, conceit, boastfulness, arrogance, or haughtiness. All of these are elements of the sin, but the heart, or core, is still missing. The central feature of pride is enmity—enmity toward God and enmity toward our fellowmen. *Enmity* means 'hatred toward, hostility to, or a state of opposition.' It is the power by which Satan wishes to reign over us [Moses 4:1]" (Ibid.). When pride infects the heart of priesthood leadership, then great damage occurs, as the Prophet Joseph Smith warned in his epistle from Liberty Jail in March 1839: "That they [the rights of the priesthood] may be conferred upon us, it is true; but when we undertake to cover our sins, or to gratify our pride, our vain ambition, or to exercise control or dominion or compulsion upon the souls of the children of men, in any degree of unrighteousness, behold, the heavens withdraw themselves; the Spirit of the Lord is grieved; and when it is withdrawn, Amen to the priesthood or the authority of that man" (D&C 121:37).

If pride is the universal sin, then the universal antidote is humility. Humility is the essence of godliness, just as pride is truly the downfall of mankind. It is an eternal principle that pride and humility cannot exist in the heart at the same time. Knowing that the ease of the way often causes us to forget the goodness of God (see Hel. 12:2–3), we can devote ourselves to overcoming pride and gaining humility. By supplanting every vestige of pride with a governing measure of humility, we will come unto God, always acknowledging our unworthiness before Him (see Alma 38:14) and committing ourselves to obey Him with a broken heart and a contrite spirit. In humility we will find the answer to many of our problems by seeking the will of the Lord and setting our view on eternal blessings.

You can avoid pride and embrace humility as a way of life by engaging systematically in the following kinds of activities:

*1. **Tune your attitude to the Spirit** by listening for the warning signs of pride, cultivating gratitude, and letting charity abound in your thoughts.*
*2. **Set up and follow a system of regular defenses**, including praying daily for protection against pride, cultivating modesty in dress and behavior, reading the scriptures often, paying an honest tithe and a generous fast offering, and visiting the temple often.*
*3. **Serve with devotion** by focusing on the family, magnifying Church callings, and serving in the community.*

Real-life Stories for Heart and Mind

The Wisdom Tooth. For many years a woman's impacted tooth had been dormant—a phantom object barely protruding from the gum. From time to time various dentists had warned that it really should come out. But it hadn't caused any problems—no pain, no discomfort. It had just continued its valueless existence as a kind of bothersome condition that she worried about under the surface of daily life. Eventually, one dentist told her, "This looks like it might be getting some decay," but still the woman took no action. Finally she was told that the wisdom tooth was headed for trouble—and that this time, the tooth could seriously affect her health and well-being. She scheduled an appointment with an oral surgeon—and within half an hour the decades-old problem was history. It would have taken the same half hour decades earlier. Procrastination didn't help.

In a spiritual context, we have invisible "wisdom teeth"—spiritual conditions that call for review, correction, rejuvenation. Sometimes there is a history of transgression that calls for action that leads to the miracle of forgiveness. Sometimes the old impacted memories need to be brought forward so that they can be subjected to spiritual correction: "For godly sorrow worketh repentance" (2 Cor. 7:10). Instead of carrying an impacted burden for decades, we find that concerted and decisive action based on

sincere, prayerful penitence and with the guidance of the Spirit and loving ecclesiastical leaders can bring about a wondrous effect, leading to peace and solace. That troublesome "wisdom tooth" decaying below the surface can be gone—forever—opening up the channels of pure communication once more with our Father in Heaven. It is true that some conditions may take longer than others to heal, but action leading to eventual healing can be taken immediately.

A member of a stake presidency recalls the day an individual approached him in the hallway of a meetinghouse to share a burden he had been carrying around for many, many decades—a spiritual "wisdom tooth" that had decayed and had been festering within his soul. They found a private spot where thoughtful listening and loving counsel was given, and they shared prayerful supplication. The man was assured that His Heavenly Father loved him. There was relief and hope. Through his own courage and the blessings of the Redeemer, this good man was on his way to recovery. His face brightened. His soul was being healed. A short hour of time had led to a change of life. One is reminded of the words of Amulek: "Yea, I would that ye would come forth and harden not your hearts any longer; for behold, now is the time and the day of your salvation; and therefore, if ye will repent and harden not your hearts, immediately shall the great plan of redemption be brought about unto you" (Alma 34:31).

Are there any neglected "wisdom teeth" in your circle of fellowship? How can you help promote the blessings and joy of a repentant life?

The Light in the Eye. A delightful young couple—bright, faithful in Church participation, eager to do the right thing—was preparing for marriage. But a problem had occurred—a compromising of values and propriety. They were embarrassed and heartbroken as they sat across from the bishop, wondering what to do. The three counseled together. There was sorrowing and pondering. But there were also comforting feelings generated in the process of repentance empowered by the Atonement. Yes, there needed to be change. There needed to be prayerful and godly sorrow and faithful commitment to a better lifestyle. But the young couple had caught themselves at the edge of the precipice, and they had recoiled under the strength of conscience and now wanted to do right before the Lord. They were good young people with the desire for righteousness. The Lord loved them and wanted them to have the fullness of His blessings. There needed to be some regular appointments for a few weeks to give momentum to the new commitments. But things went very well. And there was a special plan put in place—a code just between the bishop and these two. Thereafter, when the bishop crossed paths with them each week at Church, it took only a nod of the head and a twinkle in the eye as an indication that all was well. You can't disguise the light of the gospel in the eye. It is a sure sign that the Spirit is at work. And it was at work for them. They prospered. They rebounded. They rose to new heights, and once more the age-old story of the gospel transforming lives was repeated in a Real-life setting. Thank heavens for the principles of the gospel. Thank heavens for the Atonement of Jesus Christ. "And how great is his joy in the soul that repenteth!" (D&C 18:13).

As you consider those you love so much and those you serve in the gospel, do you see the light in the eye? How can you help others to get that light and find an infinite amount of joy in this life and hope for the life to come?

"Wrong Way—Do Not Enter." A man, accompanied by his wife, was driving along a stretch of interstate highway one day when he glanced across the median strip and saw a terrifying sight. A car across the way was driving parallel to his own car, but was moving directly into a line of oncoming traffic. The man watched with utter horror as trucks and cars swerved to avoid collision with the car that was driving in the wrong direction along the inside lane. In a split second, he realized what he had to do. He accelerated to a high rate of speed and looked for the next opportunity to cross the median. Soon he came to a connecting road and maneuvered quickly toward the opposite lanes of traffic, coming to a screeching halt on the inner shoulder of the opposite lanes. Despite significant danger to himself, he then ran toward the errant car and flagged it down amid the swerving and dodging vehicles. Incredibly, the elderly couple whom he forced to stop were at first indignant at such treatment. What business did this stranger have interrupting their trip? Soon they realized, however, that he had surely saved their lives, and were grateful for his Christian act of charity and deliverance.

This true story is like a modern-day parable about how the world has reacted in nearly all ages to the prophets of God. The eternal message is one of warning: the call to repentance, the admonition to heed the word of God and be saved. In modern terms, it is the alarm sounded when one foolishly travels down a one-way street in the wrong direction. So often this warning is met with hardness of heart and with stubborn and prideful rebellion. However, the alarm of the prophets is powered by the spirit of charity. As Samuel the Lamanite proclaimed to his obstinate Nephite audience from the walls of Zarahemla, "For behold, they have been a chosen people of the Lord; yea, the people of Nephi hath he loved, and also hath he chastened them; yea, in the days of their iniquities hath he chastened them because he loveth them" (Hel. 15:3).

As you think about people navigating the wrong way down the one-way roads in life, what courage does it take to help people correct poor choices? How does the Spirit help reveal dangerous conditions and give ideas for loving and corrective outreach?

Pondering Prayerfully

Additional scriptures to consider and ponder:

- Isa. 43:25
- Matt. 5:44
- 1 Ne. 11:36
- 2 Ne. 2:21
- 2 Ne. 9:28–29
- Alma 32:12–14
- Alma 42:13–16
- D&C 23:1
- D&C 112:10
- D&C 121:41–44
- D&C 136:31

The following hymns inspire gratitude for repentance:
- "Come, Ye Disconsolate" (*Hymns*, 115)
- "Nay, Speak No Ill" (*Hymns*, 233)
- "Our Savior's Love" (*Hymns*, 113)

Remember and Be Sure

Our salvation, immortality, and eternal life depend on our overcoming and forsaking our sins. We are to repent—there is no other way back into the presence of our Heavenly Father. The process of repentance through the Atonement of our Savior is a wonderful gift—yet how much less painful it is to make righteous choices to begin with. Alma said it correctly when he said, "O, remember, my son, and learn wisdom in thy youth; yea, learn in thy youth to keep the commandments of God" (Alma 37:35). Jacob counseled in regard to repentance and staying on the straight and narrow path: "O be wise; what can I say more?" (Jacob 6:12). King Benjamin ended his final sermon before his people with these words: "And finally, I cannot tell you all the things whereby ye may commit sin; for there are divers ways and means, even so many that I cannot number them. But this much I can tell you, that if ye do not watch yourselves, and your thoughts, and your words, and your deeds, and observe the commandments of God, and continue in the faith of what ye have heard concerning the coming of our Lord, even unto the end of your lives, ye must perish. And now, O man, remember, and perish not" (Mosiah 4:29–30).

Through the Atonement we gain passage across the chasm from that which is worldly and dead to that which is celestial and alive—even everlasting joy in the mansions of heaven. There is only one way to happiness and peace—and it is the way of humility, born of a broken heart and a contrite spirit. It is the Lord's way, based on faith, repentance, baptism, receiving the gift of the Holy Ghost, and then enduring to the end.

CHAPTER 20
Baptism: Taking Upon Us His Name

Baptism is a sign to God, to angels, and to heaven that we do the will of God, and there is no other way beneath the heavens whereby God hath ordained for man to come to Him to be saved, and enter into the kingdom of God, except faith in Jesus Christ, repentance, and baptism for the remission of sins. . . . —Joseph Smith (*HC* 4:555)

Opening the Window of Wisdom

The Lord has given us the invitation: "Come unto me, all ye that labour and are heavy laden, and I will give you rest" (Matt. 11:28). The way we come unto the Lord is by exercising faith unto repentance, taking upon us His name through the ordinance of baptism, receiving the gift and cleansing power of the Holy Ghost, and keeping the commandments—that we might in the strength of the Lord overcome temptation and endure to the end. This is the way of the Lord. He and His prophets have counseled us repeatedly to repent and be baptized. Upon the foundation of the fundamental principles and ordinances of the gospel, the sons and daughters of God can build their lives in righteousness in accordance with the example of the Savior: They can put on the "whole armour of God" (Eph. 6:13–18) to fortify themselves against evil; they can selflessly help prepare

the way for others to join the flock of God; and they can take up their cross (3 Ne. 12:30), resolutely enduring to the end in faith and devotion.

The gospel of Jesus Christ is anchored in eternal principles that are revisited and reinforced in every dispensation of time under the guidance of the Lord's anointed prophets. A choice summary of these principles is given by Mormon in an epistle to his son Moroni: "And the first fruits of repentance is baptism; and baptism cometh by faith unto the fulfilling the commandments; and the fulfilling the commandments bringeth remission of sins; And the remission of sins bringeth meekness, and lowliness of heart; and because of meekness and lowliness of heart cometh the visitation of the Holy Ghost, which Comforter filleth with hope and perfect love, which love endureth by diligence unto prayer, until the end shall come, when all the saints shall dwell with God" (Moro. 8:25–26).

The gospel of Jesus Christ is a miraculous transformative system whereby we become born again through the covenant of baptism. We undergo the "mighty change" (Alma 5:14) that makes of us a new person, spiritually reborn and rendered clean before the Lord. Jesus demonstrated the pattern in His dealings with John the Baptist. Though perfect, Jesus submitted Himself to the divinely ordained practice of entering into the covenant of baptism, thus serving as a model for all to follow: "Then cometh Jesus from Galilee to Jordan unto John, to be baptized of him. But John forbad him, saying, I have need to be baptized of thee, and comest thou to me? And Jesus answering said unto him, Suffer it to be so now: for thus it becometh us to fulfil all righteousness. Then he suffered him" (Matt. 3:13–15). So important was this milestone that the Spirit of God descended upon Jesus immediately thereafter "like a dove" (Matt. 3:16) and the voice of the Father Himself bore witness of the Savior's divine identity, saying, "This is my beloved Son, in whom I am well pleased" (Matt. 3:17).

The ordinance of baptism was not new. It had been preached and practiced in all previous dispensations where authorized priesthood leadership was in place. Even though the word *baptism* (from a Greek word meaning "to immerse") is not used in the King James Version of the Bible, we know from the words of the Lord to Enoch that Adam practiced the ordinance of baptism from the beginning by commandment of the Lord:

Therefore I give unto you [Adam] a commandment, to teach these things freely unto your children, saying:

That by reason of transgression cometh the fall, which fall bringeth death, and inasmuch as ye were born into the world by water, and blood, and the spirit, which I have made, and so became of dust a living soul, even so ye must be born again into the kingdom of heaven, of water, and of the Spirit, and be cleansed by blood, even the blood of mine Only Begotten; that ye might be sanctified from all sin, and enjoy the words of eternal life in this world, and eternal life in the world to come, even immortal glory;

For by the water ye keep the commandment; by the Spirit ye are justified, and by the blood ye are sanctified" (Moses 6:58–60)

In our time, through the restoration of priesthood keys and powers and the establishment of the Church and kingdom of God in its fulness, the ordinance of baptism is once again available to God's children in response to their faith and repentance. Worthiness for this sacred ordinance is defined in the Doctrine and Covenants: "And again, by way of commandment to the church concerning the manner of baptism—All those who humble themselves before God, and desire to be

baptized, and come forth with broken hearts and contrite spirits, and witness before the church that they have truly repented of all their sins, and are willing to take upon them the name of Jesus Christ, having a determination to serve him to the end, and truly manifest by their works that they have received of the Spirit of Christ unto the remission of their sins, shall be received by baptism into his church" (D&C 20:37). The mode of baptism is divinely appointed:

The person who is called of God and has authority from Jesus Christ to baptize, shall go down into the water with the person who has presented himself or herself for baptism, and shall say, calling him or her by name: Having been commissioned of Jesus Christ, I baptize you in the name of the Father, and of the Son, and of the Holy Ghost. Amen.

Then shall he immerse him or her in the water, and come forth again out of the water. (D&C 20:73–74)

Thus the precious gift of rebirth into the kingdom of God is again available to the living sons and daughters of God and, through the vicarious work of mercy and love in the temple, it is available on behalf of those who have gone on to the spirit realm and there accept the principles and ordinances of the gospel (see D&C 128, 138).

Inspired by Latter-Day Prophets

Joseph Fielding Smith: In the waters of baptism, we covenanted that we would keep [the] commandments; that we would serve the Lord; that we would keep this first and greatest of all commandments, and love the Lord our God; that we would keep the next great commandment, we would love our neighbor as ourselves; and with all the might that we have, with all the strength, with all our hearts, we would prove to him that we would "live by every word that proceedeth forth from the mouth of God"; that we would be obedient and humble, diligent in his service, willing to obey, to hearken to the counsels of those who preside over us and do all things with an eye single to the glory of God.

We should not forget these things, for this commandment is binding upon us as members of the Church (*Doctrines of Salvation*, 2:328).

Baptism is a covenant ordinance, and love is what is expected of us: love for God, but also love for our neighbors. Our baptismal covenant is therefore also a binding covenant to serve others as the Lord has served us. When the sacrament is administered to help us renew our baptismal covenant, we can remember our promise to love others and serve their needs. How can you help others see this broader interpretation of the baptismal covenant to love others as well as the Lord (see Mosiah 18:8–10)?

Spencer W. Kimball: Baptism is a covenant with God. All members have been baptized by immersion in water and have received the Holy Ghost by the laying on of hands by properly authorized men who hold the holy priesthood. We all have been received by baptism into The Church of Jesus Christ when we have humbled ourselves before God, have desired to be baptized, have come forth with broken hearts and contrite spirits, and when we have witnessed before the Church that we are truly repentant of our sins and are willing to take upon us the name of Jesus Christ, having a determination to serve him to the end and thus manifest by our works that we have received the Spirit of Christ unto the remission of our sins (*The Teachings of Spencer W. Kimball*, 112).

Upon being baptized, we receive a new name—the same name that King Benjamin promised his people upon their experiencing the mighty change in their lives: "And now, because of the covenant which ye have made ye shall be called the children of Christ, his sons, and his daughters. . . . There is no other name given whereby salvation cometh" (Mosiah 5:7–8). How do you feel about having a name by which you can be identified with honor at the right hand of the Lord? How can you teach others to honor and hold sacred the name of Christ—by which they are also known as members of The Church of Jesus Christ of Latter-day Saints?

Bruce R. McConkie: John, who bore testimony of Jesus, did so for one reason and one reason only: he was seeking to persuade men to believe in Christ, to come unto him, to accept him as the Son of God, and to be saved by obedience to the laws and ordinances of his gospel. When John baptized for the remission of sins, he was not seeking disciples who would follow him, except as he guided them to the one who should come after. . . . John's whole purpose was to persuade his disciples to follow, not himself, but the Lord Jesus whose witness he was (*The Mortal Messiah: From Bethlehem to Calvary*, 1:438).

The baptism of water and fire are inseparably connected, as the Prophet Joseph Smith confirmed: "Baptism by water is but half a baptism, and is good for nothing without the other half—that is, the baptism of the Holy Ghost" (HC 5:499). Fire is a purifying agent, and the Holy Ghost literally cleanses us of impurities collected through sin. How does the blessing of the Comforter continue the process of purification, based on continual repentance, following baptism? How have you experienced the ongoing cleansing process of the Spirit in your own life?

Truths to Liken

Mosiah 27:25—"And the Lord said unto me: Marvel not that all mankind, yea, men and women, all nations, kindreds, tongues and people, must be born again; yea, born of God, changed from their carnal and fallen state, to a state of righteousness, being redeemed of God, becoming his sons and daughters."

- Alma testified of his miraculous conversion and spiritual awakening after being visited by an angel and spending a long period of time physically immobilized and incapacitated but still open to instruction from the Lord.
- The commandment is clear. We are all to be born again and experience the "mighty change" (Alma 5:14). We are to strive to become like Christ so that when He appears we will indeed see that we are like Him (see Moro. 7:48). This is why we are on earth—to keep the Lord's commandments as we travel the pathway leading to life eternal. If you encounter people not of our faith who "marvel" about the simplicity and yet indispensable nature of baptism, how can you present the doctrine in

a spiritual light that will inspire them and encourage them to move forward in their study of the Church and its teachings?

3 Ne. 12:2—"And again, more blessed are they who shall believe in your words because that ye shall testify that ye have seen me, and that ye know that I am. Yea, blessed are they who shall believe in your words, and come down into the depths of humility and be baptized, for they shall be visited with fire and with the Holy Ghost, and shall receive a remission of their sins."

- After giving authority to His twelve disciples in the New World to baptize and bring people into the fold, the resurrected Lord instructed the multitude to bear witness of what they had seen and to testify to others about the truths of the gospel. This statement—which opens with the words "blessed are they"—serves as a kind of preface to the material given immediately thereafter: a rendition of the "blessed are they" Beatitudes given earlier by the Savior in the Sermon on the Mount. The added dimension in the New World, then, included believing the testimony about the truths of the gospel and responding by accepting the ordinance of baptism.
- By bearing witness of the gospel and the eternal blessings of the baptismal covenant, you can extend the canopy of the Beatitudes to others, helping them merit the Savior's promise of "blessed are they."

Moro. 6:2–3—"Neither did they receive any unto baptism save they came forth with a broken heart and a contrite spirit, and witnessed unto the church that they truly repented of all their sins. And none were received unto baptism save they took upon them the name of Christ, having a determination to serve him to the end."

- As he concluded the Book of Mormon chronicle, Moroni added information about how baptism was conducted in the Church of his day.
- The ordinance of baptism was central to gospel practice in all dispensations, as

Joseph Smith declared: "The ancients who were actually the fathers of the church in the different ages, when the church flourished on the earth, . . . were initiated into the kingdom by baptism, for it is self evident in the scripture—God changes not" (*Teachings of Presidents of the Church: Joseph Smith*, 92). As you consider the consistent and harmonious pattern of priesthood principles and ordinances administered through all dispensations of time, how do you feel knowing that you have been baptized in the same way, and for the same purpose and meaning, as Adam and all of the faithful Saints of God through the ages, including the Savior Himself?

Moro. 8:10–12—"Behold I say unto you that this thing shall ye teach—repentance and baptism unto those who are accountable and capable of committing sin; yea, teach parents that they must repent and be baptized, and humble themselves as their little children, and they shall all be saved with their little children. And their little children need no repentance, neither baptism. Behold, baptism is unto repentance to the fulfilling the commandments unto the remission of sins. But little children are alive in Christ, even from the foundation of the world."

- Moroni quoted from an epistle sent to him by his father Mormon concerning the misguided practice of baptizing little children who have not reached the age of accountability.
- The phrase *little children are alive in Christ* is an inspiring witness of the mercy and love of the Savior and confirms that infant baptism reflects blindness to the principles of mercy, love, agency, and the emergence of accountability in an individual. How can you help those who believe in infant baptism to understand the beauty of the gospel plan that ensures that little children who perish before the age of accountability will have a place in the celestial kingdom? (See Matt. 19:14; D&C 137:10.)

D&C 68:25—"And again, inasmuch as parents have children in Zion, or in any of her stakes which are organized, that teach them not to understand the doctrine of repentance, faith in Christ the Son of the living God, and of baptism and the gift of the Holy Ghost by the laying on of the hands, when eight years old, the sin be upon the heads of the parents."

- These words were included in a revelation given through the Prophet Joseph Smith at Hiram, Ohio, in November 1831.
- How great the responsibility of parents and guardians to help prepare children in mind and spirit for the grand blessing of baptism when eight years of age! Before that time the children are "alive in Christ" (Moro. 8:12), and the grace of our Lord and Savior Jesus Christ covers any misdeeds they have committed as they approach the age of accountability. At age eight, they are to be prepared and ready for baptism through the love and instruction of parents and others in the Church who teach and serve. We are all to become as little children as we come into the fold of Christ.

Rejoicing and Reasoning Together

How Did the Savior Explain the Meaning of Being "Born Again"?

The setting is extraordinary: a contemplative and reasonable ruler among the Jews, a leading Pharisee by rank, engages in a dialogue with the Creator of the world and Author of eternal salvation. Nicodemus has come to Jesus by night, no doubt to avoid detection by his ultra-conservative colleagues, and confesses to the Savior that his belief that He, Jesus Christ, is "a teacher come from God" (John 3:2). Upon hearing the confession, the Savior makes the mind-stopping statement: "Verily, verily, I say unto thee, Except a man be born again, he cannot see the kingdom of God" (John 3:3). There then ensues a remarkable exchange of ideas at two separate but related levels: the everyday level of physical reality and the higher level of spiritual truth—birth in the mortal sense and renewal in the spiritual sense. A second birth—"How can these things be?" (John 3:9) Nicodemus wants to

know. Then the Savior chides him (and his school of thought) for failing to comprehend the simple truth of spiritual matters. Just as Moses lifted up a brass serpent in the wilderness as an emblem of the Redeemer (Num. 21:8–9), so must the Savior be lifted up on the cross to bring about the atoning sacrifice on behalf of all who have faith in Him (see John 3:14). And that is the key to rebirth: *faith*.

Then the Savior makes this timeless statement: "For God so loved the world, that he gave his only begotten Son, that whosoever believeth in him should not perish, but have everlasting life" (John 3:16). The lesson—which embraces the foundational imperatives for baptism, or spiritual rebirth—ends when Jesus gives Nicodemus the secret for understanding the doctrine being taught: *action*. "But he that doeth truth cometh to the light, that his deeds may be made manifest, that they are wrought in God" (John 3:21)—a statement anticipating the well-known formula that Christ would later pronounce: "If any man will do his will, he shall know of the doctrine, whether it be of God, or whether I speak of myself" (John 7:17).

> *There is no greater teacher on baptism than Jesus Christ. The ordinance of baptism signifies the commitment on the part of a person of faith and penitence to be spiritually reborn through the "merits, and mercy, and grace of the Holy Messiah" (2 Ne. 2:8). It is instructive that the celebrated statement beginning "For God so loved the world . . ." is part of the same dialogue in which being born again is explained. Baptism and love go together, because Atonement and love go together. As you think about your own baptism, what thoughts and experiences concerning love come to mind?*

One Is Born Again through the Waters of Baptism, But How Does One Partake of the "Living Water"?

The Lord states: "But unto him that keepeth my commandments I will give the mysteries of my kingdom, and the same shall be in him a well of living water, springing up unto everlasting life" (D&C 63:23). It is one thing to know about the "living water" and its accompanying blessings; it is another thing entirely to continually drink from the eternal spring of living water unto everlasting life. To drink enduringly of the living water means that we will keep the commandments of God, including baptism by immersion in water (a form of the "living water"), followed by the baptism of fire and the Holy Ghost. In broad terms, the living water encompasses the knowledge, doctrines, principles, covenants, and ordinances of the gospel of Jesus Christ that lead to eternal and everlasting life. In specific terms, the living water is Jesus Christ Himself, the source of the saving and exalting power. How did He explain this principle?

Close to the main road from Judaea to Galilee, near the ancient city of Shechem (now Nablus), was a well called Jacob's well. It was at the site of this well that Jesus encountered a woman of Samaria and had a far-reaching discussion with her, the implications of which still resonate in the hearts of all those who are seekers of truth (see John 4:1–42). The Samaritans were an ancient people of mixed heritage, deriving partly from foreign colonists who occupied central and northern Israel after captivity by the Assyrians (see 2 Kgs. 17:5–6) and later by the Babylonians; they derive partly from Israelites who escaped at the time of the captivity. An enduring antagonism smoldered between the Samaritans and the Jews, stemming partly from the exclusion of the Samaritans from the temple-building enterprise during the ministry of Ezra and Nehemiah in the mid-fifth century BC.

But the Savior felt no such antagonism. He knew that the message of truth would soon be preached among the Samaritans and other non-Jewish peoples by His emissaries. For Him, this woman of Samaria was a daughter of God—and He could read her heart and know full well of her history and disposition. He therefore made the prophetic statement: "Whosoever drinketh of this water shall thirst again: But whosoever drinketh of the water that I shall give him shall never thirst; but the water that I shall give him shall be in him a well of water springing up into everlasting life" (John 4:13–14). In this manner the Savior spoke symbolically on two different but harmonizing levels: everyday reality and eternal truth. The water of which He spoke is the water of salvation, imparted to those who "worship [the Father] in spirit and in truth" (John 4:24), no matter their heritage and descent. Because the Savior had been able to reflect back to this woman of Samaria the facts of her life—things that a stranger could not have known—she believed Him: "Sir, I perceive

that thou art a prophet" (John 4:19). The Savior then identified Himself as the promised Messiah. The woman subsequently delivered this news to her family and associates, many of whom accepted Jesus with open and believing hearts. Thus the gateway to the fold of Christ was beginning to open for these people, and the steps of faith, repentance, baptism, and receiving the gift of the Holy Ghost were coming into view—as they would for the entire world when the resurrected Savior gave the ultimate commission to His disciples to teach all nations (see Matt. 28:19–20).

A newborn child depends from its first breath on the nurture of its mother for life-giving sustenance. So it is when one is reborn through the baptism of water and fire. Heaven continues to feed and nourish. The living water (see John 4:10–11) and the bread of life (see John 6:35, 48) provide spiritual succor to preserve strength and vitality. In addition, the "angels on earth" surrounding all newly baptized members add nourishment and fellowship (see Moro. 6:4). How have you been able to discern manifestations of the living water and the bread of life that have exceeded all of your expectations? How can you help others discern such blessings in their lives?

Real-life Stories for Heart and Mind

The Covenant of Comfort. Alma the Elder, having been touched by the Spirit as he feasted on the word of truth delivered by the prophet Abinadi, had pleaded with wicked King Noah to spare the life of this holy man. In so doing, he placed himself in mortal peril and had to flee for his life and take refuge in the wilderness. The account of his secret worship at the waters of Mormon with a small group of enthusiastic and receptive followers is one of the most celebrated accounts of conversion and baptism in all of the scriptures. The landscape was one of great beauty and provided "a fountain of pure water" (Mosiah 18:5) to carry out the ordinance of baptism: "yea, the place of Mormon, the waters of Mormon, the forest of Mormon, how beautiful are they to the eyes of them who there came to the knowledge of their Redeemer; yea, and how blessed are they, for they shall sing to his praises forever" (Mosiah

18:30). Alma gathered the faithful around him in seclusion to teach faith, repentance, and redemption through the Lord Jesus Christ. He explained to the eager congregants the commitment required in one's life to honor the baptismal covenant:

And now, as ye are desirous to come into the fold of God, and to be called his people, and are willing to bear one another's burdens, that they may be light;

Yea, and are willing to mourn with those that mourn; yea, and comfort those that stand in need of comfort, and to stand as witnesses of God at all times and in all things, and in all places that ye may be in, even until death, that ye may be redeemed of God, and be numbered with those of the first resurrection, that ye may have eternal life—

Now I say unto you, if this be the desire of your hearts, what have you against being baptized in the name of the Lord, as a witness before him that ye have entered into a covenant with him, that ye will serve him and keep his commandments, that he may pour out his Spirit more abundantly upon you?

And now when the people had heard these words, they clapped their hands for joy, and exclaimed: This is the desire of our hearts. . . .

And after this manner he did baptize every one that went forth to the place of Mormon; and they were in number about two hundred and four souls; yea, and they were baptized in the waters of Mormon, and were filled with the grace of God. (Mosiah 18:8–11, 16)

Being a true converted disciple requires that we genuinely love and care for our brothers and sisters as we bear one another's burdens, mourn with those that mourn, comfort those who stand in need of comfort, and seek their welfare by standing as a willing witness of the truth in all places and circumstances (see Mosiah 28:3; Alma 36:24). In a dramatic way, Alma demonstrated his commitment to serve His people according to the baptismal covenant he had made, for, with great risk to his own life, he soon arranged to liberate

the little colony from the lethal grip of enemy forces and lead them to safety in Zarahemla (see Mosiah 23, 24). In the same way, the Lord liberates those who enter His fold through baptism, freeing them from the captivating grip of sin so they might abound in joy and happiness. How have you been able to follow in the footsteps of Alma to help others become liberated and comforted through the blessings of the gospel and membership in the Lord's Church and kingdom? How have you been able to spread the good news about the "covenant of comfort"?

Pondering Prayerfully

Additional scriptures to consider and ponder:
- Mark 1:4
- Rom. 6:3–5
- Ether 4:18
- D&C 13:1
- D&C 20:46
- D&C 49:13

The following hymns inspire gratitude about baptism:
- "Father in Heaven, We Do Believe" (*Hymns,* 180)
- "Jesus, Mighty King in Zion" (*Hymns,* 234)
- "Lord, Accept into Thy kingdom" (*Hymns,* 236)

Remember and Be Sure

Cleansing, renewal, rebirth as a new individual, liberation from the effects of sin, spiritual adoption into the family of Christ—these are the beautiful and refreshing factors involved in baptism, the third step in the sequence of gospel principles and ordinances. Through baptism—which follows faith and repentance—we enter into a covenant with the Lord to become His sons and daughters, taking upon ourselves His sacred name forever, and promising to keep His commandments and endure to the end.

Baptism is the gateway to God's kingdom on earth, where individuals and families are "nourished by the good word of God, to keep them in the right way" (Moro. 6:4). Baptism is symbolic of the Lord's death, burial, and coming forth through the power of the resurrection, just as we are buried in the water to leave behind the old person and emerge as a new person, reborn to eternal life through the grace and mercy of the Lord and through our obedience and faithfulness in keeping His commandments.

CHAPTER 21
Laying on of Hands: The Gift of the Holy Ghost

When people believe and repent and are baptized by divine authority, and the Holy Ghost is conferred upon them as a gift, they receive the everlasting gospel. . . . the "gift of the Holy Ghost," the Holy Spirit that proceeds from the Father through the immensity of space, which guides, directs, enlightens, which is light in and of itself, which is the Spirit of intelligence, the light of truth. —Joseph Fielding Smith (*Answers to Gospel Questions*, 3:99)

Opening the Window of Wisdom

The word of the Lord in the latter days defines His gospel plan in all its simplicity and glory: "And this is my gospel—repentance and baptism by water, and then cometh the baptism of fire and the Holy Ghost, even the Comforter, which showeth all things, and teacheth the peaceable things of the kingdom" (D&C 39: 6).

The gift of the Holy Ghost is a matchless, supreme blessing from on high bestowed upon all those who are "the children of God by faith in Christ Jesus" (Gal. 3:26) and who enter the fold by baptism as "the children of the covenant" (3 Ne. 20:26). The blessing is one of light, truth, and divine witness: "And whoso believeth in me believeth in the Father also; and unto him will the Father bear record of me, for he will visit him with fire and with the Holy

Ghost. And thus will the Father bear record of me, and the Holy Ghost will bear record unto him of the Father and me; for the Father, and I, and the Holy Ghost are one" (3 Ne. 11:35–36).

We know that the Holy Ghost "has not a body of flesh and bones [like the Father and the Son], but is a personage of Spirit. Were it not so, the Holy Ghost could not dwell in us" (D&C 130:22). Yet, what is the nature of the light and power that makes it possible for the Holy Ghost to illuminate our lives with a portion of the eternal glory of God? From latter-day revelation we get an inkling of the immense and magnificent light and power that sustains the Creation and the unfolding of God's design for the blessing of His children:

> And the light which shineth, which giveth you light, is through him who enlighteneth your eyes, which is the same light that quickeneth your understandings;
>
> Which light proceedeth forth from the presence of God to fill the immensity of space—
>
> The light which is in all things, which giveth life to all things, which is the law by which all things are governed, even the power of God who sitteth upon his throne, who is in the bosom of eternity, who is in the midst of all things. (D&C 88:11–13)

What is being described is identified as "the light of Christ" (D&C 88:7), the living energy of the universe that enlivens everything. It creates all, perpetuates all life, governs all, gives us our reasoning power, quickens our sense of right and wrong (our conscience), and illuminates the pathway of salvation through the "enticings of the Holy Spirit" (Mosiah 3:19). By virtue of a continual blessing called the gift of the Holy Ghost, it brings us magnificent endowments: comfort through the forgiveness of sins, peace in the Lord, solace in overcoming tribulations, saving knowledge, and a growing abundance of rejuvenating light radiating from the Savior through the power of the Atonement, according to our capability of receiving it (see D&C 50:24).

We see in this broad spectrum representing "the light of Christ" that the gift of the Holy Ghost is manifested at the upper range of blessings made available to the sons and daughters of God. The sequence is glorious: we have, in turn, life, reasoning power, the guidance of our conscience, initial shafts of inspiration from the Holy Ghost, and finally—as the culmination of the covenant process of faith, repentance, and baptism by water—a marvelous gift bestowed by the laying of hands of those in authority: "Behold, then shall ye receive the Holy Ghost; yea, then cometh the baptism of fire and of the Holy Ghost; and then can ye speak with the tongue of angels, and shout praises unto the Holy One of Israel" (2 Ne. 31:13).

We are not left alone in a world of confusion and shadows. The Lord has prepared a way to guide the prayerful at decisive moments through His Holy Spirit. In His intercessory prayer, the Savior uttered these words: "And this is life eternal, that they might know thee the only true God, and Jesus Christ, whom thou hast sent" (John 17:3). It is essential that we come to know our Father in Heaven and His Son—that Jesus is the Christ, the Savior and Redeemer of the world. The only way to know this is through revelation by the power of the Holy Ghost (see 1 Cor. 12:3). This power is available to us forever when we have received the gift of the Holy Ghost and keep our covenants faithfully. The sacrament prayer confirms the blessing reserved unto all who "witness unto thee, O God, the Eternal Father, that they are willing to take upon them the name of thy Son, and always remember him and keep his commandments which he has given them"—that blessing is "that they may always have his Spirit to be with them. Amen" (D&C 20:77).

Inspired by Latter-Day Prophets

Joseph Smith: A man is saved no faster than he gets knowledge, for if he does not get knowledge, he will be brought into captivity by some evil power in the other world, as evil spirits will have more knowledge, and consequently more power than many men who are on the earth. Hence it needs revelation to assist us, and give us knowledge of the things of God (*HC* 4:588).

> *Knowledge is power. Knowledge through the Spirit gives us a vast advantage over evil forces. How can you increase your internal reservoir of "pure knowledge" (D&C 121:42) as a defense against influences opposed to the gospel? How does such knowledge work to defend you?*

Brigham Young: No person can receive a knowledge of this work except by the power of revelation. . . . The spirit of revelation, even the spirit of eternal life, is within that person who lives so as to bear properly the yoke of Jesus. The heavens are open to such persons, and they see and understand things that pertain to eternity, and also the things that pertain to this earth (*Discourses of Brigham Young*, 35).

> *The Spirit makes sacred things understandable to our minds as it resides within us and opens up a new channel of spiritual perception—as confirmed by the people whose lives were changed through the exhortations of King Benjamin: "And we, ourselves, also, through the infinite goodness of God, and the manifestations of his Spirit, have great views of that which is to come; and were it expedient, we could prophesy of all things" (Mosiah 5:3). How has the blessing of the gift of the Holy Ghost given you "great views" of the gospel plan of happiness and the coming world of eternal glory?*

Lorenzo Snow: We know that it is our right to have the manifestations of the Spirit every day of our lives (*The Teachings of Lorenzo Snow*, 111).

> *Our baptismal covenant is made only once, but it is renewed weekly through the ordinance of the sacrament and refreshed continually through our daily supplications to our Father*

in Heaven, in the name of the Son, to bless us with the Holy Spirit of revelation. How has this principle, as explained by President Lorenzo Snow, served to bless your life and the lives of your loved ones?

Harold B. Lee: Eternal blessings can come by yielding to the Holy Ghost. I am aware of the fact that for us to gain a testimony and, yes, beyond that, a knowledge, and finally the privilege of dwelling in the presence of God the Father and His Son . . . can only be had because of our yielding obedience to the Spirit of the Holy Ghost, which is given to the baptized members of the Church, in which light we shall walk forward until we shall have accomplished all things and shall be numbered among the faithful, with those who shall inherit celestial glory (*The Teachings of Harold B. Lee*, 100).

The gift of the Holy Ghost remains with the faithful throughout all their days—guiding them until they enter the celestial glory. The key is to obey the promptings of the Holy Ghost and thus harvest the light of eternal life. What are your thoughts about the meaning of the word yielding? *How is it related to the following reference concerning the more humble part of the Church in the days of Helaman, son of Helaman? "Nevertheless they did fast and pray oft, and did wax stronger and stronger in their humility, and firmer and firmer in the faith of Christ, unto the filling their souls with joy and consolation, yea, even to the purifying and the sanctification of their hearts, which sanctification cometh because of their yielding their hearts unto God" (Hel. 3:35).*

Truths to Liken

John 14:26—"But the Comforter, which is the Holy Ghost, whom the Father will send in my name, he shall teach you all things, and bring all things to your remembrance, whatsoever I have said unto you."

- As the time drew near for the Crucifixion, Jesus spoke to His Apostles, saying: "If ye love me, keep my commandments. And I will pray the Father, and he shall give you another Comforter, that he may abide with you for ever" (John 14:16). Then, using the words given above, He shared with them the miraculous nature of the Comforter's blessing.

- Through obedience we show our love to the Savior; through His love He sends the Holy Ghost to teach us and remind us of His sayings. The Apostles were about to lose the immediate companionship of the Savior, but they would receive a marvelous blessing to remind them of all that He had taught them. How does the Holy Ghost help you remember the truths of the gospel and put them into practice?

John 15:26—"But when the Comforter is come, whom I will send unto you from the Father, even the Spirit of truth, which proceedeth from the Father, he shall testify of me."

- The Savior continued to instruct His Apostles, prior to the hour of the atoning sacrifice, about the sacred mission of the Holy Ghost.

- A central role of the Holy Ghost in our lives is to witness of the divinity of Christ and to edify us with the light of all truth (see D&C 50:17–22; Moro. 10:4–5). Paul taught: "Wherefore I give you to understand . . . that no man can say that Jesus is the Lord, but by the Holy Ghost" (1 Cor. 12:3). How has the witness of the Holy Spirit confirmed your faith and witness of Jesus Christ as the Son of God and the Redeemer of mankind?

John 16:13–14—"Howbeit when he, the Spirit of truth, is come, he will guide you into all truth: for he shall not speak of himself; but whatsoever he shall hear, that shall he speak: and he will shew you things to come. He shall glorify me: for he shall receive of mine, and shall shew it unto you."

- Once more, the Savior confirmed to His Apostles that the blessings of the Holy Ghost are of a universal and glorious nature, appropriate as a consoling force for the time when He would no longer be able to be among them.

- The Holy Ghost is the divine Agent of communication of truth from the Savior to His people. He is the divine Agent for disseminating to the honest at heart the light of Christ in the degree to which they are receptive of that light. In so doing, the Holy Ghost glorifies Christ by receiving all truth and then sharing it with the faithful and obedient. How can you also follow this pattern to glorify the Lord by receiving in gratitude His truths through the Holy Spirit and then sharing them with others?

1 Cor. 2:9–10—"But as it is written, Eye hath not seen, nor ear heard, neither have entered into the heart of man, the things which God hath prepared for them that love him. But God hath revealed them unto us by his Spirit: for the Spirit searcheth all things, yea, the deep things of God."

- These words of Paul to the Corinthian Saints echo the words of Isaiah: "For since the beginning of the world men have not heard, nor perceived by the ear, neither hath the eye seen, O God, beside thee, what he hath prepared for him that waiteth for him" (Isa. 64:4). Paul gave the concluding dimension of this theme: the Spirit reveals to us the glories that lie ahead.
- The key to wisdom is an enduring commitment to spiritual growth; by seeking after and cultivating the gifts and blessings of the Spirit, one transcends the transitory learning of the world and discerns the uplifting and transforming patterns of godliness leading to the blessings of eternity. How can you share with your family and other loved ones your vision of the magnificent blessings of eternal life that await the faithful? How has the Holy Ghost allowed you to view such grand future blessings so often obscured by the burdens of worldly care? (See 1 Cor. 1:27–31; 2:14–16.)

1 Ne. 4:6—"And I was led by the Spirit, not knowing beforehand the things which I should do."

- Despite the trepidation and murmuring of his elder brothers, Nephi sets out courageously to obtain the plates of Laban and thus preserve the written record of God's covenant dealings with His people through the ages.
- Often it is unclear precisely how we are to proceed in magnifying our callings, but the Spirit will lead us if we will but listen and heed. When we are worthy, we can always depend on the Spirit to direct our lives, showing us the things to do (see 2 Ne. 32:5) and prompting us what to say (see D&C 100:5–6). What experiences have you or members of your family had that confirm the blessings of guidance through the Holy Ghost?

2 Ne. 31:13—"By following your Lord and your Savior down into the water, according to his word, behold, then shall ye receive the Holy Ghost; yea, then cometh the baptism of fire and of the Holy Ghost; and then can ye speak with the tongue of angels, and shout praises unto the Holy One of Israel."

- Nephi was speaking to us, his future readers—"unto all those that shall receive hereafter these things which I write" (2 Ne. 25:3).
- Through baptism and the gift of the Holy Ghost, we become conversant in a new language—the language spoken by angels in declaring the truth: "Angels speak by the power of the Holy Ghost; wherefore, they speak the words of Christ" (2 Ne. 32:3). How has your language "changed" as a result of your coming into the fold of Christ? How do you speak differently, in words and tones far above the din of worldly clamor, using words that testify of Jesus Christ and His goodness (see John 15:26)? How can you help others around you adopt and use this kind of language through obedience to the gospel plan?

2 Ne. 32:5—"For behold, again I say unto you that if ye will enter in by the way, and receive the Holy Ghost, it will show unto you all things what ye should do."

- Nephi gave his final counsel to his future readers concerning the gift and power of the Holy Ghost.
- In this simple but powerful statement, Nephi makes an extraordinary promise: the Holy Ghost will show the faithful and obedient not just *some* things to do, but *all* things to do in keeping their covenants. Is there any aspect of your life that does not come under the canopy of this grand promise for guidance? How has the Holy Ghost guided you and your loved ones in the past? How do you gain hope and confidence from the fact that the same promise holds true of the future?

Alma 5:45–47—"And this is not all. Do ye not suppose that I know of these things myself? Behold, I testify unto you that I do know that these things whereof I have spoken are true. And how do ye suppose that I know of their surety? Behold, I say unto you they are made known unto me by the Holy Spirit of God. Behold, I have fasted and prayed many days that I might know these things of myself. And now I do know of myself that they are true; for the Lord God hath made them manifest unto me by his Holy Spirit; and this is the spirit of revelation which is in me. And moreover, I say unto you that it has thus been revealed unto me, that the words which have been spoken by our fathers are true, even so according to the spirit of prophecy which is in me, which is also by the manifestation of the Spirit of God."

- Alma, high priest over the Church, resigned his office as chief judge over the land in order to preach the gospel to his people. In these verses, he proclaimed to them the authority for his testimony of the gospel.
- As you study the words of Alma concerning the source of his testimony, what stated process emerges for obtaining certainty about the truths of the gospel? How has this process been effective for you and your loved ones? How can you share this process with others who want to know more about the Church?

Moro. 8:26—"And the remission of sins bringeth meekness, and lowliness of heart; and because of meekness and lowliness of heart cometh the visitation of the Holy Ghost, which Comforter filleth with hope and perfect love, which love endureth by diligence unto prayer, until the end shall come, when all the saints shall dwell with God."

- These words are from an epistle written by Mormon to his son Moroni concerning the fundamental principles of the gospel of faith and repentance. Moroni included the epistle in his final compilation of the records of his people later known as the Book of Mormon.
- The Holy Ghost fills us with hope and a perfect love that endures forever through the power of prayer. We are counseled to include in our prayers a continuing request that the Holy Ghost will fill us with love—forever! How can you share this counsel with others so that they may have hope and love abounding in their lives without cease as a preparation for returning home to their Creator?

Moro. 10:4–5—"And when ye shall receive these things, I would exhort you that ye would ask God, the Eternal Father, in the name of Christ, if these things are not true; and if ye shall ask with a sincere heart, with real intent, having faith in Christ, he will manifest the truth of it unto you, by the power of the Holy Ghost. And by the power of the Holy Ghost ye may know the truth of all things."

- Moroni concluded his portion of the Book of Mormon record with this celebrated counsel to his future readers—*all of us!*
- This covenant advice is given in plainness: if we ask sincerely, with authentic purpose, with a firm faith in the Savior, then we have the promise that we can know the truth of all things through the Holy Ghost, including the truth of the Book of Mormon. What are your thoughts about the indispensable role of the Holy Ghost in the plan of happiness?

Rejoicing and Reasoning Together

What Is the Essence of Having a Testimony?

A testimony is the priceless personal possession of certain knowledge, obtained by the power of the Holy Ghost, concerning the eternal truths of the gospel of Jesus Christ. We can have a witness of many eternal truths: God is our Father, Jesus is the Christ, revelation is the pattern for God's dealing with man, Joseph Smith was and is the Prophet of the Restoration, the gospel truths were indeed restored through the Book of Mormon, which was translated by the gift and power of God—and many other related matters. We can know that The Church of Jesus Christ of Latter-day Saints is the Lord's Church once again established on the earth and that a living prophet leads us today. We can know these things are true by the power of the Holy Ghost. This is pure testimony. This is certain knowledge. When we bear our testimonies, we bear witness of these things by the power of the Holy Ghost, and it is the Spirit that confirms the witness of all truths. Each of us should seek to have our own personal testimony of these eternal truths.

Our testimony gives us the assurance that the purpose of Heavenly Father's magnificent plan of salvation is to enable His children to be happy and enter into a state of never-ending joy (see Mosiah 2:41). This gift—even eternal life—is the greatest of all the gifts of God (see D&C 14:7), given to us if we will but choose to obey and keep His commandments. It is made possible through the grace of God, manifested by the infinite and eternal Atonement and Resurrection of our beloved Savior, Jesus Christ—performed on our behalf so that we might be saved by grace, "after all we can do" (2 Ne. 25:23). We have been given a most priceless companion from our Heavenly Father to help us in our quest for happiness (see Alma 27:18)—the Holy Ghost, the third member of the Godhead. The power and gifts of the Spirit are innumerable and all-encompassing (see D&C 46:11–26; Moro. 10:6–19). These gifts can add magnificent blessings to our life as we become worthy of the influence and power of the Spirit (see 1 Ne. 10:17). We can humbly plead for the Spirit in all of our undertakings (see 3 Ne. 19:9), and it will show us all things to do (see 2 Ne. 32:5) and kindle within our hearts

and minds an abiding testimony of the gospel (see John 14:26; 1 Cor. 12:3).

Why is it that when we share our testimony with others it grows stronger and more vibrant? What role does the Holy Ghost play in confirming our testimony to others (see D&C 100:8)? What effect does your testimony have in heaven (see D&C 62:3)?

What Is Meant by the Word *Rock* as Used in Connection to Revelation?

On one very special occasion, the Savior taught His disciples an unforgettable lesson on the subject of how to gain a testimony based on the rock-solid foundation of revelation. As He came to the coasts of Caesarea Philippi (a town near the source of the Jordan River, at the foot of Mount Herman), He asked His disciples to tell Him who the people were saying that He, the Son of Man, was. Their responses provided the framework for the Master's lesson:

And they said, Some say that thou art John the Baptist: some, Elias; and others, Jeremias, or one of the prophets.

He saith unto them, But whom say ye that I am?

And Simon Peter answered and said, Thou art the Christ, the Son of the living God.

And Jesus answered and said unto him, Blessed art thou, Simon Bar-jona: for flesh and blood hath not revealed it unto thee, but my Father which is in heaven.

And I say also unto thee, That thou art Peter, and upon this rock I will build my church; and the gates of hell shall not prevail against it.

And I will give unto thee the keys of the kingdom of heaven: and whatsoever thou shalt bind on earth shall be bound in heaven: and whatsoever thou shalt loose on earth shall be loosed in heaven. (Matt. 16:14–19)

In this manner the Lord confirmed that essential knowledge of spiritual things comes through the channel of revelation through the Holy Ghost—providing a foundation for the operation of priesthood leadership in the kingdom of

God. This foundation of revelation ensures eternal integrity and everlasting consistency within the kingdom. What is the rock and chief cornerstone thereof? Christ Himself is the Stone of Israel (see Acts 4:10–12; 1 Cor. 3:10–12; 10:4; Eph. 2:20; D&C 50:44; 128:10). Thus both revelation and Jesus Christ together constitute the "rock" upon which the gospel and Church are founded (see Joseph F. Smith, *From Prophet to Son: Advice of Joseph F. Smith to His Missionary Sons*, 87).

The Rock of our personal salvation is the Lord Jesus Christ (see 2 Sam. 22:47; Ps. 62:2, 6; 1 Ne. 13:36; 2 Ne. 4:30; Jacob 7:25). He is the chief cornerstone on which we build our spiritual foundation. We can come to know this by personal revelation through the Holy Ghost, which revelation is the bedrock of the Church and the vital light that makes of it a "living Church" (D&C 1:30). How are revelation and Jesus Christ a perfect blend as the substance of your testimony?

What Is the Meaning of the Word *Saint*?

We become "Saints" as we enter into the covenant of baptism and receive the Holy Ghost. We change in fundamental ways because we are converted to Jesus Christ and His gospel. We take upon us the name of Jesus Christ. We are members of The Church of Jesus Christ of Latter-day Saints—and because of this we should think and act differently. We become a Saint according to the pattern described by King Benjamin: "He yields to the enticings of the Holy Spirit, and putteth off the natural man and becometh a saint through the atonement of Christ the Lord, and becometh as a child, submissive, meek, humble, patient, full of love, willing to submit to all things which the Lord seeth fit to inflict upon him, even as a child doth submit to his father" (Mosiah 3:19). This is a process of becoming, not an event. We become holy and without blemish, even unspotted from the world, as we apply the Atonement to our lives through faith unto repentance (see Alma 34:15–17). We reflect a "godly walk and conversation" (D&C 20:69) in all that we do. To make the mighty change and be born again requires great faith, which is the foundation of all righteousness. By so doing we become Saints, even "joint-heirs with Christ" (Rom. 8:17). We can press forward in saintly fashion "with a steadfastness in Christ, having a perfect brightness of hope, and a love of God and of all men" (2 Ne. 31:20).

The name of the Church is instructive. It is not only "The Church of Jesus Christ," but the Church of the "Latter-day Saints." What a grand blessing to be involved with, and jointly own, the kingdom of God as prospective "joint-heirs with Christ" (Rom. 8:17). What supreme mercy is shown by the Savior to give the Church to His sons and daughters, His Saints, "even The Church of Jesus Christ of Latter-day Saints" (D&C 115:4). What are your thoughts about the obligation we all have to act as and be Saints in the highest sense of this word?

What Is Meant by the Term *Justification*?

To Enoch the Lord revealed the pattern of gospel principles and ordinances given to Adam from the very beginning:

For by the water ye keep the commandment; by the Spirit ye are justified, and by the blood ye are sanctified;

Therefore it is given to abide in you; the record of heaven; the Comforter; the peaceable things of immortal glory; the truth of all things; that which quickeneth all things, which maketh alive all things; that which knoweth all things, and hath all power according to wisdom, mercy, truth, justice, and judgment.

And now, behold, I say unto you: This is the plan of salvation unto all men, through the blood of mine Only Begotten, who shall come in the meridian of time. (Moses 6:60–62)

These are the actual words of the Lord to our first father, and they give us a beautiful summary of the plan of salvation, including the sacred stewardship of the Comforter. Through baptism we show our obedience; through the Holy Ghost we are justified (declared by the Spirit to be worthy before God, based on our righteousness); and through the blood of the Lamb of God we are sanctified (made holy through the "merits, and mercy, and grace of the Holy Messiah"—2 Ne. 2:8).

Through justification, then, we stand approved before the Lord as confirmed by the Holy Ghost, with the demands of justice being satisfied through the power and mercy of the Atonement as we exercise our faith in Jesus Christ and bring forth good works. In this way, we manifest our devotion and commitment to the cause of building up the kingdom of God, "For not the hearers of the law are just before God, but the doers of the law shall be justified" (Rom. 2:13). How can this be, seeing that no one is perfect in abiding by the law of God? It is possible because the Atonement makes up the difference, and mercy satisfies the demands of justice through grace (see Mosiah 15:9; Alma 34:16). The Holy Ghost puts His seal of approval on our status of compliance with the law, and we are then "justified" before the Almighty and worthy of His blessings. The Holy Ghost acting in this capacity is referred to as the "Holy Spirit of promise" (see D&C 132:7, 18, 19, 26). Those who keep the commandments of faith, repentance, baptism, and receiving the gift of the Holy Ghost by the laying on of hands by one in authority are then in a position to receive the ratifying blessing from the Holy Ghost that ensures that their obedience is recognized in heaven as well as on earth (see D&C 76:53–55).

What are your thoughts about the magnificent blessings of the Spirit in confirming our justification and worthiness before the Lord as we keep the commandments in faith and obedience?

Real-life Stories for Heart and Mind

Blessings in Reserve. A stake priesthood leader was setting apart several individuals to serve as local missionaries. After having set apart one middle-aged sister, he noticed that she was in tears. Following the session, he asked her if all was well. She told him the story behind her emotion. She had been called to serve a full-time mission many years previous to that, but circumstances had prevented her from going. She had always felt that she had relinquished important blessings from her Heavenly Father, since a mission call had originally been mentioned in her patriarchal blessing. Her tears were tears of joy, since the setting apart blessing included statements that were, as she put it, "word-for-word" from her patriarchal blessing.

From this experience, she knew that her Father in Heaven loved her and had reserved for her the very blessings He wanted her to have through faithful service.

Truly the Lord watches over us and wants us to know, through the Spirit, of His love and concern. When circumstances beyond our control don't allow us at the moment to begin a specific assignment, the Lord will accept our offering of sincere desire (see D&C 105:19; 124:51). Blessings are reserved for the faithful. What experiences have you had that confirm the promises and blessings of the Lord?

The Strange Book. Parley P. Pratt told a compelling story about how the Holy Ghost confirmed to him the truthfulness of the Book of Mormon the first time he began searching its pages:

We visited an old Baptist deacon by the name of Hamlin. After hearing of our appointment for evening, he began to tell of a *book,* a STRANGE BOOK, a VERY STRANGE BOOK! in his possession, which had been just published. This book, he said, purported to have been originally written on plates either of gold or brass, by a branch of the tribes of Israel; and to have been discovered and translated by a young man near Palmyra, in the State of New York, by the aid of visions, or the ministry of angels. . . . Next morning I called at his house, where, for the first time, my eyes beheld the "BOOK OF MORMON"—that book of books—that record which reveals the antiquities of the *"New World"* back to the remotest ages, and which unfolds the destiny of its people and the world for all time to come;—that Book which contains the fulness of the gospel of a crucified and risen Redeemer;—that Book which reveals a lost remnant of Joseph, and which was the principal means, in the hands of God, of directing the entire course of my future life.

I opened it with eagerness, and read its title page. I then read the testimony of several witnesses in relation to the manner of its being found and translated. After this I commenced its contents by course. I read all day; eating was a burden, I had no desire for food; sleep was a burden when the night came, for I preferred reading to sleep.

As I read, the spirit of the Lord was upon me, and I knew and comprehended that the book was true, as plainly and manifestly as a man comprehends and knows that he exists. My joy was now full, as it were, and I rejoiced sufficiently to more than pay me for all the sorrows, sacrifices and toils of my life. (*Autobiography of Parley P. Pratt, 36–37*)

Parley P. Pratt was subsequently baptized in September 1830 by Oliver Cowdery and became one of the stalwart priesthood leaders of the restored Church. As you consider how the Holy Ghost inspired him with a testimony of the truthfulness of the Book of Mormon and the work of the Restoration, how does this account compare with your own experiences of the blessings of inspiration given by the Spirit of the Lord? How can you let your own testimony be an inspiration to your loved ones and those you serve in the Church?

Pondering Prayerfully

Additional scriptures to consider and ponder:
- John 8:12
- Acts 2:2–4
- 1 Cor. 2:5
- 2 Ne. 28:31
- 2 Ne. 25:23
- Mosiah 4:3
- Alma 5:14
- Moro. 7:13
- D&C 11:12
- D&C 11:13
- D&C 45:57
- D&C 130:23

The following hymns inspire gratitude for the gift of the Holy Ghost:
- "I Know My Father Lives" (*Hymns,* 302)
- "The Spirit of God" (*Hymns,* 2)

Remember and Be Sure

All who seek divine guidance can know through the Spirit that Jesus is the light and life of the world, and that His atoning sacrifice opens up the way for all to return to the presence of our Father and His Son. The Holy Ghost comforts, teaches, testifies, enlightens our mind, and leads us to do good, to walk humbly, to do justly, and to judge righteously; it shows us all things to do and brings us love, peace, gentleness, goodness, and a whole host of other righteous feelings, qualities, and blessings (see John 14:26; 15:26; 16:13–14; Gal. 5:22–23; D&C 11:12–13; 2 Ne. 32:5). Having been granted the gift of the Holy Ghost, we are to seek its promptings and heed its counsel.

Revelation through the Holy Ghost is the rock upon which we build a sure foundation, the Lord Jesus Christ being the chief cornerstone of our spiritual edifice. Through the Holy Ghost we can know that our Heavenly Father and His Son live and that Jesus is the Christ. We can know that They love us and bless us with words of truth through the scriptures and the voice of living prophets. We can know that the Church and kingdom of God have been restored in these latter days through the Prophet Joseph Smith, unfolding the fulness of the gospel of salvation and exaltation for all who will receive it. Without revelation through the gift of the Holy Ghost, we would lose not only the precious knowledge of God, but also the light of heaven to direct our lives today. We cannot live and gain eternal life without the blessings of the Spirit sent to testify of the Father and the Son and to give guidance for our mortal journey back home.

The sacred knowledge given us by the Spirit becomes our testimony. We can be valiant in our testimony in order to enjoy the promised blessings from our loving Heavenly Father. We can continue to have a desire to strengthen our testimony as we study, pray, serve, and bear witness of the truthfulness of the gospel of Jesus Christ. As we seek to do these things, the grace of God will enable us to be instruments in His hands for doing good as we testify and witness to the world of these eternal truths. The Apostle Paul made clear that "no man can say that Jesus is the Lord, but by the Holy Ghost" (1 Cor. 12:3). Let us therefore live so as to invite the sacred influence of the Holy Ghost into our lives, granting us continually a fervent, abiding testimony of the Savior, His Atonement, and the saving truths of the gospel, and strengthening our covenant commitment to bless the lives of our "fellowcitizens with the saints" (Eph. 2:19).

CHAPTER 22
Gifts of the Spirit to Profit All

The Holy Ghost is the Spirit of the Lord and issues forth from himself and may properly be called God's minister to execute His will in immensity. —Brigham Young (*JD* 1:50)

Opening the Window of Wisdom

As the third member of the Godhead, the Holy Ghost performs magnificent and indispensable services in support of the plan of salvation and exaltation, encompassing the following categories:

- **Word of the Lord.** As primary Agent for the light of Christ, the Holy Ghost disseminates and confirms the word and voice of the Lord: "I, the Lord, have spoken it, and the Spirit beareth record" (D&C 59:24).
- **Ordinances.** The Holy Ghost is the confirming central figure involved with the ordinances of salvation and exaltation, including baptism by water and by fire: "And this is my gospel— repentance and baptism by water, and then cometh the baptism of fire and the Holy Ghost, even the Comforter, which showeth all things, and teacheth the peaceable things of the kingdom" (D&C 39:6).

- **Missionary Work.** The Holy Ghost is the spiritual guide for the gathering of the Saints through missionary work: "Go your way whithersoever I will, and it shall be given you by the Comforter what you shall do and whither you shall go" (D&C 31:11; see also D&C 100:6).
- **Personal Revelation.** The Holy Ghost is the key to personal revelation, as we have already seen in Chapter 21: "Yea, behold, I will tell you in your mind and in your heart, by the Holy Ghost, which shall come upon you and which shall dwell in your heart. Now, behold, this is the spirit of revelation" (D&C 8:2–3).
- **Organization of the Church.** The Holy Ghost is the inspirational force to guide the organizational work of the Church, under the direction of the Lord, in the following ways: giving direction to the living prophet (see D&C 21:2), empowering the ordination of priesthood bearers (see D&C 20:60), directing all meetings (see D&C 46:2), bestowing the gifts of the Spirit "that all may be profited thereby" (see D&C 46:12), and giving guidance to "expound the scriptures, and to exhort the church" (see D&C 25:7).
- **Peace and Comfort.** The Holy Ghost is the ongoing source of peace and

comfort for the Saints as they endure to the end (see for example D&C 19:23).

- **Seal of Approval.** The Holy Ghost, acting as the Holy Spirit of Promise, places the seal of divine approval on the ordinances leading to eternal life and exaltation for the faithful and obedient (see for example D&C 132:7, 18, 19, 26).

In this extraordinary array of services rendered by the Holy Ghost, there is a key blessing known as *the gifts of the Spirit.* Related to the various gifts of the Spirit is, of course, personal revelation through the gift of the Holy Ghost bestowed upon each individual of faith and repentance who is baptized by water and fire and receives the ongoing companionship of the Holy Ghost. But the gifts of the Spirit encompass a vast range of additional blessings that contribute to the vitality and well-being of the Church and kingdom of God. Many of these gifts of the Spirit are outlined in D&C 46:10–26; 1 Cor. 12:4–11; and Moro. 10:8–18. The seventh Article of Faith opens the door: "We believe in the gift of tongues, prophecy, revelation, visions, healing, interpretation of tongues, and so forth." A fuller accounting of such gifts includes knowing of the divinity of Christ, belief in the testimony of others, administrative capability, being able to judge between divine and false influences, wisdom and how to teach it, knowledge and how to teach it, faith to be healed, faith to heal, the working of miracles, power of prophecy, discerning of spirits, tongues, interpretations of tongues, and many other gifts that come to the Saints through the Holy Ghost as circumstances and needs arise.

The word of the Lord relative to our involvement and responsibility concerning such gifts is clear: "And again, verily I say unto you, I would that ye should always remember, and always retain in your minds what those gifts are, that are given unto the church. For all have not every gift given unto them; for there are many gifts, and to every man is given a gift by the Spirit of God" (D&C 46:10–11). Paul confirms: "Now there are diversities of gifts, but the same Spirit. And there are differences of administrations, but the same Lord" (1 Cor. 12:4–5). Moroni emphasizes the purpose for the bestowal of such gifts: "And again, I exhort you, my brethren, that ye deny not the gifts of God, for they are many; and they come from the same God. And there are different ways that these gifts are administered; but it is the same God who worketh all in all; and they are given by the manifestations of the Spirit of God unto men, to profit them" (Moro. 10:8).

Every member of the Church has access to the gift of revelation as the foundation for personal testimony through the gift of the Holy Ghost. But every member is not blessed with all the other gifts of the Spirit. Why? So that we can prosper and flourish in an interactive and dynamic relationship where we depend on one another and where the several gifts distributed among the members individually can generate mutually shared blessings of inspiration, leadership, teaching, learning, and miracles. Thus, collectively, "all may be profited thereby" (D&C 46:12). To recognize the importance of seeking and cultivating the gifts of the Spirit is to imbue our lives with untold blessings from heaven.

Inspired by Latter-Day Prophets

Lorenzo Snow: Those things which are of the greatest importance to the Latter-day Saints are derived through the revelations of the Holy Spirit (*JD* 23:288).

The Holy Ghost is active in the personal lives of individuals, but also in congregations of the Church and in the family gatherings of Zion as the word of the Lord is being preached. In your opinion, how is it that the promptings of the Spirit are often magnified and augmented when we gather together to worship and learn of our responsibilities?

Joseph F. Smith: I believe that every individual in the Church has just as much right to enjoy the spirit of revelation and the understanding from God which that spirit of revelation gives him, for his own good, as the bishop has to enable him to preside over his ward. Every man has the privilege to exercise these gifts and these privileges in the conduct of his own affairs (*Gospel Doctrine: Selections from the Sermons and Writings of Joseph F. Smith,* 34).

Through the lovingkindness of a merciful Father, the inspiration and gifts of the Spirit flow to each son and daughter of God as a support in raising and nurturing families according to righteous principles. The Lord has declared: "Wherefore, verily I say unto you that all things unto me are spiritual, and not at any time have I given unto you a law which was temporal" (D&C 29:34). Thus even matters of provident living and professional productivity are governed within a spiritual framework. What has been your experience being guided by inspiration to support and care for your family?

Marion G. Romney: As we contemplate the virtue of these gifts and fruits, let me, by way of caution, emphasize the fact that there is nothing spectacular, magical, or fanatical about the working of these gifts. Under their influence one behaves perfectly normally. They do not excite. They calm and comfort. Their influence is as natural and refreshing as a gentle breeze (*Learning for the Eternities,* 126).

When the Savior taught Nicodemus about the need to be born again, He said: "The wind bloweth where it listeth, and thou hearest the sound thereof, but canst not tell whence it cometh, and whither it goeth: so is every one that is born of the Spirit" (John 3:8). The Holy Ghost is a being of peace and comfort, solace and confirmation. The Holy Ghost operates as naturally as the sun, giving its light where nurture and vitality are welcomed by those seeking to grow and unfold in their spiritual well-being. What are your thoughts about the quiet and calming influence of the Spirit as the source of spiritual gifts?

Bruce R. McConkie: Spiritual gifts come from God. They are the gifts of God; they originate with him and are special blessings that he bestows upon those who love him and keep his commandments. Because they come by the power of the Holy Ghost, they are also called the gifts of the Spirit. Hence, they are received only by those who are in tune with the Spirit.

These gifts are infinite in number and endless in their manifestations because God himself is infinite and endless, and because the needs of those who receive them are as numerous, varied, and different as there are people in the kingdom. All saints are commanded to seek earnestly the best gifts (*A New Witness for the Articles of Faith,* 270).

An infinite God can bestow an infinite number of gifts of the Spirit. What kinds of gifts of the Spirit have you experienced beyond those listed in the scriptures (see D&C 46; 1 Cor. 12; Moro. 10)?

Truths to Liken

Acts 3:6—"Then Peter said, Silver and gold have I none; but such as I have give I thee: In the name of Jesus Christ of Nazareth rise up and walk."

- Following the Crucifixion and Resurrection of the Lord, the Holy Spirit was poured out upon the multitude on the day of Pentecost as Peter, the chief Apostle, was preaching the truths of the gospel. Many were baptized and joined the fold of Christ at that time. Soon thereafter, Peter and John encountered an invalid near the temple who begged alms from them. Peter responded using the words given above. The crippled man was healed miraculously.

- When inspired by the Holy Ghost, holders of the Melchizedek Priesthood can act according to the will of God to bless those with special needs. Just as Peter did, those who bear this holy priesthood can, under the direction of the Holy Ghost, perform miracles according to the operation of faith (see Ether 12:16). When the resurrected Lord visited His Saints in the New World, He discerned the faith of the people and compassionately healed all of their afflicted family members (see 3 Ne. 17:1–10). How does the gift of healing reflect the love of the Savior?

1 Cor. 12:28–31—"And God hath set some in the church, first apostles, secondarily prophets, thirdly teachers, after that miracles, then gifts of healings, helps, governments, diversities of tongues. Are all apostles? are all prophets? are all teachers? are all workers of miracles? Have all the gifts of healing? do all speak with tongues? do all interpret? But covet earnestly the best gifts: and yet shew I unto you a more excellent way."

- Paul taught the Corinthians concerning the operation of the Church, depending as it does on the blending together of the various gifts and talents of the membership, "In whom all the building fitly framed together groweth unto an holy temple in the Lord: In whom ye also are builded together for an habitation of God through the Spirit" (Eph. 2:21–22).

- As you ponder the various people in your own ward and stake, how is a blending of the gifts of the Spirit being made manifest so as to profit everyone involved? Why is it often effective in the process of reactivating less-active members to ask them to participate in Church activities using their special talents and gifts?

Mosiah 23:14—"And also trust no one to be your teacher nor your minister, except he be a man of God, walking in his ways and keeping his commandments."

- Alma the Elder had led a group of followers to safety away from the murderous influence of wicked King Noah and his priests. In their newly established colony, Alma's followers desired that he should become their king. In response, Alma declined to reestablish a kingdom, and reminded the people of the importance of having ecclesiastical leaders who reflect spiritual qualities. Subsequently, leaders were installed and consecrated who "did watch over their people, and did nourish them with things pertaining to righteousness" (Mosiah 23:18).

- The system of government in the kingdom of God is set up to nourish the membership in righteousness under the direction of the priesthood, using diverse gifts of the Spirit to bless lives and strengthen testimonies. Think of those who are leaders in your midst, and ponder with gratitude their various spiritual gifts of leadership and edification.

Moro. 6:9—"And their meetings were conducted by the church after the manner of the workings of the Spirit, and by the power of the Holy Ghost; for as the power of the Holy Ghost led them whether to preach, or to exhort, or to pray, or to supplicate, or to sing, even so it was done."

- In the closing supplements to the Book of Mormon chronicle, Moroni confirmed that the meetings of the Church in his day were conducted using precisely the same process of spiritual guidance we use in our meetings today. Thus the gifts of the Spirit concerning administrative leadership, the teaching and learning of wisdom and knowledge, the expression of testimonies, and the exercise of faith in all spiritual matters were of central importance then as they are now.

- Everything we do—from being led by the Spirit when we seek to learn the will of the Lord (see 1 Ne. 4:6) to structuring and conducting meetings—should be directed by the Spirit. In this way, our meetings will be fruitful and achieve their intended purpose (see D&C 43:8–10). How does the Spirit of the Lord help you prepare for meetings or to provide service when called on to do so?

D&C 11:12–13—"And now, verily, verily, I say unto thee, put your trust in that Spirit which leadeth to do good—yea, to do justly, to walk humbly, to judge righteously; and this is my Spirit. Verily, verily, I say unto you, I will impart unto you of my Spirit, which shall enlighten your mind, which shall fill your soul with joy."

- These words were included in a revelation given through the Prophet Joseph Smith to his brother Hyrum Smith at Harmony, Pennsylvania, in May 1829.

- As you seek the best spiritual gifts in order to serve others more effectively, you can consider them within the beautiful framework given to Hyrum Smith—a framework of trust, goodness, justice, humility, and righteous judgment. All gifts of the Spirit reflect such qualities. How do the gifts granted to you relate to these qualities? Clearly, when we live by the Spirit we are directed and blessed in all things.

D&C 42:14—"And the Spirit shall be given unto you by the prayer of faith; and if ye receive not the Spirit ye shall not teach."

- These words are part of a revelation given through the Prophet Joseph Smith at Kirtland, Ohio, February 9, 1831, and designated by the Prophet as "embracing the law of the Church."
- To teach by the Spirit requires prayerfulness and the exercise of faith. Why? Because it is the Spirit that teaches and testifies of the truth. Truth without the testimony of the Spirit is hollow. To qualify for the Spirit is extremely important in the teaching process. As you teach your family and others in the Church, how have you experienced the blessings of the Spirit as a result of earnest prayer, with the application of faith, nothing doubting?

Rejoicing and Reasoning Together

How Can We Know Which Gifts of the Spirit We Are to Be Blessed With?

Some gifts are universal. The gift of the Holy Ghost is given to all who come into the fold of Christ through faith, repentance, and baptism. The guidance of the Spirit is therefore a blessing granted to all as the spiritual foundation for a testimony of the gospel of Jesus Christ, since "no man can say that Jesus is the Lord, but by the Holy Ghost" (1 Cor. 12:3). But what of the many others gifts bestowed by the Spirit? Which of these are intended for you to have? How can you find out? The Savior gives the answer: "Draw near unto me and I will draw near unto you; seek me diligently and ye shall find me; ask, and ye shall receive; knock, and it shall be opened unto you. Whatsoever ye ask the Father in my name it shall be given unto you, that is expedient for you" (D&C 88:63–64). Based on this counsel, the following may help you identify the gifts of the

Spirit that might be given you now or in the future:

- **Draw near to the Lord**—You can prepare yourself spiritually to learn the will of the Lord, having a firm commitment to follow His divine guidance: "And faith, hope, charity and love, with an eye single to the glory of God, qualify him for the work" (D&C 4:5). These qualities will place you in His hands. He knows you—your strengths and weaknesses, your talents and gifts, your needs and desires. He loves you and wants to bless you.

- **Seek**—Use diligence in learning about the gifts of the Spirit. The Lord has promised that answers will be given.
  - Study the scriptures concerning the gifts of the Spirit (especially D&C 46, 1 Cor. 12, and Moro. 10). Examine each gift in light of your own experience, responsibilities, and aspirations: "And again, verily I say unto you, I would that ye should always remember, and always retain in your minds what those gifts are, that are given unto the church" (D&C 46:10). "But covet earnestly the best gifts" (1 Cor. 12:31).
  - Note the gifts of the Spirit manifested in the lives of the prophets in special ways: Enoch, the gift to bring unity among the people; Melchizedek, the gift to bring peace; Abraham, the gift of obedience; Joseph, the gift of leadership and vision; Isaiah, the gift of majestic expression; Daniel, the gift of vision; Nephi, the gift of faith; Mosiah, the gift of prophecy and translation; Abinadi, the gift of courage; Alma, the gift of discourse; the brother of Jared, the gift of faith; Joseph Smith, the gift of revelation and translation—and on it goes. How can you learn from their example? How can you aspire to some of these same gifts through the blessing of the Lord?
  - Seek guidance through your patriarchal blessing. A patriarchal blessing sometimes refers to gifts of the Spirit

that have been reserved for you as you act in faith and obedience to the commandments.

- **Ask**—Reach out actively for answers, for the Lord has promised that you shall receive.
  - Ask yourself what you love to do. What activities bring fulfillment and satisfaction? Is it music, writing, art, counseling, team-building, or health-related activities? What are your productive hobbies? What talents and gifts emerge in all of this? Look at your personal journal for hints and promptings. You can be grateful to your Father in Heaven for the gifts and potential that you have.
  - Ask Heavenly Father. Pray and ask in faith and righteousness to know what you should do and how to bring it about. The sons of Mosiah were blessed with the gift of prophecy and revelation and the gift of teaching with power and authority about God. How did they receive these gifts? "They had searched the scriptures diligently, that they might know the word of God. But this is not all; they had given themselves to much prayer, and fasting" (Alma 17:2–3). The Lord told Joseph Smith: "For thou shalt devote all thy service in Zion; and in this thou shalt have strength. . . . And in temporal labors thou shalt not have strength, for this is not thy calling" (D&C 24:7, 9). The prophet's gifts were in spiritual service, not in commercial affairs.
  - Ask your loved ones what gifts they see manifest in you. Ask them what added gifts would be helpful to the family. Moses was weak in the gift of delegation, but his father-in-law, Jethro, taught him the principle of delegation with good outcomes (see Ex. 18:13–27).
  - Ask your Church leaders. A viable answer comes in the form of callings extended to you over time. Leaders may be impressed to call you on the basis of your record of achievement or your potential for service.
  - Ask the professionals. Sometimes well-established personality tests can reveal patterns of strength that you can aspire to cultivate. Do you have special capability in seeing the big picture and conceiving broad plans and strategies? Are you skilled in the mastery of detail? Do you have gifts in social relationships and networking? Are you accomplished at getting things done and inspiring others to action? Or do you have certain combinations of these traits? How can you bring forth talents that need improvement?
  - Above all, ask the Spirit. Listen to promptings and whisperings that guide you in the development of gifts and talents that will help others and bless their lives—as well as your own.

- **Knock**—The Lord has promised that the door will be opened unto you. But it takes action on your part, for the Lord has declared: "Verily I say, men should be anxiously engaged in a good cause, and do many things of their own free will, and bring to pass much righteousness; For the power is in them, wherein they are agents unto themselves. And inasmuch as men do good they shall in nowise lose their reward" (D&C 58:27–28).
  - When you knock with faith and trust in the Lord, the needed gifts and talents will emerge to enable you to accomplish worthy goals, as Nephi confirmed: "I will go and do the things which the Lord hath commanded, for I know that the Lord giveth no commandments unto the children of men, save he shall prepare a way for them that they may accomplish the thing which he commandeth them" (1 Ne. 3:7).
  - Move forward by depending on the Lord: "In the strength of the Lord you can do all things" (Alma 20:4). "And Jesus looking upon them saith, With men it is impossible, but not with God: for with God all things are possible" (Mark 10:27).

- Be patient as you act: "And inasmuch as they follow the counsel which they receive, they shall have power after many days to accomplish all things pertaining to Zion" (D&C 105:37).

How Can We Learn to Teach and Learn By the Spirit?

The Lord's grand blessing to mankind is the ability to communicate and learn through the Spirit. The foundation for all learning is the word of God as recorded in the scriptures and given by the voice of living prophets. The Spirit of the Lord confirms the truth of the word of God and brings peace and light into the lives of those who study the gospel and desire to learn more of the Lord and His ways: "Therefore, why is it that ye cannot understand and know, that he that receiveth the word by the Spirit of truth receiveth it as it is preached by the Spirit of truth?" (D&C 50:21).

The Doctrine and Covenants is the Lord's confirming handbook for seeking and receiving the gifts of the Spirit and also for teaching and learning by the Spirit. The gifts of the Spirit "are given for the benefit of those who love me and keep all my commandments, and him that seeketh so to do; that all may be benefited" (D&C 46:9). Through the Spirit we can add light and truth to our lives and strengthen our families by giving them greater access to the blessings of the Lord: "That which is of God is light; and he that receiveth light, and continueth in God, receiveth more light; and that light groweth brighter and brighter until the perfect day" (D&C 50:24). With faith and diligence, we can seek the blessings of the Spirit in our teaching and learning opportunities so that we may come to "know the truth of all things" (Moro. 10:5).

How can you achieve a more spiritual approach to teaching and learning? Missionaries understand that the Spirit does the teaching. They establish a spiritual learning environment and assist learners to open their hearts to the influence of the Spirit. How have you observed that the process of learning and teaching by the Spirit brings grand blessings into the lives of those involved? By contrast, how have you observed that the process of teaching and learning based solely or predominantly on personal judgment and reasoning does not change lives for the better with anywhere near such a high degree of success? How can you make sure you teach in a way that the light is expanded and people are blessed?

What Is Meant by the Gifts of Knowing the "Differences of Administration" and the "Diversities of Operations" (D&C 46:15–16)?

There is a depth of meaning and purpose associated with each of the gifts of the Spirit. Most of those mentioned in Section 46 of the Doctrine and Covenants (verses 13–26) are fairly understandable; several, however, might require additional explanation. For example, what is meant by the gift to know "the differences of administration" (verse 15)? This seems to refer to understanding the various offices and callings in the priesthood and how they function harmoniously to bring about the designs of the Almighty in blessing His sons and daughters. A related gift, "to know the diversities of operations, whether they be of God, that the manifestations of the Spirit may be given to every man to profit withal" (D&C 46:16), seems to refer to the ability to discern between influences that are of divine origin and opposing influences of an evil origin (such as naysayers like Sherem, Nehor, Amlici, and Korihor in the Book of Mormon). Surely the ability to discern such influences is essential in preserving the sanctity of the kingdom of God and protecting Zion.

In your experience, how have you observed the grand governance system of the Church (differences of administration) working through the inspiration of the Spirit? How can you contribute to that wonderful system? Also, all those who embark in the service of God will from time to time encounter contrary spirits who tend to belittle divine truth and disparage the good news of the gospel of Christ. The Lord has made clear that the most powerful strategy to use in all such cases is to follow the Spirit. When encountering influences of a misguided nature, how have you been able to detect and fend off such influences through the power of the Spirit?

Real-life Stories for Heart and Mind

The Lord Had Made the Choice. A stake presidency considered the assignment of selecting a new bishop to be a solemn and sacred task, not one to be accomplished without first praying and fasting for the Spirit. Several candidates were interviewed, one after the other—all good and noble men with great talent and capability, all men of God. But the Spirit whispered clearly, not once but several times in a row: "Not these, but him." The person identified by the Spirit was not on the short list at all. All three members of the presidency independently felt the prompting. What a joy to disclose to each other after the interviews that the same prompting had come to each, and that the Lord had made the choice. They needed only to obey. Subsequently the good brother who had somehow at first been placed in the background was then dutifully called and served faithfully as a bishop. He had the gifts of the Spirit needed to serve the ward over which he presided. The Lord makes these calls. It is His Church. He looks upon the heart and reads the measure of talent and ability needed for a given mission. When the Lord extends the call, it is a divine call, attended with heavenly blessings of a very specific kind for His children: "According as his divine power hath given unto us all things that pertain unto life and godliness, through the knowledge of him that hath called us to glory and virtue" (2 Pet. 1:3).

As you consider the callings you have received in the Church, what are your thoughts about the fact that these callings came from the Lord? How did He bless you with the gifts of the Spirit needed to prosper and succeed in these callings?

No Word Was Said. He was a tall, impressive young man, one of the stalwarts in the ward—and now the bishop had the task of trying to comfort him at the unexpected loss of his sweetheart. What can a young bishop say in circumstances like that? The answer: nothing. The Spirit prompted silence. The bishop stood eye-to-eye with this noble brother, clasping his hand, and they simply shed a few mutual tears together. The Spirit did the talking. It whispered that this mortal experience sometimes involves great trials and always involves death, sometimes sooner than expected. It is all part of the plan. It will be all right. There will be a reunion. The Atonement provides the way for life to be restored and couples to be together. Through faithfulness and devotion, families are forever. No word was said on that occasion. But the two men both knew the truth.

When have you experienced the power of silence in this way—the kind of silence and listening that permits the Holy Ghost, the Comforter, to do the talking with power and peace?

Angels on Earth. A young couple was discouraged. First of all, they were in a new environment far away from their extended families. Second of all, the matchbox student apartment lost in that vast city was rather sparse, bleak, and noisy. The two sat glumly pondering their options. Suddenly there was a knock on the door. Who could that be? A look through the peephole revealed their newly assigned home teacher. He exuded his normal jolly enthusiasm. "I was just driving along the street," he said, "and had the feeling I should stop by! How are you?" Since melancholy cannot long survive in an atmosphere of sincere friendship, the couple quickly fell in with the spirit of rejuvenation.

I had the feeling I should stop by! The gospel is like that. In moments when you are staring downward, the Spirit suddenly illuminates your soul and you are able to look upward instead—with hope and cheer. In moments when the shadows are gathering, the light suddenly enters your heart and fills you with radiance. In the Lord's plan, there are unseen angels who bear you up, just as there are angels on earth who just happen to stop by when the Spirit whispers to them that you have a need. The light of the gospel is strong enough to break through all of life's challenges with its warmth and peace.

Think of the "angels on earth" who may have used the gifts of the Spirit to encourage you, cheer you up, edify you, and strengthen your hope and resolve. How have you been able to follow their example in helping others with the gifts of the Spirit that have been given to you?

Gifts of the Kingdom. He was somewhat older than the average missionary, but his enthusiasm to preach the gospel was no less vibrant and energetic. He arrived with a group of new missionaries at the mission home in a distant German city, anxious to go to work. It was the custom in that mission to introduce new missionaries to proselyting work by having them participate in a street meeting soon after their arrival. So the senior missionaries accompanied these new elders, none of whom could speak German, to a popular square in the center of the city to hold a street meeting for small gatherings of curious passersby and to distribute tracts about the Church. The new missionaries bore their testimony in English, and the veteran missionaries translated for the German listeners. But when it came time for this older missionary to speak, he smiled with a glowing countenance and said, "I won't need you to translate." Then he bore his testimony in German, speaking fluently and expressively, witnessing of the truthfulness of the gospel and the restored Church to an attentive audience. The rest of the missionaries were amazed. Afterwards, the senior missionary asked him whether he had ever studied the German language, and he responded that he had heard some of his relatives speak a few words years earlier. On this occasion, however, he felt inspired to speak to the people in their own language—and so he did. It was a heartwarming display of the gifts of the Spirit at work in a faithful and humble servant of God.

The Prophet Joseph Smith explained that the gift of tongues "was particularly instituted for the preaching of the Gospel to other nations and languages" (HC 2:162)—a phenomenon in widespread evidence among the many tens of thousands of missionaries who are on the Lord's errand in countries where they need to teach in a foreign tongue. How have you observed the gift of tongues at work in the missionary force of the Lord's Church?

Pondering Prayerfully

Additional scriptures to consider and ponder:
- Rom. 8:6
- 1 Cor. 12:21–7
- Gal. 5:22–3
- Alma 1:26
- 3 Ne. 12:13–16
- D&C 20:60
- D&C 46:7
- D&C 88:118

The following hymns might contribute to understanding the gifts of the Spirit:
- "God of Power, God of Right" (*Hymns,* 20)
- "Lord, Accept Our True Devotion" (*Hymns,* 107)
- "Scatter Sunshine" (*Hymns,* 230)

Remember and Be Sure

Achieving spirituality is necessary in order to live a life in harmony with the gospel of Jesus Christ. The blessings and gifts of the Spirit are essential in all that we do. We simply cannot achieve righteousness without the Spirit. Such a state of being is one of humility where we submit our will to the will of the Father by the power of the Holy Ghost. In doing this, we become more spiritual by nature.

The fruits of spirituality are the Christlike qualities of goodness and compassion, with a disposition to serve others—without even the slightest hint of gaining recognition for personal position, station, or calling. Spirituality is the gateway to understanding God, for whom all things have a spiritual foundation (see D&C 29:34). Let us therefore commit ourselves to cultivating a more spiritual lifestyle in keeping with the commandments of God. Let us seek the best gifts of the Spirit and apply them in charity and service for the good of our families, neighbors, and fellow members of the Church.

CHAPTER 23
Of These Emblems: The Sacrament

Order, reverence, attention to divine promises—the promise to enter into the fold of Christ, to cherish virtues mentioned in the gospel of Christ, to keep them ever in mind, to love the Lord wholeheartedly, and to labor, even at the sacrifice of self, for the brotherhood of man—these and all kindred virtues are associated with the partaking of the sacrament. —David O. McKay (*Gospel Ideals: Selections from the Discourses of David O. McKay*, 146–147)

Opening the Window of Wisdom

The sacrament of the Lord's supper is a beautiful and hallowed ordinance in which the majesty of the Atonement and our obedient acceptance of the Lord's sacrifice on our behalf are made a central part of our worship. The sacrament is an extension of our covenant promises to our Father in Heaven and His Only Begotten Son, the Lamb of God. The blessings we receive on this earth come from God our Father through and because of His Beloved Son, Jesus Christ, our Lord and Savior. By partaking of the sacrament, we symbolically partake of His atoning sacrifice with all of its accompanying blessings. We take His name upon us and covenant to remember Him always and keep His commandments, thus qualifying to have His Spirit with us continually.

The commandments of God are designed to bring us happiness and joy and lead us to immortality and eternal life according to the work and glory of God (see Moses 1:39). As we begin to acquire the divine nature of Christ, we will be full of charity, we will love one another and we will treat others according to the pattern shown us by the Lord. We look to our Savior for all things. He is "the light and the life of the world" (Mosiah 16:9; 3 Ne. 9:18), "the word of truth and righteousness" (Alma 38:9)—even "the true vine" (John 15:1) that gives us sustenance and strength. He is our rock and foundation upon which we can build (see Hel. 5:12). His gospel of redemption is the power to draw us to Him and is the foundation of His Church (see 3 Ne. 27:8–15). He is the light that we look to and hold up (see 3 Ne. 18:24; 12:15; 15:12–16). He is the strength through which we can do all things (see Alma 20:4). It is His word and His Spirit that will tell us all that we should do (see 2 Ne. 32:3, 5).

On our own, we are nothing (see Mosiah 4:5, 11)—but in the strength and goodness of the Lord we can do all things (see Alma 26:11–12). Our Heavenly Father does everything through His Beloved Son, Jesus Christ (see D&C 50:27; 76:13). The sacrament is the key to remembering who we are, who the Savior is, and how we can honor our covenants through obedience to the commandments, thus having the Holy Ghost to guide our footsteps forward on the pathway to eternal life and exaltation. As the "living bread" (John 6:51) and the "fountain of living waters" (Jer. 17:13), the Savior is commemorated in the sacrament as all who partake renew their covenants and commit to live lives worthy of His Spirit. The sacrament is a profoundly sacred ordinance instituted to help us remember.

Inspired by Latter-Day Prophets

George Albert Smith: The sacrament is of great importance. The Lord himself ordained that we partake of these emblems. . . . It was regarded of such importance by our Father in Heaven that, through his Beloved Son, and the Apostles and prophets, as recorded in the scriptures, the Saints were admonished to partake of it regularly (*The Teachings of George Albert Smith*, 95).

The Spirit we receive by remembering to honor our covenants through the sacrament ordinance will give us spiritual strength and will help us influence those around us for good. One reason for this is that by partaking worthily of the bread of life and the living water, we bring into our life light that can be perceived by others. How does this bring a new perspective concerning the experience of the sacrament?

Joseph Fielding Smith: To "always remember him," does not mean simply to remember that he was crucified; but to keep in mind constantly the reasons why, and what blessings have come to each of us through his death and resurrection. We are to remember the great suffering and what it cost him to make the great atonement. We are to remember that he did it because of his love, not only for those who believe on him, but also for the whole world (*Answers to Gospel Questions*, 3:4).

Focusing on the "why" of the divine sacrifice reminds us of the grand blessings of the Atonement. As you focus on the "why," what special blessings come to mind in your own life and that of your family?

Spencer W. Kimball: Remembering covenants prevents apostasy. That is the real purpose of the sacrament, to keep us from forgetting, to help us to remember. I suppose there would never be an apostate, there would never be a crime, if people remembered, really remembered, the things they

had covenanted at the water's edge or at the sacrament table and in the temple. . . . The Nephites forgot (*The Teachings of Spencer W. Kimball*, 112).

The Lord in His mercy uses a common, everyday activity—taking nourishment—to remind us of sacred obligations. We partake of the sacrament frequently because we as mortals tend to forget frequently. What other reminders can you think of that the Lord has placed before us so that we will remember?

Howard W. Hunter: To make a covenant with the Lord to always keep his commandments is a serious obligation, and to renew that covenant by partaking of the sacrament is equally serious. The solemn moments of thought while the sacrament is being served have great significance. They are moments of self-examination, introspection, self-discernment—a time to reflect and to resolve (*The Teachings of Howard W. Hunter*, 110).

We have a choice as to what occupies our thoughts and sentiments during the sacrament. President Hunter suggests that we focus on God and our commitment to keep the commandments. What "solemn moments of thought" and resolutions do you strive to have during the sacrament?

Truths to Liken

Matt. 26:26–28—"And as they were eating, Jesus took bread, and blessed it, and brake it, and gave it to the disciples, and said, Take, eat; this is my body. And he took the cup, and gave thanks, and gave it to them, saying, Drink ye all of it; For this is my blood of the new testament, which is shed for many for the remission of sins."

- The Savior instituted the sacrament among His disciples just before His experience in Gethsemane and Golgotha. This "new testament" or "new covenant" was established by the Savior that we might remember Him and apply the Atonement in our lives through repentance and by following gospel principles. Since the scripture above was given before His atoning sacrifice, so He had not yet been "broken," He blessed the bread first and then broke it. When the resurrected Lord visited the Saints on the American continent, He broke the bread first—because He had already accomplished His atoning sacrifice—and then He blessed it (see 3 Ne. 18:3).

- The sacrament ordinance is directly in step with the sacrificing of the Lamb of God. Only by always remembering this can we also become attuned to the love of the Redeemer in performing such an act of mercy. Amulek taught that the Atonement was necessary to bring "means unto men that they may have faith unto repentance" (Alma 34:15). How does the sacrament help you to increase your faith unto repentance?

3 Ne. 18:10–12—"And when the Disciples had done this, Jesus said unto them: Blessed are ye for this thing which ye have done, for this is fulfilling my commandments, and this doth witness unto the Father that ye are willing to do that which I have commanded you. And this shall ye always do to those who repent and are baptized in my name; and ye shall do it in remembrance of my blood, which I have shed for you, that ye may witness unto the Father that ye do always remember me. And if ye do always remember me ye shall have my Spirit to be with you. And I give unto you a commandment that ye shall do these things. And if ye shall always do these things blessed are ye, for ye are built upon my rock."

- Having instituted the sacrament among His Saints in ancient America, the resurrected Lord blessed His disciples for administering the sacrament obediently and declared that in their faithfulness they were built upon His rock.
- In what ways are you built upon the rock of Christ in partaking worthily of the sacrament and renewing your covenants faithfully?

Rejoicing and Reasoning Together

Lessons of History: How Is the Sacrament a Timeless Ordinance?

It is a matter of tender poignancy that the Savior instituted the sacrament during the celebration of the Passover—with its unleavened bread and offering of the sacrificial lamb—because it was on this particular occasion that He Himself was shortly to become the sacrificial Lamb of God. The Savior sent Peter and John to prepare the Passover supper, telling them to go in quest of a man bearing a pitcher of water within the city who would guide them to a place where they could gather in privacy. At the appointed hour, the Savior and His Twelve Apostles celebrated the last of their suppers together: "And he took bread, and gave thanks, and brake it, and gave unto them, saying, This is my body which is given for you: this do in remembrance of me. Likewise also the cup after supper, saying, This cup is the new testament in my blood, which is shed for you" (Luke 22:19–20).

On that occasion the Savior announced the disconcerting news that one among them would betray Him: "But, behold, the hand of him that betrayeth me is with me on the table" (Luke 22:21). In the wake of that devastating revelation, the disciples discussed who might be the greatest among them. The Savior provided the key: he who *serves* is the chief—a reference to His divine role as atoning servant for all mankind, being the Exemplar in whose footsteps all should follow. As reported by John, the Savior washed the feet of the disciples following the supper (see John 13:4–10). When Peter proclaimed his unshakable allegiance to the Master, he heard the troubling prophecy that even he would deny the Savior three times before the crowing of the cock (see Luke 22:34). Thereafter the Savior retired to the Mount of Olives. His hour had come.

Not long after that, the resurrected Lord visited His Saints in the New World and instituted there also the sacrament of the Lord's supper—an ordinance that was perpetuated for many generations. The story of how Moroni, the final curator and contributor to the sacred records, gave an additional witness concerning the sacrament is a moving confirmation of his loyalty and obedience. Having completed the abridgement of the Book of Ether, he continued with his perilous existence, moving about on the battlefield alone and secretively among contending Lamanite factions. He knew that he would be killed if he were captured—unless he openly denied the Christ. He refused to deny the Christ, so he avoided being discovered at all costs. Within this framework of threatened existence, he still focused on what he might do to add value to the lives of his anchorless Lamanite brethren and others who might in the future receive the history of his people. Therefore, he determined to add somewhat to the record he had already made by including choice and uplifting instructions on the sacramental prayers, the requirements for baptism, our nurturing responsibility as members, the doctrine of fasting and prayer, the commandment to meet together often to partake of the sacrament, the constant need for repentance, and how to ensure that our meetings are conducted by the Spirit (see Moro. 1–6). We can feel deep gratitude to the Lord for these precious truths. In regard to the sacrament, there is confirmation in the sacramental prayers provided (Moro. 4:3; 5:2)—these prayers being the same as provided in D&C 20:77, 79—that this is a timeless ordinance, consistently administered in all settings subsequent to the mortal ministry of the Savior.

Just as the sacrament is a timeless ordinance, having been introduced by our Lord and Master as a permanent rite of worship in the kingdom of God, so is the essential need to remember our covenants of timeless importance. As you partake of the sacrament and remember our Lord, you might also remember from time to time the imperiled existence of Moroni as he labored continually to preserve the sacred record and bear witness to his future readers of the truthfulness of the gospel—including the Atonement and all related principles and ordinances, such as the sacrament. In a way, we too live an imperiled life—assaulted as we are on all sides by unrighteous influences and temptations. Let us stand firm like Moroni and keep the commandments of the Lord! How can you use the sacrament to remember your commitments to Heavenly Father and His Son and thus, in the strength of the Lord and through the blessings of His Spirit, remain faithful to the end?

Real-life Stories for Heart and Mind

The Lesson of the Hands. While visiting a branch of the Church in an outlying area, a member of a stake presidency sat on the stand observing the young Aaronic Priesthood brethren as they prepared to administer the sacrament. They were impressive in their Sunday attire, doing their best to fulfill their duty while on the Lord's errand. The sacrament song that day was a well-known hymn with the opening line "While of these emblems we partake, In Jesus' name and for his sake." As the congregation sang the words, "Let us remember and be sure our hearts and hands are clean and pure," the visitor from the stake presidency happened to be looking down at one of the young deacons. He was leaning forward, elbows on knees, with both hands outstretched in front of him, palms facing upward toward his countenance. This young deacon was gazing at his hands intently as if to find reassurance that he was, indeed, a worthy servant of the Lord about to participate in a sacred ordinance. The image of the young man with his extended hands was unforgettable. Our hands are, indeed, a constant reminder that we should be continually engaged in the Lord's errand, ever intent on keeping His commandments, ever vigilant that our hearts and hands remain unsullied by the world's ungodly practices, ever committed to that which is ennobling and edifying. "Be ye clean, that bear the vessels of the Lord" (Isa. 52:11).

The sacrament is the Lord's special ordinance to help us remember our covenants in honoring the Atonement through humble obedience. To partake of the sacrament we must, of course, use our hands. Should we not also think of our hands as a constant, ever-present lesson in remembering who we are as sons and daughters of God, reaching out to our Savior in gratitude? Look at your hands. Remember the hands of the Savior who hung on the cross to do the will of the Father. Reach out to others. Hold their hands. Listen to the Spirit. "Learn of me, and listen to my words; walk in the meekness of my Spirit, and you shall have peace in me" (D&C 19:23).

Looking Forward. Every Sunday, members of the Church have the singular opportunity to participate in the sacrament, a blessing and an opportunity of exceptional depth and reverence. We can watch those young men each week bearing the vessels of the Lord with such humility and care. Alma explained that participating in priesthood service imparts a unique perspective—one that is forward-looking and future-centered: "Now these ordinances were given after this manner, that thereby the people might look forward on the Son of God, it being a type of his order, or it being his order, and this that they might look forward to him for a remission of their sins, that they might enter into the rest of the Lord" (Alma 13:16). What a marvelous blessing for these young men, participating in the administration of the sacrament and preparing for their future priesthood duties, to be called by the Lord and thus blessed with the means of looking forward to Him in love and righteousness, having a clear view of their future pathway. Through their priesthood service they can anticipate with the eye of faith their ultimate state of becoming the sons of God who will one day receive a reward of glory and immortality in keeping with Alma's admonition: "Having faith on the Lord; having a hope that ye shall receive eternal life; having the love of God always in your hearts, that ye may be lifted up at the last day and enter into his rest" (Alma 13:29).

The sacrament allows all of us—men, women, and children—to look forward with hope to the blessings of a future life in the mansions of heaven as part of the eternal family of God. Think of your experience participating in the sacrament. How does it help you to look forward with faith and joy?

Pondering Prayerfully

Additional scriptures to consider and ponder:
- 1 Cor. 11:26–29
- D&C 20:77
- D&C 20:79
- D&C 27:2

The following hymns contribute to an understanding of and gratitude for the sacrament:
- "O God, the Eternal Father" (*Hymns,* 175)
- "While of These Emblems We Partake" (*Hymns,* 173)

Remember and Be Sure

The sacrament is a vital part of Heavenly Father's plan to help us keep the commandments and become perfected in Christ (see Moro. 10:32–33). The Atonement of our Savior draws us to Him (see 3 Ne. 27:14–15), and when we partake of the sacrament, we can remember Him and renew our covenants. The sacrament is the "bread of life" (John 6:35, 48) and the "living water" (John 4:10). It is a sacred way to show our reverence for and love to our Father and His Son. The sacrament prayers are covenant prayers, for they promise us, through our grateful obedience, that we will have the blessing of the Spirit to be with us always.

The sacrament is an ordinance performed not in private, but in congregations of the Saints, emphasizing unity and fellowship in honoring our covenants. The sacrament uses the plural form of the pronouns: "we ask thee," "that they may eat," "that they are willing," "that they may always have his Spirit." The principle of togetherness through the sacrament helps us focus on being "fellowcitizens with the saints, and of the household of God" (Eph. 2:19). It is a weekly reminder that we are truly part of the family of God, for which we can be eternally grateful.

CHAPTER 24
The Sabbath: The Lord's Day

The purpose of the Sabbath is for spiritual uplift, for a renewal of our covenants, for worship, for rest, for prayer. It is for the purpose of feeding the spirit, that we may keep ourselves unspotted from the world by obeying God's command. (D&C 59:9.) —Ezra Taft Benson (*The Teachings of Ezra Taft Benson,* 438)

Opening the Window of Wisdom

The Sabbath is the Lord's day. He made it for us, commanding: "Remember the sabbath day, to keep it holy" (Ex. 20:8). The purpose of the Sabbath day is to worship God, rest from our daily labors, renew our covenants, pray together, receive instruction in the ways of the Lord through the word of God, and receive edification to our spirits—all in order to become more pure and grateful before the Lord. The Sabbath is a reminder that we should practice pure religion by keeping ourselves unspotted from the world and by caring for those who need help (see James 1:27). Honoring the Sabbath is not only one of the Ten Commandments, but signifies our enduring covenant with God and our willing dependence on Him: "Verily my sabbaths ye shall keep: for it is a sign between me and you throughout your generations; that ye may know that I am the Lord that doth sanctify you" (Ex. 31:13).

On one occasion the Savior was passing through the fields of the countryside with His followers. Because His disciples were hungry, they plucked ears of corn (that is, heads of grain) to eat. Such behavior caused concern among the Pharisees, who judged it to be a violation of the law that provided stringent rules for keeping the Sabbath day holy. The Savior responded by referring them to instances in the scriptures where leaders apparently violated the Sabbath day without punishment or consequence. Then the Savior stated the truth of the matter: "For the Son of man is Lord even of the Sabbath" (Matt. 12:8).

Later the Savior healed the withered hand of a man on the Sabbath, reminding the concerned priests who sought to find a cause against Him: "What man shall there be among you, that shall have one sheep, and if it fall into a pit on the sabbath day, will he not lay hold on it, and lift it out? How much then is a man better than a sheep? Wherefore it is lawful to do well on the sabbath days" (Matt. 12:11–12).

On another occasion the Lord healed a woman of a serious infirmity on the Sabbath day, much to the indignation of the ruler of the synagogue. The Savior responded: "Thou hypocrite, doth not each one of you on the sabbath loose his ox or his ass from the stall, and lead him away to watering? And ought not this woman, being a daughter of Abraham, whom Satan hath bound, lo, these eighteen years, be loosed from this bond on the sabbath day? And when he had said these things, all his adversaries were ashamed: and all the people rejoiced for all the glorious things that were done by him" (Luke 13:15–17).

The Sabbath is a day of rest, as Moses learned early in his ministry (see Moses 3:2–3). It is ordained of God that we should rest from our temporal duties on His holy day, ensuring that we consecrate our lives to the God who gave us life: "Six days shalt thou labour, and do all thy work: But the seventh day is the sabbath of the LORD thy God: in it thou shalt not do any work, thou, nor thy son, nor thy daughter, thy manservant, nor thy maidservant, nor thy cattle, nor thy stranger that is within thy gates" (Ex. 20:9–10). We can honor the Sabbath by renewing our covenant of obedience through the sacrament and celebrating God's goodness and mercy. We can elevate our minds to God through edifying expressions of praise and celebration. Songs of glory, poetry of honor, sayings of truth, artwork of beauty and dignity—all these are reminders of our divine heritage and our noble birthright.

Moses taught his people to cultivate the highest form of expression in remembering and celebrating God's goodness. He taught them songs of praise that kept the covenant ideas and commitment alive in their hearts. He taught them to think in terms of the "rock of their salvation" (in other words, Jesus Christ—see Deut. 32:15, 18, 30–31). He used words that edified and lifted. He rehearsed God's mercy and triumph in unforgettable terms: "For the LORD's portion is his people; Jacob is the lot of his inheritance. He found him in a desert land, and in the waste howling wilderness; he led him about, he instructed him, he kept him as the apple of his eye. As an eagle stirreth up her nest, fluttereth over her young, spreadeth abroad her wings, taketh them, beareth them on her wings: So the Lord alone did lead him" (Deut. 32:9–12). Moses also was explicit in his images of warning for Israel, that they might be stirred up to remembering the Lord their God (see Deut. 32:15–43). We can learn from these ancient patterns of keeping the Sabbath day holy and fill our Latter-day Sabbaths with veneration and reverence, honor and peace.

There are grand blessings in store when we keep the Sabbath day holy. When we enter into the Sabbath, we enter into a holy state of being—one in which rich blessings lie in store for those who serve the Lord in righteousness and bring Him gifts of devotion and prayerful worship. The blessings of the Sabbath include peace, spirituality, unity with family and friends, enhanced understanding of the plan of salvation, humility, spiritual awakenings, escape from the fetters of earthly burdens and pressures, and the satisfaction of knowing that one is abiding by the will of the Lord.

Inspired by Latter-Day Prophets

David O. McKay: Sunday is a day of rest, essential to the true development and strength of the body, and that is a principle which we should publish more generally abroad and practise (*Gospel Ideals: Selections from the Discourses of David O. McKay*, 397).

> *It is revealing to hear a prophet of the Lord teach that honoring the day of rest is essential for our health—both physical and spiritual. It is also revealing to remember that the Sabbath day commemorates the resurrection of the Great Healer, even Jesus Christ, who rose on the first day of the week, now celebrated as the Sabbath day (see Acts 20:7; 1 Cor. 16:2). What are your thoughts about placing the Sabbath day in the context of health and healing? How does it help you to view the commandment to keep the Sabbath day holy not as a restriction but as the gateway to great blessings of well-being and spiritual vitality?*

Spencer W. Kimball: The Sabbath is a holy day in which to do worthy and holy things. Abstinence from work and recreation is important but insufficient. The Sabbath calls for constructive thoughts and acts, and if one merely lounges about doing nothing on the Sabbath, he is breaking it. To observe it, one will be on his knees in prayer, preparing lessons, studying the gospel, meditating, visiting the ill and distressed, sleeping, reading wholesome material, and attending all the meetings of that day to which he is expected. To fail to do these proper things is a transgression on the omission side (*The Miracle of Forgiveness*, 96–97).

> *It is helpful to have a prophet define rest as it pertains to the Sabbath. The Sabbath is indeed a day of action as well as repose,*

service as well as prayer. It is a day of balance and harmony, not one of laziness and emptiness. What is the pattern that you and your loved ones tend to follow on the Sabbath? How might this pattern be enriched and augmented with actions that will produce even greater joy and happiness for you and those you serve?

Harold B. Lee: Reverence defined is profound respect, mingled with love and awe, for a holy being, place, or exalted thing. . . . We reverence that which we love, adore, or respect. Reverence is a quality of the soul which needs a proper climate in which to flourish (*The Teachings of Harold B. Lee,* 202).

How have you been able to cultivate and encourage reverence as the quality most appropriate to the Sabbath day?

Bruce R. McConkie: The Sabbath is a day of worship. It is the Lord's day, a day on which we renew our allegiance to that Lord on whose errand we serve. On the Sabbath day we feed our spirits, we feast upon the word of Christ, and we renew our covenants to serve him with all our might, mind, and strength (*A New Witness for the Articles of Faith,* 300).

To love the Lord and refresh our promises to Him in obedience is the essence of Sabbath worship. What are your thoughts about the nourishment and spiritual vitality that come from honoring the Sabbath day?

Truths to Liken

Mark 2:27—"And he said unto them, The sabbath was made for man, and not man for the Sabbath."

- When the Pharisees observed the Lord's disciples picking ears of corn (heads of grain) in the fields on the Sabbath, they were offended. The Lord reminded them that David, when hungered, was offered hallowed bread by the high priest of the Lord, something that was appropriate but not according to the letter of the law. When this happened, David and his followers were fleeing the murderous plots of King Saul and needed help.

- The Savior shed light on the genuine spirit of the Sabbath. Too many times the Sabbath day is viewed as a day of "do nots" rather than an opportunity to do many things that are holy and uplifting: worship, pay homage to our Heavenly Father and Savior, rest from our daily labors, be filled with the words of truth, bless our brothers and sisters, and be with the family. How can you help others remove the Sabbath day from a context of restrictions and prohibitions and place it into a context of doing good, creating joy, and blessing lives?

3 Ne. 18:6–7—"And this shall ye always observe to do, even as I have done, even as I have broken bread and blessed it and given it unto you. And this shall ye do in remembrance of my body, which I have shown unto you. And it shall be a testimony unto the Father that ye do always remember me. And if ye do always remember me ye shall have my Spirit to be with you."

- The resurrected Lord established the sacrament among the Saints in the New World, reminding them that the great blessing of honoring the Sabbath is to receive His Spirit.
- The Sabbath and the sacrament are anchored fundamentally in the process of becoming worthy to receive the Spirit of the Lord. To remember the Lord in obedience is to receive of His Spirit—a glorious blessing of eternal consequence. We are promised that the Holy Ghost will show us "all things" that we should do (see 2 Ne. 32:5). How does the Sabbath open the gateway of spiritual wisdom for you, revealing all that you should do? How can you help others to see the Sabbath in this way—as a blessing from God to guide us toward salvation and exaltation?

D&C 59:8–16—"Thou shalt offer a sacrifice unto the Lord thy God in righteousness, even that of a broken heart and a contrite spirit. And that thou mayest more fully keep thyself unspotted from the world, thou shalt go to the house of prayer and offer up thy sacraments upon my holy day; For verily this is a day appointed unto you to rest from your labors, and to pay thy devotions unto the Most High; Nevertheless thy vows shall be offered up in righteousness on all days and at all times; But remember that on this, the Lord's day, thou shalt offer thine oblations and thy sacraments unto the Most High, confessing thy sins unto thy brethren, and before the Lord. And on this day thou shalt do none other thing, only let thy food be prepared with singleness of heart that thy fasting may be perfect, or, in other words, that thy joy may be full. Verily, this is fasting and prayer, or in other words, rejoicing and prayer. And inasmuch as ye do these things with thanksgiving, with cheerful hearts and countenances, not with much laughter, for this is sin, but with a glad heart and a cheerful countenance—Verily I say, that inasmuch as ye do this, the fulness of the earth is yours."

- These magnificent words were included in a revelation given through the Prophet Joseph Smith in Zion (Jackson County, Missouri) on August 7, 1831.
- The Sabbath is a day of latter-day sacrifice where we come before the Lord humbly, with broken hearts and contrite spirits, ready to receive blessings of joy and spiritual nourishment from "the bread of life" (John 6:35, 48) and the "living water" (John 4:10). How can you more fully make the Sabbath a day of rejoicing and happiness? What are your thoughts about the injunction to "confess thy sins" to others on the Sabbath? How is the Sabbath a high point of worship that overflows into all the days of the week?

Rejoicing and Reasoning Together

How Can We Enhance Reverence on the Sabbath Day?

Listed below are three things you can do to cultivate reverence and help others to do likewise:

1. Decide in your heart what it is you truly revere in life. Without reverence for Heavenly Father and His Son, there is no reverence for life. To come to know of Their exalted goodness is to be filled with reverence for Their eternal work on behalf of all mankind. Reverence nurtures humility; humility brings dependence on the Lord; dependence on the Lord ensures the unfolding of charitable deeds in the service of others—all based on the values and principles we hold dear. Moreover, when we cultivate reverence for the word of God we will come to understand the blessing and power of the scriptures in our lives, for the word enhances faith, and faith is the power by which all good things are accomplished. Reverence for the handiwork of God is also a staple in our spiritual growth, for there is dignity in all of God's magnificent creations. In addition, reverence for life itself and the inborn freedom that all should enjoy here on earth brings courage and hope. When we have reverence and respect for others, we will be more Christlike in our attitudes and actions.

Take time to ponder, meditate, savor the peaceful silence, and cultivate a feeling of thanks in your heart for the blessings of life. The Sabbath day brings an opportunity to ponder the work and greatness of God, His almighty word, the Creation, life itself, the gift of agency, the goodness of our fellow travelers on the pathway to salvation and exaltation—and all things worthy of our reverence. What values and principles do you hold most dear in the spirit of the Sabbath? Is it truth, integrity, honor, courage, respect for the dignity of life, unity, harmony, peace? How can you let others know that you revere and respect such values, and thus confirm for them your testimony of eternal principles?

2. Set an example of reverence for others. You can demonstrate by your language and manner of speaking that you have reverence for others and their beliefs. You can teach others by precept and example the concepts and principles of genuine reverence. You can set an example of reverence for the spiritual aspects of life. You can do this through prayer, dignified worship, reading the scriptures regularly, partaking of the sacrament, preparing for and participating in gospel classes, listening carefully to Sabbath discourse, and giving praise to God through sacred music. There is no greater way to show that you revere and respect people than by serving them willingly. Some have even given their lives for their family or for others—a sacrifice that represents the deepest form of reverence.

As you think of the quality of reverence, especially as it is related to the Sabbath day, which individuals do you admire as examples of reverent worship? If these individuals are still living, how can you express gratitude and admiration for their example? How can you emulate their example?

3. Exercise leadership in cultivating reverence in society. If the Sabbath day is a day of practicing reverence for all the higher things of life, how can you practice that kind of reverence throughout the remainder of the week? Wherever you detect reverence and respect in the community, you can recognize it, reinforce it, and reward it. Watch for examples of young people being reverent and respectful and thank them for their courtesy. You can be reverent and respectful of the environment by doing your part to care for and beautify your space on earth, and then teach others to do the same. You can respect and obey the law. You can be supportive and respectful of the institutions of government that secure to individuals their rights and privileges. You can do this by playing an active role in the community, studying the issues, contributing to civic dialogue, and voting regularly. Above all, you can make the home a place of reverence by cultivating courtesy and respect among family members, fostering uplifting discourse and music, limiting the incursions of raucous and debasing television programs, and maintaining an environment that is peaceful and clean.

Reverence for God and all spiritual matters becomes a stream of living water that flows into all aspects of life: homes, neighborhoods, communities, workplaces. The Sabbath is a day for renewing our commitment to reverence, peace, harmony, and charity. As you examine your life experiences, how can you discern the blessing of Sabbath day reverence flowing to you in unexpected ways throughout the week—especially through the influence of the Spirit of the Lord?

Real-life Stories for Heart and Mind

A Towering Example. One ward enjoys a frequent visitor from the stake high council who cuts a rather unusual figure—if you can call a towering 340-pound gentleman unusual. In his mild and humble way he carries out his business on the Lord's errand with dispatch and self-deprecating modesty. But Eli Herring is special. As a former BYU senior offensive lineman with a 3.5 grade-point average, he declined a potentially lucrative deal with the Oakland Raiders in 1995 because he chose not to play professional football on Sunday. Instead, he decided to become a high school coach and teacher and carry on his service to the Lord in ways aligned more closely with his deeply held values. When he was asked from what source he drew the strength to make such a far-reaching decision, he mentioned four things: (1) his mother, (2) the scriptures and the word of modern prophets, (3) prayer and the strength of his wife—since they had made this decision together, and (4) the example of other men in similar situations. Not too many years later he was called as bishop in his ward and continues to reflect qualities of spiritual valor.

What impact does this kind of spiritual leadership have on others—especially young people? The kind of courage that enables an individual to uphold principles that he or she considers inviolate engenders profound respect. What are your thoughts about being a "hero of the Sabbath" and a "hero of eternal principles"?

The Home Game. He was a bright young man, pleasant and articulate, with a charming wife and a growing family—just the kind of person a bishop would want to have as one of his ward clerks. When the Spirit whispered a quiet confirmation to the bishop one day, he went to visit the young man and extend him an invitation to join the circle of leadership in the ward. The young man was honored by the calling, but somewhat reserved in his response. "Bishop," he said, "I want to be of help. But you know, there is something I need to explain." *Oh-oh,* the bishop thought to himself, preparing to hear a confession. "Ever since I joined the Church a few years ago," he continued, "I have tried to do my duty and attend my meetings, but I have always had season tickets to see our major league team play on Sundays. That's why you don't see me at the meetings sometimes."

The bishop thought about the situation for a few seconds, then felt impressed to offer him a special arrangement. The Lord wanted him to be a part of the team. Therefore, he would complete his

Church assignment to the best of his ability and the bishopric would work around his schedule. When the team was in town with a home game, he would be away, and the bishopric would understand. He accepted the assignment, but the bishop could see that he had a struggle going on inside—and that is just as it should be when one is learning. For the next few months, every time the bishop and his wife drove past the football stadium on the way to their Church meetings, the bishop thought of this young man's struggle.

One Sunday when there was a home game, the bishop was surprised when this young man showed up at his office. He was energized, with a kind of glow about him and a sparkle in his eyes. "Bishop," he said, "I have decided to give up my season tickets. The gospel is more important. I will always be here on the Sabbath." The bishop put his arm around the young man's shoulders and bore witness to the strength and courage of his correct decision. Then the bishop thanked the Lord in his heart for the patient way in which the Spirit works. The words of the Savior came to his mind: "If any man will do his will, he shall know of the doctrine, whether it be of God, or whether I speak of myself" (John 7:17).

There is always a "home game" going on. It takes place within the heart of every individual as he or she engages in the choices of life—the choices that define character and honor and devotion to the cause of building up the kingdom of God. How have you resolved the "home games" in your life, and how has the Spirit blessed you accordingly?

Pondering Prayerfully

Additional scriptures to consider and ponder:
- Ex. 20:11
- Deut. 5:12
- Mark 3:4–6
- Luke 14:5
- Heb. 12:9
- Heb. 12:28
- Mosiah 18:23
- D&C 59:20–21

The following hymns inspire gratitude for the Sabbath:
- "Gently Raise the Sacred Strain" (*Hymns,* 146)
- "Sweet Is the Work" (*Hymns,* 147)
- "Thanks for the Sabbath School" (*Hymns,* 278)
- "Welcome, Welcome, Sabbath Morning" (*Hymns,* 280)

Remember and Be Sure

If a Church member were asked what he or she was hoping for or aspiring to become, the answer would probably be: "I am seeking eternal life and to be like our Savior." We would all agree. We should use our Sabbath days to come closer to our Heavenly Father and our Savior. We need to study and pray. We need to make every effort to acquire those attributes that will help us not only keep the commandments, but in reality become more like the Savior. We should be about our Father's work—bringing "to pass the immortality and eternal life of man" (Moses 1:39). The Sabbath day should surely be spent in this cause. In this way we can sanctify it and keep it holy for the betterment of all of Heavenly Father's children. We will be renewed and strengthened in doing so, thus living throughout the week in harmony with the teachings of the gospel. The Sabbath day is thus not only a day of "rest" (a term related to a Hebrew word of this meaning), but also a day of "becoming," for we become more like the Savior by honoring His sacred day.

Why did the Lord command us to keep the Sabbath day holy? That we might better become holy ourselves: "Whereby are given unto us exceeding great and precious promises: that by these ye might be partakers of the divine nature, having escaped the corruption that is in the world through lust" (2 Pet. 1:4). The Sabbath offers to us an ongoing opportunity to renew our covenants through the sacrament, and to show ourselves worthy to receive greater spiritual blessings—especially the blessing of having access to the Spirit of the Lord to guide and direct us on the pathway of life.

CHAPTER 25
Law of the Fast

Parents who provide a home where gospel principles are lived will have, as the Lord has said, "a house of prayer, a house of fasting, a house of faith, a house of learning, . . . a house of order, a house of God" (D&C 88:119). Regardless of how modest or humble that home may be, it will have love, happiness, peace, and joy. Children will grow up in righteousness and truth, and will desire to serve the Lord. —Ezra Taft Benson (The Teachings of Ezra Taft Benson, 525–526)

Opening the Window of Wisdom

Fasting and giving a generous fast offering for those in need is one of our most holy offerings to God. To fast with joy and humility is to remember things spiritual and to confirm our willingness to place our own desires and needs beneath the will of the Father. To pay our fast offerings with gladness and charity is a step toward true discipleship, because is allows us to practice, if only in a modest way, the redeeming walk that belongs to the kingdom of God: "And on this day thou shalt do none other thing, only let thy food be prepared with singleness of heart that thy fasting may be perfect, or, in other words, that thy joy may be full. Verily, this is fasting and prayer, or in other words, rejoicing and prayer" (D&C 59:13–14).

The faithful who sincerely practice a prayerful fast gain great blessings from God in the form of strengthening, healing, or an increase of understanding. The blessings of the Spirit and the power to teach by that same Spirit come through fasting and prayer (see Alma 17:3, 9). Fasting helps us develop a more contrite disposition in accordance with heavenly principles: "Nevertheless they did fast and pray oft, and did wax stronger and stronger in their humility, and firmer and firmer in the faith of Christ, unto the filling their souls with joy and consolation, yea, even to the purifying and the sanctification of their hearts, which sanctification cometh because of their yielding their hearts unto God" (Hel. 3:35).

The law of the fast, when practiced sincerely, endows us with spiritual power to rise above earthly desires and become more like the Savior. When we pay our fast offerings, we practice the great commandment of love. The Lord is explicit if we fail to care for the needy, saying through His servant Amulek, "And now behold, my beloved brethren, I say unto you, do not suppose that this is all; for after ye have done all these things, if ye turn away the needy, and the naked, and visit not the sick and afflicted, and impart of your substance, if ye have, to those who stand in need—I say unto you, if ye do not any of these things, behold, your prayer is vain, and availeth you nothing, and ye are as hypocrites who do deny the faith" (Alma 34:28).

The Lord in His almighty power stands waiting to bless mankind. It is His agenda that governs the flow of life upon the earth. Through fasting and prayer we can learn of His will and see His hand at work as He manifests Himself and blesses His children. We can literally call down the powers of heaven through the practice of fasting and prayer, for it allows us to overcome and avoid temptation (see 3 Ne. 18:15, 18), gain and strengthen our testimony (see Alma 5:46), bring about the restoration of health (see 2 Sam. 12:15–16), worship with thanksgiving (see Luke 2:37), enjoy the Spirit of revelation and prophecy (see Alma 17:3), bless those who know not God (see Alma 6:6), mourn in righteous sorrow when loved ones depart (Alma 28:2–6), and become sanctified in faith and humility (see Hel. 3:35). The regular practice of fasting and prayer unleashes a dynamic force in our lives, allowing us to tap into the power of God to enrich our lives and make us more valiant servants.

Inspired by Latter-Day Prophets

Joseph F. Smith: The Lord has instituted the fast on a reasonable and intelligent basis, and none of his works are vain or unwise. His law is perfect in this as in other things. Hence, those who can are required to comply thereto; it is a duty from which they cannot escape; but let it be remembered that the observance of the fast day by abstaining twenty-four hours from food and drink is not an absolute rule, it is no iron-clad law to us, but it is left with the people as a matter of conscience, to exercise wisdom and discretion. Many are subject to weakness, others are delicate in health, and others have nursing babies; of such it should not be required to fast. Neither should parents compel their little children to fast. I have known children to cry for something to eat on fast day. In such cases, going without food will do them no good. Instead, they dread the day to come, and in place of hailing it, dislike it; while the compulsion engenders a spirit of rebellion in them, rather than a love for the Lord and their fellows. Better teach them the principle, and let them observe it when they are old enough to choose intelligently, than to so compel them.

But those should fast who can, and all classes among us should be taught to save the meals which they would eat, or their equivalent, for the poor. None are exempt from this; it is required of the Saints, old and young, in every part of the Church.

It is no excuse that in some places there are no poor. In such cases the fast donation should be forwarded to the proper authorities for transmission to such stakes of Zion as may stand in need.

So shall we gain favor in the sight of God, and learn the acceptable fast before him (*Gospel Doctrine: Selections from the Sermons and Writings of Joseph F. Smith*, 243–244).

> *Fasting is a principle that is carried out with wisdom and thanksgiving. The Lord seeks from us an "acceptable offering" (see D&C 84:31; 124:104). If conditions are such that fasting would compromise health, then the person should wait for a better day, just as little children can be allowed to grow into the spirit of fasting as they mature and gain a fuller understanding of gospel principles. When the Saints in Missouri were prevented by circumstances beyond their control from building the temple required of them, the Lord understood and accepted their offering to that point, consoling them in their affliction (see D&C 124:51–53). In terms of fasting, all who are able to fast should enjoy this sacred privilege and be accounted worthy through their "acceptable offering." How are you able to guide others in kindness and love, especially young people, to learn the process of fasting and prayer in order to receive the blessings of the Spirit and gain favor in the sight of God?*

Spencer W. Kimball: Generous fast offering develops unselfishness. We wish to remind all the Saints of the blessings that come from observing the regular fast and contributing as generous a fast offering as we can. . . . This principle of promise, when lived in the spirit thereof, greatly blesses both giver and receiver. Upon practicing the law of the fast, one finds a personal wellspring of power to overcome self-indulgence and selfishness (*The Teachings of Spencer W. Kimball*, 145).

> *How have you experienced the "wellspring of power" to gain self-mastery in your own life through fasting and paying fast offerings?*

Harold B. Lee: Before we can have the windows of heaven open to us, we must keep the law. The way by which we can keep on speaking terms with God is by observing the law of fasting (*The Teachings of Harold B. Lee,* 610).

The process of becoming "perfect in Christ" (Moro. 10:33) involves learning to become obedient to many eternal principles. What do you think President Lee means when he says that observing the law of fasting can keep you "on speaking terms with God"?

Bruce R. McConkie: Fasting, with prayer as its companion, is designed to increase spirituality; to foster a spirit of devotion and love of God; to increase faith in the hearts of men, thus assuring divine favor; to encourage humility and contrition of soul; to aid in the acquirement of righteousness to teach man his nothingness and dependence upon God; and to hasten those who properly comply with the law of fasting along the path to salvation (*Mormon Doctrine,* 275).

This checklist of blessings that come from fasting and prayer is a reminder of God's mercy and lovingkindness to all of His children. As you consider this list, what experiences have you had that confirm the fulfillment of these covenant promises?

Truths to Liken

Matt. 6:16–18—"Moreover when ye fast, be not, as the hypocrites, of a sad countenance: for they disfigure their faces, that they may appear unto men to fast. Verily I say unto you, They have their reward. But thou, when thou fastest, anoint thine head, and wash thy face; That thou appear not unto men to fast, but unto thy Father which is in secret: and thy Father, which seeth in secret, shall reward thee openly."

- In His Sermon on the Mount the Lord taught the people the principle of how to fast with an attitude of authentic purity and the spirit of personal communion with Heavenly Father.
- We fast not to gain the honors of the world, but to show devotion to God and to plead that the blessings of heaven will flow to our families as well as those who need special help. When you pay your fast offerings, you do so quietly, with private donations known only to your bishopric and to Heavenly Father. How does paying a generous fast offering bring you the rewards of heaven?

Isa. 58:6–11—"Is not this the fast that I have chosen? to loose the bands of wickedness, to undo the heavy burdens, and to let the oppressed go free, and that ye break every yoke? Is it not to deal thy bread to the hungry, and that thou bring the poor that are cast out to thy house? when thou seest the naked, that thou cover him; and that thou hide not thyself from thine own flesh? Then shall thy light break forth as the morning, and thine health shall spring forth speedily: and thy righteousness shall go before thee; the glory of the LORD shall be thy rereward. Then shalt thou call, and the LORD shall answer; thou shalt cry, and he shall say, Here I am. If thou take away from the midst of thee the yoke, the putting forth of the finger, and speaking vanity; And if thou draw out thy soul to the hungry, and satisfy the afflicted soul; then shall thy light rise in obscurity, and thy darkness be as the noonday: And the LORD shall guide thee continually, and satisfy thy soul in drought, and make fat thy bones: and thou shalt be like a watered garden, and like a spring of water, whose waters fail not."

- In this magnificent passage of scripture from Isaiah, we begin to capture the joyful essence and profoundly holy nature of the fast as a process of sharing in the redeeming nature of the Lord. Those who fast begin to understand what it means to cultivate and bestow gifts of charity to others, just as Christ has done for us.
- When we participate in the fast as a truly Christian act of blessing the lives of others, we have the assurance that we are following in the footsteps of the Master. How have you been able to confirm that fasting in the Lord's way brings joy, light, and nurture into your life and the lives of your loved ones?

Alma 5:46—"Behold, I say unto you they are made known unto me by the Holy Spirit of God. Behold, I have fasted and prayed many days that I might know these things of myself. And now I do know of myself that they are true; for the Lord God hath made them manifest unto me by his Holy Spirit; and this is the spirit of revelation which is in me."

- When Alma set aside his calling as chief judge to devote his full energy to preaching the gospel to his people, his objective was to "stir them up in remembrance of their duty, and that he might pull down, by the word of God, all the pride and craftiness and all the contentions which were among his people, seeing no way that he might reclaim them save it were in bearing down in pure testimony against them" (Alma 4:19). We have his exact words because he personally recorded them (see Alma 5:2), including the testimony above concerning how he knew of the truths of the gospel with certainty.
- Devoted fasting and prayer are the keys to building testimony. If any individuals you know are seeking to strengthen their testimonies, what counsel would you have for them, including encouraging them to follow the example of Alma?

Alma 17:3—"But this is not all; they had given themselves to much prayer, and fasting; therefore they had the spirit of prophecy, and the spirit of revelation, and when they taught, they taught with power and authority of God."

- On his travels as the ministering high priest, Alma encountered the sons of Mosiah returning from their extensive mission among the Lamanites. He was able to confirm the noble character of his former colleagues, who are wonderful examples of the principle of fasting and prayer.
- What are your thoughts about fasting and prayer resulting in the spirit of prophecy and revelation (see 1 Cor. 12:3)? Why is it the case that monthly testimony meetings always occur on fast Sunday?

D&C 59:15–16—"And inasmuch as ye do these things [fasting and prayer] with thanksgiving, with cheerful hearts and countenances, not with much laughter, for this is sin, but with a glad heart and a cheerful countenance—Verily I say, that inasmuch as ye do this, the fulness of the earth is yours."

- These words were included in a revelation given through the Prophet Joseph Smith in Zion (Jackson County, Missouri) on August 7, 1831, at a time when the Saints had consecrated the land as the future site for Zion and for the house of the Lord.
- Fasting and prayer are covenant actions of obedience that lead to the fulfillment of heavenly promises. In this case, the Lord promised the "fulness of the earth" in exchange for the Saints' obedience in gladness and cheerfulness. Clearly all things are to be done with pure motives, with joy, and with an eye single to the glory of our Heavenly Father. How do you feel about the fact that simple and cheerful obedience will result in blessings of such abundance that it would take the whole earth to accommodate them? The Saints in Missouri lost all that they had through persecution and tribulation. How then would the "fulness of the earth" be theirs (see D&C 59:16)?

D&C 109:8—"Organize yourselves; prepare every needful thing, and establish a house, even a house of prayer, a house of fasting, a house of faith, a house of learning, a house of glory, a house of order, a house of God."

- These words were spoken during the prayer of the Prophet Joseph Smith at the dedication of the Kirtland Temple on March 27, 1836, which he received through revelation.
- Among other important things, the temple is declared to be a house of fasting. What are your thoughts about characterizing the temple in this way?

Rejoicing and Reasoning Together

How Is the Law of the Fast a Way to Unearth Hidden Wisdom and Spiritual Truth?

On May 17, 1845, nearly a year after the martyrdom of Joseph and Hyrum, the Twelve issued a general letter to the Church to convey special instructions, stating among other things:

> Beloved Brethren: Our whole souls bless you; and we are happy in the privilege of communicating to you a few thoughts. Much more would we rejoice were it our privilege to be in your midst the coming Sabbath and tell you all that is in our hearts; but we are pilgrims in a world of sorrow and woe. In our journeyings to proclaim the gospel and bring about salvation to the honest in heart, God is with us and we prosper; though weary, we are not cast down nor discouraged, for we know that victory is with the upright.
>
> We are happy to hear of the great union and love manifested at your recent fast, which also the Spirit bore witness of to us, and of your liberality towards the poor, and may the abundance which you have so liberally contributed in your penury in dealing your bread to the hungry be the omen of an abundant harvest of the fruits of the earth into your granaries the present and all future seasons.
>
> Since we commenced our journey we have discovered some letters from Brother Joseph Smith to Bishop Partridge from which we extract the following for your edification and instruction. . . .
>
> The Principle of Fasts Defined—
>
> Let this be an ensample to all saints, and there will never be any lack for bread: When the poor are starving, let those who have, fast one day and give what they otherwise would have eaten to the bishops for the poor, and every one will abound for a long time; and this is one great and important principle of fasts approved of the Lord. And so long as the saints will all live to this principle with glad hearts and cheerful countenances they will always have an abundance. (*HC* 7:412–413)

In discovering and publishing missing letters from the Prophet Joseph, including this choice statement about the law of the fast, the Twelve had retrieved a hidden gem of wisdom for the enrichment of the spiritual life of the Saints. This discovery is symbolic, for the law of the fast is itself a means of unearthing hidden wisdom and spiritual truth. As we participate in fasting and prayer, we are often blessed to find within ourselves, through the blessings of the Lord, hidden strength and unexpected insight to facilitate our journey through mortal life.

The word *fast* itself comes from a Middle English antecedent word meaning "firm" or "fixed." As we remain firm in the faith, with our eye "fixed" on the goal of spiritual perfection, our fasting and prayer will edify our natures and lift us higher toward our quest for perfection as servants of God.

How can you remain firm and fixed in obedience to the law of the fast—and therefore harvest rich blessings of abundance and spiritual joy?

Real-life Stories for Heart and Mind

The Humility of the Fast. The story of how the prophet Elijah talked with the Lord is a confirmation of the power of fasting and prayer. After Elijah had called down fire to consume the idolatrous priests of Baal (see 1 Kgs. 18), the prophet went into hiding to avoid the treacherous hand of Queen Jezebel. He was sustained by an angel and then fasted for forty days and forty nights—like Moses did on Mount Sinai (see Ex. 34:28) and the mortal Messiah would also do in the wilderness (see Matt. 4:2)—before going up on Mount Horeb to speak with the Lord. The account is magnificent:

> And he came thither unto a cave, and lodged there; and, behold, the word of the LORD came to him, and he said unto him, What doest thou here, Elijah?
>
> And he said, I have been very jealous for the LORD God of hosts: for the children of Israel have forsaken thy covenant, thrown down thine altars, and slain thy prophets with the sword; and I, even I only, am left; and they seek my life, to take it away.

And he said, Go forth, and stand upon the mount before the LORD. And, behold, the LORD passed by, and a great and strong wind rent the mountains, and brake in pieces the rocks before the LORD; but the LORD was not in the wind: and after the wind an earthquake; but the LORD was not in the earthquake:

And after the earthquake a fire; but the LORD was not in the fire: and after the fire a still small voice.

And it was so, when Elijah heard it, that he wrapped his face in his mantle, and went out, and stood in the entering in of the cave. And, behold, there came a voice unto him, and said, What doest thou here, Elijah? (1 Kgs. 19:9–13)

The Lord then instructed Elijah and unfolded to him the course of action he was to follow to promote the designs of heaven for the people of the Lord. Through fasting and prayer, the prophet knew the will of the Lord and how to carry it out with the blessing of heaven.

The story of Elijah's humble way of approaching the Lord through fasting and prayer shows how our own patterns of living can proceed if we seek to know the will of the Lord through revelation. Though we are not prophets, yet we are all favored to have the promise of revelation in our lives through the operation of the Holy Ghost. Moses declared: "Would God that all the LORD's people were prophets, and that the LORD would put his spirit upon them!" (Num. 11:29). Paul declared: "No man can say that Jesus is the Lord, but by the Holy Ghost" (1 Cor. 12:3). What are your thoughts about how fasting and prayer result in personal revelation?

Pondering Prayerfully

Additional scriptures to consider and ponder:

- Acts 13:2–3
- Mosiah 4:26
- Alma 17:9
- 3 Ne. 27:1–3
- Moro. 6:5–6
- D&C 95:16

The following hymns might inspire gratitude for the fast:

- "Because I Have Been Given Much" (*Hymns,* 219)
- "Bless Our Fast, We Pray" (*Hymns,* 138)
- "In Fasting We Approach Thee" (*Hymns,* 139)

Remember and Be Sure

The law of the fast, when practiced sincerely, empowers us with the sustaining strength of heaven. When we pay our fast offerings, we practice the great commandment of love. The power of fasting and prayer has been shown throughout the scriptures; today the Lord continues to bless us as we humble ourselves in prayer and fasting, pay our fast offerings, and seek blessings at His hand.

Within our own families we should testify of the blessings that we have received through fasting and prayer. Like Elijah, we can show the Lord our humility and devotion through fasting and prayer, and thus prepare ourselves to receive the inspiration of the Spirit to ensure our safety and spiritual welfare, and that of our families. We are counseled always to align our fast with a spiritual purpose: to improve ourselves in righteousness, to seek a worthy blessing, to express our love and gratitude, to seek blessings for others in need, to sanctify our visits to the house of the Lord, and to serve our God and our fellowman. Great blessings flow from God to the faithful who sincerely practice a prayerful fast with an eye single to His glory.

CHAPTER 26
Law of Sacrifice and Consecration

Let us here observe, that a religion that does not require the sacrifice of all things never has power sufficient to produce the faith necessary unto life and salvation; for, from the first existence of man, the faith necessary unto the enjoyment of life and salvation never could be obtained without the sacrifice of all earthly things. —Joseph Smith (*Lectures on Faith,* 6:7)

Opening the Window of Wisdom

Sacrifice is at the heart of the gospel of Jesus Christ. In comparison with the transcendent atoning sacrifice of the Savior, there is nothing that man can do to balance the scales—except to make obedient sacrifice the heart and soul of his life: "Verily I say unto you, all among them who know their hearts are honest, and are broken, and their spirits contrite, and are willing to observe their covenants by sacrifice—yea, every sacrifice which I, the Lord, shall command—they are accepted of me" (D&C 97:8). Thus the sacrifice of all things in devotion to the cause of immortality and eternal life is never too high a price to pay, for even the sacrifice of all things leaves man a debtor before God (see Mosiah 2:21).

Before the Atonement of the Savior, the children of God offered a blood sacrifice as a symbol of their reverence and devotion to God (see Moses 5:5–7). Today, according to the higher law given by the Savior, we offer a broken heart and contrite spirit: "And whoso cometh unto me with a broken heart and a contrite spirit, him will I baptize with fire and with the Holy Ghost" (3 Ne. 9:20). Offering a broken heart and contrite spirit is literally offering your very self—you give yourself, your will, and your decisions to the will of God. When our hearts are broken, we are entwined with our Savior and His sacrifice at Calvary, for He most likely "died of a broken heart" (James E. Talmage, *Jesus the Christ,* 620).

Through the spirit of sacrifice, we enter a condition of profound change: we are in a state of humility; we depend on God; we are easily entreated; we have no pride or ego to maintain; we are willing to learn and change in this time of testing. In short, we fully accept the Lord's magnificent, infinite, and eternal Atonement. The law of sacrifice requires that we, as disciples of Jesus Christ, give all that we have—our time, talents, and all we possess, even our lives if necessary—in order to build up the kingdom of God and to gain exaltation (see D&C 98:13–15).

One sacrifices by giving up something of value for something of a higher value, especially on behalf of the children of God. Sacrifice becomes an exalting principle, flowing as it does from love and obedience. A sacrificial attitude requires that we want nothing more than to do the will of God. We want to make sacrifices that will bless His children so that they also might gain eternal life.

Associated with the law of sacrifice is the law of consecration. The law of consecration is a gift to the Saints based on the eternal pattern of governance established by the Lord as the model for a Zion people: "And thus I grant unto this people a privilege of organizing themselves according to my laws" (D&C 51:15). The Lord states His objective for inaugurating this organizing principle: "That through my providence, notwithstanding the tribulation which shall descend upon you, that the church may stand independent above all other creatures beneath the celestial world" (D&C 78:14). Being organized under the law of God ensures total self-sufficiency and organizational integrity for the Saints. To the extent we are able to live according to the law of consecration, we rise in attainment ever closer to the heavenly goal of being prepared to be received by the Lord into His celestial domain.

The Doctrine and Covenants is the Lord's handbook on key principles of heavenly governance, including the law of consecration. The law of consecration is one of the pillars of a Zion society, which must of necessity operate according to the will of the Lord, with the Saints demonstrating an enduring commitment to benevolence, brotherly love, unity, equality, orderliness, and submission to the Almighty. The Lord has asked His righteous people to consecrate their lives for the building up of the kingdom of God (see JST, Matt. 6:38). When we consecrate our lives, we dedicate and set apart our time, talents, and material goods for the Lord's purposes. Consecration is uniquely related to the depth of our conversion to our Savior Jesus Christ. Through consecration we truly sacrifice all things for the Lord. We begin the process of purification of our own lives and in turn we are better able to bless our brothers and sisters that they too might enjoy eternal life—this truly being the way to build up the kingdom of God. Part of this law, as we now live it, requires us to provide for our family in the spirit of genuine providence and be an instrument in the Lord's hands to bless our family and all those we associate with. Consecration is an attitude as well as an observable act of goodness.

Inspired by Latter-Day Prophets

Lorenzo Snow: We have found the treasure in the field, we have found the pearl of great price, and now we have got to give all that we have for it, at one time or another. The Lord has said that He will prove us even unto death, to see whether we will stand by the covenants we have made with Him (*The Teachings of Lorenzo Snow*, 115).

We have the choice of identifying ourselves with the transitory world of temporal things or with the eternal work of redemption. How is our choice confirmed? Through sacrifice—sacrifice of the highest order. As you consider your own life and the lives of your forebears, how has sacrifice been the key to opening the door of joy in the gospel and confidence before God for covenants honored?

Joseph Fielding Smith: We read in the Pearl of Great Price how Enoch was called to cry repentance, and through his diligent labors he gathered together those who were willing to make covenant to serve the Lord. These made covenant to obey the celestial law, or the law of consecration, for this is a celestial law, and the celestial kingdom is governed by it. They were willing to give all that they had, even their lives to the kingdom of God. The result was that they became so righteous that they walked with God (*The Way to Perfection*, 274).

Obeying and living the law of consecration—giving all that we have for the purposes of Zion—enables a people to walk with God and to participate in a Zion society that is redeemed of God. What are your thoughts about the transcendent blessings that lie ahead for the Saints as they learn to live according to the same pattern as the people of Enoch? What do you need to do to prepare to live the celestial law more fully and thus become worthy to walk with God?

Spencer W. Kimball: Saints must keep the covenant of consecration. The Lord has blessed us as a people with a prosperity unequaled in times past. The resources that have been placed in our power are good, and necessary to our work here on the earth. But I am afraid that many of us have been surfeited with flocks and herds and acres and barns and wealth and have begun to worship them as false gods, and they have power over us. Do we have more of these good things than our faith can stand? Many people spend most of their time working in the service of a self-image that includes sufficient money, stocks, bonds, investment portfolios, property, credit cards, furnishings, automobiles, and the like to *guarantee* carnal security throughout, it is hoped, a long and happy life. Forgotten is the fact that our assignment is to use these many resources in our families and quorums to build up the kingdom of God—to further the missionary effort and the genealogical and temple work; to raise our children up as fruitful servants unto the Lord; to bless others in every way, that they may also be fruitful. Instead, we expend these blessings on our own desires, and as Moroni said, "Ye adorn yourselves with that which hath no life, and yet suffer the hungry, and the needy, and the naked, and the sick and the afflicted to pass by you, and notice them not" (Mormon 8:39) (*The Teachings of Spencer W. Kimball*, 357).

President Kimball reminds us of our assignment to use our abundance to build up the kingdom of God, raise our families in service to the Lord, and bless the lives of others. How can you sacrifice more of the fruit of your labors to ensure the fruitful outcomes of the Lord's design for His sons and daughters? How can you learn to be satisfied in filling your needs, rather than your wants, and thus find joy in honoring the principles of sacrifice and consecration?

Ezra Taft Benson: The law of consecration is a law for an inheritance in the celestial kingdom. God, the Eternal Father, His Son Jesus Christ, and all holy beings abide by this law. It is an eternal law. It is a revelation by God to His Church in this dispensation. Though not in full operation today, it will be mandatory for all Saints to live the law in its fulness to receive celestial inheritance (*The Teachings of Ezra Taft Benson*, 123).

Why do we need to learn to live the law of consecration? Because the Father and Son live this law and are waiting to receive us into Their presence if we are willing to live according to celestial patterns. Just as the Law of Moses was a "schoolmaster to bring us unto Christ, that we might be justified by faith" (Gal. 3:24) and thus live the higher law introduced by the Savior, even so we have what might be called the "schoolmaster" of sacrifice in the form of paying tithing, giving

fast offerings, and providing devoted service to others—all for the purpose of building the kingdom, helping to prepare us for living the celestial law of consecration in its fulness, and inheriting a place in the celestial kingdom. What are your thoughts about how to improve in your current covenant obligations (tithing, fast offerings, service) in order to prepare for a future time when you will be called on to live in full accordance with the celestial law of consecration?

Truths to Liken

Matt. 6:33—"But seek ye first the kingdom of God, and his righteousness; and all these things shall be added unto you." (Compare JST, Matt. 6:38: "Wherefore, seek not the things of this world but seek ye first to build up the kingdom of God, and to establish his righteousness, and all these things shall be added unto you.")

- In the Sermon on the Mount, the Lord taught the principle of priorities with respect to seeking wealth.
- As we seek to live the law of consecration we can ask ourselves, *Will what I do bless lives, bring others closer to God and Christ, and build up the kingdom of God?* These are the things a consecrated life can do. In our complex world, there are many overlapping priorities that compete for our attention. What are your thoughts about cultivating harmony and peace by setting priorities based on sacrificing for the Lord and His children?

2 Ne. 2:7—"Behold, he offereth himself a sacrifice for sin, to answer the ends of the law, unto all those who have a broken heart and a contrite spirit; and unto none else can the ends of the law be answered."

- Lehi taught Jacob and his other sons about the indispensable gift of grace and mercy brought about through the Atonement of Jesus Christ.
- The demands of justice require an infinite Atonement. Through the grace and mercy of our Savior we qualify ourselves for the blessings of the Atonement by

offering the sacrifice of a broken heart and a contrite spirit. We are welded together by His atoning sacrifice and our repentance, love, and obedience. How can you teach others, especially youth, the same principles of willing sacrifice that Lehi taught his sons?

Mosiah 4:21—"And now, if God, who has created you, on whom you are dependent for your lives and for all that ye have and are, doth grant unto you whatsoever ye ask that is right, in faith, believing that ye shall receive, O then, how ye ought to impart of the substance that ye have one to another."

- In his final address to the people, King Benjamin reminded them that sacrifice for others is a central part of the gospel of Jesus Christ.
- Consecrating ourselves requires overcoming any obsession with worldly goods and power, as well as overcoming idleness. When we are "anxiously engaged in a good cause" (D&C 58:27), being of one heart and equal in worldly things, then the blessings of the Spirit can flow more fully into our lives. How can you become the very answer to the prayers sent to heaven by those in distress and in need of relief?

D&C 78:6—"For if ye are not equal in earthly things ye cannot be equal in obtaining heavenly things."

- These words are part of a revelation given through the Prophet Joseph Smith at Hiram, Ohio, in March 1832 concerning the need to establish a storehouse for the poor.
- The Lord has given us in the scriptures a compelling checklist to help us prepare for the Second Coming. Are we actively engaged in a committed effort to care for the poor and needy around us? Have we established for ourselves and our families a pattern of living that places spiritual things above earthly things in the order of priority—thus placing material gain below our interest

in building the kingdom of God? Do we truly have an eye single to the glory of God? What are your thoughts about the people of Zion needing to be equal in earthly things in order to become worthy of obtaining heavenly things?

D&C 82:3, 10—"For of him unto whom much is given much is required. . . . I, the Lord, am bound when ye do what I say; but when ye do not what I say, ye have no promise."

- These memorable sentences were included in a revelation given to the Prophet Joseph Smith in Jackson County, Missouri, on April 26, 1832, on the occasion of a general council of the Church at which Joseph Smith was sustained as the President of the High Priesthood.
- Our blessings from on high are overwhelming. Should we not sacrifice all that is required of us in return? The promise of eternal life is magnificent. Should we not obey the Lord in all dimensions of our covenant activities to merit such a blessing? What is required of you in return for "the merits, and mercy, and grace of the Holy Messiah" (2 Ne. 2:8)?

D&C 98:13–15—"And whoso layeth down his life in my cause, for my name's sake, shall find it again, even life eternal. Therefore, be not afraid of your enemies, for I have decreed in my heart, saith the Lord, that I will prove you in all things, whether you will abide in my covenant, even unto death, that you may be found worthy. For if ye will not abide in my covenant ye are not worthy of me."

- This counsel of the Lord was included in a revelation given through the Prophet Joseph Smith at Kirtland, Ohio, on August 6, 1833, at a time of great suffering by the Saints at the hands of their persecutors.
- Sacrifice—even of our own lives, if necessary—is a means of proving our loyalty to the Lord. The Prophet, who received these words of revelation,

would indeed sacrifice his own life just a decade later. Many of the ancient prophets also laid down their lives for the cause of the Lord. If you are not required to *die* for the Lord, how can you more fully *live* for the Lord?

D&C 105:5—"And Zion cannot be built up unless it is by the principles of the law of the celestial kingdom; otherwise I cannot receive her unto myself."

- These words were part of a revelation given through the Prophet Joseph Smith at Fishing River, Missouri, on June 22, 1834, during the advance of Zion's Camp, which was organized to bring relief to the Saints suffering at the hands of the Missouri mobs.

- Sacrifice and consecration are celestial laws, keys to building up the kingdom of God in preparation for the Second Coming. In times of oppression and adversity the need to sacrifice for the good of Zion is magnified even more. How can you help your family and those you serve in the Church—especially when they are faced with overwhelming challenges—grasp more fully the need to abide by the principles of the celestial law, so that the Lord may pour down such a rich blessing of abundance "that there shall not be room enough to receive it" (Mal. 3:10)?

Rejoicing and Reasoning Together

What Is the Greatest Among All the Examples of Sacrifice and Consecration?

True disciples of Jesus Christ follow the Savior, doing the things that He would have them do and investing all that they have to support the cause of building up the kingdom of God. The Savior of the world took up a mortal tabernacle and lived among God's children in the meridian of time. What better authority to speak about the dichotomy of earthly and heavenly things than Jesus Christ, who was at the same time mortal and immortal? His abiding theme was the need to rise above the worldly and transient and attain the eternal and everlasting. Through His Atonement, He manifested the supreme degree of sacrifice and consecration for the good of all mankind.

So often in His discourses He taught the principle of investing one's all in that which leads to immortality and eternal life, rather than squandering one's loyalty by giving allegiance to the fleeting and shallow things of the world. Jesus counseled the man who had been compliant with God's laws to go one further step—by selling all that he had to provide resources for the poor, and by taking up his cross and following the Lord. But the man was sad, "for he had great possessions" (Mark 10:22). On another occasion, the Savior expressed great satisfaction with the poverty-stricken widow who donated her pittance to the treasury, for "she of her want did cast in all that she had, even all her living" (Mark 12:44).

Those who seek the kingdom are disposed toward humility and meekness, not pride and station: "For whosoever exalteth himself shall be abased; and he that humbleth himself shall be exalted" (Luke 14:11). It is the poor and the beggars—those who are devoid of the trappings of luxury and extravagance—that are invited to the "great supper" of the Lord (Luke 14:16), while those who are distracted with worldly entanglements remove themselves from the venue of eternal blessings. Like the builder of a house or the king governing his armies, the aspiring disciple of Christ is to lay a solid foundation for action and calculate the sacrificial cost of discipleship in advance, before taking up his cross: "So likewise, whosoever he be of you that forsaketh not all that he hath, he cannot be my disciple" (Luke 14:33).

Are you prepared for an invitation to the "great supper" of the Lord? How do you still need to prepare?

What Will Be Your Sacrificial Test? Ask What Thing Is Most Dear to You!

To Abraham the Lord gave this command: "Take now thy son, thine only son Isaac, whom thou lovest, and get thee into the land of Moriah; and offer him there for a burnt offering" (Gen. 22:2). Abraham then took Isaac—the thing most dear to him—and two other young men on the journey to Moriah, where he was to offer Isaac as a burnt offering, a sacrifice to the Lord.

On the third day Abraham and Isaac went to worship. Isaac carried the wood as they journeyed. Isaac asked about the sacrifice, and Abraham replied, "My son, God will provide himself a lamb for a burnt offering" (Gen. 22:8). Abraham then bound Isaac (who must have complied willingly) and laid him on the altar, preparing for the ultimate sacrifice.

It was at that moment in time that Abraham was put to the supreme test. Would he shrink from the awesome task, or would he rise in majesty as a figure of unforgettable valor and unshakeable obedience? As Abraham took the knife, an angel of the Lord forbade him, saying, "For now I know that thou fearest [in other words, show unyielding reverence to] God, seeing thou hast not withheld thy son" (Gen. 22:12). A ram was subsequently provided, and the Lord promised Abraham, "in thy seed shall all the nations of the earth be blessed" (Gen. 22:18). The willingness of Abraham to sacrifice the thing most dear to him was a frontrunner of the coming sacrifice by the Father of His Only Begotten Son for the sake of mankind. Only through a commitment to sacrifice all that we have, if required to do so, can we manifest to the Lord that our enduring love for Him and His divine cause is perfect.

We can see reflected in the life of Abraham the exemplary pattern of spiritual growth that all of God's righteous children can strive for as part of the mortal experience. From his early youth, Abraham's faith and devotion were schooled on experiences of adversity and oppression (he being put in mortal danger by his own father—see Abr. 1:30), and the lessons of obedience and valor he learned carried him through life on the wings of divine support and blessing. Never losing the vision of his destined calling as a key participant in the grand design of the Lord, he set a peerless example of one willing to do everything asked of him by God—without hesitation and without question. In many ways, the life journey of Abraham shows that our mortal experience consists of a continuing cycle of trial, sacrifice, and deliverance, followed repeatedly by trial, sacrifice, and deliverance—all without end. As we go through this cycle again and again, our progress is traced by a spiral that carries us higher and higher, according to our diligence and willingness to keep the commandments. The motion is an upward cycle, ever closer to the objective of being more like our Father in Heaven and His Son, Jesus Christ.

How have you been tested and tried "even as Abraham" to this point in your life? What lessons and manifestations of God's support have you observed as you willingly sacrificed for the cause of Zion? How might you be tested and tried in times to come? How will you respond "in the strength of the Lord" (Alma 20:4)?

Real-life Stories for Heart and Mind

"The Coat." A faithful husband had quietly saved up enough money to buy his wife a much-needed winter coat. Then, during sacrament meeting one Sunday, the bishop called for donations to help a needy local couple go on a service mission. Graciously, the husband contributed the coat fund for this purpose. Decades later, he rejoiced in learning that those same missionaries had saved a whole branch of the Church that was struggling to achieve greater cohesion and unity. Their efforts succeeded admirably, and the branch prospered under their leadership. The father later commented to his children that it was a source of much satisfaction to him to know that the coat had had such a protective and useful influence in building the kingdom of God. As for his wife, an opportunity presented itself for her to obtain a fine new coat after all—just a year after the donation was made—and thus all were served well. As the Savior taught during His ministry: "But seek ye first the kingdom of God and his righteousness, and all these things shall be added unto you" (3 Ne. 13:33).

We are not always made aware of how our sacrifices are transformed into blessings for others. But we can have joy knowing that the Lord and His servants will put our offerings to good use in building Zion. How have the sacrifices of others blessed your life without measure? How can you encourage others to see in the principle of sacrifice a liberating and edifying source of joy?

The King Is Risen. The most important event in all of the history of mankind took place when the King of Heaven sacrificed His life for us and then took it up again through the Resurrection. His death and Resurrection enabled God's children to transcend temporal death with ultimate immortal renewal and, through faith and obedience, achieve salvation and eternal life. No earthly king could do what the Heavenly King did for us. He testified to the ancient Americans at the time of His post-resurrection visit to Bountiful: "Behold, I am Jesus Christ, whom the prophets testified shall come into the world. And behold, I am the light and the life of the world; and I have drunk out of that bitter cup which the Father hath given me, and have glorified the Father in taking upon me the sins of the world, in the which I have suffered the will of the Father in all things from the beginning" (3 Ne. 11:10–11).

The Savior's act of eternal consecration and sacrifice makes all mortal sacrifices seem modest in scope and measure. How does your love for the Redeemer unfold and expand as you prayerfully consider the infinite love that He has for you and your family?

Pondering Prayerfully

Additional scriptures to consider and ponder:
- 1 Sam. 15:22
- John 13:34–35
- 1 Ne. 3:7
- Mosiah 17:20
- 4 Ne. 1:2–3
- D&C 19:26–27
- D&C 42:30–31
- D&C 42:40–42
- D&C 82:19–20
- Moses 7:16–18

The following hymns can help us ponder sacrifice:
- "I'll Go Where You Want Me to Go" (*Hymns,* 270)
- "Lead Me into Life Eternal" (*Hymns,* 45)
- "Though Deepening Trials" (*Hymns,* 122)

Remember and Be Sure

The sacred counsel reflected in the records of the Savior's mortal ministry is clear: Trust in things of heaven rather than in things of the earth, seek treasures in heaven rather than treasures of the world, and dedicate your all to the building up of the kingdom of God. Wealth is a fundamental part of the gospel of Jesus Christ—wealth of the eternities. Jacob, brother of Nephi, expressed this doctrine as follows: "But before ye seek for riches, seek ye for the kingdom of God. And after ye have obtained a hope in Christ ye shall obtain riches, if ye seek them; and ye will seek them for the intent to do good—to clothe the naked, and to feed the hungry, and to liberate the captive, and administer relief to the sick and the afflicted" (Jacob 2:18–19). In our day, the Lord has renewed the call for the Saints to keep their priorities focused on things pertaining to salvation: "Now, as you have asked, behold, I say unto you, keep my commandments, and seek to bring forth and establish the cause of Zion; Seek not for riches but for wisdom, and behold, the mysteries of God shall be unfolded unto you, and then shall you be made rich. Behold, he that hath eternal life is rich" (D&C 6:6–7).

Through sacrifice and the spirit of consecration we receive many blessings—patience here and now, blessings of eternal life in the life to come, compassion for others, self-esteem, and self-reliance, among many others. We can teach the principles of sacrifice and consecration to our children in ennobling ways. The family will be strengthened and the entangling philosophy of "instant gratification" will gradually be replaced with the ethic of work and sacrifice for the betterment of self, family, and our "fellowcitizens" in the kingdom of God, now and in the future. Ultimately every sacrifice we make in the name of the Savior is but a shadow and hint of the transcendent eternal sacrifice He made, willingly, to enable us to return to our heavenly home one day. Let us sacrifice for future generations just as those before us have sacrificed for us—especially just as the Savior has given His life for our sakes.

Even though the Lord loves all of His children, His honor is reserved for those who honor Him, as the scriptures attest (see D&C 76:5). We honor Him by keeping His commandments. We honor him by teaching our children to follow in His footsteps. As parents and leaders in Zion, we honor Him by infusing our lives with the light of the gospel. We consecrate our time, talents, and resources to the building up of His kingdom. We fulfill our missions with diligence and valor. We teach allegiance to our Heavenly King rather than to worldly practices not based on eternal principles. All of this brings glory to our Heavenly Father and blessings of light and truth into our family circles. The families of Zion are the units of eternal increase in the Lord's plan, the places where holiness is learned and practiced—but it must be done in the Lord's way (see D&C 104:16), and according to the principles of spiritual truth: "Therefore, O ye that embark in the service of God, see that ye serve him with all your heart, might, mind and strength, that ye may stand blameless before God at the last day" (D&C 4:2).

CHAPTER 27
Work and Self-Reliance

Work hard educationally and in your vocation. Put your trust in the Lord, have faith, and it will work out. The Lord never gives a commandment without providing the means to accomplish it. —Ezra Taft Benson (*Come, Listen to a Prophet's Voice*, 53)

Opening the Window of Wisdom

The quality of self-reliance is rooted in the reality of agency. God created mankind with the inherent blessing of choice, the freedom to apply the principles of initiative under the inspiration of the Almighty: "For the power is in them, wherein they are agents unto themselves. And inasmuch as men do good they shall in nowise lose their reward" (D&C 58:28). This agency extends both to temporal as well as to spiritual matters, for God's children can prayerfully use their talents, skills, and energy to improve their situation and increase their spirituality. Such was a key part of the design of God's plan for the blessing of His children. From the beginning, He commanded His offspring to sustain themselves through productive enterprise: "In the sweat of thy face shalt thou eat bread, till thou return unto the ground" (Gen. 3:19; compare Moses 4:25).

Parents work with great devotion to support their children: "All children have claim upon their parents for their maintenance until they are of age. And after that, they have claim upon the church, or in other words upon the Lord's storehouse, if their parents have not wherewith to give them inheritances" (D&C 83:4). This obligation was confirmed in "The Family: A Proclamation to the World."

We work to achieve a provident lifestyle for the sake of our own family circle, but also for the well-being of others who might need assistance. Service to others—in particular to those who are wanting in material necessities and in the fundamentals of a spiritual life—is anchored in a defining attitude of selflessness and mercy. The key to such service is that it mirrors in essence the all-embracing charity of the Redeemer. We work and serve because He works and serves (see John 5:17); we give because He gives; we love unconditionally because of His abiding example of unconditional love: "And behold, thou wilt remember the poor, and consecrate of thy properties for their support that which thou hast to impart unto them, with a covenant and a deed which cannot be broken. And inasmuch as ye impart of your substance unto the poor, ye will do it unto me" (D&C 42:30–31). We are to do all in our power to help relieve suffering and to eliminate conditions that cause pain and misery. As Brigham Young declared, at the beginning of the exodus to the West: "Let each company bear an equal proportion, according to the dividend of their property, in taking the poor, the widows, the fatherless, and the families of those who have gone into the army, that the cries of the widow and the fatherless come not up into the ears of the Lord against this people" (D&C 136:8).

The Lord's design to care for His children is centered in industry and self-reliance. "Thou shalt not be idle; for he that is idle shall not eat the bread nor wear the garments of the laborer" (D&C 42:42). He also commanded, "Cease to be idle" (D&C 88:124). Nevertheless, those who remain wanting after striving with all their heart and might to lift themselves from need are fully embraced by the spirit of service and charity on the part of their companions.

In great measure, charitable service includes also reaching out to teach principles of self-reliance and self-sufficiency. Often those who want for life's basics lack principally in the knowledge of how to open doorways of opportunity. As one hand of the giver reaches out to feed and nurture, the other points the way and gives insight into strategies of self-care and self-nurture for individuals and families. The Lord appointed man to "have dominion over all the beasts of the field, and to eat his bread by the sweat of his brow" (Moses 5:1). The same principle is reflected in the realm of spiritual need, as Nephi declared: "For we labor diligently to write, to persuade our children, and also our brethren, to believe in Christ, and to be reconciled to God; for we know that it is by grace that we are saved, after all we can do" (2 Ne. 25:23). "After all we can do" is the simple, profound lever for the implementation of the endowment of divine grace unto salvation. Because the Savior is full of grace, we strive to be gracious to our fellows. Because the Savior is full of saving love, we strive to do all in our power to save our fellows and elevate them to a higher level of joy and self-reliance.

The ethic of work (being diligent) is the price of success—essential in the building of character and the building up of the Lord's kingdom. The natural immune system to protect us from the consequences of idleness is simple: work, work, work—that is the key. Yes, productive work is and will always be the standard of excellence in any chosen field. When you exhibit a positive attitude, a trust within, a certainty of your abilities, with a hope and assurance that you can perform well, you indeed have self-confidence and the capacity for self-reliance. You can depend on yourself to do what is expected of you. People who have this quality—even though they may not have achieved mastery in all aspects of their lives—have the ability to succeed in difficult situations. When you truly believe in yourself, you will always do better. One of the great things you can do for others, especially your children, is to help them grow up with self-confidence. This will contribute, in turn, to their resourcefulness and self-reliance—especially if they are trained to depend on the Lord and follow the promptings of His Spirit.

To be meaningful, work needs to be directed toward essential goals and objectives. Work needs to proceed on the basis of careful design and preparation. When the vision and desire are in place, preparation becomes the master. Preparation precedes power. If you are prepared, you will not suffer from anxiety—or, as the Lord expressed it, "If ye are prepared ye shall not fear" (D&C 38:30). Preparation has a price. It takes time, effort, dedication, and often sacrifice to prepare well. Many want to be the best, to overcome challenges, to support and nurture loved ones with excellence and devotion. The hard question is: How many want to *prepare* to be the best, and thus to gain mastery over the challenges of life? Preparation is key to self-reliance and provident living.

In the spiritual context, our prototype in this kind of undertaking is the Master Himself: "Nevertheless, glory be to the Father, and I partook and finished my preparations unto the children of men" (D&C 19:19). In emulating the Savior's example, we should don the armor of God: "Stand, therefore, having your loins girt about with truth, having on the breastplate of righteousness, and your feet shod with the preparation of the gospel of peace, which I have sent mine angels to commit unto you" (D&C 27:16). Then we should work in all diligence to prepare our families for the times to come: "Wherefore the decree hath gone forth from the Father that they shall be gathered in unto one place upon the face of this land, to prepare their hearts and be prepared in all things against the day when tribulation and desolation are sent forth upon the wicked" (D&C 29:8). Having done that, we can rest assured that we shall be ready, as the Lord has commanded: "Prepare ye, prepare ye for that which is to come, for the Lord is nigh" (D&C 1:12). May we all prepare ourselves to serve well, build the kingdom with valor, work productively and with purpose, and take our places at the banquet table of the Lord.

Inspired by Latter-Day Prophets

Stephen L Richards: It is said that Jesus had more to say about man's attitude toward money and property than about any other one thing. In sixteen of thirty-eight parables Jesus made this his theme. We all need to make a living, but a living does not always make a life. Money is a means to an end, not a worthy end in itself. And money alone is not security. It may be that enough of it will keep the wolf from the door but not from the heart (*Where Is Wisdom?* 71–72).

Our work in this life is blessed and edified through balance—a balance of nurture and support of our families' temporal needs on the one hand, and the cultivation of spiritual well-being on the other. At the same time, self-reliance is magnified through devoted reliance on the Spirit to guide and direct our quest to satisfy the needs of life and fulfill our potential as sons and daughters of God. What do you think Elder Richards meant when he referred to keeping the wolf "from the heart"? What wolves gain access when priorities begin to shift from spiritual objectives to purely worldly objectives? What can be done in your life to achieve an ongoing balance between temporal and spiritual aspirations?

Marion G. Romney: Self-reliance is not the end, but a means to an end. It is very possible for a person to be completely independent and lack every other desirable attribute. One may become wealthy and never have to ask anyone for anything, but unless there is some spiritual goal attached to this independence, it can canker his soul ("The Celestial Nature of Self-reliance," *Ensign,* Nov. 1982, 91).

There are only two verses of scriptures where the word independent *is used (the word* Independence *being used only to refer to the city in Missouri): (1) "That through my providence, notwithstanding the tribulation which shall descend upon you, that the church may stand independent above all other creatures beneath the celestial world" (D&C 78:14); and (2): "All truth is independent in that sphere in which God has placed it, to act for itself, as all intelligence also; otherwise there is no existence" (D&C 93:30). Both*

of these references are relevant to the subject of work and self-reliance, since devoted work is required to achieve deliverance from temporal needs, and since divinely appointed agency permits the children of God to rise to their potential by applying eternal principles in productive ways. What are your thoughts about the process of using faith and industry to call down heavenly blessings that will bring independence of a worthy kind into your life and the lives of your loves ones?

Ezra Taft Benson: Every accountable child of God needs to set goals, short- and long-range goals. . . . When we set goals we are in command. If we know where we are going, we can judge more accurately where we are now and make effective plans to reach our destination. If we keep a goal firmly in mind, we will know when we have reached it. This gives us a sense of accomplishment and the challenge of establishing fresh, new goals—always keeping the long-range objective in mind (*The Teachings of Ezra Taft Benson,* 384).

How would you describe your short-, intermediate-, and long-term goals? How is your life brought "into focus" by having goals that are "clearly understood"?

Harold B. Lee: We should each live so when that time comes we will be prepared to meet our maker and have him say to us, "Well done my good and faithful servant" (*The Teachings of Howard W. Hunter,* 15).

When the young Alma was confronted by an angelic messenger and commanded to reform his life, he was unable to move for three days and three nights and was racked with agonizing torment: "The very thought of coming into the presence of my God did rack my soul with inexpressible horror. Oh, thought I, that I could be banished and become extinct both soul and body, that I might not be brought to stand in the presence of my God, to be judged of my deeds" (Alma 36:14–15). Then, when he remembered his father's words about the Savior and turned his heart to God, he went through a mighty transformation: "And oh, what joy, and what marvelous light I did behold; yea, my soul was filled with joy as exceeding as was my pain!" (Alma 36:20). Thereafter he filled his life with devoted work and service on behalf of the well-being of his people, the children of God. What are your thoughts about the transformation that comes when we fill our lives with the love of God and perform devoted service to achieve the well-being of our immediate family as well as the family of God?

Truths to Liken

2 Ne. 5:11, 17—"And the Lord was with us; and we did prosper exceedingly; for we did sow seed, and we did reap again in abundance. And we began to raise flocks, and herds, and animals of every kind. . . . And it came to pass that I, Nephi, did cause my people to be industrious, and to labor with their hands."

- For purposes of safety, Nephi and his followers separated themselves from his elder brothers and their murderous designs. Thus the Nephites were able to establish a community of their own where they could honor their covenants with the Lord: "And it came to pass that we lived after the manner of happiness" (2 Ne. 5:27).
- Self-reliance is an important aspect of happiness. When we are industrious, we are engaged in productive work, and we become diligent, steady, and self-confident. These attributes serve us well in all facets of life. Nephi was an advocate of work, having taught his people principles of provident living with such effectiveness that soon the entire nation embraced self-reliant practices. How have you been able to emulate Nephi by teaching these principles through example and encouragement?

D&C 10:4–5—"Do not run faster or labor more than you have strength and means provided to enable you to translate; but be diligent unto the end. Pray always, that you may come off conqueror; yea, that you may conquer Satan, and that you may escape the hands of the servants of Satan that do uphold his work."

- The Lord counseled the Prophet Joseph Smith in a revelation given at Harmony, Pennsylvania, in the summer of 1828, subsequent to the tragic event in which Martin Harris lost the first 116 pages of the translation of the Book of Mormon.
- Diligence is to be balanced by prudence and wisdom in laboring within one's strength and means (see also Mosiah 4:27). Prayer is the key to victory, for the Lord will provide deliverance from evil. Every noble and righteous labor is a target for the forces of Satan. If we know this and prepare for it through wisdom, diligent labor, and continual prayer, depending on the Lord in all things, then we will "come off conqueror"—for, as the Lord promised, "I will fight your battles" (D&C 105:14). What has been your experience following the above formula—diligence, wisdom, and prayer—in accomplishing worthy goals for family, Church, and community? What are your thoughts about the following related passage and how it gives hope for the accomplishment of all worthy goals? "But the Lord knoweth all things from the beginning; wherefore, he prepareth a way to accomplish all his works among the children of men; for behold, he hath all power unto the fulfilling of all his words. And thus it is. Amen" (1 Ne. 9:6).

D&C 75:28–29—"And again, verily I say unto you, that every man who is obliged to provide for his own family, let him provide, and he shall in nowise lose his crown; and let him labor in the church. Let every man be diligent in all things. And the idler shall not have place in the church, except he repent and mend his ways."

- These words were included in a revelation given through the Prophet Joseph Smith at Amherst, Ohio, on January 25, 1832, on the occasion of a Church conference in which the elders wanted to learn more about how to proceed with their duties.

- We need to achieve balance as we work to support our families and the Church, and we are to be "diligent in all things." Idleness is a sin so serious that it would displace the unrepentant individual from the circle of the Church (see also D&C 60:13). Clearly the Lord upholds faithful diligence as a central principle for a Zion society. There can and will never be a substitute for work. Our blessings are predicated on the primary principle of self-reliance. The model in this regard is the Savior Himself, who said to His detractors: "My Father worketh hitherto, and I work" (John 5:17). How have you been able to balance your work in the family, Church, and community with good outcomes? How can you improve in this regard?

Rejoicing and Reasoning Together

How Can Temporal Work Be Made a Spiritual Activity?

The Savior said: "Behold, I stand at the door, and knock: if any man hear my voice, and open the door, I will come in to him, and will sup with him, and he with me" (Rev. 3:20). He can be called the "Portal of Providence." Through the guidance of the Lord—our divine Portal of Providence—we can consecrate ourselves and all that we have—our time, our talents, our resources—to provide for our families and assist in building the kingdom of God. In doing so, we receive abundant blessings from the Lord, enabling us to give even more to the cause of Zion. Giving and then receiving, receiving and then giving—this is the eternal cycle of providence yielding a harvest of everlasting joy. The Lord has stated: "All things unto me are spiritual" (D&C 29:34)—thus our quest for temporal well-being and self-reliance also depends on how well we cultivate the spiritual qualities of the divine nature. Consider the ten grand qualities of the divine nature of the Savior: "Remember faith, virtue, knowledge, temperance, patience, brotherly kindness, godliness, charity, humility, diligence" (D&C 4:6). These qualities provide the key for making our temporal stewardship a spiritual endeavor as we follow the example of Jesus Christ:

1. Faith—With faith in yourself, you can do many good things; with faith in God, you can do all things "in the strength of the Lord" (Alma 20:4). With a spirit of hope, you can "be of good cheer" (D&C 61:36) and overcome all fear and doubt—not just for now, but forever.

How are you using faith and hope to overcome the temporal challenges of life? The Savior said, "In the world ye shall have tribulation: but be of good cheer; I have overcome the world" (John 16:33). How can you follow His example? Good cheer is a sign of faith. How are you manifesting good cheer to yourself and others? How does the "fear of God" strengthen your faith (see D&C 122:9)?

2. Virtue—Purity of thought and action will tune your heart and mind to the Spirit. The Lord said, "If ye will enter in by the way, and receive the Holy Ghost, it will show unto you all things what ye should do" (2 Ne. 32:5). Thus you can "stand in holy places, and . . . not be moved" (D&C 45:32).

In what ways are you supplicating the Lord for guidance by the Spirit in your professional and temporal needs and challenges? How are you ensuring that your professional involvements remain completely honorable and upright? How are you teaching virtue and honor to your children and all who depend on you for livelihood? How are you manifesting your obedience by paying tithes and offerings?

3. Knowledge—Stewardship, both spiritual and temporal, takes knowledge and understanding. Through the scriptures you gain access to the "power of God unto salvation" (D&C 68:4); through "all good books" (D&C 90:15) and other avenues of continuing education, you gain career skills to support your family.

How important is continuing education in your life? What avenues of continuing education (books, seminars, certificate and degree programs, Internet, internships, use of mentors, and so on) are most helpful to you? How can studying and pondering the scriptures help you in your career and professional life? How can continuing learning help you and your family enjoy greater health?

4. Temperance—By "being temperate in all things" (Alma 7:23), you can awaken the spirit of vitality and safety in your family and avoid any tendency to "have it all right now." Being provident rather than extravagant is the pathway to peace and joy.

How are you doing at practicing and teaching the principle of saving for a rainy day? What is the status of your food storage program? What kind of produce garden do you have? (Even modest residences can accommodate small indoor and/or outdoor garden projects.) How can you learn to find joy in life by taking care of needs rather than focusing on wants?

5. Patience—"And seek the face of the Lord always, that in patience ye may possess your souls, and ye shall have eternal life" (D&C 101:38). Likewise, patience in temporal matters—avoiding all excess—will allow you to possess confidence and the respect of your family.

The Lord advised, "And he who receiveth all things with thankfulness shall be made glorious; and the things of this earth shall be added unto him, even an hundred fold, yea, more" (D&C 78:19). How does that help you cultivate patience in temporal concerns? How can you teach family members the value of patience in seeking for desired blessings? How does preparing with patience give you security?

6. Brotherly kindness—The spirit of loving encouragement, team-building, unity, and kindness fills the provident home, leaving no room for fault-finding, selfishness, or "unrighteous dominion" (D&C 121:39). Kindness is a treasure you can freely give to all others.

The eternal cycle of providence is expressed as "Give and then receive; receive and then give." How does this operate in your life, and how can you apply this principle more fully? The Lord said, "And remember in all things the poor and the needy, the sick and the afflicted, for he that doeth not these things, the same is not my disciple" (D&C 52:40).

How do you balance that task with your need to care for your own family?

7. Godliness—Provident living depends on seeing with a higher vision. We can "look to God and live" (Alma 37:47), or we can look to worldliness and lose sight of our spiritual and temporal well-being. Let us look up to God, follow His counsel, and visit Him often in His holy house.

To the suffering Prophet Joseph Smith the Lord said: "Know thou, my son, that all these things shall give thee experience, and shall be for thy good" (D&C 122:7). How can you make a new context for your own tribulation by seeing it from a godly perspective? How can the triumph of the Lord help you overcome your own challenges? Consider this: "The Son of Man hath descended below them all. Art thou greater than he?" (D&C 122:8).

8. Charity—A provident person is one who serves others—even in his or her time of need. Charity is "the pure love of Christ" (Moro. 7:47)—demonstrated in how we show our love in helping others (see Matt. 25:40). The word *providence* relates to the action of "providing" for others as well as for ourselves.

As you seek to provide for your own family in challenging times, how can you remember and apply the counsel of James? "Pure religion and undefiled before God and the Father is this, To visit the fatherless and widows in their affliction, and to keep himself unspotted from the world" (James 1:27). How can you help bring joy to widows, the lonely, those with special needs, and the homeless or near homeless?

9. Humility—A humble heart is a grateful heart—not one that is prideful or self-obsessed. "By humility and the fear of the LORD are riches, and honour, and life" (Prov. 22:4). Humility is not a weakness, but a key to heavenly power. In our humility we see more clearly the operation of the Lord's grace in lifting us beyond our weaknesses.

In the past, how has the Lord blessed you to overcome your trials? He said: "I give unto men weakness that they may be humble; and my grace is sufficient for all men that humble themselves before me; for if they humble themselves before me, and have faith in me, then will I make weak things become strong unto them" (Ether 12:27). How will the Lord bless you today to transform humility into strength?

10. Diligence—Diligence dispels idleness and opens up the gateway to self-reliance and provident living. Men and women are "agents unto themselves" with power to "bring to pass much righteousness" (D&C 58:28). The diligent are by nature provident, for "the laborer is worthy of his hire" (D&C 31:5).

The Lord has promised that His "providence" will make us "independent" (self-sustaining and self-reliant) "notwithstanding the tribulation which shall descend upon you" (D&C 78:14). How will your own diligence help your loved ones become independent of temporal concerns? "Thrust in your sickle with all your soul, and . . . your family shall live" (D&C 31:5). How does this promise give you confidence to proceed?

The Savior said, "Be of good cheer, for I will lead you along. The kingdom is yours and the blessings thereof are yours, and the riches of eternity are yours. And he who receiveth all things with thankfulness shall be made glorious; and the things of this earth shall be added unto him, even an hundred fold, yea, more" (D&C 78:18–19). In this, we perceive the manifestation of the power of love. Heavenly Father loves you. His Son, Jesus Christ, loves you. When you consecrate your time, talents, and resources to provide for all who depend on you and work diligently to build up the kingdom, the Lord will open the windows of heaven and pour out an abundance of blessings—"that there shall not be room enough to receive it" (Mal. 3:10). Through your work and toil you can lay the foundation for a godly preparation, for the Lord has promised the faithful, "If ye are prepared ye shall not fear" (D&C 38:30).

How Can We Use Our Time More Wisely?

Time is a most precious commodity. It is what life is made up of. It can't be stored or saved; it can only be used. The truth is: Everyone could use it more wisely. Often we simply let life take us down the "river of time." We simply partake of whatever is going on today. However, the pivotal idea about the use of time is that you can choose how to use it—you can plan what you want to have happen. If you can control your time, you can control your productivity. Most of all, you'll enjoy life more and have better self-esteem. In terms of ultimate goals, the most productive use of time was identified by the Savior: "But seek ye first the kingdom of God, and his righteousness; and all these things shall be added unto you" (Matt. 6:33; see also 3 Ne. 13:33). If our time is spent fulfilling that commission faithfully and valiantly, then we will have mastered time in the way the Lord has ordained.

Here are four strategies to help you be more efficient and effective with the use of your time:

- **Commit your time to things that matter most.** Idleness is impossible when you are passionate about life. *Focus energetically on key priorities*—set a few top-priority goals for your life, and concentrate on the daily and weekly actions that will bring you closer to the realization of these objectives. Most of your other time-consuming activities can be eliminated or held to a minimum. *Plan well*—make plans based on gospel values and standards. Cut down on things that use time unproductively (excessive television watching, long telephone conversations, or too much texting, for example). *Filter wisely*—try to de-emphasize those things in life that have no lasting value. Place the accent on family, friends, and relationships rather than worldly possessions.
- **Use a few wise and proven methods of time management.** Prioritize carefully and follow through with exactness on what really matters. *Delegate*—learn the art and science of teamwork, delegation, and accountability. Those who "do it all" by themselves lose the opportunity to leverage their time and energy and fail to accelerate their rate of success through effective teamwork. *Layer your time*—where appropriate, try to derive multiple benefits from the same activity. An example would

be combining business and pleasure on the same trip, or using commute time to accomplish important professional tasks. In the "waiting moments," have something to read or write. Often a meditative moment will decrease stress. *Use the best tools*—plan and organize your activities using a suitable organizer (electronic or print). Schedule necessary functions so that you can keep unplanned interruptions to a minimum. Use succinct email or texting when appropriate rather than time-consuming correspondence or endless phone calls. Keep meetings to a minimum. *Keep score*—evaluate the results of all important activities. If you can't measure it, it's probably not serving useful ends. Assessment and stock-taking are indispensable time savers. Midcourse corrections may make all the difference in the world to the outcomes. *Avoid procrastination*—do the important things now.

- **Don't forget to have fun**. *Stay flexible and resilient*—don't become a slave to the routine daily tasks. *Stay flexible*—make time for the family. Be flexible enough to enjoy life. Don't become a slave to your planner; sometimes a little spontaneity can reap a harvest of good memories. *Avoid perfectionism*—some things need to be done adequately, not perfectly. We can become obsessed with perfection in the "routine daily tasks." This is not the best use of time. *Relax*—save time for meditation, exercise, and recreation. It is time used wisely because it will make you more productive in your other pursuits.

- **Remember the Lord's time**. *Measure with a higher clock*—during our busy day-to-day life, we sometimes forget to measure with the clock of heaven. We may become so efficient with mortal time-management that we forget to include those things that bring success on a higher plane of existence. Make time for scripture study, family activities, personal time, expressions of love, and service. It is a most valuable use of time. *Pray*—express gratitude. Ask for guidance. Ask for wisdom in the use of your time. Invest your time in the house of the Lord. Take time to hope and express gratitude. There are great dividends to such activities.

Real-life Stories for Heart and Mind

"You Haven't Lost Much." A stake president, extending a call to a local high priest, learned that the brother had just gone through a devastating loss of his source of income. "If you lose everything," said the president, "but retain your testimony of the gospel of Jesus Christ, you haven't lost much." And so it is. Our greatest anchor in times of trial is the spiritual witness that God lives and that we have hope through the Redeemer. That is the pearl of great price. That is the gospel treasure.

> *In times of financial reversal and distress, how does it help to anchor one's soul and disposition in the eternal values of the gospel? How is that the surest foundation for self-reliance and achieving a state of adequacy with respect to food, shelter, and the necessities of life?*

The Joy of Education. A young mother of a special-needs child spent several years going to evening school to obtain a degree in psychology. Why? She wanted to learn how to serve the needs of this special son, as well as the needs of her other children. The long nightly commute, the hours spent poring over books, and the investment of time and effort yielded a harvest of joy in being able to better serve her family. At the same time, she also served well in the Church and community.

> *The Lord said through the Prophet Joseph Smith: "The glory of God is intelligence, or, in other words, light and truth" (D&C 93:36). When we work to gain intelligence for the purpose of serving with love and compassion, is that not a measure of eternal glory in our lives? When we gather light in order to shed it charitably in the lives of loved ones, is that not the light of the eternities? How have you found that your diligence in learning worthwhile things generates the light of wisdom and authentic purpose in your life?*

Legacy of Work. A stalwart and successful medical practitioner and priesthood holder remembered always having to pull weeds as a little boy. Just when he would finish his chores and start to play, his father would tell him to go pull burdock (a large weed). Even though he tried to hide, his father always knew where he was. He couldn't escape, so he pulled burdock. He thought this was too much for a nine-year-old boy. The following year the family moved to the city, and two years later his father passed away. Life went on. He grew up and married a lovely woman, and they had eight beautiful children over the years. One day when musing on life's experiences, he realized that his father had given him one of life's greatest blessings. He had taught the most important lessons of life—obedience and work. Idleness was not tolerated in any form. He then realized that all he had accomplished in life was due to his work ethic.

From whom have you learned similar lessons of diligence and hard work? With whom have you shared these important principles as a blessing in their lives?

Pondering Prayerfully

Additional scriptures to consider and ponder:
- Ex. 20:17
- 1 Thes. 5:11–13
- 1 Tim. 5:8
- 1 Tim. 5:13
- Alma 34:32
- D&C 64:27
- D&C 78:13–15
- D&C 88:119
- D&C 104:78–80
- D&C 107:100

The following hymns inspire gratitude for work and self-reliance:
- "I Have Work Enough to Do" (*Hymns,* 224)
- "Let Us All Press On" (*Hymns,* 243)
- "Put Your Shoulder to the Wheel" (*Hymns,* 252)
- "We Are Marching On to Glory" (*Hymns,* 225)

Remember and Be Sure

The great welfare program of the Church is centered on the principle of self-sufficiency and work. Work is key to success and accomplishment in all human endeavor, and "the laborer is worthy of his hire" (D&C 31:5). As the Lord taught, "Verily I say, men should be anxiously engaged in a good cause, and do many things of their own free will, and bring to pass much righteousness; For the power is in them, wherein they are agents unto themselves. And inasmuch as men do good they shall in nowise lose their reward" (D&C 58:27–28).

In life, self-confidence and self-reliance play a vital role in improving performance and self-perception through hope, faith, and depending on the Lord. "Jesus said unto him, If thou canst believe, all things are possible to him that believeth" (Mark 9:23). And again, "With men this is impossible; but with God all things are possible" (Matt. 19:26). Therefore, let us help ourselves—and everyone else—become more diligent and self-reliant in faith and trust. When our life is in harmony with our deepest values, and when these values are eternal in nature, we will feel peace and achieve our goals. Above all, let us use our time wisely for celestial pursuits, such that we can say, with Paul, on that day of accountability, "I have fought a good fight, I have finished my course, I have kept the faith" (2 Tim. 4:7).

We are endowed with infinite capacity, sensed only faintly in this mortal state, but nonetheless present in our emerging and God-given potential—if we will but lift ourselves to the throne of industry, creativity, commitment to worthwhile purposes, and devotion to the cause of righteous endeavor. Let us all put our shoulder to the wheel and root out idleness from every facet of our lives. Let us place our focus on spiritual matters and remove ourselves from the entanglements of materialism and unnecessary debt. Let us commit valiantly to productive effort in building the kingdom of God and lifting ourselves and others to higher levels of achievement and spiritual refinement through focused planning, hard work, and covenant valor.

CHAPTER 28
Service: The Test of a True Disciple

Live in all things outside yourself by love. As you serve others, the children around you, your father, your mother, your associates, ever striving to make yourself and the world better, then will your souls grow in wisdom. Therein you will find the guide to the happy life. —David O. McKay (*Pathways to Happiness*, 161)

Opening the Window of Wisdom

True service is based on love. Love is the ultimate concern that brings about righteous service and good works on behalf of others—in the family, in the Church, and in the community. Nothing is as fulfilling as honorable and caring service. Nothing lifts and inspires as much as working for the good of others. Serving those who cannot help themselves is a vicarious act of goodness—one of the greatest expressions of love. By losing yourself in the service of others, you discover your authentic self, for it is only through service that your divine potential as a son or daughter of God can unfold in full measure with an abundant harvest of joy and happiness. The Savior said: "He that findeth his life shall lose it: and he that loseth his life for my sake shall find it" (Matt. 10:39). As you serve others in the spirit of the gospel, they will, in turn, have a desire to serve. It becomes not just

contagious, but exponential in its power to affect lives throughout the world. With the motive of love being expressed through service, we truly have the capacity to bless lives.

Serving is more than a duty—it is an opportunity. The test of a true disciple is in serving God willingly and submitting to His will in all things. The Savior admonished the people to enter in through the gate and follow the pathway leading to eternal life (see Matt. 7:13–14). He counseled them to become as good trees, bringing forth good fruit: "Wherefore by their fruits ye shall know them" (Matt. 7:20). In all things, the disciples of the Savior were to do the will of the Father (see Matt. 7:21), that they may one day return to His presence of eternal rest, "which rest is the fulness of his glory" (D&C 84:24). In this, the Savior Himself was the pattern, saying, "I am among you as he that serveth" (Luke 22:27). Service was to be the measure of greatness in the kingdom: "But whosoever will be great among you, let him be your minister; And whosoever will be chief among you, let him be your servant" (Matt. 20:26–27).

The Savior offered a parable that encapsulated all that He was teaching the people about faithful obedience and devoted service: Those who follow His sayings are like the man who wisely builds his house upon the rock so that the winds and tempest will have no power to bring it down. By contrast, those who do not follow His sayings are like the man who foolishly builds his house upon the sand, where there is no security and no longevity (see Matt. 7:24–28). Following in the footsteps of the Savior leads one through the divinely ordained steps of gospel obedience and heartfelt service and into a state of being where the promised blessings of joy and eternal life are realized.

Of special importance in rendering service is to watch out for the lost sheep and bless the wayward and struggling. "Remember the worth of souls is great in the sight of God; For, behold, the Lord your Redeemer suffered death in the flesh; wherefore he suffered the pain of all men, that all men might repent and come unto him" (D&C 18:10–11). Reaching out to help those who need spiritual sustenance is the source of great joy (see D&C 18:15–16). In our day, the Lord has said: "Wherefore, be faithful; stand in the office which I have appointed unto you; succor the weak, lift up the hands which hang down, and strengthen the feeble knees" (D&C 81:5). As Saints of the latter days, we have entered into a covenant through baptism to help people with their burdens and to comfort them in their hour of need and mourning (see Mosiah 18:8–9). We are therefore to reach down and lift up all those around us in all circumstances and at all times.

The kingdom of God is organized under the banner of service, with a wondrous network of interrelated stewardships and callings in the priesthood, Relief Society, and other auxiliaries designed to extend service in a systematic and productive way. The operant motto is: "Wherefore, now let every man learn his duty, and to act in the office in which he is appointed, in all diligence" (D&C 107:99). This scripture also applies to the sisters of Zion who serve with diligence and charity in their various callings. In addition, all members serve on their own initiative to help family members and neighbors enjoy the blessings of the gospel in fuller measure, based on principles of faith and obedience.

Synergy and mutual support are reflected in the process of building up the kingdom of God through service, with offices and callings being blended "for the perfecting of the saints, for the work of the ministry, for the edifying of the body of Christ: Till we all come in the unity of the faith, and of the knowledge of the Son of God, unto a perfect man, unto the measure of the stature of the fulness of Christ" (Eph. 4:12–13). Shared leadership and shared responsibility are key ingredients for the furtherance of the gospel of Jesus Christ. When the burdens are shared the load is lightened, and there is exhilarating joy in working together.

Genuine encouragement and praise are pure sunshine in the process of rendering service. Some of the greatest blessings in life lie in the expression of approval for something someone else has done. People need approval. People need to feel accepted. People need to know they are all right. People need to know that they are of worth and can do meaningful things. Genuine praise and encouragement become some of the greatest motivating tools in the world. As a central part of serving, let us say something good about our family, friends, and coworkers. It will bless our lives as well as theirs. If we are in a leadership position, we should continually praise, instruct, and then encourage. We will have a better relationship and all involved will find joy in the work. Remember that this is always motivated by the pure love of Christ with genuine concern for the welfare of others. Honest and genuine praise and encouragement can change the soul. Thanksgiving and gratitude expressed bring so much joy to the receiver as well as the giver. As you look to see the good in others, you will live the thirteenth Article of Faith: "If there is anything virtuous, lovely, or of good report or praiseworthy, we seek after these things." Our service should continually reflect the practice of giving praise and encouragement, resulting in a harvest of abundance and unity.

Inspired by Latter-Day Prophets

Brigham Young: Let every man and woman be industrious, prudent, and economical in their acts and feelings, and while gathering to themselves, let each one strive to identify his or her interests with the interests of this community, with those of their neighbor and neighborhood, let them seek their happiness and welfare in that of all (*Discourses of Brigham Young,* 303).

> *Where do we find happiness and welfare? In the happiness and welfare of all. Happiness is never an isolated state of being; welfare is never faring well alone. Service to all is the key. How has the truth of this principle been manifested to you over the years? How can you ensure that all within your circle of friendship are blessed, and that no one is forgotten?*

Joseph F. Smith: If I do my duty, according to my understanding of the requirements that the Lord has made of me, then I ought to have a conscience void of offense; I ought to have satisfaction in my soul, in the consciousness that I have simply done my duty as I understand it, and I will risk the consequences. With me it is a matter between me and the Lord; so it is with every one of us (*Gospel Doctrine: Selections from the Sermons and Writings of Joseph F. Smith,* 249).

In what ways is our service to others truly a matter between ourselves and the Lord? How does the covenant of baptism represent a commitment to the Lord that we will serve others? (See Mosiah 18:8–10; D&C 90:24.)

John A. Widtsoe: Those who have authority should not be rulers, nor dictators; they should not be arbitrary; they should gain the hearts, the confidence and love of those over whom they preside, by kindness and love unfeigned, by gentleness of spirit, by persuasion, by an example that is above the reproach and above the reach of unjust criticism. In this way, in the kindness of their hearts, in their love of their people, they lead them in the path of righteousness, and teach them the way of salvation, by saying to them, both by precept and example: Follow me, as I follow our Head. This is the duty of those who preside (*Priesthood and Church Government,* 68–69).

Whether we lead in the family, in the Church, or in the community, there is eternal logic in following the principle: "Follow me as I follow the Lord." We commit to following the pathway of righteousness and charity, obedience and love—and those we serve will discern that we genuinely have their interests at heart and will abide with us in this process of being perfected in Christ (see Moro. 10:32–33). As you consider those who have served as your leaders over the years, how did your confidence in their Christlike patterns of living give you confidence in following their example? How can you present yourself to loved ones and those you serve as one who follows the Lord in all ways?

Ezra Taft Benson: Reach out to others. Rather than turning inward, forget self and really serve others in your Church callings, in personal deeds of compassionate service, in unknown, unheralded personal acts of kindness (*Come, Listen to a Prophet's Voice,* 59).

The reach of love moves outwardly, not just inwardly. As you have practiced this principle over the years, what has been your experience performing good deeds of service anonymously— in "unknown, unheralded" ways?

Truths to Liken

Matt. 25:21—"His lord said unto him, Well done, thou good and faithful servant: thou hast been faithful over a few things, I will make thee ruler over many things: enter thou into the joy of thy lord."

- In the Savior's parable of the talents, we catch a glimpse of the grand feelings of satisfaction we will experience if we can endure to the end in valor and righteousness, having served in faith and devotion, and at last be welcomed by the Lord and Master with acceptance and rejoicing.
- Ultimately, the Savior will welcome the good and faithful home again with confirming acceptance and blessings of greater joy. In smaller but still significant measure, we can lift up and encourage others along the highways and byways of life by frequently recognizing their good desires and efforts and by praising them with sincerity and genuine respect for their service in Zion. How have you been able to bless the lives of others by recognizing the ways in which they have been a "good and faithful servant"?

Matt. 25:40—"And the King shall answer and say unto them, Verily I say unto you, Inasmuch as ye have done it unto one of the least of these my brethren, ye have done it unto me."

- In the Savior's parable of the sheep and the goats, we learn that our service to God's children is truly our service to God.
- When we serve one of the "least," we serve one of the greatest, for *all* of God's

children—even the most marginal and forgotten—are majestic sons and daughters of the Almighty, worthy in every respect of our attention and love. To remember them and serve them is to remember and serve the Lord. In His ministry, the Savior went out of His way to serve the downtrodden, the rejected, those despised of the leading classes: "But their scribes and Pharisees murmured against his disciples, saying, Why do ye eat and drink with publicans and sinners? And Jesus answering said unto them, They that are whole need not a physician; but they that are sick" (Luke 5:30–31). In what ways have you occasionally been able to give service to "one of the least of these my brethren"? How did this give you the comforting feeling of serving the Lord?

James 2:26—"For as the body without the spirit is dead, so faith without works is dead also."

- The celebrated counsel of James concerning the need to be an exemplar of righteous service is a reminder that faith is power unto action: "Even so faith, if it hath not works, is dead, being alone. Yea, a man may say, Thou hast faith, and I have works: shew me thy faith without thy works, and I will shew thee my faith by my works" (James 2:17–18).
- Good works and charitable service are at the heart of a covenant life. Faith is power leading to good works. As you observe others around you and note that many are demonstrating admirable works of service, what does that say about the strength of their faith? How do your own acts of service provide a measure of your own faith in the truths of the gospel?

Mosiah 2:17—"And behold, I tell you these things that ye may learn wisdom; that ye may learn that when ye are in the service of your fellow beings ye are only in the service of your God."

- The aging King Benjamin taught this powerful principle to his people as

part of his final act of service in the kingdom.
- As we serve others we literally serve our Savior. When we truly believe that, we will serve others out of our inherent goodness and find great joy in doing so. How have you been able to prepare a legacy of service for the coming generation? What will you be remembered for in the years to come?

D&C 108:7–8—"Therefore, strengthen your brethren in all your conversation, in all your prayers, in all your exhortations, and in all your doings. And behold, and lo, I am with you to bless you and deliver you forever. Amen."

- These are words from a short revelation given through the Prophet Joseph Smith at Kirtland, Ohio, on December 26, 1835, on behalf of a priesthood brother requesting to know what the Lord would have him do.
- If you could ask the Lord through His prophet what you should be doing, the counsel might be very similar to the words given above: serve others and know that the Lord is with you. Truly we should seek to bless others at all times, thus helping perfect the Saints. There are many ways to help others who stand in need—visiting them, praying for them personally, putting their names on the prayer roll in the temple, encouraging and admonishing them by the power of the word, and showing them a sweet example of goodness. As moved by the Spirit, we can be directed in all things to bless and strengthen our brothers and sisters. How has the Spirit helped you to serve others? Has your patriarchal blessing given you counsel and direction on how to use your gifts and talents in the service of others?

D&C 128:15—"And now, my dearly beloved brethren and sisters, let me assure you that these are principles in relation to the dead and the living that cannot be lightly passed over, as pertaining to our salvation. For their salvation is necessary and essential to our salvation, as Paul says concerning the fathers—that they without us cannot be made perfect—neither can we without our dead be made perfect."

- These are words from an inspired epistle on vicarious temple work for the dead written to the Church on September 6, 1842, by the Prophet Joseph Smith. He was at the time in hiding to avoid falling into the hands of authorities seeking to take him captive on false charges.

- Our service is not only to the living, but also to the dead. We have been encouraged and admonished to seek out our kindred dead and to help our brothers and sisters who are beyond the veil by doing vicarious temple work for them. In this way we can help them gain their exaltation. It is our sacred duty (see D&C 138:54, 58). How has temple service for the deceased been a source of joy and satisfaction to you and your extended family circle? What are your thoughts about the process of perfection depending on the mutual relationships and bonds within the family circle— past, present, and future?

Rejoicing and Reasoning Together

How Can Our Service to Wayward Children Be Accounted as a Worthy Offering?

Please read the following sequence of quotations from the prophets, and then consider the question that follows:

- "The Prophet Joseph Smith declared— and he never taught a more comforting doctrine—that the eternal sealings of faithful parents and the divine promises made to them for valiant service in the Cause of Truth, would save not only themselves, but likewise their posterity. Though some of the sheep may wander, the eye of the Shepherd is upon them, and sooner or later they will feel the tentacles of Divine Providence reaching out after them and drawing them back to the fold. Either in this life or the life to come, they will return. They will have

to pay their debt to justice; they will suffer for their sins; and may tread a thorny path; but if it leads them at last, like the penitent Prodigal, to a loving and forgiving father's heart and home, the painful experience will not have been in vain. Pray for your careless and disobedient children; hold on to them with your faith. Hope on, trust on, till you see the salvation of God." —Orson F. Whitney (*Conference Report,* April 1929, 110)

- "Let the father and mother, who are members of this Church and kingdom, take a righteous course, and strive with all their might never to do a wrong, but to do good all their lives; if they have one child or one hundred children, if they conduct themselves towards them as they should, binding them to the Lord by their faith and prayers, I care not where those children go, they are bound up to their parents by an everlasting tie, and no power of earth or hell can separate them from their parents in eternity; they will return again to the fountain from whence they sprang." —Brigham Young (quoted in *Doctrines of Salvation,* 2:90–91)

- "God has fulfilled His promises to us, and our prospects are grand and glorious. Yes, in the next life we will have . . . our sons and daughters. If we do not get them all at once, we will have them some time. . . . You that are mourning about your children straying away will have your sons and your daughters. If you succeed in passing through these trials and afflictions and receive a resurrection, you will, by the power of the Priesthood, work and labor, as the Son of God has, until you get all your sons and daughters in the path of exaltation and glory. This is just as sure as that the sun rose this morning over yonder mountains. Therefore, mourn not because all your sons and daughters do not follow in the path that you have marked out to them, or give heed to your counsels. Inasmuch as we succeed in securing eternal glory, and stand as saviors, and as kings and priests to our God, we will save our posterity." —John Taylor (*Millennial Star*, 22 January 1894, 51–52)

What hope and consolation, faith and assurance do you feel as you consider these statements by the prophets of God? God loves us. He loves these children. Through mercy and grace and accountability things will work out in the Lord's due time.

What Is Our Service Role as "Under-Shepherds" in the Kingdom?

Prior to His Crucifixion, the Savior taught His disciples: "I am the good shepherd: the good shepherd giveth his life for the sheep" (John 10:11). Later, just before His Ascension, the resurrected Lord used the same symbolism in teaching a precious lesson on service, saying to Peter:

> Simon Peter, Simon, son of Jonas, lovest thou me more than these? He saith unto him, Yea, Lord; thou knowest that I love thee. He saith unto him, Feed my lambs.
> He saith to him again the second time, Simon, son of Jonas, lovest thou me? He saith unto him, Yea, Lord; thou knowest that I love thee. He saith unto him, Feed my sheep.
> He saith unto him the third time, Simon, son of Jonas, lovest thou me? Peter was grieved because he said unto him the third time, Lovest thou me? And he said unto him, Lord, thou knowest all things; thou knowest that I love thee. Jesus saith unto him, Feed my sheep. (John 21:15–17)

In latter-day revelation, the Lord renewed this imagery, with a promise: "Wherefore, I am in your midst, and I am the good shepherd, and the stone of Israel. He that buildeth upon this rock shall never fall" (D&C 50:44).

If the Lord is the Good Shepherd, then we are commissioned and called as His "under-shepherds" to watch over the flock under His direction. The parable of the lost sheep provides a timeless job description for our service (see Luke 15:4–7): "I

say unto you, that likewise joy shall be in heaven over one sinner that repenteth, more than over ninety and nine just persons, which need no repentance" (Luke 15:7). Each and every soul is precious to our Heavenly Father and our Savior—and to us as well (see Moses 1:39; Mosiah 28:3; D&C 18:10–16). Every effort needs to be made to find and reclaim, through loving service, our brothers and sisters who have strayed (see Matt. 18:14).

The under-shepherds who fail to honor their covenant callings are rebuked of the Lord with the words: "Son of man, prophesy against the shepherds of Israel, prophesy, and say unto them, Thus saith the Lord GOD unto the shepherds; Woe be to the shepherds of Israel that do feed themselves! should not the shepherds feed the flocks?" (Ezek. 34:2; compare John 10:1–2, 10). By contrast, those who rise in valor to guard and guide the flock shall harvest eternal joy (see D&C 18:15–17).

We as under-shepherds of the Lord have the same purpose as the Lord Himself. We should have ultimate concern for all mankind in the spirit of love and service. Let us perform our personal stewardships—which cannot be delegated—with diligence and honor. President Ezra Taft Benson has provided the following checklist for the fathers in Zion (and by extension to the mothers as well) to assess their success as under-shepherds:

Shepherds—fathers in Israel:
- Are you holding family prayer with your family, morning and evening?
- Do you hold a regular, consistent, inspiring family home evening once a week?
- Do you lead out in spiritual matters?
- Is your example what it should be before those whom you lead?
- Do you ask and pray for the welfare of your own?
- Do you love them?
- Would you give your life for them? . . .

Today our Lord repeats the same charge He gave Peter. He repeats it with the same emphasis, the same repetition: "Feed my lambs. . . . Feed my sheep. . . . Feed my sheep!" —Ezra Taft Benson (*Come unto Christ*, 68)

As you consider these questions in relation to your own stewardship, review also the counsel of President Benson in the following broad sweep of the territory of service in the kingdom of God: "With a shepherd's care, our new members, those newly born into the gospel, must be nurtured by attentive fellowshipping as they increase in gospel knowledge and begin living new standards. Such attention will help to ensure that they will not return to old habits. With a shepherd's loving care, our young people, our young lambs, will not be as inclined to wander. And if they do, the crook of a shepherd's staff, a loving arm and an understanding heart, will help to retrieve them. With a shepherd's care, many of those who are now independent of the flock can still be reclaimed. Many who have married outside the Church and have assumed the life-styles of the world may respond to an invitation to return to the fold" (The Teachings of Ezra Taft Benson, 231–232).

How Can We Improve Our Service to the Lord?

Here are some ideas to consider as we strive to bless and serve those who are lost, wayward, or struggling:

- **Love everyone**—It is given to us that we should love everyone with the pure love of Christ (see John 13:34–35). It is a commandment (see John 15:12) with a precious blessing that we shall never fall if we remain obedient (see 2 Pet. 1:10). In order to love with a perfect, unfailing love we are to seek to possess the pure love of Christ (see Moro. 7:48), which will provide strength and support as we seek to bless those who have strayed. We can have an overwhelming desire to seek them out (see John 21:15–17) and then we can number them and name them so they can be nurtured with the good word of God (see Moro. 6:1–4). We can seek to understand their situation, each person coming with different perceptions and challenges. We can be careful not to judge except righteously (see JST, Matt. 7:1–2), showing forth love with empathy and patience. Once their needs are identified and understood, we are better able to assist them. Sometimes they do not perceive their needs and are blinded. Resolving this kind of situation takes time and patience and total reliance on the Lord (see Prov. 3:4–5).

- **Seek counsel and strength from the Lord and the Spirit**—We can seek direction through prayer (see 3 Ne. 14:7), the guidance of the Spirit (see 2 Ne. 32:5), the counsel of the Lord (see Jacob 4:10), the scriptures (see 2 Ne. 3:23), and our leaders (see D&C 108:1). The Lord is always there to help us and strengthen us in all things (see Alma 26:11–12). Those we serve need to feel our love and caring spirit. We can be their true friend. When love is felt, people are drawn by its magnificent motivating power (see 3 Ne. 27:13–15).

- **Get them involved**—A concerted effort on their part is also essential. It is imperative that they accept responsibility and make some form of commitment to change. Real growth requires commitment. Love can be manifested to them through kindly encouragement and instruction, but they need to step forward with a desire to improve. We can follow through and be their support in trying times. We can utilize all the resources available—family, friends, ward leaders, ward council, and everything that the Lord inspires us to do. All of this is to be done in wisdom, at the proper pace according to their capacity to change. This is an expression of never-deviating love and concern for the welfare of our brothers and sisters. It is a program of effectiveness in leadership and charity.

- **Seek to strengthen their faith in Christ**—The Savior is their rock (see Hel. 5:12). Let us do all we can to increase their faith in Him (see Luke 17:5) so that their faith might become perfect in Him (see 2 Ne. 9:23). We can focus on the one. As directed by the Spirit, one-on-one contact can be very effective even as the Savior demonstrated His love for the Nephite people one by one (see 3 Ne. 11:15). Never give up; never give in; and never give out. The test of life is surely endurance. Enduring to the end in all things is the key, especially as we act as instruments in the hands of the Lord to bless struggling Saints who desperately need our help. We can press forward with "unwearyingness" (see Hel. 10:4–5). Patience and time are our allies. Through exercising our faith, we can have hope in all things through the Atonement of our Savior Jesus Christ (see Moro. 8:26).

What About Civic Duty and Volunteer Service?

As members of society we have a moral and civic responsibility to our neighborhood, community, county, state, nation, and the world at large. We are children of a loving Heavenly Father; therefore, all of us are brothers and sisters—and we should be our brothers' and sisters' keeper. We need to understand our unique role and capacity to help humanity. As Saints, our overwhelming concern should be for our fellowman—hence we should serve them with compassion (see Matt. 25:40; 1 Ne. 1:5; Mosiah 2:17). We seek to make the world a better place to live, that all might enjoy freedom and the pursuit of happiness. Concerning the appointment and election of leaders, the Lord has counseled: "Wherefore, honest men and wise men should be sought for diligently, and good men and wise men ye should observe to uphold; otherwise whatsoever is less than these cometh of evil" (D&C 98:10). It is incumbent upon all, at all costs, to seek righteous men and women to serve in leadership positions that affect our community and nation. When people choose unrighteous leaders, the people suffer. The twelfth Article of Faith states: "We believe in being subject to kings, presidents, rulers, and magistrates, in obeying, honoring, and sustaining the law." The people should uphold the government where they reside, "while protected in their inherent and inalienable rights by the laws of such governments" (D&C 134:5). If there is something with respect to government that needs changing, then the people should work within the law to establish something better.

Exercising civic duty and carrying out volunteer service should be a natural expression of a Latter-day Saint acting as a disciple of Jesus Christ.

Our vision of becoming like our Savior should include the vision of love of country, concern with how we can help those in need, a focus on whom we can serve today, and a motivation rooted in our desire to serve and bless. Surely we need not be commanded in all things. We need to be about our Father's business—blessing His children, our brothers and sisters.

As you consider your role in community service, you might use the following checklist to guide your assessment: (1) be informed by studying the issues and seeking information from reputable sources; (2) support the election process for local, state, and national leaders; be proactive in mind and deed; always vote; involve your family in discussion to teach service principles and responsibility; (3) be active in volunteer service; use personal leadership by picking a cause or projects where your service, expertise, energy, and leadership can be applied; cooperate with organized civic efforts; (4) attend community meetings: town meetings, school board meetings, PTA gatherings, and informative lectures on current issues; (5) stand for something; cultivate the mindset of a civic leader; remember that one person can make the difference; stand on values; seek to uphold principles of truth in the government arena; concentrate on things that matter, choosing causes that make a difference in people's lives; (6) make civic duty a lifelong pursuit: learn from the past; act in the present; plan for the future; seek wisdom through experience; let us grow from it and promote action that is positive and helpful to the community.

Real-life Stories for Heart and Mind

Holiness to the Lord. There are countless ways to sing praises to God for His protecting hand and merciful blessings. Some express their praise through the medium of painting or sculpture, some through poetry or discourse, some in personal journals, and still others through quiet acts of selfless service when they "succor the weak, lift up the hands which hang down, and strengthen the feeble knees" (D&C 81:5). Elder Theodore M. Burton often shared the story about his Grandfather Moyle, who had been a skillful craftsman. The gentleman had lost his leg on a farm in Alpine, Utah, after being kicked by a cow, and had great difficulty hobbling about. But he nevertheless traveled many miles each day to reach the construction site of the Salt Lake Temple, where his appointed mission was to chisel in the walls of granite the phrase, "Holiness to the Lord." Those simple words of praise have inspired countless thousands who visit the temple and its sacred grounds. Genuine praise for God, in all of its forms, is a means to lift the one who praises, to edify the community of those giving thanks, and to magnify the joy of the gospel. It is a way to give utterance to the transcendent concept of "Holiness to the Lord" in our lives of service.

In your own life, how have you found that service to the Lord and His children is the best way to overcome melancholy or disappointment, or to transcend the burdens that sometimes come with the mortal experience?

The Dusting Wand. A noble and devoted high priest of senior age had a long history of service in the Church. Despite severe and crippling medical challenges, he was constantly reaching out to express concern for others and help them in any way possible. When his name came up on the schedule of those appointed to take their turn cleaning the chapel, he insisted on participating—even though his condition made it difficult to walk, let alone operate one of the vacuum cleaners. "What can I do to help?" he asked. The captain of the cleaning team thought for a moment, then suggested that he might want to try using one of the dusting wands to clean the picture frames that hung along the hallways of the building. He smiled and cheerfully went about his duties—slowly though devotedly— not ceasing until every picture was completely clean. His associates watched him throughout the cleaning period, dragging his lame foot along as he reached up and attended to his duties. His demeanor reminded them of the scripture: "Wherefore, now let every man learn his duty, and to act in the office in which he is appointed, in all diligence" (D&C 107:99). If our duty at the moment is to dust pictures in the meetinghouse, then we can do so with valor and dedication, and feel the pride of accomplishment and service.

Since that time, this devoted high priest has gone to his heavenly reward, yet he has left behind an example of one who did his duty in all diligence. Sometimes we are called on to serve in leadership offices; sometimes we are called on to teach and counsel; sometimes we are called on to go to the house of the Lord and offer up our oblations and sacraments to the Most High (D&C 59:12); and sometimes we are called on to dust the pictures in the meetinghouse. All of this is part of the Lord's work when done willingly and with an eye single to the glory of God.

How does this example remind you that everyone is important in the process of building the kingdom of God? How have your services over the years contributed to the unfolding of God's design for happiness and salvation in the latter days?

"They Don't Have to Be Perfect—They Just Have to Come." Some time ago a couple reported a situation to the high priest group leader in their ward. Home teaching visits to their home had become somewhat sporadic, and the family was sensing a deficit in the priesthood encouragement and support that can come from the faithful discharge of home teaching responsibilities. The wife's job description of a home teacher was a classic: "They don't have to be perfect—they just have to come." Her memorable comment was the ideal metaphor for the greater human condition as viewed in the context of the plan of salvation and the law of justification. We are not justified through perfect obedience to the commandments (since no mortal measures up to the law in perfection). However, we *can* be justified through "the merits, and mercy, and grace of the Holy Messiah" (2 Ne. 2:8)—"after all we can do" (2 Ne. 25:23). In effect, the Lord says: "They don't have to be perfect—they just have to come." It is in the "coming" before Him with a broken heart and a contrite spirit, in faith and obedience, that we can aspire through our service to achieve the essential state of justification through grace and service, and thus enter into His presence once again.

What are your thoughts about the need to serve in diligence and faithfulness, even though our service is not at the level of perfection? How does this relate to the words of Ammon: "Yea, I know that I am nothing; as to my strength I am weak; therefore I will not boast of myself, but I will boast of my God, for in his strength I can do all things" (Alma 26:12)?

Pondering Prayerfully

Additional scriptures to consider and ponder:
- 1 Cor. 12:25–26
- Col. 3:23–24
- 1 Tim. 4:12
- Alma 31:34–35
- Moro. 9:6
- D&C 58:27–28

The following hymns help inspire us regarding service:
- "Called to Serve" (*Hymns,* 249)
- "Dear to the Heart of the Shepherd" (*Hymns,* 221)
- "Who's on the Lord's Side?" (*Hymns,* 260)

Remember and Be Sure

If we are following the Savior's admonitions as laid out for us in the Sermon on the Mount—the greatest of all gospel sermons—then we will find ourselves leading the lives of true disciples of Christ. We will be acting out of pure motivation—doing the right things for the right reason. We will be following the Savior's example by praying and fasting with sincere purpose, submitting our own will to the will of the Father in all things. We will exercise charity, compassion, and forgiveness in our dealings with others. And we will make service to God and His children the governing philosophy of our lives, building our house on the solid foundation of eternal principles and saving doctrines.

When we become service-oriented people, life's greatest blessing—happiness—will flow to us. Happiness is the byproduct of expressing love. As we consider our lives and where we are and what we can do, we can strive to remember that service is multifaceted, giving us an endless variety of opportunities to assist others and add value to their lives in pure devotion and selflessness. If we make service an integral part of our life, then life will serve us well. We will have a life filled with the joy of serving. We will follow in the footsteps of the Savior, the paragon of loving compassion and service.

CHAPTER 29
The Word of Wisdom

No official member in this Church is worthy to hold an office, after having the Word of Wisdom properly taught him, and he, the official member, neglecting to comply with or obey it. . . . —Joseph Smith (*HC* 2:35)

Opening the Window of Wisdom

Who can better guide us in the prudent use of the earth's resources for our good and well-being than the omniscient and benevolent Creator? We are wise, then, to obey the Lord's counsel on health by avoiding that which harms the body and by promoting the wise use of nature's abundance to improve and preserve our health. There are grave physical and spiritual consequences when we stray from the Lord's counsel on health, just as there are magnificent physical and spiritual advantages awaiting those who heed the word of the Lord in humble gratitude.

The riches of the earth, given through the grace and blessing of God, allow us to choose that which will have the most beneficial impact on health and well-being. The Lord has given us the resources of the earth for nurture and sustenance during our days of probation: "For, behold, the beasts of the field and the fowls of the air, and that which cometh of the earth, is ordained for the use of man for food and for raiment, and that he might have

in abundance" (D&C 49:19). Yet these things are to be used with wisdom. From earliest times, the inspiration of the Spirit has prompted those with receptive hearts to walk in pathways of prudence when it comes to health. The prophet Daniel responded with courage in the Babylonian halls of royalty: "But Daniel purposed in his heart that he would not defile himself with the portion of the king's meat, nor with the wine which he drank: therefore he requested of the prince of the eunuchs that he might not defile himself" (Dan. 1:8). When Daniel and his colleagues chose instead to nourish themselves with "pulse" (Dan. 1:12)—in other words, wholesome seeds and grains—their health improved: "And at the end of ten days their countenances appeared fairer and fatter in flesh than all the children which did eat the portion of the king's meat" (Dan. 1:15).

In Book of Mormon times, the people learned to depend on the medicinal qualities of certain herbs for enhancing health "because of the excellent qualities of the many plants and roots which God had prepared to remove the cause of diseases, to which men were subject by the nature of the climate" (Alma 46:40). In the latter days, the Lord has given similar counsel: "And whosoever among you are sick, and have not faith to be healed, but believe, shall be nourished with all tenderness, with herbs and mild food, and that not by the hand of an enemy" (D&C 42:43).

By far the most complete statement from the Lord concerning health is found in Section 89 of the Doctrine and Covenants, given through the Prophet Joseph Smith on February 27, 1833, in the translating room at the Whitney Store in Kirtland, Ohio (see *HC* 1:327–329). In this "Word of Wisdom," the Lord reveals His counsel—a principle with a promise—concerning "the temporal salvation" (verse 2) of the Saints in the last days. Wine, strong drink, tobacco, and hot drinks (tea and coffee) are not for the use of man. Wholesome herbs and every fruit "in the season thereof" (verse 11) are ordained for the use of man. Meat is to be used "sparingly" (verse 12). Grains and the fruit of the vine are for the use of man. The Saints who remember and do these sayings, "walking in obedience to the commandments" (verse 18), are promised health, wisdom, knowledge, strength, and deliverance from the "destroying angel" (verse 21).

Brigham Young gives this background for the revelation:

> I think I am as well acquainted with the circumstances which led to the giving of the Word of Wisdom as any man in the Church, although I was not present at the time to witness them. The first school of the prophets [according to the instructions given in D&C 88:127, December 27, 1832] was held in a small room situated over the Prophet Joseph's kitchen, in a house which belonged to Bishop Whitney, and which was attached to his store, which store probably might be about fifteen feet square. In the rear of this building was a kitchen, probably ten by fourteen feet, containing rooms and pantries. Over this kitchen was situated the room in which the Prophet received revelations and in which he instructed his brethren. The brethren came to that place for hundreds of miles to attend school in a little room probably no larger than eleven by fourteen. When they assembled together in this room after breakfast, the first they did was to light their pipes, and, while smoking, talk about the great things of the kingdom, and spit all over the room, and as soon as the pipe was out of their mouths a large chew of tobacco would then be taken. Often when the Prophet entered the room to give the school instructions he would find himself in a cloud of tobacco smoke. This, and the complaints of his wife at having to clean so filthy a floor, made the Prophet think upon the matter, and be inquired of the Lord relating to the conduct of the Elders in using tobacco, and the revelation known as the Word of Wisdom was the result of his inquiry. (*JD* 12:157)

The Word of Wisdom as outlined in Section 89 is a covenant law with blessings predicated on our obedience. The revelation itself outlines specific dietary guidelines, but by logical extension, the spirit of the Word of Wisdom also counsels against the use of non-prescribed drugs that could have harmful and addictive effects (see President Howard W. Hunter's admonition in "Let Lives Reflect the Gospel," *LDS Church News,* December 17, 1994). The Word of Wisdom does not specifically allude to unwise extremes in regard to a specific dietary regimen, counseling only that we do things "with prudence and thanksgiving" (verse 11).

We all seek feelings of well-being and vitality. In all aspects of life—mental, social, emotional, intellectual, and physical—we want to be healthy. The price of good health includes proper nutrition, regular exercise, adequate rest and relaxation, and consulting as needed with skilled medical professionals. The promises for those who follow the Lord's counsel on health are extraordinary:

> And all saints who remember to keep and do these sayings, walking in obedience to the commandments, shall receive health in their navel and marrow to their bones;
> And shall find wisdom and great treasures of knowledge, even hidden treasures;
> And shall run and not be weary, and shall walk and not faint.
> And I, the Lord, give unto them a promise, that the destroying angel shall pass by them, as the children of Israel, and not slay them. Amen. (D&C 89:18–21)

Inspired by Latter-Day Prophets

Heber J. Grant: Health is one of the most precious gifts of God to man. All the wealth in the world cannot produce health. . . . Health of body and of mind, and hidden treasures of knowledge from God are all predicated upon keeping this simple law of the Word of Wisdom (*Gospel Standards: Selections from the Sermons and Writings of Heber J. Grant*, 48).

> *The price to pay for the treasure of enhanced health of mind and body is very modest, consisting of obedience to fundamental principles revealed by God through His Prophet. In this age of rapidly escalating health costs, it is widely understood that the vast majority of debilitating medical problems are directly related to unwise lifestyle choices. In your own extended family circle, how can you help others to enjoy greater health and well-being by more fully applying all aspects of the Lord's law of health?*

J. Reuben Clark, Jr.: The word of wisdom is not a rule of conduct; it is a law—the Lord's law—of health. It was promulgated by Him. The law existed before He told it to us; it would exist if the revelation were blotted out from the book. The Church authorities have nothing to do with the law. God, speaking through the forces of the physical world, has prescribed it, and so long as those forces exist the law will remain (cited in *The Teachings of Ezra Taft Benson*, 477–478).

> *The Lord's law of health is universal and eternal. He has shared aspects of it with His children by revelation as a way to bless their lives. It is not an organizational directive, nor a cultural preference. It is a law. What blessings have you experienced in relationship to obeying this law of health? How have your loved ones been blessed through obedience to the law?*

N. Eldon Tanner: For many years after the [Word of Wisdom] was given, people thought the Mormons peculiar because they abstained from these seemingly harmless substances. Then scientists began to discover many harmful effects of tobacco, and today we are made increasingly aware of the health hazards caused by the use of tobacco, tea, coffee, and alcohol, with additional warnings about the risks involved for the unborn children of pregnant women. Latter-day Saints should be able to accept the words of the prophets without having to wait for science to prove the validity of their words. We are most fortunate to have a living prophet at the head of the Church to guide us, and all who heed

his counsel will be partakers of the promised blessings which will not be enjoyed by those who fail to accept his messages ("The Debate Is Over," *Ensign*, Aug. 1979, 2).

> *Keeping the Word of Wisdom is an exercise in faith. The early Saints did not have the benefit of scientific discovery to confirm the harmful effects of using certain substances, such as tobacco, alcohol, and addictive drugs. The Word of Wisdom also counsels the use of wholesome herbs, fruits, and grains—plus the use of meats in moderation ("sparingly"— D&C 89:12). To what extent does it require faith to cultivate a lifestyle in which this latter counsel becomes a central part of one's diet?*

Ezra Taft Benson: The condition of the physical body can affect the spirit. That is why the Lord gave us the Word of Wisdom. . . . The Word of Wisdom leads to clean habits, thoughts, and actions. It will make you more receptive to the Spirit of God which cannot dwell in an unclean tabernacle (see Hel. 4:24) (*The Teachings of Ezra Taft Benson*, 475–476).

> *The Word of Wisdom is not simply a temporal or physical law. It is linked to one's spiritual and emotional health as well. The Lord declared: "Wherefore, verily I say unto you that all things unto me are spiritual, and not at any time have I given unto you a law which was temporal; neither any man, nor the children of men; neither Adam, your father, whom I created" (D&C 29:34). How has your spiritual, mental, emotional, and intellectual well-being been improved as a result of obeying the Word of Wisdom? How can you help your loved ones and those you teach in the Church make the connection between obedience to the Word of Wisdom in its physical dimensions and achieving the spiritual and mental blessings that follow?*

Truths to Liken

Rom. 14:17—"For the kingdom of God is not meat and drink; but righteousness, and peace, and joy in the Holy Ghost."

- The Mosaic Law as recorded in Leviticus listed many dietary restrictions. Here

Paul tried to teach his audience that there is more to religion and spirituality than simply what one eats and drinks under the Law of Moses. The Lord suggested the same thing (see Mark 7:18–19).

- How can we avoid going to extremes regarding the Word of Wisdom? How can we balance our obedience to the Word of Wisdom with our obedience to all of the commandments of the Lord?

1 Cor. 3:16–17—"Know ye not that ye are the temple of God, and that the Spirit of God dwelleth in you? If any man defile the temple of God, him shall God destroy; for the temple of God is holy, which temple ye are."

- In these well-known words of Paul to the Corinthians, he reminded his audience of their sacred station as sons and daughters of God, with the obligation of keeping themselves pure and untainted.
- When we understand the sacredness of our mortal tabernacle, we will be more diligent in keeping it healthy, strong, and pure. The blessings of the Spirit can be ours if we are pure and clean (see 1 Cor. 6:19–20). How can obedience to the Word of Wisdom help you qualify for magnificent blessings from God through the Spirit?

D&C 59:18–20—"Yea, all things which come of the earth, in the season thereof, are made for the benefit and the use of man, both to please the eye and to gladden the heart; Yea, for food and for raiment, for taste and for smell, to strengthen the body and to enliven the soul. And it pleaseth God that he hath given all these things unto man; for unto this end were they made to be used, with judgment, not to excess, neither by extortion."

- These words are part of a revelation given through the Prophet Joseph Smith in Zion (Jackson County, Missouri) on August 7, 1831.
- Gratitude for all gifts from God, given for the nourishment and clothing of His children, should fill our souls with

joy. When we know that it pleases God to have blessed us with the abundance of the earth, we are reminded to accept these gifts with humility, moderation, thankful hearts, and total aversion to misusing or abusing these resources. Think about this admonition: "And in nothing doth man offend God, or against none is his wrath kindled, save those who confess not his hand in all things, and obey not his commandments" (D&C 59:21).

D&C 88:124—"Cease to be idle; cease to be unclean; cease to find fault one with another; cease to sleep longer than is needful; retire to thy bed early, that ye may not be weary; arise early, that your bodies and your minds may be invigorated."

- These words were included in a revelation given through the Prophet Joseph Smith at Kirtland, Ohio, that was designated by the Prophet as the "olive leaf . . . plucked from the Tree of Paradise, the Lord's message of peace to us." The elders of the Church were counseled to teach one another words of wisdom and to establish a house of prayer, fasting, faith, learning, glory, and order—even a house of God (a temple). They were to instruct one another in the spirit of love, charity, and fellowship "in the house of the Lord, in the school of the prophets" (verse 137). Their preparations were to include the items listed in the verse given above.
- The commandment to regulate one's sleep by retiring early and rising early is a covenant commandment, resulting in added vitality of mind and body. How has gaining adequate rest following periods of devoted activity resulted in blessings for you and for your loved ones?

D&C 89:4—"Behold, verily, thus saith the Lord unto you: In consequence of evils and designs which do and will exist in the hearts of conspiring men in the last days, I have warned you, and forewarn you, by giving unto you this word of wisdom by revelation."

- The Word of Wisdom came by way of warning to the Saints concerning evil and destructive designs in the hearts of certain individuals in the last days.
- What individuals or groups do you think might be viewed by the Lord as destructive and conspiring? How can you help your loved ones and those you serve in the Church avoid such influences?

Rejoicing and Reasoning Together

How Can We Use the Word of Wisdom with *Wisdom*—Avoiding Imbalance and Speculation?

President Joseph F. Smith warned against the practice of having "religious hobbies" that would become obsessions and lead to "holier than thou" attitudes. As an example, he cited preoccupation with the Word of Wisdom at the expense of the full panorama of God's law: "We have noticed this difficulty: that Saints with hobbies are prone to judge and condemn their brethren and sisters who are not so zealous in the one particular direction of their pet theory as they are. The man with the Word of Wisdom only in his brain, is apt to find unmeasured fault with every other member of the Church who entertains liberal ideas as to the importance of other doctrines of the gospel" (*Gospel Doctrine: Selections from the Sermons and Writings of Joseph F. Smith*, 117).

Moreover, President Harold B. Lee cautioned against what he called "speculative interpretations of the Word of Wisdom," saying: "Even gospel principles, like the Word of Wisdom, if I might say it discreetly, are undergoing some strange dietary interpretations which I fancy would startle our early leaders and cause even the Omnipotent to smile indulgently in His dwelling place as He contemplates the spectacle of the many uninspired interpretations of His holy laws and speculations on sacred matters which for reasons of His own He has never seen fit to reveal to man" (*The Teachings of Harold B. Lee*, 204). He then recounted an experience where one member of the Church was persuaded that the use of pork in the summertime was contrary to the Word of Wisdom: "I said, 'Oh, where did he say that? I haven't read that.' 'Why, in the Word of Wisdom.' I said, 'Not in my Doctrine and Covenants, it doesn't

say that. Will you open the Doctrine and Covenants and read me what you have just said?'" When the visitor tried to justify her position, she was directed to read Section 49 of the Doctrine and Covenants, where the Lord made it clear that forbidding the use of meats is not ordained of Him (see D&C 49:18). In regard to the reference about using meats only in times of "famine" (D&C 89:13), he told her that he "was not sure what a famine was as mentioned in section 89. We should eat meat sparingly, yes, as the Lord counsels. But when we reach a hard and fast conclusion contrary to what the Lord has said, be careful" (ibid.).

Some have raised questions about the reference to eating herbs and fruits "in the season thereof" (D&C 89:11). President Joseph Fielding Smith has provided this counsel:

> Some have stumbled over the meaning of the expression "in the season thereof," and have argued that grains and fruits should only be used in the season of their growth and when they have ripened. This is not the intent, but any grain or fruit is out of season no matter what part of the year it may be, if it is unfit for use. The apple under the tree bruised and decaying is out of season while the good fruit is waiting to be plucked from the tree. (*Church History and Modern Revelation*, 2:148)

> *As you consider these and similar issues regarding the Word of Wisdom, how have you personally been able to maintain a wise balance in applying the Lord's law of health? How can you assist others to use the Word of Wisdom wisely and harvest the blessings associated with it?*

How Can We Make Sure That We Follow the Word of Wisdom Consistently?

Here are three ideas to help us keep the Word of Wisdom faithfully:

- **Set goals and make plans**. You can organize your meals to include those foods that are recommended and specified in the Word of Wisdom. You can make and keep a commitment to abstain from alcohol, tobacco, hot drinks (tea and coffee), and drugs. (Those with problems concerning the Word of Wisdom can seek counsel from their Church leaders, ask for a priesthood blessing, seek medical help, and do everything in their power to overcome hurtful habits.)

- **Count the blessings**. By following the Word of Wisdom, you will be healthier in every respect. You are the temple of God—purity in this regard enables you to receive the inspiration of the Lord. You can find grand treasures of wisdom, knowledge, and strength (see D&C 89:19–20). You can have economic benefits—those who maintain a healthy lifestyle can realize enormous monetary savings over a lifetime. You can have clarity of thought and judgment by controlling what you take into your body. You can avoid depression and despair. You can be a self-starter with a winning attitude, not depending slavishly on harmful chemicals to get going. You can enjoy temple blessings— keeping the commandments with valor, including the Word of Wisdom, will allow you to have a temple recommend and go to the house of the Lord.

- **Depend on the Lord**. Praying with devotion and heeding the whisperings of the Holy Ghost will lift your spirit, edify your mind, and enable you to do all things "in the strength of the Lord" (Alma 20:4).

What specific actions can you personally take regarding proper diet, adequate rest, and pacing yourself wisely in order to have greater blessings of health and well-being?

Real-life Stories for Heart and Mind

"**I Brewed It Myself.**" A member of the Church learned firsthand that honoring God as well as honoring your fellowmen in the world is much less challenging if you have wise allies looking out for you. His senior faculty advisor in graduate school, a world-renowned scholar, was also a careful student of human affairs and human values. He regularly convened seminars in his home, where he served the graduate students coffee and tea. At his first such

event, the Church member was pleasantly surprised when the professor, after serving all the others their usual coffee and tea, offered him something quite different—a cup of herbal tea. "It's rose hips," he said, with a friendly twinkle in his eyes. "I brewed it myself from my rose plants. I know you don't drink coffee or regular tea, so this is for you." His generosity was matched only by his magnanimous respect for one's values and standards. Thereafter, at each such occasion, he hospitably prepared and served his LDS student a portion of delicious and nutritious rose-hips tea. Members of the Church never know how many eyes are watching, or how many hearts can be influenced for good when one strives in all diligence to keep the commandments.

As you have honored the Word of Wisdom, how has your obedience made you stand out as someone of principle? How has your obedience served to cast good light on the restored gospel of Jesus Christ?

"**The Higher Word of Wisdom.**" The Cooper Aerobics Center—a beautiful thirty-acre complex located in Dallas, Texas—is among the most recognized health institutions today, featuring what is arguably the leading preventive medicine program in the world. Dr. Kenneth H. Cooper, the founder, CEO, and president of the Center, is celebrated throughout the world for his pioneering work as the father of *aerobics,* a word he coined for his bestselling 1968 book of the same name. Now, many books later, he is single-handedly responsible for galvanizing tens of millions of people in more than fifty countries to increase their regular exercise regimen and thus partake of the benefits of increased health and wellness. His most famous statement proclaims the indisputable truth: "It is easier to maintain good health through proper exercise, diet, and emotional balance than it is to regain it once it is lost." What is notable about Dr. Cooper is not only his strategic drive and organizational genius, but his faith in God. On one occasion, for example, he told a group of Latter-day Saints that he could not possibly have survived the challenges and daunting difficulties he faced over the years of growth and progress without providential input and support.

Launched as a modest clinic in 1970, The Cooper Aerobics Center, with its eight service and research divisions, represents a vanguard movement for health and vitality. And yet there is another institution located only a few hundred yards to the east of the Cooper Campus that has a similar but even higher mission. It is an imposing "campus" of a spiritual nature, featuring a magnificent multi-spired edifice with a central door bearing the words "The House of the Lord." It is the Dallas Texas Temple of The Church of Jesus Christ of Latter-day Saints. There, as in the other temples of the Church throughout the world, the focus is likewise on health and wellness—of a spiritual and godly nature. There, life-changing truth of a healing kind is imparted to those who attend these sacred precincts—truth that transcends the here and now and opens up vistas for eternal well-being and divine nurture. The same Holy Being who revealed through the Prophet Joseph Smith in 1833 the Word of Wisdom to ensure that His children would "receive health in their navel and marrow to their bones; And shall find wisdom and great treasures of knowledge, even hidden treasures; And shall run and not be weary, and shall walk and not faint" (D&C 89:18–20)—that same Being continues the endowment of truth today by teaching faithful men and women in the house of the Lord the keys for returning to their heavenly home through the power and efficacy of the atoning sacrifice of Jesus Christ and the majestic sealing protocols of the holy priesthood. There is imparted the higher word of wisdom, the most potent "preventive medicine" regimen of the universe.

As the "temple of God" (1 Cor. 3:16), how does your body serve as an emblem of the house of the Lord? What steps can you take to continue to preserve it and in all things endure faithfully to the end?

Pondering Prayerfully

Additional scriptures to consider and ponder:
- Prov. 23:20–21
- 1 Cor. 6:19–20
- Mosiah 4:27
- D&C 49:18
- D&C 136:24

The following hymns contribute to a spirit of understanding and gratitude about the Word of Wisdom:
- "In Our Lovely Deseret" (*Hymns,* 307)
- "Keep the Commandments" (*Hymns,* 303)

Remember and Be Sure

All counsel from the Lord is a commandment to the righteous (see Jacob 4:10). Keeping the Word of Wisdom is a requirement for enjoying the blessings of the temple. The prophets have made it clear that it is a commandment for us to obey. The Lord's beneficial law of health is "given for a principle with promise, adapted to the capacity of the weak and the weakest of all saints, who are or can be called saints" (D&C 89:3).

The principle for harvesting the rich blessings of this Word of Wisdom is the principle of "remembering." It is well to review the promises in the context of remembering: "And all saints who remember to keep and do these sayings, walking in obedience to the commandments, shall receive health in their navel and marrow to their bones; And shall find wisdom and great treasures of knowledge, even hidden treasures; And shall run and not be weary, and shall walk and not faint. And I, the Lord, give unto them a promise, that the destroying angel shall pass by them, as the children of Israel, and not slay them. Amen" (D&C 89:18–21).

We can keep the Word of Wisdom in the strength of the Lord. He will provide a way for us so long as we have a desire, exercise our faith, and are willing to work diligently at keeping this, the Lord's law of health (see Ether 12:27; 1 Ne. 3:7; 17:2–3; Alma 26:11–12; Moro. 7:33). Let us therefore remember and be physically and spiritually edified and enriched.

CHAPTER 30
Charity: The Pure Love of Christ

Love is one of the chief characteristics of Deity, and ought to be manifested by those who aspire to be the sons of God. A man filled with the love of God, is not content with blessing his family alone, but ranges through the whole world, anxious to bless the whole human race. —Joseph Smith (*HC* 4:227)

Opening the Window of Wisdom

The essence of the gospel is to cultivate faith in the Lord Jesus Christ, through whose atoning sacrifice and mercy we can be sustained in our hope for salvation, and to confirm this hope through our own charity and works of covenant righteousness. Charity is the ultimate attribute of godliness. It constitutes obtaining the divine nature of Christ through faith, virtue, knowledge, temperance, patience, brotherly kindness and godliness, with all humility and diligence (see D&C 4:6). This pure love of Christ is total, complete, enduring, and characteristic of the divine Being. When one is possessed of this love, his or her desires are like our Savior's—to bless and serve mankind.

"Charity never faileth" (1 Cor. 13:8). Christ did not fail his Father, nor did He fail us; His pure love motivated His great sacrifice—the eternal, infinite, vicarious Atonement. When we possess that love, we act in our lives according to the principles of the

Atonement. When we possess charity—the "pure love of Christ" (Moro. 7:47), this love for all men, this desire to bless and serve—we then possess the qualities of genuine charity, and we never fail. For in the strength of the Lord we can do all things, just as Ammon demonstrated (Alma 26:12). In the strength of charity, through the Atonement of Christ, we begin to acquire an unconditional godly love, the divine nature of Christ, centered in love.

Love is a word we use repeatedly in the English language. It implies affection and strong heartfelt feelings. The Greek language uses three forms of love: *eros*—physical love; *philia*—brotherly and reciprocatory love; and *agape*—godly love. Since the English language uses a single word to express love, we might suggest a broader meaning for the word, one that embraces charity—ultimate concern that brings about righteous service. Charitable love is about caring, empathy, service, and kindness.

In kindness, one shows the qualities of goodness manifested in being gentle, thoughtful, sympathetic, cordial, pleasant, benevolent, and showing true love and respect to mankind—all the qualities leading to inner peace. Kindness of a charitable nature requires a character based on gospel principles. It becomes an outward expression of our love of God, a demonstration of a pure heart and genuine concern for others through authentic friendship. In the world where everyone needs love and acceptance, friendship is absolutely imperative. When friendship and charity are blended, forgiveness abounds. Charity remembers the saying: "JUDGE not, that ye be not judged" (Matt. 7:1). True disciples seek to be full of charity, abounding in good works and demonstrating Christlike love to everyone—showing forgiveness, brotherly kindness, and the spirit of gratitude for all of God's blessings.

The Sermon on the Mount is ultimately a discourse about charity. The Savior uses the occasion to teach the people that a person of charity is not given to judging others for their faults, but rather focuses on the process of self-cleansing through repentance and godly practice. The person of charity is not possessive and selfish, but gives to others freely out of love and compassion—just as parents willingly and lovingly serve the interests of their children. The epitome of charity is the Father, for we can approach the Father with full faith in His ability and desire to bless our lives: "Ask, and it shall be given you; seek, and ye shall find; knock, and it shall be opened unto you: For every one that asketh receiveth; and he that seeketh findeth; and to him that knocketh it shall be opened" (Matt. 7:7–8). How disposed are we to emulate the Father in how we practice charity in our lives? The Savior gives the key, which has come to be known as the "Golden Rule": "Therefore all things whatsoever ye would that men should do to you, do ye even so to them: for this is the law and the prophets" (Matt. 7:12).

On one occasion, a lawyer, thinking to tempt the Savior, asked Him the question, "What shall I do to inherit eternal life?" (Luke 10:25). Discerning the devious thoughts and motives of the lawyer, the Savior asked him: "What is written in the law? how readest thou? And he answering said, Thou shalt love the Lord thy God with all thy heart, and with all thy soul, and with all thy strength, and with all thy mind; and thy neighbour as thyself. And he said unto him, Thou hast answered right: this do, and thou shalt live" (Luke 10:26–28).

But the lawyer was not satisfied with truth and divine counsel. So he posed a second question: "And who is my neighbour?" (Luke 10:29). To this the Savior responded by reciting one of His most celebrated parables, that of the Good Samaritan. A man had been robbed, beaten, and left for dead along the road from Jerusalem to Jericho. In turn, he was ignored by a priest traveling along the same road, and then by a Levite. But a Samaritan came to his rescue in compassion and charity. When He had finished the parable, the Savior asked the lawyer, "Which now of these three, thinkest thou, was

neighbour unto him that fell among the thieves? And he said, He that shewed mercy on him. Then said Jesus unto him, Go, and do thou likewise" (Luke 10:36–37).

Loving one another in the spirit of charity is a commandment—the motive for every righteous act and the source of true joy. During the last hours with His Apostles before His Crucifixion, the Savior taught them magnificent lessons concerning the doctrines of the kingdom. In a display of gracious humility, He washed the feet of His anointed servants. At first, Peter objected: "Thou shalt never wash my feet. Jesus answered him, If I wash thee not, thou hast no part with me. Simon Peter saith unto him, Lord, not my feet only, but also my hands and my head" (John 13:8–9). The Lord assured him: "He that is washed needeth not save to wash his feet, but is clean every whit: and ye are clean, but not all" (John 13:10). The latter phrase, of course, was a reference to Judas, who would betray the Lord. In contrast to the vile deceit of Judas, the Lord expounded a doctrine of mutual loyalty and charity: "If I then, your Lord and Master, have washed your feet; ye also ought to wash one another's feet. For I have given you an example, that ye should do as I have done to you. Verily, verily, I say unto you, The servant is not greater than his lord; neither he that is sent greater than he that sent him. If ye know these things, happy are ye if ye do them" (John 13:14–17).

The Lord then pronounced a commandment superseding all others as a demonstration of fidelity to the divine cause: "A new commandment I give unto you, That ye love one another; as I have loved you, that ye also love one another. By this shall all men know that ye are my disciples, if ye have love one to another" (John 13:34–35). The Savior promised to send them the Comforter: "Peace I leave with you, my peace I give unto you: not as the world giveth, give I unto you. Let not your heart by troubled, neither let it be afraid" (John 14:27). Finally, "This is my commandment, That ye love one another, as I have loved you. Greater love hath no man than this, that a man lay down his life for his friends" (John 15:12–13). In these words, the Savior expressed the essence of charity.

Inspired by Latter-Day Prophets

Brigham Young: Only a few men on the earth understand the charity that fills the bosom of our Savior. We should have charity; we should do all we can to reclaim the lost sons and daughters of Adam and Eve, and bring them back to be saved in the presence of our Father and God. If we do this, our charity will extend to the utmost extent that it is designed for the charity of God to extend in the midst of this people (*Discourses of Brigham Young*, 273).

How expansive is the reach of charity? Enough to reach from the here and now into the distant eternities. When we serve in love to bring our neighbors into the fold of Christ, our modest deed of charity becomes infinite in scope, for the blessings that come from it are everlasting. As you consider your acts of charity over the years, how have these seeds grown into a harvest of thanksgiving and joy for those you have served? How can this harvest extend forever as a blessing to those you love?

Joseph F. Smith: The Latter-day Saints possess the spirit of salvation, and not the spirit of destruction; the spirit of life, not the spirit of death; the spirit of peace, not the spirit of disunion; the spirit of love for their fellow beings, not the spirit of hate (*Gospel Doctrine: Selections from the Sermons and Writings of Joseph F. Smith*, 75).

If we are charitable, full of peace and love, we can thank God from whom these blessings flow. Whenever we extend the hand of charity to others, it is because the Spirit of our Father in Heaven is prompting us to serve in humility, kindness, and love. Like Ammon, we do not take credit for our accomplishments, but rather we recognize the influence of the Lord (see Alma 26:12). How can you remember to thank your Father in Heaven in gratitude every time you render service to others?

George Albert Smith: I pray that the love of the gospel of our Lord will burn in our souls and enrich our lives, that it will cause husbands to be kinder to wives, and wives to be kinder to husbands, parents to children, and children to parents because of the gospel of Jesus Christ, which is a gospel of love and kindness. It will cause us, if we are living as we should, to love our neighbors as ourselves, and go out of our way, if possible, to help them understand

better the purpose of life (*The Teachings of George Albert Smith*, 136).

Charity is infectious and creates an aura— an environment with a certain kind of ambiance—that expands and touches all within its unfolding influence. If we radiate the spirit of charity, then others feel it and respond (inwardly, outwardly, or both) with the same life force and disposition. Think of those in your circle of activity who seem to radiate a special spirit of charity and benevolence. How do you feel in their presence? How can you also become to a greater degree the source of a charitable spirit that will engender in others the desire to serve and grow in the gospel?

Ezra Taft Benson: The final and crowning virtue of the divine character is charity, or the pure love of Christ (see Moro. 7:47). If we would truly seek to be more like our Savior and Master, learning to love as He loves should be our highest goal (*The Teachings of Ezra Taft Benson*, 275).

Charity is no small thing. Among the grand qualities of the divine nature (see D&C 4; 2 Pet. 1:4–8), charity rises to the zenith of importance. It is the quality that confirms the worth of man: "For if he have not charity he is nothing" (Moro. 7:44). If someone were to ask you what the objective of your life might be, or what would constitute the achievement of your highest potential, what would you say?

Truths to Liken

Ps. 142:4—"I looked on my right hand, and beheld, but there was no man that would know me: refuge failed me; no man cared for my soul."

- The Psalmist expressed the loneliness of life when we are without an anchor in the gospel. He continued: "I cried unto thee, O LORD: I said, Thou art my refuge and my portion in the land of the living" (Ps. 142:5).
- The gospel dispels loneliness, and charity comforts the downhearted. There is no worse feeling than being lonely or

unloved. We as disciples of Christ are to love one another (see John 13:34–35) and feed His sheep (see John 21:15–17). If we fail to do so, we relinquish our role as disciples: "And remember in all things the poor and the needy, the sick and the afflicted, for he that doeth not these things, the same is not my disciple" (D&C 52:40). Our joy and glory in life is to help people come unto Christ (see Alma 29:9–10). How do these thoughts confirm for you the counsel of the Lord: "Verily I say unto you, Inasmuch as ye have done it unto one of the least of these my brethren, ye have done it unto me" (Matt. 25:40)?

Matt. 22:37–39—"Jesus said unto him, Thou shalt love the Lord thy God with all thy heart, and with all thy soul, and with all thy mind. This is the first and great commandment. And the second is like unto it, Thou shalt love thy neighbour as thyself."

- This was the celebrated response of the Savior to one of the Pharisees, a lawyer who attempted to manipulate Him by asking what the greatest commandment was in the law. To love God embraces the first portion of the Ten Commandments, just as to love our neighbor covers the second. The inquiring Pharisee was left speechless after the statement quoted above, because the Savior was expressing inviolate and incontestable truth.
- We are to love God with all our heart, might, mind, and soul—and then show others the same kind of love. This fulfills all the law and the prophets (see Matt. 22:40). How can you make love the motive for obedience to God (see John 14:15) and service to others (see Mosiah 2:17)?

Col. 3:12–14—"Put on therefore, as the elect of God, holy and beloved, bowels of mercies, kindness, humbleness of mind, meekness, longsuffering; Forbearing one another, and forgiving one another, if any man have a quarrel against any: even as Christ forgave you, so also do ye. And above all these things put on charity, which is the bond of perfectness."

- In his epistle to the Colossians, Paul counseled them to "put on the new man, which is renewed in knowledge after the image of him that created him" (Col. 3:10). That image is reflected in the qualities of mercy, kindness, and the others listed above.
- In your opinion, what does Paul mean by the word *bond* in the expression "bond of perfectness"? How does this relate to the latter-day scripture that counsels us to "search diligently, pray always, and be believing, and all things shall work together for your good, if ye walk uprightly and remember the covenant wherewith ye have covenanted one with another" (D&C 90:24)?

1 Jn. 4:7–11—"Beloved, let us love one another: for love is of God; and every one that loveth is born of God, and knoweth God. He that loveth not knoweth not God; for God is love. In this was manifested the love of God toward us, because that God sent his only begotten Son into the world, that we might live through him. Herein is love, not that we loved God, but that he loved us, and sent his Son to be the propitiation for our sins. Beloved, if God so loved us, we ought also to love one another."

- John shared sublime truths about the nature of God and how we can know God though love. The measure of the Father's love for us is His gift of the Lamb of God, given to bring to pass the "immortality and eternal life of man" (Moses 1:39). The measure of our love for God is how we love one another in following the pattern of divine love.
- What are your thoughts about love being the key for knowing God? We are taught: "And this is life eternal, that they might know thee the only true God, and Jesus Christ, whom thou hast sent" (John 17:3). Could we interject John's witness by saying, "And this is life eternal, that they might *love, and thereby* know thee the only true God, and Jesus Christ, whom thou hast sent" (John 17:3)? How important, therefore, is love to our eternal salvation?

3 Ne. 12:44–45—"But behold I say unto you, love your enemies, bless them that curse you, do good to them that hate you, and pray for them who despitefully use you and persecute you; That ye may be the children of your Father who is in heaven; for he maketh his sun to rise on the evil and on the good."

- The resurrected Lord included this counsel in His discourse—similar to the Sermon on the Mount—given to the Saints at Bountiful in the New World.
- To be children of our Father in Heaven, we are to follow His example of showing mercy and love to all. Loving our enemies becomes the test of life. Do we love them? Do we care for their well-being? The sons of Mosiah not only cared for their Lamanite brethren, but went to them, served them, and brought them to Christ. Why? Because "they could not bear that any human soul should perish; yea, even the very thoughts that any soul should endure endless torment did cause them to quake and tremble" (Mosiah 28:3). This is love. How can you more fully practice this principle and help others find greater joy by doing so as well?

Moro. 7:48. "Wherefore, my beloved brethren, pray unto the Father with all the energy of heart, that ye may be filled with this love, which he hath bestowed upon all who are true followers of his Son, Jesus Christ; that ye may become the sons of God; that when he shall appear we shall be like him, for we shall see him as he is; that we may have this hope; that we may be purified even as he is pure. Amen."

- This is the concluding statement in Mormon's sermon on faith, hope, and charity included by his son Moroni in the final portion of the Book of Mormon chronicle. This is one of the most sublime presentations on charity in all of scripture.
- Christ is love incarnate. To prepare ourselves to meet Him one day, we are to become as He is by receiving from the Father a full measure of love reserved for those who are true followers of Christ. Love will know love; purity will know purity; the Christlike will know Christ. How can you cultivate the hope of being made pure and worthy of the divine presence of God?

D&C 121:41–42, 45—"No power or influence can or ought to be maintained by virtue of the priesthood, only by persuasion, by long-suffering, by gentleness and meekness, and by love unfeigned; By kindness, and pure knowledge, which shall greatly enlarge the soul without hypocrisy, and without guile— . . . Let thy bowels also be full of charity towards all men, and to the household of faith, and let virtue garnish thy thoughts unceasingly; then shall thy confidence wax strong in the presence of God."

- These words are from the inspired epistle written to the Church by the Prophet Joseph Smith in March 1839 from within the walls of Liberty Jail, where he and his colleagues were being subjected to wanton acts of cruelty and abuse.
- Kindness, charity, and love unfeigned are among the key attributes that should characterize all priesthood stewardships—and any callings—in the Church. Charity is to be an indwelling quality that governs thoughts and deeds and becomes manifested through pure service to others. In your opinion, how could Joseph Smith have brought forth such a transcending statement about kindness and charity when he was being subjected to such a high degree of brutality and ruthless mistreatment?

Rejoicing and Reasoning Together

Can You Identify These Prophets of Charity?

1. Forgiveness and Charity—He was the target of attempted murder by his brothers, then subsequently sold by them into slavery in a foreign realm, where his qualities of vision and leadership elevated him to the top level of governance. When his brothers came seeking help during an acute famine in their region, he forgave them tearfully and completely, choosing to become their rescuer and deliverer: "Now therefore be not grieved, nor angry with yourselves, that ye sold me hither: for God did send me before you to preserve life. . . . And God sent me before you to preserve you a posterity in the earth, and to save your lives by a great deliverance" (Gen. 45:5, 7).

2. Respect and Charity—He was chosen of God to rise up and lead the people in the stead of a wayward and proud sovereign who attempted continually to murder him and prevent his ascendancy. When the newly anointed leader had the chance to terminate these murderous attacks, he charitably refused, saying, "I will not put forth my hand against my lord, for he is the Lord's anointed" (1 Sam. 24:10). He thus manifested the spirit of respect for an anointed office and ultimate forgiveness as the paragon of mercy and clemency among the Lord's chosen.

3. Understanding and Charity—As prophet-leader of a vast empire of Israelite extraction, he was deposed by conspirators and forced to organize a recovery movement in exile. While fighting to restore the liberty and rights of his oppressed people, he received an epistle from his commanding general struggling in a different part of the realm to withstand the assaults of the enemy. The epistle accused the prophet-leader of gross tyranny, slothfulness, negligence—and even treason—in not sending critically needed supplies to the armies in the theater of engagement (see Alma 60:14–80). How did the prophet-leader respond to these accusations? In his letter to the general, he reveals the details of the insurrection, then says, "And now, in your epistle you have censured me, but it mattereth not; I am not angry, but do rejoice in the greatness of your heart. I . . . do not seek for power, save only to retain my judgment-seat that I may preserve the rights and the liberty of my people. My soul standeth fast in that liberty in the which God hath made us free" (Alma 61:9).

4. Faith and Charity—Obeying the command of God, this prophet-leader organized a small contingent of committed rescuers to travel by wagon to a distant part of the realm for the purpose of bringing charitable relief to their fellow Saints, who were being persecuted and tormented by violent mobs (see D&C 103:30–34). At one point a mob of nearly 400 men was converging on

the rescue camp, vowing to kill the leader and his group. When some wanted to rise up in defensive action, the leader ordered them to desist, saying: "Stand still and see the salvation of God" (see *Church History in the Fulness of Times,* 1993], 148). Soon "a small cloud like a black spot appeared in the north west, and it began to unroll itself like a scroll, and in a few minutes the whole heavens were covered with a pall as black as ink" (*HC* 2:104). The ensuing storm, of unprecedented violence, entirely frustrated the schemes of the scattering mob so that the rescue camp could proceed on its charitable mission.

You were probably able to identify the prophet figures described above. It may take somewhat more thought and pondering to answer the following question: How can I cultivate similar qualities of courage, leadership, and charity in order to carry out my own stewardship in the family and in the Church?

Real-life Stories for Heart and Mind

The Elixir of Charity. An elderly man had devoted all his days to service and building up the kingdom of God on earth. Now the toll of mortality was showing up more frequently in his life in the form of recurring illnesses and chronic discomforts. This time pneumonia had set in, together with a worrisome blood infection. He was lying in his hospital bed when the high priests group leader stopped by to greet him, fully expecting to hear of the struggles that come with advancing years. But the patient would have none of that. His number-one worry—despite the obvious dangers of his condition—was not his health, but rather his home teaching. Prior to his hospitalization, he and his companion had completed two of the three family visits assigned to them. One family remained. The good brother had made repeated calls from the hospital to try to arrange for backup assistance, but he had not been able to connect. When the visiting group leader asked about the remaining family, he mentioned an elderly widow who lived alone. "Oh," said the leader, "it turns out that, by coincidence, we of the high priests group leadership visited her just three days ago and left a spiritual message. Consider the visit done!" Immediately the eyes of the venerable high priest brightened and a look of peace washed over him. What a potent medicine is the divine elixir of charity in the heart of good people such as this older brother.

What better sign of gospel charity is there than a loving disposition that transcends one's own needs? Things turned out well for this older brother in the hospital, for he was living the principle so well articulated by Mormon: "But charity is the pure love of Christ, and it endureth forever; and who is found possessed of it at the last day, it shall be well with him" (Moro. 7:47). In what circumstances have others displayed genuine charity to you and your loved ones over the years? How can you help others more fully subscribe to the principle of charity, and thus reap a harvest of joy and satisfaction in life?

When Charity Calls. Two full-time missionaries of the Church were ministering to the needs of investigator families in a remote part of their mission field. Poverty was rampant. Many families had insufficient means for their daily needs. One family was destitute, so the missionary companions took everything they had—all of their reserve funds—and gave everything to the family so that these poor people might have food for survival. The elders were acting on pure faith, for they did not know how they would be able to support themselves until the next regular mission payment would come many days later. When they arrived back home that day they found a letter from the grandmother of one of the missionaries. Many days earlier she had sensed that her grandson was in need of additional support. She was well aware that the missionaries received funds regularly through the contribution channels funded by missionary families and friends, but she could not shake off the feeling that something extra was needed. Finally she responded to the prompting and mailed off the letter containing a check. The missionaries gratefully thanked their Father in Heaven for His goodness and the faithful and charitable response of the grandmother.

The prophet Isaiah put the principle into these words: "And it shall come to pass, that before they call, I will answer; and while they are yet speaking, I will hear" (Isa. 65:24). The divine directive to love one's fellows and care for their needs—"both spiritually and temporally" (Mosiah 4:26)—is integral to the gospel plan. On what occasions have you or others in your family circle been prompted to reach out in charity to help another? What was the harvest of joy and peace?

The Key to Life's Burdens. A father sat down next to his seven-year-old autistic son in Primary opening exercises and leaned over to whisper something to the boy's teacher that he and his wife felt they should be more involved during the class itself as well as opening exercises and sharing time. "It is quite a burden for you," he said, referring to the task of not only handling her regular class, but also this young boy with challenging autistic behaviors. Her response was unforgettable. She whispered back, "It is no burden when you love."

How have you found that love and charity remove the burdens of life in a wondrous and enduring way?

The Milk of Kindness. A priesthood brother recalls with utter clarity the scene he saw through the front porch windows of his childhood home one blistering-hot summer day. A gruff-looking stranger who was cutting down weeds along the edge of the street paused to mop his brow from time to time. The boy's father was also watching. Suddenly the father went to the kitchen and retrieved a new, unopened quart bottle of milk and went directly outside to speak with the stranger. The boy watched with fascination as his father and the stranger exchanged a few words. Then the father handed the milk bottle to the man, who gratefully accepted it, opened it, and immediately drank down the contents. Two things about this memory stood out for the boy. One was seeing a total stranger drink down a quart of milk right from the jar—quite a feat in itself. The other was the grateful look on his face, which was matched only by the glow of satisfaction on his father's face after having done a kind deed for a total stranger. The man has thought about that scene repeatedly in the intervening years, considering it—for all of its simplicity—to be a lasting legacy from his father concerning the milk of human kindness and a vivid reminder to be generous and charitable to others in their need.

Those who reach out willingly, even to strangers in need, are true disciples of Christ. King Benjamin counseled: "And ye will not suffer that the beggar putteth up his petition to you in vain, and turn him out to perish" (Mosiah 4:16). Have there been times where you have extended the arm of charity to strangers? What feelings of inner joy were generated?

Pondering Prayerfully

Additional scriptures to consider and ponder:
- Prov. 17:17
- JST, Matt. 7:2–5
- Matt. 25:40
- Gal. 5:6
- Eph. 2:19
- Eph. 4:32
- 1 Pet. 4:8
- 1 Jn. 5:2
- Moro. 7:45
- Moro. 8:26
- D&C 121:9

The following hymns help us understand charity:
- "God Is Love" (*Hymns,* 87)
- "God Loved Us, So He Sent His Son" (*Hymns,* 187)
- "Have I Done Any Good?" (*Hymns,* 223)
- "Love at Home" (*Hymns,* 294)

Remember and Be Sure

Christ's love for us endures forever. When we are possessed of it, it endures in our lives. What are the decisive questions? Do we desire charity? Do we want to be possessed with love? Can we see the benefits and the blessings of love exercised in our life? Let us with all the energy of our hearts, with all our souls, with all our minds, and in all of our decisions seek to be full of charity. Life will be beautiful and we will find peace as only the Lord can give. "And now abideth faith, hope, charity, these three; but the greatest of these is charity" (1 Cor. 13:13).

When you have a goal to be a friend to others you will have a generous number of friends. One of the joys of life is the memories you share with people you love—your family and friends. You can never have too many friends and you never are a friend to too many people. The Lord said to His servants in the latter days: "I will call you friends, for you are my friends, and ye shall have an inheritance with me" (D&C 93:45). Similarly, should we not make the cultivation of friendships and the bestowing of sincere charity and service on our friends a central part of our lives? Expressions of love and service are the hallmark of true disciples of Christ. It is love that brings about righteous service. The love that our Savior taught was a godlike, perfect, and unconditional love that never fails. Indeed, the motto for a lifetime is simply this: "Charity never faileth" (1 Cor. 13:8).

CHAPTER 31
A Life of Honesty

And above all things one must be honest and sincere in the performance of his religious duties. On these lines we are dealing with our conscience and with our God, but in every phase of life strict honesty is the "best policy." —Joseph F. Smith (*From Prophet to Son: Advice of Joseph F. Smith to His Missionary Sons,* 108–109)

Opening the Window of Wisdom

Honesty is the expression of one's true character. Honesty is the core of integrity. Honesty is the character trait without equal in building and maintaining relationships. When based on honesty and truthfulness, communication can be trusted. Thus in the family, school, Church, and workplace—in all of life—honesty becomes a principle that governs, a principle of trust. With trust, all relationships can be built and maintained—especially our relationship with God. The thirteenth Article of Faith begins: "We believe in being honest, true, chaste, benevolent, virtuous, and in doing good to all men."

Heavenly Father would have a Zion people that are unified in charity, service, and honesty: "I say unto you, be one; and if ye are not one ye are not mine" (D&C 38:27). We cannot be one in an environment of greed, envy, inequality, and dishonesty. All mortals are as nothing when measured against the majesty of God (see Mosiah 4:5, 11).

Thus we are to aspire through integrity and honor to serve our fellowman in the strength of the Lord and to practice honesty in all our dealings.

Integrity and honesty form the foundation of our capacity to prove ourselves worthy of returning to the presence of our Heavenly Father and His Son. The little exaggerations, the silent tongue when things need to be said, the so-called misrepresentations—all of these go against integrity and undermine honesty. Dishonesty within the bonds of matrimony is without doubt the most destructive force of all, devastating families with long-lasting effects. Trusting relationships are destroyed because of the lack of fidelity. In all situations, honesty is pivotal in maintaining a level of communication built on trust. Honesty is the best policy—the *only* policy—and should become our quest in all things.

As we heed our prophet and follow principles of honor and integrity, life will be sweet. We can make honesty the policy in family life. In our dealings with others and with the Lord, we can make integrity the flywheel of personal progress and the central principle of spiritual growth and vitality. Joseph of Egypt had the strength of character to flee the scene of temptation. We can follow his extraordinary example and do the same.

Inspired by Latter-Day Prophets

Joseph Smith: Therefore we beseech of you, brethren, that you bear with those who do not feel themselves more worthy than yourselves, while we exhort one another to a reformation with one and all, both old and young, teachers and taught, both high and low, rich and poor, bond and free, male and female; let honesty, and sobriety, and candor, and solemnity, and virtue, and pureness, and meekness, and simplicity crown our heads in every place; and in fine, become as little children, without malice, guile or hypocrisy (*Teachings of the Prophet Joseph Smith*, 137).

Honesty is an overarching principle of nobility that unites all of the character traits listed above by the Prophet Joseph Smith. All of the Ten Commandments are illuminated by the light of honesty. The Savior has told us to "become as a little child" (3 Ne. 11:37–38) in obedience to the laws of God. By doing so, we are honest with our Father in Heaven, holding nothing back, giving ourselves into His eternal care. The Prophet has told us to "crown our heads" with honesty and its related virtues. How can you rest assured that the "crown" upon your head is so characterized?

David O. McKay: And what is the crowning glory of man in this earth so far as his individual achievement is concerned? It is *character—character developed through obedience to the laws of life as revealed through the gospel of Jesus Christ, who came that we might have life and have it more abundantly.* Man's chief concern in life should not be the acquiring of gold nor fame nor material possessions. It should *not* be the development of physical prowess nor of intellectual strength, *but his aim, the highest in life, should be the development of a Christlike character* (*Man May Know for Himself: Teachings of President David O. McKay*, 29).

To become like Christ is to be spiritually and eternally honest, with no guile, no deception, no misrepresentation—just transparently honest in every way. That way we can be full of light, with no shadows of darkness to deflect the blessings of truth and love that emanate from God. How can you help disseminate this principle so that others, too, can find joy in being spiritually honest?

David O. McKay: Jesus the Christ lived a life of truth. Men have called him an enthusiast; they have

accused him of being a dreamer, an ascetic, a recluse, and other epithets have they hurled at him, but they are loath ever to say that Christ, the Redeemer, was dishonest or untrue. His life was a life of honesty, honor, uprightness (*Man May Know for Himself: Teachings of President David O. McKay*, 140).

To follow in the footsteps of the Savior, we can strive to cultivate a life of honesty, honor, and uprightness. These three related standards form the essence of our progress. As you consider your own life, how can you become even more Christlike in honesty, honor, and uprightness? How can you share these principles with those you love?

Ezra Taft Benson: Members of The Church of Jesus Christ of Latter-day Saints are to emulate the character of the Savior. And what is His character? He has identified the cardinal virtues of His divine character. . . . He said, "Remember faith, virtue, knowledge, temperance, patience, brotherly kindness, godliness, charity, humility, diligence." (Doctrine and Covenants 4:6.) These are the virtues we are to emulate. This is the Christlike character (*Come unto Christ*, 48).

Honesty before God and man is the spirit of the qualities mentioned in D&C 4:6, because honesty implies integrity of character and spiritual uprightness in all things. Look at each of the ten qualities mentioned, and ask yourself how honesty contributes to the essence in each case. Think of each of the ten qualities and identify a person you know who exemplifies for you that quality in great measure. How can you exemplify these same qualities for your loved ones to a greater extent and thus be an even better example of spiritual honesty?

Truths to Liken

Ex. 20:15—"Thou shalt not steal."

- This divine command, one of the Ten Commandments, calls for honesty in respecting the property of others and not depriving people through deception and manipulation of what is rightfully theirs. Modern scripture states it thus:

"Thou shalt not steal; and he that stealeth and will not repent shall be cast out" (D&C 42:20).

- Those who are not honorable in regard to that which belongs to others are to be expelled from the society of Zion. Modern culture tends to be rather careless by condoning acts that take things from others deceptively. How can you help others, particularly young people, respect the rights of all people and avoid stealing in any of its forms?

Ex. 20:16—"Thou shalt not bear false witness against thy neighbour."

- Honesty in our relationships with others is also part of the commandments given by the Lord though Moses. Modern scripture expresses it thus: "Thou shalt not speak evil of thy neighbor, nor do him any harm" (D&C 42:27).
- Gossiping, lying, backbiting, degrading others—all of these are manifestations of dishonesty that are hurtful and cause disunity and discord. As you chance to hear such language from time to time, how can you respond in such a way as to promote the opposite: encouragement, praise, finding goodness in others?

1 Tim. 2:1–2—"I exhort therefore, that, first of all, supplications, prayers, intercessions, and giving of thanks, be made for all men; For kings, and for all that are in authority; that we may lead a quiet and peaceable life in all godliness and honesty."

- Paul exhorted the Saints to pray for blessings to be upon all people in order that peace, godliness, and honesty might prevail. This is the only verse in the scriptures (including the King James Version of the Bible) where the word *honesty* is used (although the word *honest* is used fairly frequently).
- We all desire peace, godliness, and honesty. Do we remember to pray for everyone, including those responsible for the government of the land, so that we can have the stated blessings? How can you be an example, in giving family and congregational prayers, of praying for others—including our community, state, national, and international leaders—so that honesty and related virtues can prevail and peace can abound?

Alma 27:27—"And they were among the people of Nephi, and also numbered among the people who were of the church of God. And they were also distinguished for their zeal towards God, and also towards men; for they were perfectly honest and upright in all things; and they were firm in the faith of Christ, even unto the end."

- In Mormon's account of the migration of the converted Lamanites to the Nephite territories, we learn that these courageous people of Ammon followed the teachings of Christ without compromise. They were in all respects upright and honest.
- True conversion brings with it personal righteousness, of which honesty is an integral part. How does "zeal toward God" ensure that people are honest with their fellowmen? How does zeal for eternal principles translate into honesty in our relationships with others? What experiences have you had with those who are zealously honest and therefore have earned our admiration and respect?

D&C 8:1—"Oliver Cowdery, verily, verily, I say unto you, that assuredly as the Lord liveth, who is your God and your Redeemer, even so surely shall you receive a knowledge of whatsoever things you shall ask in faith, with an honest heart, believing that you shall receive a knowledge concerning the engravings of old records, which are ancient, which contain those parts of my scripture of which has been spoken by the manifestation of my Spirit."

- These are the words of the Lord to Oliver Cowdery in a revelation given through the Prophet Joseph Smith at Harmony, Pennsylvania, in April 1829. Oliver wanted to translate ancient records, and the Lord counseled him accordingly.
- Prayer is to be uttered with faith and "an honest heart." In what ways do you

think honesty figures into the process of praying?

D&C 42:21—"Thou shalt not lie; he that lieth and will not repent shall be cast out."

- The Ten Commandments were reiterated in this latter-day revelation given through the Prophet Joseph Smith at Kirtland, Ohio, on February 9, 1831, and designated by him as "embracing the law of the Church." This particular application of the injunction to be honest, using a reference to lying, is unique to the latter-day version of the Ten Commandments.

- Lying is not condoned in a Zion society. God uses His word with uncompromising integrity; what He says always comes to pass. He expects His children to learn the same: to speak with infallible honor, never proclaiming falsehoods, never exercising hypocrisy, always following the promptings of the Spirit. So exacting is this principle that God promises that those who proclaim truth under the influence of the Holy Ghost actually speak scripture, because they are speaking the will, the mind, the word, and the voice of the Lord and "the power of God unto salvation" (D&C 68:4). What are your thoughts about the possibility of speaking scripture within your circle of stewardship when you expound the truth through the power of the Holy Ghost? How can you teach others the sacred responsibility of always speaking with honor and truthfulness, never dissembling or misrepresenting the truth?

D&C 97:8—"Verily I say unto you, all among them who know their hearts are honest, and are broken, and their spirits contrite, and are willing to observe their covenants by sacrifice—yea, every sacrifice which I, the Lord, shall command—they are accepted of me."

- These words are part of a revelation given through the Prophet Joseph Smith at Kirtland, Ohio, on August 2, 1833, at a time when the Saints in Missouri

were undergoing severe persecution and displacement. The Lord comforted the Saints and recognized the sincere labors of those, such as Parley P. Pratt, who were conducting the School of the Prophets in that part of the vineyard.

- The Lord declares the criteria for being accepted by Him, even in times of trial and challenge: hearts that are honest and broken, spirits that are contrite, and a willingness to sacrifice in honoring the covenants—to whatever degree the Lord requires. This is the only place in the scriptures where the word *honest* is linked with the word *broken* in relation to the heart of the Saints. It is a uniquely appropriate combination, for hearts are broken and spirits contrite in recognition and acceptance of the breakage and contrition (from the Latin root meaning to crush or grind) suffered by the Lamb of God in the Atonement. And hearts are honest through a spiritual mindset and a transparency of obedience to every word of the Lord. How can you help others in your circle of influence cultivate honest and broken hearts and contrite spirits in order to be accepted of the Lord and fulfill every sacrifice He may require?

D&C 98:9–10—"Nevertheless, when the wicked rule the people mourn. Wherefore, honest men and wise men should be sought for diligently, and good men and wise men ye should observe to uphold; otherwise whatsoever is less than these cometh of evil."

- This is the word of the Lord included in a revelation given through the Prophet Joseph Smith at Kirtland, Ohio, on August 6, 1833, during times of acute persecution of the Saints in Missouri. Before giving these words, the Lord had declared that the Saints should support the Constitution of the land, which was designed to secure their rights and privileges, and was thus "justifiable before me" (D&C 98:5).

- Then as now, there is a need to use wisdom and judgment in electing people that are honest in upholding the rights and liberties of the people. When selecting those who might govern us, we should consider character above all else. If integrity is compromised, trust is destroyed. This is of primary concern for us as we elect government officials. What are your thoughts about the "diligent" exercise of constitutional privileges to place honorable and honest people in office and then support their service?

Rejoicing and Reasoning Together

How Can We Enhance and Secure Our Honesty Before God?

Here are four points for you to consider:

- **Honesty is the foundation upon which you can build your future.** Honesty is a foundational principle. A life built on dishonesty will crumble in due time, while a life built on honesty will have endurance, resilience, and vitality (see A of F 1:13). By deciding to build your character, relationships, and life's vision on the principle of honesty, you spare yourself the task of making ten-thousand-thousand future decisions—for you only have to decide to be honest once (see Job 27:5; Mal. 2:6).
- **Honesty has consequences that are highly desirable.** Honesty generates trust and peace, builds friendship and unity, attracts creative and like-minded people, enhances the vitality and staying power of organizations, and liberates the mind. The honest person has nothing to fear from the light of truth. Dishonesty enslaves. One dishonest act can lead to other acts of dishonesty in an attempt to cover the first. It is not difficult to discern the virus of dishonesty: If people will cheat in little ways, they will cheat in big ways, for they are slaves to their addiction. By contrast, honesty brings freedom and enduring dividends.
- **Honesty is the backbone of leadership.** It teaches with authenticity and integrity; it

teaches by persuasion, generating harmony and cooperation among the parties involved; it draws a line in the sand. We can stand up for the principle of honesty. The most repulsive patron of dishonesty is the liar, the gossiper, the twister of truth. It is a humane act of charity for civilization if you forcefully oppose the actions of those who chronically lie. When you discern the operation of a liar in your community or in your workplace, take steps immediately to make truth the basis for decision-making and policy-formulation—always with wisdom and care.
- **Honesty is the heart and soul of one's covenant with God.** Is there another quality that better reflects the core essence of each of the Ten Commandments? If we are honest and true in our thoughts, our desires, our relationships, our speech, our service, and our devotion, we have covered all that God requires of us. Honesty has roots in the Golden Rule: honesty will always be enhanced if we remember to treat others as we would have them treat us (see Matt. 7:12; 3 Ne. 14:12). Honesty is the absolute of character qualities, being not only the best policy—it is the *only* policy.

As you consider this short checklist, which items stand out to you as especially worthy of your attention at this time?

Real-life Stories for Heart and Mind

The Courage to Change. A young business executive was on a company assignment far away from his family. Lying on the bed of his hotel room and staring at the ceiling, he was pondering his predicament as a senior officer under strict company orders to carry out policies that he felt were increasingly at variance with the fundamental principles of honesty taught by the gospel. He sensed the deep responsibility he had to provide support for his wife and children, and yet his growing uneasiness over the nature of his professional duties brought agony to his soul. Suddenly, while lying there in prayerful meditation, he had the sensation that he must change. Instantly he made a decision. Like Joseph of Egypt, he found within himself the courage to pull away and go in a totally different direction. He made some quick telephone calls to inform his superiors and bring the welcome news to his family, then packed his bags and returned home. His pathway thereafter was marked by increased harmony, peace, and prosperity.

This man, an active priesthood bearer in the Church, went through a remarkable transformation that changed his life for the better. He was being honest with himself and with his Heavenly Father. What experiences of change have you or others in your circle of acquaintance gone through that illustrate the power and wisdom of making honest decisions?

The Keeper of the Gate. It was another glorious day at one of the temples of the Lord. The Saints were flocking into the building on the Lord's errand, being welcomed by officials on duty at the recommend desk. Two young adults then approached the desk, where they were greeted warmly by the official stationed there; he asked to see their temple recommends. As he later described it, for some reason a feeling of uneasiness came over him. As he examined the first recommend he glanced at the authorizing signatures, then back into the eyes of the individual. He felt impressed to say, "This is not the signature of your stake president, is it?" Chagrined, the young person confessed that it was not. The official then counseled the two, in a kindly but firm way, to leave and return again when they were worthy to do so, and they would be welcome in the house of the Lord.

This experience reminds us that the temples of the Most High are sacred precincts reserved for those who come cloaked with honesty, having a broken heart and a contrite spirit—those who are sincerely striving to keep all of the commandments and abide by the standards of temple-worthy Saints. The temple experience is in many respects a type pointing to our eventual return to the home from whence we have come. Jacob, brother of Nephi, made it clear that the process of admittance into our Heavenly Father's presence is by way of a very special gatekeeper: "O then, my beloved brethren, come unto the Lord, the Holy One. Remember that his paths are righteous. Behold, the way for man is narrow, but it lieth in a straight course before him, and the keeper of the gate is the Holy One of Israel; and he employeth no servant there; and there is none other way save it be by the gate; for he cannot be deceived, for the Lord God is his name" (2 Ne. 9:41).

Our Father in Heaven and His Son want us to return to Their presence. The principles and ordinances of the gospel and the holy priesthood are designed to render us worthy, through the grace of God, "after all we can do" (2 Ne. 25:23), to return to our heavenly home once again. But our homecoming will be based on our honesty in keeping all of the commandments. What are your thoughts about the supreme privilege of meeting the "Keeper of the Gate" at that ultimate hour of returning home? What remains, by way of preparation, for you to make the journey home?

Pondering Prayerfully

Additional scriptures to consider and ponder:
- Acts 6:3–4
- Rom. 12:17
- 1 Pet. 2:12
- 2 Ne. 9:34
- D&C 51:9

The following hymns help us appreciate honesty:
- "Oh Say, What Is Truth?" (*Hymns,* 272)
- "Truth Reflects upon Our Senses" (*Hymns,* 273)

Remember and Be Sure

"Sow an act, and you reap a habit; sow a habit and you reap a character; sow a character, and you reap a destiny." This statement by George D. Boardman truly puts into perspective the process of building character based on honesty. It is a process that takes time and effort, and requires a value system based on the gospel of Jesus Christ. It takes self-discipline. It takes integrity. Surely it takes all that one possesses to become a man or woman of Christ. The Savior stated with utter clarity the commission for our existence: "Therefore I would that ye should be perfect even as I, or your Father who is in heaven is perfect" (3 Ne. 12:48). He then later restated the commandment with similar unequivocal clarity: "What manner of men [and, by extension, women] ought ye to be? Verily I say unto you, even as I am" (3 Ne. 27:27). Such is the divine directive to build character and answer the call to honor and fulfill our destiny.

What you *are* truly does make your destiny. Honesty, virtue, and courage are marks of the disciple of Christ. The Apostle John summarized the essence of our quest to acquire the divine nature when he said, speaking of the lot of the valiant and obedient: "Beloved, now are we the sons of God, and it doth not yet appear what we shall be: but we know that, when he shall appear, we shall be like him; for we shall see him as he is" (1 Jn. 3:2). May we all strive with every fiber of our being to transcend the tests of mortality and rise to the challenge of becoming, in our inmost character and patterns of living, even as He is.

CHAPTER 32
Payment of Tithes and Offerings

Yes, it may take great faith to pay tithes when funds are scarce and demands are great. But we remember the promise from the Father to Malachi. We also remember the Lord's promise in our day: "I, the Lord, am bound when ye do what I say; but when ye do not what I say, ye have no promise." (D&C 82:10.)
—Spencer W. Kimball (*President Kimball Speaks Out*, 64)

Opening the Window of Wisdom

The kingdom of heaven on the earth is to be built up with the tithes of the Lord's people. Of His abundance, He will sustain the faithful Saints through their obedience to His laws and principles. Malachi, prophesying around 430 BC, taught the comforting lesson of spiritual abundance—that the Lord is prepared to open the windows of heaven in blessing the faithful who obediently support the unfolding of His kingdom through their sacrifice and consecrations: "Bring ye all the tithes into the storehouse, that there may be meat in mine house, and prove me now herewith, saith the Lord of hosts, if I will not open you the windows of heaven, and pour you out a blessing, that there shall not be room enough to receive it" (Mal. 3:10). In response to our obedience, the promise of heaven is that "all nations shall call you blessed: for ye shall be a delightsome land, saith the Lord of Hosts" (Mal. 3:12).

The context for Malachi's statement about tithing is a broad range of righteous actions called for by the Almighty. Thus Malachi taught the people of his day—and ours—that we should honor God (see Mal. 1:5), bring a "pure offering" before Him in righteousness (Mal. 1:11; 3:3), give glory to His name (see Mal. 2:2), walk with God "in peace and equity" (Mal. 2:6), remain faithfully within the covenant boundaries of marriage (see Mal. 2:11), care for the poor and needy (see Mal. 3:5), return unto God (see Mal. 3:7), pay tithes and offerings (see Mal. 3:10), fear God and always keep Him in our thoughts (see Mal. 3:16), avoid pride (see Mal. 4:1), and, under the influence of the sealing power of the priesthood, cultivate a godly and eternal disposition of oneness among families, both fathers (parents) toward their children, and children toward their fathers (see Mal. 4:5–6).

The commandment to pay tithes and offerings is therefore one in a range of key manifestations of righteousness required of the Lord. So important are the words of Malachi that the Lord brought many of them to the ancient American Saints at Bountiful during His post-resurrection visit there: "And it came to pass that he commanded them that they should write the words which the Father had given unto Malachi, which he should tell unto them. And it came to pass that after they were written he expounded them" (3 Ne. 24:1).

Offerings to the Lord are given in many forms. We offer sacrifices to the Lord of a broken heart and contrite spirit (see 3 Ne. 9:20). We offer our devotions to the Lord in all kinds of service. The important thing to remember is that we owe our Heavenly Father everything; therefore, we should not withhold our oblations from our Heavenly Father: "And it pleaseth God that he hath given all these things unto man; for unto this end were they made to be used, with judgment, not to excess, neither by extortion. And in nothing doth man offend God, or against none is his wrath kindled, save those who confess not his hand in all things, and obey not his commandments" (D&C 59:20–21). We give temporal offerings to the Lord, in particular our tithes—one tenth of our increase—and our fast offerings. Tithing is a commandment of God (see D&C 119). Payment of an honest tithe is a requirement for obtaining a temple recommend. Payment of tithes brings resultant blessings from our Heavenly Father, both temporal and spiritual. We cannot rob God in any of our tithes and offerings or else we will be cursed (see Mal. 3:8–9).

The law of tithing is a key ingredient in the Lord's divine plan for bringing about the sanctification of His sons and daughters. Paying tithing with pure intent and sincere gratitude is a confirmation of one's triumph over a self-centered and prideful attitude. It is an act of reaching out to the Lord in humility and obedience to obtain grace and empowerment—blessings the Prophet Joseph Smith yearned for the Saints to have: "Help thy servants to say, with thy grace assisting them: Thy will be done, O Lord, and not ours" (D&C 109:44). Paying tithing is an act of direct participation in the all-encompassing design of the Lord to build up the kingdom of God and spread the gospel to the four quarters of the earth in keeping with the Abrahamic covenant. It is a holy practice consonant with valiant discipleship: "And all the tithe of the land, whether of the seed of the land, or of the fruit of the tree, is the LORD's: it is holy unto the LORD" (Lev. 27:30). Likewise, observing the law of the fast and giving fast offerings on behalf of the poor and needy are an involvement in the Lord's plan for teaching and administering charity among the Saints. Both of these laws—tithing and fasting—are principal channels for experiencing joy and satisfaction in our daily lives. Let us thank the Lord for His gracious kindness in granting us the privilege of participating in such magnificent laws and learning thereby the principles of how to be more like Him.

Inspired by Latter-Day Prophets

Lorenzo Snow: The time has now come for every Latter-day Saint, who calculates to be prepared for the future and to hold his feet strong upon a proper foundation, to do the will of the Lord and to pay his tithing in full. . . . There is no man or woman that now hears what I am saying who will feel satisfied if he or she fails to pay a full tithing (*The Teachings of Lorenzo Snow*, 155).

*These stirring words from a prophet reminded the Church in his day of the sacred need to pay a full tithing. President Snow also said in that same address that "Part of tithing is no tithing at all" (*The Teachings of Lorenzo Snow*, 155). "The word of the Lord" to all of us is to pay a full and honest tithing. How is this act of obedience a way to "stand up" for truth and righteousness?*

Joseph F. Smith: By this principle (tithing) the loyalty of the people of this Church shall be put to the test. By this principle it shall be known who is for the kingdom of God and who is against it. By this principle it shall be seen whose hearts are set on doing the will of God and keeping his commandments, thereby sanctifying the land of Zion unto God, and who are opposed to this principle and have cut themselves off from the blessings of Zion. . . . [I]f a man keep all the law save one point, and he offend in that, he is a transgressor of the law, and he is not entitled to the fulness of the blessings of the gospel of Jesus Christ. But when a man keeps all the law that is revealed, according to his strength, his substance, and his ability, though what he does may be little, it is just as acceptable in the sight of God as if he were able to do a thousand times more (*Gospel Doctrine: Selections from the Sermons and Writings of Joseph F. Smith*, 225).

As an indicator of our loyalty and faithfulness, President Joseph F. Smith says that the law of tithing is "as essential" as the first four principles and ordinances of the gospel. Tithing is a measure of our obedience in doing the will of God. It is certainly among the requirements for receiving a temple recommend to enter the house of the Lord. Looking forward, what are your feelings about tithing being among the requirements to enter the celestial kingdom one day? What has been your experience with the blessings received by paying your tithes and offerings over the years?

Spencer W. Kimball: The Lord herein [Mal. 3:10] makes clear that tithing is his law and is required of all his followers. It is our honor and privilege, our safety and promise, our great blessing to live this law of God. To fail to meet this obligation in full is to deny ourselves the promises and to omit a weighty matter. It is a transgression, not an inconsequential oversight (*President Kimball Speaks Out*, 63–64).

Tithing is identified here as an honor and a privilege. It is a covenant matter, for obedience to the law brings the promise of safety and great blessings. In what way does paying an honest tithe bring safety into your life and the lives of your loved ones?

Ezra Taft Benson: One is blessed temporally for obedience to the law of tithing. But the greatest blessings of the Lord are, after all, spiritual in nature. Perhaps that is the deeper meaning to the expression, "I will open you the windows of heaven and pour you out a blessing, that there shall not be room enough to receive it" (Malachi 3:10). The late Elder Melvin J. Ballard, an Apostle, said that "the Lord has promised that the man and woman who pay their honest tithing shall be provided for, [but] He doesn't promise to make them rich, not in material things. The greatest blessings of the Lord are spiritual, and not material" (*The Teachings of Ezra Taft Benson*, 472–473).

What spiritual blessings have come into your life as a result of paying tithes and offerings? How can you assist the coming generation to participate joyfully and willingly in supporting the advance of Zion in this way?

Truths to Liken

Mal. 3:8—"Will a man rob God? Yet ye have robbed me. But ye say, Wherein have we robbed thee? In tithes and offerings."

- This reference to tithing is one of the most oft-recited scriptures on this subject,

especially the promise that the obedient will be blessed when the windows of heaven are opened unto them in such abundance "that there shall not be room enough to receive it" (Mal. 3:10). However, as with every covenant arrangement, there is the opposite possibility, based on agency. To rob God is a shocking and distressing thought. The verse implies the surprise of those so accused, meaning that they have forgotten or ignored their obligations, perhaps because of "their ease, and their exceedingly great prosperity" (Hel. 12:2).

- Heavenly Father has given us everything. He asks for so little in return. We are indebted to Him for all things, including our very life (see Mosiah 2:20–21). We should make a plan to be honest tithe-payers and generous in our donations. Honesty in paying tithes implies the opposite of "robbing God." How have you determined in your own life what it is that constitutes an "honest tithing"? How have the windows of heaven been opened to you in the form of opportunities, spiritual enlightenment, and the blessings of the earth?

D&C 59:12, 16, 20–21—"But remember that on this, the Lord's day, thou shalt offer thine oblations and thy sacraments unto the Most High, confessing thy sins unto thy brethren, and before the Lord. . . . Verily I say, that inasmuch as ye do this, the fulness of the earth is yours. . . . And it pleaseth God that he hath given all these things unto man; for unto this end were they made to be used, with judgment, not to excess, neither by extortion. And in nothing doth man offend God, or against none is his wrath kindled, save those who confess not his hand in all things, and obey not his commandments."

- These words were part of a revelation given through the Prophet Joseph Smith in Zion (Jackson County, Missouri) on August 7, 1831, outlining the commandments and laws the Saints were to obey. An *oblation* is something offered to the Lord—in this case a broken heart and a contrite spirit as well as our offerings in support of the building up of His kingdom. The promised blessing for obedience is no less than "the fulness of the earth."

- It pleases God to give abundant blessings of the earth to the Saints; the only thing He requires in return is to recognize Him and keep His commandments. In our day and age, where the Creator is too often ignored, what are your thoughts when you receive the kind of confirmation this verse gives that the Creation was expressly carried out for the benefit of mankind? How can you help others, especially those not of our faith, to look upon the earth as a gift from God and to recognize His hand in everything?

D&C 64:23—"Behold, now it is called today until the coming of the Son of Man, and verily it is a day of sacrifice, and a day for the tithing of my people; for he that is tithed shall not be burned at his coming."

- These words were included in a revelation given through the Prophet Joseph Smith to the elders of the Church at Kirtland, Ohio, on September 11, 1831. To the Saints gathered in Bountiful in the New World, the resurrected Lord cited the following relevant passage from Malachi: "FOR behold, the day cometh that shall burn as an oven; and all the proud, yea, and all that do wickedly, shall be stubble; and the day that cometh shall burn them up, saith the Lord of Hosts, that it shall leave them neither root nor branch" (3 Ne. 25:1; compare Mal. 4:1; D&C 85:3). In a manner of speaking, tithing is a form of "fire insurance" against that day of visitation of the Lord when the wicked will be destroyed. What is the benefit of such an insurance policy? It is stated clearly: "But unto you that fear my name shall the Sun of righteousness arise with healing in his wings; and ye shall go forth, and grow up as calves of the stall" (Mal. 4:2; see also 3 Ne. 25:2).
- Paying an honest tithe is an act of faith. The Lord fosters and encourages our faith by promising us rich blessings if we are obedient to this sacred law. Let us therefore respond willingly and honorably and bring joy to

the heavens. Let us pay the Lord first, and manage our affairs conscientiously, living within our means, that we might merit the kindness of a just and merciful Lord, and "abide the day of his coming" (Mal. 3:2). How does obedience to the law of tithing bring into your life the "healing" influence of the Spirit of the Lord that sustains life and vitality? (See Mosiah 2:22.)

D&C 119:1, 4, 6–7—"VERILY, thus saith the Lord, I require . . . that, those who have thus been tithed shall pay one-tenth of all their interest annually; and this shall be a standing law unto them forever, for my holy priesthood, saith the Lord. . . . And I say unto you, if my people observe not this law, to keep it holy, and by this law sanctify the land of Zion unto me, that my statutes and my judgments may be kept thereon, that it may be most holy, behold, verily I say unto you, it shall not be a land of Zion unto you. And this shall be an ensample unto all the stakes of Zion. Even so. Amen."

- These words were part of a revelation given through the Prophet Joseph Smith at Far West, Missouri, on July 8, 1838, in answer to his supplication: "O Lord, show unto thy servants how much thou requirest of the properties of thy people for a tithing." According to the heading to the revelation, "The law of tithing, as understood today, had not been given to the Church previous to this revelation. The term 'tithing' in the prayer just quoted and in previous revelations (64:23; 85:3; 97:11) had meant not just one-tenth, but all free-will offerings, or contributions, to the Church funds." This revelation established for the first time the meaning of *tithing* as we now understand it.
- Tithing is a way of "sanctifying" the land of Zion to the Lord. In what way is the paying of an honest tithe a means of "sanctifying" your own home to the Lord?

Rejoicing and Reasoning Together

How Is Tithing Used in the Church?

The law of tithing is an opportunity for faithful Saints to understand and experience the process of being edified and blessed through humble and charitable giving. After all, everything in this world belongs to the Lord, and when He blesses us with greater temporal goods, the paying of tithing is but an act of returning a portion of that which was borrowed in the first place. Tithing underwrites the building up of the kingdom of God; but even more importantly, it results in the building up of the character and Christlike nature of the Saints within the kingdom.

Tithing is accounted for with meticulous care by the leaders of the Church. President Joseph F. Smith and his counselors provided the following explanation many years ago:

Tithing is received and receipted for by the local bishops and in the respective wards, who are under the supervision of the local presidents of stakes. The whole income is accounted for to the presiding bishopric of the Church and is under their direction. Their office contains complete records of all the tithings paid during each year. Each tithepayer will find in that office his record. The entire receipts and disbursements are there accounted for in the most complete detail. An auditing committee composed of men well known in the community for their independence of character and business integrity, not of the leading authorities of the Church, chosen by the general conference, thoroughly inspect and report annually upon them. The funds thus received are not the property of the president of the Church or his associates, nor of the Presiding Bishopric, nor of the local bishops. They belong to the Church and are used for Church purposes, including the building and maintenance of temples, meetinghouses, schools, colleges, universities and other structures, the aid of the poor and afflicted, the extension of missions abroad and the help of new colonies at home, and sundry other objects and but a small amount is used for the support of persons devoting their whole time to the service of the Church, and that not out of the tithing, but from the proceeds of investments made with profit. This includes the presidency and other Church leaders. (*CR*, April 1911, 130)

How do you feel about the fact that your tithing record is a part of the records of the kingdom of God? Malachi recorded: "Then they that feared the LORD spake often one to another: and the LORD hearkened, and heard it, and a book of remembrance was written before him for them that feared the LORD, and that thought upon his name. And they shall be mine, saith the LORD of hosts, in that day when I make up my jewels; and I will spare them, as a man spareth his own son that serveth him" (Mal. 3:16–17). What do you think the connection might be between tithing records and the "book of remembrance" containing the names of those who feared the Lord and remembered Him? What feelings of joy are associated with the hope of being "spared" at the Second Coming and included among the "jewels" of the Lord? How can you teach the principle of paying an honest tithe to the coming generation?

How Does Tithing Relate to the Law of Consecration?

President Joseph F. Smith stated, "The law of tithing is the law of revenue for the Church of Jesus Christ of Latter-day Saints. Without it, it would be impossible to carry on the purposes of the Lord" (*Gospel Doctrine: Selections from the Sermons and Writings of Joseph F. Smith*, 226). How does the law of tithing relate to the law of consecration in its most specific meaning? President Joseph Fielding Smith explained:

The Lord had given to the Church the law of consecration and had called upon the members, principally the official members, to enter into a covenant that could not be broken and to be everlasting in which they were to consecrate their properties and receive stewardships, for this is the law of the celestial kingdom. Many of those who entered into this solemn covenant broke it and by so doing brought upon their heads, and the heads of their brethren and sisters, dire punishment and persecution. This celestial law of necessity was thereupon withdrawn for the time, or until the time of the redemption of Zion. While suffering intensely because of their debts and lack of means to meet their obligations Joseph Smith and Oliver Cowdery, November 29, 1834, in solemn prayer promised the Lord that they would give one tenth of all that the Lord should give unto them, as an offering to be bestowed upon the poor; they also prayed that their children, and children's children after them should obey this law. (D.H.C. 2:174–5.) Now, however, it became necessary for the law to be given to the whole Church so the Prophet prayed for instruction. The answer they received in the revelation called for the following [see D&C 119]. . . .

The people failed in the law of consecration. The Lord commanded them not to fail in this lesser law for the building up of Zion. Unfortunately we cannot boast very loudly of our faithfulness in the observance of this law. We have good reason to believe that the anger of the Lord will be kindled against all those who violate it, as his anger was kindled against those who broke the higher law. We may not receive the punishment in this life, but surely it will come to all who wilfully break it. (D. & C. 64:23–24.). . . .

It is definitely true, however, that all those who will not obey the law of tithing, will not be entitled to enter into the covenants of consecration, but when the day comes for the establishing of Zion and the redemption of the earth, such people will find themselves removed.

Tithe-paying is not a principle new to our dispensation. Whenever the Lord has had a people on the earth who were willing to observe his laws, and they were not practicing the law of consecration, they have been called upon to pay tithes and offerings. . . . This law is one binding upon members of the Church. We call it a free-will offering, and so it is, for everything in the Gospel is by free will, but nevertheless it is a law of God which to us is everlasting. (*Church History and Modern Revelation*, 3:120–21)

Real-life Stories for Heart and Mind

The Willing Convert. One day a counselor in a stake presidency and his wife invited a young woman into their home to talk about the gospel. She had been referred to them by a previous stake president as one having considerable interest in learning more about the Church. The counselor on that occasion recorded the following in his journal concerning the young visitor: "If anyone was converted, she was. She spent several hours with us, and toward the end of her stay she asked whether it was not so that Mormons paid tithing. I said yes, and asked what her understanding of that might be. She replied that it was her understanding that this meant one-third of one's income. Somewhat surprised, I asked her whether she would be willing to pay this much to the Lord. 'Certainly,' was her response, and she had the most sincere and warm spirit about her. I then explained what the law of tithing meant, and complimented her on her humble devotion and willingness to do whatever the Lord asked of her."

This young woman soon thereafter joined the Church and rendered much service in the spirit of humility and obedience. Her angelic faith and acceptance of the will of the Lord exemplified the principle taught by the Lord: "Verily I say unto you, all among them who know their hearts are honest, and are broken, and their spirits contrite, and are willing to observe their covenants by sacrifice, yea, every sacrifice which I, the Lord, shall command—they are accepted of me" (D&C 97:8).

On one occasion a ruler asked the Lord what he should do to inherit eternal life, claiming to be obedient already in all things. Responded the Lord: "Yet lackest thou one thing: sell all that thou hast, and distribute unto the poor, and thou shalt have treasure in heaven: and come, follow me" (Luke 18:22). The rich ruler was very sorrowful, not wanting to give up his worldly treasures for heavenly treasures. The Saints of today are not asked to give everything back to the Lord in the form of tithing, just "one-tenth of all their interest annually" (D&C 119:4). The young woman in the story above was prepared to give more than three times what is required of the Lord—a manifestation of her goodness and devotion. What are your thoughts about a future time when the full law of consecration—as the law of the celestial kingdom—will again be instituted, with the opportunity to give all to the Lord? How does the law of tithing serve as a kind of "schoolmaster" leading to that day of glory when a still higher law will prevail?

The Story of a Generous Man. On one occasion, President George Albert Smith was riding in a car with a member of the Church who was explaining to him how he paid his tithing:

"Well," he said, "if I make ten thousand dollars in a year, I put a thousand dollars in the bank for tithing. I know why it's there. Then when the bishop comes and wants me to make a contribution for the chapel or give him a check for a missionary who is going away, if I think he needs the money, I give him a check. If a family in the ward is in distress and needs coal or food or clothing or anything else, I write out a check. If I find a boy or a girl who is having difficulty getting through school in the East, I send a check. Little by little I exhaust the thousand dollars, and every dollar of it has gone where I know it has done good. Now, what do you think of that?"

"Well," I said, "do you want me to tell you what I think of it?"

He said, "Yes."

I said: "I think you are a very generous man with someone else's property." And he nearly tipped the car over.

He said, "What do you mean?"

I said, "You have an idea that you have paid your tithing?"

"Yes," he said.

I said: "You have not paid any tithing. You have told me what you have done with the Lord's money but you have not told me that you have given anyone a penny of your own. He is the best partner you have in the world. He gives you everything you have, even the air you breathe. He has said you should take one-tenth of what comes to you and give it to the Church as directed by the Lord. You haven't done that; you have taken your best partner's money, and have given it away."

Well, I will tell you there was quiet in the car for some time. We rode on to Salt Lake City and talked about other things.

About a month after that I met him on the street. He came up, put his arm in mine, and said: "Brother Smith, I am paying my tithing the same way you do." I was very happy to hear that. (*Sharing the Gospel with Others*, 45–47)

How is the Lord the "best partner you have in the world"? How will He open the windows of heaven and bless you abundantly if you obey the law of tithing and pay it in His ordained way?

The "Tithing Child." A young graduate student was discussing with his wife the hospital bill for the birth of their second daughter. The question was whether they should pay this bill or pay the tithing that was due—for it seemed improbable that their resources could cover both at the same time. They decided prayerfully to pay their tithing, and had a good feeling about it. The next day, the young man was called into the office of the dean at the university, who informed him that he had been selected that year to receive a certain award pertaining to graduate teaching. It was to be bestowed at the graduation ceremonies a few days later, and the young man was surprised and most gratified at the honor—especially when the dean explained that it was unusual for the award to be going to someone in the student's department this year, since another colleague in the same department had received the award the previous year.

As the graduate student was leaving the dean's office, he called him back to say, "By the way, there is a stipend that comes with the award." He then mentioned a figure that was almost exactly the same amount as the hospital bill. The student was amazed and touched by the news. His wife, who served as a secretary in the departmental office, was also overjoyed at such an unanticipated blessing. Moreover, the department unexpectedly adjusted the young man's teaching scholarship to provide more revenue than expected, allowing his wife more time to remain at home to care for the children. Thereafter, the couple often referred to their new daughter as "our tithing child," because she was paid for by the Lord.

We are all paid for in a similar way through

the Atonement: "For ye are bought with a price: therefore glorify God in your body, and in your spirit, which are God's" (1 Cor. 6:20). How have you been able to glorify the Lord through obedience to the law of tithing and therefore receive a blessing from heaven such "that there shall not be room enough to receive it" (Mal. 3:10)?

Pondering Prayerfully

Additional scriptures to consider and ponder:
- JST, Gen. 14:37–40
- Heb. 7:1–10
- Alma 13:13–16

The following hymns contribute to our understanding about tithes and offerings:
- "Choose the Right" (*Hymns,* 239)
- "We Give Thee But Thine Own" (*Hymns,* 218)

Remember and Be Sure

When we understand the law of tithing and the worthy purposes served by the gathering of tithes and offerings, we can appreciate that the Lord needs these resources in order to build up the kingdom of God here on earth. These funds go for glorious purposes in support of the three-fold mission of the Church: perfecting the Saints, preaching the gospel, and redeeming the dead. From building chapels and temples to caring for the poor and sustaining the missionary effort around the globe, we should find great joy in living the law of tithes and offerings, knowing that in this way we become part of the divine plan to build up the kingdom of God and bless all of Heavenly Father's children. Tithing and faith go hand in hand: when we open our hearts and our personal storehouse at the invitation of the Lord, and do it willingly and with thanksgiving, we stand to gain joy, satisfaction, and the marvelous blessings of heaven in such abundance "that there shall not be room enough to receive it" (Mal. 3:10).

CHAPTER 33
Preach My Gospel

*After all that has been said, the greatest and
most important duty is to preach the Gospel.*
—Joseph Smith (*HC* 2:478)

Opening the Window of Wisdom

Without exception, we can all contribute to the growth of the kingdom of God by embarking with faith, devotion, and courage on the pathway of missionary service. Nephi declared: "For we labor diligently to write, to persuade our children, and also our brethren, to believe in Christ, and to be reconciled to God; for we know that it is by grace that we are saved, after all we can do" (2 Ne. 25:23). It is within the framework of "all we can do" that the vision and opportunity of missionary work arises in its glory. The degree of our commitment to this covenant principle will in large measure determine our worthiness before the Lord when the hour of accountability arrives: "And the voice of warning shall be unto all people, by the mouths of my disciples, whom I have chosen in these last days. And they shall go forth and none shall stay them, for I the Lord have commanded them" (D&C 1:4–5).

What agenda of action will produce the greatest long-term value for the Saints of God? The Lord has answered this question with clarity: "And now, behold, I say unto you, that the thing which will be of the most worth unto you will be to declare repentance unto this people, that you may bring souls unto me, that you may rest with them in the kingdom of my Father" (D&C 16:6). Our preparation for this sacred calling was made long before we came into the mortal sphere: "Even before they were born, they, with many others, received their first lessons in the world of spirits and were prepared to come forth in the due time of the Lord to labor in his vineyard for the salvation of the souls of men" (D&C 138:56).

As we continue our schooling in the art and practice of missionary labors, we find that the heart and soul of our commission is associated with key inner qualities of discipleship:

Now behold, a marvelous work is about to come forth among the children of men.

Therefore, O ye that embark in the service of God, see that ye serve him with all your heart, might, mind and strength, that ye may stand blameless before God at the last day.

Therefore, if ye have desires to serve God ye are called to the work;

For behold the field is white already to harvest; and lo, he that thrusteth in his sickle with his might, the same layeth up in store that he perisheth not, but bringeth salvation to his soul;

And faith, hope, charity and love, with an eye single to the glory of God, qualify him for the work.

Remember faith, virtue, knowledge, temperance, patience, brotherly kindness, godliness, charity, humility, diligence.

Ask, and ye shall receive; knock, and it shall be opened unto you. Amen. (D&C 4:1–7)

Building upon such a solid foundation of faith and godliness, we take up the banner of truth with courage and devotion, knowing that we go forth in the strength of the Lord: "Open your mouths and they shall be filled, and you shall become even as Nephi of old, who journeyed from Jerusalem in the wilderness. Yea, open your mouths and spare not, and you shall be laden with sheaves upon your backs, for lo, I am with you. Yea, open your mouths and they shall be filled, saying: Repent, repent, and prepare ye the way of the Lord, and make his paths straight; for the kingdom of heaven is at hand; Yea, repent and be baptized, every one of you, for a remission of your sins; yea, be baptized even by water, and then cometh the baptism of fire and of the Holy Ghost" (D&C 33:8–11).

Such is the commission, the walk, and the glory of those who embark in the service of the Lord to proclaim the gospel and gather the sheaves of the righteous on behalf of the Lord of the harvest (see Alma 26:7). With Ammon we can rejoice, humbly, in the goodness of God to call us into a work of such magnificent joy and service (see Alma 26:12–13).

Missionary work and the joy it brings into our lives is not a new phenomenon. According to the Lord's blessings on Abraham and his seed, the privilege and opportunity to convey the message of the gospel to the world is a universal privilege given to this chosen lineage in perpetuity: "And I will make of thee a great nation, and I will bless thee above measure, and make thy name great among all nations, and thou shalt be a blessing unto thy seed after thee, that in their hands they shall bear this ministry and Priesthood unto all nations" (Abr. 2:9).

With the dawning of the Restoration in 1820 through the miraculous First Vision, the era of missionary work under the Abrahamic covenant was once again inaugurated. As the Church and kingdom of God were reestablished on the earth, including the restoration of the priesthood of God and all attendant keys and ordinances, a wave of missionary activity was inaugurated that even now flows over the earth uninterrupted, in ever-growing scope and intensity. "The field is white already to harvest" (D&C 4:4) is a pervasive theme in the pages of the Doctrine and Covenants. The call for each individual to "thrust in his sickle with his might, and reap while the day lasts" (D&C 6:3) is a repeated admonition. A careful and prayerful study of those sections of the Doctrine and Covenants outlining in detail the Lord's design for missionary service provides an inspiring and powerful action plan for success in the program of the Lord's harvest.

Service in the vineyard of the Lord requires focused and devoted preparation. The heart is prepared through the "mighty change" that King Benjamin's people experienced (Mosiah 5:2; Alma 5:13), whereby they became sons and daughters of the Lord, having cultivated a broken heart and a contrite spirit. The mind is prepared through prayerful immersion in the word of God, which aligns one with God's will and imbues one with the vision of contributing to the divine design of bringing about the immortality and eternal life of man (see Moses 1:39). Might and strength are cultivated by constantly exercising one's spiritual faculties of faith and hope, whereby one learns to depend fully on the Lord, in whom alone is centered the power of salvation. The essence of missionary work is teaching with the spirit of prophecy and revelation, gifts acquired through dedication, scripture study, fasting, and prayer—as demonstrated by the example of the sons of Mosiah (see Alma 17:2–4).

The commission of the Savior to His Apostles was to "Go ye therefore, and teach all nations, baptizing them in the name of the Father, and of the Son, and of the Holy Ghost" (Matt. 28:19). That commission has been renewed in our dispensation. We have a duty to proclaim the restored gospel of Jesus Christ to every nation, kindred, tongue, and people (see Morm. 9:22).

Why is there such emphasis on missionary work? Why do we have more than 50,000 full-time missionaries in the field at any given time sharing the gospel of Jesus Christ? Why have more than one million such missionaries engaged in this work since the dawning of the Restoration? The answer is simply that souls are precious. The purpose of Heavenly Father and our Savior is to bring about our immortality and eternal life.

We as disciples of Jesus Christ have been foreordained to do this work (see D&C 138:53–57;

Jacob 5:70–75; Alma 13:3–7)—and now is the time. We preach here with devotion during our sojourn on the earth, and when we depart we continue to preach the gospel in the spirit world, as the vision recounted by President Joseph F. Smith confirms (see D&C 138:57). Missionary work is universal and eternal. The good news never grows old. The covenant obligation extends beyond the veil. It is an everlasting duty.

Inspired by Latter-Day Prophets

David O. McKay: Every member a missionary! (*CR*, April 1959, 122).

This famous maxim of the prophet still resonates in our hearts. How has it helped remind you over the years of the opportunity that is yours to join with others in the calling to fulfill the promises and blessings of the Abrahamic covenant?

Brigham Young: Let one go forth who is careful to prove logically all he says by numerous quotations from the revelations, and let another travel with him who can say, by the power of the Holy Ghost, Thus saith the Lord, and tell what the people should believe—what they should do—how they should live, and teach them to yield to the principles of salvation,—though he may not be capable of producing a single logical argument, though he may tremble under a sense of his weakness, cleaving to the Lord for strength, as such men generally do, you will invariably find that the man who testifies by the power of the Holy Ghost will convince and gather many more of the honest and upright than will the merely logical reasoner (*Discourses of Brigham Young*, 330).

How does this confirm that the Holy Ghost—not the missionaries—do the converting? How have you found that your testimony, spoken by the Spirit, opens hearts more readily than logical argument alone?

George Albert Smith: *The Saints need to share the gospel with their neighbors.* It is my firm conviction, my brethren and sisters, that unless we stir ourselves more than we are doing, that when we go to the other side of the veil, we will meet there men and women who have been our neighbors, and

associates, and lived among us, that will condemn us because we have been so inconsiderate of them in not telling them of the truth of the gospel of our Lord (*The Teachings of George Albert Smith*, 152).

We serve our neighbors with warmth in time of cold, with food in times of scarcity, with comfort in times of loss—but unless we serve them with the truths of the restored gospel in times of spiritual want, our charity is empty, for their eternal salvation is at stake. How in the future can you make sure that every neighbor (near or far) has a chance to hear the good news of the gospel and be welcomed into the fold of the Savior now and forever?

Harold B. Lee: Develop a testimony and share it. The most important responsibility that we, as members of the Church of Jesus Christ, have is to see that we are converted to the truthfulness of the gospel. Then we must share this truth with others (*The Teachings of Harold B. Lee*, 589).

Missionary work begins at home—with each of us. On the eve of the Crucifixion, the Lord counseled Peter: "I have prayed for thee, that thy faith fail not: and when thou art converted, strengthen thy brethren" (Luke 22:32). When Peter responded: "Lord, I am ready to go with thee, both into prison, and to death" (Luke 22:33), the Lord told him the shocking news that he would deny knowing the Christ three times before the cock would crow that day (verse 34). It was that same Peter who, after the Atonement and Resurrection had become a reality, rose in majesty under the power of the Holy Ghost and commenced with valor and strength the missionary program of the Church (see Acts 2). What are your thoughts about how to use your conversion through the Spirit to "strengthen thy brethren" with the message of eternal life and salvation? How can we all make sure that we testify of Jesus to our neighbors before the cock should crow this very day?

Spencer W. Kimball: The proper motivation for missionary work of any kind, as for all Church service, is, of course, love for fellowmen; but always such work has its by-product effect on one's own life. Thus, as we become instruments in God's hands in changing the lives of others, our own lives cannot help being lifted. One can hardly help another to the top of the hill without climbing there himself (*President Kimball Speaks Out*, 43).

Missionary work, as Paul said, is a "work of faith, and labour of love, and patience of hope in our Lord Jesus Christ, in the sight of God and our Father" (1 Thes. 1:3). The miracle is that such love and faith are magnified for both teacher as well as listener in missionary service. How have your love and faith been strengthened and expanded through sharing the gospel with others?

Truths to Liken

Acts 4:33—"And with great power gave the apostles witness of the resurrection of the Lord Jesus: and great grace was upon them all."

- Luke's account of the Acts of the Apostles (an extension of the Gospel of Luke) confirms the courage and valor of the Apostles in moving forward with their commission to take the gospel to the entire world. When the Jewish leaders commanded Peter and his colleagues to refrain from any ministry in the name of Christ, they steadfastly refused to comply and continued undeterred with their proselyting work. Not even imprisonment or death could dissuade them from honoring the call issued to them by the Savior, for the angel of the Lord liberated them and commanded them to continue preaching the gospel in the temple (see Acts 5:19–39).
- How do we overcome any fear we might have to preach the gospel using boldness and love (as Alma counseled his son Shiblon in Alma 38:12)? We overcome fear through the "great grace" of the Lord, which sustains courage and strengthens our witness of the truth of the gospel. How have you experienced the "great grace" of the Lord in helping you put your shoulder to the wheel and participate in missionary work?

1 Cor. 12:3—"No man can say that Jesus is the Lord, but by the Holy Ghost."

- Paul's memorable confirmation of the doctrine of testimony through the Spirit reminds us that we should "say" or "speak" our knowledge of the divinity of Christ in order to share the light and joy with others.
- The supernal role of the Holy Ghost as the divine witness of the Father and the Son is the essence of all missionary work. The Holy Ghost conveys the truth of our inspired testimony to those who have hearts to listen: "And I give unto you this promise, that inasmuch as ye do this the Holy Ghost shall be shed forth in bearing record unto all things whatsoever ye shall say" (D&C 100:8). How is it a source of comfort to you to know that we need only bear witness in all sincerity, and the Holy Ghost will do the rest?

Mosiah 18:9—"Yea, and are willing to mourn with those that mourn; yea, and comfort those that stand in need of comfort, and to stand as witnesses of God at all times and in all things, and in all places that ye may be in, even until death, that ye may be redeemed of God, and be numbered with those of the first resurrection, that ye may have eternal life."

- These words of Alma the Elder to the congregation of his followers at the Waters of Mormon remind us that our baptismal covenant includes a commitment to do missionary work throughout our lives.
- On the basis of what ordinance, following baptism, do we recommit ourselves to share the gospel with others? By participating weekly in the sacrament, where we witness to the Father that we will keep the Lord's commandments, which include lifelong missionary service! What are your thoughts about being worthy to receive the Spirit in order to draw people unto Christ? Consider the following: "Therefore let your light so shine before

this people, that they may see your good works and glorify your Father who is in heaven" (3 Ne. 12:16). What is the nature of the light that you hold up (see 3 Ne. 18:24)?

Mosiah 28:3—"Now they were desirous that salvation should be declared to every creature, for they could not bear that any human soul should perish; yea, even the very thoughts that any soul should endure endless torment did cause them to quake and tremble."

- Like Alma the Younger, the sons of Mosiah had repented of their misguided obsession to work destruction against the Church (see Mosiah 27:8–10) and were filled with a desire to bless the lives of others. Having known the anguish of personal torment over disobedience and unrighteousness, they could not bear to see others suffer. Thus they were irreversibly committed to their missionary labors among the Lamanites.
- When we are truly converted, we will feel like the sons of Mosiah. We will have an overwhelming concern for the welfare of others. We will seek to serve and bless their lives (see Matt. 25:40). How committed are you to engage in the process of bringing others to Christ? How have you felt satisfaction, joy, and glory in doing so (see Alma 29:9–10)?

D&C 65:2—"The keys of the kingdom of God are committed unto man on the earth, and from thence shall the gospel roll forth unto the ends of the earth, as the stone which is cut out of the mountain without hands shall roll forth, until it has filled the whole earth."

- These are words from a revelation given through the Prophet Joseph Smith at Hiram, Ohio, in October 1831, and designated by him as "a prayer."
- What is the scope of missionary work as it has been once again restored in this, the last dispensation? Using the symbolism from Daniel 2 (verses 34–35 and 45), the Lord proclaims that the

Church and kingdom will roll forth until it fills the entire earth. What are your thoughts on being part of an undertaking that will encompass the whole world before it is finished? How does the progress of missionary work go forward not as a cultural undertaking, but rather according to the power of priesthood keys restored?

D&C 84:88—"And whoso receiveth you, there I will be also, for I will go before your face. I will be on your right hand and on your left, and my Spirit shall be in your hearts, and mine angels round about you, to bear you up."

- These words are from a revelation given through the Prophet Joseph Smith at Kirtland, Ohio, on September 22 and 23, 1832, and designated by him as a revelation on the priesthood.
- We do not undertake missionary work alone. Our companions include the Lord, the Holy Ghost, and a host of supporting angels. This is the Lord's work. He is in charge and will assist us as we seek to do His will. We can serve, trusting in the Lord that He will open for us the way and provide strength to preach His word. How does this give you hope, confidence, and courage to proceed? How have you experienced divine help as you have gone about sharing the gospel with others?

D&C 88:81—"Behold, I sent you out to testify and warn the people, and it becometh every man who hath been warned to warn his neighbor."

- These words are from a revelation given through the Prophet Joseph Smith at Kirtland, Ohio, on December 27–28, 1832. It was designated by the Prophet as the "olive leaf . . . plucked from the Tree of Paradise, the Lord's message of peace to us."
- As members of the Church and as disciples of Jesus Christ, we have an obligation to stand as witnesses of Christ at all times (see Mosiah 18:9). We are to open our mouths and share

the gospel (see D&C 33:8–11), and thus be approved of the Lord (see D&C 60:2–3). We are all to be member missionaries—instruments in the Lord's hands (see Alma 29:9–10). If we will open our mouths to bear testimony, the Lord and the Spirit will help us (see D&C 84:85–88; 100:5–6). How does this promise give peace to you and confidence to proceed in "warning" your neighbors and friends?

D&C 100:5–6—"Therefore, verily I say unto you, lift up your voices unto this people; speak the thoughts that I shall put into your hearts, and you shall not be confounded before men; For it shall be given you in the very hour, yea, in the very moment, what ye shall say."

- This counsel was given by the Lord in a revelation to the Prophet Joseph Smith and Sidney Rigdon at Perrysburg, New York, on October 12, 1833, at a time when these two were concerned about their families far away. The Lord confirmed: "Your families are well; they are in mine hands, and I will do with them as seemeth me good; for in me there is all power" (D&C 100:1). He then proceeded to give glorious promises concerning missionary service.

- When the prepared and the humble teach the gospel, the Spirit prompts them to speak the words of life as the Lord would have this message presented (see also D&C 33:8–11). What experiences have you had in knowing what to say when bearing your testimony to others not of our faith?

D&C 123:12—"For there are many yet on the earth among all sects, parties, and denominations, who are blinded by the subtle craftiness of men, whereby they lie in wait to deceive, and who are only kept from the truth because they know not where to find it."

- These words were included in an inspired statement concerning the duty of the Saints in relation to their persecutors as issued by the Prophet Joseph Smith in March 1839 while imprisoned in Liberty Jail.

- The sacrifice of those who have gone before to declare the word and preach the gospel to every nation, kindred, tongue, and people is legendary, from the stirring accounts of the missionary service of Peter and Paul in the primitive Church to the Book of Mormon accounts of magnificent missionary triumphs. Now it is our time. We can do so many simple and easy things—from placing a copy of the Book of Mormon, prayerfully setting a date for someone to accept the missionaries, praying for those who know not God (see Alma 6:6), distributing pass-along cards, and a whole host of other activities to befriend those who seek the truth but don't know about the gospel of Jesus Christ and its restoration in these latter days. We are "finders." We have an obligation to share the gospel with everyone with whom we come in contact. The Lord will provide a way. How best can you show waiting families where to find the truth?

Rejoicing and Reasoning Together

How Does the Principle of Multiple Witnesses Relate to Missionary Work?

The Lord has proclaimed, "In the mouth of two or three witnesses shall every word be established" (2 Cor. 13:1). The Book of Mormon, the Lord's fundamental missionary text, is "Another Testament of Jesus Christ" (subtitle)—"Proving to the world that the holy scriptures are true, and that God does inspire men and call them to his holy work in this age and generation, as well as in generations of old" (D&C 20:11).

Joseph Smith was accompanied by Oliver Cowdery when the priesthood and its keys were restored (see D&C 13). Nephi confirmed that his testimony of the Lord was to be blended with those of his brother Jacob and the prophet Isaiah—and that "God sendeth more witnesses, and he proveth all his words" (2 Ne. 11:3). Amulek added his witness to that of Alma: "The people began to be astonished, seeing there was more than one witness who testified of the things whereof they were accused, and also of the things which were to come, according to the spirit of prophecy which was in them" (Alma 10:12). The testimonies of the three witnesses and the eight witnesses confirm the truth of the Book of Mormon, plus we have the testimony of the Twelve Apostles concerning the truth of the Doctrine and Covenants (see the introductory sections of these books).

Full-time missionaries go two by two to bear witness of the gospel. Multiple witnesses act for the good of all in monthly testimony meetings. The conferences of the Church feature many spiritual witnesses to the truths of the gospel. In all things the Lord acts through multiple witnesses to leverage and magnify the confirming witness of the Holy Ghost to the sons and daughters of God.

To this magnificent chorus of testimonies you can add your testimony, just as Joseph Smith and Sidney Rigdon did when they received Section 76 of the Doctrine and Covenants: "And now, after the many testimonies which have been given of him, this is the testimony, last of all [i.e., most recently], which we give of him: That he lives! For we saw him, even on the right hand of God; and we heard the voice bearing record that he is the Only Begotten of the Father" (D&C 76:22–23). How has the Spirit confirmed for you "that he lives!" and that you, too, can bear solemn witness of this truth?

How Is It That When You Teach the One, You Teach the Many?

Missionary work can be a wonderful leveraging enterprise: when you bless the life of one person by bringing him or her into the fold of the Savior, that person, in turn, might bring many more into the fold over time. Thus your efforts can be magnified and multiplied in an endless process of enlarging the circle of spiritual influence, like the proverbial pebble in the pond causing positive ripples that never cease to expand.

Ammon concentrated on just one family in his initial missionary service—the family of King Lamoni. But the success of that enterprise, and the supporting work of Ammon's brethren, brought a whole nation into the fold: "And thus the work of the Lord did commence among the Lamanites; thus the Lord did begin to pour out his spirit upon them; and we see that his arm is extended to all people who will repent and believe on his name" (Alma 19:36).

Young Samuel Smith, the Prophet Joseph's brother, felt his initial missionary labors were not productive—until he later determined that his efforts within a small circle of listeners brought Brigham Young and Heber C. Kimball and their families (and posterity) into the fold (see *Church History in the Fulness of Times*, 74–75).

We never know the leveraging power of our missionary efforts. "Wherefore, be not weary in well-doing, for ye are laying the foundation of a great work. And out of small things proceedeth that which is great" (D&C 64:33). How does this principle increase and extend your faith and hope when you reach out to others who might respond favorably to the promptings of the Spirit and come into the fold of Christ?

What Is the Lord's Choicest Missionary Resource?

The Book of Mormon is the textbook of conversion. One of its principal figures and teachers, Alma the Younger, compares faith to a seed and inspires his listeners to undertake a most practical strategy in spiritual horticulture: "But behold, if ye will awake and arouse your faculties, even to an experiment upon my words, and exercise a particle of faith, yea, even if ye can no more than desire to believe, let this desire work in you, even until ye believe in a manner that ye can give place for a portion of my words" (Alma 32:27). He then unfolds his memorable counsel for understanding the magnificent principle of how the Lord cultivates within us the power and strength to rise to our divine potential based on faith.

The sprouting seeds that come from a sincere study of the Book of Mormon lead to the growth and maturation of a tree of faith: "Behold, by and by ye shall pluck the fruit thereof, which is most precious, which is sweet above all that is sweet, and which is white above all that is white, yea, and pure above all that is pure; and ye shall feast upon this fruit even until ye are filled, that ye hunger not, neither shall ye thirst" (Alma 32:42).

Is it any wonder that the Lord has commanded us to share the Book of Mormon with our friends and colleagues so that they, too, can learn divine truth through spiritual confirmation? What a profound insight is offered to anyone who is enabled to see through the spiritual lens of truth provided by this volume of scripture. By studying the Book of Mormon prayerfully, with real intent, with a sincere desire to know the truth, any individual can receive the blessing of spiritual insight whereby the Lord "will manifest the truth of it unto you, by the power of the Holy Ghost. And by the power of the Holy Ghost ye may know the truth of all things" (Moro. 10:4–5). Truly this experience will confirm one's testimony of the truth and give strength to seek the will of the Lord in all things.

"The Book of Mormon is the great, the grand, the most wonderful missionary that we have," declared Heber J. Grant (*CR*, April 1937, 123). President Ezra Taft Benson stated: "I have a conviction: The more we teach and preach from the Book of Mormon, the more we shall please the Lord and the greater will be our power of speaking. By so doing, we shall greatly increase our converts, both within the Church and among those we proselyte. The Lord expects us to use this book, and we remain under His condemnation if we do not (see D&C 84:57)" (*The Teachings of Ezra Taft Benson*, 58). Moroni himself confirmed this principle: Through the Book of Mormon we obtain a clear vision of the magnanimous dealings of the Lord with our forebears in the past, the vital role of covenant fidelity in the present, the hope of enjoying the blessings of the Atonement in the future, and—most importantly—the assurance of the divinity of Jesus Christ, "the Eternal God, manifesting himself unto all nations" (see Title Page).

What role does the Book of Mormon play in your own program to help spread the gospel of Jesus Christ? How can you make greater use of the Book of Mormon in this regard?

How Can You Measure Your Desire to Do Missionary Work?

One priesthood leader gives a dependable answer to this question:

A number of years ago it was my privilege to serve in a branch presidency at the Missionary Training Center in Provo. You just had to love the young Elders and Sisters as they arrived and began the

process of learning what it meant to give their "all" to the Lord as His ambassadors. One of the things we liked to watch for was what the new missionaries had to say about the people living in the areas where they were being sent. Their feelings about these people gave an important clue about how they were equipping themselves spiritually for the errand of the Lord. Often you would find missionaries who would articulate their sincere love for these people—even though they had never met any of them. And that was a sure sign that the missionaries were in tune with the Spirit, because, as Paul taught: "And hope maketh not ashamed; because the love of God is shed abroad in our hearts by the Holy Ghost which is given unto us" (Rom. 5:5). Others may also have felt this love budding in their hearts, but were still learning how to discern it, identify it, and express it to others. They were learning that "the fruit of the Spirit is love" (Gal. 5:22). A key part of becoming a missionary—in fact a key part of becoming a faithful Latter-day Saint—is to pray for this love to flourish in our hearts: "Wherefore, my beloved brethren, pray unto the Father with all the energy of heart, that ye may be filled with this love, which he hath bestowed upon all who are true followers of his Son, Jesus Christ; that ye may become sons of God" (Moro. 7:48). By purifying our minds and hearts, we prepare ourselves to be a suitable dwelling place for the Spirit, which can plant within us the love for God and, in turn, the love for all of His children. Anyone who is called to service in the kingdom of God, who embraces this duty with humility and full purpose of heart, experiences an unfolding love for the people served. Thus Nephi understood the meaning of the tree in his father's vision: "Yea, it is the love of God, which sheddeth itself abroad in the hearts of the children of men; wherefore, it is the most desirable above all things" (1 Ne. 11:22).

Your neighbors, your friends close and far away, the stranger on the street, your professional contacts and associates—how do you feel about these people, and all others who may not be of our faith or who may be less active in the Church? If the fundamental feeling is one of love, then the Spirit of missionary work abides and flourishes in your heart. How can you increase your love for others?

How Can You Prepare More Fully for Missionary Service in the Kingdom of God?

The scriptures give glorious accounts of missionary service, including the journeys of Paul in the New Testament and the missionary experiences of Alma and the sons of Mosiah in the Book of Mormon. The work of the sons of Mosiah among the Lamanites (see especially Mosiah 27–28; Alma 17–26) is an excellent account of the triumph of a commitment to spread the gospel in the face of overwhelming odds—then as well as now. It is a rich tapestry of doctrine and practical advice concerning how to build the kingdom in the Lord's way. A reading of the indicated chapters in Mosiah and Alma will identify the following key questions and guide you to the answers based on the key words indicated in parentheses:

- **Are you prepared?** (repentance, a desire to serve, spiritual priorities, scripture study, fasting and prayer)
- **Are you called of the Lord?** (divine approval and empowerment)
- **Do you have the right purpose at heart?** (service, commitment to a great cause)
- **Do you have the essential missionary qualities?** (patience and long-suffering, courage, trust, persistence, humility, wisdom, innocence)
- **Have you sought and obtained the appropriate missionary gifts?** (prophecy and revelation, teaching with the power and authority of God, discernment)
- **Do you proceed according to a careful plan?** (follow the Spirit, leverage your time, be a servant, be a friend, appeal to the deepest values, apply talents, show leadership and initiative, be positive, commit people to action, be bold when appropriate, use questions effectively,

teach only fundamentals, teach from the scriptures, bear testimony, teach prayer, confirm the workings of the Spirit, use multiple witnesses)
- **Do you follow through?** (give thanks, perform ordinances, do fellowshipping and ongoing teaching, offer protection and guidance)

As you study Mosiah 27–28 and Alma 17–26, you will discover once again the marvelous guidance for missionary work given in the Book of Mormon. Concerning the issues listed above, how can you strengthen your own capability to do missionary work? Of special importance is the ability to follow the Spirit in all things: "And they went forth whithersoever they were led by the Spirit of the Lord, preaching the word of God" (Alma 21:16).

Real-life Stories for Heart and Mind

"**My Sheep Hear My Voice.**" When do investigators of the restored gospel first know that it is true? Elder Alvin R. Dyer, at one time president of the Central States Mission, often shared with missionaries an important discovery he had made based on a mission-wide research poll among all of the converts of the mission. Several thousand participated in the project and were asked to declare when they first knew the gospel was true. Elder Dyer found that 82 percent of the converts knew the gospel was true the *first time they heard the missionaries bear witness of it.* In most cases, then, the transforming witness came not after a period of experience with the Church, but *immediately* upon hearing the message for the first time as the missionaries spoke with the power of the Spirit. Elder Dyer testified that this phenomenon validated the Savior's statement: "My sheep hear my voice, and I know them, and they follow me" (John 10:27). It is a reminder that the missionaries of the Church are sent with a divine charge: "Again I say, hearken ye elders of my church, whom I have appointed: Ye are not sent forth to be taught, but to teach the children of men the things which I have put into your hands by the power of my Spirit" (D&C 43:15).

How does this story give you confidence to bear witness more often of the truthfulness of the gospel when prompted by the Holy Ghost? How does the gift of the Holy Ghost following baptism bless converts to have a continuing influence of spiritual strength and conviction?

"Why Are You Here?" While in the mission field, a mission president always asked newly arriving missionaries: "Why are you here?" The answers varied. Some missionaries said they were following in the footsteps of their fathers; some were there out of duty; some did not know. For those who seemed uncertain, the mission president had this follow-up question: "Have you asked the Lord? Have you been on your knees to ask Him if the gospel is true?" What the mission president discovered was that many missionaries who came into the mission field had indeed been on their knees and knew precisely why they were there. They had a clear focus about their calling. They were there to participate in the spiritual harvest that the Lord spoke about (see John 4:31–38).

One such missionary from a very large family arrived virtually penniless. "Why are you here?" asked the mission president, in his kindly way. The young elder said: "I have followed what the Prophet Joseph Smith did. I prayed about it and I know it's true. And I want to share this message with the world." This young elder had a light in his eyes and a firm testimony in his heart—but he had scant financial support for his labors. The mission president said to him, "We will pray and see what the Lord wants." The very next day a family from the area called the mission home to say, "We have been greatly blessed in our business and we want to support a missionary. Do you have someone who needs help?" That was the answer to the prayer. As a result of the kindness and charity of the family, the young missionary received the support he needed to carry on his missionary labors. He advanced quickly in his calling, from district leader to zone leader to assistant to the president. He was an extraordinarily devoted and successful emissary for the Lord, always acting in the strength of the Lord with complete faith, because he knew why he was there.

After his mission, the young man moved to his home state and opened up a business that flourished under his leadership to the point where he needed to expand his staff. A family had moved into the area from a neighboring state after the 9–11 tragedy had caused their business to fail. The father needed employment and, as it turned out, was hired by the returned missionary. It was the same family who had stepped forward to support the young missionary when he needed help—and a reminder of the Lord's counsel: "Search diligently, pray always, and be believing, and all things shall work together for your good, if ye walk uprightly and remember the covenant wherewith ye have covenanted one with another" (D&C 90:24).

Why are you involved in missionary work? How can you ensure that the Spirit will guide you in all that you do?

"The Least I Could Do." A young elder departing on his mission stood at the Missionary Training Center and said with a quiver in his voice, "I have been a convert now for three years. After my conversion and baptism I came to realize the goodness of God and the magnificence of my Savior's sacrifice. I was so happy. The first year went by so slowly. I could hardly wait to get my mission call. It was the least I could do for my Savior." He expressed his joy over his Savior, the Atonement, and the feeling he had in preaching the word of God to his brothers and sisters. He had partaken of the joy of bringing souls unto Christ.

Relative to the magnificent blessings of the Atonement and the transcendent joy of the gift of eternal life, our service unto the Lord, in whatever capacity and scope, is "the least we can do." What are your thoughts about the fact that we are always indebted to the Lord for His love and redemptive grace?

"By Your Very Presence." A number of years ago, two full-time missionaries assigned to a newly opened European city wanted to gain acceptance in the community. They met with the local high school officials to request an opportunity to lecture to the students about American culture and give English lessons. The principal in charge hesitated. The missionaries responded by gladly agreeing not to make any mention of Church matters whatsoever. The principal's response was memorable: "I understand that you will not present any doctrine here. However, by your very presence you may influence my students." Thus he showed his clear understanding that the missionaries were conveying by their

---

deportment, appearance, attitude, language, and spirit something of the message that their words were intended to convey.

What happened in that European city was both bad and good—bad because the missionaries were denied the opportunity to become acquainted with the youth of the community, but good because it confirmed that preaching the truth has several dimensions, including radiating the spirit and light of the gospel through one's presence. "Therefore let your light so shine before this people, that they may see your good works and glorify your Father who is in heaven" (3 Ne. 12:16). How can you ensure that all who come under your influence will conduct themselves with the "godly walk and conversation" (D&C 20:69) worthy of those who gather under the ensign of truth to preach the gospel?

Pondering Prayerfully

Additional scriptures to consider and ponder:
- Mark 16:15
- Acts 1:8
- Rom. 1:16
- 2 Tim. 1:8
- Jacob 5:71
- Alma 17:2–3
- Hel. 3:27–30
- 3 Ne. 9:22
- Moro. 6:4–5
- D&C 11:21
- D&C 29:7
- D&C 49:11–13
- D&C 90:11
- D&C 133:36–38

The following hymns inspire gratitude for missionary work:
- "Behold! A Royal Army" (*Hymns,* 251)
- "Called to Serve" (*Hymns,* 249)
- "We Are Sowing" (*Hymns,* 216)

Remember and Be Sure

In these latter days the Church has come forth out of obscurity to take its place as "the only true and living church upon the face of the whole earth, with which I, the Lord, am well pleased,

speaking unto the church collectively and not individually" (D&C 1:30). It is now our duty as members of the Church to take the gospel to all the world in keeping with the Abrahamic covenant and promise. Furthermore, we are to labor diligently to fellowship and nurture new converts as they enter the kingdom of God and move forward toward spiritual perfection.

What a glorious opportunity is ours to achieve covenant valor in contributing to the building up of the Lord's kingdom in the dispensation of the fullness of times in preparation for the Second Coming: "Verily I say unto you all: Arise and shine forth, that thy light may be a standard for the nations; And that the gathering together upon the land of Zion, and upon her stakes, may be for a defense, and for a refuge from the storm, and from wrath when it shall be poured out without mixture upon the whole earth" (D&C 115:5–6).

Let us do all in our power to gather our families and converts together in holy places and be found worthy of the Lord's blessings and protection in full measure (see D&C 101:22). The gospel of Jesus Christ is a universal gospel. The Lord encourages all people to repent and come unto Him. He will receive them in love "as a hen gathereth her chickens under her wings" (3 Ne. 10:6). The mission of The Church of Jesus Christ of Latter-day Saints, the kingdom of God, is to invite all to come unto Christ that they might have life everlasting.

We have a sacred work to do in helping build up the kingdom of God and bringing the gospel to every nation, kindred, tongue, and people using every means at our disposal, including the wonders of modern communications technology (see Spencer W. Kimball, "When the World Will Be Converted," *Ensign,* Oct. 1974, 2). This work is our responsibility and blessing. It is our privilege to be "saviours . . . on mount Zion" (see Obad. 1:21) and share the gospel of everlasting life with the world. Thus we can personally see the fulfillment of the Lord's promise: "Look unto me, and be ye saved" (Isa. 45:22).

CHAPTER 34
Talents: Gifts from God

We developed spiritual talents before we came to earth. While on earth, we are dual beings comprised of a physical body and a spirit. Our bodies are of recent origin and come to us from mortal elements. Our spirits were begotten by God and have had an extensive period of growth and development in the spirit world, where we came to know God and to comprehend the nature of spiritual realities. Some of our Father's sons developed spiritual talents to a marked degree, and they were foreordained to spiritual callings in mortality whereby their talents would be utilized to administer salvation to our Father's children. —Howard W. Hunter (*Teachings of Howard W. Hunter, 12*)

Opening the Window of Wisdom

One of the greatest tests of character is how we use the talents, gifts, and means with which the Lord has blessed us. The better part of wisdom is to aspire to outcomes of service and honor that will merit the judgment cited by the Savior in His parable of the talents: "Well done, thou good and faithful servant; thou hast been faithful over a few things, I will make thee ruler over many things: enter into the joy of thy lord" (Matt. 25:21).

Few among mortals have been blessed with gifts and means greater than those of Solomon, the son of David. When he used these resources to bless the lives of others and further God's purposes—such as rendering sound judgment among the people and erecting the temple of the Lord—he prospered and enjoyed the blessings of heaven. When he lost balance in his life and elevated worldly goods and honors above the principles of heaven, he was replaced.

The Lord declared during His mortal ministry: "Ye cannot serve God and mammon" (Matt. 6:24). If we cultivate and use our talents and gifts for the glory of God and to promote harmony, peace, and righteous endeavors, then our devotion and valor earn the favor of God. By way of contrast, if we devote our talents and gifts purely for self-aggrandizement and gaining the honors of men, then our devotion to the cause of righteousness fades away, and we lose harmony, peace, and the favor of God.

We all have roles and assignments in our different stewardships in Zion. We can measure and monitor our progress. We can seek the best gifts and apply our talents for the good of others with increasing skill. As we learn more, we can report our progress to our leaders and to the Lord. We can watch ourselves grow and take courage in our progress. We can build our self-confidence. A well-known hymn makes it clear that "Angels above us are silent notes taking Of ev'ry action; then do what is right!" (*Hymns*, 237). The Lord is even more candid: "For it is required of the Lord, at the hand of every steward, to render an account of his stewardship, both in time and in eternity" (D&C 72:3).

The kingdom of God is an interdependent network of stewards applying their God-given talents to leverage the spiritual yield of the enterprise as a whole. Every management expert knows that progress measured regularly—and rewarded—expands. It is that way in the Church as well, where the spiritual blessings of stewardship and service are being compounded every day without cease and without limit. We have a solemn responsibility as stewards of God to account for the gifts and endowments that He bestows upon us for the purpose of building up His kingdom and nurturing and guiding His children. To magnify our talents is to invoke the comforting confirmation of God's satisfaction with our service. To confine and bury our talents slothfully, and with trepidation, is to invoke the severe judgments of God upon us as ungrateful and unprofitable servants in His cause: "For unto every one that hath shall be given, and he shall have abundance: but from him that hath not shall be taken away even that which he hath" (Matt. 25:29). As the Only Begotten Son of God, Jesus Christ served as the consummate Exemplar of one who perfectly magnified His calling as Redeemer and Advocate with the Father. He asks only that we do our part in following His example in all diligence and faith.

Just as the Lord "grew, and waxed strong in spirit, filled with wisdom: and the grace of God was upon him" (Luke 2:40), and just as He "continued from grace to grace, until he received a fulness" (D&C 93:13), we too can take the measure of light and talent given to us and magnify it for the good of all. We can seek "out of the best books words of wisdom; seek learning, even by study and also by faith" (D&C 88:118). We can cultivate talents with an attitude of service and charity. We can consecrate our abilities—whether in art, music, athletics, speech, writing, teaching, research, leadership, and many other fields—to the process of lifting, encouraging, guiding, praising, inspiring, and blessing the lives of others according to the guidance of the Spirit.

The word *talent* is related to a Greek root meaning to "balance" or "weigh"—as in the process of measuring assets used as money. In a similar way, the talents we receive from the Lord are indeed treasures that can be expended to "pay for," or contribute to, the happiness of others. In the scales of righteousness, Belshazzar, the reveling prince-regent in Babylon at the time of Daniel, saw his destiny written on a wall: "Thou art weighed in the balances, and art found wanting" (Dan. 5:27). By contrast, Job prayed, "Let me be weighed in an even balance, that God may know mine integrity" (Job 31:6). Let us put our talents to good use and look forward, with hope and faith, to the hour when we are weighed in the scales of heaven and found worthy in the eyes of the Great Judge.

Inspired by Latter-Day Prophets

Brigham Young: If you give anything for the building up of the kingdom of God, give the best you have. What is the best thing you have to devote to the kingdom of God? It is the talents God has given you. How many? Every one of them (*Discourses of Brigham Young*, 445).

> *Some might feel they don't have any special talent. But when you join in any sincere and uplifting conversation about the beauties and truths of the gospel, you participate in a wonderful display of talent—the ability to share testimonies with others through the Spirit. Bearing your testimony is a divine talent that cannot be surpassed by any other. Add to that the other abilities and gifts you have received from heaven, and you have a medley of talents that manifest the love of God in your life and allow you to give the best that you have for building up the kingdom of God. How does the application of talent for good purposes bring more joy and satisfaction into your life?*

George Q. Cannon: Every defect in the human character can be corrected through the exercise of faith and pleading with the Lord for the gifts that He has said He will give unto those who believe and obey His commandments (*Gospel Truth: Discourses and Writings of President George Q. Cannon*, 155).

> *What are your thoughts about "pleading with the Lord" for gifts and talents to improve your character and sanctify your spirit? How has the Lord blessed you with the power to strengthen and magnify your gifts and talents for the good of your family and the perfecting of your stewardship in Zion? How has*

your patriarchal blessing given you guidance, perhaps in reference to gifts and talents?

J. Reuben Clark, Jr.: Remember the parable of the talents where the man who failed to improve the talent given him, had it taken from him? I ask you brethren, and myself, are we magnifying our Priesthood in such a way, are we living close enough to the Lord and in obedience to his commandments that we may exercise this power, or shall it be wholly or in part taken away from us? You would better think about it. It is worth thinking about. It is the greatest power that has been revealed to man (*Behold the Lamb of God*, 286).

How are the blessings of the priesthood part of our inventory of "talents"—or treasures—from the Lord? How can we magnify our callings by supporting the work of the priesthood as the means for bringing people onto the pathway of salvation and guiding them toward ultimate eternal life and exaltation?

Bruce R. McConkie: Every man must use such talents as he may have or they will be lost. If a man cannot compose music, perhaps he can sing in the choir; if he cannot write books, at least he can read them; if he cannot paint pictures, he can learn to appreciate the artistry of others; if he cannot achieve preeminence in one specific field, so be it, he still can succeed in his own field; for each man has some talent, and he will be judged on the basis of how he uses what he has. It is an eternal law of life that men either progress or retrogress; they either increase their talents and abilities, or those they have wither and die. No one stands still; there is no such thing as pure neutrality (*Doctrinal New Testament Commentary*, 1:689).

How we use what we have received is the measure of judgment in the hour of accountability. What are your thoughts about the choice of progression or retrogression, gain or loss, in regard to our talents?

Truths to Liken

Prov. 23:7—"For as he thinketh in his heart, so is he."

- There is wisdom in connecting the power of thought with the power of accomplishment and achievement.
- The heart is the center of the soul, the mirror of the mind, and the affective center of our very being. We eventually become the results of the feelings and yearnings of our hearts. We act on our thoughts and our feelings. The question is: Where will your thoughts take you today? How is the capacity to think in productive ways a talent from God? How can you learn to cultivate worthy and creative thoughts that will produce desired outcomes according to the pattern of the Creator? Remember: "There is nothing that the Lord thy God shall take in his heart to do but what he will do it" (Abr. 3:17).

Matt. 25:15—"And unto one he gave five talents, to another two, and to another one; to every man according to his several ability; and straightway took his journey."

- In the parable of the talents, the Lord made clear that each individual receives an appropriate endowment of talents and gifts. It is not the quantity of talents that counts, but the results—in other words, how they are applied, in wisdom, according to independent agency, in order to enlarge the initial endowment and magnify the results.
- The Lord has expectations for each of us according to that which we have been given. This is not a comparison test. It is a test of doing our very, very best with what the Lord has given us and then magnifying it with all our heart, might, mind, and soul. All can be exalted if they keep the commandments. High station or position does not exalt—only the grace of God after all we can do (see 2 Ne. 25:23). How does "all we can do" relate to our talents, gifts, and capacities?

2 Ne. 9:28–29—"O that cunning plan of the evil one! O the vainness, and the frailties, and the foolishness of men! When they are learned they think they are wise, and they hearken not unto the counsel of God, for they set it aside, supposing they know of themselves, wherefore, their wisdom is foolishness and it profiteth them not. And they shall perish. But to be learned is good if they hearken unto the counsels of God."

- Jacob, the brother of Nephi, called his people to repentance and taught them the principles of the gospel that he had learned through prayer, study, and the operation of the Spirit.
- The capacity to learn is a talent from God. Knowledge gained through learning is a talent (a treasure) that can be applied to bring about much good, provided such knowledge is acquired and invested in righteous endeavors. Let us remember that the learning (knowledge) of man is desirable and useful as long as it is consistent with enduring principles and brings about worthwhile purposes. At the same time, we can remember that the counsel and knowledge given from God is ultimate saving truth of an eternal nature. As you observe cultural patterns of learning in the world today, where is it apparent that people and groups have diverged from the teachings of the Savior? What can you do to help your loved ones and those you serve in the Church to balance secular learning with the truths of the gospel in order to place an emphasis on eternal principles?

2 Ne. 28:30—"For behold, thus saith the Lord God: I will give unto the children of men line upon line, precept upon precept, here a little and there a little; and blessed are those who hearken unto my precepts, and lend an ear unto my counsel, for they shall learn wisdom; for unto him that receiveth I will give more; and from them that shall say, We have enough, from them shall be taken away even that which they have."

- Nephi was addressing his people (and his future readers) by citing the prophet Isaiah (see Isa. 28:13) and expounding on the expansive nature of wisdom and truth. He emphasized that those who receive wisdom and truth with gratitude

and faithfulness will receive even more. (see also Alma 12:9–11).

- Learning is a process that builds on each concept we internalize. We are encouraged to learn by study and by faith (see D&C 88:118). How can this doctrine be applied to talents? As we receive one talent and nurture it with care, we can expect through the blessing of God to receive another talent, and then another, as we progress in our stewardship for the good of the Church and kingdom. By contrast, those who fail to invest their talents with care and devotion stand to be cut short. This principle is confirmed in the parable of the talents: "For unto every one that hath shall be given, and he shall have abundance: but from him that hath not shall be taken away even that which he hath" (Matt. 25:29). In terms of the gifts of the Spirit, the Lord counsels, "Seek ye earnestly the best gifts, always remembering for what they are given" (D&C 46:8). We too can seek after the best talents if they are to be anchored in righteous endeavors. When you are given assignments in the Church and feel inadequate to perform them with quality, how can you approach the Lord for strength and skill to do your duty?

D&C 60:13—"Thou shalt not idle away thy time, neither shalt thou bury thy talent that it may not be known."

- This counsel was given in a revelation through the Prophet Joseph Smith in Jackson County, Missouri, on August 8, 1831, in response to a request from a group of elders who wanted to know how to proceed with their missionary assignments.
- Idleness has no place in our stewardships for the Lord, nor should we "bury" our talents (as the parable of the talents warns in Matt. 25:18, 25). When we bury our talents, they will be given to another (see Matt. 25:28). To unfold and manifest one's talents is an exercise in following the Spirit. How does the

Spirit make known how best to use your talents on behalf of others—whether in the family, in the Church, or in the community? How does the instruction "Let your light so shine" (Matt. 5:16) apply to talents and gifts?

Rejoicing and Reasoning Together

How Does Willing and Devoted Use of Our Talents Help Us Magnify Our Callings?

One of the ward leaders stopped by the home to ask that a six-year-old boy participate in an upcoming sacrament meeting program. After listening to his request, the boy pondered for a moment about the intimidation of having to appear before such a large congregation and said that he would prefer not to do it. The leader was very kind and gentle. He thanked the boy for considering it, and then went on his way.

That's when the lesson started. For the next few days, the boy felt ashamed for having turned down the calling when it would have been relatively easy to fulfill. Not wanting to confess to his parents about his shortcoming, he kept the circumstances to himself (though they probably knew all about it). The most burdensome experience was sitting through the sacrament meeting a few weeks later and watching as another boy performed very well the part that he should have taken. It made him feel rather small and inadequate. At the time he did not understand that this feeling was diametrically opposite to what the prophet Jacob described when he talked about how to "magnify our office" (Jacob 1:19).

Constriction, reduction, limitation, isolation, shrinking—the things the boy felt at that time—are the opposite of magnifying, radiating, expanding, enveloping, illuminating, blessing, unfolding—the feelings that come when we accept service in the kingdom of God by using our talents with devotion, enthusiasm, and a willing heart. As the young boy later learned through an endless array of positive experiences on the errand of the Lord, the process is one of "magnifying." That is the essence of righteous service. It is part of applying and enlarging one's gifts and talents for spiritual profit, as the Savior taught in the parable of the talents (see Matt. 25:14–30).

To *magnify* means to make greater, to make more splendid. There are really three kinds of magnifying evidenced in the gospel. First, there is the process of magnifying an office by accepting it with humility, gratitude, soberness, and devotion—as Jacob exemplified when he spoke of "taking upon us the responsibility, answering the sins of the people upon our own heads if we did not teach them the word of God with all diligence" (Jacob 1:19; 2:2). A similar usage is reflected in the revelation given to Joseph Smith and Oliver Cowdery in July 1830: "Attend to thy calling and thou shalt have wherewith to magnify thine office, and to expound the scriptures, and continue in laying on of the hands and confirming the churches" (D&C 24:9). Perhaps the most celebrated usage of this kind is found in the oath and covenant of the priesthood: "For whoso is faithful unto the obtaining these two priesthoods of which I have spoken, and the magnifying their callings, are sanctified by the Spirit unto the renewing of their bodies" (D&C 84:33).

Second, the principal purpose of gospel service is to bring glory to God, to magnify Him and His Son, and to cause others to do the same: "Remember that thou magnify his work, which men behold" (Job 36:24). The Psalmist said, "I will praise the name of God with a song, I will magnify him with thanksgiving" (Ps. 69:30). Nephi declared: "Wherefore, my soul delighteth to prophesy concerning him, for I have seen his day, and my heart doth magnify his holy name" (2 Ne. 25:13). Perhaps the most famous of such instances was uttered by the mother of the Redeemer: "And Mary said, my soul doth magnify the Lord, And my spirit hath rejoiced in God my Saviour" (Luke 1:46–47).

Third, gospel service causes people themselves to be magnified personally or rendered more splendid in the spiritual sense. "And the Lord said unto Joshua, This day will I begin to magnify thee in the sight of all Israel, that they may know that, as I was with Moses, so I will be with thee" (Joshua 3:7).

There is a continual process implied with such references. We *magnify* our calling by *magnifying* the Lord and enlarging His holy name before the world; and thus we are, in turn, *magnified* through His blessings to us. This triad of enlargement—this eternal circle of service and the willing application of one's talents—is a lifting force. When the three stages are completed, the cycle starts again at a higher level. Thus we see emerging a *magnificent spiral* that carries us ever upward as we contribute to, and are nurtured by, the process of magnification. What a grand and magnanimous blessing it is to have part in such a program of enlargement and building as the kingdom of God expands and grows like the stone that was cut from the mountain without hands and rolls forth to fill the whole world (Dan. 2:34–35, 45).

There are, of course, circumstances where it might be difficult or impossible to respond to a calling. At such times the Lord, in His compassion, may judge the heart of those involved and confirm that they "cease not their diligence"—and thus He will "require that work no more" of them, but "accept of their offerings" (D&C 124:49). And perhaps the Lord, in His lovingkindness, will forgive a six-year-old boy who did not yet have an inkling of the divine process of growth and development that comes when the Saints of God display a devoted "heart and a willing mind" (D&C 64: 34).

As you ponder the various callings that you have received in the Church or might yet receive, how has the willing cultivation and application of your talents and gifts contributed to the magnificent spiral just described? That is, you magnify your calling by magnifying the Lord and enlarging His holy name before the world; and thus you are, in turn, magnified through His blessings to you.

Real-life Stories for Heart and Mind

First Things First. A delightful young couple that had recently joined the Church was telling some Church friends about their first experience watching general conference on television. "We were all assembled downstairs in front of the TV, waiting with great excitement—all except our young son, who was still upstairs busy with his playthings," they recounted. "We kept calling up to him to remind him, but he didn't come. When the broadcast started, we called once more, saying the Tabernacle Choir and General Authorities were coming on. In response, he called down, in all sincerity, saying, 'When God comes on, let me know.'" Here was a young man wise beyond his years. Even though he had not yet learned much about the role of prophets in the Lord's kingdom, he was certainly putting his Father in Heaven at the top of his priority list, above everything else—even his toys. The Savior said, "Suffer little children, and forbid them not, to come unto me: for of such is the kingdom of heaven" (Matt. 19:14). If only all

of us could have a child's innocent focus and commitment and apply ourselves fully to the Lord by putting first things first.

When it comes to your talents and gifts, you can decide that when you have a choice to use them for worldly gain or for the Lord, you will always put the Lord first. How has the consecration of your talents brought you joy and spiritual growth?

Hidden Wisdom. It began as a routine statement about education but ended as a life-changing demonstration about wisdom. The presenter, a representative of one of the large publishing houses in America, stood on the stage before a vast audience of educators and writers. Behind him was a gigantic banner that stretched from wall to wall, emblazoned with the words "Education is the acquisition of knowledge." As he delivered his message about acquiring learning, it seemed he was simply preaching to the choir, restating the age-old message about the need to expand one's inventory of facts and figures. The audience was on the verge of getting sleepy.

But then, just at the right moment, he asked whether his thesis was actually true. That caught the attention of the audience. At the same time, he walked back to the banner and pointed out a fold in it. He and several assistants opened the fold, revealing the full banner—which now read, "Education is the acquisition of *the art of the utilization of* knowledge." The statement, a quote from British philosopher Alfred North Whitehead, was a clear reminder that education without application was a shallow exercise. What truly counts is learning that can profitably be applied to good ends.

That demonstration reminds us that isolated knowledge is of little value, just as unused talents are without merit. Only when learning and capability are turned to helpful and wise applications of service can they be deemed useful. In fact, applied learning leads, in time, to that most desirable quality—wisdom. It was King Benjamin who stated the case most succinctly: "And behold, I tell you these things that ye may learn wisdom; that ye may learn that when ye are in the service of your fellow beings ye are only in the service of your God" (Mosiah 2:17).

The greatest example of this kind of applied learning was the Savior Himself, whom Isaiah characterized in this manner: "And the Spirit of the Lord shall rest upon him, the spirit of wisdom and understanding, the spirit of counsel and might, the spirit of knowledge and of the fear of the Lord" (2 Nephi 21:2). It is this kind of proactive and goal-centered learning that constitutes wisdom, and "Happy is the man that findeth wisdom, and the man that getteth understanding" (Prov. 3:13).

Talent is ability applied in doing good for others. How have you been able to confirm this principle in your experience on the pathway of life? How can you help others come to an understanding that their talents and gifts, wisely applied in service to others, will grow and expand as a blessing from God?

Spiritual Compounding. Over the years one LDS leader enjoyed helping neighborhood children improve their reading skills. One young deacon was about three grade levels behind; reading didn't fascinate him as much as sports and other activities. So his mentor tried something different—they decided to start keeping score. Every few days the young man would spend an hour reading out loud to his teacher from a book or article in which he was interested—and that was above his current reading level. There was a catch: he had to correct each and every error before going on. They timed each session carefully and calculated the number of words read, then plotted the score on a sheet of graph paper after each session. They set a goal and settled on an appropriate reward for success. By following the line, the student could see how he was doing over time. The line started to rise consistently—even dramatically. A light went on. He was not accounting to his teachers anymore; he was accounting to himself. That was different. Being highly competitive, he started to enjoy the exercise more and more, and actually took satisfaction from seeing his results improve rapidly.

Over a span of just fourteen sessions, he brought his reading skill up three grade levels—where he needed to be. He was able to read without making any errors, and his comprehension improved significantly as his fluency rose. It was a matter of changing his perspective on things—and giving him a little self-confidence. He had gotten hooked on self-improvement. It's an example of stewardship and accountability—line upon line. It

works with anyone, in both temporal and spiritual avenues of development.

As you consider this illustration of improving a specific talent, how could you adapt and apply this to other kinds of talents and activities? How could you help others cultivate a passion for self-improvement and self-mastery—and thus become more fully engaged in the discovery and cultivation of God-given talents for the good of the family, the Church, and the community?

Pondering Prayerfully

Additional scriptures to consider and ponder:
- Ex. 31:3
- 1 Sam. 17:45–49
- 1 Pet. 4:11
- Alma 37:35
- D&C 25:12
- D&C 93:36–37
- D&C 131:6

The following hymns inspire gratitude for talents:
- "Do What Is Right" (*Hymns*, 237)
- "Improve the Shining Moments" (*Hymns*, 226)
- "Today, While the Sun Shines" (*Hymns*, 229)
- "You Can Make the Pathway Bright" (*Hymns*, 228)

Remember and Be Sure

The Lord stands ready to bless us as we come to Him in meekness and humility desiring to serve and bless our fellowmen. Let us aspire to seek and gain the knowledge and talents that will help us live righteously and serve nobly, thus qualifying ourselves for eternal life.

We may be blessed with a special talent for understanding and gaining things spiritual; we may be blessed with musical or artistic ability; we may be blessed with the ability to bear our testimony with compelling inspiration; we may be blessed with vision and wisdom; we may be blessed with inventiveness and technical skills; or we may be blessed with capability in languages, a gift the Prophet Joseph Smith said was "particularly instituted for the preaching of the Gospel to other nations and languages" (*HC* 2:162). Whatever our talent or gift, we can magnify it through obedience to the promptings of the Holy Ghost and use it to bless others and find favor with our Father in Heaven and His Son, Jesus Christ.

If we aspire to the best gifts and talents in order to accomplish a higher level of service to others; if we stand in holy places such as homes of devotion, unified congregations of Zion, and sacred temples; and if we are able, through the guidance of the Spirit, to maintain an eye single to the glory of God, then we can truly look forward to the day of judgment when the valiant will hear the Savior's words: "Well done, thou good and faithful servant; thou hast been faithful over a few things, I will make thee ruler over many things: enter into the joy of thy lord" (Matt. 25:21).

CHAPTER 35
Obedience to the Commandments

Happiness is the object and design of our existence; and will be the end thereof, if we pursue the path that leads to it; and this path is virtue, uprightness, faithfulness, holiness, and keeping all the commandments of God. —Joseph Smith (*HC* 5:134–135)

Opening the Window of Wisdom

Heavenly Father, through His beloved Son, Jesus Christ, has given us the laws and commandments essential for gaining eternal life. Obedience to the commandments enables us to achieve happiness here and everlasting joy in the hereafter (see Mosiah 2:41). We are to "live by every word that proceedeth forth from the mouth of God" (D&C 84:44). The commandments have been established according to divine design, and when we fail to keep them, we break ourselves against them and suffer the consequences.

When we truly love God, we will keep His commandments (see John 14:15; Moses 5:13), for that is the test of mortality (see Eccl. 12:13; D&C 93:1; Abr. 3:25). We are given blessings in accordance with our obedience. And likewise, blessings are withheld in the case of disobedience (see D&C 82:10; 130:19–21). King Benjamin declared: "And moreover I would desire that ye should consider on the blessed and happy state of those that keep the commandments of God. For behold, they are blessed in all things, both temporal and spiritual; and if they hold out faithful to the end they are received into heaven, that thereby they may dwell with God in a state of never-ending happiness. O remember, remember that these things are true; for the Lord God hath spoken it" (Mosiah 2:41).

The commandments are central to the Lord's covenant with His people. The Ten Commandments—eternal requirements from the beginning—were given to guide Israel into the proper pathways for honoring that covenant. These commandments are repeated in the Book of Mormon (see Mosiah 12:33–36), the Doctrine and Covenants (see D&C 42:18–27), and the New Testament (see Matt. 5:17–37). They deal with relationships of eternal significance—God, family, and fellowman. The Gospel of John records, "And this is life eternal, that they might know thee the only true God, and Jesus Christ, whom thou hast sent" (John 17:3). Eternal life is indeed establishing an eternal relationship with our Heavenly Father and our Savior.

It is clear what blessings come through obedience to the commandments—life eternal in the presence of our Heavenly Father and His Son and eternal increase through the blessings of the Abrahamic covenant. Through obedience, we become the sons and daughters of God. Obedience, in fact, is the first law of heaven, and all blessings are predicated on this law (see D&C 130:20–21).

When we gain mastery over our conduct through obedience to the Lord, then by nature we desire that which is good and we behave in a Christlike manner, thus being worthy to have the Spirit with us always (see D&C 20:77, 79).

The greatest example of godly obedience is the Savior, who, in perfect and humble submission to the will of the Father, offered Himself as Redeemer: "Father, thy will be done, and the glory be thine forever" (Moses 4:2). To follow the Lord valiantly, we too can continue to submit humbly to God's will throughout our mortal probation, just as we chose to do in the premortal realm. The pattern of our existence is righteousness—that state of being in which one is blameless, full of faith, seeks the will of the Father with an eye single to His glory, is full of good works, and is exactly, immediately, and courageously obedient to the laws and commandments of the Lord.

We can seek to be righteous—that is our compass and our charge. Righteousness is the oil of our lamp. Righteousness is happiness (see 2 Ne. 2:13). Righteousness is the pathway to salvation and exaltation.

Inspired by Latter-Day Prophets

Brigham Young: Every son and daughter of God is expected to obey with a willing heart every word which the Lord has spoken, and which he will in the future speak to us. It is expected that we hearken to the revelations of his will, and adhere to them, cleave to them with all our might; for this is salvation, and any thing short of this clips the salvation and the glory of the Saints (*Discourses of Brigham Young*, 220).

> *Salvation is something we seek in its wholeness and completeness. If we fail to have complete obedience—even in regard to the least of the commandments—then our salvation is "clipped" to that extent and our joy is incomplete. As you consider the totality of your performance before the Lord, which areas need improvement? How can you help your loved ones see their happiness in the context of obeying all the commandments?*

Joseph Fielding Smith: Some people have the idea that the Ten Commandments were first given by Moses when he directed the children of Israel and formulated their code of laws. This is not the case. These great commandments are from the beginning and were understood in righteous communities in the days of Adam (*Doctrines of Salvation*, 1:96).

> *The commandments of God are eternal. They are administered by the Lord according to our capacity to grow into a state of obedience in doing His will. Even the Ten Commandments were given twice during the days of Moses (see Ex. 20; Deut. 5), once in their fulness, and once in a form that still incorporated the law but provided a system of carnal commandments in place of the higher priesthood and its ordinances (see JST, Ex. 34:1–2). We are privileged to live in a time when the fulness of the gospel and its saving principles, ordinances, and commandments are in force. How can you show gratitude to the Lord for the revelation of the commandments in their fulness?*

Spencer W. Kimball: Righteousness requires action. People tend often to measure their righteousness by the absence of wrong acts in their lives, as if passivity were the end of being. But God has created "things to act and things to be acted upon" (2 Ne. 2:14), and man is in the former category. He does not fill the measure of his creation unless he acts, and that in righteousness (*The Teachings of Spencer W. Kimball*, 148).

> *John the Revelator proclaimed the judgment of God upon one of the churches in his day: "So then because thou art lukewarm, and neither cold nor hot, I will spue thee out of my mouth" (Rev. 3:16). How can you make sure that personal initiative and bold obedience to the commandments of the Lord will serve as the antidote to the perilous state of being "lukewarm"? How can you help others to increase their commitment and enthusiasm for doing the will of the Lord and thus achieve eternal joy and happiness for themselves and their loved ones?*

Ezra Taft Benson: We must put God in the forefront of everything else in our lives. He must come first, just as He declares in the first of His Ten Commandments: "Thou shalt have no other gods before me" (Ex. 20:3.) (*The Teachings of Ezra Taft Benson*, 349).

In our list of priorities, God comes first. What has been your experience in having all other things of importance fall into their proper place when we elevate to the pinnacle of all values our faith in, and obedience to, God?

Truths to Liken

Eccl. 12:13–14—"Let us hear the conclusion of the whole matter: Fear God, and keep his commandments: for this is the whole duty of man. For God shall bring every work into judgment, with every secret thing, whether it be good, or whether it be evil."

- The author of Ecclesiastes, traditionally believed to be Solomon, gave the bottom line to his treatise on the "vanities of vanities" (Eccl. 1:2)—to be humbly obedient to the commandments of God.
- The worldly life of mankind is shaped by vanity and superficiality. To rise above the the temporal and fleeting values of the world, one looks to God in obedience, with a commitment to take on the divine nature and come forth as a son or daughter of God in righteousness. What are your thoughts about how best to make the transition to that higher level and remain steadfast once there?

Ps. 111:10—"The fear of the LORD is the beginning of wisdom: a good understanding have all they that do his commandments: his praise endureth for ever."

- The Psalmist gave a succinct definition of what it means to fear God: understand His gospel plan, keep His commandments, and praise Him forever.
- There are many references in the scriptures to *the fear of the Lord.* Proverbs contains this statement: "The fear of the LORD is the beginning of wisdom: and the knowledge of the holy is understanding" (Prov. 9:10). The essence of the principle is obedience—based on the knowledge that to obey brings joy and results in eternal life. How can you help your family members

and those you teach in the Church understand that we do not obey because we are "afraid," but instead out of love, reverence, gratitude, and the wise use of our agency?

Luke 4:8—"And Jesus answered and said unto him, Get thee behind me, Satan: for it is written, Thou shalt worship the Lord thy God, and him only shalt thou serve."

- During the Savior's forty-day fast in the wilderness, He was tempted by Satan, who tried to persuade Him to apply His divine power and agency in inappropriate ways. This was His response to that temptation.
- The motto *Get thee behind me, Satan* provides a wonderful governing principle for our lives. It is a command, an order from one in charge of the situation. It is necessary for us to experience opposition in all things (see 2 Ne. 2:11) and to be tempted as a trial of our faith (see D&C 29:39). Our goal is to learn how to withstand and overcome temptation. How have you found it effective to take an active and commanding position against the tempter in order to stay on the right course?

1 Ne. 22:31—"Wherefore, if ye shall be obedient to the commandments, and endure to the end, ye shall be saved at the last day. And thus it is. Amen."

- Having read extensively to his brethren from the plates of brass (essentially the Old Testament of his day), Nephi gave them this final exhortation, which summarized his presentation.
- The simple truth of life is that if we lovingly obey the commandments of God, we will be exalted. It is refreshing to have in one single line a summary of an entire book of scripture. If you were to give those you love a single-line version of what you have learned in your lifetime to this point, what would it be? What would you like to leave as a legacy of wisdom for those who follow in your footsteps?

D&C 11:20—"Behold, this is your work, to keep my commandments, yea, with all your might, mind and strength."

- This is a portion of the counsel the Lord gave to Hyrum Smith in a revelation through the Prophet Joseph Smith at Harmony, Pennsylvania, in May 1829.
- We are to do all in our power to strengthen our commitment to keep our covenants with the Lord. The work and glory of the Lord is to "bring to pass the immortality and eternal life of man" (Moses 1:39). The work and glory of man is to keep the Lord's commandments as part of this grand divine design. What are your thoughts about the central role of obedience in your own personal journey back to the presence of the Father and the Son? How can you help your family focus on obedience as their central duty before God?

D&C 130:20–21—"There is a law, irrevocably decreed in heaven before the foundations of this world, upon which all blessings are predicated— And when we obtain any blessing from God, it is by obedience to that law upon which it is predicated."

- These words are among the items of inspired instruction given by the Prophet Joseph Smith at Ramus, Illinois, on April 2, 1843.
- The law of the harvest is simple: we are blessed with glorious rewards by practicing true principles and obeying the commandments of God. Ammon expressed this promise and assurance to his brothers following their highly successful fourteen-year mission among the Lamanites: "But behold, they are in the hands of the Lord of the harvest, and they are his; and he will raise them up at the last day" (Alma 26:7). What are your feelings about the opportunity to be "in the hands of the Lord of the harvest" through obedience to His commandments?

Rejoicing and Reasoning Together

How Can We Know That the Commandments Are of God?

In His discourse at the temple during the Feast of Tabernacles (John 7), the Savior disclosed to the sinister and plotting clergy an infallible key for establishing the truth of the doctrine of salvation that He was preaching: "If any man will do his will, he shall know of the doctrine, whether it be of God, or whether I speak of myself" (John 7:17). Long before the Savior's mortal ministry, King Benjamin had made the same invitation: "And again, believe that ye must repent of your sins and forsake them, and humble yourselves before God; and ask in sincerity of heart that he would forgive you; and now, if you believe all these things see that ye do them" (Mosiah 4:10). Alma, too, had encouraged the people to actively experiment with the word of truth so that it could spring up in them as a living tree and bear precious fruit (see Alma 32). As the prophets down through time have made clear, the gospel of Jesus Christ is an action plan with a built-in way to verify its truth. Doctrine plus sincere application yields certainty; concept plus devoted action yields revealed testimony. In other words, do it and you will know that it is true.

Based on the spirit and tone in John 7, here is a short, action-oriented checklist of seven points that show how this process can work in daily life. These points might help you strengthen your testimony that applying gospel doctrine in real life lets you know that it is of God. In essence, you know the gospel is true and the commandments are of divine origin when you:

- ***Discern the light of understanding*** *as you search the scriptures and learn—line upon line and precept upon precept—the pattern of liberation given us by the Author of eternal salvation;*
- ***Perceive the beacon of hope*** *penetrating the blackness of night as you repent of your sins and experience the mighty change of heart (see Mosiah 5:2–3; Alma 5:13–14);*
- ***Sense the buoyancy of pure truth*** *lifting you out of the depression of doubt as you pray for, and receive, the confirmation of the Holy Spirit;*

- *Detect the joy of spiritual security* overcoming the insidious influences of evil as you gather in holy places—home, stake, temple (see D&C 87:8; 101:22)—and worship with your family and friends in truth, purity, and humility;
- *Feel the dawning glow of peace* dispersing the darkness of resentment each time you forgive another of a supposed offense;
- *Experience the glow of charity* dispelling the isolation of selfishness as you serve others with sincere devotion;
- *Behold the majesty of God's lovingkindness* overpowering the fleeting pretenses of worldliness as you strive day-by-day to do a little better, act with a little more kindness, and move a little closer to the "godly walk and conversation" prescribed for disciples of Christ (D&C 20:69).

How Can We Strengthen Our Resolve to Keep the Commandments?

These seven key ideas may help you keep the commandments:

- **Knowledge**: You can increase your knowledge and understanding of the commandments by studying the scriptures (see 2 Ne. 32:3; D&C 84:43–44) and listening to the living prophets; by pondering prayerfully to gain a fuller understanding and appreciation of gospel truths (see 1 Ne. 11:1; D&C 138:1–11); by visiting the temple often, since performing vicarious service refreshes your mind concerning your covenants and allows you to be taught by the Lord (see D&C 97:13–14); by seeking counsel and instruction from your loved ones and leaders; and by following the Spirit, remembering that the Holy Ghost can teach you all things (see Moro. 10:4–5; D&C 50:17–22).
- **Prayer**: You can pray for strength, remembering that we are nothing without the Lord, and that in our finite and mortal state we need strength from the Lord to rise to our potential (see Alma 26:11–12).
- **Humility**: Humility is a protective shield and is imperative in order to keep the commandments (see Alma 7:23; Ether 12:27).
- **Holy Ghost**: You can live worthy of the Spirit and pray for guidance in being obedient (see 2 Ne. 32:5; D&C 46:10–33).
- **Love**: You can seek to love God with all your heart, might, mind, and strength (see John 14:15)—and to love your neighbor as yourself (see Matt. 22:37–39).
- **Remember**: Simple reminders can remind you to keep the commandments—some examples include little signs, pictures on the wall, a penny in your shoe, calendar items for prayer and study, smiles from loved ones, and CTR rings.
- **Spiritual blessings**: You can savor the blessings of obedience—peace, joy, confidence, enlightenment—when you keep the commandments. This will give momentum and spiritual confirmation for the future, as in the sacrament prayers (see D&C 20:77, 79).

What Can We Learn About Obedience from Lehi's Tree of Life Vision?

Lehi's vision of the tree of life was an uplifting allegory about God's overarching plan of love and redemption, as well as a template for action in one's immediate life. What Lehi saw came from the highest reaches of the spiritual firmament, yet it provides a compass for the real experiences of the moment. Lehi was wise enough to see that his vision had meaning not just in relation to concept and principle, but especially when applied to himself, his wife, and his own family. And so it is with us all. The tree of life is not an abstract model to be admired like a tapestry, but a roadmap that becomes all the more compelling when we use it as a mirror in which to see ourselves in the very act of striving to gain perfection.

In seeking eternal life, we need to stay on the straight and narrow path, hold to the iron rod, and press forward steadfastly to partake of the tree of life. It takes great effort and perseverance to remain among the faithful and obedient and avoid casting our lot with those who either fail to grab hold of the iron rod, or, having once chosen it, eventually having lost their way, wander off and are lost (see 1 Ne. 8:20–23).

In the vision of the tree of life we are granted a clear and unmistakable view of the types of people ever present in mortality, and the different strategies each might use in their quest to attain what they perceive to be a fulfilling lifestyle. Let's look at the four types of travelers in mortality, and determine which type we might be at any given moment:

- **Group 1. The Vagrants**—Some never get to the iron rod or fail to hold on to it; these lose their way in the mists of darkness, wander off, and are lost (see 1 Ne. 8:21–23). This shows that we need to search the word daily, diligently nourish ourselves with it, and live according to every word that proceeds forth from the mouth of God—or else we are doomed.
- **Group 2. The Vacillators**—These hold to the iron rod and start to enjoy the fruit of the tree, but when they find themselves mocked and ridiculed, they are unable to stand against the persecution; they fall away and are lost (see 1 Ne. 8:24–28). We need to continually stand for truth and righteousness and live as Paul described: "For I am not ashamed of the gospel of Christ: for it is the power of God unto salvation to every one that believeth; to the Jew first, and also to the Greek" (Rom. 1:16).
- **Group 3. The Vain**—These wander in strange roads and eventually feel their way to the spacious building, where they become its mocking tenants (see 1 Ne. 8:31–33). Regrettably, this group represents a vast multitude of Heavenly Father's children who succumb to pride and vanity and, like the others who stray from the pathway leading to truth, become separated from the things of God.
- **Group 4. The Valiant**—These hold to the iron rod, press forward with steadfastness, partake of the fruit of the tree, and—like Lehi, Sarah, Nephi, and Sam—remain faithful (see 1 Ne. 8:30). This is how faithful Latter-day Saints should live.

As you consider this array of travelers, how can you ensure that you remain among the valiant who move forward and partake of the fruit of the tree, which is "most precious and most desirable above all other fruits; yea, and it is the greatest of all the gifts of God" (1 Ne. 15:36)?

Real-life Stories for Heart and Mind

The Noble Birthright. A bright and capable young man with a young family held a responsible position as choir director with one of the local Christian congregations and was affiliated with a prestigious local music conservatory. He had talked about the restored Church several times with a friend who was a priesthood leader in a local stake. As he read the Book of Mormon, he sent his friend a note in which he bore witness that he knew he had found the truth. His friend felt that the Spirit was working with him to bring about a "mighty change of heart," as among the people of King Benjamin. The young man's interest was keen and searching. He was attending the Church meetings. But the young man voiced hesitation, asking questions about this doctrine or that aspect of Church history. The priesthood leader knew that the young man's focus was being distracted by some other issue. What was it? And then he discerned what the investigator's concern might be: the young man was sensing that a commitment to the gospel could very well cause him to lose his job as choir director. The priesthood leader encouraged him to move forward with faith, but he gradually drew back. Later correspondence the priesthood leader sent the young man remained unanswered.

As you consider this close encounter with eternal joy, what are your thoughts about helping others who are still just outside the gateway and who need love and encouragement?

How Happy Can You Be? He was a legend in the ward—a noble gentleman, close to eighty years old, always smiling and friendly. Everyone loved him. His southern expressiveness, unpretentious demeanor, and infectious enthusiasm endeared him to young and old alike. He never missed sharing his love for the Savior on the first Sunday of each month, and people looked forward to his testimony, because they always felt good afterwards—uplifted and inspired, confirmed in their conviction about the goodness of life and the love of the Lord. Though not wealthy in worldly goods, this senior gentleman never left anyone in doubt that he was happy. He was a perfect example of someone who keeps the Lord's commandments—all of them. He exemplified joy, as if to demonstrate every day of his life the truth that "men are, that they might have joy" (2 Ne. 2:25). He would lean his head back, peer through his glasses, then grin and say the words—that line that everyone was listening for and knew would inevitably come—"I know the gospel is true, because it makes me happy. I am just as happy as a toad in a crock of buttermilk." Then everyone would chuckle and sigh, relieved that the truth had once more been revealed from the lips of one who was a master at being happy, and a master at infecting everyone else with the spirit of joy in life and gratitude for the blessings of the Lord.

It may be hard for the rest of us to visualize the implied reality of a toad doing blissful backstrokes through that crock of buttermilk—but we can take it for what it's worth: a metaphor of the joy that comes from obedience to the commandments of God. How would you describe, in your own terms, the authentic nature of the joy of obedience to the commandments as you have experienced it?

The Courage to Do What Is Right. A small group of college students was being trained to qualify for summer work as licensed tour-bus drivers in a Rocky Mountain resort area. The young students were taken on dangerous switchbacks to learn the skills needed for maneuvering a large passenger vehicle safely in the mountains. One day the trainer surprised them with an unexpected question: "Imagine that you are driving a fully loaded bus on the outside lane of a mountain highway with a steep granite wall rising to your left and a deep precipice dropping to your right. Suddenly you round a curve and find that a car is racing toward you in the middle of the road. What would you do?"

The instinct is to veer out of the way—but that would be catastrophic. Any attempt to veer to the right or left, out of the way of the oncoming car, might take you too close to the edge and place your forty-five passengers in even greater danger—with the possibility of certain death. The answer the trainer was looking for was simply this: "You hold to your lane and hit the oncoming car directly. The

enormous weight and size of the bus will give you a powerful advantage against the much smaller car—and will provide the greatest safety for your passengers." While such a strategy seemed drastic, it soon became obvious that it was the only possible solution to such a crisis.

A similar thing happens when honor collides with moral compromise. There are times in every person's life when a sudden and unexpected confrontation with the oncoming dangers of evil demand a head-on stand for what is right and true. At such times of choice there can be no compromise. To leave the well-marked pathway and veer to right or left to avoid taking a stand can only make the crisis worse and lead to tragic consequences. The model to follow is the Lord Himself: "For God doth not walk in crooked paths, neither doth he turn to the right hand nor to the left, neither doth he vary from that which he hath said, therefore his paths are straight, and his course is one eternal round" (D&C 3:2).

Our commission in life is much like that of the bus driver. We journey along the highways of life with the responsibility to guide our families safely to the destination of sanctity and righteousness. There are many dangerous curves to maneuver. There are countless distractions to divert our vision from the course straight ahead. Our duty and our honor demand constant attention and the never-ending exercise of correct principles in keeping the commandments at all times. When on occasion we come upon a sudden challenge in the road, we are then prepared and ready to take a stand for the sake of our families, our Church, our peace, and our faith. We stay in tune with the Spirit and follow the promptings that come.

You have responsibilities for others—especially your family members. You are at the wheel on the journey of life, responsible for the attainment of the destination in safety and honor. How can you ensure the security and happiness of those who depend on you? How does keeping the commandments with honor invite the Spirit to attend the journey with you so that you can know the correct route and apply eternal principles successfully?

Pondering Prayerfully

Additional scriptures to consider and ponder:
- Deut. 6:17
- 1 Sam. 15:22
- Matt. 19:21
- 1 Tim. 6:10–11
- 2 Ne. 5:20–21
- 2 Ne. 31:10
- Jarom 1:9
- D&C 29:35
- D&C 29:39

The following hymns inspire gratitude for the commandments:

- "Come, Let Us Anew" (*Hymns,* 217)
- "I Have Work Enough to Do" (*Hymns,* 224)
- "With Humble Heart" (*Hymns,* 171)
- "We'll Sing All Hail to Jesus' Name" (*Hymns,* 182)

Remember and Be Sure

In life, we are free to choose, but we need to remember that there are rewards or consequences for every decision. Every person has experienced the blessings that come from obedience to eternal principles and laws. That kind of experience brings mounting conviction that to keep the commandments of God is for our best good. As we go about our daily lives, we can always remember that the commandments are given by God in love, for He knows that obedience will bring great blessings to us—blessings of joy, happiness, and eternal life.

We cannot be true disciples of Christ until we learn to obey. Consider the example of the Savior: "Though he were a Son, yet learned he obedience by the things which he suffered; And being made perfect, he became the author of eternal salvation unto all them that obey him" (Heb. 5:8–9). We can strive each day to honor His atoning sacrifice by accepting Him as our Savior and following with faith and courage every word with which He has blessed our lives. The more we obey, the more we have the Spirit; the more we have the Spirit, the more righteous we become; the more righteous we become, the greater is our capacity to serve and bless others; the more we bless others and build up the kingdom of God through charity, the more abundant is happiness and joy for all, and the more we will become like our Savior.

CHAPTER 36
Families Can Be Forever

A Latter-day Saint who has no ambition to establish a home and give it permanency has not a full conception of a sacred duty the gospel imposes upon him. —Joseph F. Smith (*Gospel Doctrine: Selections from the Sermons and Writings of Joseph F. Smith,* 301)

Opening the Window of Wisdom

Marriage is a divinely ordained institution. Parenthood within marriage is a divinely ordained aspect of this institution—a sublime opportunity to participate in the ongoing creative process associated with God's work and glory.

The Lord taught Moses that it is crucial to the Father's eternal plan that man and woman be together, that they be one, and that they have joy in their posterity by multiplying and replenishing the earth. Paul stated the principle as follows: "Nevertheless neither is the man without the woman, neither the woman without the man, in the Lord" (1 Cor. 11:11). Eternal marriage is imperative in order for mankind to receive all the blessings of God (see D&C 131:1–4). Eve was created to be a helpmeet for Adam—a companion, an equal partner having an eternal relationship of fellowship and love, a counselor and friend to her husband. As husband and wife, they were commanded to bring forth children in keeping with the design of the Almighty.

Marriage and family thus form the basis of Heavenly Father's plan for bringing spirit children to the earth, providing for them physical tabernacles, and teaching and training them to live by the eternal principles of the gospel of Jesus Christ. Families are the basic unit of the Church and kingdom of God here on earth. The devil and all his angels seek to destroy marriage and the sanctity of the family. Marriage and family are at risk in a culture where eternal values take a back seat to worldly interests and philosophies.

Despite what the world would say, there is no question about the central importance of marriage and family in regard to life here on earth and throughout all eternity. Family life is the proper place for the gospel to be taught and practiced. The home is a refuge from the world. We are to do all that we can to maintain a strong marriage and happy families by living the gospel of Jesus Christ and by participating in the covenants and ordinances of exaltation. Fostering and cultivating an edifying covenant relationship within the family—and with the Lord—will lead to greater happiness and joy in this life and eternal blessings in the life to come.

"The Family: A Proclamation to the World," prepared by the First Presidency and Council of the Twelve Apostles, is a glorious statement of divine truth that encapsulates and confirms with uncompromising boldness and beautiful simplicity the central role of the family in God's plan of salvation. It teaches that the key to having good relationships within the family, and particularly between husband and wife, is to live the doctrines of the gospel. When we come to understand and apply the doctrines, principles, ordinances, and covenants of the gospel, our attitudes and behaviors are transformed, lifting us to a higher level of spiritual fulfillment. This is especially evident within the family unit.

The relationship and companionship we have here on earth in our families will go with us into the eternities (see D&C 130:2). It is to this state of happiness and never-ending joy that we aspire as we look forward to eternal life with our Heavenly Father, our Savior, and our loved ones, knowing that all blessings are predicated on our obedience (see Mosiah 2:41; D&C 130:20–21).

The family unit is a timeless aspect of the plan of happiness, extending from the premortal realm (where the spirit children of Heavenly Father were associated within His vast family circle) to the mortal realm (where family units are organized according to the pattern of enduring relationships) and extending into the postmortal sphere (where eternal families have the cherished opportunity to be together forever through the sealing keys and powers of the priesthood). In premortal life we became the children of God the Eternal Father. Heavenly Father's plan was presented and we accepted it under the leadership of Jesus Christ, the Son of the Almighty. We were valiant in our premortal estate and were sent to earth as mortals to work out our salvation through the gospel plan. Earth life is a test (see Abr. 3:25) during which we are given enabling power and nurturing blessings through the grace of God. Christ's Atonement makes possible not only forgiveness of sins if we repent, but provides for immortality and eternal life. Eternal life is given to those who qualify by entering into sacred covenants and ordinances and remaining true and faithful to them so as to enjoy the blessings of exaltation as everlasting family units.

The power to create life in mortality is sacred and involves a sacred partnership with the heavens. The Lord provides the system of life, with its sustaining vitality, and we provide the family relationships within which pure souls can come to earth to be nurtured and cared for in love. The power to call forth new life in this way is a solemn and beautiful commission from God that requires purity, devotion, courage, and a constant commitment to remember the covenants in faith and gratitude: "And all thy children shall be taught of the LORD; and great shall be the peace of thy children" (Isa. 54:13). The uniting of families forever through the blessings of the sealing covenants is a choice and magnificent framework for the work of the ministry of God and the building up of His kingdom in the latter days.

Inspired by Latter-Day Prophets

David O. McKay: No other success can compensate for failure in the home. This is the one thing of limitless potentialities on earth. The poorest shack of a home in which love prevails over a united family is of greater value to God and future humanity than the richest bank on earth. In such a home God can work miracles and will work miracles (*CR*, April 1935, 116).

> *Throughout his ministry, President David O. McKay emphasized the principle of making the home the top priority of life, and the maxim he quoted has become a watchword of Church counsel on the family. In a follow-up promise, President McKay said that "Pure hearts in a pure home are always in whispering distance of heaven." How has your own experience fulfilled that promise?*

Harold B. Lee: The most important part of the Lord's work that you will do, is the work that you do within the walls of your own home ("Doing the Right Things for the Right Reasons," *Brigham Young University Speeches of the Year*, April 19, 1961, 5).

> *The family is the supreme stewardship for everyone, transcending all other temporal and spiritual obligations. What are your thoughts about how to balance the complex array of demands of mortality in such a way that family happiness and integrity rise to the zenith of worthy goals?*

Harold B. Lee: Remember that great love is built on great sacrifice and that a daily determination in each other to please in things that are right will build a sure foundation for a happy home. That determination for the welfare of each other must be mutual and not one-sided or selfish. Husband and wife must feel equal responsibilities and obligations to teach each other (*The Teachings of Harold B. Lee,* 252).

How can you better serve as a witness and example of the principle of togetherness and equal partnership of husband and wife within the family union?

Ezra Taft Benson: Did the God of heaven who created and intended marriage and family to be the source of man's greatest joy, his dearest possession while on this earth, intend that it end at death? Do marriage and families pertain only to this transitory state? Are all our sympathies, affections, and love for each other a thing of naught, to be cast off in death? . . . Through [Joseph Smith], God revealed the eternity of the marriage covenant and the timelessness of the family (*This Nation Shall Endure,* 127).

What confirming comfort has been planted in your heart and soul though the restoration of the doctrine and ordinances relating to the eternal family?

Truths to Liken

1 Cor. 7:3—"Let the husband render unto the wife due benevolence: and likewise also the wife unto the husband."

- In answering questions about marriage, the Apostle Paul emphasized the mutual covenant of love and respect that should abound in the marital relationship.
- When our first concern is the well-being of our spouse, we show compassion and empathy; we are warmhearted and understanding, charitable in all things. The word *benevolent* derives from the Latin words "bene" (well) and "volens" (a form of the verb *velle,* meaning "to wish"). If we are benevolent, then, our first wish is for the well-being of our spouse. How have you confirmed in your experience that "benevolence" is a rewarding and charitable way of governing relationships?

Eph. 5:25, 27–8, 33—"Husbands, love your wives, even as Christ also loved the church, and gave himself for it; . . . that it should be holy and without blemish. So ought men to love their wives as their own bodies. He that loveth his wife loveth himself. . . . Nevertheless let every one of you in particular so love his wife even as himself; and the wife see that she reverence her husband."

- Paul's counsel on loving relationships within marriage draws its power from a comparison with the love that Christ has for His Church (using Christ's symbolism of the bridegroom/bride relationship as in Matt. 9:15; 25:1–10).
- From "The Family: A Proclamation to the World," we read: "Husband and wife have a solemn responsibility to love and care for each other and for their children." Love is that ultimate concern that brings about righteous service. All the Lord has ever done for us has been motivated by His love for us (see 2 Ne. 26:24). Husbands are to love their wives even as Christ has loved the Church. Christ did everything for us, so likewise should husbands do everything for their wives. Love translates into caring concern that serves others. In reverencing their husbands, wives are involved in giving back—as each honors, respects, and treats the other with deference and kindness.

D&C 75:28—"And again, verily I say unto you, that every man who is obliged to provide for his own family, let him provide, and he shall in nowise lose his crown; and let him labor in the church."

- These words are included in a revelation given through the Prophet Joseph Smith at Amherst, Ohio, on January 25, 1832, on the occasion of a conference where the Prophet was sustained and ordained as President of the High Priesthood. At that conference, he was asked by the elders to give counsel concerning their duties in preaching the gospel and caring for their families.
- As we labor in the Church we are likewise responsible for the temporal welfare of our families. This is part

of our eternal role. If we fulfill our duties to our family while building up the kingdom of God, we will receive blessings and strength from on high. How have you been able to harmonize family and Church responsibilities in the strength of the Lord? How has the principle of eternal families enabled you to more fully balance family, Church, and work responsibilities?

Moses 5:11—"And Eve, his wife, heard all these things and was glad, saying: Were it not for our transgression we never should have had seed, and never should have known good and evil, and the joy of our redemption, and the eternal life which God giveth unto all the obedient."

- Eve had the capacity to weigh choices and act in ways to support the ultimate design of God for His children. When she was "beguiled" by Satan to partake of the forbidden fruit, she, as "the mother of all living" (Gen. 3:20; Moses 4:26), realized that the consequences of transgressing would be in the best interests of her children—for they could not "live" in the eternal sense unless the plan of happiness were enacted, based on the agency of man. In careful consideration of what was at stake, Eve made the conscious decision to partake of the forbidden fruit and also have Adam partake (see Moses 4:6–13). As she later described her position with respect to this decision—having learned of the great plan of salvation from the Lord—Eve articulated her profound insight as seen in Moses 5:11.
- The blessing of mortality that came from Adam and Eve provides for us the sacred opportunity to procreate and provide a mortal experience for the spirit children of Heavenly Father. Married couples sealed in the temple receive this sacred obligation and blessing, rejoicing in their children as an eternal posterity ordained and given to them by Heavenly Father.

Abr. 2:11—"And I will bless them that bless thee, and curse them that curse thee; and in thee (that is, in thy Priesthood) and in thy seed (that is, thy Priesthood), for I give unto thee a promise that this right shall continue in thee, and in thy seed after thee (that is to say, the literal seed, or the seed of the body) shall all the families of the earth be blessed, even with the blessings of the Gospel, which are the blessings of salvation, even of life eternal."

- The Lord established His covenant with Abraham, the father of nations, with an obligation to carry the priesthood and the gospel to the world and the promise of eternal life.
- By participating in the work and mission of the Abrahamic covenant, how have you been able to remind your loved ones and all you meet that everything in the gospel plan points to the exaltation of families? Those who are of the seed of Abraham, or who are adopted into the family of Abraham through gospel ordinances, are to do all in their power to help families be forever. How have you been able to further this message in your service in the Church and the community?

Rejoicing and Reasoning Together

How Can Husbands Contribute More Fully to the Cause of Eternal Families?

The role of husband and father should be the most prominent one in every man's life. The greatest fulfillment in life lies within the family unit. Many men today surrender their marital roles—and families suffer. Children are left without a father figure to help give them direction and leadership. Husbands need to realize that their role can have no substitute—no one can take their place. Each husband can make a commitment to be the best husband for his wife and the best father for his children. Each husband can place the cause of the eternal family uppermost in his thoughts, plans, and actions. Here is a checklist that can remind husbands of their most significant roles and duties:

- **Build from within.** Build your family relationships on a gospel foundation of honor, honesty, service, harmony, and truth—enduring principles that will help your relationships endure. Make being a husband and father the highest priority and goal in your life. Your spouse will rise to the level of your love for her. Treat her as a princess, and she will be a princess. Treat her as a queen, and she will be a queen. Treat her as a "goddess," and she will be a "goddess." Treat her as all three, and she will be all three. It is your choice.

- **Use constructive strategies with long-term benefits.** Provide for your wife and family in the best possible way so that your wife can be a true mother for your children. Honor her role, recognizing her as your loving partner and the mother of your children. Use tenderness; be forgiving; be an example of love; and recognize your differences (women have different needs—help them fulfill them).

- **Find common ground and common purpose.** Have many common goals: health, companionship, spiritual growth, and leaving a legacy of honor and harmony for the children. Here are some of the key objectives for husband and wife to keep in mind: fidelity in all things, loyalty, charity, selflessness, communication, happiness, togetherness, empathy, gratitude, service; praise, privacy (giving each other space—for friends, hobbies, meditation, and so on), affection, uniqueness (recognizing that each has a unique and vital role in the marriage), and worshiping together (scripture reading, prayer, family home evening, Church service).

How Can Wives Contribute More Fully to the Cause of Eternal Families?

The role of wife and mother is without equal in the world today. The wife is a companion and partner to her husband. One of the primary purposes in matrimony is to have a family. In this role, the wife is not only a loving partner to her husband, but the mother of their children. Among all those who influence the family, wives and mothers have the most dynamic effect. They are the source of life; they are the ones who are usually always "there" when needed; they are the ones to whom the chil-

dren go when they are hurt. In his vision of the spirit world, President Joseph F. Smith beheld "our glorious Mother Eve, with many of her faithful daughters who had lived through the ages and worshiped the true and living God" (D&C 138:39). This sacred view reminds us all that faithful and honorable women hold an exalted place among God's children. Consider these four strategies that can help a woman more fully fulfill her eternal role as wife and mother:

- **Improve the inner reality.** Elevate your vision, knowing that you are a partner with God in the Creation. You, in concert with your husband, are key to the vital process of bringing new life into the world. There is nothing to equal it, nothing to surpass it in its significance. Choose correct principles by anchoring your actions and decisions to rock-solid values of integrity, honor, selflessness, loyalty, service, trustworthiness, and love. Set aside any excessive allegiance to things that fade: fads, fashions, or momentary pleasures. Establish priorities in keeping with your eternal stewardship as wife and mother. If you are not blessed with wifehood or motherhood in this life, then look forward in hope and faith to the fulfillment of these roles in the eternal reach of God's grace and love.

- **Foster positive actions that bring benefits to you, your spouse, and your children.** Work toward long-term results by cultivating harmony, peace, contentment, and joy in your functions as wife and mother. No one can have a more profound influence on the well-being of your children than you. Be fit by cultivating optimum health in all of its aspects; remember that beauty is in the radiance of well-being. Learn always: from the best books, through meaningful conversations with chosen role models, via positive media and Internet sources, and by taking workshops and courses. Cultivate unity of purpose and action.

- **Strengthen relationships.** Foster dialogue by communicating your needs and feelings frankly to your spouse. Remember that sometimes the male ego prefers to remain aloof and self-contained. Help your husband communicate freely. Support him in his occupation by helping him enhance his career as much as possible. If you must also help earn the living, then work toward a fair sharing of domestic responsibilities. This counsel applies to both husband and wife. Be of good cheer. Understanding will go a long way toward fostering unity and cooperation. Praise and honor your husband—then your children will do so as well, being more respectful and obedient. Take initiative in teaching your children the gospel and correct principles of behavior in patience and kindness.

- **Find common ground and common purpose.** Follow a plan of action such as that suggested above in the checklist for husbands.

How Can Husbands and Wives Achieve Excellence in Their Eternal Family Progress?

Ten qualities of excellence will help you achieve greater success in life—particularly in your family relationships and accomplishments:

- **Excellence is a state of mind**—It begins as a special way of looking at yourself and life with the highest regard. Cultivate a desire for excellence, with a plan to achieve excellence in every given task.
- **Excellence is rooted in principle**—It thrives on tested and proven gospel principles. If you cultivate excellence within, then excellence will pervade your external actions and deeds.
- **Excellence is balanced**—In your pursuit of excellence in professional and community life, never make the goal so important that your loved ones and others around you are hurt, neglected, or destroyed emotionally at the expense of the so-called "project."
- **Excellence is realistic**—Be sure that your goal is truly achievable; at the same time, "stretch" yourself as much as you can.
- **Excellence is measurable**—Make

sure your goals can be broken down into actions you can measure day-by-day. How else will you know you are succeeding? The game isn't exciting if you don't keep score. Tracking your progress draws you onward and upward.
- **Excellence is resourceful**—Use all the available resources to create excellence in all aspects of your life—family, Church, career, and community. Reach out to others for ideas and strategies. Be creative and innovative.
- **Excellence is teachable**—Find the best role models for each of your chosen pursuits, and aim to emulate and even surpass them. Stay humble, never prideful, always looking for ways to learn, always viewing achievement as an opportunity to serve others and be a good example.
- **Excellence is tireless**—Excellence depends on diligence and hard work. When you look at a champion, you see triumph before you—but it's not as easy to see the years of devoted practice and effort. Take the time to train and prepare well so that excellence is a byproduct of your efforts, not just a hoped-for result.
- **Excellence is resilient**—It cultivates the ability to cross over barriers and transcend adversity, never giving up until the highest goal is reached. Strive for patience rather than mere "efficiency."
- **Excellence serves others**—Praise others with genuine compliments for their work; such encouragement creates an atmosphere of excellence.

As you review this checklist for excellence, identify one or two aspects of your family life that might benefit from improvement. How can you help others to achieve a higher level of excellence in their worthy goals?

Real-life Stories for Heart and Mind

An Interview with the Prophet. When the Prophet Joseph Smith journeyed to Washington, D.C., to meet with President Martin Van Buren in February 1840, he was not able to get redress for the sufferings of the Saints at the hands of the Missouri mobs. President Van Buren, sensitive about the Missouri vote, said: "Gentlemen, your cause is just, but I can do nothing for you" (*HC* 4:80).

The Prophet had more success in Philadelphia during that same trip when he met with a large public audience of some three thousand people to explain the doctrines and blessings of the restored gospel. Parley P. Pratt was on hand to witness how "the entire congregation were astounded; electrified, as it were, and overwhelmed with the sense of the truth and power by which he spoke, and the wonders which he related; many souls were gathered unto the fold" (*Autobiography of Parley P. Pratt*, 260–261). During the Prophet's stay in Philadelphia, Parley P. Pratt had a number of private conversations with the Prophet in which they discussed the glories of the eternal family. Parley P. Pratt reported:

> In Philadelphia I had the happiness of once more meeting with President Smith, and of spending several days with him and others, and with the Saints in that city and vicinity.
>
> During these interviews he taught me many great and glorious principles concerning God and the heavenly order of eternity. It was at this time that I received from him the first idea of eternal family organization, and the eternal union of the sexes in those inexpressibly endearing relationships which none but the highly intellectual, the refined and pure in heart, know how to prize, and which are at the very foundation of everything worthy to be called happiness.
>
> Till then I had learned to esteem kindred affections and sympathies as appertaining solely to this transitory state, as something from which the heart must be entirely weaned, in order to be fitted for its heavenly state.
>
> It was Joseph Smith who taught me how to prize the endearing relationships of father and mother, husband and wife; of brother and sister, son and daughter.
>
> It was from him that I learned that the wife of my bosom might be secured to me for time and all eternity; and that the refined sympathies and affections which endeared us to each other emanated from the fountain of divine eternal love. It was from him that I learned that we might cultivate these affections, and grow and increase in the same to all eternity; while the result of our endless union would be an offspring as numerous as the stars of heaven, or the sands of the sea shore.
>
> It was from him that I learned the true dignity and destiny of a son of God, clothed with an eternal priesthood, as the patriarch and sovereign of his countless offspring. It was from him that I learned that the highest dignity of womanhood was, to stand as a queen and priestess to her husband, and to reign for ever and ever as the queen mother of her numerous and still increasing offspring.
>
> I had loved before, but I knew not why. But now I loved—with a pureness and intensity of elevated, exalted feeling, which would lift my soul from the transitory things of this grovelling sphere and expand it as the ocean. I felt that God was my heavenly Father indeed; that Jesus was my brother, and that the wife of my bosom was an immortal, eternal companion; a kind ministering angel, given to me as a comfort, and a crown of glory for ever and ever. In short, I could now love with the spirit and with the understanding also.
>
> Yet, at that time, my dearly beloved brother, Joseph Smith, had barely touched a single key; had merely lifted a corner of the veil and given me a single glance into eternity. (*Autobiography of Parley P. Pratt*, 259–260)

In this fervent and touching witness of the everlasting nature of the family, Parley P. Pratt uses the terms eternity *and* eternal *no fewer than nine times. He succeeds in elevating our perspective from the everyday view of family life to the never-ending perspective of enduring family relationships based on heavenly principles. How has the principle of the eternal family helped you and your loved ones transcend the taxing daily challenges of family routines and grasp the vision of glory and exaltation awaiting the faithful and patient sons and daughters of God?*

A Lesson in Patience. A priesthood leader remembers the time when he repented of being one-sided in establishing a harmonious balance between service in the family and service in the Church. He reported:

> On that Saturday morning I said good-bye to my wife and young family and started the hour-long drive to attend stake leadership meeting. As I drove alone down the highway, I thought about how many such meetings I had attended in the past, and I lost count. A spirit of narrowness came upon me and I struggled to maintain my positive attitude. How I missed my family at that moment. I must not have been attending to the time adequately, for as I drove in to the parking lot of the stake center, I noticed that the hour had already arrived. Hurriedly I gathered up my materials and rushed into the building. Then it happened. The strains of a familiar song greeted my ears. "O that I were an angel, and could have the wish of mine heart." These were the words of Alma I was hearing, set to a beautiful melody and sung by a chorus. As I neared the chapel doors and then took my place among the assembled crowd, I heard the rest: "O that I were an angel, and could have the wish of mine heart, that I might go forth and speak with the trump of God, with a voice to shake the earth, and cry repentance unto every people" (Alma 29:1).
>
> It was the fervent prayer of the prophet Alma as he sought strength and guidance to bring his people closer to the Lord "that there might not be more sorrow upon all the face of the earth" (Alma 29:2). I remembered that his prayer was answered shortly thereafter as he found the inspiration to protect his flock from the treacherous mistruths of the anti-Christ Korihor. His prayer was answered again as he found the inspiration to "try the virtue of the word of God" (Alma 31:5) in teaching the ostracized Zoramites one of the greatest lessons on faith ever uttered (see Alma 32).
>
> I was dramatically reminded of the need for prayerful preparation in carrying out our duties as Latter-day Saints. There is a balance that comes through inspiration and faith to manage one's affairs with work and Church and family. There is a time and a season for all needful things leading to the joy of gospel living. I repented for being jealous of a few hours of time when the founding elders of the Church were often called on to spend years away from their families in the building up of the kingdom of God. I repented for my narrowness of heart when the Lord was waiting to expand, edify, nurture, nourish, and exalt—if only the people would let Him. That Saturday morning I learned a lesson in patience: "Therefore it is expedient in me that mine elders should wait for a little season, for the redemption of Zion" (D&C 105:13). When we wait faithfully on the Lord, we can look forward to the joy of salvation and the glory of eternal life.

How have you been able to find a joyful balance between service in the family and service in the Church—through the strength and grace of the Lord?

Pondering Prayerfully

Additional scriptures to consider and ponder:
- Col. 3:19
- Jacob 2:31
- D&C 64:33
- Abr. 3:25–26

The following hymns help inspire gratitude for the eternal family:
- "Families Can Be Together Forever" (*Hymns,* 300)
- "Love One Another" (*Hymns,* 308)

Remember and Be Sure

The family is an eternal institution. The light of this truth penetrates through the darkness of a world in which the divine role of the family is under assault. The eternal family will triumph and prevail. The unfolding of families of covenant valor has been decreed by God. His covenant is once again restored to the earth, with all the rights, privileges, powers, and keys needed to secure and nurture the eternal family: "Verily I say unto you, blessed are you for receiving mine everlasting covenant, even the fulness of my gospel, sent forth unto the children of men, that they might have life and be made partakers of the glories which are to be revealed in the last days, as it was written by the prophets and apostles in days of old" (D&C 66:2).

The greatest commission from God to us as His children is to raise up our families in righteousness and truth. May we all make the covenant of the eternal family the center and core of our very existence and thus reap a harvest of everlasting joy in the halls of glory above. As one wise bishop counseled: "Hang on the walls of your mind the memory of your successes. Take counsel of your strength, not your weakness. Think of the good jobs you have done. Think of the times when you rose above your average level of performance and carried out an idea or a dream or a desire for which you had deeply longed. Hang these pictures on the walls of your mind and look at them as you travel the roadway of life" (Sterling W. Sill, *CR*, April 1971, 35).

The Lord gives us power as we keep the covenants and ordinances of the gospel of Jesus Christ and work toward building a Zion family. We honor our covenants and ordinances by keeping the commandments and renewing our commitments in partaking of the sacrament each week. By doing so, we find that the Lord "doth immediately bless" us (see Mosiah 2:24), in that we can always have His Spirit to guide, direct, and comfort us in our lives and to give us the appropriate gifts and wisdom necessary to bless and serve our families and our fellowmen.

CHAPTER 37
The Zion Family

The building up of Zion is a cause that has interested the people of God in every age; it is a theme upon which prophets, priests and kings have dwelt with peculiar delight; they have looked forward with joyful anticipation to the day in which we live; and fired with heavenly and joyful anticipations they have sung and written and prophesied of this our day; but they died without the sight; we are the favored people that God has made choice of to bring about the Latter-day glory. —Joseph Smith (*HC* 4:609–610)

Opening the Window of Wisdom

Once a family has been established, the design of heaven is that it should be cultivated through faith and obedience as an eternal family—one whose members are worthy and prepared to be accepted into the mansions of heaven. Zion is comprised of a magnificent array of such families founded and governed by eternal laws: "And Zion cannot be built up unless it is by the principles of the law of the celestial kingdom; otherwise I cannot receive her unto myself" (D&C 105:5).

The ultimate purpose of the Lord is plainly manifest through the voice of His latter-day prophet: "For I will raise up unto myself a pure people, that will serve me in righteousness" (D&C 100:16).

The pure people—"THE PURE IN HEART" (D&C 97:21)—constitute Zion, the future of which the Lord has secured through His proclaimed word: "For, behold, I say unto you that Zion shall flourish, and the glory of the Lord shall be upon her; And she shall be an ensign unto the people, and there shall come unto her out of every nation under heaven. And the day shall come when the nations of the earth shall tremble because of her, and shall fear because of her terrible ones. The Lord hath spoken it. Amen" (D&C 64:41–43).

But the people must first cultivate the nature and qualities of a Zion people. Only those who have overcome sin through the Atonement of the Savior can be citizens of Zion and heirs to the riches of eternity: "But no man is possessor of all things except he be purified and cleansed from all sin" (D&C 50:28). Similarly, Zion must of necessity be a people unified in the discipleship of the Redeemer, like unto the people of Enoch: "And the Lord called his people ZION, because they were of one heart and one mind, and dwelt in righteousness; and there was no poor among them" (Moses 7:18).

What are the promises given to such a people? The main promise is the unspeakable gift of being elevated above the plane of mortal existence and admitted into the presence of the Lord forever: "And Enoch and all his people walked with God, and he dwelt in the midst of Zion; and it came to pass that Zion was not, for God received it up into his own bosom; and from thence went forth the saying, ZION IS FLED" (Moses 7:69). To us falls the ongoing assignment to prepare ourselves with devotion for the transition—line upon line, precept upon precept—toward becoming a Zion people, comprised of worthy Zion families, being willing in all respects to take upon ourselves the qualities of purity, unity, and covenant valor that alone can qualify a people as the people of the Lord.

Family success is a pervasive duty that depends on the interaction and mutual support of many people and institutions. Nevertheless, it falls to the parents (and sometimes to the single parent) to take the lead in building up the family in righteousness. The principles of righteousness form the basis for success in marriage and family life: "But I have commanded you to bring up your children in light and truth" (D&C 93:40). We cannot hope to enjoy enduring relationships in the family without a foundation of gospel light and truth, nor enjoy spiritual prosperity without the guiding influence of the Holy Ghost, nor experience eternal lives without the covenant blessings received in worthiness in the temples of God. It is only through valor, courage, and obedience to God's commandments that we have the right to call down from heaven the healing and sustaining influence of the Lord in magnifying our office as parents and edifying our increase as families of God. It is through the divine perspective—that we are truly partners with our Father in Heaven and his Only Begotten Son in bringing about their glorious work—that we find purpose, dignity, and meaning in life.

The Book of Mormon is one of the Lord's greatest tools for teaching parents how to counsel their children in righteousness. From the loving concern of Lehi and Sariah for their children at the outset of the chronicle to the cherished partnership of Mormon and his son Moroni at the end, there is in these pages an endless flow of inspiring examples about parent-child relationships. Consider Alma's anxiety and ultimate joy in his son Alma. Consider Alma the Younger's splendid legacy of instruction for his own sons (see Alma 36–42). Think also of the indomitable faith and courage of the sons of Helaman founded in the counsel of their mothers (see Alma 56:47–48).

The blessings of the covenant bond flow from our Father in Heaven to His sons and daughters. In resonance with this pattern, fathers and mothers are commissioned to reinforce the word of truth as they instruct their children in the operation of covenant principles. Jacob's legacy of blessings for his twelve sons (see Gen. 49) is essentially no different from the blessings of truth that all fathers in Zion are able to bestow on their children as part of the Lord's plan of edification and teaching. Mothers in Zion have the same sacred commission to impart principles of righteousness to their children.

There is no greater duty or obligation than for parents to teach their children the principles of a Zion family. Parents are accountable: "And again, inasmuch as parents have children in Zion, or in any of her stakes which are organized, that teach them not to understand the doctrine of repentance, faith in Christ the Son of the living God, and of baptism and the gift of the Holy Ghost by the laying on of the hands, when eight years old, the sin be upon the heads of the parents. And they shall also teach their children to pray, and to walk uprightly before the Lord" (D&C 68:25, 28). The greatest legacy that parents can leave for their children is to teach them the truths of salvation in clear and loving ways and to model these truths in the form of a righteous life.

We will ever be in debt to our Father in Heaven for the gift of eternal life and eternal families. There is no way to repay this gift of love, except to do our humble part by following His will and being obedient to His commandments. Gifts of love flow to us from God in many forms: the grand design for immortality and eternal life, the light of the gospel, principles for a Zion society, the compassionate power of the Atonement, the treasures of the holy scriptures, and the comforting guidance of the Holy Ghost. In turn, gifts of love flow back to God from us in many forms: an acceptable offering in righteousness, obedience to the prophets and the whisperings of the Holy Spirit, unity and purity, gratitude and thanksgiving, and, above all, the cultivation of eternal Zion families.

Inspired by Latter-Day Prophets

Brigham Young: If the law of Christ becomes the tradition of this people, the children will be brought up according to the law of the celestial kingdom, else they are not brought up in the way they should go (*Discourses of Brigham Young*, 207).

Entire libraries could be filled with books on parenting and child-rearing. But this one-sentence curriculum says it all: use the celestial law of Christ. How can we be sure of understanding it? Study the word of God from the scriptures and the living prophets, then pray for guidance and follow the promptings of the Spirit. As you look back on your method of guiding loved ones, how has the celestial law of Christ figured into the curriculum you have used? How can you more fully use this law in your future teaching and guidance?

Harold B. Lee: In all leadership situations in which we seek to improve human behavior, it is difficult to overestimate the power of example—whether it consists of parents both showing and telling their children about the value of temple marriage or a returned missionary who shines forth as a result of the changes and maturation the gospel has wrought in him (*The Teachings of Harold B. Lee,* 508).

The power of example is supreme in lifting others to a higher degree of spirituality. Which people in your experience have been the most influential examples of Christlike living? Who might be looking to you as an example to follow? How can you ensure that such are never disappointed?

Spencer W. Kimball: Mothers have a sacred role. They are partners with God, as well as with their own husbands, first in giving birth to the Lord's spirit children, and then in rearing those children so they will serve the Lord and keep his commandments. Could there be a more sacred trust than to be a trustee for honorable, well-born, well-developed children? (*The Teachings of Spencer W. Kimball,* 326).

Describing mothers and fathers as "trustees" for children reminds us of the trust our Father in Heaven has placed in us to partner with Him in bringing about "the immortality and eternal life of man" (Moses 1:39). In your opinion, what are the duties of faithful and honorable trustees?

Ezra Taft Benson: Remember, the family is one of God's greatest fortresses against the evils of our day. Help keep your family strong and close and worthy of our Father in Heaven's blessings. As you do, you

will receive faith and strength, which will bless your lives forever (*Come, Listen to a Prophet's Voice,* 15).

The home is truly a fortress. Concerning the future state of Zion, Isaiah prophesied: "And the LORD will create upon every dwelling place of mount Zion, and upon her assemblies, a cloud and smoke by day, and the shining of a flaming fire by night: for upon all the glory shall be a defence. And there shall be a tabernacle for a shadow in the daytime from the heat, and for a place of refuge, and for a covert from storm and from rain" (Isa. 4:5–6). How much of this sacred prophecy can be applied to your home? How can you enhance the quality of your home as a source of light, glory, and refuge from the storm?

Truths to Liken

Isa. 54:13—"And all thy children shall be taught of the LORD; and great shall be the peace of thy children."

- The resurrected Lord repeated these words of Isaiah when He visited the Saints at Bountiful (see 3 Ne. 22:13). Isaiah was describing the state of affairs during the last days of the gathering of the Saints and giving the promise of the Lord.
- What are your thoughts about the coming day when your children will be taught of the Lord and will be at peace, far from oppression, protected and secure, full of righteousness, blessed with eternal heritage? How can you contribute to these very conditions today, while there is turmoil and temptation on all sides? The knowledge of the Lord brings peace to one's soul. Your children find peace in righteousness as they live the doctrines and principles you teach them.

John 13:15—"For I have given you an example, that ye should do as I have done to you."

- When Jesus knew that His hour had come, He washed the feet of His disciples and gave them counsel, including this definitive statement on how they should conduct themselves once He was gone.

- We have our perfect example in the Lord Jesus Christ. Our goal should be to do as He has done as we build our Zion family. He will help us and provide a way (see D&C 84:88; 1 Ne. 3:7; Moro. 7:33). How has the pattern of the Savior been the key example you have followed in your family relationships and activities?

2 Ne. 2:30—"And I [Lehi] have none other object save it be the everlasting welfare of your souls."

- Lehi gave final counsel to Jacob and his other sons as he approached the final days of his life. He explained to them the principle of agency and encouraged them to choose the better part (see 2 Ne. 2:28–29). Lehi confirmed to them in the passage quoted above that his central motivation was the everlasting welfare of their souls.
- We can help our children realize that our joy is in their righteousness, just as Heavenly Father's joy is in the welfare of all His children. We, like Heavenly Father and His Son, seek only the happiness of our children. When our children fully internalize this truth, they often listen with a softened heart because they understand our true purpose. How have you been able to help your loved ones understand that their everlasting welfare is the central concern of your life?

2 Ne. 25:23, 26—"For we labor diligently to write, to persuade our children, and also our brethren, to believe in Christ, and to be reconciled to God; for we know that it is by grace that we are saved, after all we can do. . . . And we talk of Christ, we rejoice in Christ, we preach of Christ, we prophesy of Christ, and we write according to our prophecies, that our children may know to what source they may look for a remission of their sins."

- Toward the end of his ministry, Nephi gave inspiring counsel concerning the legacy he hoped to leave for the coming generation. The process of conveying saving truths to our families and fellow Saints is clear: When we *talk* of Christ in our family circles and congregations, then our souls are moved to *rejoice* in the gospel plan, enabling us to *preach* and expound the truth for one another, *prophesying* of the great blessings that will be brought into our lives through obedience, and giving us the motivation to record our testimonies in *writing* as the source of inspiration and counsel for our children in the coming years. All of this is part of the process of performing "all we can do" to merit the redeeming grace of our Lord.
- How close are you coming to the standard of contributing "all [you] can do" for the sake of the family and the building up of Zion? Of the key actions listed—talking, rejoicing, preaching, prophesying, writing, doing—are there some that need strengthening in your family circle and extended family circle?

Mosiah 4:14–15—"And ye will not suffer your children that they go hungry, or naked; neither will ye suffer that they transgress the laws of God, and fight and quarrel one with another, and serve the devil, who is the master of sin, or who is the evil spirit which hath been spoken of by our fathers, he being an enemy to all righteousness. But ye will teach them to walk in the ways of truth and soberness; ye will teach them to love one another, and to serve one another."

- King Benjamin gave this pertinent counsel for parents in his grand discourse at the end of his ministry. It is noteworthy that all of his listeners had gathered in a huge congregation made up of separate families, each united with its family members in a group, with tents pitched "round about the temple, every man having his tent with the door thereof towards the temple, that thereby they might remain in their tents and hear the words which king Benjamin should speak unto them" (Mosiah 2:6).
- Parents have the responsibility of providing food, clothing, and shelter for their children, and also of nurturing them with the bread of life and the

living water of the gospel. What are your thoughts about how best to sustain and nurture your family both temporally and spiritually? How can you pitch your "tent" toward the house of the Lord so that the principles of salvation and exaltation will have full influence on your family members and fill their hearts with the joy of eternal truth?

3 Ne. 18:21—"Pray in your families unto the Father, always in my name, that your wives and your children may be blessed."

- The resurrected Lord gave this admonition to the fathers of Zion on behalf of their wives and children.
- Prayer is the strength of the family; we cannot build a Zion family without Heavenly Father's help. We receive all things as we pray with real intent, in humility and by exercising our faith, always in the name of Christ. How has prayer been the source for your family of unity, faith, hope, and the power to do the Father's will?

D&C 24:8—"Be patient in afflictions, for thou shalt have many; but endure them, for, lo, I am with thee, even unto the end of thy days."

- These words of comfort and counsel were given to Joseph Smith in a revelation at Harmony, Pennsylvania, in July 1830, at a time of intense persecution against the rising Church—at the time fewer than four months old. The Lord had told Joseph: "For thou shalt devote all thy service in Zion; and in this thou shalt have strength" (D&C 24:7). How would he have strength? Because the Lord promised to be with him, "even unto the end of thy days."
- If we are likewise to devote all our service in Zion, centrally for the blessing of our families, then how can we endure the afflictions that will surely come? The answer is: through the same blessings that the Lord prepared for the Prophet Joseph—by the Lord being with him "even unto the end of thy days." How

have you felt the strength of heaven flowing into your life as a result of devoted service to your family and the Church? Enduring our trials and tribulations with patience is part of the test, part of the perfecting process (see D&C 67:13).

D&C 38:26–27—"For what man among you having twelve sons, and is no respecter of them, and they serve him obediently, and he saith unto the one: Be thou clothed in robes and sit thou here; and to the other: Be thou clothed in rags and sit thou there—and looketh upon his sons and saith I am just? Behold, this I have given unto you as a parable, and it is even as I am. I say unto you, be one; and if ye are not one ye are not mine."

- This admonition to be unified was part of a revelation given to a conference of the Church through the Prophet Joseph Smith at Fayette, New York, on January 2, 1831.
- The Lord loves all of His children and does not discriminate against any of them in their obedience. He is just to all of them, and He wants us to follow that same principle. If we are not unified through unconditional love and charity for our faithful and devoted sons and daughters, then we are not the Lord's. Through obedience, mutual respect, and love, the family is blessed, having made an acceptable offering to the Lord. What are your thoughts about the source of unity in the family circle—and how can that unity be maintained?

D&C 93:42–43—"You have not taught your children light and truth, according to the commandments; and that wicked one hath power, as yet, over you, and this is the cause of your affliction. And now a commandment I give unto you—if you will be delivered you shall set in order your own house, for there are many things that are not right in your house."

- These stern words of censure were given to Frederick G. Williams in a revelation received through the Prophet Joseph Smith at Kirtland, Ohio, on May 6, 1833. Similar words were given to the Prophet Joseph, Sidney Rigdon, and Newel K. Whitney. At the time Newel K.

Whitney was serving as bishop and the others constituted the First Presidency of the Church.

- The Lord holds us accountable for cultivating Zion families in obedience to His commandments. If the First Presidency and the bishop were called to repentance, then surely we have to be vigilant in guiding our own families down the pathway of righteousness. We can never delegate our parental duties and responsibilities. What specific counsel might the Lord give you in regard to your own family?

Rejoicing and Reasoning Together

How Can You Teach Repentance to Youth?

Youth need to learn the principle of repentance from their parents so they can participate in the divine blessings of the Atonement. Parents have this solemn obligation (see D&C 68:25–28). One of the great examples of how to teach repentance is the approach used by Alma with his wayward son Corianton (see Alma 39–42). With tenderness, yet firmness, Alma admonished his son to repent of his misdeeds while in the mission field (see Alma 39:2–3). He provided the context for repentance by teaching him the key doctrines most relevant to the occasion: Atonement, resurrection, and restoration according to one's righteousness. He declared the celebrated formula that "wickedness never was happiness" (Alma 41:10). Alma, himself an authority on the process of repentance, was precisely the right person to counsel his son on this subject, and his patriarchal admonition and testimony served to redirect this young man into the right channels so that Corianton could once again be called to the ministry (see Alma 42:31).

Alma used kindness, love, and persuasion—an approach confirmed and recommended in our day by President Joseph F. Smith: "You can't force your boys, nor your girls into heaven. You may force them to hell, by using harsh means in the efforts to make them good, when you yourselves are not as good as you should be. The man that will be angry at his boy, and try to correct him while he is in anger, is in the greatest fault; he is more to be pitied and more to be condemned than the child who has done wrong. You can only correct your children by love, in kindness, by love unfeigned, by persuasion, and reason" (*Gospel Doctrine: Selections from the Sermons and Writings of Joseph F. Smith*, 317).

The words of President Smith are reminiscent of the inspired counsel given by the Prophet Joseph Smith in March 1839 while suffering in the squalor of Liberty Jail:

> *No power or influence can or ought to be maintained by virtue of the priesthood, only by persuasion, by long-suffering, by gentleness and meekness, and by love unfeigned;*
>
> *By kindness, and pure knowledge, which shall greatly enlarge the soul without hypocrisy, and without guile—*
>
> *Reproving betimes [immediately] with sharpness, when moved upon by the Holy Ghost; and then showing forth afterwards an increase of love toward him whom thou hast reproved, lest he esteem thee to be his enemy;*
>
> *That he may know that thy faithfulness is stronger than the cords of death. (D&C 121:41–44).*

How has this counsel of the Prophet been helpful to you as you have guided your loved ones in the pathway of righteousness?

What Can You See in the Mirror of Motherhood?

Our Father in Heaven is mindful of every precious spirit leaving His presence to embark on his or her earthly quest. As such, He is surely mindful of every mother in her travail and sacrifice—serving as the sacred gateway of life to bring a new child of God into the world. The scriptures extend a mirror of motherhood into our view, celebrating the honor and triumph of the women who were chosen to be the mothers of mighty servants of God, and in some cases, mothers of nations: Eve ("the mother of all living"), Sarah (mother of Isaac), Rebekah (mother of Jacob or "Israel"), Rachel (mother of Joseph), Sariah (mother of Nephi and his brothers), and a myriad of other exemplary figures, extending to Elisabeth and Mary in the meridian of time. President Joseph F. Smith was privileged to perceive such noble women among the concourses of the righteous abiding in the spirit realm: "Among the great and mighty ones who were assembled in this vast congregation of the righteous were Father Adam, the Ancient of Days and father of all, And our glorious Mother Eve, with many of her faithful daughters who had lived through the ages and worshiped the true and living God" (D&C 138:38–39).

The Abrahamic covenant is born of priesthood power and authority, but the seed of Abraham is born of the mothers of Israel. All life is dependent on mothers. For that reason the commandment from Sinai did not say alone "honor thy father," but "Honour thy father and thy mother: that thy days may be long upon the land which the LORD thy God giveth thee" (Ex. 20:12). The Savior's final words on the cross included the poignant evidence of His relationship with His mother, and His concern for her welfare: "When Jesus therefore saw his mother, and the disciple standing by, whom he loved, he saith unto his mother, Woman, behold thy son! Then saith he to the disciple, Behold thy mother! And from that hour that disciple took her unto his own home" (John 19:26–27).

In the mirror of motherhood we all see reflected the pristine love of a mother for her offspring. It is from that fountain of insight that we all draw our first sublime lessons of love and what it means to care for another enough to place one's life in jeopardy for that person's vitality and well-being. Sometimes the life of a mother is cut short. Sometimes she is called home in the very hour of giving birth to a new child. It is through such an ultimate sacrifice of a mother that we remember the divine act of giving manifested in the Savior's ultimate sacrifice, He being "the life and the light of the world" (D&C 11:28).

Motherhood, like Saviorhood, is sustained through eternal nurture and unconditional love. How inspired was Eliza R. Snow when she articulated the heartfelt hopes of those who place motherhood on a divine pedestal: "In the heav'ns are parents single? No, the thought makes reason stare! Truth is reason; truth eternal Tells me I've a mother there" (Hymns, 292). Our mothers confirm the faith that life is worth living and that our mission on earth is of such import that we are buoyed up in the commitment to do all in our power to merit the blessings of heaven.

As you look into the "mirror of motherhood," what do you see that strengthens your faith, confirms your love, and gives you hope in the eternal family?

How Can Single Parents Carry On with Their Great Responsibilities?

Life is hard with all the trials, tribulations, and seemingly overwhelming problems facing families—especially those who are single parents. There is hope as we trust in the Lord (see Prov. 3:5–6), and there is a way as we follow Heavenly Father's plan. We can remember that His plan is motivated by His love for us. There are gospel principles that will, when applied, bring power into our lives. We can measure our success by eternal standards and not the apparent values of society. Our true priorities are more focused because of our situation in loving and serving our children. This, too, is the governing priority of our Father in Heaven and our Savior (see Moses 1:39).

The difficulty often lies in the inability to understand and cope with situations: Why? Why me? Why now? What did I do wrong? How can this be fair? Can't Heavenly Father make things all better right now? My children deserve better—why should they be the victims of this? And the questions keep coming. There can be only one response: we are to press forward with faith, hope, and charity, with an eye single to God's glory, knowing full well that in the strength of the Lord He will bless us and support us in our hour of need and in our times of pain and suffering—for He has paid the price (see Alma 7:11–12). We can wisely learn from the past, diligently striving to start where we stand, moving forward into the future with courage. We can act with faith, believing in the Lord, for life can be fulfilling. We don't have to simply live with the expectation of hope in the long-distant future; we can enjoy the fruits of the gospel of Jesus Christ in our lives *today*. We can choose—and in all of this we come to know our Heavenly Father and our Savior, for this is life eternal (see John 17:3). Remember that you can make the difference, for the power of God is within you.

Here are some ideas that might help you as a single parent:

- **Hope is the key to persevere and move forward.** Find power in the grace of God and Christ's atoning sacrifice, the very source that gives you strength to carry on. He will support you in this sacred work and holy calling. He will ease your burdens (see Mosiah 24:14–15). You are endowed with divine power. You have power within your very being as you act diligently and with a positive attitude. Time is your ally. Remember that others have gone through this and have created a wonderful family and are presently enjoying life to its fullest, free from guilt and pain. Use support groups in the family and the Church. Do fun and enjoyable activities. Even a modest budget can stretch far enough to include fun and unifying activities.

- **Set goals and make plans using wisdom.** Organize every needful thing. Set realistic and measurable goals. Schedule for success. Budget wisely with resources and time. Balance your life with opportunities for self, family, friends, and work (as required). Make lasting memories.

- **Deal with personal concerns and responsibilities.** You can make the difference. Lift yourself out of loneliness through the strength of the Lord. Use the power of uplifting "self-talk." Seek to enhance self-esteem, self-worth, self-respect, and self-confidence. Use sacrifice and service—you are responsible and accountable. You can do it. Use loving discipline with yourself and your children. Forgive and move on.

- **Live by gospel principles and standards.** Make the gospel of Jesus Christ your Liahona. Teach the gospel to your children. Use family councils to make your gospel study program a reality within your family. It can be done, and you can do it. The Lord will never let you down.

Real-life Stories for Heart and Mind

The Wooden Splinter. A priesthood holder and father reported an experience of how he had to repent and learn more wisdom in parenting:

In a special location at home I keep handy a small reminder of a big lesson I learned one time as a young father. It is a sharp wooden splinter about an inch-and-a-half long that was pulled from the tire of our family car many years ago when one of our daughters was learning to drive. One day while she was driving that particular car alone, she rounded a corner and bumped up over the curb. Soon after that the tire went flat, and I had to go rescue her. Assuming the impact had caused the problem, I admonished her on being more careful. It was, I thought, the perfect teaching moment—and so it was, but for the *father* rather than the *daughter*. The repairman soon discovered the problem with the tire: it was not the bump over the curb, but rather an imbedded wooden splinter that caused the flat tire. I apologized to my daughter for the misplaced blame (she was always very forgiving) and resolved to be less judgmental in the future.

As parents teach, they need to remember constantly that they, too, are imperfect and have need of continuing education and constant correction. The Savior reminded us: "And why beholdest thou the mote that is in thy brother's eye, but considerest not the beam that is in thine own eye?" (Matt. 7:3). Parents as teachers would do well to clothe truth in humility, doctrine in compassion, principles in charity, and chastening in love. What have you learned in your lifetime about such principles, and how has this helped you build a Zion family?

An Awakening. A Church leader and father had just arrived home from work. Feeling tired, he sat down to read the evening paper for a minute. All of a sudden his four-year-old son burst into his room wanting to make paper airplanes *that minute*. The father said, "We'll do it later." The little boy persisted and begged, and still the father put him off. The little boy kept at his father until the man made a mistake. He said, "Leave me alone. We'll do it when I'm ready." The little boy left the room with tears rolling down his cheeks. The father threw down the paper and ran after his son, crying, "We'll build them right now! We'll build them right now—this very minute!" A smile spread across his face, and the two built paper airplanes for a long time. They had fun. They were happy together. That day, the father made a promise that when he came home each day, he would be King Daddy—like King Benjamin—servant of all and friend to his children.

Such awakenings tend to happen as a blessing in our parental roles and callings. How have such awakenings helped you confirm that the Lord has called you to a sacred duty to build, sustain, and maintain a Zion family where all can be blessed?

Pondering Prayerfully

Additional scriptures to consider and ponder:
- Ps. 127:3
- Prov. 22:6
- Amos 3:3
- Matt. 18:6
- Luke 21:19
- John 13:34–35
- John 17:11
- Eph. 6:4
- Col. 3:20
- 1 Tim. 3:4–5
- Heb. 12:9
- 1 Pet. 3:8
- 1 Ne. 1:1
- Jacob 2:35
- Mosiah 3:19
- Mosiah 23:14
- Alma 36:3
- Alma 57:21
- Moro. 7:45–47
- D&C 25:14
- D&C 42:14
- Moses 6:57

The following hymns inspire us in building a Zion family:
- "I Am a Child of God" (*Hymns,* 301)
- "More Holiness Give Me" (*Hymns,* 131)
- "O My Father" (*Hymns,* 292)
- "Teach Me to Walk in the Light" (*Hymns,* 304)

Remember and Be Sure

When the Savior visited the Saints in ancient America following His Resurrection, He provided His disciples with the consummate counsel for the unending process of family development and covenant service: "Therefore, what manner of men ought ye to be? Verily I say unto you, even as I am" (3 Ne. 27:27). His example is the ultimate model we are to follow in building a Zion family. His example is the pinnacle of the "godly walk and conversation" (D&C 20:69) we are striving to acquire and practice. Let us all be committed to the process of improving our lives in conformity with divine example. Let us strive to cultivate within our family circle the qualities of unity, love, cooperation, trust, harmony, patience, mutual respect, the cultivation of good cheer, and obedience to the commandments of the gospel.

CHAPTER 38
Celestial Marriage

Except a man and his wife enter into an everlasting covenant and be married for eternity, while in this probation, by the power and authority of the Holy Priesthood, they will cease to increase when they die; that is, they will not have any children after the resurrection. But those who are married by the power and authority of the priesthood in this life, and continue without committing the sin against the Holy Ghost, will continue to increase and have children in the celestial glory. —Joseph Smith (*HC* 5:391)

Opening the Window of Wisdom

The union of man and woman in marriage brings together God's greatest creations. Marriage and sealing in the temples of God is for time and all eternity. This ultimate ordinance and covenant makes possible exaltation and "eternal lives" (D&C 132:24, 55). If we are true and faithful to the new and everlasting covenant of marriage, we can have eternal increase (see D&C 131; 132:19). The purpose of this union is to create an eternal family. With that purpose in mind, the family should live in love and harmony to help each member become a disciple of Jesus Christ and build up the kingdom of God here on earth.

Early in the scriptures we learn sacred truths about the ordained marriage relationship: "And the LORD God said, It is not good that the man should be alone; I will make him an help meet for him. . . . Therefore shall a man leave his father and his mother, and shall cleave unto his wife: and they shall be one flesh" (Gen. 2:18, 24). Adam and Eve were married in the Garden of Eden before they were sent into the world, so their marriage was celestialized by the hand of God.

At its fundamental level, the kingdom of God is made up of families. Celestial marriage, through the priesthood, is ordained of God in order to maximize the opportunities for eternal blessings to be poured out on His children at the highest level possible in this life and in the life to come. Celestial marriage is the key to eternal lives. Celestial marriage is divine marriage, endless marriage, eternal marriage:

> IN the celestial glory there are three heavens or degrees;
> And in order to obtain the highest, a man must enter into this order of the priesthood [meaning the new and everlasting covenant of marriage];
> And if he does not, he cannot obtain it.
> He may enter into the other, but that is the end of his kingdom; he cannot have an increase. (D&C 131:1–4)

Without the new and everlasting covenant of celestial marriage, individuals cannot enter into the highest degree of glory and perfection promised by God to His chosen faithful. But through the blessings of this holy covenant, marriage partners, through a process of perfection, can rise in majesty, sealed to this relationship by the powers of the priesthood, to attain a continuity of lives and be gods in the heavenly realm: "Then shall they be gods, because they have no end; therefore shall they be from everlasting to everlasting, because they continue; then shall they be above all, because all things are subject unto them. Then shall they be gods, because they have all power, and the angels are subject unto them" (D&C 132:20). What a glorious and transcendent view this gives us as we work to overcome the challenges of life! The Restoration of the gospel of Jesus Christ has brought to mankind once again the opportunity to enjoy this most sacred and holy of blessings, even the blessing of eternal marriage.

In many ways the jewel in the crown of exaltation is eternal marriage in the temples of God. Isaiah said, "I will greatly rejoice in the Lord, my soul shall be joyful in my God; for he hath clothed me with the garments of salvation, he hath covered me with the robe of righteousness, as a bridegroom decketh himself with ornaments, and as a bride adorneth herself with her jewels" (Isa. 61:10).

All blessings of God relating to eternal marriage are bestowed by covenant in the house of the Lord, performed by those with the sealing authority of the holy priesthood, attended with marvelous promises that are conditioned on our faithfulness and obedience. Eternal marriage unfolds matchless blessings to those who live by this covenant in devotion and faithfulness: a vision of the eternal destiny of joy and glory, an outpouring of knowledge and truth concerning the continuation of the sacred relationship of parents and children, gifts and powers to raise a Zion family, the ability to deflect and triumph over evil, and a full measure of sealing blessings from the Comforter, the Holy Spirit of Promise (see Eph. 1:13; D&C 76:53; 88:3; 124:124; 132:7, 19, 26).

Inspired by Latter-Day Prophets

Heber J. Grant: I believe that no worthy young Latter-day Saint man or woman should spare any reasonable effort to come to the house of the Lord to begin life together. The marriage vows taken in these hallowed places and the sacred covenants entered into for time and all eternity are proof against many of the temptations of life that tend to break homes and destroy happiness (*Gospel Standards: Selections from the Sermons and Writings of Heber J. Grant*, 359).

> *Eternal marriage is a fortress against the onslaught of evil influences in the world today. Preserved and sanctified by obedience and honor, it deflects temptation and strengthens resolve to endure to the end in valor. Why do you think this is so? What is the power behind eternal marriage?*

Harold B. Lee: You young women advancing in years who have not yet accepted a proposal of marriage, if you make yourselves worthy and ready to go to the house of the Lord and have faith in this sacred principle, even though the privilege of marriage does not come to you now, the Lord will reward you in due time and no blessing will be denied you. You are not under obligation to accept a proposal from someone unworthy of you for fear you will fail of your blessings. Likewise you young men who may lose your lives in a terrible conflict [war] before you have had an opportunity for marriage, the Lord knows the intents of your hearts and in his own time will reward you with opportunities made possible through temple ordinances instituted in the Church for that purpose (*Decisions for Successful Living*, 129–130).

> *It is a comfort to the soul and a confirmation of the mercy and grace of the Lord that no one will be denied the opportunities afforded through the new and everlasting covenant—in all of its dimensions. What are your thoughts about the all-encompassing love of God for all of His children, in all circumstances of mortality?*

Ezra Taft Benson: Marriage, designed to be an eternal covenant, is the most glorious and most exalting principle of the gospel of Jesus Christ. Faithfulness to the marriage covenant brings the fullest joy here and glorious rewards hereafter. The abuse of this sacred ordinance despoils the lives of individuals, wrecks the basic institution of the home, and causes the downfall of nations (*The Teachings of Ezra Taft Benson*, 533–534).

There is glory associated with the promises and blessings of the celestial marriage covenant. How can you bear witness of these truths to your friends who are not members of the Church in order to touch their hearts with the concept of everlasting family relationships?

Howard W. Hunter: There is no more powerful principle of life to promote love, forbearance, and devotion in the home than that of eternal marriage. . . . The principle of eternal marriage is a most powerful stabilizing influence in promoting the kind of home needed to rear children who are happy and well adjusted (*The Teachings of Howard W. Hunter,* 131).

The Lord has commanded: "Behold, it is my will, that all they who call on my name, and worship me according to mine everlasting gospel, should gather together, and stand in holy places" (D&C 101:22). Those places are the homes of holiness in Zion, the congregations of the Saints in the stakes of Zion, and the sacred temples of Zion. Eternal marriage is the binding force that unites all three of these places, for it sanctifies and edifies the home environment, gives unity and vision to the congregations of the Saints, and constitutes the most sublime manifestation of the sealing powers in the temples of God. Parents and children sealed together for time and all eternity in the temple can return to their home, a place of purity and peace, comfort and solace. In what ways does this kind of home facilitate the acquiring of the divine nature on the part of family members (see D&C 4:6; 2 Pet. 1:3–8)?

Truths to Liken

D&C 132:19–21—"And again, verily I say unto you, if a man marry a wife by my word, which is my law, and by the new and everlasting covenant, and it is sealed unto them by the Holy Spirit of promise, by him who is anointed, unto whom I have appointed this power and the keys of this priesthood; and it shall be said unto them—Ye shall come forth in the first resurrection; and if it be after the first resurrection, in the next resurrection; and shall inherit thrones, kingdoms, principalities, and powers, dominions, all heights and depths—

then shall it be written in the Lamb's Book of Life, that he shall commit no murder whereby to shed innocent blood, and if ye abide in my covenant, and commit no murder whereby to shed innocent blood, it shall be done unto them in all things whatsoever my servant hath put upon them, in time, and through all eternity; and shall be of full force when they are out of the world; and they shall pass by the angels, and the gods, which are set there, to their exaltation and glory in all things, as hath been sealed upon their heads, which glory shall be a fulness and a continuation of the seeds forever and ever. Then shall they be gods, because they have no end; therefore shall they be from everlasting to everlasting, because they continue; then shall they be above all, because all things are subject unto them. Then shall they be gods, because they have all power, and the angels are subject unto them. Verily, verily, I say unto you, except ye abide my law ye cannot attain to this glory."

- These breathtaking lines are from a revelation given through the Prophet Joseph Smith at Nauvoo, Illinois, recorded on July 12, 1843, in relation to the new and everlasting covenant, including eternal marriage. The essence of these doctrines was apparently made known to the Prophet as early as 1831.
- What are your thoughts about the magnificent capability of men and women involved in the new and everlasting covenant of marriage to become gods according to the design of the Almighty? Is it not logical that the offspring of God should have the destiny to become as He is? The covenant promises in the verses cited above are the most lofty imaginable: blessings of the first resurrection, thrones, kingdoms, principalities, powers, dominions, exaltation, glory in all things, continuation of seeds forever and ever (eternal increase), and becoming gods (in the footsteps of Abraham, Isaac, and Jacob, who have already entered into this state—see D&C 132:37). The key question is this: What do we have to do be worthy of such blessings?

Rejoicing and Reasoning Together

How Does One Prepare for Eternal Marriage?

Temple marriage is an objective to be reached after patient and devoted preparation have elevated and expanded the soul to a state of readiness. Isaiah characterized the process of spiritual advancement in these terms: "For precept must be upon precept, precept upon precept; line upon line, line upon line; here a little, and there a little" (Isa. 28:10). Nephi confirmed this doctrine: "For behold, thus saith the Lord God: I will give unto the children of men line upon line, precept upon precept, here a little and there a little; and blessed are those who hearken unto my precepts, and lend an ear unto my counsel, for they shall learn wisdom; for unto him that receiveth I will give more; and from them that shall say, We have enough, from them shall be taken away even that which they have" (2 Ne. 28:30). In modern times, the Lord has reiterated the process of preparing carefully for greater blessings: "For he will give unto the faithful line upon line, precept upon precept; and I will try you and prove you herewith" (D&C 98:12; compare D&C 128:21).

Preparing for temple marriage is perhaps the most critically important channel of spiritual development, for it encompasses, quite literally, all of the key aspects of eternal progression. Our values and standards are forged early; that's why it is so important to teach our children the purpose and blessing of temple marriage when they are young. All of the Church auxiliaries emphasize personal worthiness and preparation for temple marriage. The Young Women's Theme, the Aaronic Priesthood Goals, and the "For the Strength of Youth" pamphlet all admonish youth to live worthy and prepare for the temple. Preparing for the temple encompasses, quite literally, all of the key aspects of eternal progression and requires a degree of worthiness in keeping with the temple recommend questions.

How can you help others to aspire to, and be worthy of, the ordinance of eternal marriage by preparing line upon line, precept upon precept, until they are ready for this sacred opportunity?

What Does It Mean to Be Sealed by the Holy Spirit of Promise?

The Apostle Paul communicated with the Saints about the process of being "sealed with that holy Spirit of promise" (Eph. 1:13), a doctrine manifested again in the restored gospel concerning those of a celestial order: "And who overcome by faith, and are sealed by the Holy Spirit of promise, which the Father sheds forth upon all those who are just and true" (D&C 76:53). Section 132 of the Doctrine and Covenants refers four times to the process of being sealed by the Holy Spirit of Promise (see D&C 132:7, 18, 19, 26). Elder Bruce R. McConkie explains the principle:

> The Holy Spirit of Promise is the Holy Spirit promised the saints, or in other words the Holy Ghost. This name-title is used in connection with the sealing and ratifying power of the Holy Ghost, that is, the power given him to ratify and approve the righteous acts of men so that those acts will be binding on earth and in heaven. . . .
>
> Thus an act which is sealed by the Holy Spirit of Promise is one which is ratified by the Holy Ghost; it is one which is approved by the Lord; and the person who has taken the obligation upon himself is justified by the Spirit in the thing he has done. The ratifying seal of approval is put upon an act only if those entering the contract are worthy as a result of personal righteousness to receive the divine approbation. (*Mormon Doctrine*, 361)

It is a glorious doctrine that the Holy Ghost, as the Holy Spirit of Promise, would seal and ratify priesthood ordinances performed on behalf of worthy Saints who have done all in their power to honor their covenants and obligations before the Lord. Why does this sacred sealing, as recognized by heaven, always depend on continuing worthiness?

Real-life Stories for Heart and Mind

Eternal Joy. A priesthood leader who served for many years as a temple sealer bears witness to the joy of the eternal marriage ordinance:

Nothing in mortality has a greater effect upon one's life than marriage for time and all eternity. It seals a man and a wife and their family forever. It was my privilege to serve for some time in performing this sacred ordinance.

I would visit with the couple prior to the ceremony and then go into the sealing room, where friends and loved ones gathered for this most sacred covenant.

I can still see the joy in the parents and grandparents, family and friends, as they witnessed the ceremony. The tears of joy from their mothers have left an indelible impression on my mind, and especially my heart.

I remember as a father praying for this most important event in my children's lives—and like all parents, my joy became full because of the faith of my children and knowing they were walking in truth (see 3 John 1:4).

Joy is the essence of the eternal marriage covenant. Togetherness on earth in anticipation of eternal togetherness is sublimely rewarding. What have been your experiences with the influence of this sacred relationship and the covenant associated with it?

The Decision. How does one make the commitment for eternal marriage? One priesthood brother shared the following personal experience of how he came to make this eternally important decision many years ago:

I recall as a young man asking this very question of my bishop long ago—how do you decide on your partner for celestial marriage? His counsel is as good today as it was then: "Study it out in your mind. Fast and pray." Everyone who goes through this process should record the details of the experience, as it is truly one of the most far-reaching decisions of one's life. I share here a few excerpts from my journal only to illustrate how Heavenly Father blesses and guides us in these kinds of covenant decisions:

"Wednesday and Thursday, the twelfth and thirteenth of July, were set aside as special fast days. I had prayed all along that I might learn of the sanction of our continuing with our relationship. On Thursday morning as I was walking down some steps of the campus en route to a class, I was struck by the beauty of a small garden and pool nearby. It was certainly a pleasant day and the comfort of the surroundings invited meditation. I stayed. Thoughts seemed to come quickly to mind from all areas. Was it the thing to do? Would she be happy with me? Should I ask her? When? Factors came clearly and forcibly before my mind. Things became logical and sound. I knew she was the one. No voice spoke and no light appeared—certainly no outward manifestation was given to me on that beautiful morning—but the inward calm and peace, the heartfelt conviction that all areas of importance had been explored and successfully answered—this was indeed overwhelming.

"For anyone who has never experienced a prayer being answered in the way only the Lord can answer a prayer, this indeed would be hard to fathom. But I knew that the Lord would have it so, that she was to be my wife. Seldom have I been blessed with so powerful an outpouring of truth through the Spirit of the Lord. What a joy to pray to the Lord, thanking him later for His attention to my problem, and for His testimony of prayer given to me. This I record with the hope that any who might peruse these pages will be able to share with me the profound knowledge we enjoy of God in the Church that prayer is based on very definite principles just as repentance or faith or sanctification or any doctrine in the gospel. One must pray always to God for guidance and help in decisions."

How have you found that the Lord answers prayers for those of faith and humility? How have you been able to teach others the power of prayer, particularly those who are pondering the important decision concerning eternal marriage?

The Mirror of Majesty. A senior couple reflected in the epitome of the righteousness to which all

Saints should aspire. The friendly glow in their countenances was always consistently the same, whether they were seen in public places or in the privacy of their home. They were a celestial pair who had devoted their years to service—service to others as well as to each other. In visiting them one day, their home teacher asked about the unusual mirror mounted high on the wall of the entrance to their home opposite a lofty upper window. The husband explained that his wife couldn't see the majestic mountain peak from the lower windows of the house, so he had mounted the large mirror so that she could look up and see the towering summit of the mountain. He had mounted another mirror in the small fenced garden behind the house at just the right angle so that his wife could look through the window facing the garden and catch a glimpse of a second inspiring mountain vista, allowing her to feel edified and liberated from the confines of the condo walls.

Celestial marriage is like that—each partner taking every opportunity to discover ways of lifting the other, strengthening faith, illuminating the pathway, giving encouragement, and opening the view to higher aspirations and blessings of a heavenly nature. Both partners in a celestial marriage have the commission of helping one another keep in view the future goal of glory and eternal lives promised to the valiant and obedient. With the eyes of faith, the covenant pair can view in the mirror of truth "the things which God hath prepared for them that love him" (1 Cor. 2:9). What is seen now with but limited earthly vision will eventually be viewed in resplendent actuality, for the righteous will transition "to their exaltation and glory in all things, as hath been sealed upon their heads, which glory shall be a fulness and a continuation of the seeds forever and ever. Then shall they be gods, because they have no end" (D&C 132:19–20).

How have you and your loved ones been able to keep in view the glories and joys of your future home in the presence of the Father and the Son through the power and blessings of the new and everlasting covenant of marriage?

Pondering Prayerfully

Additional scriptures to consider and ponder:
- Gen. 2:21–24
- 1 Cor. 11:11
- D&C 42:22
- D&C 49:15–16
- D&C 68:28
- Moses 3:24

The following hymns inspire gratitude for eternal marriage:
- "High on the Mountain Top" (*Hymns,* 5)
- "Now Let Us Rejoice" (*Hymns,* 3)
- "The Morning Breaks" (*Hymns,* 1)

Remember and Be Sure

Marriage for time and all eternity is necessary in order for us to enter the highest degree of celestial glory. Early preparation is essential in order for temple marriage to become a reality as aspiring couples progress in all worthiness and sanctity. The promised blessings flowing from eternal marriage are necessarily based on honoring our holy covenant vows in all respects.

Heavenly Father's desire is that we might gain immortality and eternal life (see Moses 1:39), and celestial marriage is key to our becoming exalted. This knowledge—along with that of all other gospel truths, when understood and lived—will bring all the blessings of God into our lives so that we receive "all that my Father hath" (D&C 84:38).

The ordinance of temple marriage brings to bear all the blessings of Heavenly Father and our Savior as an eternal enrichment for our lives. In faithfulness, we receive the blessings of Abraham, Isaac, and Jacob. If we are true and loyal, our families will be sealed by the Holy Spirit of Promise, and all the blessings of the Father can be ours. Celestial marriage is heavenly marriage, eternal marriage—sanctioned and commissioned by the Almighty, anchored in covenant fidelity, vitalized by the Holy Spirit, infused with lasting bonds of love, and edified by the saving and enduring principles of the gospel of Jesus Christ.

If we are faithful in abiding by the new and everlasting covenant of marriage, sealed in the temples of God, we qualify ourselves for the highest gifts of exaltation and eternal lives. Our personal and family stewardship, as well as our stewardship within the Church and kingdom of God, is anchored in the sacred obligation to aspire to, prepare for, enter into, and maintain in righteousness the celestial marriage covenant and relationship. There is no more solemn duty for parents than to teach these principles to their children, and to use their ordained stewardship to prepare the way for their children to follow in the footsteps of those who honor their birthright and covenant obligations. Through obedience and humble prayer, the supreme gift of personal revelation will illuminate the way for these divine decrees to be obeyed. Then we will inherit the continuation of our fondest relationships on earth: "And that same sociality which exists among us here will exist among us there, only it will be coupled with eternal glory, which glory we do not now enjoy" (D&C 130:2).

CHAPTER 39
Chastity: The Pure in Heart

That the Church's stand on morality may be understood, we declare firmly and unalterably, it is not an outworn garment, faded, old-fashioned, and threadbare. God is the same yesterday, today, and forever, and his covenants and doctrines are immutable; and when the sun grows cold and the stars no longer shine, the law of chastity will still be basic in God's world and in the Lord's church. Old values are upheld by the Church not because they are old, but rather because through the ages they have proved right. It will always be the rule. —Spencer W. Kimball (*The Teachings of Spencer W. Kimball*, 265)

Opening the Window of Wisdom

The thirteenth Article of Faith provides a constitution for our moral behavior: "We believe in being honest, true, chaste, benevolent, virtuous, and in doing good to all men; indeed, we may say that we follow the admonition of Paul—We believe all things, we hope all things, we have endured many things, and hope to be able to endure all things. If there is anything virtuous, lovely, or of good report or praiseworthy, we seek after these things." A key part of this code for righteous living is chastity, the cultivation of a moral and virtuous character. The Lord will have a pure house and pure servants. Purity and cleanliness of mind and body are absolutely essential to qualify for the Spirit in one's life. Immorality in any of its forms has a devastating effect on the mind and spirit of individuals and families.

The media seems to parade or glamorize all types of immorality, the lack of integrity, and all manner of crime and violence. It is sad to witness this commentary on society. Society today suffers from the lack of purity and virtue. How can we be subject to sin in our mortal state and yet seek to be pure?

The dictionary tells us that *purity* means to be free from moral or physical defilement, to be chaste, to be free from pollution, to be blameless—even to the point of being sinless. This seems almost overwhelming: *We are to be perfect.* How can we be completely pure and virtuous, while we are mortal? The answer is that we can aspire to absolute purity in the strength of the Lord and through the help of the Spirit. We can make a difference through repentance and spiritual endurance. We can bear witness of the joy and blessings of moral goodness. We can testify to it. We can live it. We can stand for purity and virtue.

In a famous statement, Paul uses an effective metaphor to encourage a renewed commitment to be morally clean and holy: "Know ye not that ye are the temple of God, and that the Spirit of God dwelleth in you? If any man defile the temple of

God, him shall God destroy; for the temple of God is holy, which temple ye are" (1 Cor. 3:16–17). Later on in his epistle, Paul reemphasizes this same principle with these words: "What? know ye not that your body is the temple of the Holy Ghost which is in you, which ye have of God, and ye are not your own? For ye are bought with a price: therefore glorify God in your body, and in your spirit, which are God's" (1 Cor. 6:19–20).

Virtue and purity are essential attributes of those who labor in the vineyard of the Lord. As Alma counseled his righteous son, Shiblon: "See that ye bridle all your passions, that ye may be filled with love" (Alma 38:12). The Spirit can abide only in temples of holiness and purity. When one chooses to abide by the highest standards of virtue and decency, great blessings flow to sanctify and lift up lives. Even in a world of evaporating values, we can stand forth in courage to practice virtue and valor. We can be in the world, but not of the world. In His grand intercessory prayer on the eve of the Crucifixion, the Redeemer prayed for His followers with these words:

I pray not that thou shouldest take them out of the world, but that thou shouldest keep them from the evil.

They are not of the world, even as I am not of the world.

Sanctify them through thy truth: thy word is truth.

As thou hast sent me into the world, even so have I also sent them into the world.

And for their sakes I sanctify myself, that they also might be sanctified through the truth. (John 17:15–19)

Inspired by Latter-Day Prophets

Brigham Young: The sooner an individual resists temptation to do, say, or think wrong, while he has light to correct his judgment, the quicker he will gain strength and power to overcome every temptation to evil (*Discourses of Brigham Young*, 266).

From the beginning, the Lord warned: "My Spirit shall not always strive with man" (Gen. 6:3). In our day, the Lord has repeated: "And he that repents not, from him shall be taken even the light which he has received;

for my Spirit shall not always strive with man, saith the Lord of Hosts" (D&C 1:33). It is wisdom, then, to use the light within to deflect the darkness from without and thus overcome sin through the strength and power of the Lord. What are your thoughts about kindling the light within through purity and then using it to draw added strength from the Almighty to resist temptation?

David O. McKay: Infidelity and sexual immorality are two principal evils that threaten to weaken and to wreck present-day civilization. Unfortunately, the trends of modern life are tending to disintegrate the very foundation of the Christian home. . . . When family life disintegrates, the foundation and bulwark of human society is undermined (*Gospel Ideals: Selections from the Discourses of David O. McKay*, 487).

The home is the centerpiece of Zion, the bastion of the "godly walk and conversation" (D&C 20:69) characteristic of those who enter the Lord's fold. What can you do to preserve the values of integrity and morality in the homes of Zion?

Ezra Taft Benson: We covenant to live the law of chastity. The law of chastity is virtue and sexual purity. This law places us under covenant to live this commandment strictly. . . . A reason for virtue—which includes personal chastity, clean thoughts and practices, and integrity—is that we must have the Spirit and the power of God in our lives to do God's work (*The Teachings of Ezra Taft Benson*, 278).

The light of the Spirit within the lives of the Saints is part of the ensign that will come forth in the last days: "For, behold, I say unto you that Zion shall flourish, and the glory of the Lord shall be upon her; And she shall be an ensign unto the people, and there shall come unto her out of every nation under heaven" (D&C 64:41–42). Virtue is therefore a beacon to help gather the dispersed from the four corners of the earth and bring them into the fold of Christ. In what ways have you observed the power of virtue in the lives of members of the Church drawing attention in positive ways to the gospel of Jesus Christ and its blessings?

Truths to Liken

Matt. 5:8—"Blessed are the pure in heart: for they shall see God."

- In His Sermon on the Mount, the Savior included this glorious covenant promise that those who are pure will be able to come into the presence of God one day and thus behold His glory (see also 3 Ne. 12:8).
- Purity of heart is reflected in our behavior, our thoughts, our intentions, and our noblest affections towards God. The "mighty change" of heart (Alma 5:14) includes a transformation toward purity and cleanliness, with the resulting blessing of being able to have the influence of the Spirit to keep us on the pathway of becoming worthy to be in the presence of God. Moroni said, "Yea, come unto Christ, and be perfected in him, and deny yourselves of all ungodliness; and if ye shall deny yourselves of all ungodliness, and love God with all your might, mind and strength, then is his grace sufficient for you, that by his grace ye may be perfect in Christ; and if by the grace of God ye are perfect in Christ, ye can in nowise deny the power of God" (Moro. 10:32). We cannot be made pure and perfect on our own, but with the help of Christ we can be made pure and perfect. What are your thoughts concerning this sacred process of purification and perfection through the grace and power of the Lord?

Moro. 7:48—"Wherefore, my beloved brethren, pray unto the Father with all the energy of heart, that ye may be filled with this love, which he hath bestowed upon all who are true followers of his Son, Jesus Christ; that ye may become the sons of God; that when he shall appear we shall be like him, for we shall see him as he is; that we may have this hope; that we may be purified even as he is pure. Amen."

- In his account on the plates of the Book of Mormon, Moroni included these words of his father, Mormon, from a sermon concerning faith, hope, and charity.
- Purity is intimately connected to prayer, love, and hope. When we accept the Savior as the perfect model of purity, then we will strive to become like Him and become worthy of seeing Him someday. How can you remember to include in your prayers a supplication that Heavenly Father will fill you with love and the capacity to follow the Savior, thus enabling you to be made pure?

D&C 88:67–68—"And if your eye be single to my glory, your whole bodies shall be filled with light, and there shall be no darkness in you; and that body which is filled with light comprehendeth all things. Therefore, sanctify yourselves that your minds become single to God, and the days will come that you shall see him; for he will unveil his face unto you, and it shall be in his own time, and in his own way, and according to his own will."

- These words were included in a revelation given through the Prophet Joseph Smith at Kirtland, Ohio, in December 1832 and January 1833, and designated by him as the "olive leaf . . . plucked from the Tree of Paradise, the Lord's message of peace to us" (D&C 88, section heading).
- Being sanctified and pure is a condition that allows one to be filled with light, being attuned perfectly with the things of God and thus enabled to comprehend all things. In this capacity we are made ready to behold the Lord in accordance with His will. What are your thoughts concerning the relationship between chastity and light, between purity and the power to behold one day the Father and His Beloved Son? (See D&C 137 for a vision of the celestial glory.)

D&C 88:74–75—"And I give unto you, who are the first laborers in this last kingdom, a commandment that you assemble yourselves together, and organize yourselves, and prepare yourselves, and sanctify yourselves; yea, purify your hearts, and cleanse your hands and your feet before me, that I may make you clean; That I may testify unto your Father, and your God, and my God, that you are clean from the blood of this wicked generation; that I may fulfil this promise, this great and last promise, which I have made unto you, when I will."

- These words from the revelation known as "the olive leaf" connect purity with a "great and last promise" made by the Lord. What is this promise? In regard to this passage, Elder Bruce R. McConkie stated: "To those of understanding we say: The purpose of the endowment in the house of the Lord is to prepare and sanctify his saints so they will be able to see his face, here and now, as well as to bear the glory of his presence in the eternal worlds" (*The Promised Messiah: The First Coming of Christ*, 583).

- Purity of mind and heart enables us to participate in the sacred ordinances of the temple, where we learn how to return to the presence of God. The purpose of the temple is to ensure that we are empowered—through the endowment of priesthood blessings—to be able to return to our heavenly home as eternal families in dignity and worthiness, having fulfilled the measure of our creation and answered the ends of the law through obedience and the mercy of salvation. In perhaps the most celebrated statement concerning this divine process, Brigham Young declared: "Let me give you a definition in brief. Your endowment is, to receive all those ordinances in the house of the Lord, which are necessary for you, after you have departed this life, to enable you to walk back to the presence of the Father, passing the angels who stand as sentinels, being enabled to give them the key words, the signs and tokens, pertaining to the holy Priesthood, and gain your eternal exaltation in spite of earth and hell" (*Discourses of Brigham Young*, 416).

How can you make it your all-encompassing purpose in life to be worthy of the temple and help your loved ones do the same, thus harvesting the blessings of celestial glory forever and ever?

Rejoicing and Reasoning Together

How Can We Make the Home a Temple of Purity?

The home, like a garden, is a place where nourishing things are cultivated and grown. What is cultivated in the home is love—love for Heavenly Father and His Son, love for one another, and love for the gospel and its principles of honor and purity. We can establish in the home a standard of behavior that is moral and upright, based on the true and ennobling principles of the gospel. We can make a commitment to be clean in all ways—emotionally, physically, and intellectually, allowing nothing to enter the mind or body that is impure.

In the home we are honest with one another, and project that honesty into our dealings with everyone outside the home in order to promote a community spirit that is upright and acceptable before God. We are committed to a lifestyle of charity as well as chastity, for that is how the Spirit will feel comfortable residing with us in our home. In the home we can establish an environment where purity and holiness can unfold and endure.

What we read and see on television or on the Internet is a matter of choice, and purity comes through correct choices. If virtue is the seed, then virtuous thoughts and ideas are the seedbed, and virtuous and positive discourse is the nurturing element. When we control our environment, we control the unfolding of our lives. We can read uplifting books, watch decent television shows and movies, and use the Internet to expand the mind rather than debase it. We can speak in positive and honorable terms with one another, and cultivate the fruit of purity and virtue with care and patience. We can decorate and beautify the home with uplifting things that promote virtuous thoughts and desires. We can purify the environment so that it reflects the kind of order that will encourage good ideas, clear thinking, and upright behavior. In this way, we can bring into our pattern of living the principles and standards that will ensure that we will avoid situations leading to immorality and promiscuity in any form.

The home is a place to teach and cultivate the principles of purity and chastity, knowing that these lead to the glorious alliance of freedom, strength, and honor. How does this work? Virtue is liberating, while immorality is enslaving. If freedom is a principle we want to live by, then virtue is the gateway, for virtue leads to harmony, peace, balance, and long-term rewards. By contrast, those who capitulate to the never-abating hunger for momentary pleasures and titillation will pass through the gateway of immorality—and suffer the consequences. The home is the place where true freedom, based on purity and honor, is taught and learned.

Virtue is strong, while immorality is weak. It takes strength of character to lead a life of virtue and integrity, while a life of lax morals is shallow and weak. If strength is a principle we want to live by, then virtue is the gateway. On the other hand, those who think there is joy in weakness and surrendering to shallow desires or the abuse of others pass through the gateway of immorality—and suffer the consequences.

Virtue attracts respect and honor, while immorality repels respect. If respect and honor are principles we wish to cultivate, then virtue is our gateway. By contrast, those who wish to leave behind a legacy of selfishness and loneliness for the coming generation will choose to pass through the gateway of immorality—and suffer the consequences. It is a choice. We can make the home a place where virtue and purity lead to freedom, strength, and honor. The harvest is peace, joy, and confidence: "Let virtue garnish thy thoughts unceasingly; then shall thy confidence wax strong in the presence of God" (D&C 121:45).

Virtue is a family effort. We do it "for them." We keep our lives pure for the sake of our loved ones—our spouse and our children and grandchildren—because that gives them a life and a legacy they can build on. The Savior said in His grand intercessory prayer, "And for their sakes I sanctify myself, that they also might be sanctified through the truth" (John 17:19). We leave behind for the coming generations the good seeds of wholesome behavior, harmony, peace, and love. We leave behind memories of courage and honor. We keep the marriage sacred—understanding and appreciating the sacred bonds of matrimony. We make and keep promises of fidelity and chastity. We make and keep covenants to be pure in language, thought, and deed. We teach leadership principles of setting worthy goals, allowing virtue to govern the way we create, plan, organize, and build enduring relationships with others. And we teach patience, remembering that maintaining virtue is a lifetime goal, one that depends on the strength of

the Lord. We can pray for that strength every day, since purity and virtue flow from God. We can seek the direction of the Holy Spirit to rise to the challenge of being pure and chaste.

The essence of morality is the wondrous insight that each of us is a child of God. Moral living begins in realizing and internalizing our divine heritage. Knowing that we bear the image of the Creator within us and on us lifts our view to a higher plane, elevates our vision to higher possibilities, and instills within us the desire—the responsibility—to act according to the highest standards of decency and honor.

As you study this portrait of a home of purity, what are your thoughts about making your own home an even better place for the spirit of purity to flourish, a place where the Holy Ghost will always abide as a blessing to you and your loved ones?

Real-life Stories for Heart and Mind

Integrity of Heart—Joseph in Egypt. Joseph's example of integrity and moral uprightness in Egypt is among the most celebrated instances of strength of character in all of scripture. Joseph had made the Lord his God and the Lord was with him. We learn from the scriptural account: "And the LORD was with Joseph, and he was a prosperous man; and he was in the house of his master the Egyptian. And his master saw that the LORD was with him, and that the LORD made all that he did to prosper in his hand. And Joseph found grace in his sight, and he served him: and he made him overseer over his house, and all that he had he put into his hand" (Gen. 39:2–4).

Joseph's devoted effort and performance with his assigned duties brought favor with Potiphar. Joseph was a faithful servant, even while his allegiance was to the Lord. As the story unfolds, Joseph was approached and tempted by Potiphar's scheming wife. In response, Joseph said, "How then can I do this great wickedness, and sin against God?" (Gen. 39:9). Because of his sterling character and moral strength, Joseph took immediate action "and fled, and got him out" (Gen. 39:12).

Potiphar's wife then accused him falsely and reported him to her husband. As a consequence, Joseph was put in prison. But again the hand of the Lord preserved him. He invoked the power of the Lord to interpret the dreams of Pharaoh, King of Egypt, concerning the seven years of plenty followed by the seven years of famine (see Gen. 41). Pharaoh then rewarded Joseph with a great honor: "Thou shalt be over my house, and according unto thy word shall all my people be ruled: only in the throne will I be greater than thou . . . and he made him ruler over all the land of Egypt" (Gen. 41:40, 43).

Joseph's strength of character and his dependence on the Lord were forces for good in his life and opened the gateway to future service. Joseph's flight at the adulterous overtures of Potiphar's wife stands in stark contrast with the moral weakness of some of his own brothers. The story of his integrity is a beacon of light that still shines today in our world. Joseph's resiliency, positive leadership, and creative problem-solving caused him to be elevated in stature and office in Egypt, thus laying the groundwork for his future role of preserver of his heritage under the Abrahamic covenant. When your heart is right with the Lord, you will be true to the faith and the Lord will strengthen you and bless you in all facets of your life.

To learn from Joseph we need to view his personal integrity of heart as an inner strength. His personal righteousness empowered him so that the Lord was with him. He was anchored in a clear vision of the Lord's design for His covenant people. Because of Joseph's moral integrity and leadership, he stood the test and laid the foundation for a continuation of the covenant blessings to millions upon millions of people in the future. How can you use the example of Joseph in strengthening your own resolve to help your family and those you serve in the Church become what the Lord would have them be in purity and honor?

Pondering Prayerfully

Additional scriptures to consider and ponder:
- Isa. 52:11
- Matt. 5:27
- 2 Cor. 7:1
- Philip. 4:8
- James 1:27
- 1 Pet. 1:22
- 2 Pet. 1:5–8
- 3 Ne. 12:27
- D&C 63:16

The following hymns remind us of the blessings of chastity and purity:
- "More Holiness Give Me" (*Hymns*, 131)
- "Sweet Is the Peace the Gospel Brings" (*Hymns*, 14)
- "True to the Faith" (*Hymns*, 254)

Remember and Be Sure

Recognizing that we are the divine offspring of God should give us hope and build our self-esteem. Knowing who we really are empowers us to realize that we need to be clean and pure in order to enjoy the Spirit in our lives (see Mosiah 2:37; Hel. 4:24). The process of cleansing and purification prepares the way for the operation of the Spirit, with its attendant blessings of peace, love, harmony, and joy in the gospel.

Immorality may give fleeting "moments of pleasure," but it does not result in enduring joy and happiness. "For what is a man profited, if he shall gain the whole world, and lose his own soul?" (Matt. 16:26). Integrity is required to maintain a state of morality—individually and collectively. The gospel standard is our moral law. In society as a whole, we have the opportunity to be courageous in fighting for that which is morally right. When the majority has no concern for morality, all suffer. Standards are not upheld. Wickedness is the result—all because of the lack of society's integrity in upholding high moral standards. By embracing and sustaining a moral lifestyle, we can make a difference—for ourselves, our families, our neighborhoods, our cities and states, and even the nation and the world.

The quality of purity and virtue is something we continually strive for. It becomes manifest in our lives on a daily basis as we strive to uphold eternal principles of honor and righteousness. In the strength of the Lord each of us can become a person of noble character, of exemplary behavior, full of integrity and espousing moral goodness as well as committed to living the principles of righteousness continually. May we make a solemn promise to stand for virtue and make a difference in the world. We can make a firm commitment to a moral and pure lifestyle. We can take time to get involved in promoting a moral environment in our community. Consider the magnificent blessings that flow to the pure in heart: "But behold, I,

Jacob, would speak unto you that are pure in heart. Look unto God with firmness of mind, and pray unto him with exceeding faith, and he will console you in your afflictions. . . . O all ye that are pure in heart, lift up your heads and receive the pleasing word of God, and feast upon his love; for ye may, if your minds are firm, forever" (Jacob 3:1–2).

CHAPTER 40
The House of the Lord

These [temple] ordinances have been revealed unto us for this very purpose, that we might be born into the light from the midst of this darkness—from death into life. —Joseph F. Smith (*JD* 19:265)

Opening the Window of Wisdom

The kingdom of God is a kingdom of order, power, and transcendent glory, organized by our Father in Heaven for the blessing of all who belong to this earthly sphere. As such, the Father, in His mercy, has prepared a plan to extend every opportunity for spiritual growth and salvation to every soul who has ever lived or who will ever live on earth—including those who have departed this life without the opportunity to learn of or embrace the gospel of Jesus Christ. The activation of this plan can take place only upon the bestowal of divine keys and the authorization of the sealing ordinances required for such ordinances to be in effect beyond the veil. The Savior said to Peter: "And I will give unto thee the keys of the kingdom of heaven: and whatsoever thou shalt bind on earth shall be bound in heaven: and whatsoever thou shalt loose on earth shall be loosed in heaven" (Matt. 16:19). Peter and his associates clearly understood the breadth and majestic reach of the gospel plan: "For for this cause was the gospel preached also to them that are dead, that they

might be judged according to men in the flesh, but live according to God in the spirit" (1 Pet. 4:6).

To this end, the Lord commissioned the prophet Elijah to administer the sealing keys for priesthood ordinances—including temple ordinances—for all dispensations. The angel Moroni, citing Malachi, taught this principle to Joseph Smith during his visits of September 21, 1823: *"Behold, I will reveal unto you the Priesthood, by the hand of Elijah the prophet, before the coming of the great and dreadful day of the Lord. . . . And he shall plant in the hearts of the children the promises made to the fathers, and the hearts of the children shall turn to their fathers. If it were not so, the whole earth would be utterly wasted at his coming"* (JS–H 1:38–39). Consequently, the sealing keys were bestowed and activated once again through the appearance of Elijah on April 3, 1836, in the Kirtland Temple (see D&C 110:13–16), inaugurating a spiritual movement of temple work that continues even to this day.

Temples are holy. They are the house of the Lord. They are erected and dedicated as sacred precincts where we can worship God and receive sacred ordinances of exaltation pertaining to the living and the dead. Within the walls of the temple are made available all of the exalting ordinances, covenants, and blessings for the children of God. Temple work and family history concern the eternal destiny of the family. Families can be forever through the blessings of the temple. The restoration of the priesthood sealing powers through

Elijah has truly caused the children and their fathers to turn towards each other (see D&C 2). This power makes possible the eternal family. As we search out our ancestors and do their temple work, we can be made perfect with them, and they with us (see D&C 128:15). An important part of our family history work is doing genealogical research to identify family members who need temple ordinances and then ensuring that these ordinances are performed. Truly the temple draws families toward their promised eternal covenant destiny. As such, the temple is a place of peace and revelation, glory and joy. It is:

> A place of thanksgiving for all saints, and for a place of instruction for all those who are called to the work of the ministry in all their several callings and offices;
>
> That they may be perfected in the understanding of their ministry, in theory, in principle, and in doctrine, in all things pertaining to the kingdom of God on the earth, the keys of which kingdom have been conferred upon you.
>
> And inasmuch as my people build a house unto me in the name of the Lord, and do not suffer any unclean thing to come into it, that it be not defiled, my glory shall rest upon it;
>
> Yea, and my presence shall be there, for I will come into it, and all the pure in heart that shall come into it shall see God. (D&C 97:13–16)

We should look to the temple of God as the enduring icon of God's mission to bring about the immortality and eternal life of mankind. By keeping our eye on the temple and remembering our covenant promises, we prepare the way for great spiritual blessings to flow into our lives continually.

To enter the sacred places where the eyes and heart of Deity are present is to receive magnificent blessings of light and glory. Temple work affords the faithful and devoted Saints of God the supreme opportunity to partake of the nature of redeeming and saving love in doing for their progenitors what these deceased persons could not do for themselves. In this way, those who come to the temples of the Most High with the records of their dead to participate in vicarious ordinances are fulfilling the prophecy of the ancient prophet Obadiah, who declared, in relationship to the unfolding work of the Lord: "And saviours shall come up on mount Zion" (Obad. 1:21). We learn from a careful study of the scriptures that the height of the Lord's design for His children is the holy temple, with its sealing ordinances, its washings and anointings, and its sacred endowments. The Kirtland

Temple, first in the dispensation of the fullness of times, holds a singularly important place in the history of the Restoration. It inaugurated the unfolding of temple work in the latter days and marked the initial milestone beyond which lay the establishment of many other houses of the Lord in all quarters of the earth—a process that still moves forward.

We, the children of God in this last dispensation, have been called to help in laying the foundation of this great latter-day work: proclaiming the gospel, perfecting the Saints, and redeeming the dead. We build temples. We go there in worthiness to receive sealing ordinances and endowments from on high. We do vicarious work for the dead. We spread the word throughout the world about the restoration of these essential truths. We will continue the work on the other side of the veil so that the spirits residing and waiting there can enjoy the blessings of the ordinances of the temple vicariously (see D&C 138:57–58).

There is a grand work to do, and we are the ones to do it. Our work and glory is to help Heavenly Father in bringing to pass His eternal plan of happiness—the immortality and eternal life of His children, lifted and redeemed through the Atonement of Jesus Christ. Temple work and family history service are the culminating triumphs of His plan to prepare us fully for our future roles in the worlds to come.

The spirit of Elijah is the consummate power to unite fathers and sons, mothers and daughters, the living and the dead—that the family of God can be sealed His according to the covenants, principles, and saving ordinances of the gospel of Jesus Christ. Such could not occur without the sealing powers and the spiritual motivation associated with the spirit of Elijah, upon whom this divine commission has been bestowed. The Spirit of Elijah causes us to think of our kindred dead with a sense of appreciation and gratitude, thus giving us the desire to do the necessary temple work for them. It turns our hearts to our living family. Recognizing this great power and blessing in our lives reinforces the importance of family both here and in the hereafter. The family is truly the basic unit of the kingdom of God, and we should do all in our power to strengthen it through the blessings of the temple.

Inspired by Latter-Day Prophets

Joseph Smith: Every man that has been baptized and belongs to the kingdom has a right to be baptized for those who have gone before; and as soon as the law of the Gospel is obeyed here by their friends who act as proxy for them, the Lord has administrators there to set them free (*HC* 6:365–366).

What are your thoughts to learn that you have "a right" in the gospel plan to participate in vicarious work for the dead? How does it increase your joy to know that your temple service is a partnership with the Lord through which individuals will be set free on the basis of your proxy work and their having satisfied the principles and ordinances of the gospel?

John A. Widtsoe: Only once are the endowments taken for himself by any one person. To refresh his memory, and to place him in close touch with the spirit of the work, a person may enter the temple as frequently as he desires and take endowments for the dead. In that way both he and the dead are benefited. . . . Temple work is the safety of the living and the hope of the dead (*A Rational Theology*, 129).

Heavenly Father love us. He has entrusted us with the sacred opportunity to be involved actively in temple work, not alone for the blessing and salvation of the departed, but also to kindle over and over again within our own consciousness the truths of the temple covenants and activate our memory and understanding of things eternal. Alma taught his son Helaman concerning the purpose of the scriptures: "And now, it has hitherto been wisdom in God that these things should be preserved; for behold, they have enlarged the memory of this people, yea, and convinced many of the error of their ways, and brought them to the knowledge of their God unto the salvation of their souls" (Alma 37:8). In what way is the temple a "living scripture" to bring about the same purpose for each of us participating in the joy of temple work?

Spencer W. Kimball: Missionary work is not limited to proclaiming the gospel to every nation, kindred, tongue, and people now living on the earth. Missionary work is also continuing beyond the veil among the millions and even billions of the children of our Heavenly Father who have died either without hearing the gospel or without accepting it while they lived on the earth. Our great part in this aspect of missionary work is to perform on this earth the ordinances required for those who accept the gospel over there. The spirit world is full of spirits who are anxiously awaiting the performance of these earthly ordinances for them. I hope to see us dissolve the artificial boundary line we so often place between missionary work and temple and genealogical work, because it is the same great redemptive work! (*The Teachings of Spencer W. Kimball*, 540)

President Kimball reminds us that our service in all aspects of the kingdom of God is seamless—it is fully unified, coordinated, and harmonized. How can you help others catch this same vision of temple work being, in essence, missionary work? How is all the work of the Church truly missionary work?

Ezra Taft Benson: I promise you that, with increased attendance in the temples of our God, you shall receive increased personal revelation to bless your life as you bless those who have died ("The Book of Mormon and the Doctrine and Covenants," *Ensign*, May 1987, 85).

The prophet gives us a promise on how to receive personal revelation. The key word is increased—revelation takes added devotion and added commitment. How have you found that the level of inspiration and revelation increases with "increased attendance"?

Truths to Liken

2 Ne. 21:12—"And he shall set up an ensign for the nations, and shall assemble the outcasts of Israel, and gather together the dispersed of Judah from the four corners of the earth." (Compare Isa. 11:12.)

- Nephi included in his record many such words of Isaiah concerning the latter days, saying, "for my soul delighteth in his words" (2 Ne. 11:2).
- By the power of multiple witnesses, the Lord establishes the truth of His plan of salvation. A central part of the ensign to be set up in the latter days is the program of temple work—a magnificent light of truth emanating from the Church as part of the gathering of Israel. Temples are visual signs of invitation to the world to come and find the truth. How have you been able to use temples as

a way of adding your witness of the blessing of those who are seeking the truth? We are all part of the ensign of the Lord—the Church, the priesthood, the temples. It is our duty to do temple work and spread the light of the gospel (see D&C138:47–53; Jacob 5:70–77).

D&C 88:119 "Organize yourselves; prepare every needful thing; and establish a house, even a house of prayer, a house of fasting, a house of faith, a house of learning, a house of glory, a house of order, a house of God."

- These words were included in a revelation given through the Prophet Joseph Smith at Kirtland, Ohio, in late December 1832 and early January 1833, designated by the Prophet as the "olive leaf . . . plucked from the Tree of Paradise, the Lord's message of peace to us" (D&C 88, section heading).
- The divine directive to build a temple is indeed related to the process of obtaining heavenly peace. What we learn in the temples of God is the pinnacle of spiritual truth that will lift us, through faith and devotion, ever closer to our heavenly home. The temple is truly the Lord's house. It is a place of empowerment as we are endowed with blessings from on high. The Lord is present in His house, and if we are prepared to learn, being pure in heart, we can be taught concerning our callings and stewardships for building up the kingdom of God. The temple is indeed a house where we may learn of the mysteries of God and about life everlasting. What have you learned through temple service that has immeasurably blessed your life and that of your loved ones?

D&C 109:44 "But thy word must be fulfilled. Help thy servants to say, with thy grace assisting them: Thy will be done, O Lord, and not ours."

- The inspired dedicatory prayer for the Kirtland Temple on March 27, 1836, contained this supplication of the Prophet Joseph Smith.
- Through the grace of the Lord, it is never difficult to follow His will. It is

only difficult when we would act solely on our own. Let us remember to pray, as the Prophet Joseph did on our behalf, that we might have the courage, the humility, the strength, the inspiration, and the faith to follow the will of the Lord always—His grace assisting us continually. What are your thoughts concerning the will of the Lord for you and your family at the present time? What would He have you do? How can you do it, in the strength of the Lord?

D&C 110:11–16. "After this vision [of the Savior] closed, the heavens were again opened unto us; and Moses appeared before us, and committed unto us the keys of the gathering of Israel from the four parts of the earth, and the leading of the ten tribes from the land of the north.

After this, Elias appeared, and committed the dispensation of the gospel of Abraham, saying that in us and our seed all generations after us should be blessed. After this vision had closed, another great and glorious vision burst upon us; for Elijah the prophet, who was taken to heaven without tasting death, stood before us, and said: Behold, the time has fully come, which was spoken of by the mouth of Malachi—testifying that he [Elijah] should be sent, before the great and dreadful day of the Lord come—To turn the hearts of the fathers to the children, and the children to the fathers, lest the whole earth be smitten with a curse—Therefore, the keys of this dispensation are committed into your hands; and by this ye may know that the great and dreadful day of the Lord is near, even at the doors."

- These words were included in several visions manifested to the Prophet Joseph Smith and Oliver Cowdery on the Sabbath day in the Kirtland Temple on April 3, 1836—just a few days after its dedication. That particular day was Easter for the Christian world; it was also the time of the Passover for the Jewish people—the time of the year, according to their tradition, when the long-awaited Elijah would return at some future date.
- The restoration of the priesthood keys enables and empowers the great purpose of the kingdom of God—to invite all to come unto Christ by proclaiming the gospel,

perfecting the Saints, and redeeming the dead. This is our work, to build up the kingdom of God (see JST, Matt. 6:38). Concerning these extraordinary events, President Joseph Fielding Smith said, "Among the keys of authority and power which were bestowed, there are none of more far reaching or greater significance than the keys of authority bestowed by Elijah. . . . We have been given the record of the coming of Moses, with the keys of the gathering of Israel and the restoration of the ten tribes; the coming of Elias, who lived in the days of Abraham, with the restoration of the covenants and authorities given to Abraham and in his day; and the coming of Elijah who was spoken of by Malachi as having the authority to restore the power of turning the hearts of the fathers to the children, and the hearts of the children to their fathers. This was to come before the great and dreadful day of the Lord and to save the earth from being smitten with a curse" (*Doctrines of Salvation*, 3: 127).

What impact does it have on your heart and mind to know that the keys of the last dispensation have been committed into the hands of the priesthood leadership of the Church?

D&C 128:24—"Behold, the great day of the Lord is at hand; and who can abide the day of his coming, and who can stand when he appeareth? For he is like a refiner's fire, and like fuller's soap; and he shall sit as a refiner and purifier of silver, and he shall purify the sons of Levi, and purge them as gold and silver, that they may offer unto the Lord an offering in righteousness. Let us, therefore, as a church and a people, and as Latter-day Saints, offer unto the Lord an offering in righteousness; and let us present in his holy temple, when it is finished, a book containing the records of our dead, which shall be worthy of all acceptation."

- These are words from an inspired epistle on vicarious temple work for the dead written to the Church on September 6, 1842, by the Prophet Joseph Smith, who at the time was in hiding to avoid falling into the hands of authorities seeking to take him captive on false charges.

- We are to act on the inspiration planted in our hearts through the restored keys and powers of Elijah, causing us to seek after those who have gone before and to turn to our living family members with increased compassion and love. What is the "book" that constitutes an "offering in righteousness"? It is the record of our forebears that confirms the temple work done on their behalf. Let us never forget that the earth would be wasted if there is not a recognized and authorized link from the children to their fathers. Do we have the spirit of Elijah in our hearts? Can we do more to further this celestial cause with greater faith and devotion? What are your thoughts on this essential dimension of the work of salvation and exaltation?

D&C 138:53–54, 57—"The Prophet Joseph Smith, and my father, Hyrum Smith, Brigham Young, John Taylor, Wilford Woodruff, and other choice spirits who were reserved to come forth in the fulness of times to take part in laying the foundations of the great Latter-day work, Including the building of the temples and the performance of ordinances therein for the redemption of the dead, were also in the spirit world. . . . I beheld that the faithful elders of this dispensation, when they depart from mortal life, continue their labors in the preaching of the gospel of repentance and redemption, through the sacrifice of the Only Begotten Son of God, among those who are in darkness and under the bondage of sin in the great world of the spirits of the dead."

- These words describe a remarkable vision given to President Joseph F. Smith in Salt Lake City, Utah, on October 3, 1918, concerning the work of the Lord in the spirit world.
- The veil is thin. The family of our Heavenly Father—whether in the premortal realm, the mortal realm (this earth), or the postmoral spirit realm following death—constitutes the continuity of His greatest creation. The work continues with precision and urgency in the world of the spirits under the direction of great leaders who act in the authority and power of Jesus Christ—the very one who inaugurated this work of liberation following His Crucifixion (see 1 Pet. 4:6). How do these doctrines and principles strengthen

your testimony of the universal love and mercy of our Father in Heaven and His Son, our Redeemer? How does it give you increased hope and joy to know that your stewardship to save souls will be continued in the hereafter?

Rejoicing and Reasoning Together

What Is the History of Temples?

Joseph Smith stated: "The Church is not fully organized, in its proper order, and cannot be, until the Temple is completed, where places will be provided for the administration of the ordinances of the Priesthood" (*HC* 4:603). From the beginning of time there have always been places provided for the ordinances of exaltation. The Garden of Eden itself was a holy place in which celestial marriage could be performed (see Moses 2:28; 3:23–25; 4:26–29). Mountain tops served as a site for the endowment of truth when so ordained of the Lord (see Moses 1:1; Ex. 19:3; Matt. 17:1). Following the Exodus, the Tabernacle served as a kind of portable temple for sacred priesthood rites in ancient Israel (see Ex. 25:8; D&C 124:38).

The Lord promised David that his son would build a temple (see 1 Kgs. 5:5), and Solomon followed through by erecting a magnificent temple complex for sacred worship. The dedicatory program for that temple (see 1 Kgs. 8)—around a millennium before the birth of Christ—is filled with pleas for the Lord to accept His people as His own and prosper their way as long as they heeded His word and kept His commandments—thus making the temple a continual reminder of their covenant commitments (see 1 Kgs. 9:3–4). The resplendent temple became renowned throughout the region, and rulers came from all around to admire it and bask in the opulence and wisdom of Solomon's court.

Temple services were restored in the days of Hezekiah and Isaiah (in the eighth century BC), but the edifice was destroyed in the Babylonian conquest around 587 BC (see Jer. 44:30; 52:12–13; 2 Kgs. 25:8–10). It was later rebuilt by Zerubbabel, appointed by the Persians as governor over the Holy Land, and dedicated in 516 BC (see Ezra 6:15–16). Herod reconstituted this temple during the days of Jesus, but it was completely destroyed by the Romans in 70 AD, thus interrupting the tradition of temple service in that part of the world until the days of the Restoration. Meanwhile, the branch of Israel guided to the New World in the days of Lehi constructed temples for sacred rites and gatherings: "And I, Nephi, did build a temple; and I did construct it after the manner of the temple of Solomon save it were not built of so many precious things" (2 Ne. 5:16; also Jacob 1:17; Mosiah 2:5–7; 3 Ne. 11:1).

The prophet Isaiah foresaw our day in terms of the glories of temple work: "And it shall come to pass in the last days, that the mountain of the LORD's house shall be established in the top of the mountains, and shall be exalted above the hills; and all nations shall flow unto it. And many people shall go and say, Come ye, and let us go up to the mountain of the LORD, to the house of the God of Jacob; and he will teach us of his ways, and we will walk in his paths: for out of Zion shall go forth the law, and the word of the LORD from Jerusalem" (Isa. 2:2–3).

In the foothills leading to such a visionary, yet very real, mountain, lies Kirtland, Ohio, where the first of the Lord's temples in the dispensation of the fullness of times came into service on March 27, 1836. That experience was the culmination of a groundswell of extraordinary events comprising the Restoration to that point—from the First Vision to the return of the priesthood, the coming forth of the Book of Mormon, and the organization of the Church. With the Lord's temple once again rising toward the heavens, the first bastion of the process by means of which the hearts of the fathers and the hearts of the children should be once again melded together became a reality. The Kirtland Temple is a simple though dignified structure; however, the implication of what transpired there rises beyond the modest scope of this edifice to reach astounding heights of importance for the plan of salvation and the emergence of the Church from obscurity and into the light of its divine mission. It was in that temple that Jesus Christ Himself appeared to Joseph Smith and Oliver Cowdery to accept the sacrifice and offering of the Saints (see D&C 110:7), followed by the ministration of Moses, Elias, and Elijah restoring essential keys for the work of the kingdom.

After the Saints were forced to leave Kirtland, and were then prevented by mobs from building temples in Zion (Missouri), they moved onward to Nauvoo, where the divine commission was renewed: "And again, verily I say unto you, I command you again to build a house to my name, even in this place, that you may prove yourselves unto me that ye are faithful in all things whatsoever I command you, that I may bless you, and crown you with honor, immortality, and eternal life" (D&C 124:55). The chronology of how temple work unfolded in that city is of great interest:

DATE	EVENT
August 15, 1840	First mention is made by the Prophet Joseph Smith of baptism for the dead at the funeral for Seymour Brunson (see *Teachings of Presidents of the Church: Joseph Smith*, 403); first performance of the ordinance is done in the Mississippi River; others are performed in the ensuing weeks in the river or in nearby streams (see *Church History in the Fulness of Times*, 251).
Late 1840	Hyrum Smith is baptized for his deceased brother Alvin (see *Teachings of the Presidents of the Church: Joseph Smith*, 403).
January 19, 1841	D&C 124 is given, in which the Lord orders that baptisms for the dead can be performed only in the temple, except in times of poverty (see D&C 124:30).
October 3, 1841	As the basement of the Nauvoo Temple nears completion, Joseph Smith announces that no more baptisms for the dead could be performed until done in the Lord's house (see *HC* 4:426).
October 1841	Joseph Smith sends an epistle to those of the Twelve laboring in England, mentioning baptism for the dead (see *HC* 4:231).
November 8, 1841	The temporary baptismal font of the Nauvoo Temple (which was still under construction) is dedicated by Brigham Young with Joseph Smith in attendance (see *HC* 4:446).
November 21, 1841	First baptisms for the dead are performed in the font in the basement of the Nauvoo Temple (which was still under construction). (See *HC* 4:454.)

DATE	EVENT
May 4, 1842	Joseph Smith introduces the endowment ordinance for the living to a trusted few in the upper room of his red brick store in Nauvoo; over the next two years, he introduces the ordinance to some ninety other men and women (see *Church History in the Fulness of Times*, 254).
September 1, 1842	D&C 127 is provided in the form of an inspired epistle by the Prophet Joseph Smith concerning records to be kept at baptisms for the dead.
September 6, 1842	D&C 128 is provided in the form of a second inspired epistle by the Prophet Joseph Smith concerning the doctrine of baptism for the dead, "that they without us cannot be made perfect—neither can we without our dead be made perfect" (D&C 128:15).
June 27, 1844	Joseph Smith and Hyrum Smith are martyred.
December 1845	The Nauvoo Temple is completed enough to have the endowment ordinance for the living performed there (see *Church History in the Fulness of Times*, 254).
May 1, 1846	"The temple was dedicated publicly by Orson Hyde. In all, nearly 6,000 Latter-day Saints had received their temple ordinances in Nauvoo during the course of the previous winter" (William G. Hartley, "The Pioneer Trek: Nauvoo to Winter Quarters," *Ensign*, June 1997, 31).

For a brief but shining moment, the work in the house of the Lord was the consummation of the Saints' labor of love in obeying the voice of the Lord to build unto Him a house worthy of all acceptation. Following the exodus to the West beginning in 1847, the Saints continued the divine program for building, dedicating, and placing temples in service: St. George, 1877; Logan, 1884; Manti, 1888; Salt Lake City, 1898; Hawaii, 1919; Alberta, 1923; Mesa, 1927; Idaho Falls, 1945; Swiss, 1955; and on to the present day. On June 27, 2002, the rebuilt Nauvoo Temple was dedicated as a memorial to the mission of Joseph Smith, the Prophet of the Restoration. Temple building continues at a steady pace throughout the world, with the count to reach 150 in not too many years.

The courage and devotion of the Saints and their prophet-leaders in establishing temples in the wilderness of Deseret is a chronicle of unparalleled sacrifice and faith. There is no better theme for what transpired in the valleys of the Rocky Mountains after the exodus from Nauvoo and the arrival in the Salt Lake Valley on July 24, 1847, than what Nephi memorialized in his famous pronouncement: "I will go and do the things which the Lord hath commanded, for I know that the Lord giveth no commandments unto the children of men, save he shall prepare a way for them that they may accomplish the thing which he commandeth them" (1 Ne. 3:7).

You are part of this unfolding history of glory. How are you and your extended family contributing to the Church's "Book of Remembrance" as it applies to the house of the Lord?

Why Are Records and Personal Journals So Important?

The journals, diaries, and writings of our ancestors are a source of inspiration and guidance to our lives. Such records bring to our hearts understanding for the trials and tribulations of the past, inspire gratitude for the exemplary lives of our loved ones, and constitute a legacy of love for our own lives. We come to know and appreciate our forebears for what they valued and lived for. Nephi's family history in the Book of Mormon, together with the remembrances of succeeding prophet-historians, has brought the fullness of the gospel into our lives. Our individual journals and writings can be the source of saving souls we have yet to meet among our own posterity. Our personal record can bless their lives forever.

The operational foundation of temple work is an authorized record of all that transpires relative to the house of the Lord. From the foundation of the world it was decreed that the history of mankind—the deeds and works of all individuals—would be memorialized as a chronicle to guide the ultimate judgments of God (see Moses 6:5–8). John the Revelator saw clearly the importance of the content

of the records of posterity: "And I saw the dead, small and great, stand before God; and the books were opened: and another book was opened, which is the book of life: and the dead were judged out of those things which were written in the books, according to their works" (Rev. 20:12).

Through latter-day revelation, much additional light has been shed on the importance of record-keeping as a key priesthood practice in the kingdom of God: "And all they who are not found written in the book of remembrance shall find none inheritance in that day, but they shall be cut asunder, and their portion shall be appointed them among unbelievers, where are wailing and gnashing of teeth. These things I say not of myself; therefore, as the Lord speaketh, he will also fulfil. And they who are of the High Priesthood, whose names are not found written in the book of the law, or that are found to have apostatized, or to have been cut off from the church, as well as the lesser priesthood, or the members, in that day shall not find an inheritance among the saints of the Most High" (D&C 85:9–11).

Keeping a journal is part of the process of witnessing—of bearing our testimony about the worth and goodness of life and the blessings of our Heavenly Father. It is an exercise in blending together the generations and melding hearts into one. It is an expression of gratitude to the Lord. It is in many respects a prayer in written format. When Moroni completed his supplement to the sacred record of the Book of Mormon, he added a title page that currently appears as the preface. In his title page he lays down the principles that guided his work and can serve to guide our own journal writing: "Which is to show unto the remnant of the House of Israel what great things the Lord hath done for their fathers; and that they may know the covenants of the Lord, that they are not cast off forever—And also to the convincing of the Jew and Gentile that JESUS is the CHRIST, the ETERNAL GOD, manifesting himself unto all nations."

This criteria for recordkeeping is a reminder for us to let our own writings confirm the following: (1) the great things the Lord has done for us and our family in the past, (2) the priceless value and worth that our covenants have for us in the present, (3) the sustaining hope we have for the future, and (4) our belief that everything we do rests on the sure foundation of our own personal witness of the living reality of the Lord Jesus Christ and His redeeming Atonement. May we all improve in our keeping of personal and family records as a blessing to the present and future generations.

In what ways does your own personal journal provide the kind of permanent record suggested above? How can you use your journal as a means to record the inspiration and personal revelation that might come to you from time to time through the Holy Ghost? President Spencer W. Kimball counseled: "No one is commonplace, and I doubt if you can ever read a biography from which you cannot learn something from the difficulties overcome and the struggles made to succeed. These are the measuring rods for the progress of humanity. . . . What could you do better for your children and your children's children than to record the story of your life, your triumphs over adversity, your recovery after a fall, your progress when all seemed black, your rejoicing when you had finally achieved? . . . Get a notebook, . . . a journal that will last through all time, and maybe the angels may quote from it for eternity. Begin today and write in it your goings and comings, your deepest thoughts, your achievements and your failures, your associations and your triumphs, your impressions and your testimonies" ("The Angels May Quote from It," New Era, October 1975, 4–5).

How Can We Utilize Modern Technology to Enhance Family History Research?

The Church is at the forefront of family history recordkeeping and record access. Most wards and stakes have family history consultants who can be of help to those researching genealogical sources for data needed in vicarious temple work. The Church website, familysearch.org, is an important resource in this regard.

Real-life Stories for Heart and Mind

"**Angels on Earth.**" The expression "angels on earth" is an apt reminder that brothers and sisters, mothers and fathers, extended family members, and caring friends and associates are continually involved in a "labour of love" (Heb. 6:10)—sometimes manifest, but often invisible,

to support, encourage, sustain, heal, and guide in ways that promote our well-being and happiness, particularly in regard to temple work and family history. One good "angel on earth" was revered by members of her extended family circle as the dependable source of family history materials that enlarged their understanding of the roots from which their branch of Israel had sprung.

On one occasion many years ago she related to her loved ones a story about a special kind of "angel on earth" who played an important role in opening up one of the genealogical channels that had long remained hidden. The family organization had retained a professional genealogist and sent her to Wales to see if a particular parish might not hold the key for a breakthrough in research. Since the local curators of the records were rather particular about protocol, she had prepared the way by writing ahead concerning a particular volume of records she needed to see, knowing that she would be permitted to see only that which she had ordered ahead of time. On the appointed day, she was ushered into the reading room, and the priceless volume was placed before her. However, when she examined it, she noted, much to her disappointment, that it was not the volume she had requested, but another one.

As she thought about traveling so far without the opportunity to see the precious records, she looked around and caught the eye of an older gentleman seated in a corner of the same room. He was smiling pleasantly at her—and his countenance seemed somehow to be familiar to her. Then for an instant she looked back at the volume before her and noted from its index that though it was not the requested volume, it was precisely the one that contained the needed information. Overjoyed, she looked back toward the older gentleman, but he had disappeared. She smiled, remembering who he was—a venerated member of the family organization who had labored long to further the cause of family history and temple work—until he had died several years earlier. "Have miracles ceased?" asks Mormon. "Behold, I say unto you, Nay; neither have angels ceased to minister unto the children of men" (Moro. 7:29). And the Psalmist declared: "For he shall give his angels charge over thee, to keep thee in all thy ways" (Ps. 91:11).

What experiences have you had with temple service and family history work have that confirmed for you that you are not alone, and that this is truly the work of the Lord?

"Messengers of the Lord." Melvin J. Ballard, a member of the Quorum of the Twelve Apostles, recorded the following story:

I recall an incident in my own father's experience. How we looked forward to the completion of the Logan Temple! It was about to be dedicated. My father had labored on that house from its very beginning, and my earliest recollection was carrying his dinner each day as he brought the rock down from the quarry. How we looked forward to that great event! I remember how in the meantime father made every effort to obtain all the data and information he could concerning his relatives. It was the theme of his prayer night and morning that the Lord would open up the way whereby he could get information concerning his dead.

The day before the dedication while writing recommends to the members of his ward who were to be present at the first service, two elderly gentlemen walked down the streets of Logan, approached my two young sisters, and, coming to the older one of the two placed in her hands a newspaper and said:

"Take this to your father. Give it to no one else. Go quickly with it. Don't lose it."

The child responded and when she met her mother, her mother wanted the paper. The child said, "No. I must give it to father and to no one else."

She was admitted into the room and told her story. We looked in vain for these travelers. They were not to be seen. No one else saw them. Then we turned to the paper. The newspaper, *The Newbury Weekly News,* was printed in my father's old English home, Thursday, May 15th, 1884, and reached our hands May 18, 1884, three days after its publication. We were astonished, for by no earthly means could it have reached us, so that our curiosity increased as we examined it. Then we discovered one page devoted to the writings of a reporter of the paper,

who had gone on his vacation, and among other places had visited an old cemetery. The curious inscriptions led him to write what he found on the tombstones, including the verses. He also added the names, date of birth, death, etc., filling nearly an entire page.

It was the old cemetery where the Ballard family had been buried for generations, and very many of my father's immediate relatives and other intimate friends were mentioned.

When the matter was presented to President Merrill of the Logan Temple he said, "You are authorized to do the work for those, because you received it through messengers of the Lord" (*Three Degrees of Glory* [Salt Lake City: Magazine Printing Co., 1922].

It is instructive that Elder Ballard's father had prayed "night and morning that the Lord would open up the way whereby he could get information concerning his dead." How have your prayers on behalf of temple work opened up avenues of success through the workings of the Spirit? How can your prayers in the presence of family members strengthen their faith and resolve to be of service to their Father in Heaven?

Mountains May Come and Go. Edward J. Wood, the first president of the Cardston Alberta Temple, was a leader of legendary vision and spirituality during his many years of service in the house of the Lord. One priesthood leader told the following story about President Wood:

On one occasion I was in the Cardston Alberta Temple with my wife. She noticed in one of the corridors a painting of Chief Mountain, a nearby famous landmark in Southern Alberta and Northern Montana. At the same time, she noticed that this craggy granite mountain peak is plainly visible through one of the temple windows. President Wood happened to be passing by at the time and she asked him, "Why would we have a painting of Chief Mountain hanging here in the temple when we can look through the window and see the actual mountain?" Without hesitation, President Wood responded, "Because this temple is going to be here longer than that mountain, and we want to remember what it looked like." His point, taken in the spirit of faith and hope, is that the temple is our most apparent evidence of the eternity of lives and the grand bonding that takes place among faithful families—present, past, and future—by virtue of the sealing powers of the priesthood of God. Families under the new and everlasting covenant of eternal marriage are intended to endure forever, far beyond the frontiers of mortality.

What are your thoughts about the everlasting nature of temple work and the enduring blessings of the sealing covenants? Mountains may come and go, but the children of God and their covenant relationships are to be secured through sanctification and sealing keys and made to last forever. The scriptures concerning the Second Coming make clear the dramatic transformation that will take place: "And he shall utter his voice out of Zion, and he shall speak from Jerusalem, and his voice shall be heard among all people; And it shall be a voice as the voice of many waters, and as the voice of a great thunder, which shall break down the mountains, and the valleys shall not be found" (D&C 133:21–22). Safety derives from righteous compliance with the commandments of God; security flows from temple covenants and ordinances; refuge is found in holy places of Zion (homes, stakes, and temples) where the Spirit of the Lord can guide and direct the affairs of men, women, and children bought with the sacred blood of the Redeemer and characterized by broken hearts and contrite spirits.

Pondering Prayerfully

Additional scriptures to consider and ponder:
- John 17:17–19
- 1 Cor. 1:2
- 1 Ne. 1:1
- 2 Ne. 9:41

- 2 Ne. 25:23
- Moro. 7:1
- D&C 43:9
- D&C 43:16
- D&C 124:39
- D&C 128:23
- D&C 133:62
- D&C 137:1–3

The following hymns contribute to our gratitude for the temple:
- "Holy Temples on Mount Zion" (*Hymns*, 289)
- "O Ye Mountains High" (*Hymns*, 34)
- "The Spirit of God" (*Hymns*, 2)

Remember and Be Sure

Among all the doctrines and practices that distinguish The Church of Jesus Christ of Latter-day Saints from all other churches of the world, perhaps the most unique and compelling is the vast, encompassing work of the temples of God. Temple work is the evidence that God has extended to every individual who has ever lived upon the earth, and who will ever be born into this mortal experience, the blessings and opportunities of salvation, immortality, and eternal life. The Lord's holy house is a place of peace, safety, and love. It is a place where the Spirit resides. It is a place of instruction in the ways of the Lord. It is a place of sacred covenants that open the gateway to the presence of the Father and the Son in the everlasting eternities.

The temples of God are truly buildings of light and radiance. They are the architectural reminders that we, too, are temples of the Most High and places for the Spirit to abide. "Know ye not that ye are the temple of God, and that the Spirit of God dwelleth in you. If any man defile the temple of God, him shall God destroy; for the temple of God is holy, which temple ye are" (1 Cor. 3:16–17).

Each of us is the architect of his or her own life, and each has the opportunity to build that life and unfold it with a vision of the finished edifice being in the likeness of the Master Architect of our salvation, even the Lord Jesus Christ (see Heb. 5:8–9). We plan, we prepare, we work, and we gather into our house all the elements of vitality and growth. We dedicate ourselves to the glory and honor of God, and we invite the Spirit to visit often to give comfort and truth and peace to our life, just as in a temple of God. And when the final chapter of our life draws to a close, it will reflect the spirit of honor and righteousness to the same degree we are able to align it with the motto on the walls of God's temples: "Holiness to the Lord."

The importance of building temples and partaking of the life-saving and exalting ordinances is evident as the prophets and the Saints of the past sought with such vigor and determination to build temples. Living prophets in our day have escalated the effort. Now it is up to us to be worthy as well as diligent in moving forth the work of the Lord to advance the work of the temples. There is no greater work than helping people come unto Christ. This is our work and our glory: to help Heavenly Father in bringing to pass His eternal plan of happiness—the immortality and eternal life of His children. Family history and temple work is the culmination of His plan, because it perfects the family and prepares us for our future roles in the worlds to come. Let us all take the time to make family history and temple work the central focus of our lives, for as the Lord has said: "This is eternal lives—to know the only wise and true God, and Jesus Christ, whom he hath sent. I am he. Receive ye, therefore, my law" (D&C 132:24).

CHAPTER 41
After Death: The Spirit World

When the breath leaves the body, your life has not become extinct; your life is still in existence. And when you are in the spirit world, everything there will appear as natural as things now do. Spirits will be familiar with spirits in the spirit world—will converse, behold, and exercise every variety of communication with one another as familiarly and naturally as while here in tabernacles. There, as here, all things will be natural, and you will understand them as you now understand natural things. —Brigham Young (*Discourses of Brigham Young*, 380)

Opening the Window of Wisdom

The great plan of happiness encompasses all stages of life: premortal, mortal, and postmortal. It is all part of the Lord's universal design for His children: "For he is the same yesterday, to-day, and forever; and the way is prepared for all men from the foundation of the world, if it so be that they repent and come unto him. For he that diligently seeketh shall find; and the mysteries of God shall be unfolded unto them, by the power of the Holy Ghost, as well in these times as in times of old, and as well in times of old as in times to come; wherefore, the course of the Lord is one eternal round" (1 Ne. 10:18–19). We learn in the scriptures that "Adam fell that men might be; and men

are, that they might have joy" (2 Ne. 2:25). We also learn the indispensable nature and role of the Atonement for empowering the plan for achieving that joy: "And now, the plan of mercy could not be brought about except an atonement should be made; therefore God himself atoneth for the sins of the world, to bring about the plan of mercy, to appease the demands of justice, that God might be a perfect, just God, and a merciful God also" (Alma 42:15). Through modern-day revelation we have marvelous confirmation of these truths in ways that inspire the mind and strengthen our resolve to prepare for our introduction into the spirit world following our mortal experience. In this dispensation, God has again spoken with power and forcefulness of His plan of salvation and redemption—and the urgent need to conform to His will with thanksgiving and devotion in keeping His commandments.

Meanwhile, life is full of situations that we may not fully understand. One of the most trying is death. In our finite mortal minds, death is difficult and seemingly final. The sorrow is deep when we lose loved ones and suffer the interruption of relationships. But all who come to earth must die, for it is part of the plan (see 2 Ne. 9:6). Temporal death is a temporary separation of the body and spirit, for the spirit never dies. Through the power of the Resurrection, the spirit and the body are inseparably reunited in preparation for a final judgment and consignment to a place in the mansions of the Father's house (see John 14:2; D&C 98:18). Every soul will need to render an accounting before God for every desire, thought, and deed pertaining to the mortal experience. Given that knowledge, we should seek to live life to its fullest by keeping the commandments and preparing to meet God.

"Where will we go after death?" is a question that either haunts the mind or fills the heart with sweet anticipation and hopeful yearning. Every individual ponders the question and seeks a satisfying answer. In the worldly philosophies of man there is no answer. It is only through the gospel of Jesus Christ that we know enough to view our destiny in the coming state. And what a panorama of forward-reaching truth is unfolded to us through the scriptures and the words of the living prophets! Consider, for example, "But as it is written, Eye hath not seen, nor ear heard, neither have entered into the heart of man, the things which God hath prepared for them that love him. But God hath revealed them unto us by his Spirit: for the Spirit searcheth all things, yea, the deep things of God. For what man knoweth the things of a man, save the spirit of man which is in him? even so the things of God knoweth no man, but the Spirit of God" (1 Cor. 2:9–11).

It is through the Spirit that we begin to have an inkling of the pathway beyond this sphere of existence. For example, we learn from Alma's counsel to his son Corianton much about the destination of mortals following death (see Alma 40:11–14), and we can learn from the vision of the spirit world, received by President Joseph F. Smith in 1918, a fuller measure of truth concerning the divine order of things in that realm as established by the visit of Jesus Christ. What emerges is a panoramic view of the postmortal spirit world that confirms the love and mercy of our Father in Heaven, operating through the Atonement of the Redeemer. Every son and daughter of God will have a chance to embrace the gospel to its fullest and come forth, based on righteous choices, into a post-resurrection state that will for most provide glories of unimaginable scope and measure—all in keeping with the level of obedience demonstrated during the probationary stages of existence.

Inspired by Latter-Day Prophets

Brigham Young: Where is the spirit world? It is right here. Do the good and evil spirits go together? Yes, they do. Do they both inhabit one kingdom? Yes, they do. Do they go to the sun? No. Do they go beyond the boundaries of the organized earth? No, they do not. They are brought forth upon this earth, for the express purpose of inhabiting it to all eternity. . . . Can you see it with your natural eyes? No. Can you see spirits in this room? No. Suppose the Lord should touch your eyes that you might see, could you then see the spirits? Yes, as plainly as you now see bodies, as did the servant of Elijah. If the Lord would permit it, and it was his will that it should be done, you could see the spirits that have departed from this world, as plainly as you now see bodies with your natural eyes (*Discourses of Brigham Young*, 376).

*The spirit world is here—all around us. We cannot see the inhabitants of the spirit world with our mortal eyes, but the just spirits among them have awareness of our lives, as the Prophet Joseph Smith taught: "The spirits of the just are exalted to a greater and more glorious work; hence they are blessed in their departure to the world of spirits. Enveloped in flaming fire, they are not far from us, and know and understand our thoughts, feelings, and motions, and are often pained therewith" (*Teachings of the Prophet Joseph Smith*, 326). How does the near proximity of the world of the spirits, and the knowledge that the more exalted of the spirits know of our thoughts and dealings, increase your motivation to do well in obeying the covenants and encourage your loved ones to do the same?*

Joseph Fielding Smith: We all lived in the presence of God before we came here. When we die, our spirits will still exist, and in that spirit world the wicked will suffer torment for their sins (*Answers to Gospel Questions*, 3:132).

We are created as eternal beings, passing through the several states of existence in preparation for the promised blessings of everlasting lives. Our spirits came from the presence of God to receive mortal tabernacles here; they return to the spirit world when we die; and they will be raised to a state of immortality through the grace and gift of the Resurrection inaugurated by the risen Lord. The righteous escape suffering and torment in the post-spirit world and beyond. How have you been able to encourage the coming generation to live the gospel of faith and repentance in order to savor the liberating spirit of forgiveness and prepare themselves to go to the spirit world free from sin? (For ideas see Alma's masterful discourse to Corianton concering the principle of restoration, see Alma 40–42.)

Spencer W. Kimball: If we look at mortality as a complete existence, then pain, sorrow, failure, and short life could be a calamity. But if we look upon life as an eternal thing stretching far into the pre-earth past and on into the eternal post-death future, then all happenings may be put in proper perspective. Is there not wisdom in his giving us trials that we might rise above them, responsibilities that we might achieve, work to harden our muscles, sorrows to try our souls? Are we not permitted temptations to test our strength, sickness that we might learn patience, death that we might be immortalized and glorified? . . . If mortality be the perfect state, then death would be a frustration, but the gospel teaches us there is no tragedy in death, but only in sin (*The Teachings of Spencer W. Kimball,* 38–39).

We anguish when loved ones depart—particularly when their departure comes without warning. But the gospel gives hope and comfort. The Apostle Paul declared: "O death, where is thy sting? O grave, where is thy victory? The sting of death is sin; and the strength of sin is the law" (1 Cor. 15:55–56). Death itself has no sting because the resurrection of all mortals will triumph over death. The only sting that remains is the effects of sins not repented of, not taken care of through obedience to the saving principles and ordinance of the gospel of Jesus Christ. We can do all in our power to prepare ourselves for a pure departure from this life, so that our loved ones are freed of both kinds of "sting" on our behalf through the blessings of the Atonement. How can you help your family members, young and old alike, prepare worthily for the end to their mortal probation and the transition to the spirit realm of paradise?

Ezra Taft Benson: There were two grand divisions in the world of spirits. Spirits of the righteous (the just) had gone to paradise, a state of happiness, peace, and restful work. The spirits of the wicked (the unjust) had gone to prison, a state of darkness and misery. (See Alma 40: 12–15.) Jesus went only to the righteous—to paradise (*The Teachings of Ezra Taft Benson,* 37).

The spirit world comprises two states: one of light, by nature a paradise reserved for the righteous, and another of darkness reserved for the wicked (see D&C 138:22). In a sense, both realms represent a "prison," for after they have left their mortal state all spirits look upon the separation from their bodies "to be a bondage" (D&C 45:17). However, the wicked in the world of spirits were in a deeper sense imprisoned, for they were not able to receive the presence and teachings of the Savior during His visit to the righteous in the spirit world between the time of His Crucifixion and the time of His Resurrection (see D&C 138:20–21). Instead, the Savior commissioned righteous spirits to present the gospel plan to the wicked so that those who would repent and reform themselves might be freed from their confinement (see D&C 138:31).

God, in His mercy and love, extends to all individuals in the spirit world the blessings of the gospel of Jesus Christ, even to those who are in the spirit "prison" of darkness and remorse. How does this knowledge instill within you the desire to be an instrument in the hands of God—now as well as later in the spirit world—to share the joy and light of the gospel to those who await deliverance and peace?

Truths to Liken

1 Pet. 3:18–20; 4:6—"For Christ also hath once suffered for sins, the just for the unjust, that he might bring us to God, being put to death in the flesh, but quickened by the Spirit: By which also he went and preached unto the spirits in prison; Which sometime were disobedient, when once the longsuffering of God waited in the days of Noah, while the ark was a preparing, wherein few, that is, eight souls were saved by water. . . . For for this cause was the gospel preached also to them that are dead, that they might be judged according to men in the flesh, but live according to God in the spirit."

- These words of Peter confirm the Savior's ministry in the spirit world to provide all individuals with the opportunity to embrace the principles of the gospel of faith, repentance, and (through the coming work of the temples) vicarious ordinances for redemption. Concerning these words from Peter, President Joseph F. Smith said: "As I pondered over these things which are written, the eyes of my understanding were opened, and the Spirit of the Lord rested upon me, and I saw the hosts of the dead, both small and great" (D&C 138:11). After that, he received the vision of the spirit world recorded in Section 138 of the Doctrine and Covenants.
- How has the knowledge of this program served to strengthen your testimony of the mission of the Savior and the perfection of both the Father and the Son?

Alma 40:11–14—"Now, concerning the state of the soul between death and the resurrection—Behold, it has been made known unto me by an angel, that the spirits of all men, as soon as they are departed from this mortal body, yea, the spirits of all men, whether they be good or evil, are taken home to that God who gave them life. And then shall it come to pass, that the spirits of those who are righteous are received into a state of happiness, which is called paradise, a state of rest, a state of peace, where they shall rest from all their troubles and from all care, and sorrow. And then shall it come to pass, that the spirits of the wicked, yea, who are evil—for behold, they have no part nor portion of the Spirit of the Lord; for behold, they chose evil works rather than good; therefore the spirit of the devil did enter into them, and take possession of their house—and these shall be cast out into outer darkness; there shall be weeping, and wailing, and gnashing of teeth, and this because of their own iniquity, being led captive by the will of the devil. Now this is the state of the souls of the wicked, yea, in darkness, and a state of awful, fearful looking for the fiery indignation of the wrath of God upon them; thus they remain in this state, as

well as the righteous in paradise, until the time of their resurrection."

- Alma was counseling his son Corianton, who was troubled about the doctrine of the resurrection. In a kindly way, Alma set the stage for a discussion of the resurrection by giving his son the broad picture of the stages of man's existence, including the world of the spirits to which all mortals go following death. The world of spirits is separated into two states of existence—one for the righteous, who enjoy happiness, rest, and peace, and one for the wicked, who experience outer darkness, weeping, wailing, gnashing of teeth, captivity, and fear. Clearly Alma, as a loving father, was guiding his wayward son into a realization that his behavior was aligning him with the captive spirits in outer darkness and fear.
- Heavenly Father wants to give us enough understanding about the coming stages of our existence that we can make wise choices in our lives. When mortals die, they "are taken home to that God who gave them life" (Alma 40:11), meaning they are brought under the direct jurisdiction of the Almighty, although not yet into His presence (see Joseph Fielding Smith, *Answers to Gospel Questions,* 2:86). We do not know all details about the spirit world, but we do know that a form of preliminary judgment occurs when the spirits arriving there are placed either in association with the righteous in paradise or with the wicked in the realm of darkness and remorse.

How does this understanding help you choose the right and look forward to a relationship with the righteous in the coming world of spirits? How can you guide your loved ones to choose the right by pondering and understanding the principle of accountability and the consequences of one's actions?

Alma 41:10, 13–15—"Do not suppose, because it has been spoken concerning restoration, that ye shall be restored from sin to happiness. Behold, I say unto you, wickedness never was happiness. . . . the meaning of the word restoration is to bring back again evil for evil, or carnal for carnal, or devilish for devilish—good for that which is good; righteous for that which is righteous; just for that which is just; merciful for that which is merciful. Therefore, my son, see that you are merciful unto your brethren; deal justly, judge righteously, and do good continually; and if ye do all these things then shall ye receive your reward; yea, ye shall have mercy restored unto you again; ye shall have justice restored unto you again; ye shall have a righteous judgment restored unto you again; and ye shall have good rewarded unto you again. For that which ye do send out shall return unto you again, and be restored; therefore, the word restoration more fully condemneth the sinner, and justifieth him not at all."

- Alma continued to advise his son Corianton about the principle of restoration: we take into the spirit world the same disposition and character we have cultivated in this life. We are therefore advised to establish a pattern of living consistent with the qualities of the Savior, for we are to be even as He is (see 3 Ne. 27:27). There will be no miraculous transformation from wickedness to righteousness after we cross the threshold into the spirit realm. We will arrive there just as we left here. As it turned out, Corianton heeded the warnings and counsel of his father and reformed his life, returning to his missionary assignment with honor (see Alma 49:30).
- There is no such thing as deathbed repentance; what we send out is what we get back. Noted scholar Joseph McConkie, son of Elder Bruce R. McConkie, regularly included in his lessons and lectures a comment that the doctrine of restoration might well be designated the doctrine of "same ole/ same ole." This always brought a smile to the listeners, but they understood the truth of the matter—that we are what we are by choice. We can choose to set aside the imperfect state of "same ole" and replace it with something new and better according to the gospel of Jesus Christ. What are your thoughts about

the doctrine of restoration and how it determines which state of being we will be assigned to in the spirit world—one of light and peace, or one of darkness and remorse?

D&C 131:7—"There is no such thing as immaterial matter. All spirit is matter, but it is more fine or pure, and can only be discerned by purer eyes."

- This statement was among a series of instructions the Prophet Joseph Smith gave to associates in Ramus, Illinois (east of Nauvoo), on May 16–17, 1843 (see *HC* 5:392–393). The Prophet gave this clarification: "Difference Between Body and Spirit. In tracing the thing to the foundation, and looking at it philosophically, we shall find a very material difference between the body and the spirit; the body is supposed to be organized matter, and the spirit, by many, is thought to be immaterial, without substance. With this latter statement we should beg leave to differ, and state the spirit is a substance; that it is material, but that it is more pure, elastic and refined matter than the body; that it existed before the body, can exist in the body; and will exist separate from the body, when the body will be mouldering in the dust; and will in the resurrection, be again united with it" (*Teachings of the Prophet Joseph Smith*, 207).
- What are your thoughts concerning the nature of spirit? As you ponder, review the miraculous account of the brother of Jared and how his mighty faith enabled him to view the spirit body of Jesus Christ (see Ether 3).

D&C 138:18–19—"While this vast multitude waited and conversed, rejoicing in the hour of their deliverance from the chains of death, the Son of God appeared, declaring liberty to the captives who had been faithful; And there he preached to them the everlasting gospel, the doctrine of the resurrection and the redemption of mankind from the fall, and from individual sins on conditions of repentance."

- This statement from the vision of the spirit world received by President Joseph F. Smith describes the appearance of the Savior—as a spirit Being prior to His Resurrection—among those in paradise who were still "captives" in the sense that they were awaiting the resurrection and the deliverance from their bodiless state. We can only imagine the transcendent joy of those He visited, for He represented the key of redemption and freedom soon to bless their lives.

- Through a modern-day prophet, the Lord has blessed us with precious additional light and understanding about the plan of salvation and how it applies to those departed hosts who wait upon Him in the spirit realm. The blessings of a righteous life allow us the privilege of being with the righteous in the spirit world and enjoying the peace, light, and joy that abounds there as a result of the plan of happiness. How does this truth increase your hope and faith in the justice and mercy and grace of the Lord? How can you help others come to this understanding?

Rejoicing and Reasoning Together

How Is the Work of Redemption Organized in the Spirit World?

The 1918 vision of President Joseph F. Smith concerning the world of the spirits recounted the visit there of the Lord Jesus Christ, just prior to His Resurrection, to organize and empower the forces of good for spreading the gospel message within that realm. The righteous received Him with humble gratitude: "And the saints rejoiced in their redemption, and bowed the knee and acknowledged the Son of God as their Redeemer and Deliverer from death and the chains of hell. Their countenances shone, and the radiance from the presence of the Lord rested upon them, and they sang praises unto his holy name" (D&C 138:23–24). The Lord did not go among the wicked who had rejected the truth, but sent His message to them through a host of the righteous commissioned to act in His name: "from among the righteous, he organized his forces and appointed messengers, clothed with

power and authority, and commissioned them to go forth and carry the light of the gospel to them that were in darkness, even to all the spirits of men; and thus was the gospel preached to the dead. And the chosen messengers went forth to declare the acceptable day of the Lord and proclaim liberty to the captives who were bound, even unto all who would repent of their sins and receive the gospel" (D&C 138:30–31).

This was a supreme milestone in the history of mankind on behalf of those in the spirit world who "had died in their sins, without a knowledge of the truth, or in transgression, having rejected the prophets" (D&C 138:32). The Savior, in effect, bridged the "great gulf" between the wicked and the righteous that had existed in the realm of the spirits up until that time. What were the prisoners taught when the righteous were dispatched to reach them by crossing over the bridge of truth? "These were taught faith in God, repentance from sin, vicarious baptism for the remission of sins, the gift of the Holy Ghost by the laying on of hands, And all other principles of the gospel that were necessary for them to know in order to qualify themselves that they might be judged according to men in the flesh, but live according to God in the spirit" (D&C 138:33–34).

The spreading of the gospel of deliverance in the world of the spirits was a universal campaign—for all residents of that realm:

And so it was made known among the dead, both small and great, the unrighteous as well as the faithful, that redemption had been wrought through the sacrifice of the Son of God upon the cross.

Thus was it made known that our Redeemer spent his time during his sojourn in the world of spirits, instructing and preparing the faithful spirits of the prophets who had testified of him in the flesh;

That they might carry the message of redemption unto all the dead, unto whom he could not go personally, because of their rebellion and transgression, that they through the ministration of his servants might also hear his words. (D&C 138:35–37)

President Smith beheld the vast throng of leaders inducted into the program of missionary work in the spirit realm, including Adam, Eve and many of her faithful descendant daughters, Abel, Seth, Noah, Shem, Abraham, Isaac, Jacob, Moses, Isaiah, Ezekiel, Daniel, Elias, Malachi, Elijah, the prophets who dwelt among the Nephites, the Prophet Joseph Smith, Hyrum Smith, Brigham Young, John Taylor, Wilford Woodruff, and "other choice spirits who were reserved to come forth in the fulness of times to take part in laying the foundations of the great latter-day work" (D&C 138:53). President Smith beheld that these same figures were appointed to their offices in the premortal realm, and "Even before they were born, they, with many others, received their first lessons in the world of spirits and were prepared to come forth in the due time of the Lord to labor in his vineyard for the salvation of the souls of men" (D&C 138:56). Moreover, he observed that Saints in this dispensation will carry on the work of redemption when they reach the spirit world:

I beheld that the faithful elders of this dispensation, when they depart from mortal life, continue their labors in the preaching of the gospel of repentance and redemption, through the sacrifice of the Only Begotten Son of God, among those who are in darkness and under the bondage of sin in the great world of the spirits of the dead.

The dead who repent will be redeemed, through obedience to the ordinances of the house of God,

And after they have paid the penalty of their transgressions, and are washed clean, shall receive a reward according to their works, for they are heirs of salvation. (D&C 138:57–59)

There is more truth and detail about the work of redemption in the world of spirits in this revelation (D&C 138) than in any other segment of scripture. We can be forever grateful to the Lord for making these glorious truths known; they inspire us with an awareness of the universal reach of the plan of happiness and a confirmation of the limitless grace and mercy of God on behalf of His children. Brigham Young taught: "Compare those inhabitants on the earth who have heard the Gospel in our day, with

the millions who have never heard it, or had the keys of salvation presented to them, and you will conclude at once as I do, that there is an almighty work to perform in the spirit world. . . . Every faithful man's labor will continue as long as the labor of Jesus, until all things are redeemed that can be redeemed, and presented to the Father. There is a great work before us" (Discourses of Brigham Young, *377–378). How does the knowledge of the ongoing work in the spirit world confirm your testimony of the greatness and omniscience of the Almighty, who is full of grace and truth? How does this shed new light on the universal scope of the doctrines and principles in the Church manual* Preach My Gospel *(2004), which, in truth, prepares us for our work in the next phase of existence, as well as in mortality?*

Real-life Stories for Heart and Mind

"**A**re You in Trouble?" President Hugh B. Brown shared this story of a woman's unfailing belief in the truth of the spirit world and the reunion of loved ones there:

I should like to introduce a story coming out of the first world war. I had a companion, a fellow officer, who was a very rich man, highly educated. He was a lawyer, had great power, was self-sufficient, and he said to me as we often talked of religion (because he knew who I was), "There is nothing in life that I would like to have that I cannot buy with my money."

Shortly thereafter he and I with two other officers were assigned to go to the city of Arras, France, which was under siege. It had been evacuated, and upon arrival there we thought there was no one in the city. We noted that the fire of the enemy was concentrated on the cathedral. We made our way to that cathedral and went in. There we found a little woman kneeling at an altar. We paused, respecting her devotion. Then shortly she arose, wrapped her little shawl around her frail shoulders, and came tottering down the aisle. The man among us who could speak better French said, "Are you in trouble?"

She straightened her shoulders, pulled in her chin, and said, "No, I'm not in trouble. I was in trouble when I came here, but I've left it there at the altar."

"And what was your trouble?"

She said, "I received word this morning that my fifth son has given his life for France. Their father went first, and then one by one all of them have gone. But," straightening again, "I have no trouble; I've left it there because I believe in the immortality of the soul. I believe that men will live after death. I know that I shall meet my loved ones again."

When the little soul went out, there were tears in the eyes of the men who were there, and the one who had said to me that he could purchase anything with money turned to me and said, "You and I have seen men in battle display courage and valor that is admirable, but in all my life I have never seen anything to compare with the faith, the fortitude and the courage of that little woman."

Then he said, "I would give all the money I have if I could have something of what she has." (*CR,* October 1969, 106–107)

The king of the Lamanites—a very rich man indeed—said in his prayer to God after Aaron had taught him the truths of the gospel: "O God, Aaron hath told me that there is a God; and if there is a God, and if thou art God, wilt thou make thyself known unto me, and I will give away all my sins to know thee, and that I may be raised from the dead, and be saved at the last day" (Alma 22:18). Such was the right attitude—the same attitude that President Brown's colleague was starting to understand. How can you help others not of our faith, or those of our faith who need a strengthening of their testimony, to appreciate the plan of salvation, prepare to go to the spirit world in worthiness, and continue the work of love and service on behalf of God's children?

Pondering Prayerfully

Additional scriptures to consider and ponder:
- Ps. 142:7
- Ps. 146:7–9
- Luke 23:42–43
- John 11:25–26
- 1 Cor. 15:22
- Alma 12:24
- D&C 76:22–24
- D&C 76:73

The following hymns inspire appreciation for the work of redemption in the spirit world:
- "God Loved Us, So He Sent His Son" (*Hymns,* 187)
- "I Stand All Amazed" (*Hymns,* 193)
- "Ye Elders of Israel" (*Hymns,* 319)

Remember and Be Sure

There is a great work going on in the spirit world at this very moment. It has been unfolding since the gateway was opened by the Savior as part of His atoning mission, established from before the foundation of the world, "To open the blind eyes, to bring out the prisoners from the prison, and them that sit in darkness out of the prison house" (Isa. 42:7). As the Prophet Joseph Smith exclaimed in gratitude to the Almighty for the revelation of doctrines and ordinances pertaining to the vicarious temple work for the dead: "Brethren, shall we not go on in so great a cause? Go forward and not backward. Courage, brethren; and on, on to the victory! Let your hearts rejoice, and be exceedingly glad. Let the earth break forth into singing. Let the dead speak forth anthems of eternal praise to the King Immanuel, who hath ordained, before the world was, that which would enable us to redeem them out of their prison; for the prisoners shall go free" (D&C 128:22).

Every son and daughter of God will have the opportunity to hear the good news of the gospel and respond, using divinely appointed agency, either unto eternal life and exaltation, or unto a lesser level of glory and sanctity. The Savior "glorifies the Father, and saves all the works of his hands, except those sons of perdition who deny the Son after the Father has revealed him" (D&C 76:43).

God is just and merciful, being "no respecter of persons" (Acts 10:34): "Behold, he sendeth an invitation unto all men, for the arms of mercy are extended towards them, and he saith: Repent, and I will receive you" (Alma 5:33). That invitation resounds through the valleys of mortality as well as the halls of the spirit world until the last tenant has crossed the frontier of the resurrection into immortality and the work is done. We sing praises to the Father and the Son for the magnificent plan of salvation, for unfolding the mystery of the pathway of existence from stage to stage in enough detail of pure knowledge to ensure the exaltation of the faithful and the pure in glory and eternal rest.

CHAPTER 42
The Gathering: Fulfillment of Prophecy and Covenant

You and I live in a day in which the Lord our God has set His hand for the last time, to gather out the righteous and to prepare a people to reign on this earth,—a people who will be purified by good works, who will abide the faith of the living God and be ready to meet the Bridegroom when He comes to reign over the earth, even Jesus Christ . . . and be prepared for that glorious event—the coming of the Son of Man—which I believe will not be at any great distant day. —Joseph F. Smith (*Millennial Star* 36:220)

Opening the Window of Wisdom

The tenth Article of Faith states: "We believe in the literal gathering of Israel and in the restoration of the Ten Tribes; that Zion (the New Jerusalem) will be built upon the American continent; that Christ will reign personally upon the earth; and, that the earth will be renewed and receive its paradisiacal glory." According to the dynamics of the grand covenant design, the Lord scatters and gathers His people for the ultimate blessing of mankind. The scattering process may serve to *protect* (as when Lehi's family was guided away from Jerusalem in the wake of torment and abuse), *correct* (because of iniquity or wickedness, as in the scattering of the ten tribes by the Assyrians or the dispersal of the Jewish people by the Babylonians), or *connect* (as with the modern-day dispatching of missionaries throughout the world to spread the gospel message among the honest at heart). The gathering process is much the same: to *protect* the Saints by bringing them to holy places of refuge within the stakes of Zion where houses of the Lord abound (both sacred temples as well as chapels and righteous homes), to *correct* the Saints in a continual way through inspired instruction by the prophets of God to the assembled congregations of Zion, and to *connect* the Saints one with another and with the Holy Spirit through the unifying and purifying process of daily gospel living.

The Lord has a divine strategy for preserving the temporal and spiritual well-being of His children through the process of scattering and gathering, while allowing them to exercise their innate and God-given moral agency. That strategy is anchored in the *Word*—who is the Only Begotten.

The message of the gospel of Jesus Christ has been taught by holy prophets throughout all the dispensations of time. The central core of the message is repentance based on faith, covenanted through baptism, confirmed through the gift of the Holy Ghost, and proven by a willingness to endure to the end. The invitation of the Lord to all peoples is to come unto Him and gather in places of protection and security, united through gospel bonds. Places of refuge are established to receive the obedient, including lands of promise ordained for the abode of the righteous, stakes and homes of Zion in which the faithful can congregate for counsel and protection, and sacred temples where ordinances of exaltation are provided. When the "children of the covenant" (3 Ne. 20:26) obey and follow the will of the Lord, wherever it might take them, they are blessed with safety under His protecting hand. When they rebel and take counsel from their pride, the Lord at times scatters them for correction and to dispel their prideful ambitions.

Through prayer, study, and obedience, we can begin to discern the hand of the Lord in our lives as He works His miraculous design for our eternal blessing and good. The object is for us to be found worthy to bear the name of His Son, Jesus Christ, in whose name alone we can ultimately be gathered home, in company of our loved ones, forever secure in the rest of the Lord.

One of the Savior's choice images for the blessings of the Atonement is the reference to a hen desiring to gather her chicks under her wings (see Matt. 23:37). This image is often used in the scriptures to convey the Lord's profound wish to nourish and nurture His sons and daughters—if only they would humble themselves and obey His commandments. His message has perpetually been the same in all ages: "O Israel, return unto the Lord thy God" (Hosea 14:1). To the Saints of the New World, the resurrected Lord sounded the theme of following His invitation to gather together according to His word:

> And I command you that ye shall write these sayings after I am gone, that if it so be that my people at Jerusalem, they who have seen me and been with me in my ministry, do not ask the Father in my name, that they may receive a knowledge of you by the Holy Ghost, and also of the other tribes whom they know not of, that these sayings which ye shall write shall be kept and shall be manifested unto the Gentiles, that through the fulness of the Gentiles, the remnant of their seed, who shall be scattered forth upon the face of the earth because of their unbelief, may be brought in, or may be brought to a knowledge of me, their Redeemer.
>
> And then will I gather them in from the four quarters of the earth; and then

will I fulfil the covenant which the Father hath made unto all the people of the house of Israel. . . .

> And then shall the remnants, which shall be scattered abroad upon the face of the earth, be gathered in from the east and from the west, and from the south and from the north; and they shall be brought to the knowledge of the Lord their God, who hath redeemed them. (3 Ne. 16:4–5; 20:13)

The Savior taught the people about the scattering and gathering of Israel as part of the Father's plan for saving and exalting His children. He prophesied of the spiritual and the literal gathering of the house of Israel in the latter days. There would be signs and events heralding the beginning of the ultimate phase of preparation for the Second Coming: "And verily I say unto you, I give unto you a sign, that ye may know the time when these things shall be about to take place—that I shall gather in, from their long dispersion, my people, O house of Israel, and shall establish again among them my Zion" (3 Ne. 21:1). What was the sign? "And behold, this is the thing which I will give unto you for a sign—for verily I say unto you that when these things which I declare unto you, and which I shall declare unto you hereafter of myself, and by the power of the Holy Ghost which shall be given unto you of the Father, shall be made known unto the Gentiles that they may know concerning this people who are a remnant of the house of Jacob, and concerning this my people who shall be scattered by them" (3 Ne. 21:2). The sign, therefore, is the glory of the Restoration in our day, including the dissemination of the fulness of the gospel through the Book of Mormon (see D&C 20:8–14). The grand and final gathering is presently underway in full force, directed by those holding the keys of the priesthood and sustained by the miraculous coming forth of the Book of Mormon among the nations as part of "a great and a marvelous work" (3 Ne. 21:9) to restore the word of God and the fulness of the gospel.

How do we engage in the gathering? Christ's injunction to those seeking the truth was simple and direct: "come, follow me" (Luke 18:22). All the Lord requires is that we obey His commandments in all humility of heart, and He will establish us as His people once again through the process of gathering and restoration: "My sheep hear my voice, and I know them, and they follow me: And I give unto them eternal life" (John 10:27–28).

The fold of the Shepherd offers light, truth, security, and a protection against the circling packs of "ravening wolves" (Matt. 7:15). The righteous homes, congregations, and temples of Zion offer the only enduring refuge from the oppression and tyranny of iniquity and evil. The gospel of Jesus Christ is the only resort of eternal safety for all mankind: "And the Lord will create upon every dwelling place of mount Zion, and upon her assemblies, a cloud and smoke by day, and the shining of a flaming fire by night: for upon all the glory shall be a defence" (Isa. 4:5). The tent of Zion, with its securing stakes and reinforcing cords, is the abiding image of refuge afforded by the kingdom of God (see Isa. 54:2).

The gathering is a manifestation of the fulfillment of the Abrahamic covenant. The Lord promised Abraham: "in thy seed after thee . . . shall all the families of the earth be blessed, even with the blessings of the Gospel, which are the blessings of salvation, even of life eternal" (Abr. 2:11). According to this royal covenant, the faithful stewards of Israel were assured magnificent blessings: a homeland on the earth and an inheritance in the mansions of the heaven; a bounteous earthly offspring and, in keeping with the new and everlasting covenant of marriage, eternal increase in the hereafter; the blessings of the fulness of gospel truth on earth, followed by salvation and exaltation for the faithful and obedient in the coming world of glory.

By divine decree, the obligation under this magnificent covenant was that Israel was to convey priesthood blessings to the entire world and spread the gospel of saving ordinances to the receptive children of God in all lands. That process of gathering is taking place before our very eyes. The ensign of the Lord has been raised in its majesty in the four quarters of the earth, causing people to flow unto it and be fed with spiritual truth. "And he will lift up an ensign to the nations from far, and will hiss unto them from the end of the earth; and behold, they shall come with speed swiftly; none shall be weary nor stumble among them" (2 Ne. 15:26).

Inspired by Latter-Day Prophets

Bruce R. McConkie: The place of gathering for the Mexican Saints is in Mexico; the place of gathering for the Guatemalan Saints is in Guatemala; the place of gathering for the Brazilian Saints is in Brazil; and so it goes throughout the length and breadth of the whole earth. Japan is for the Japanese; Korea is for the Koreans; Australia is for the Australians; every nation is the gathering place for its own people (*CR*, 1972, 45).

During the infancy of the restored Church, Saints were directed to gather to specific locations: Ohio, Missouri, Illinois, and Utah. Now that the Church has expanded into a worldwide organization, places of gathering are established in many lands, with the establishment of stakes and temples closer to the homes of the Saints. What are your thoughts about the purpose in having multiple places of gathering throughout the world? (You might want to ponder the parable of the wheat and the tares in Matt. 13:24–30.)

Ezra Taft Benson: We will live in the midst of economic, political, and spiritual instability. When these signs are observed—unmistakable evidences that His coming is nigh—we need not be troubled, but "stand in holy places, and be not moved, until the day of the Lord come" (D&C 87:8). Holy men and women stand in holy places, and these holy places consist of our temples, our chapels, our homes, and stakes of Zion, which are, as the Lord declares, "for a defense, and for a refuge from the storm, and from wrath when it shall be poured out without mixture upon the whole earth" (D&C 115:6) (*The Teachings of Ezra Taft Benson*, 106).

It is a commandment of the Lord to "gather together, and stand in holy places" (D&C 101:22). In your opinion, how is this commandment evidence of the love of the Lord for His children?

Howard W. Hunter: Without doubt there are significant challenges facing the Latter-day Saints, both here and elsewhere in the world. We hope that you will not be overcome with discouragement in your attempts to raise your families in righteousness. Remember that the Lord has commanded this: "But my disciples shall stand in holy places, and shall not be moved" (D&C 45:32). While some interpret this to mean the temple, which surely it does, it also represents the homes in which we live. If you will diligently work to lead your families in righteousness, encouraging and participating in daily family prayer, scripture reading, family home evening, and love and support for each other in living the teachings of the gospel, you will receive the promised blessings of the Lord in raising a righteous posterity. In an increasingly wicked world, how essential it is that each of us "stand in holy places" and commit to be true and faithful to the teachings of the gospel of Jesus Christ (*The Teachings of Howard W. Hunter*, 155).

President Hunter lists some of the patterns of living that render the home a "holy place": daily family prayer, scripture reading, family home evening, loving encouragement to live the gospel, and a commitment to be obedient. How have these and similar actions contributed to the joy, peace, and security of your home? How can you help your children and grandchildren live up to these standards of the gathering of Zion?

Bruce R. McConkie: Why is the Lord gathering Israel in these last days? It is to fulfil the covenant made with Abraham and renewed with Isaac and Jacob and others. . . . What is that covenant? . . . Jehovah promised—covenanted with—his friend Abraham that in him and in his seed, meaning the literal seed of his body, should "all families of the earth be blessed, even with the blessings of the Gospel, which are the blessings of salvation, even of life eternal" (Abr. 2:8–11) (*The Mortal Messiah: From Bethlehem to Calvary*, 4:337–338).

The gathering is not just a vast cultural movement in the latter days, but rather the fulfillment of a divine plan established before the foundation of the world to prepare for God's children to move into His presence—first as Saints of the kingdom of God in the stakes of Zion, then as citizen-Saints of the millennial kingdom, and finally as "joint-heirs with Christ" (Rom. 8:17) in the celestial kingdom. The Prophet Joseph Smith said this of a vision given him in the Kirtland Temple on January 21, 1836: "I saw the transcendent beauty of the gate through which the heirs of that kingdom will enter, which was like unto circling flames of fire; Also the blazing throne of God, whereon was seated the Father and the Son" (D&C 137:2–3). How does this process of gathering in ever higher stages of glory give you hope and joy in the ultimate destiny that has been established for you by our Father in Heaven and His Only Begotten Son? How can you encourage your family to prepare themselves as active and worthy participants in this grand gathering process?

Truths to Liken

2 Ne. 12:2–3—"And it shall come to pass in the last days, when the mountain of the Lord's house shall be established in the top of the mountains, and shall be exalted above the hills, and all nations shall flow unto it. And many people shall go and say, Come ye, and let us go up to the mountain of the Lord, to the house of the God of Jacob; and he will teach us of his ways, and we will walk in his paths; for out of Zion shall go forth the law, and the word of the Lord from Jerusalem."

- Jacob, brother of Nephi, rejoiced in reading his people the prophecies of Isaiah concerning the gathering in the latter days (compare Isa. 2:2–3). The reference to the "mountain of the Lord's house" serves as a symbol for those places in the kingdom of God where temples are built to carry on the work of salvation and exaltation—whether in the Rocky Mountains beginning in the pioneer era, the future New Jerusalem in Jackson County (see D&C 84:2–5), the rebuilding of the temple in the Old Jerusalem (see D&C 133:13), or in all other places where the house of the Lord rises as an ensign of the truth and an emblem of God's eternal love for His children.
- To "go up to the mountain of the Lord" is to gather to holy places of Zion where the ordinances of exaltation are accessible to worthy Saints. How has the opportunity to "go up to the mountain of the Lord" been a great blessing for you and your loved ones? How can you help others follow this pathway upward and be gathered to Zion?

2 Ne. 5:5–6, 16—"And it came to pass that the Lord did warn me, that I, Nephi, should depart from them [Laman and Lemuel] and flee into the wilderness, and all those who would go with me. . . . And all those who would go with me were those who believed in the warnings and the revelations of God; wherefore, they did hearken unto my words. . . . And I, Nephi, did build a temple; and I did construct it after the manner of the temple of Solomon save it were not built of so many precious things."

- Nephi reported on the wisdom of the Lord to "gather" the faithful to a territory away from the murderous designs of Laman and Lemuel and their group. In his new place of refuge, one of Nephi's earliest initiatives was to build a temple for the blessing of the people—a wonderful illustration of the process of gathering to the house of the Lord.
- The gathering is a continual process of liberation and preservation in the context of covenant honor. How has the Lord blessed you from time to time in guiding you away from environments of danger and evil and toward environments of safety and righteousness?

2 Ne. 10:7–8—"But behold, thus saith the Lord God: When the day cometh that they shall believe in me, that I am Christ, then have I covenanted with their fathers that they shall be restored in the flesh, upon the earth, unto the lands of their inheritance. And it shall come to pass that they shall be gathered in from their long dispersion, from the isles of the sea, and from the four parts of the earth; and the nations of the Gentiles shall be great in the eyes of me, saith God, in carrying them forth to the lands of their inheritance."

- Jacob, brother of Nephi, was diligent in teaching his people the doctrine of the gathering as the fulfillment of the divine covenant between God and His people. The "long dispersion" of the scattering would in the latter days be resolved unto the blessing of the Saints who, remembering their promises to the Lord, would be gathered to Him in joy.
- For the people of Jacob and his posterity,

who were "wanderers in a strange land" (Alma 13:23), these prophecies might have sounded like distant and faint tidings of gladness. But to us, they are very real, for they are underway in our time in full power and glory. How does it make you and your loved ones feel to participate in the fulfillment of ancient prophecy? As you look at your four-generation ancestors (or even earlier), from which lands have they been gathered, and by what process of enlightenment, guidance, and blessing? How does this process of the gathering contribute to your feelings of gratitude to your Father in Heaven and His "angels of earth" who laid the foundation for your inheritance in Zion?

2 Ne. 29:14—"And it shall come to pass that my people, which are of the house of Israel, shall be gathered home unto the lands of their possessions; and my word also shall be gathered in one. And I will show unto them that fight against my word and against my people, who are of the house of Israel, that I am God, and that I covenanted with Abraham that I would remember his seed forever."

- Nephi included this divine prophecy in his final discourses to his people and the future readership of the Book of Mormon. The words are a reminder that all things are to be gathered in one—not only the Saints of the covenant, but also the doctrine, principles, and words of truth from all generations. Brigham Young taught: "All the knowledge, wisdom, power, and glory that have been bestowed upon the nations of the earth, from the days of Adam till now, must be gathered home to Zion" (*JD* 8:279).
- How is the coming forth of the Book of Mormon a fulfillment of this prophecy that "all things are to be gathered in one"? (See Isa. 29.)

Jacob 5:23, 77—"But, behold the tree. I have nourished it this long time, and it hath brought forth much fruit; therefore, gather it, and lay it up against the season, that I may preserve it unto mine own self. . . . And when the time cometh that evil fruit shall again come into my vineyard, then will I cause the good and the bad to be gathered; and the good will I preserve unto myself, and the bad will I cast away into its own place. And then cometh the season and the end; and my vineyard will I cause to be burned with fire." (Compare 1 Ne. 15:12–17.)

- Jacob included in his writings Zenos's allegory of the olive tree concerning the design of the Lord for the scattering and gathering of His people in connection with the gospel plan of happiness. Concerning this passage of scripture, President Joseph Fielding Smith said: "One of the most interesting and significant parables ever written is that revealed to Zenos and recorded in the fifth chapter of Jacob in the Book of Mormon. It is a parable of the scattering of Israel. If we had the full key to the interpretation, then we would have in detail how Israel was transplanted in all parts of the earth. Thus through this scattering the Lord has caused Israel to mix with the nations and bring the Gentiles within the blessings of the seed of Abraham" (*Answers to Gospel Questions*, 2:57).

- We might say, with the spirit of good cheer: Get out your pruning shears and your gardening tools! Through missionary labors we are "grafting" the honest at heart into the tree of Zion, into the home base of spiritual growth and development. What a blessing it is to further the gathering and support the building up of the kingdom of God. How have you experienced the joy and happiness of serving in the vineyard of the Lord to assist in the gathering of His people—beginning with yourself, then your family circle, then those with whom you have shared the gospel message?

3 Ne. 16:1–3—"AND verily, verily, I say unto you that I have other sheep, which are not of this land, neither of the land of Jerusalem, neither in any parts of that land round about whither I have been to minister. For they of whom I speak are they who have not as yet heard my voice; neither have I at any time manifested myself unto them. But I have received a commandment of the Father that I shall go unto them, and that they shall hear my voice, and shall be numbered among my sheep, that there may be one fold and one shepherd; therefore I go to show myself unto them."

- The resurrected Lord told the Saints at Bountiful that He had other sheep—not of their fold, nor of the fold in Jerusalem—who would hear His voice, meaning enjoy His direct ministry of truth among them. Who are these "other sheep"? They are certainly among the lost tribes of Israel, as Nephi implied: "And it shall come to pass that the Jews shall have the words of the Nephites, and the Nephites shall have the words of the Jews; and the Nephites and the Jews shall have the words of the lost tribes of Israel; and the lost tribes of Israel shall have the words of the Nephites and the Jews" (2 Ne. 29:13). When the record of the Savior's visit to these "other sheep" of the lost tribes comes forth in a future day, we will be blessed with a further witness of the divinity of the Lord's work; but until then, He is testing our faith and obedience in savoring the truths of that portion of His word that we have. Mormon explained that he included not even a hundredth part of what Christ taught the people (see 3 Ne. 26:6), saying, "Behold, I was about to write them, all which were engraven upon the plates of Nephi, but the Lord forbade it, saying: I will try the faith of my people" (3 Ne. 26:11).

- What are your thoughts about the opportunity someday, based on faith and obedience, to receive the "greater things" not included in the Book of Mormon account—as well as the record of Christ's visit to the "other sheep" among the lost ten tribes? How might the Book of Mormon and the Bible be the instrumentality for conveying "the words of the Nephites and the Jews" among the scattered tribes of Israel throughout the world as part of the gathering?

3 Ne. 22:2—"Enlarge the place of thy tent, and let them stretch forth the curtains of thy habitations; spare not, lengthen thy cords and strengthen thy stakes."

- To the people in the New World, the Lord quotes Isaiah 54 concerning the gathering of the Saints to the stakes of Zion in the last days. The symbolism here compares the establishment of the kingdom of God to a large canopy or tent. The tent is literally held up and strengthened by the individual cords and stakes, the stakes being likened to the organizational units of the kingdom that are multiplying throughout the earth as the canopy of Zion is enlarged. The first stake of Zion in the last days was established at Kirtland, Ohio, on February 17, 1834, with Joseph Smith as president, he being at the time also president of the Church (see *Church History in the Fulness of Times*, 122). Since that time, the number of stakes has progressively grown as the gathering has progressed.

- The ongoing work of gathering the Saints to Zion is continually enlarging the tent and curtains of the kingdom of God on the earth. But there remains much work to be done in expanding the number of stakes around the world. In his visions of the future, Nephi was blessed to see the growth of the Church of God, yet, relative to the size of the world at large, the Church across the globe was small because of the influence of the forces of worldliness: "And it came to pass that I beheld the church of the Lamb of God, and its numbers were few, because of the wickedness and abominations of the whore who sat upon many waters; nevertheless, I beheld that the church of the Lamb, who were the saints of God, were also upon all the face of the earth; and their dominions upon the face of the earth were small, because of the wickedness of the great whore whom I saw" (1 Ne. 14:12).

How can the "dominions" of Zion (administrative units, such as stakes), though relatively small in number, achieve greater success in carrying the message of the gospel to all quarters of the earth? How can you as one individual help enlarge the tent of Zion through your devoted service? How can you teach and encourage others to increase their service in gathering the Saints to Zion?

D&C 110:11—"After this vision closed, the heavens were again opened unto us; and Moses appeared before us, and committed unto us the keys of the gathering of Israel from the four parts of the earth, and the leading of the ten tribes from the land of the north."

- The priesthood keys of the gathering were restored on April 3, 1836, being committed to Joseph Smith and Oliver Cowdery in a heavenly manifestation in the Kirtland Temple. In conjunction with the keys bestowed by Moses, associated keys related to the gathering were restored by Elias, who "committed the dispensation of the gospel of Abraham, saying that in us and our seed all generations after us should be blessed" (D&C 110:12) and Elijah, who restored the sealing keys of the priesthood (see D&C 110:15). All such keys are essential to the gathering in the last days—the keys from Moses to empower the organizational process, the keys from Elias to restore the work of the Abrahamic covenant, and the keys from Elijah to ratify and confirm in heaven the efficacy of all priesthood ordinances, including temple ordinances used in gathering the Saints to Zion. The summary statement of this extraordinary process is given in these words: "Therefore, the keys of this dispensation are committed into your hands; and by this ye may know that the great and dreadful day of the Lord is near, even at the doors" (D&C 110:16).

- What are your thoughts about how Heavenly Father has provided knowledge, powers, keys, and blessings in such abundance so that the gathering of Zion can occur in preparation for the Second Coming? How would you characterize and describe your role and function in this process? How have you and your loved ones been blessed beyond measure to participate in this unique and divinely ordained movement for the last days?

Rejoicing and Reasoning Together

How Is the Gathering Proceeding Today?

Nephi foresaw in grand detail the panorama of the vast gathering process of the latter days: "Wherefore, the Lord God will proceed to make bare his arm in the eyes of all the nations, in bringing about his covenants and his gospel unto those who are of the house of Israel. Wherefore, he will bring them again out of captivity, and they shall be gathered together to the lands of their inheritance; and they shall be brought out of obscurity and out of darkness; and they shall know that the Lord is their Savior and their Redeemer, the Mighty One of Israel" (1 Ne. 22:11–12). This gathering started at Kirtland, expanded for a season to Missouri, transitioned to Illinois, and then broadened through the westward migration of the Saints to the Salt Lake Valley—"unto the utmost bound of the everlasting hills" (Gen. 49:26). Tens of thousands streamed in from many countries during this process. Just as the Lord tested and tried His people throughout the mighty latter-day exodus, He also ultimately granted them the supreme blessing of "arrival"—accomplishing their journey and attaining the refuge they so dreamed about. The Salt Lake Valley was a relatively desolate place, but it afforded a protected environment where they could make the desert blossom as a rose (see Isa. 35:1) and once again build up a temple: "And there shall be a tabernacle for a shadow in the daytime from the heat, and for a place of refuge, and for a covert from storm and from rain" (Isa. 4:6).

From there, the gathering continues even to this day in the assembling of the faithful at the stakes of Zion and in her temples in all regions of the world: "I have kept in store a blessing such as is not known among the children of men, and it shall be poured forth upon their heads. And from thence [Ohio] men shall go forth into all nations" (D&C 39:15).

The Lord has said: "Behold, it is my will, that all they who call on my name, and worship me according to mine everlasting gospel, should gather together, and stand in holy places" (D&C 101:22).

Thus in our day, the call to "stand in holy places" serves to expand the boundaries of Zion as numerous congregations of the Lord's Saints, established in growing measure in homes of faith and stakes of strength, work to obey the divine directive to build temples to the Most High.

According to prophetic vision in all dispensations of time, the latter days would be marked by a monumental and massive gathering of the Saints to places of refuge and worship in preparation for the Millennium. How many such places of gathering are there in the world today? At recent count there are more than 2,800 stakes and 28,000 wards and branches, with nearly 350 missions and more than 600 districts! In what measure is the word gathering *an appropriate action word to describe your pattern of living as part of this Zion society? How often do you and your loved ones "gather" for prayer and family home evening? How often do you "gather" for family reunions? How often do you "gather" with the Saints to learn more of the gospel and renew your covenants? How often do you and your loved ones "gather" to the house of the Lord? How often do you speak with friends and associates not of our faith about "gathering" (learning more about coming into the fold of the Savior through the principles and ordinances of the gospel)?*

How Is the Book of Mormon the Handbook of the Gathering?

One of the grand themes of the Book of Mormon is the "everlasting kindness" and "great mercies" of the Lord in watching over and lifting up Israel (see 3 Ne. 22:7–8). Records of the Lord's dealing with His people over the millennia always contain the promise and hope of the ultimate gathering together of the House of Israel in the latter days and the establishment of an enduring society of Zion with the Lord Himself as the Lawgiver and Head. During His post-resurrection visit in the New World, the Savior recited extensively from Isaiah concerning the house of Israel and how the Lord's people will overcome their past iniquities and participate in the building up of Zion in the latter days. Scattered Israel and those without the gospel are to be gathered into Zion and endowed with truth (see Isa. 33:20; D&C

82:14). The Savior emphasized that He would forgive scattered Israel for her wickedness as she returns to Him in faithfulness. He reassured the people that He will not forget Israel and the covenant promises He has made. The city of Zion shall be built up and the gospel taught. Righteousness will prevail. No one will harm Israel.

Nephi, in his fledgling but prospering circle of Saints in the promised land, must have had in his bosom a feeling of dispersal, of being scattered—considering how far he was from his native Jerusalem, and the fact that he was now separated from his elder brothers because of their rejection of righteous ways. Is it any wonder that he was attracted to the writings of Isaiah, one of whose major themes was the scattering and eventual gathering of Israel? How Nephi must have yearned for the security of his people, for their adherence to the principles of covenant integrity so that they might be gathered and preserved as a community of faithful servants to the Lord. How he must have anguished over his visions of his people's future apostasy and decline. How he must have rejoiced at his vision of the latter-day Restoration and gathering in of the remnants of his lineage in a future age as confirmed by Isaiah (see 2 Ne. 20:21). Nephi clearly perceived, like Isaiah, the coming "times of refreshing" (Acts 3:19) when the Lord would raise up an ensign to signal the ushering in of the last days (see 2 Ne. 25:17). Thus Nephi lays out plainly the design of the Lord in preserving these very records for the blessing of coming generations: "Wherefore, he shall bring forth his words unto them, which words shall judge them at the last day, for they shall be given them for the purpose of convincing them of the true Messiah" (2 Ne. 25:18).

From the higher perspective of the Lord's dealings with His people over the generations, a consistent pattern emerges: He moves and scatters both the righteous as well as the wicked according to His far-reaching plan to maximize the blessings of redemption for the greatest number of souls. Thus we have seen the influence of His hand in removing Lehi and his family from the dangers of impending bondage in Jerusalem (where the wicked were to be scattered shortly by the Babylonians) to the security of the promised land. And yet, only a generation later, Nephi and his faithful few are again removed from the perils of unrighteousness to the safety of a refuge where they could live in peace "after the manner of happiness" (2 Ne. 5:27). Not

many generations later, we see the first Mosiah and his people again warned of the Lord to flee from the wrath of their enemies (see Omni 1:12). Thus he and his righteous group are led from the land of Nephi northward to Zarahemla, where they come upon yet another group (the Mulekites) who have likewise been guided by the hand of the Lord to a place of safety. In turn, this new group had come upon the last survivor of yet an earlier nation (the Jaredites) that had followed the Lord's counsel in removing themselves from the dislocations associated with the Tower of Babel (see Omni 1:20–22).

The principle of scattering is part of the Lord's agenda for His people, just as the principle of gathering is an instrument of strategic restoration for building, strengthening, and enlarging the tent of Zion. Thus it should not surprise us in the Book of Mormon to see this divine process of dispersion and recovery played out many times, in greater or smaller measure, as evidence of the Lord's compassionate intervention. All of these patterns make the Book of Mormon the most precious instrument of the gathering in our day.

The first step of the gathering for any individual is confirmation by the Spirit that these things are true—in Moroni's famous words: "And when ye shall receive these things, I would exhort you that ye would ask God, the Eternal Father, in the name of Christ, if these things are not true; and if ye shall ask with a sincere heart, with real intent, having faith in Christ, he will manifest the truth of it unto you, by the power of the Holy Ghost. And by the power of the Holy Ghost ye may know the truth of all things" (Moro. 10:4–5). Those who are prompted in this way will feel motivated to pass through the open gateway via baptism of water and fire, and thus become part of the gathering of Zion.

As you study the Book of Mormon and gain greater understanding of the process of scattering and gathering, how can you use this sacred text as a means for helping others—either not of our faith or less active in the Church—to gather together for blessings of joy and liberation?

What Are the Leadership Principles for the Gathering?

The gathering is a central part of the Lord's design to establish His kingdom once again on the earth, never again to be diminished or removed. The gathering is accomplished according to leadership principles defined and confirmed from before the foundation of the earth. Since all of us are stewards in the gathering, much like the servants portrayed in Zenos's allegory of the olive trees (see Jacob 5), we would do well to understand the principles and procedures followed by the "Lord of the vineyard" so that we might, as He says, "have joy with me because of the fruit of my vineyard" (Jacob 5:75).

Even though the purpose of Zenos's narrative may not have been to teach leadership principles, we can see from the masterful leadership of the Lord of the vineyard specific ways and means by which we can improve and advance in our own various roles as stewards of the gathering—whether that be in the family, in the wards and stakes of the Church, or in missionary endeavors. Each of the questions in the following checklist reflects a leadership principle contained in the narrative of the allegory. You might want to score yourself and then go back through Jacob 5 to determine how the Lord acted in order to maximize the harvest. What better leadership model is there than the Lord Himself?

1. General Principles

- Do you have a governing sense of purpose and mission in what you do? (See verses 9, 49, 54, 61.)
- Do you maintain focus without ever losing sight of the objective? (See verses 13, 35, 61.)
- Do you understand and remain aligned with the "root" values of your enterprise? (See verse 59.)
- Are you firm in your commitment to action? (See verses 14, 75; compare Abr. 3:17; 2 Ne. 24:24.)
- Is your engagement total and "impassioned"? (See the entire allegory; compare Mark 12:30; 2 Ne. 25:29; D&C 4:2.)
- Do you maintain an attitude of faith and hope? (See verses 53–54, 60.)

2. Leadership Structure and Style

- Do you plan before taking action? (See the entire allegory.)
- Do you follow through with the steps of your plan? (See verses 37, 61–62, 71–72, 74–75.)

- Do you understand the time frame within which you operate? (See verses 29, 47, 71.)
- Are you a team builder? (See verses 15, 19, 61, 70.)
- Do you delegate effectively? (See verses 12, 72, 75.)
- Do you understand how to apply rewards effectively? (See verses 53–54, 60, 71, 75.)
- Do you participate as a leader and work alongside team members? (See verse 72.)
- Are you an effective listener? (See verses 27, 33, 47–48, 50.)
- Do you take responsibility for your decisions? (See verses 27, 29, 45.)
- Do you discipline effectively? (See verse 22.)

3. Effective Leadership Strategies

- Are you adaptable and resilient? (See verses 22, 48.)
- Do you operate from a contingency perspective, always with a careful fallback position? (See verse 13.)
- Do you constantly evaluate and monitor results? (See verse 31.)
- Are you able to deal resourcefully with crises? (See verses 34, 36.)
- Do you understand the techniques and process of vitality and growth? (See verses 61, 64.)
- Is your approach balanced and fine-tuned? (See verses 48, 65, 74.)
- Do you harvest as you go—"against the season"? (See the entire allegory.)
- Are you integrative and able to "close the circle"—to restore, to complete, to resolve, to bring things to a successful conclusion? (See verses 63, 68, 75.)

Every servant and steward in the Lord's vineyard is enjoined to "learn his duty, and to act in the office in which he is appointed, in all diligence" (D&C 107:99).

Real-life Stories for Heart and Mind

When a Prophet Weeps For Joy. On Wednesday, April 12, 1843, the steamer *Amaranth*—the first up the Mississippi River that season—arrived in Nauvoo about noon, at a time when a special three-day conference of the priesthood (including most of the Quorum of the Twelve) was being conducted. While the conference was busy ordaining elders and sending nearly ninety missionaries into the field (see *HC* 5:347–349), the ship was delivering 240 immigrant convert Saints from England, under the leadership of Lorenzo Snow. The Prophet Joseph Smith greeted them in person with great joy. A few hours later, at five o'clock PM, the steamer *Maid of Iowa* arrived with around 200 more Saints from England, under the leadership of Levi Richards and Parley P. Pratt (whose thirty-sixth birthday happened to be that day). The Prophet noted in his journal: "I was present at the landing and the first on board the steamer, when I met Sister Mary Ann Pratt (who had been to England with Brother Parley) and her little daughter, only three or four days old. I could not refrain from shedding tears. So many friends and acquaintances arriving in one day. . . . I was rejoiced to meet them in such good health and fine spirits; for they were equal to any that had ever come to Nauvoo" (*HC* 5:353–354). Thus the fledgling Church sustained a beehive of activity spreading the gospel and gathering in the Saints of Zion, as the Lord had commanded.

These are moments of truth that remind us to labor diligently to spread the "good news" so that others might also obtain the blessings of the gospel. Gathering brings joy. Joseph Smith, the Prophet of the Restoration, shed tears of joy over the gathering. How can you shed tears of joy in your success as a builder of the kingdom and gatherer after the manner of the Savior: "And Jesus said unto them, Come ye after me, and I will make you to become fishers of men" (Mark 1:17)?

Not Cast Off. Many years ago a family went through a traumatic experience when their young son, who has complex disabilities, became separated from his parents at a busy mall and got lost. There was deep anxiety as the family marshaled the help of neighbors and security officers to scour the hallways and stores for what seemed like endless hours in an attempt to find the missing boy. Finally he was located, disoriented but safe. He could not communicate his feelings, but observers could certainly imagine how he must have felt, being torn unexpectedly from his family moorings and somehow cast adrift and alone among strangers for

so long a period of time.

Such an experience is not completely foreign, for all of us from time to time have feelings of separation and disconnection from our roots and our home base of operation. In many respects, life is an experience of finding our way repeatedly back home to the familiar shores of our sustaining connections. This is particularly true when our detours and separations occur because of sin or wayward behavior. The Savior's parable of the prodigal son (see Luke 15:11–32) illustrates the anxiety a family feels when a loved one chooses to depart from the pathways of secure and tested bonds. The parable also celebrates the joy that attends a homecoming after unfortunate choices have led to separation and anguish. The younger Alma is a case in point, having been gathered back into the arms of his family after repenting of his destructive campaign against the Church (see Mosiah 27:27).

Gathering is the opposite and reversal of being *cast off*, a term that occurs repeatedly in the Book of Mormon. On the title page itself the theme of being "cast off" is used in the context of the four-dimensional formula that characterizes the full message of the Book of Mormon: "Which is to show unto the remnant of the House of Israel what great things the Lord hath done for their fathers; and that they may know the covenants of the Lord, that they are not cast off forever—And also to the convincing of the Jew and Gentile that Jesus is the Christ, the Eternal God, manifesting himself unto all nations." Thus we are taught four important lessons: what great things the Lord has done for our forefathers, how the covenant promises apply to us personally today, and how we can have hope for the future (in other words, not be "cast off")—and that all is because of the merits, mercy, and grace of the atoning Redeemer, even Jesus Christ. These are what enable the "gathering" of the Saints in the latter days.

What are your thoughts about the blessings of the gathering for your family—that they are not "cast off," but have the opportunity through the gospel plan to join you as an eternal family in the life ahead?

The Seeds of Greatness. A number of years ago a Church youth leader developed a training retreat for the youth of his ward who were serving in leadership positions. One of the themes was to strengthen the wards and stakes by seeing the value of each person. As the youth leaders were assembling on the bus in preparation for the journey to the retreat site, they were reminded that "man looketh on the outward appearance, but the Lord looketh on the heart" (1 Sam. 16:7). They were asked to watch for opportunities that day to serve others without regard to outward appearance.

A mile or two down the road, the bus passed a homeless person walking along the road, disheveled, unkempt, and tattered. The group leader asked the driver to pull over and stop about half a block beyond the vagabond. "Should we interrupt our retreat to help this person?" he asked the youth. Clearly some were wondering if that would be the appropriate thing to do—after all, the whole day was already planned around a fun program. After some discussion, however, the group was unanimous in the decision to stop and help the homeless person. By then, he had caught up with the bus, and the door was opened to extend to him the invitation to climb aboard. With some difficulty he mounted the steps of the vehicle and then stood there somewhat embarrassed under the silent watchful gaze of several dozen young people. He began to express his appreciation for their help, and it did not take the young people long to discern that this was indeed a special person hidden under the dirty and torn rags of clothing he was wearing. In fact, it was the bishop himself—and his brief and loving remarks about seeing the value in every person cast a spiritual glow over the rest of the day.

What greater way to strengthen wards and stakes and facilitate the gathering than to perceive within all members, or potential members, the seeds of greatness as sons and daughters of God? The Savior said: "For inasmuch as ye do it unto the least of these, ye do it unto me" (D&C 42:38). How can you assist in the gathering of the Lord's children by looking beyond appearances and focusing on who they are: sons and daughters of God?

Pondering Prayerfully

Additional scriptures to consider and ponder:
- Deut. 30:1–5
- Isa. 35:8–10
- Isa. 40:11
- Isa. 40:31
- Isa. 43:5–7
- Jer. 23:3
- Ezek. 11:17
- 1 Ne. 22:12
- 3 Ne. 20:13
- Morm. 5:14
- Ether 2:5–8
- Ether 13:10–12
- D&C 10:58–62
- D&C 57:1–3
- D&C 133:26

The following hymns increase understanding about the gathering:
- "Behold, the Mountain of the Lord" (*Hymns,* 54)
- "Hail to the Brightness of Zion's Glad Morning!" (*Hymns,* 42)
- "Israel, Israel, God Is Calling" (*Hymns,* 7)

Remember and Be Sure

The Lord has given to the Saints of the Restoration a sacred charge: "And ye are called to bring to pass the gathering of mine elect; for mine elect hear my voice and harden not their hearts" (D&C 29:7). The world waits for the Saints of the House of Israel to fulfill their destiny under the Abrahamic covenant—to take the blessings of the gospel to all the earth by preaching the word of God and by providing the temples for living and vicarious work for the dead so that the faithful can return to our Heavenly Father's presence. Under provisions of the Abrahamic covenant, all of Israel is called into service to carry the gospel of light and the blessings of the priesthood throughout the world. Through the process of spiritual adoption, all mankind has access to the covenant blessings. Great joy is reserved for those who help in the gathering: "And now, if your joy will be great with one soul that you have brought unto me into the kingdom of my Father, how great will be your joy if you should bring many souls unto me!" (D&C 18:16).

The Lord uses the gathering to bless His sons and daughters of the covenant. Regarding the Kirtland Temple, the Lord said: "Yea the hearts of thousands and tens of thousands shall greatly rejoice in consequence of the blessings which shall be poured out, and the endowment with which my servants have been endowed in this house" (D&C 110:9).

Each of us in this, the last dispensation, should participate with full heart and mind in the gathering of the Lord's people, who may come to learn the truth only through our righteous service. That will happen when we take the time to guide our friends to the banquet of the Lord: "For there are many yet on the earth among all sects, parties, and denominations, who are blinded by the subtle craftiness of men, whereby they lie in wait to deceive, and who are only kept from the truth because they know not where to find it" (D&C 123:12). Let us show them where to find the truth, that they also may be gathered into the fold: "But behold, they are in the hands of the Lord of the harvest, and they are his; and he will raise them up at the last day" (Alma 26:7).

CHAPTER 43
The Second Coming: Signs of the Times

We will live in the midst of economic, political, and spiritual instability. When these signs are observed—unmistakable evidences that His coming is nigh—we need not be troubled, but "stand in holy places, and be not moved, until the day of the Lord come" (D&C 87:8). . . . We must heed the Lord's counsel to the Saints of this dispensation: "Prepare yourselves for the great day of the Lord" (D&C 133:10).
—Ezra Taft Benson (*The Teachings of Ezra Taft Benson,* 106)

Opening the Window of Wisdom

In the last days signs will indicate that the time is near for the Second Coming of the Lord Jesus Christ. We are living in the last days. We have a duty to warn people (see D&C 88:81) and help them to prepare for the Second Coming of the Lord (see D&C 1:12). Elder Bruce R. McConkie lists fifty-one events or signs that will take place prior to or at the advent of the Second Coming; of those, forty-three have been completed or are in the process of being completed (see *Mormon Doctrine,* 715–734).

Since no man knows the date and hour of His coming or the date and time that we as individuals may leave this earthly existence, we should simply ask, *Are we doing all we can in our preparation to meet our Savior and our Heavenly Father?* These are our

days of probation, and every day is precious—each represents one more day to prepare to meet God.

The dispensation of the fullness of times is the final episode in mortal history prior to the Second Coming. The Lord's voice of warning is proclaimed to all the world through the mouthpiece of His prophets as recorded in scripture in the form of commandments and revelations. The Lord's voice of warning in the opening section of the Doctrine and Covenants makes clear the sober and compelling truth that the latter-day work is the ultimate directive to all mankind to repent and come unto the Lord Jesus Christ, that He might heal the wounds of the faithful and penitent and teach them how to abide the day of His coming (see D&C 1:1–5).

The Lord gives His word of warning as a blessing to all mankind to help them prepare for His coming by doing that which is right and just. President Harold B. Lee has recommended that we avoid listening to misguided speculators about the time of the Second Coming, and instead focus on the "sure word of prophecy" concerning the signs of the times given by the Lord Himself in the inspired version of Matthew 24 contained in the Pearl of Great Price, as well as in Sections 38, 45, 101, and 133 of the Doctrine and Covenants (see *The Teachings of Harold B. Lee,* 398–399). To know the word of the Lord concerning the signs of the times will guide our preparations day by day.

Significant challenges lie ahead, "but if ye are prepared ye shall not fear" (D&C 38:30).

The battle of good versus evil in the final chapters of human history will see the triumph of the Almighty for the immortality and eternal life of His children. Our Father in Heaven controls the destinies of nations as the course of human events moves forward toward the consummation of the preadvent period and the ushering in of the millennial reign. All of God's laws include consequences, both blessings and cursings. The Gentiles who hearken to the Lord will be blessed through His manifestations of truth and power. They will be numbered among the House of Israel. Those who seek to destroy—in other words, the adherents of the great and abominable church—will fill the pit that they prepared for the destruction of others (see 1 Ne. 14:3). The Saints of God will rise above the massive tribulations of that day through the blessings of heaven: "And it came to pass that I, Nephi, beheld the power of the Lamb of God, that it descended upon the saints of the church of the Lamb, and upon the covenant people of the Lord, who were scattered upon all the face of the earth; and they were armed with righteousness and with the power of God in great glory" (1 Ne. 14:14).

The fundamental commandment of the Lord, declared from the foundation of the earth, is strictly plain: "And seek the face of the Lord always, that in patience ye may possess your souls, and ye shall have eternal life" (D&C 101:38). The face of the Lord will be revealed to all the world upon His Second Coming: "And there shall be silence in heaven for the space of half an hour; and immediately after shall the curtain of heaven be unfolded, as a scroll is unfolded after it is rolled up, and the face of the Lord shall be unveiled; And the saints that are upon the earth, who are alive, shall be quickened and be caught up to meet him" (D&C 88:95–96). To meet the Lord within a framework of honorable and valiant compliance with His gospel principles is the purpose of our existence, leading to a glorious reunion of joy and a sweet welcoming into the millennial era of life under the direct nurture and leadership of the Savior. How important it is to conduct our individual affairs on earth in such a way that the Second Coming will be a time of rejoicing and eternal peace, rather than a time of eternal regret and bitter shame.

When the great Jehovah extended the arm of love toward the ancient Israelites abiding at the foot of Sinai and beckoned them to prepare to see His face, they pulled back in fear and sought to cover themselves in the shallow mantel of golden-calf worship. In His wrath at their idol worship, the Lord denied them His presence and instituted an interim way of life that would serve to prepare them for greater blessings as they matured in their spiritual growth. The lesson from that episode is clear: "Harden not your heart, as in the provocation, and as in the day of temptation in the wilderness" (Ps. 95:8; compare Heb. 3:8, 15). The prophet Jacob reinforced this lesson in his day: "Wherefore we labored diligently among our people, that we might persuade them to come unto Christ, and partake of the goodness of God, that they might enter into his rest, lest by any means he should swear in his wrath they should not enter in, as in the provocation in the days of temptation while the children of Israel were in the wilderness" (Jacob 1:7; compare Alma 12:36).

The Doctrine and Covenants serves as a modern-day handbook on how to prepare ourselves and our families to "seek the face of the Lord always" (D&C 101:38) and experience a blissful reunion at the Second Coming of the Lord Jesus Christ. The signs and milestones leading to this transcendent event serve to warn us and guide us, encourage us and thrill us with the assurance that the Bridegroom is already at the door, and that a better world, a glorious world, is about to be ushered in.

Inspired by Latter-Day Prophets

Joseph Smith: I will prophesy that the signs of the coming of the Son of Man are already commenced. One pestilence will desolate after another. We shall soon have war and bloodshed. The moon will be turned into blood. I testify of these things, and that the coming of the Son of Man is nigh, even at your doors. If our souls and our bodies are not looking forth for the coming of the Son of Man; and after we are dead, if we are not looking forth, we shall be among those who are calling for the rocks to fall upon them (*Teachings of the Prophet Joseph Smith*, 160).

The Prophet of the Restoration counseled us to "look forth." To look forth is to be in tune with the unfolding of the events leading to the Second Coming. To look forth is to get prepared in every needful way to meet the Lord upon His return. To look forth is to gather our families around us and ensure that all are living according to the teachings of the gospel so that the Second Coming will be a time of rejoicing with the "rock of our salvation" (Ps. 95:1), rather than a time of yearning for "the rocks and the mountains to fall upon us to hide us from his presence" (Alma 12:14). Looking forward in joy, rather than looking backward or downward in shame, is to have our "confidence wax strong in the presence of God" (D&C 121:45). What qualities should you cultivate to bring you the confidence you need to prepare for the Second Coming (see D&C 121:41–46)?

Hugh B. Brown: While all is not well in the world, we testify that God is still in heaven, that Christ will defeat anti-Christ, that the millennium will be ushered in, that Satan will be bound, and there will be a new heaven and a new earth, and you are to join with us in helping to build that new world and prepare for the second coming of the Lord. You are the harbingers and builders of a new and better world (*Continuing the Quest*, 14).

There is an office associated with the process of observing the signs of the times—it is the office of harbinger of things to come and builder of a better world. How do the signs of the times serve to confirm this office for you and your family? Every time you mark the presence of a prophetic sign of the Second Coming, you can remind yourself of the obligation to warn others and serve God well, for in this there are grand blessings in store.

Bruce R. McConkie: These are the last days; the signs of the times are now being shown forth on every hand; and the coming of the Lord is not far distant. . . . Prepare for the pestilence and plagues and sorrows of the last days. Prepare for the second coming of the Son of Man. Prepare to abide the day, to stand when he appeareth, and to live and reign with him on earth for a thousand years. Prepare for the new heaven and the new earth whereon dwelleth righteousness. Prepare to meet thy God (*The Millennial Messiah: The Second Coming of the Son of Man*, 570).

What are we preparing for? To meet the Savior as He comes adorned in red apparel,

with a presence of glory far exceeding that of the sun (see D&C 133:48–49). How can you be ready today to meet the Savior? We don't know when He will return, but there is wisdom in being ready today; if we are, the signs of the times are simply comforting confirmations of our preparedness, not discomforting signals of work yet to be done.

Bruce R. McConkie: In the dispensation of the fulness of times, the members of the true Church are directed by the Lord to warn the world of the desolation and destruction that is to be poured out without measure upon the wicked and ungodly (*Mormon Doctrine*, 828).

If we are prepared, we need not fear for ourselves (see D&C 38:30), but we still need to fear for the eternal well-being of others—whether of our own family circle or of the circle of humanity not yet part of the fold of Christ. How can you share the signs of the times with others who are still in need of knowledge—doing it in a kindly and loving way, but still with the boldness of a sure witness?

Truths to Liken

JST, Matt. 1:38–40, 47–48—"Now learn a parable of the fig-tree—When its branches are yet tender, and it begins to put forth leaves, you know that summer is nigh at hand; So likewise, mine elect, when they shall see all these things, they shall know that he is near, even at the doors; But of that day, and hour, no one knoweth; no, not the angels of God in heaven, but my Father only. . . . But know this, if the good man of the house had known in what watch the thief would come, he would have watched, and would not have suffered his house to have been broken up, but would have been ready. Therefore be ye also ready, for in such an hour as ye think not, the Son of Man cometh."

- Jesus instructed His disciples privately on the Mount of Olives concerning the signs of the times and the need to be prepared for the Second Coming.
- Only the Father knows the time of the Second Coming, yet the angels of heaven await word as they stand ready

to perform their labors. We should likewise be prepared for that ultimate event. What do you believe the Savior meant in saying He would return "in such an hour as ye think not"? On your checklist of things to do in preparing for the Second Coming, what still needs to be done?

D&C 38:30–31, 42—"I tell you these things because of your prayers; wherefore, treasure up wisdom in your bosoms, lest the wickedness of men reveal these things unto you by their wickedness, in a manner which shall speak in your ears with a voice louder than that which shall shake the earth; but if ye are prepared ye shall not fear. And that ye might escape the power of the enemy, and be gathered unto me a righteous people, without spot and blameless. . . . And go ye out from among the wicked. Save yourselves. Be ye clean that bear the vessels of the Lord. Even so. Amen."

- These words were included in a revelation given through the Prophet Joseph Smith at Fayette, New York, on January 2, 1831, on the occasion of a conference of the Church. An imposing and chilling sign of the times is the rampant culture of wickedness that will prevail prior to the Second Coming. The defensive armor against the invasion of wickedness includes (1) continual prayer; (2) wisdom based on truth that allows you to discern danger, thus escaping untainted and unharmed; (3) gathering to the congregations of the righteous in Zion; and (4) moral cleanliness. All of this constitutes the preparation needed to overcome fear and save yourself.

- What are your thoughts about this divine formula for surviving the dangers rampant on the eve of the Second Coming? How can you help others to don such armor and thus be prepared without fear?

D&C 45:28–32, 34–35, 39–40—"And when the times of the Gentiles is come in, a light shall break forth among them that sit in darkness, and it shall be the fulness of my gospel; But they receive it not; for they perceive not the light, and they turn their hearts from me because of the precepts of men. And in that generation shall the times of the Gentiles be fulfilled. And there shall be men standing in that generation, that shall not pass until they shall see an overflowing scourge; for a desolating sickness shall cover the land. But my disciples shall stand in holy places, and shall not be moved; but among the wicked, men shall lift up their voices and curse God and die. . . . And now, when I the Lord had spoken these words unto my disciples, they were troubled. And I said unto them: Be not troubled, for, when all these things shall come to pass, ye may know that the promises which have been made unto you shall be fulfilled. . . . And it shall come to pass that he that feareth me shall be looking forth for the great day of the Lord to come, even for the signs of the coming of the Son of Man. And they shall see signs and wonders, for they shall be shown forth in the heavens above, and in the earth beneath."

- These words are from a revelation given through the Prophet Joseph Smith to the Church at Kirtland, Ohio, on March 7, 1831. The Restoration of the gospel is one of the glorious signs of the times. A subsequent sign of the times includes scourges and sickness throughout the world—but the Savior counsels His disciples not to be troubled by such desolation, for it serves as a reminder that the promises of glory will also shortly be fulfilled for all who stand in holy places, fearing the Lord and awaiting His presence.

- What are your thoughts about viewing the signs of the times as milestones of joy and confirmations of the promised rewards to come—even though some signs come in the form of alarming events of horror and desolation? How can you help others prepare themselves for the Second Coming and thus follow the counsel of Nephi: "Wherefore, ye must press forward with a steadfastness in Christ, having a perfect brightness of hope, and a love of God and of all men. Wherefore, if ye shall press forward, feasting upon the word of Christ, and endure to the end, behold, thus saith the Father: Ye shall have eternal life" (2 Ne. 31:20)?

D&C 101:11–16, 22—"Mine indignation is soon to be poured out without measure upon all nations; and this will I do when the cup of their iniquity is full. And in that day all who are found upon the watch-tower, or in other words, all mine Israel, shall be saved. And they that have been scattered shall be gathered. And all they who have mourned shall be comforted. And all they who have given their lives for my name shall be crowned. Therefore, let your hearts be comforted concerning Zion; for all flesh is in mine hands; be still and know that I am God. . . . Behold, it is my will, that all they who call on my name, and worship me according to mine everlasting gospel, should gather together, and stand in holy places."

- These words were included in a revelation given to the Prophet Joseph Smith at Kirtland, Ohio, on December 16, 1833, at a time when the Saints in Missouri were being subjected to widespread persecution and threats of death.
- The Lord is teaching His suffering Saints to gain perspective on the sufferings they are experiencing, which belong to the signs of the times leading up to the Second Coming. How can they gain this kind of higher perspective and know that their rewards are imminent? From the holy places where they are to stand in readiness and silence to know of the glories to come and the Lord's love for them. What are these holy places? The homes, congregations, and temples of God. How can you help loved ones in your extended family circle, or those you serve in the Church, to be comforted in their suffering, to stand receptively in holy places and know that the Lord will nurture and preserve them?

D&C 133: 57–58, 62—"And for this cause, that men might be made partakers of the glories which were to be revealed, the Lord sent forth the fulness of his gospel, his everlasting covenant, reasoning in plainness and simplicity—To prepare the weak for those things which are coming on the earth, and for the Lord's errand in the day when the weak

shall confound the wise, and the little one become a strong nation, and two shall put their tens of thousands to flight. . . . And unto him that repenteth and sanctifieth himself before the Lord shall be given eternal life."

- These words are from a revelation given through the Prophet Joseph Smith at Hiram, Ohio, on November 3, 1831, in response to a request from the elders to know how to gather the Saints and do the will of the Lord. The revelation was originally included in the Doctrine and Covenants as an appendix, but was later assigned a section number.
- Of all the signs of the times leading up to the Second Coming, the Restoration of the gospel with its sacred covenants is the most glorious and comforting. The weak are to be brought into the fold and from there dispatched to the ends of the earth to do their mighty work in warning all to repent and come unto Christ. In this capacity, *you* are one of the signs of the times! Your service on the Lord's errand is a sign of the times. What are your thoughts concerning this office and calling to be a sign of the Second Coming to all those who see your shining light (see Matt. 5:16) and listen to your witness of the truth? How can you impress on your family members that they, too, are wonderful signs of the times to bless others and help them prepare for things to come?

Rejoicing and Reasoning Together

How Can We Respond in Courage and Faith to the Signs of the Second Coming?

Here is a partial list of some major events and signs to help us prepare for the last days before the Second Coming of the Lord:

The establishment of a free land. The founding of a free nation with an inspired Constitution to protect the inalienable rights of its people enabled the gospel to go forth throughout the entire world (see 2 Ne. 10:9–19; 3 Ne. 21:4; D&C 101:80).

In what ways can we do our part to ensure the continuing preservation of liberty and justice for all?

The fulness of the gospel restored through the Book of Mormon (see Isa. 29:2–4, 9–18; Ezek. 37:15–20; 2 Ne. 3; 29; 3 Ne. 21; Morm. 8:12–17).

How can we do better at feasting on these words of eternal life and sharing them with others as we prepare for the Second Coming (see 2 Ne. 32:3; Alma 32)? How can we ensure that we live by every word that proceeds forth from the mouth of God (see Matt. 4:4)?

Restoration of the priesthood and essential keys. The priesthood constitutes the power and authority of God delegated to man to act in all things pertaining to the well-being and eternal salvation of mankind (see D&C 13).

Preparing for the Second Coming requires that we learn our duty (see D&C 107:99–100). How can we more fully magnify our callings (see D&C 24:9), fulfill the three-fold mission of the Church (see D&C 110), and bless our fellowman (see D&C 68:3–7)?

The Church is reestablished on the earth (see D&C 20).

How can we exercise more devotion and sacrifice in building up the Church and kingdom of God?

Gathering of Israel. With the restoration of the keys of the gathering, the re-establishment of the work of the Abrahamic covenant, and the bringing back of the sealing keys of priesthood ordinances and the spirit of family history work (see D&C 110), the work of the gathering was able to unfold in all of its majesty and authority through missionary work designed to prepare the faithful for the Second Coming and warn the rest of the people of the judgments to come.

How can we enhance and magnify our service on behalf of missionary work and the gathering of the elect to the stakes and temples of Zion? Think of giving invitations to friends, hosting missionary discussions, using pass-along cards, distributing copies of the Book of Mormon, praying for those who don't know the Lord, and any other worthy strategy for being on the Lord's errand.

Temples and family history work. Elijah restored the keys for genealogical and temple work on April 3, 1836 (see D&C 110:14–15). The temples of the Lord throughout the world are beautiful and majestic signs of the Second Coming.

How can we enhance our efforts to search our family lines and perform temple work for our ancestors so that they might enjoy the blessings of eternal life? We can faithfully remember the words of Paul, concerning the fathers, that "they without us cannot be made perfect—neither can we without our dead be made perfect" (D&C 128:15).

The signs will proliferate. Disease, commotion, and wickedness will abound. Peace will be taken from the earth. Wars and rumors of wars will happen. Famines will occur. False churches will arise, and many more signs will be seen.

If we are prepared, such signs will remind us that the Second Coming, with its attendant blessings of eternal life, is at the door. Our hearts can be filled with comfort and hope to meet our Lord and Savior soon.

Real-life Stories for Heart and Mind

Preparing for That Which Is to Come. How keenly must the Prophet Joseph Smith have sensed the awesome burden as the mouthpiece of the Lord in proclaiming the message of warning to a world languishing in a state of spiritual famine! With the Second Coming "nigh" (see D&C 1:12), there was an atmosphere of urgency about the service that the Prophet and his stalwart priesthood colleagues were rendering under the inspiration of the Almighty. Not only were they engaged in a campaign to spare the faithful and valiant from the coming calamity (see D&C 1:17), they knew they were fulfilling the word of the Lord just as surely as if from His own mouth (see D&C 1:38).

Joseph Smith, as the principal articulator of the spiritual truths encompassed by the Doctrine and

Covenants, was the Redeemer's instrument of salvation in the latter-day dispensation of time leading up to the Second Coming. The entire world depended on him as the Lord's prophet of the Restoration. Like Captain Moroni, one of the heroes of the covenant he had referenced in the Book of Mormon, he was laboring without cease to rescue his brothers and sisters from calamity (see Alma 48:12).

One of the celebrated episodes in the life of the Prophet illustrates his nature as a man of rescuing instincts. On Wednesday, November 27, 1839, he was en route to Washington, D.C., to speak with President Martin Van Buren and seek redress for the persecution of the Saints. After stopping to rest, the coachman stepped away for a drink, and the horses ran away at full speed with the crowded coach. "I persuaded my fellow travelers to be quiet and retain their seats," wrote the Prophet in his journal, "but had to hold one woman to prevent her throwing her infant out of the coach. The passengers were exceedingly agitated, but I used every persuasion to calm their feelings; and opening the door, I secured my hold on the side of the coach the best way I could, and succeeded in placing myself in the coachman's seat, and reining up the horses, after they had run some two or three miles, and neither coach, horses, or passengers received any injury. My course was spoken of in the highest terms of commendation, as being one of the most daring and heroic deeds, and no language could express the gratitude of the passengers, when they found themselves safe, and the horses quiet. There were some members of Congress with us, who proposed naming the incident to that body, believing they would reward such conduct by some public act" (HC 4:23–24). However, when they learned who Joseph was—the "Mormon Prophet"—they promptly forgot their gratitude. Nevertheless, General Smith, like Captain Moroni, was skillful in securing the safety of his colleagues—not only physically, but, of greater consequence, spiritually.

We all have the opportunity to assume the role of "rescuer" as we prepare for the Second Coming. Section 1 of the Doctrine and Covenants is a call to rescue, a charge to prepare the world for the ensuing return of the Master, a proclamation of the Lord's agenda of salvation during the eleventh hour of the world's history. The canon of sacred truth restored through modern-day prophets is the blueprint for surviving the challenges that lie ahead. It is urgent to lean on the Lord's arm for understanding and heed the word of modern prophets. In our runaway world, there is no sure rescue other than following the Lord's chosen servants in the pathway of security and deliverance. How can you better serve as a "rescuer" for your family and those you serve in the Church? How can you be a "rescuer" for those not of our faith who are thirsty for truth and hungry for spiritual sustenance?

Pondering Prayerfully

Additional scriptures to consider and ponder:
- D&C 34:6
- D&C 34:11
- D&C 133:1–5

The following hymns can help us understand the signs of the Second Coming:
- "Guide Us, O Thou Great Jehovah" (*Hymns*, 83)
- "I Saw a Mighty Angel Fly" (*Hymns*, 15)
- "Saints, Behold How Great Jehovah" (*Hymns*, 28)
- "The Day Dawn Is Breaking" (*Hymns*, 52)

Remember and Be Sure

We are in the last days. The time of the Second Coming is approaching: "For the time is at hand; the day or the hour no man knoweth; but it surely shall come. And he that receiveth these things receiveth me; and they shall be gathered unto me in time and in eternity" (D&C 39:21–22).

Our commission in life is to prepare in all soberness and conviction to meet the Savior and enter into His rest. The ancient prophet Micah encapsulated the entire process in a single sentence: "He hath shewed thee, O man, what is good; and what doth the LORD require of thee, but to do justly, and to love mercy, and to walk humbly with thy God?" (Micah 6:8). This philosophy of righteous living is reflected repeatedly in plainness in the Doctrine and Covenants and in the other scriptures. It is for us to read and savor the words of life and bring them with clarity before our families, that we might together prepare to endure the glory of the Second Coming with joy and thanksgiving.

CHAPTER 44
The Hour Is Nigh: The Savior's Second Coming

When I contemplate the rapidity with which the great and glorious day of the coming of the Son of Man advances, when He shall come to receive His Saints unto Himself, where they shall dwell in His presence, and be crowned with glory and immortality; when I consider that soon the heavens are to be shaken, and the earth tremble and reel to and fro; and that the heavens are to be unfolded as a scroll when it is rolled up; and that every mountain and island are to flee away, I cry out in my heart, What manner of persons ought we to be in all holy conversation and godliness!
—Joseph Smith (*HC* 1:442)

Opening the Window of Wisdom

The Second Coming of our Lord is a reality soon to take place. The tenth Article of Faith confirms that "Christ will reign personally upon the earth; and, that the earth will be renewed and receive its paradisiacal glory." His return will be amidst overwhelming power and all-encompassing glory. When He first came to live among mortals, the Savior was born into humble circumstances and cloaked in modesty. By contrast, when He returns at His Second Coming, cloaked in the brilliance of His red robes of judgment (see D&C 133:48) and surrounded by the consuming glory of His presence, He will instill in all the inhabitants of

the world, at an instant, the awe of His majesty. At that time, all will proclaim His Saviorhood—either by constraint or by joyful witnessing, for "every knee shall bow, and every tongue shall confess, while they hear the sound of the trump, saying: Fear God, and give glory to him who sitteth upon the throne, forever and ever; for the hour of his judgment is come" (D&C 88:104). The message of the Lord of Hosts is clear:

> For the hour is nigh and the day soon at hand when the earth is ripe; and all the proud and they that do wickedly shall be as stubble; and I will burn them up, saith the Lord of Hosts, that wickedness shall not be upon the earth;
> For the hour is nigh, and that which was spoken by mine apostles must be fulfilled; for as they spoke so shall it come to pass;
> For I will reveal myself from heaven with power and great glory, with all the hosts thereof, and dwell in righteousness with men on earth a thousand years, and the wicked shall not stand." (D&C 29:9–11)

At the time of the Second Coming, the millennium is to be ushered in, accompanied by enormous upheaval and cataclysmic change—a nightmare for the wicked and a blessed dream fulfilled for the faithful. The Son of Man is to return in power and sanctity to perform His final labors at the dawning of the millennium of peace. He will fulfill His commission to judge the inhabitants of the earth and receive the faithful in a cloud of angelic choirs.

How do we prepare for the Second Coming? We can search the word of God to learn what counsel He gives us to prepare the way. Within the pages of the Doctrine and Covenants we find enlightenment and rich detail concerning the Second Coming—especially in Sections 29, 34, 45, 88, 101, and 133.

The signs of the times, concerning the final hours of the earth's history prior to the Second Coming, constitute a call to action. These signs are more than mileposts along the way to a final and ultimate renewal of heaven and earth: they are signals and prompts that galvanize the faithful to a state of readiness, a state that will be characterized by peace, not fear. In our time, the Lord has said: "But if ye are prepared ye shall not fear" (D&C 38:30). Luke recorded the following counsel from the Lord: "And take heed to yourselves, lest at any time your hearts be overcharged with surfeiting, and drunkenness, and cares of this life, and so that day come upon you unawares. For as a snare shall it come on all them that dwell on the face of the whole earth. Watch ye therefore, and pray always, that ye may be accounted worthy to escape all these things that shall come to pass, and to stand before the Son of man" (Luke 21:34–36). The ultimate refuge, in the face of these signs of the times, is the process of gathering to holy places to await the Second Coming (see D&C 45:32; 87:8; 101:22).

If at the Second Coming we are prepared and ready, with oil in our lamps, then blessings of glory will rain down upon our heads and a place of honor will be reserved for us at the wedding of the Bridegroom. "For they that are wise and have received the truth, and have taken the Holy Spirit for their guide, and have not been deceived—verily I say unto you, they shall not be hewn down and cast into the fire, but shall abide the day. And the earth shall be given unto them for an inheritance; and they shall multiply and wax strong, and their children shall grow up without sin unto salvation. For the Lord shall be in their midst, and his glory shall be upon them, and he will be their king and their lawgiver" (D&C 45:57–59).

As individuals, we do not know the hour when we will be called home, so we do not know the timing of our first judgment—whether it will be at death or at the time of the Second Coming of the Lord. It behooves us, therefore, to be ready by living righteously according to the whisperings of the Spirit, doing the very best we can in all things, and seeking to build up the kingdom of God—thus proving ourselves worthy to be on the Lord's side.

Inspired by Latter-Day Prophets

Lorenzo Snow: Faithfulness will prepare us for the Second Coming. If you are on a moving train of cars, as long as you sit still and occupy your seat that train will take you to the point you wish to go; but if you step off the cars it will be dangerous, and it may be a long time before another train will come along. It is the same with us—if we are living right, doing our work, we are going along, and if we are keeping our covenants, we are doing the work of God and accomplishing His purposes, and we will be prepared for the time when Jesus the Son of God will come in honor and glory, and will confer upon all those who prove faithful all the blessings that they anticipate, and a thousand times more (*The Teachings of Lorenzo Snow*, 149).

In the modern world there are endless superhighways for transportation and countless pathways of communication using the latest technologies—all taking people to myriad destinations. How can you help yourself and your loved ones stay on the straight and narrow pathway leading to the only destination of eternal significance: a place of covenant security where the blessings of heaven can prepare you to meet the Savior in worthiness when He returns in glory?

Heber J. Grant: The mission of the Church of Jesus Christ of Latter-day Saints is one of peace. It aims to prepare the peoples of the world for the second coming of Christ, and for the inauguration of that blessed day when the millennium shall come and Christ shall reign as King of kings, standing at the head of the universal brotherhood of man (*Gospel Standards: Selections from the Sermons and Writings of Heber J. Grant*, 79).

Though the signs of the times include unlimited turmoil, dislocation, chaos, wars, earthquakes, and pestilence, the core message of the Church is peace—peace that can come only when one has done everything possible to honor the covenants and look forward with joy and serenity to the advent of the millennial reign. What is the role of peace in your life? How can you help your family and those you teach in the Church to plan for peace, cultivate peace, and preserve peace in these trying times?

Howard W. Hunter: *Preparation for the Second Coming does not require a preoccupation with the future.* Jesus taught his disciples to watch and pray; however, he taught them that prayerful watching does not require sleepless anxiety and preoccupation with the future, but rather the quiet, steady attention to present duties (*The Teachings of Howard W. Hunter*, 201).

How can "quiet, steady attention to present duties" reflect more wisdom than a preoccupation with things to come? What duties should we attend to in order to be prepared?

Bruce R. McConkie: It is true that no man knoweth the day nor the hour of his return . . . but those who treasure up his word will not be deceived as to the time of that glorious day, nor as to the events to precede and to attend it. (Jos. Smith 1:37.) The righteous will be able to read the signs of the times. To those in darkness he will come suddenly, unexpectedly, "as a thief in the night," but to "the children of light" who "are not of the night, nor of darkness," as Paul expressed it, that day will not overtake them "as a thief." They will recognize the signs as certainly as a woman in travail foreknows the approximate time of her child's birth. (1 Thess. 5:1–6.) (*Mormon Doctrine*, 688).

How can we read the signs of the times accurately and thus not be surprised at the Second Coming? The answer: Treasure up the word of the Lord and live righteously! How can you more fully treasure up the words of truth and live worthy of the Spirit? "For behold, again I say unto you that if ye will enter in by the way, and receive the Holy Ghost, it will show unto you all things what ye should do" (2 Ne. 32:5).

Truths to Liken

Dan. 7:13–14—"I saw in the night visions, and, behold, one like the Son of man came with the clouds of heaven, and came to the Ancient of days, and they brought him near before him. And there was given him dominion, and glory, and a kingdom, that all people, nations, and languages, should serve him: his dominion is an everlasting dominion, which shall not pass away, and his kingdom that which shall not be destroyed."

- Among the visions of Daniel after he had been led away captive to Babylon was a prophetic view of a future priesthood gathering of great importance involving the Son of Man and the "Ancient of Days" (Adam, or Michael—see D&C 27:11). This refers to the gathering at Adam-ondi-Ahman where the Savior, on the eve of His millennial reign, will receive back the keys dispensed to various prophets through the ages, beginning with Adam (see D&C 107:53–56). The Prophet Joseph Smith said of this council: "Daniel in his seventh chapter speaks of the Ancient of Days; he means the oldest man, our Father Adam, Michael, he will call his children together and hold a council with them to prepare them for the coming of the Son of Man. He (Adam) is the father of the human family, and presides over the spirits of all men, and all that have had the keys must stand before him in this grand council. This may take place before some of us leave this stage of action. The Son of Man stands before him, and there is given him glory and dominion. Adam delivers up his stewardship to Christ, that which was delivered to him as holding the keys of the universe, but retains his standing as head of the human family" (*Teachings of the Prophet Joseph Smith*, 157).

- There are multiple returns of the Savior to His people prior to His grand Second Coming in glory. The Savior came with His Father in the spring of 1820 to the boy Joseph at the dawning of the Restoration. He came to the Kirtland

Temple on April 3, 1836, to preside at the bestowing of sacred priesthood keys essential to the work of the ministry. He will return to Adam-ondi-Ahman for the council referenced above. And when all is in place for His millennial reign on the basis of various appearances with His chosen leaders, He will appear to the whole world in glory at the Second Coming. There is great logic in the preparatory visits of the Savior prior to the Second Coming. How can you help others not of our faith to understand the supreme mercy of the Lord in preparing His sons and daughters for the Second Coming by visiting them repeatedly as part of the Restoration so that they may be ready and active in helping others to prepare as well?

D&C 34:4–12—"And blessed are you because you have believed; And more blessed are you because you are called of me to preach my gospel—To lift up your voice as with the sound of a trump, both long and loud, and cry repentance unto a crooked and perverse generation, preparing the way of the Lord for his second coming. For behold, verily, verily, I say unto you, the time is soon at hand that I shall come in a cloud with power and great glory. And it shall be a great day at the time of my coming, for all nations shall tremble. But before that great day shall come, the sun shall be darkened, and the moon be turned into blood; and the stars shall refuse their shining, and some shall fall, and great destructions await the wicked. Wherefore, lift up your voice and spare not, for the Lord God hath spoken; therefore prophesy, and it shall be given by the power of the Holy Ghost. And if you are faithful, behold, I am with you until I come—And verily, verily, I say unto you, I come quickly. I am your Lord and your Redeemer. Even so. Amen."

- These words were given to Orson Pratt, a nineteen-year-old convert, in a revelation through the Prophet Joseph Smith at Fayette, New York, on November 4, 1830.
- The Second Coming provides a major context for missionary work. With the voice of prophesy given by the Holy Ghost, we are to warn our neighbors to repent and prepare for the return of the

Savior. Imagine that the words given to Orson Pratt, young brother of Parley P. Pratt, were given to you personally. How might you go about applying this counsel in your own life as you spread the gospel message to others? How has the Holy Ghost prompted you with words of inspiration in speaking to your friends about the restored gospel?

D&C 45:48, 51–53—"And then shall the Lord set his foot upon this mount, and it shall cleave in twain, and the earth shall tremble, and reel to and fro, and the heavens also shall shake. . . . And then shall the Jews look upon me and say: What are these wounds in thine hands and in thy feet? Then shall they know that I am the Lord; for I will say unto them: These wounds are the wounds with which I was wounded in the house of my friends. I am he who was lifted up. I am Jesus that was crucified. I am the Son of God. And then shall they weep because of their iniquities; then shall they lament because they persecuted their king."

- These heart-rending words from the account of the Second Coming were given at Kirtland, Ohio, on March 7, 1831; they mark the moment in time when the Jewish nation as a whole will know that their long-awaited Messiah is indeed the one they at first rejected, even Jesus Christ.
- The Savior mercifully calls the Jews His "friends." He has delivered them from their enemies. His arms are open to receive them in their remorse and repentance. This applies not just to the Jewish people, because most in the world will have rejected the Lord. All will need to come to terms with their actions. The wicked (those of a telestial nature) will be destroyed at His coming, but a vast multitude of those surviving the upheavals at the time of the Second Coming (those terrestrial) will need to hear the message of the fulness of the gospel from the servants of the Lord (those celestial souls caught up to meet Him at His descent upon the earth) as the millennial era unfolds. What are your thoughts about the choice

opportunities opened up through the Second Coming to become missionaries and teachers to the terrestrial nations?

D&C 82:14–15—"For Zion must increase in beauty, and in holiness; her borders must be enlarged; her stakes must be strengthened; yea, verily I say unto you, Zion must arise and put on her beautiful garments. Therefore, I give unto you this commandment, that ye bind yourselves by this covenant, and it shall be done according to the laws of the Lord."

- These words were included in a revelation given to the Prophet Joseph Smith in Jackson County, Missouri, on April 26, 1832, at a general council of the Church at which Joseph Smith was sustained as the president of the high priesthood. Jackson County is the very place where the future New Jerusalem will be raised up as one of the two centers (along with the restored Jerusalem of old) for the government of God during the millennial reign.

- As a people aspiring for the conditions of Zion, there are many things we can and should do to establish Zion— purify our hearts, seek to lift and bless others, and live a righteous life. We have covenanted to do these things. Zion is not a dream but rather a destiny; not a wish but a commandment of God. God will have a pure and righteous people to meet Him upon His return in glory. Where such a society emerges in the strength of the Lord, nourished by the blessings of the Almighty, there is Zion. What are your thoughts and feelings concerning your own duties in relation to this covenant commission to build up Zion? How can you help others be more active in preparing a Zion society for the arrival of the Lord?

D&C 133:20–25—"For behold, he shall stand upon the mount of Olivet, and upon the mighty ocean, even the great deep, and upon the islands of the sea, and upon the land of Zion. And he shall utter his voice out of Zion, and he shall speak from Jerusalem, and his voice shall be heard among all people; And it shall be a voice as the voice of many waters, and as the voice of a great thunder, which shall break down the mountains, and the valleys shall not be found. He shall command the great deep, and it shall be driven back into the north countries, and the islands shall become one land; And the land of Jerusalem and the land of Zion shall be turned back into their own place, and the earth shall be like as it was in the days before it was divided. And the Lord, even the Savior, shall stand in the midst of his people, and shall reign over all flesh."

- These words were contained in a revelation given through the Prophet Joseph Smith at Hiram, Ohio, on November 3, 1831; they were initially used as an appendix to the Doctrine and Covenants but were later designated as Section 133.

- In scope difficult to imagine, the earth will go through a monumental continental and geological restructuring at the time of the Second Coming, being restored to its original configuration before the division mentioned in the Old Testament (see 1 Chron. 1:19; Gen. 10:25). Mountains will be lowered and valleys removed; the "islands" (continents) will become "one land." Jerusalem and Zion will be situated as center points for the government of the millennial King to rule the affairs of the world during the thousand-year period.

What are your thoughts concerning such a revolutionary adjustment of the earth? How does the account of the upheavals in the New World incident to the death of the Savior (see 3 Ne. 8) serve as an anticipation of these future events? How does the voice of the Lord heard across the land at that time and His subsequent appearance among the survivors in the New World (see 3 Ne. 9–11) illustrate the transformations to come upon the entire world at the time of the Second Coming? Could it be that Mormon was inspired to include in his account graphic references to these catastrophic events—and the eventual triumph of the emerging forces of peace and glory—as a rehearsal of precisely what lies ahead in the near future?

Rejoicing and Reasoning Together

What Is the Timing and the Process of the Resurrection?

The resurrection is the permanent reuniting of the body and the spirit following death in mortality. Through the miracle of the resurrection we become immortal. We are restored to a state of existence (capacity for glory) according to our works of righteousness (see 2 Ne. 9:13). The resurrection was made possible through the grace of God because of the infinite and eternal Atonement of the Lord Jesus Christ (see 2 Ne. 9:22). We will be resurrected whole, restored to our perfect frame (see Alma 11:43–44). We will take with us all that we have learned through our experiences on earth (see D&C 130:18–19). In addition to the blessing of the resurrection (immortality), there is the magnificent blessing of eternal life and celestial exaltation that we can look forward to through our obedience. If we hold out faithful to the end and endure well—following strictly in the pathway of the Savior—we will eventually receive "all that my Father hath" (D&C 84:38).

A sublime aspect of the Second Coming is that it empowers and brings about the miracle of the resurrection for a host of the righteous who lived up to that point, subsequent to the time of Christ, and are awaiting the eternal reunion of body and spirit: "Now, verily I say unto you, that through the redemption which is made for you is brought to pass the resurrection from the dead. And the spirit and the body are the soul of man. And the resurrection from the dead is the redemption of the soul" (D&C 88:14–16). The timing of the resurrection as a key dimension of the Second Coming is explained in a revelation to the Church given through the Prophet Joseph Smith at Kirtland, Ohio, on March 7, 1831:

> And before the day of the Lord shall come, the sun shall be darkened, and the moon be turned into blood, and the stars fall from heaven.
>
> And the remnant shall be gathered unto this place; And then they shall look for me, and, behold, I will come; and they shall see me in the clouds of heaven, clothed with power and great glory; with all the holy angels; and he that watches not for me shall be cut off.
>
> But before the arm of the Lord shall fall, an angel shall sound his trump, and the saints that have slept shall come forth to meet me in the cloud.
>
> Wherefore, if ye have slept in peace blessed are you; for as you now behold me and know that I am, even so shall ye come unto me and your souls shall live, and your redemption shall be perfected; and the saints shall come forth from the four quarters of the earth.
>
> Then shall the arm of the Lord fall upon the nations.
>
> And then shall the Lord set his foot upon this mount, and it shall cleave in twain, and the earth shall tremble, and reel to and fro, and the heavens also shall shake. (D&C 45:42–48)

Christ was the first to be resurrected: "For as in Adam all die, even so in Christ shall all be made alive. But every man in his own order: Christ the firstfruits; afterward they that are Christ's at his coming" (1 Cor. 15:22–23). Subsequent to the Resurrection of the Lord following His Crucifixion, other righteous individuals who had lived previously were brought forth from the grave in the Holy Land (see Matt. 27:52–53) and in the New World (see Hel. 14:25; 3 Ne. 23:9–14; D&C 133:54–56). The process of the resurrection of the righteous who lived after Christ will continue at the time of His Second Coming, prior to His triumphal descent upon the mount in Jerusalem to end the massive assault against Israel by her enemies.

Four trumpet signals will announce the unfolding of the resurrection according to the order established from before the foundation of the world, timed according to each individual's level of obedience and righteousness. The first two trumps will announce the resurrection of the just at the time of the Second Coming (see D&C 88:96–99), and the second two trumps will announce the resurrection of the unjust after the thousand-year period has ended (see D&C 88:100–102).

Those resurrected at the sound of the first trump are part of the "first resurrection" (see Rev. 20:5–6; D&C 76:64), a celestial resurrection reserved for those who are "just men made perfect through Jesus the mediator of the new covenant, who wrought out this perfect atonement through the shedding of his own blood. These are they whose bodies are celestial, whose glory is that of the sun, even the glory of God, the highest of all, whose glory the sun of the firmament is written of as being typical" (D&C 76:69–70). In patriarchal blessings this resurrection is often described as the "morning of the first resurrection." The Book of Mormon also makes reference to a "first resurrection" that took place shortly after the Resurrection of Christ involving those righteous individuals who lived prior to His day (see Mosiah 15:21–22).

Those resurrected at the sound of the second trump are also part of the first resurrection, but come forth in what is typically designated as the afternoon of the first resurrection to a terrestrial status. These are they who "died without law; And also they who are the spirits of men kept in prison, whom the Son visited, and preached the gospel unto them, that they might be judged according to men in the flesh; Who received not the testimony of Jesus in the flesh, but afterwards received it. These are they who are honorable men of the earth, who were blinded by the craftiness of men. These are they who receive of his glory, but not of his fulness. These are they who receive of the presence of the Son, but not of the fulness of the Father. Wherefore, they are bodies terrestrial, and not bodies celestial, and differ in glory as the moon differs from the sun" (D&C 76:72–78). At this same time "shall the heathen nations be redeemed, and they that knew no law shall have part in the first resurrection; and it shall be tolerable for them" (D&C 45:54).

Those resurrected at the sound of the third trump are the wicked who come forth in the beginning of the second, or final resurrection, being the resurrection of the unjust after the end of the thousand years (see D&C 76:81–90). These have a telestial resurrection. Last of all, at the end of the second resurrection, the sons of perdition come forth in a resurrection that gives them immortality, as all the rest, but outside the reach of Christ's redemption and without any glory: "Having denied the Holy Spirit after having received it, and having denied the Only Begotten Son of the Father, having crucified him unto themselves and put him to an open shame" (D&C 76:35).

The Second Coming will coincide with the miracle of the first resurrection. The Prophet Joseph Smith has given us a clearer view of the process of this resurrection. On the occasion of the death of Lorenzo D. Barnes at Bradford, England, on December 20, 1842—the first elder to die on a foreign mission—the Prophet Joseph made the following remarkable commentary concerning the resurrection (as recorded by Willard Richards and Wilford Woodruff):

I will tell you what I want. If tomorrow I shall be called to lie in yonder tomb. In the morning of the resurrection let me strike hands with my father, and cry, "My father," and he will say, "My son, my son," as soon as the rock rends and before we come out of our graves.

And may we contemplate these things so? Yes, if we learn how to live and how to die. When we lie down we contemplate how we may rise in the morning; and it is pleasing for friends to lie down together, locked in the arms of love, to sleep and wake in each other's embrace and renew their conversation.

Would you think it strange if I relate what I have seen in vision in relation to this interesting theme? Those who have died in Jesus Christ may expect to enter into all that fruition of joy when they come forth, which they possessed or anticipated here.

So plain was the vision, that I actually saw men, before they had ascended from the tomb, as though they were getting up slowly. They took each other by the hand and said to each other, "My father, my son, my mother, my daughter, my brother, my sister." And when the voice calls for the dead to arise, suppose I am laid by the side of my father, what would be the first joy of my heart? To meet my father, my mother, my brother, my sister; and when they are by my side, I embrace them and they me.

It is my meditation all the day, and more than my meat and drink, to know how I shall make the Saints of God comprehend the visions that roll like an overflowing surge before my mind.

Oh! how I would delight to bring before you things which you never thought of! But poverty and the cares of the world prevent. But I am glad I have the privilege of communicating to you some things which, if grasped closely, will be a help to you when earthquakes bellow, the clouds gather, the lightnings flash, and the storms are ready to burst upon you like peals of thunder. Lay hold of these things and let not your knees or joints tremble, nor your hearts faint; and then what can earthquakes, wars and tornadoes do? Nothing. All your losses will be made up to you in the resurrection, provided you continue faithful. By the vision of the Almighty I have seen it.

More painful to me are the thoughts of annihilation than death. If I have no expectation of seeing my father, mother, brothers, sisters and friends again, my heart would burst in a moment, and I should go down to my grave.

The expectation of seeing my friends in the morning of the resurrection cheers my soul and makes me bear up against the evils of life. It is like their taking a long journey, and on their return we meet them with increased joy.

God has revealed His Son from the heavens and the doctrine of the resurrection also; and we have a knowledge that those we bury here God will bring up again, clothed upon and quickened by the Spirit of the great God; and what mattereth it whether we lay them down, or we lay down with them, when we can keep them no longer? Let these truths sink down in our hearts, that we may even here begin to enjoy that which shall be in full hereafter.

Hosanna, hosanna, hosanna to Almighty God, that rays of light begin to burst forth upon us even now. I cannot find words in which to express myself. I am not learned, but I have as good feelings as any man.

O that I had the language of the archangel to express my feelings once to my friends! But I never expect to in this life. When others rejoice, I rejoice; when they mourn, I mourn. (*HC* 5: 361–362)

The miracle of the resurrection is not unlike the miracle of the coming forth of a new life from the mother's womb in mortality. What are your thoughts about the joy that comes to the heart and mind of one who loves his or her family with a never-ending love, and looks forward to a heavenly family reunion of resurrected souls in the hereafter with such fervor and rapture that these feelings fully overpower any fear of the destructive events associated with the Second Coming? How can you cultivate such joy and contentment as you prepare for the Second Coming? The miraculous event of the first resurrection is not far in the future. The Second Coming brings amazing gifts of light, life, liberation, restoration, cleansing, deliverance, and the inauguration of peace across the world after a period of acute dislocation and frenzy. What are your thoughts and feelings concerning the imminent resurrection of loved ones from the ranks of your righteous ancestors?

Real-life Stories for Heart and Mind

The Clouds of Heaven. We all take a moment, now and again, to look up into the heavens and admire the panorama of the clouds moving across the sky before our eyes like living phantoms of the Creation. Each day is different; each season has its recurring canvasses of beauty. At times these cloud formations are so marvelously shaped and colored that one has to take a deep breath and look again in order to confirm that they are real—and not the figment of some great artist's imagination.

We are told that at His Second Coming the Lord will appear "in a cloud with power and great glory" (Luke 21:27). There are several places in the scriptures that speak about the faithful being thus caught up at the last day to meet the Savior—"gathered with the saints, to be caught up unto the church of the Firstborn, and received into the cloud" (D&C 76:102). Paul stated it thus: "Then we which are alive and remain shall be caught up together with them in the clouds, to meet the Lord in the air: and so shall we ever be with the Lord. Wherefore comfort one another with these words" (1 Thes. 4:17–18).

The image of the cloud is used often in the scriptures as a reference for the presence and glory of the Lord. But it is also used to imply many other things or individuals. Paul speaks of "so great a cloud of witnesses" (Heb. 12:1). Ezekiel foresaw the great final battle of Gog and Magog where the enemies of the kingdom of God would come in numberless hordes "like a cloud to cover the land, thou, and all thy bands, and many people with thee" (Ezek. 38:9). Could it be that the "clouds" spoken of in association with the Second Coming are not merely natural phenomena, but the numberless concourses of the righteous Saints caught up to meet the Redeemer at His advent, along with the returning city of Enoch (see Moses 7:63)? In his inspired translation, Joseph Smith rendered the opening part of the Book of Revelation this way: "For behold, he cometh in the clouds with ten thousands of his saints in the kingdom, clothed with the glory of his Father" (JST, Rev. 1:7).

It is our challenge to remain on the pathway of righteousness and to prepare ourselves for this final coming, that we might be caught up in the "clouds of heaven" (D&C 45:16) on that grand day: "And then they shall look for me, and, behold, I will come; and they shall see me in the clouds of heaven, clothed with power and great glory; with all the holy angels; and he that watched not for me shall be cut off" (D&C 45:44).

What are your thoughts about being caught up in the "clouds" to greet the Savior at His Second Coming? Isaiah pronounced the word of the Lord: "But they that wait upon the LORD shall renew their strength; they shall mount up with wings as eagles; they shall run, and not be weary; and they shall walk, and not faint" (Isa. 40:31). Strength to fly and move without fainting! Are you prepared to ascend in power and worthiness before the Lord upon His return? How can you more fully prepare for this event?

Hope Is Rooted in Christ. A long-time teacher of religion classes shared this experience:

As a teacher for many years, I have witnessed the change of heart of many students. It occurs as they embrace the gospel by making sacred covenants and receiving lifesaving ordinances that can bring them back to the presence of our Heavenly Father. This happens when they are full of hope. This change occurs when gratitude is felt and then expressed through loving obedience to God and service to their fellowmen. I followed an underlying principle when

I taught: be sure they leave the classroom with hope. Hope is rooted in Christ and in the anticipation of eternal life. You really can't exist on this earth and overcome temptation without hope. If one is hopeless, sin lieth at the door. Hope is preceded by, and part of, our personal righteousness, for faith and hope are so intertwined they cannot be separated. They truly are the foundation of all righteousness. This is why we as parents and teachers need to be positive. We need to give people hope to carry on—hope for eternal life according to the plan provided by God before the world began (see Titus 1:2). Isaiah truly prophesied of the Second Coming of the Lord Jesus Christ and of His millennial reign. We are the generation assigned to prepare the people for these glorious events. Those who are faithful and endure to the end are surely filled with hope (see Isa. 64:4; D&C 133:45). As our minds reflect on these things, it surely awakens a sense of hope, and above all, great gratitude for the Lord our God. Hope is a power that causes one to endure. Gratitude for the blessings of God is exemplified in the change of our attitude and behavior as we prepare, in faith, for the Second Coming of our Lord.

How can you help your loved ones and others around you cultivate a greater sense of hope and gratitude while looking forward to the Second Coming?

Pondering Prayerfully

Additional scriptures to consider and ponder:

- Ps. 50:1–6
- Ezek. 37:4, 11–12, 14
- Zech. 13:6
- Luke 14:14
- 2 Ne. 9:6–8
- Alma 11:43–44
- Alma 40:23
- Alma 41:3
- Morm. 8:22–23
- D&C 14:6
- D&C 33:16–17
- D&C 34:6

The following hymns inspire gratitude toward the Second Coming:

- "Christ the Lord Is Risen Today" (*Hymns,* 200)
- "I Know That My Redeemer Lives" (*Hymns,* 136)
- "Joy to the World" (*Hymns,* 201)
- "Lo, the Mighty God Appearing!" (*Hymns,* 55)
- "The Happy Day at Last Has Come" (*Hymns,* 32)
- "We Will Sing of Zion" (*Hymns,* 47)

Remember and Be Sure

The Lord has a great work for us to do in this, the dispensation of the fullness of times. We are to be worthy to take the gospel to every kindred, tongue, and people. This is the last time He will set His hand to recover and gather His people prior to the Second Coming that will usher in the millennial reign.

We are to watch and be ready. The gospel message sounds with clarion echoes: Hold to the iron rod, pray with faith, listen to the Spirit, and follow the living prophets. The agenda for preparing to meet the Lord upon His return in glory is simple but forthright: Commune with the Lord regularly and sincerely; be humble, avoiding pride and self-serving attitudes; be charitable toward others, loving the Lord and your neighbor with all your heart; cultivate unity; walk in the light of truth; gather in holy places (the homes, congregations, and temples of Zion); uphold the Lord's anointed in word and deed; cultivate love and mutual confidence within the home; listen for the personal revelations of God; be virtuous and morally clean; remember your sacred covenants. This is the agenda of courage and readiness: "but if ye are prepared ye shall not fear" (D&C 38:30).

God is all-powerful in His ability to restore and render dynamic and alive all aspects of man's existence—including the restoration of the body and its reunion with the spirit in a resurrected state, the restoration of the spirit of hope within the breast of His struggling children, and the restoration of His chosen people to holy places—including the millennial realm of peace and security and the ultimate mansions of exaltation in the presence of Father and Son. Of this we can be sure.

We are not involved in a work of the hour, nor in a work of the month or year. We are involved in a work that stretches from the foundations of the earth to the ushering in of Christ's imminent return and beyond. We are the servants in the Lord's vineyard who have the charge to help cultivate, nurture, and harvest the covenant crop. Through faith and diligence we can be wise and honor our promises to the Lord. We can prevail over the forces of evil that would undermine and discredit the doctrine of Christ. We can rise valiant and victorious to hear one day the blessed words in the Savior's parable: "Well done, thou good and faithful servant: thou hast been faithful over a few things, I will make thee ruler over many things: enter thou into the joy of thy lord" (Matt. 25:21).

CHAPTER 45
The Millennial Reign of the Savior

The world has had a fair trial for six thousand years; the Lord will try the seventh thousand Himself. . . . Satan will be bound, and the works of darkness destroyed; righteousness will be put to the line and judgment to the plummet, and "he that fears the Lord will alone be exalted in that day." —Joseph Smith (*HC* 5:63–64)

Opening the Window of Wisdom

The Millennium will be ushered in with the dawning glory of the Second Coming of our Lord and Savior Jesus Christ (see D&C 29:11). No man knows the time of this grand event (see Matt. 24:36). We can be prepared by keeping our lamps full of oil—the oil of righteousness.

The Millennium is the time when judgment will come upon the children of God. The wicked will be consumed by fire (see Isa. 13:9–14), while the righteous will be caught up to meet the Lord and "the earth will be renewed and receive its paradisiacal glory" (A of F 10).

The Lord has ordained that the seat of the millennial government will be in a glorious capital called the New Jerusalem, the inheritance of Joseph on the American continent, as well as in the rebuilt and renewed Jerusalem in the Holy Land, the inheritance of the Jewish people and other Israelite tribes of the covenant. It is to these centers and

associated regions that the faithful and righteous "whose garments are white through the blood of the Lamb" (Ether 13:10) are to be gathered in the days of the Second Coming and beyond (see Ether 13:4–5).

During the Millennium, Satan will be bound for a season until the end of the thousand years (see Rev. 20:1–3, 7; D&C 43:31; 88:110–111), having no "power to tempt any man" (D&C 101:28). Nephi characterized this period as follows:

> And the Holy One of Israel must reign in dominion, and might, and power, and great glory.
>
> And he gathereth his children from the four quarters of the earth; and he numbereth his sheep, and they know him; and there shall be one fold and one shepherd; and he shall feed his sheep, and in him they shall find pasture.
>
> And because of the righteousness of his people, Satan has no power; wherefore, he cannot be loosed for the space of many years; for he hath no power over the hearts of the people, for they dwell in righteousness, and the Holy One of Israel reigneth. (1 Ne. 22:24–26)

Consequently, the obedient under Christ who have "taken the Holy Spirit for their guide" (D&C

45:57) will enjoy glorious blessings: "And the earth shall be given unto them for an inheritance; and they shall multiply and wax strong, and their children shall grow up without sin unto salvation. For the Lord shall be in their midst, and his glory shall be upon them, and he will be their king and their lawgiver" (D&C 45:58–59). There will be peace on the earth and all enmity will cease. The Lord has said, "And there shall be no sorrow because there is no death. In that day an infant shall not die until he is old; and his life shall be as the age of a tree; And when he dies he shall not sleep, that is to say in the earth, but shall be changed in the twinkling of an eye, and shall be caught up, and his rest shall be glorious" (D&C 101:29–31). The great family of God will be organized as a resplendent Zion society commissioned to carry the gospel to their millennial fellowcitizens not yet part of the kingdom of God and to complete temple ordinances for all who are worthy. At the end of the thousand years, Satan will be loosed for a season (see Rev. 20:2–3, 7–10; D&C 29:22–29; D&C 43:31) before he is removed forever through the victory of Michael (Adam) over the hosts of evil:

> And then he shall be loosed for a little season, that he may gather together his armies.
> And Michael, the seventh angel, even the archangel, shall gather together his armies, even the hosts of heaven.
> And the devil shall gather together his armies; even the hosts of hell, and shall come up to battle against Michael and his armies.
> And then cometh the battle of the great God; and the devil and his armies shall be cast away into their own place, that they shall not have power over the saints any more at all.
> For Michael shall fight their battles, and shall overcome him who seeketh the throne of him who sitteth upon the throne, even the Lamb. (D&C 88:111–15)

Our Father in Heaven knows the future. We can only peer dimly forward with hope and a measure of happiness as we rely on the Lord and His mercy and grace and follow the promptings of the Comforter. We know that the plan of happiness cannot be frustrated by the devil. If we but

keep the commandments, we have been promised everlasting life in the presence of the Father and the Son. When the earth is celestialized at the end of the millennial period, all pain and sorrow as we know it will pass away and the righteous shall inherit all things in glory and eternal life (see D&C 88:18–20). The outcome of the final judgment for the valiant and obedient is the blessing of eternal lives in everlasting glory.

Inspired by Latter-Day Prophets

Joseph Smith: Christ and the resurrected Saints will reign over the earth during the thousand years. They will not probably dwell on the earth, but will visit it when they please or when it is necessary to govern it. There will be wicked men on the earth during the thousand years. The heathen nations who will not come up to worship will be visited with the judgments of God, and must eventually be destroyed from the earth (*HC* 5:212).

> *Being in a terrestrial realm during the Millennium, the global society will be a blending of the covenant righteous belonging to the kingdom of God and those not yet within the kingdom who are "wicked" in the sense that they have not yet come unto Christ to enjoy the blessing of the gospel of faith, repentance, baptism, and the gift of the Holy Ghost (see D&C 84:49–53). A great missionary work will occur during the millennium with the purpose of inviting all, including the heathen nations, to come to Christ to become what He called "the children of the covenant" (3 Ne. 20:26) and heirs to the celestial glory. In what measure will your experience in mortality as a lifelong missionary for the Lord serve as a rehearsal for the continuing missionary labors to come in the millennial period? How will the nature of missionary work change in a mission field freed of the evil of telestial influences (these having been purged completely at the Second Coming)? It will surely still be a challenge, as Brigham Young confirmed:*

>> *When Jesus comes to rule and reign, King of nations, as he now does, King of Saints, the veil of the covering will be taken from all nations, that all flesh*

may see his glory together, but that will not make them all Saints . . . the veil of the covering may be taken from before the nations, and all flesh see his glory together, and at the same time declare they will not serve him. . . . In the Millennium men will have the privilege of their own belief, but they will not have the privilege of treating the name and character of Deity as they have done heretofore. No, but every knee shall bow and every tongue confess to the glory of God the Father that Jesus is the Christ. (Discourses of Brigham Young, *116, 118)*

Brigham Young: In the Millennium, when the kingdom of God is established on the earth in power, glory and perfection, and the reign of wickedness that has so long prevailed is subdued, the Saints of God will have the privilege of building their temples, and of entering into them, becoming, as it were, pillars in the temples of God, and they will officiate for their dead. Then we will see our friends come up, and perhaps some that we have been acquainted with here. . . . And we will have revelations to know our forefathers clear back to Father Adam and Mother Eve, and we will enter into the temples of God and officiate for them. Then man will be sealed to man until the chain is made perfect back to Adam, so that there will be a perfect chain of Priesthood from Adam to the winding-up scene. . . . This will be the work of the Latter-day Saints in the Millennium (*Discourses of Brigham Young,* 116).

As an extension of missionary work in the Millennium, the central commission of the Saints will be temple work. What sense of joy do you receive knowing that you will have a stewardship with those known as the "pillars in the temples of God"? It will take a millennium of time to perfect the work, even with the blessing of revelation to complete the chain of individuals from the end to the beginning, and from the beginning to the end. Why will temple work ensure a prevailing spirit of joy and gratitude during the Millennium?

John Taylor: When the will of God is done on earth as it is in heaven, that priesthood will be the only legitimate ruling power under the whole heavens; for every other power and influence will be subject to it. When the millennium . . . is introduced, all potentates, powers, and authorities—every man, woman, and child will be in subjection to the kingdom of God; they will be under the power and dominion of the Priesthood of God: then the will of God will be done on the earth as it is done in heaven (*JD* 6:25–26).

The government during the millennial reign will be the theocratic government of Christ, operating according to the eternal principles and powers of the holy priesthood. Those who rule will be the Saints of the Most High, who "hath made us kings and priests unto God and his Father; to him be glory and dominion for ever and ever" (Rev. 1:6). There will be duties of both an ecclesiastical as well as an administrative nature placed upon the shoulders of the servants of God during the Millennium. What are your thoughts about the expanded nature of millennial leadership that will be placed upon the Saints of God in the future? How is your current set of duties within the Church—as well as in the community, state, and nation—a rehearsal for what is to come? How does this give new meaning to the reference in the Lord's prayer: "Thy kingdom come. Thy will be done in earth, as it is in heaven" (Matt. 6:10)?

Bruce R. McConkie: Both Jew and Gentile shall build the New Jerusalem. The remnant of Jacob in the Americas (meaning the Lamanites), and the gathered remnants of the whole house of Israel—indeed, all people from all nations who are righteous and pure and believing, all who keep the commandments—all shall join in building the Holy City. And the Jews (other than the Lamanite Jews) who believe and repent and purify themselves shall build up anew the Jerusalem of old (*The Mortal Messiah: From Bethlehem to Calvary,* 4:358).

One of the great signs of the times leading up to the millennial era will be the emergence of the New Jerusalem and the restored and rebuilt Old Jerusalem, built under the direction of the priesthood of God. What are your thoughts and feelings about these future events? How do you feel about the importance of staying focused on the needs and obligations we have in our current day-to-day service even as we look toward tomorrow? How can we maintain a worthy and wholesome balance in our pondering of all things divine and holy and still get today's work done?

Truths to Liken

Isa. 2:4–5—"And he shall judge among the nations, and shall rebuke many people: and they shall beat their swords into plowshares, and their spears into pruninghooks: nation shall not lift up sword against nation, neither shall they learn war any more. O house of Jacob, come ye, and let us walk in the light of the LORD."

- The prophet Isaiah, prophesying in the time period of around 740 BC to 701 BC—the same period in which the ten tribes were carried away captive by the Assyrian forces—described the last phase of the earth's history involving temple building, the gathering of Israel, and conditions of peace during the Millennium.
- The famous metaphors about swords being converted into plowshares (the cutting blades of the plow) and spears into pruning hooks convey the transformation from a dominantly military culture into one that is peaceful and domesticated. Even more important is the image of walking in the light of the Lord. In the millennial world, enmity will cease (see D&C 101:26), and the light of the Lord will penetrate the entire world. Can you imagine a world in which there is no enmity or aggression? How can you use your influence to promote goodwill and charitable relationships in the present world? How is the gospel the most effective force for peace in the world today?

Isa. 11:6–9—"The wolf also shall dwell with the lamb, and the leopard shall lie down with the kid; and the calf and the young lion and the fatling together; and a little child shall lead them. And the cow and the bear shall feed; their young ones

shall lie down together: and the lion shall eat straw like the ox. And the sucking child shall play on the hole of the asp, and the weaned child shall put his hand on the cockatrice' den. They shall not hurt nor destroy in all my holy mountain: for the earth shall be full of the knowledge of the LORD, as the waters cover the sea."

- Isaiah described conditions during the Millennium. Peace among all species of living things will abound because the "knowledge" of the Lord will fill the entire earth.
- There is surely prevailing peace and calm in a world in which an infant can interact with formerly poisonous serpents, just as there is peace and calm when the enmity between Satan and the seed of the woman (Christ—see Gen. 3:15; Moses 4:21) is suspended during the millennial period. In your opinion, how does the "knowledge of the Lord" create conditions of peace? Note how Nephi interprets this principle after citing the words of Isaiah: "Wherefore, all things which have been revealed unto the children of men shall at that day be revealed; and Satan shall have power over the hearts of the children of men no more, for a long time" (2 Ne. 30:18).

3 Ne. 22:13–14—"And all thy children shall be taught of the Lord; and great shall be the peace of thy children. In righteousness shalt thou be established; thou shalt be far from oppression for thou shalt not fear, and from terror for it shall not come near thee."

- The Savior quoted from Isaiah 54 to the Saints in the New World at the time of His visit there (see Isa. 54:13–14), characterizing the peace and serenity of the learning environment in the millennial kingdom of God.
- What greater teacher than the Lord Himself? What greater environment for learning than one of righteousness, absent of all oppression and fear? How can you cultivate a similar learning environment for your loved ones right now—one of righteousness centered in

Christ, one of peace, with no hint of oppression or terror?

D&C 29:11—"For I will reveal myself from heaven with power and great glory, with all the hosts thereof, and dwell in righteousness with men on earth a thousand years, and the wicked shall not stand."

- This promise was included in a revelation given through the Prophet Joseph Smith in the presence of six elders at Fayette, New York, in September 1830, shortly before a conference of the Church. The statement is a succinct and powerful summary of the nature and purpose of the Millennium.
- Note the key dimensions of the millennial era: revelation, power, glory, hosts (congregating of the Saints), dwelling (being in close proximity with the Lord), righteousness, and judgment (the "wicked shall not stand"). To what degree are these dimensions characteristic of life today in the Church? (See D&C 130:2.)

D&C 29:22–28—"And again, verily, verily, I say unto you that when the thousand years are ended, and men again begin to deny their God, then will I spare the earth but for a little season; And the end shall come, and the heaven and the earth shall be consumed and pass away, and there shall be a new heaven and a new earth. For all old things shall pass away, and all things shall become new, even the heaven and the earth, and all the fulness thereof, both men and beasts, the fowls of the air, and the fishes of the sea; And not one hair, neither mote, shall be lost, for it is the workmanship of mine hand. But, behold, verily I say unto you, before the earth shall pass away, Michael, mine archangel, shall sound his trump, and then shall all the dead awake, for their graves shall be opened, and they shall come forth—yea, even all. And the righteous shall be gathered on my right hand unto eternal life; and the wicked on my left hand will I be ashamed to own before the Father; Wherefore I will say unto them—Depart from me, ye cursed, into everlasting fire, prepared for the devil and his angels."

- The revelation given through the Prophet Joseph Smith at Fayette, New York, in September 1830 includes important

insights into events at the conclusion of the thousand-year period. Even in an environment of ongoing millennial tranquility, men will again begin to deny their God, according to their agency, despite the presence of His influence for good in the administration of global affairs. The Lord will then cause the final episode of the resurrection to take place, bringing forth the remainder of the waiting hosts—all of them unjust—into a state of immortality. The final judgment will separate all the souls into two camps: the righteous on the right hand of the Lord, destined for eternal life, and the wicked on the left, who are consigned to everlasting fire. All things in heaven and earth will be renewed and the work of the millennium will be done.

- Why is it that men can choose to deny God even in an environment where His power and light are made manifest continually? (Consider D&C 29:36.) How is it that the principle of moral agency is honored eternally by the Lord, in this case right up until the very end of the Millennium?

D&C 63:50–53—"And he that liveth when the Lord shall come, and hath kept the faith, blessed is he; nevertheless, it is appointed to him to die at the age of man. Wherefore, children shall grow up until they become old; old men shall die; but they shall not sleep in the dust, but they shall be changed in the twinkling of an eye. Wherefore, for this cause preached the apostles unto the world the resurrection of the dead. These things are the things that ye must look for; and, speaking after the manner of the Lord, they are now nigh at hand, and in a time to come, even in the day of the coming of the Son of Man."

- These words about the millennial era were included in a revelation given through the Prophet Joseph Smith at Kirtland, Ohio, late in August 1831, at a time when "there was a great anxiety to obtain the word of the Lord upon every subject that in any way concerned our salvation" (*HC* 1:207).
- We learn that the transition from death

to immortality will happen in a different way during the Millennium, occurring in "the twinkling of an eye" without any death or burial (see also 1 Cor. 15:51–52; 3 Ne. 28:8; D&C 101:29–31). There is no separation caused by death, as in the current state of existence. Death is overcome instantly through the grace of the Messiah. How will this fundamental change in the human condition contribute to the aura of peace and tranquility during the Millennium?

D&C 101:32–38—"Yea, verily I say unto you, in that day when the Lord shall come, he shall reveal all things—Things which have passed, and hidden things which no man knew, things of the earth, by which it was made, and the purpose and the end thereof—Things most precious, things that are above, and things that are beneath, things that are in the earth, and upon the earth, and in heaven. And all they who suffer persecution for my name, and endure in faith, though they are called to lay down their lives for my sake yet shall they partake of all this glory. Wherefore, fear not even unto death; for in this world your joy is not full, but in me your joy is full. Therefore, care not for the body, neither the life of the body; but care for the soul, and for the life of the soul. And seek the face of the Lord always, that in patience ye may possess your souls, and ye shall have eternal life."

- These are words from a revelation given to the Prophet Joseph Smith at Kirtland, Ohio, on December 16, 1833, at a time when the Saints in Missouri were suffering great losses due to persecution and mob action. The spirit of these words gives the promise of coming knowledge and glory to be granted to the faithful, creating a fullness of joy—something that was not available in the mortal realm during that time of persecution and abuse. The counsel is to focus on spiritual things and look forward to seeing the face of the Lord and receiving eternal life.
- In a world of tribulation, the Lord seeks to give comfort to His faithful children, granting them the promise of future joy. The Millennium is but a stepping stone

to the resplendent gateway of celestial glory, where suffering and sacrifice will be rewarded by everlasting peace in the presence of the Father and the Son (see D&C 137). How do these principles serve to give comfort to you and your loved ones even now in the face of life's inevitable tribulations and trials? As Joseph Smith suffered in Liberty Jail, the Lord told him, "Know thou, my son, that all these things shall give thee experience, and shall be for thy good. The Son of Man hath descended below them all. Art thou greater than he? Therefore, hold on thy way . . . for God shall be with you forever and ever" (D&C 122:7–9).

Rejoicing and Reasoning Together

What Are the Special Blessings of the Millennium?

Though the Millennium is in the future, we can still make it a comforting and validating theme for our daily living. The following ideas help us gain increased appreciation for the Millennium and the accompanying resurrection as part of our daily thinking and behavior:

- **Dynamics of being alive**—The Millennium is the era of the resurrection. We can ponder each day the blessing of being alive, and we can savor the thought that this blessing will continue through the resurrection at the beginning of the millennial period—whether we return to mother earth and then come forth again at the Second Coming, or whether we are alive at the Second Coming and are caught up to meet Him (see 1 Thes. 4:17). As we have noted already, those whose lives extend into the Millennium will be transformed to a state of immortality "in the twinkling of an eye" (see 1 Cor. 15:51–52).
- **Transcending mortal infirmities**—We can look forward with joy to the millennial phase of our eternal progression when we are delivered from all physical infirmities, illnesses, and natural imperfections. "The spirit and the body shall be reunited

again in its perfect form . . . every thing shall be restored to its perfect frame." (Alma 11:43–44).

- **Nurturing of our departed children**—We can rejoice in the blessing of being able to see our children who may have died before growing to maturity coming forth in the millennial resurrection to be nurtured by us and raised to adulthood. An entry in the *History of the Church* confirms this blessing: "In the Improvement Era for June, 1904, President Joseph F. Smith in an editorial on the Resurrection said: 'The body will come forth as it is laid to rest, for there is no growth or development in the grave. As it is laid down, so will it arise, and changes to perfection will come by the law of restitution. But the spirit will continue to expand and develop, and the body, after the resurrection will develop to the full stature of man.' This may be accepted as the doctrine of the Church in respect to the resurrection of children and their future development to the full stature of men and women; and it is alike conformable to that which will be regarded as both reasonable and desirable" (see *HC* 4:555–557, footnote).

- **Inheritance of celestial glory**—Even though the resurrection is given to all by the grace of the Lord, the obedient can look forward to a resurrection of particular significance—the resurrection of the just who inherit a celestial glory (see D&C 76:69–70). By obedience to the Lord's commandments, we can come forth in the morning of the first resurrection and enjoy the resurrection unto eternal life.

- **Gratitude**—We are indebted to our Heavenly Father and our Savior Jesus Christ for the resurrection. We can thank Heavenly Father each day in our thoughts and prayers for this endowment of immortality through His grace and love and the sacrifice of His Son: "Wherefore, how great the importance to make these things known unto the inhabitants of the earth, that

they may know that there is no flesh that can dwell in the presence of God, save it be through the merits, and mercy, and grace of the Holy Messiah, who layeth down his life according to the flesh, and taketh it again by the power of the Spirit, that he may bring to pass the resurrection of the dead, being the first that should rise" (2 Ne. 2:8).

- **Knowledge of all things**—The Millennium will open up to us the mysteries of God in all of their dimensions from the beginning of time—including personal communion with the Savior (see D&C 101:32–38). Therefore, the present day is the time to prepare to meet God (see Alma 34:32). It is a time of probation and a time to repent and perfect our lives through the Lord Jesus Christ (see Moro. 10:32).

- **Daily remembrance**—In anticipation of the millennial era about to unfold, let us ponder our state of preparation and ask the Spirit for a blessing of guidance to ensure that we can endure to the end and be ready, as Moroni said in the last words of the Book of Mormon, for our elevation in the clouds of glory at the Second Coming: "And now I bid unto all, farewell. I soon go to rest in the paradise of God, until my spirit and body shall again reunite, and I am brought forth triumphant through the air, to meet you before the pleasing bar of the great Jehovah, the Eternal Judge of both quick and dead. Amen" (Moro. 10:34).

Real-life Stories for Heart and Mind

"**Just a Hint of the Millennium.**" An LDS scholar who directed a BYU Semester Abroad Program before the Iron Curtain came down reported an unusual event:

We were behind the Iron Curtain. We were in the hands of the leadership of the Communist Youth Movement. We worried: Would we be subjected to heartless propaganda and find ourselves locked in a hard-nosed debate with our political foes? It didn't turn out that way at all. Our BYU Semester Abroad group was on tour to learn more about Eastern European mores and culture, and the consensus among our students, as well as the members of our young welcoming delegation, was that we should have a party and a dance. So that's what we did. As I looked on peacefully with my wife and other faculty members, the young people from both sides simply related to each other as human beings, as young people seeking new friendships and new dialogue, as energetic, fun-loving citizens of one grand human family. They danced and laughed and shared insights about life and the hope of the future. For an hour or two, all potential acrimony about important differences in principles of government was suspended—replaced by a dance. There was no enmity. Hope flourished. Peace abounded. Friendship took root. It was just a hint of the Millennium, an anticipatory microcosm of the millennial era when borders would dissolve and the government would be in the hands of a divine Ruler with infinitely more wisdom than anyone on earth.

Imagine a time when the spirit of aggression will vanish from off the face of the earth, when there will be no threats of terror, no prideful aggrandizement of power, no warfare or wanton destruction. Imagine a time like that, and that you are in the Millennium. The Nephite nation had peace and unity for several generations following the visit of the resurrected Lord (see 4 Nephi). Imagine the state of affairs when the Lord rules in the millennial period for a thousand years and "the earth shall be full of the knowledge of the LORD, as the waters cover the sea" (Isa. 11:9). What would you do to inherit such a world? What would you do to ensure that your loved ones will also be prepared and worthy to participate at the highest level of valor during that peaceful phase of existence leading to the ultimate renewal of heaven and earth when the millennial work has been completed?

Pondering Prayerfully

Additional scriptures to consider and ponder:
- Isa. 12:1–6
- D&C 34:6
- D&C 43:29–35
- D&C 133:19

The following hymns inspire gratitude about the Millennium:
- "Beautiful Zion, Built Above" (*Hymns*, 44)
- "Come, All Ye Saints of Zion" (*Hymns*, 38)
- "Come, O Thou King of Kings" (*Hymns*, 59)

Remember and Be Sure

The Millennium is the final period of earth's history, lasting a thousand years following the Second Coming of the Lord in His majesty (see Rev. 20:4; D&C 29:11). During the Millennium, "Christ will reign personally upon the earth" (A of F 10). Peace—that illusive state of being so desired by God's children throughout history—will finally be established on the earth. Righteousness will prevail among the peoples of the earth. The Lord has revealed through His prophets that "in that day the enmity of man, and the enmity of beasts, yea, the enmity of all flesh, shall cease" (D&C 101:26). Satan will be "bound, that he shall have no place in the hearts of the children of men" (D&C 45:55).

Missionary work will flourish. Not all those who remain after the cleansing of the Second Coming will have yet received the fulness of the gospel, though they will be good and honorable in their character and behavior. As a result, there will be grand opportunities during the Millennium for the Saints to preach the gospel and spread the good news about the Atonement and the saving and exalting ordinances of the gospel.

Temple work will also abound, and the Saints will be immersed in this sacred service to an extent never realized before as they continue to build temples and receive ordinances on behalf of their kindred dead. Under the guidance of revelation, they will research the records of their ancestors extending all the way back to our first parents, Adam and Eve, and continue in their family service until the work is finally done.

The millennial conditions of righteousness and peace will continue until the end of the thousand-year period, when Satan "shall be loosed for a little season, that he may gather together his armies" (D&C 88:111). Then there will be an ultimate and final battle between the armies of Satan and the hosts of heaven, led by Michael (Adam). Satan and his followers will be defeated and consigned to their place of darkness forever (see D&C 88:111–115).

The prospect of the coming millennial period should be one of hope and inspiration for the righteous. It can also inspire fear in the souls of those who know they must prepare more fully, with a higher measure of devotion and valor. We can strive to live each day in such a way that we might have hope rather than fear, confidence rather than anxiety, always abounding in good works and holding fast to the iron rod of God's word. When we understand and appreciate the blessings and power of the resurrection that will begin with the Second Coming and the unfolding of the millennial era, we should be motivated to righteousness. If we remember these divine blessings each day, we will be filled with gratitude that will inspire us to live worthily of coming forth in the morning of the first resurrection. Each of us will become a just person with all the accompanying blessings (see D&C 76:69). We will be made perfect in Christ and become joint-heirs with Him in glory (see Rom. 8:17).

The peace of the Millennium is something we can work toward here and now. We can have peace in the Lord Jesus Christ. The Lord has said, "Learn of me, and listen to my words; walk in the meekness of my Spirit, and you shall have peace in me" (D&C 19:23). The peace yet to come in the millennial reign can come to us now, for we can have peace in and through our Savior Jesus Christ. This gift of peace unfolds as we come to the knowledge of the word of God and come to know our Heavenly Father and our Savior Jesus Christ—for this is life eternal (see John 17:3).

CHAPTER 46
The Last Judgment

You will be responsible for your own sins; it is a desirable honor that you should so walk before our heavenly Father as to save yourselves; we are all responsible to God for the manner we improve the light and wisdom given by our Lord to enable us to save ourselves. —Joseph Smith (*HC* 4:606)

Opening the Window of Wisdom

Our time in the premortal realm of existence lasted until the moment of our birth into mortality. Our mortal experience extends until our death. Our time in the postmortal world of spirits ends with our resurrection (or in the case of some, when they are "changed in the twinkling of an eye from mortality to immortality"). The millennial experience ends with the celestialization of the earth at the end of the thousand-year period and the final judgment.

All of these phases of our existence have boundaries. While they are all indispensable, they are still temporary and transitory. Only the ultimate phase of our existence, the infinite expanse of our being entered into following the last judgment, will be without end. That's why our thoughts, desires, and actions leading to the last judgment are so important, for the record of our performance along the way will determine forever our destiny in the eternities—including the level of glory and joy

we harvest and the nature of our relationships with loved ones and with Deity.

There is much contained in the word of God concerning His judgments, including the final judgment at the end of the Millennium. In many ways, this final judgment will not be a day of surprises, since judgment is a process as much as a final verdict. Every accountable individual is aware at every step along the pathway of life how he or she is measuring up to the degree of light and truth provided by the Almighty. The Spirit of Christ that activates our conscience in mortality serves as a measure of how we are doing at any given moment: "For behold, my brethren, it is given unto you to judge, that ye may know good from evil; and the way to judge is as plain, that ye may know with a perfect knowledge, as the daylight is from the dark night. For behold, the Spirit of Christ is given to every man, that he may know good from evil" (Moro. 7:15–16). Thus we are aware of our performance, as measured against the standards given by the Lord, at any given moment. When the fulness of the gospel is presented to us, and we accept it in full faith, we know the degree to which we make and keep sacred covenants. When we use our moral agency to remain obedient to God's commands and serve Him with diligence, we know the score.

At the final and last judgment, we will be judged out of the books—for the books will reveal at every stage of our existence how we have magnified our talents and advanced in our quest to become more like our Heavenly Father and His Son. If we prove ourselves worthy, becoming just men and women and obtaining a state of enduring righteousness, we will receive the gift of eternal life and dwell with God forever: "And whoso is found a faithful, a just, and a wise steward shall enter into the joy of his Lord, and shall inherit eternal life" (D&C 51:19).

The vision of John the Revelator concerning the last days concludes with the account of the final judgment: "And I saw the dead, small and great, stand before God; and the books were opened: and another book was opened, which is the book of life: and the dead were judged out of those things which were written in the books, according to their works" (Rev. 20:12). Those not written in the book of life were "cast into the lake of fire" (Rev. 20:15). The glorious blessings enjoyed by those found to be righteous surpass all understanding:

And I heard a great voice out of heaven saying, Behold, the tabernacle of God is with men, and he will dwell with them, and they shall be his people, and God himself shall be with them, and be their God.

And God shall wipe away all tears from their eyes; and there shall be no more death, neither sorrow, nor crying, neither shall there be any more pain: for the former things are passed away.

And he that sat upon the throne said, Behold, I make all things new. And he said unto me, Write: for these words are true and faithful.

And he said unto me, It is done. I am Alpha and Omega, the beginning and the end. I will give unto him that is athirst of the fountain of the water of life freely.

He that overcometh shall inherit all things; and I will be his God, and he shall be my son. (Rev. 21:3–7)

John ends his account of the revelation granted to him by outlining the promises that await the faithful and valiant of the Lord's children, promises that are beyond comprehension for their glory and the supernal joy they bring:

And they shall see his face; and his name shall be in their foreheads.

And there shall be no night there; and

they need no candle, neither light of the sun; for the Lord God giveth them light: and they shall reign for ever and ever.

And he said unto me, These sayings are faithful and true: and the Lord God of the holy prophets sent his angel to shew unto his servants the things which must shortly be done.

Behold, I come quickly: blessed is he that keepeth the sayings of the prophecy of this book. . . .

And, behold, I come quickly; and my reward is with me, to give every man according as his work shall be.

I am Alpha and Omega, the beginning and the end, the first and the last.

Blessed are they that do his commandments, that they may have right to the tree of life, and may enter in through the gates into the city. . . .

And the Spirit and the bride say, Come. And let him that heareth say, Come. And let him that is athirst come. And whosoever will, let him take the water of life freely. (Rev. 22:4–7, 12–14, 17)

Likewise, Isaiah proclaimed the word of a just eternal Judge: "Look unto me, and be ye saved, all the ends of the earth: for I am God, and there is none else. I have sworn by myself, the word is gone out of my mouth in righteousness, and shall not return, That unto me every knee shall bow, every tongue shall swear" (Isa. 45:22–23). Before God, the Great Magistrate, and before His Son, our Advocate with the Father, we will be judged. How daunting is this prospect—yet how comforting and soothing to know that Their judgments are just and pure, and that through faith and godly sorrow in repentance we can look forward to the outcomes of the judgment process with the assurance and hope that the cleansing and purification made possible through the Atonement will have prepared us for this ultimate event. How can we show our gratitude to God for His justice and equity? By living His commandments and by showing to our fellowmen and to our family members similar justice and equity in how we relate to them and tender our love and compassion to them as they strive to perfect themselves in faith and devotion.

The judgment process is a function of the justice and mercy of God. Mercy is the benevolent kindness and grace of God shown to His children through the infinite Atonement that pays the debt for our sins if we but repent. Mercy overpowers justice and provides the way whereby mankind can exercise faith unto repentance and be forgiven (see Alma 34:15–17). In a masterful process of divine balance—the center being the Atonement of Jesus Christ—justice and mercy are eternally harmonized for the "truly penitent" (Alma 42:24). It is through the balancing grace of our Lord that we are saved—"after all we can do" (2 Ne. 25:23).

In the final analysis, the Lord looks upon the heart in His judgments. While mankind tends to evaluate based on outward appearance and temporal standards, the Lord discerns one's potential for doing good and judges by the heart (the desire and capacity for righteous service). Recall the surprise of the Prophet Joseph Smith when he saw in vision in January 1836 that his deceased older brother, Alvin, had obtained an inheritance in the celestial realm even though he had not had the opportunity to partake of the restored gospel: "Thus came the voice of the Lord unto me, saying: All who have died without a knowledge of this gospel, who would have received it if they had been permitted to tarry, shall be heirs of the celestial kingdom of God; Also all that shall die henceforth without a knowledge of it, who would have received it with all their hearts, shall be heirs of that kingdom; For I, the Lord, will judge all men according to their works, according to the desire of their hearts. And I also beheld that all children who die before they arrive at the years of accountability are saved in the celestial kingdom of heaven" (D&C 137:7–10).

We can be grateful for the majestic mercy and perfect justice of God. He judges righteously. The judgment process extends along the causeway of man's existence from beginning to end, with the grand ratifying seal of divine judgment being pronounced at the end of the vast probationary cycle when each individual is consigned to the everlasting destiny earned on the basis of moral agency and "the merits, and mercy, and grace of the Holy Messiah" (2 Ne. 2:8). Said the Savior: "And none of them that my Father hath given me shall be lost" (D&C 50:42). The grand sweep of judgment is that "through him all might be saved whom the Father had put into his power and made by him; Who glorifies the Father, and saves all the works of his hands, except those sons of perdition who deny the Son after the Father has revealed him" (D&C 76:42–43).

Inspired by Latter-Day Prophets

Joseph Smith: Men not unfrequently forget that they are dependent upon heaven for every blessing which they are permitted to enjoy, and that for every opportunity granted them they are to give an account (*HC* 2:23–24).

One aspect of the judgment is a measure of how well we acknowledge our blessings from the Lord: "And it pleaseth God that he hath given all these things unto man; for unto this end were they made to be used, with judgment, not to excess, neither by extortion. And in nothing doth man offend God, or against none is his wrath kindled, save those who confess not his hand in all things, and obey not his commandments" (D&C 59:20–21). Gratitude and obedience go hand in hand, and it is in the blending of the two that we make an accounting to the Lord. In what ways can you confess the Lord's hand in all things that enrich and bless your life?

John Taylor: The Savior thus becomes the master of the situation—the debt is paid, the redemption made, the covenant fulfilled, justice satisfied, the will of God done, and all power is now given into the hands of the Son of God—the power of the resurrection, the power of the redemption, the power of salvation, the power to enact laws for the carrying out and accomplishment of this design. Hence life and immortality are brought to light, the Gospel is introduced, and He becomes the author of eternal life and exaltation (*The Mediation and the Atonement,* 171).

The Savior is our supreme Advocate and Judge. Consider the merits outlined in the statement above from President Taylor and then ponder the following statement by Jacob: "O then, my beloved brethren, come unto the Lord, the Holy One. Remember that his paths are righteous. Behold, the way for man is narrow, but it lieth in a straight course before him, and the keeper of the gate is the Holy One of Israel; and he employeth no servant there; and there is none other way save it be by the gate; for he cannot be deceived, for the Lord God is his name" (2 Ne. 9:41). The Master of the gate—both at baptism as well as at the gateway to exaltation—is Jesus Christ. Why will His judgment be precise and thorough—not capable of deception? What are your thoughts about how to become "perfect in Christ" (Moro. 10:32–33) and thus prepared and worthy to be judged by Him in all things?

Joseph Fielding Smith: Therefore, if a person is for any cause denied the privilege of complying with any of the covenants, the Lord will judge him or her by the intent of the heart (*Answers to Gospel Questions*, 2:37).

The goodness of the heart transcends the barriers of mortality that are beyond our control. The mercy and understanding of the Lord as eternal Judge are without limit in such circumstances. When the Saints in Missouri were prevented from complying with the will of the Lord because of the atrocities of their enemies, the Lord said, "Verily, verily, I say unto you, that when I give a commandment to any of the sons of men to do a work unto my name, and those sons of men go with all their might and with all they have to perform that work, and cease not their diligence, and their enemies come upon them and hinder them from performing that work, behold, it behooveth me to require that work no more at the hands of those sons of men, but to accept of their offerings" (D&C 124:49). What circumstances have you experienced in your lifetime that have rendered it difficult or impossible to comply with any aspect of the covenants? How have you been able to transcend such disappointments and feel the influence of the Comforter as you have done your best?

Ezra Taft Benson: Yes, life is eternal. We live on and on after earth life, even though we ofttimes lose sight of that great basic truth. . . . This is but a place of temporary duration. We are here to learn the first lesson toward exaltation—obedience to the Lord's gospel plan ("Life Is Eternal," *Ensign*, Aug. 1991, 2).

Mortality is but a temporary phase of life, affording us the opportunity to learn "the first lesson toward exaltation"—obedience. How does obedience gain higher meaning in the eternal context? How have you found that obedience causes your confidence to

"wax strong in the presence of God" (D&C 121:45)? How can you help others to come to a fuller understanding that because all will gain immortality through the gift of the resurrection, all will account directly before God for their obedience?

Truths to Liken

2 Nephi 9:6–7, 15, 18—"For as death hath passed upon all men, to fulfil the merciful plan of the great Creator, there must needs be a power of resurrection, and the resurrection must needs come unto man by reason of the fall; and the fall came by reason of transgression; and because man became fallen they were cut off from the presence of the Lord. Wherefore, it must needs be an infinite atonement—save it should be an infinite atonement this corruption could not put on incorruption. Wherefore, the first judgment which came upon man must needs have remained to an endless duration. . . . And it shall come to pass that when all men shall have passed from this first death unto life, insomuch as they have become immortal, they must appear before the judgment-seat of the Holy One of Israel; and then cometh the judgment, and then must they be judged according to the holy judgment of God. . . . But, behold, the righteous, the saints of the Holy One of Israel, they who have believed in the Holy One of Israel, they who have endured the crosses of the world, and despised the shame of it, they shall inherit the kingdom of God, which was prepared for them from the foundation of the world, and their joy shall be full forever."

- Jacob, brother of Nephi, presents to his listeners a masterful discourse on the plan of salvation (2 Nephi 9), including these words about the infinite Atonement, which liberates all mankind from the shackles of death. Save for the Atonement, the death of mortals, which Jacob refers to as the "first judgment" (verse 7)—meaning a transition into one of two states in the spirit world, either "the paradise of God" (verse 13) or the state of those "who are filthy" (verse 16)—would have consigned mankind to an endless separation from their bodies (a temporal death) as well as from God (a spiritual death). But through the

Atonement, all will be resurrected and those who are righteous will inherit the kingdom of God and return to the presence of the Lord (verse 18).

- Without the Atonement, our sojourn in the spirit world (whether among the righteous or among the wicked) would have been an endless imprisonment, with no relief in the eternities. Because the Atonement was infinite, this otherwise endless imprisonment is rendered temporary, to cease with the resurrection and final judgment—either to endless joy or to endless misery. How does this outcome help to explain the word "infinite" used in conjunction with the Atonement? How will the final judgment be an event of everlasting joy for the righteous?

Alma 12:14–15—"For our words will condemn us, yea, all our works will condemn us; we shall not be found spotless; and our thoughts will also condemn us; and in this awful state we shall not dare to look up to our God; and we would fain be glad if we could command the rocks and the mountains to fall upon us to hide us from his presence. But this cannot be; we must come forth and stand before him in his glory, and in his power, and in his might, majesty, and dominion, and acknowledge to our everlasting shame that all his judgments are just; that he is just in all his works, and that he is merciful unto the children of men, and that he has all power to save every man that believeth on his name and bringeth forth fruit meet for repentance."

- Alma is contending with Zeezrom, the hard-hearted lawyer in the apostate city of Ammonihah, warning him that his way of life and that of his wayward colleagues constitutes prima facie evidence of guilt that will condemn him before the judgment bar of the Almighty.
- How does the record of our lives (including our thoughts, words, and works) constitute a continual "judgment" that we ourselves will bring with us when we give an accounting of our mortal experience? By what power and means can this record be cleansed and rendered pure? (See D&C 58:42.)

Alma 41:3—"And it is requisite with the justice of God that men should be judged according to their works; and if their works were good in this life, and the desires of their hearts were good, that they should also, at the last day, be restored unto that which is good."

- Alma is teaching his wayward son Corianton about the principle of restoration, that our disposition upon death will carry over with us into the next realm, evil staying evil and good staying good. Thus the importance of cultivating a righteous lifestyle in keeping with eternal principles, so that we might be found worthy before the judgment bar of God and be rewarded with the goodness and treasures of eternity.
- If we know of the gospel and its eternal principles, then the judgment of God will not be in the nature of a surprise, since we are continually aware of the quality of our own lifestyle as it relates to His commandments. How can you help others to understand the emergent nature of the judgment, i.e., that we judge ourselves along the pathway of life in terms of the kind of person we choose to be? "For behold, they are their own judges, whether to do good or do evil" (Alma 41:7).

Alma 42:15—"And now, the plan of mercy could not be brought about except an atonement should be made; therefore God himself atoneth for the sins of the world, to bring about the plan of mercy, to appease the demands of justice, that God might be a perfect, just God, and a merciful God also."

- In his counsel to his son Corianton, Alma, as a loving father, explains the requisite balance of mercy and justice in the plan of salvation, the Atonement satisfying the demands of justice (the requirement to live the law perfectly—something that is beyond the capacity of all who have lived, save only the Savior—see 2 Nephi 2:5–8) by bringing grace before the judgment bar of God for all who repent of their imperfections and place themselves in the hands of their Advocate with the Father. Nephi expressed this principle perfectly: "For we labor diligently to write, to persuade our children, and also our brethren, to believe in Christ, and to be reconciled to God; for we know that it is by grace that we are saved, after all we can do" (2 Nephi 25:23).

- As you look toward the ultimate judgment of a just and merciful God, how does the charitable element of grace on the part of the Redeemer serve to give you the assurance that you are forgiven of your sins through repentance and obedience? Note the words of Peter: "And above all things have fervent charity among yourselves: for charity shall cover the multitude of sins" (1 Peter 4:8). How does our charity cover sins? The Redeemer is charitable and forgiving to us just as we confirm our obedience and righteousness by showing charity to others. When we come to understand the mercy of the Lord for us, we too will be more merciful to others as part of our repentance (see 3 Nephi 12:7)—and a multitude of sins can thus be "covered."

3 Nephi 27:13–17—"Behold I have given unto you my gospel, and this is the gospel which I have given unto you—that I came into the world to do the will of my Father, because my Father sent me. And my Father sent me that I might be lifted up upon the cross; and after that I had been lifted up upon the cross, that I might draw all men unto me, that as I have been lifted up by men even so should men be lifted up by the Father, to stand before me, to be judged of their works, whether they be good or whether they be evil—And for this cause have I been lifted up; therefore, according to the power of the Father I will draw all men unto me, that they may be judged according to their works. And it shall come to pass, that whoso repenteth and is baptized in my name shall be filled; and if he endureth to the end, behold, him will I hold guiltless before my Father at that day when I shall stand to judge the world. And he that endureth not unto the end, the same is he that is also hewn down and cast into the fire, from whence they can no more return, because of the justice of the Father."

- These words of the resurrected Lord to His disciples in the New World constitute one of the most memorable expressions concerning the judgment of God as the culminating aspect of the gospel of Jesus Christ.
- What are your thoughts about the principle of being "drawn" to the Son and "lifted up" by the Father to stand before the Son to be judged? What does the Savior mean when He says the obedient "shall be filled"? Why does the justice of the Father require that those who do not endure to the end will be dispatched without the ability to return?

D&C 138:14–19—"All these had departed the mortal life, firm in the hope of a glorious resurrection, through the grace of God the Father and his Only Begotten Son, Jesus Christ. I beheld that they were filled with joy and gladness, and were rejoicing together because the day of their deliverance was at hand. They were assembled awaiting the advent of the Son of God into the spirit world, to declare their redemption from the bands of death. Their sleeping dust was to be restored unto its perfect frame, bone to his bone, and the sinews and the flesh upon them, the spirit and the body to be united never again to be divided, that they might receive a fulness of joy. While this vast multitude waited and conversed, rejoicing in the hour of their deliverance from the chains of death, the Son of God appeared, declaring liberty to the captives who had been faithful; And there he preached to them the everlasting gospel, the doctrine of the resurrection and the redemption of mankind from the fall, and from individual sins on conditions of repentance."

- In his remarkable vision of the spirit world, received in 1918, President Joseph F. Smith provides much detail about the glorious ministry of the Lord among the righteous spirits held captive in the state between death and resurrection—the very state being experienced by the Savior (see D&C 138:27). The coming of the Lord brought joy and relief to the faithful through the light of the gospel of repentance and deliverance.

- As those spirits in paradise anxiously awaited the word of truth, how did the advent of the Savior give them assurance that the judgment of God would be in their favor? What were the conditions of their deliverance?

Rejoicing and Reasoning Together

What Is the Timeline of the Judgments of God?

The judgments of devoted parents extend throughout the lifetime of each child as they observe, guide, prompt, discipline, and render feedback about the progress of the child. Among the last words of Lehi to his children were these: "And I have none other object save it be the everlasting welfare of your souls. Amen" (2 Ne. 2:30). Similarly, the judgments of a merciful and just God extend throughout the lifetime of each of His created sons and daughters, culminating in that final judgment when the work of this earth will be completed and all inhabitants thereof will have been consigned to their place in the eternities, based on their record of obedience to eternal laws and commandments.

What are the milestones of divine judgment that the children of God encounter along the pathway of their existence? The following list might be helpful to consider in the context of the principle that judgment is an extended *process* leading up to the final and last judgment at the conclusion of the Millennium:

- **The Premortal Realm.** Most of the spirit children of Heavenly Father were faithful and devoted, yet a third of them followed Lucifer, the rebellious son of the morning (see Isa. 14:12) and gave up the opportunity to come to earth as mortals and advance in their growth toward perfection (see D&C 29:36). That was a judgment of God, based on eternal principles: "And they who keep their first estate shall be added upon; and they who keep not their first estate shall not have glory in the same kingdom with those who keep their first estate; and they who keep their second estate shall have glory added upon their heads for ever and ever" (Abr. 3:26).

At the same time, righteous spirits were foreordained to serve in specific roles of service and leadership in their second estate (mortality). Joseph Smith taught: "Every man who has a calling to minister to the inhabitants of the world was ordained to that very purpose in the Grand Council of heaven before this world was. I suppose I was ordained to this very office in that Grand Council" (*Teachings of the Prophet Joseph Smith*, 365). That was also a judgment of God, based on the promise and devotion of His children and their manner of applying the talents and gifts granted to them. How they follow through with these stewardships will constitute an important part of the books from which they will be judged.

- **The Mortal Realm.** Faithful spirit children were sent to earth at a specific time and in a specific place—very likely in connection with the stewardships they were assigned in the premortal realm. As Paul declared on Mars' Hill concerning God: "And hath made of one blood all nations of men for to dwell on all the face of the earth, and hath determined the times before appointed, and the bounds of their habitation; That they should seek the Lord, if haply they might feel after him, and find him, though he be not far from every one of us: For in him we live, and move, and have our being; as certain also of your own poets have said, For we are also his offspring" (Acts 17:26–28). If the Lord determines the times and the bounds of our habitation, is that not a form of judgment with regard to our potential and our role of service in mortality? Peter referred to the Saints as constituting "a chosen generation, a royal priesthood, an holy nation, a peculiar people; that ye should shew forth the praises of him who hath called you out of darkness into his marvellous light" (1 Pet. 2:9).

How is our progress documented? What are the records of "judgment" along the way? The records of the

Church on our behalf are part of our official "judgment" (see Rev. 20:12), just as our temple recommend is a sacred document of judgment attesting to our worthiness. Our own memory is a meticulous record of all our thoughts, desires, words, and actions—and constitutes a form of judgment concerning our devotion to the cause of the Lord. We are, indeed, our own judge in this regard (see Alma 41:7).

While on earth, we are subjected to the judgments of God according to worthiness (or lack thereof). The scattering and gathering of nations comes at the hand of the Almighty. The flood during the days of Noah represented a monumental act of judgment by God (see Gen. 7:11–24). He often brings about His corrective measures to cleanse and reprove: "But, behold, the judgments of God will overtake the wicked; and it is by the wicked that the wicked are punished; for it is the wicked that stir up the hearts of the children of men unto bloodshed" (Morm. 4:5). At the same time, His judgments bless and lift the righteous with abundance, light, and glory.

- **Postmortal Spirit Realm**. It is by divine judgment that the spirits of the departed are consigned in the spirit realm either to a state of paradise or to a state of darkness, based on their level of righteousness (see Alma 40:11–14). It is also according to the judgment of God that those in the realm of darkness can transition to the realm of light according to their acceptance of the gospel of faith and repentance being preached to them by the servants of Jesus Christ commissioned to gather the elect (see 1 Pet. 4:6). The process of bringing the receptive spirits into the light is made clear: "And the chosen messengers went forth to declare the acceptable day of the Lord and proclaim liberty to the captives who were bound, even unto all who would repent of their sins and receive the gospel. Thus was the gospel preached to those who had died in their

sins, without a knowledge of the truth, or in transgression, having rejected the prophets. These were taught faith in God, repentance from sin, vicarious baptism for the remission of sins, the gift of the Holy Ghost by the laying on of hands" (D&C 138:31–34). Those who repented and embraced the gospel with full devotion were welcomed into the ranks of the faithful through a favorable judgment of God.

- **The Second Coming**. The cleansing of the earth in connection with the Second Coming is a judgment of God, for all of a telestial nature will be destroyed (see Mal. 3:2–3, 5; Matt. 25:31–46; Rev. 20:3–6; 3 Ne. 8; D&C 88:95–99). The earth will become a terrestrial realm, with those of a celestial character serving as ministrants to preach the gospel and gather the faithful into the fold of Christ (see D&C 138).

- **Resurrection and Degrees of Glory**. The resurrection, empowered through the Atonement of Jesus Christ, is a form of judgment, since the type of body granted in the resurrection depends on the degree of glory attained by each individual. Those who come forth in the "morning of the first resurrection" are celestial bodies; those in the "afternoon of the first resurrection" are terrestrial bodies; those in the second resurrection at the end of the thousand years are telestial bodies. Only the sons of perdition obtain no glory. Moreover, as people living during the Millennium mature and come to the point of transition, they are changed in a twinkling of an eye and inherit that kind of terrestrial or celestial body that will be in keeping with their assigned degree of glory (see D&C 43:32; 63:51; 101:31). That, too, is a divine judgment.

- **Celestial Glory**. "IN the celestial glory there are three heavens or degrees; And in order to obtain the highest, a man must enter into this order of the priesthood [meaning the new and everlasting covenant of marriage]; And if he does not, he cannot obtain it. He may enter into the other, but that is the end of his kingdom; he cannot have an increase" (D&C 131:1–4). Thus in the highest degree of glory there is also an assignment according to merit, based on the judgment of God.

- **The Last and Final Judgment**. What is the agenda for this ultimate judgment? Is it not in a way a ratification of the judgments already confirmed? Is it not a sealing of the final verdict of the Almighty, a confirmation and activation of the blessings of everlasting glory in the degrees determined, and a final sending of the wicked to their eternal places of abode? There may be precious few surprises at the last and final judgment. The Twelve Apostles will have already judged Israel (see 1 Ne. 12:9; D&C 29:12). The twelve disciples of the New World will have judged their people (see 1 Ne. 12:8–10). The transformation of the earth into a celestial realm as home of celestial beings and families will take place. By then, all aspects of the ultimate destiny of every individual will have been determined, having unfolded throughout the sequential phases of existence already completed (see Rev. 20:11–15; 2 Ne. 9:15–16). Abraham, Isaac, Jacob, and the other chosen leaders will have already attained the stature of gods (D&C 132:29–37). The destiny of countless other righteous souls will have been sealed for all time and eternity in honor of their covenant valor, and their eons of service in the eternities will see a continuation of their progress and an eternal unfolding of their rewards. In effect, the judgment of a loving and merciful God will continue forever.

As you contemplate the panoramic scope of the judgment process, what are your feelings about your own status before the Lord? What do you and your loved ones need to focus on in order to prepare more fully for the times to come? How can you use the gifts, talents, blessings, and spiritual guidance accorded you to achieve in greater measure a favorable "judgment" from the Lord as your Supreme Advocate with the Father?

What Are the Qualifications for the Three Degrees of Glory?

The voice of the Lord in the latter days has proclaimed the ultimate destiny of mankind—of every individual who has passed through the gates of the Creation, without exception. He has revealed the all-encompassing vista of the kingdoms and realms prepared as the postmortal dwellings for all the hosts of heaven belonging to this earth, all who await the day of judgment and bestowal of their inheritance of glory or, in the case of the sons of perdition, of their irreversible consignment to outer darkness. He has promised His faithful and valiant all knowledge and wisdom: "For by my Spirit will I enlighten them, and by my power will I make known unto them the secrets of my will—yea, even those things which eye has not seen, nor ear heard, nor yet entered into the heart of man" (D&C 76:10).

A stunning and compelling glimpse into the archive of the Lord's heavenly truth is afforded to those who study the Doctrine and Covenants, especially Section 76. The vision of the hereafter recorded there is the most comprehensive presentation of the life to come contained anywhere in scripture. Of the material in Section 76, Brigham Young said: "The vision given to Joseph Smith and Sidney Rigdon is the greatest vision I ever knew given to the children of men, incorporating more in a few pages than any other revelation I have any knowledge of" (*JD*, 8:36). What was given through the Prophet Joseph Smith and his companion Sidney Rigdon concerning the pathway beyond death is an unforgettable taste of what awaits us, and a strict delineation of the qualifications that apply to the different outcomes of the judgment process. Who can ever look upon life and the plan of salvation the same way after having studied, pondered, and sought spiritual guidance concerning the ideas and concepts contained in this revelation and related passages from latter-day scriptures?

It is the will of God to bestow immortality and eternal lives upon as many of His children as will receive and practice the degree of truth needed for abiding a celestial level of glory. To such is given all that the Father has: "And he that receiveth my Father receiveth my Father's kingdom; therefore all that my Father hath shall be given unto him. And this is according to the oath and covenant which belongeth to the priesthood" (D&C 84:38–39). Not all will be worthy of so transcendent a blessing; thus lesser degrees of glory are also prepared. Through the ministry of the Prophet Joseph Smith, the Lord has outlined with clarity the kingdoms that are reserved for mankind in the hereafter, according to their several levels and qualifications. At the heart of the process of assigning individuals to such levels is the degree of righteousness, loyalty, and obedience shown to the Redeemer, Jesus Christ. It is the solemn mission of each individual in mortality to exercise faith in Jesus Christ, manifest repentance, experience baptism at the hands of authorized priesthood representatives, receive and savor the gift of the Holy Ghost in all humility and contrition, and endure to the end. Of such is the kingdom of heaven, and the ultimate placement of all souls within the courts on high will depend on their degree of spiritual refinement and enlightenment, and the quality of their "godly walk and conversation" (D&C 20:69) before the Lord.

In general terms, those who inherit the three kingdoms can be classified as follows (using verses from Section 76):

- **Telestial kingdom**: This kingdom is like the glory of the stars (see verses 81, 98). Even those who inherit this kingdom—the most persistently wicked of souls other than the sons of perdition—inherit a kingdom of such glory that it "surpasses all understanding" (verse 89). Nevertheless, they are isolated by their chosen natures, and, tragically, "where God and Christ dwell they cannot come, worlds without end" (verse 112; see also verses 81–86). Below this group in stature are the sons of perdition, who receive no glory whatsoever. At one time they knew the light of truth intimately through the Holy Ghost, but nevertheless came to deny it and declare it to be darkness—unto their utter doom and destruction (see verses 31–37; also D&C 88:32–33; Matt. 12:31–32). There is little comfort in studying the fate of the sons of perdition, except that in contrast with a state of utter darkness, the light

of the gospel shines with the greatest luminosity (see verses 31–32).

- **Terrestrial kingdom**: The glory of the moon is the image that the Lord chooses to characterize the brightness that pertains to this kingdom (see verses 71, 78, 97), by way of contrast with the starlight nature of the telestial and the sunlight nature of the celestial. Those who inherit this kingdom "are they who are not valiant in the testimony of Jesus" (verse 79). They will have the privilege of beholding the presence of the Son, but "not of the fulness of the Father" (verse 77). Though refulgent and blazing, the glory of this kingdom is no equal of the celestial. The passages of scripture that describe the terrestrial realm (see verses 71–77) offer a poignant reminder of the need for constant vigilance on the part of all sincere seekers after truth, that they might find themselves, through obedience to the laws and ordinances of the gospel, in the celestial kingdom rather than here, where the occupants include those who passed away without having the law of God, yet still declined to follow it after having received it in the spirit realm; those who rejected the gospel as mortals but accepted it in the spirit realm; and the "honorable men of the earth, who were blinded by the craftiness of men" (verse 75).

- **Celestial kingdom**: The glory of this kingdom is compared with the glory of the sun (see verses 70, 78, 96). "And let virtue garnish thy thoughts unceasingly; then shall thy confidence wax strong in the presence of the Lord" (D&C 121:45). This is the purpose for the gospel of Jesus Christ and the plan of salvation—to guide mankind to a level of righteousness that will enable them to feel fully confident in the presence of the Father and the Son, having established themselves as completely valiant in the testimony of Jesus Christ, having put all enemies beneath their feet—not the least of which is pride, worldliness, and (through the grace of the Atonement) death and sin. Such are destined to inherit the celestial kingdom, even the highest degree thereof, to live forever in the house of the Father and the Son. "Wherefore, as it is written, they are gods, even the sons of God—Wherefore, all things are theirs, whether life or death, or things present, or things to come, all are theirs and they are Christ's, and Christ is God's. And they shall overcome all things. . . . These shall dwell in the presence of God and his Christ forever and ever" (verses 58–60, 62).

As you ponder and review the nature of these degrees of glory and the qualifications that pertain to each, how is your commitment strengthened to endure to the end and be worthy of inheriting a place in the celestial kingdom of glory with your family?

Real-life Stories for Heart and Mind

Judgment Rendered. President Harold B. Lee shared the following story and counsel:

Some years ago, President Marion G. Romney and I were sitting in my office. The door opened and a fine young man came in with a troubled look on his face, and he said, "Brethren, I am going to the temple for the first time tomorrow. I have made some mistakes in the past, and I have gone to my bishop and my stake president, and I have made a clean disclosure of it all; and after a period of repentance and assurance that I have not returned again to those mistakes, they have now adjudged me ready to go to the temple. But, brethren, that is not enough. I want to know, and how can I know, that the Lord has forgiven me also."

What would you answer one who might come to you asking that question? As we pondered for a moment, we remembered King Benjamin's address contained in the book of Mosiah. Here was a group of people asking for baptism, and they said they viewed themselves in their carnal state:

And they all cried aloud with one voice, saying: O have mercy, and apply the atoning blood of Christ that we

may receive forgiveness of our sins, and our hearts may be purified;
. . . after they had spoken these words the Spirit of the Lord came upon them, and they were filled with joy, having received a remission of their sins, and having peace of conscience. . . . (Mosiah 4:2–3)

There was the answer. (*Stand Ye in Holy Places,* 184–85)

Through the Spirit we can know how we are judged of the Lord. How have you experienced the blessings of the Comforter through your diligence in honoring your covenants through faith and repentance?

Judging with Mercy. On Thursday, June 9, 1842, the Prophet Joseph Smith delivered an address regarding mercy to the sisters of the Female Relief Society in Nauvoo—one filled with delicious spiritual nourishment. Here is a sampling of his wisdom: "Nothing is so much calculated to lead the people to forsake sin as to take them by the hand, and watch over them with tenderness. When persons manifest the least kindness and love to me, O what power it has over my mind, while the opposite course has a tendency to harrow up all the harsh feelings and depress the human mind" (*HC* 5:23–24). And also, "God does not look on sin with allowance, but when men have sinned, there must be allowance made for them. All the religious world is boasting of righteousness: it is the doctrine of the devil to retard the human mind, and hinder our progress, by filling us with self-righteousness. The nearer we get to our heavenly Father, the more we are disposed to look with compassion on perishing souls; we feel that we want to take them on our shoulders, and cast their sins behind our backs. . . . if you would have God have mercy on you, have mercy on one another" (*HC* 5:24). And finally: "How oft have wise men and women sought to dictate Brother Joseph by saying, 'O, if I were Brother Joseph, I would do this and that;' but if they were in Brother Joseph's shoes they would find that men or women could not be compelled into the kingdom of God, but must be dealt with in long-suffering, till God shall bring such characters to justice. There should be no license for sin, but mercy should go hand in hand with reproof" (*HC* 5:24).

The message is clear: the Lord judges with mercy and truth. In the same way, we are to feed God's sheep with mercy and longsuffering, avoiding judging others unrighteously: "And now, verily, verily, I say unto thee, put your trust in that Spirit which leadeth to do good—yea, to do justly, to walk humbly, to judge righteously; and this is my Spirit" (D&C 11:12).

"Running Home to the Savior." Looking back over many years, one priesthood brother shares a vivid memory:

> In the power of God lies the power to restore, to make whole, to be resurrected into a newness of life. Hope truly governs our attitude, which is reflected in our behavior.
>
> It was Mother's Day 1947 and my daddy had just died of heart failure. I couldn't believe my daddy could die. He was so big—6'3," 250 pounds—and so strong. I was twelve years old and I had already been to the funeral of my grandma. Death was so final. Death was the end of life as I knew it. I had been taught of the resurrection. I knew that when people died they went to the spirit world and later would be resurrected. I had the knowledge, but my understanding and appreciation came later.
>
> When I truly realized the goodness of God, His supreme power and concern for His children, my heart was filled with gratitude. Then, oh how I wanted to live a good life so I could enjoy the blessings of coming forth in the morning of the first resurrection. I love life and I want to live a long time, but I still treasure this thought.
>
> As a little boy, I would run down the lane after school to our farmhouse and there would be my mom waiting for her boy. We would have a treat and then she would ask me about my day at school.
>
> I think of passing through the veil in the same light—running home to my Savior and Heavenly Father and them taking me in their arms and giving me their love. This fills my soul with the joy of

eternal life. It gives me hope to live a life worthy of their presence. God loves His children and His power is always used to bless our lives.

Going home to our Heavenly Father and His Son is the purpose of our mortal life. They want us to come back in joy and glory and stay forever. That is the message of the gospel of Jesus Christ. What are your feelings and thoughts and hopes as they relate to the purpose of life and the plan of happiness?

Pondering Prayerfully

Additional scriptures to consider and ponder:
- Ex. 34:6–7
- 1 Chron. 16:34
- Matt. 25:32–34
- Rom. 2:13
- 1 Cor. 15:40–42
- 1 Pet. 3:18–20
- Alma 12:34
- Alma 42:13–15, 23
- Alma 42:24–25
- Moro. 10:34
- D&C 29:27
- D&C 88:14–16

The following hymns provide understanding about the judgment of God:
- "Have I Done Any Good?" (*Hymns,* 223)
- "Lord, I Would Follow Thee" (*Hymns,* 220)

Remember and Be Sure

How much insight comes to mankind through a clear understanding of death, the spirit world, the resurrection, and the judgments of God as revealed through the scriptures! How much wisdom comes from a correct understanding of the doctrine of restoration—that our development is a process of being perfected in Jesus Christ (see Moro. 10:32–33) and that we leave this life with a disposition and character that goes with us into the spirit world!

When we understand and appreciate the blessing and power of the resurrection, we will be motivated to righteousness. In that context, how much happiness comes from a calm and purposeful understanding of the doctrines of justice and mercy. We should never forget what our fate might have been without the Atonement (see 2 Ne. 9:8–9). If we remember these things, we will be filled with gratitude, which will become a catalyst for obedience and valor in our lives. We will live worthy of coming forth in the morning of the first resurrection. We will become "just"—with all the accompanying blessings (see D&C 76:69). We will be made perfect in Christ and become joint-heirs with Him (see Rom. 8:17; Moro. 10:32–33). We can take a lesson from Thomas, who at first doubted the actuality of the resurrection until the very moment when the Lord had him touch the marks on His hands and His sides: "And Thomas answered and said unto him, My Lord and my God. Jesus saith unto him, Thomas, because thou hast seen me, thou hast believed: blessed are they that have not seen, and yet have believed" (John 20:28–29). Belief leads to obedience; obedience leads to sanctification; sanctification leads to exaltation. All will be resurrected; those who are faithful and endure to the end will participate in the resurrection of glory, even the glory of the celestial kingdom.

Our lives are a continual witness to our level of obedience and our love for the Lord. As we conduct our lives in keeping with the commandments and covenants, we can look forward to the final judgment. Perhaps the best summary of the doctrine of judgment is the statement made by the Savior: "But seek ye first the kingdom of God, and his righteousness; and all these things shall be added unto you" (Matt. 6:33; 3 Ne. 13:33).

CHAPTER 47
Exaltation: The Greatest of All the Gifts of God

The gospel embraces principles that dive deeper, spread wider, and extend further than anything else that we can conceive. . . . It "brings life and immortality to light," brings us into relationship with God, and prepares us for an exaltation in the eternal world.
—John Taylor (*JD* 16:369)

Opening the Window of Wisdom

The purpose of life for the children of God is to become like our Heavenly Father and His Only Begotten Son, who are exalted Beings of infinite power, knowledge, glory, mercy, and love. The word *exalted* means elevated to a great height (from the Latin "ex," meaning up or away, and "altus," meaning high). The plan of salvation is a divine design of transformation to lift us upward to the destined level of being truly exalted, receiving the promised fulness of the glory of God, even eternal life. The goal is precise: "Therefore I would that ye should be perfect even as I, or your Father who is in heaven is perfect" (3 Ne. 12:48).

As we strive with all our heart, mind, might, and strength to take on the divine nature and fulfill our destiny, we bring glory to our Heavenly Father and His Son. At the same time, Their work and glory is to "bring to pass the immortality and eternal life of man" (Moses 1:39). Their ultimate goal is to receive us unto Themselves forever in the celestial kingdom, having endowed us with saving knowledge, guided us by the Spirit, given us an abundance of temporal strength and spiritual power, prepared and sealed us through sacred covenant ordinances, and granted us the capacity to endure to the end—throughout our endless struggles and devoted labors—by honoring gospel principles and meriting the sublime blessings of the Atonement of Jesus Christ.

"Fulness" of the type vested in the Father and the Son is impossible to capture with mortal language. The scriptures give only hints and suggestions about the eternal blessings reserved for the faithful:

- "They who are of a celestial spirit shall receive the same body which was a natural body; even ye shall receive your bodies, and your glory shall be that glory by which your bodies are quickened. Ye who are quickened by a portion of the celestial glory shall then receive of the same, even a fulness" (D&C 88:28–29).
- "The Spirit of truth is of God. I am the Spirit of truth, and John bore record of me, saying: He received a fulness of truth, yea, even of all truth; And no man receiveth a fulness unless he keepeth his commandments. He that keepeth his commandments receiveth truth and light, until he is glorified in

truth and knoweth all things" (D&C 93:26–28).

- "And they shall pass by the angels, and the gods, which are set there, to their exaltation and glory in all things, as hath been sealed upon their heads, which glory shall be a fulness and a continuation of the seeds forever and ever. Then shall they be gods, because they have no end; therefore shall they be from everlasting to everlasting, because they continue; then shall they be above all, because all things are subject unto them. Then shall they be gods, because they have all power, and the angels are subject unto them. Verily, verily, I say unto you, except ye abide my law ye cannot attain to this glory" (D&C 132:19–21).

To follow in the footsteps of the Savior is to follow the pathway to exaltation. Such a destination is not attained quickly, nor all at once, but line upon line and grace upon grace (see D&C 93:11–14). That pattern is given to all: "I give unto you these sayings that you may understand and know how to worship, and know what you worship, that you may come unto the Father in my name, and in due time receive of his fulness. For if you keep my commandments you shall receive of his fulness, and be glorified in me as I am in the Father; therefore, I say unto you, you shall receive grace for grace" (D&C 93:19–20).

The Prophet Joseph Smith was permitted to view the flaming gateway of the celestial kingdom, with its golden streets, and "Also the blazing throne of God, whereon was seated the Father and the Son" (D&C 137:3). Isaiah asked: "Who among us shall dwell with the devouring fire? who among us shall dwell with everlasting burnings? He that walketh righteously, and speaketh uprightly . . . and shutteth his eyes from seeing evil" (Isa. 33:14–15).

The promise of celestial exaltation is magnificent: "And if your eye be single to my glory, your whole bodies shall be filled with light, and there shall be no darkness in you; and that body which is filled with light comprehendeth all things. Therefore, sanctify yourselves that your minds become single to God, and the days will come that you shall see him; for he will unveil his face unto you, and it shall be in his own time, and in his own way, and according to his own will" (D&C 88:67–68).

Love is the motive; exaltation is the ultimate state and condition; eternal life is the goal. In the strength of the Lord, we can endure and succeed, for that is the entire purpose of life.

Inspired by Latter-Day Prophets

Brigham Young: We cannot expect to receive real wealth until we receive the riches of eternity, which are eternal. . . . How vain it is in man to allow himself to think that he can make himself happy with the pleasures of this world. There is no lasting pleasure here, unless it is in God (JD 18:213–14).

Perfecting ourselves is possible only by fulfilling our assigned stewardships on behalf of others in a manner acceptable to the Lord. Rather than asking, "Am I perfect?" you can ask a more practical question: "Am I doing my duty perfectly?" What are your thoughts about the "riches of eternity"? Of what do they consist? How do we attain them in fuller measure?

John Taylor: I heard the Prophet Joseph say, in speaking to the Twelve on one occasion: "You will have all kinds of trials to pass through. And it is quite as necessary for you to be tried as it was for Abraham and other men of God, and (said he) God will feel after you, and He will take hold of you and wrench your very heart strings, and if you cannot stand it you will not be fit for an inheritance in the Celestial Kingdom of God" (JD 24:197).

Exaltation in the celestial kingdom is reserved for those who pass every test of honor, survive every trial of character, endure every hardship for the cause of Zion, and prove themselves altogether worthy of a fullness of glory—for God will have only such to be in His presence. At the same time, we can remind ourselves of the promise of the Savior: "With men this is impossible; but with God all things are possible" (Matt. 19:26). What has been your experience in overcoming challenges and tribulations in the strength of the Lord as you have worked toward exaltation?

Joseph Fielding Smith: The real purpose of mortality is twofold: first, to obtain tabernacles of flesh and bones; second, to obtain experiences which could only be had in mortality. . . . Therefore, it is essential that we come in contact with some things that are bitter that we may appreciate the sweet and our earthly education may be complete. If we did not have access to these conditions, our mortal training would be defective and lacking in many features which are essential to the exaltation which awaits us if we are faithful and true (*Answers to Gospel Questions*, 5:58).

Why does exaltation depend on experiencing the bitter dimensions of life with courage and faithfulness as part of our mortal journey?

Howard W. Hunter: If you endure to the end, and if you are valiant in the testimony of Jesus, you will achieve true greatness and will live in the presence of our Father in Heaven (*The Teachings of Howard W. Hunter*, 72).

"True greatness" is defined here in covenant terms: enduring to the end and maintaining a valiant testimony of the Savior will admit you into the presence of God. The desire to be "great" is a common quest among mortals. How can you help family members and others within your influence apply the two fundament dimensions of true greatness emphasized by President Hunter?

Truths to Liken

2 Ne. 31:19–20—"And now, my beloved brethren, after ye have gotten into this strait and narrow path, I would ask if all is done? Behold, I say unto you, Nay; for ye have not come thus far save it were by the word of Christ with unshaken faith in him, relying wholly upon the merits of him who is mighty to save. Wherefore, ye must press forward with a steadfastness in Christ, having a perfect brightness of hope, and a love of God and of all men. Wherefore, if ye shall press forward, feasting upon the word of Christ, and endure to the end, behold, thus saith the Father: Ye shall have eternal life."

- Toward the end of his ministry, Nephi gave this succinct and well-known formula for how to inherit the gift of eternal life. It is unique, not only because of the compelling language,

but also because of the unusual context. Nephi had heard the voice of the Son confirming the gospel of faith, repentance, baptism, and the gift of the Holy Ghost (see 2 Ne. 31:12, 14); remarkably, he had also heard the voice of the Father declaring: "Yea, the words of my Beloved are true and faithful. He that endureth to the end, the same shall be saved" (2 Ne. 31:15).

- When the Father spoke from heaven, testifying of Christ and confirming that enduring to the end leads to salvation, the words of Nephi ("press forward with a steadfastness in Christ") took on special divine authority. Attaining eternal life and exaltation is a process involving faith, active devotion, hope, love, and unflagging endurance. How have you found in your lifetime that this continual process generates strength and fortitude to carry on?

Mosiah 2:41—"And moreover, I would desire that ye should consider on the blessed and happy state of those that keep the commandments of God. For behold, they are blessed in all things, both temporal and spiritual; and if they hold out faithful to the end they are received into heaven, that thereby they may dwell with God in a state of never-ending happiness. O remember, remember that these things are true; for the Lord God hath spoken it."

- King Benjamin used these words to end the first section of his final discourse to his people assembled around the temple. He connected happiness to obedience, and linked never-ending happiness with never-ending obedience ("hold out faithful to the end").
- Obedience—exact, immediate, and courageous obedience—should be our quest. How have you and your loved ones found joy in keeping the commandments? What are your thoughts when you consider being able to magnify and expand those moments of joy into a state of endless joy?

D&C 14:7—"And, if you keep my commandments and endure to the end you shall have eternal life, which gift is the greatest of all the gifts of God."

- This counsel and promise was part of a revelation given through the Prophet Joseph Smith to David Whitmer at Fayette, New York, in June 1829, while the work of translating the Book of Mormon was being completed in the home of David's father, Peter Whitmer, Sr. David was later one of the three witnesses to the Book of Mormon, along with Oliver Cowdery and Martin Harris. Despite this personal revelation to David, he later apostatized and lost his membership in the Church—although he preserved his witness to the Book of Mormon. The Lord pronounced this judgment on him: "BEHOLD, I say unto you, David, that you have feared man and have not relied on me for strength as you ought. But your mind has been on the things of the earth more than on the things of me, your Maker, and the ministry whereunto you have been called; and you have not given heed unto my Spirit, and to those who were set over you, but have been persuaded by those whom I have not commanded. Wherefore, you are left to inquire for yourself at my hand, and ponder upon the things which you have received" (D&C 30:1–3).

- We can learn a lesson from the tragic case of David Whitmer. The Lord gives a grand promise in the form of a covenant: endure to the end and you will have the greatest of all gifts—eternal life. But what happens when we fear man more than God, fail to rely on the strength of the Lord, focus on the things of the earth rather than things divine, neglect our stewardship, and fail to listen to the Spirit and the leaders of the Church, heeding instead those not called of God? In that sad case, all is lost. What are your thoughts and feelings about the power of doing the *opposite*—fearing God and relying on His strength, placing a priority on the things of heaven, doing your duty

with devotion, heeding the Spirit and the living prophets, and turning away from those not called of God? To do so brings the richest of all blessings, even eternal life.

D&C 84:20–21—"Therefore, in the ordinances thereof, the power of godliness is manifest. And without the ordinances thereof, and the authority of the priesthood, the power of godliness is not manifest unto men in the flesh."

- This statement was included in a revelation given through the Prophet Joseph Smith at Kirtland, Ohio, on September 22 and 23, 1832, designated by the Prophet as a revelation on priesthood.
- Exaltation is possible for the faithful and obedient only through the administration of sacred priesthood ordinances as ordained of God, which serve as the gateway to the bestowal of greater truth. How do baptism, the bestowal of the gift of the Holy Ghost, ordinations to the priesthood (for worthy men), and temple endowments and sealings serve as essential preparatory milestones for eventual admission into the celestial kingdom?

D&C 131:1–4—"In the celestial glory there are three heavens or degrees; And in order to obtain the highest, a man must enter into this order of the priesthood [meaning the new and everlasting covenant of marriage]; And if he does not, he cannot obtain it. He may enter into the other, but that is the end of his kingdom; he cannot have an increase."

- This statement was included in a set of instructions by the Prophet Joseph Smith given at Ramus, Illinois, on May 16 and 17, 1843.
- We learn that the highest of the three levels of the celestial kingdom is accessible only for the righteous who have entered into the covenant of celestial marriage (see D&C 132:19–20). What joy does it bring you to know that the Lord, in His mercy, has arranged

for vicarious sealings to be part of the work of the temple so that those who left mortality without the opportunity to receive those ordinances might still enjoy celestial marriage?

Rejoicing and Reasoning Together

What Are the Qualities of the Celestial Realm?

The Prophet Joseph Smith said: "Could you gaze into heaven five minutes, you would know more than you would by reading all that ever was written on the subject" (*HC* 6:50). As one who was often permitted to gaze into heaven, the Prophet Joseph has given us, by inspiration of the Almighty, the most comprehensive portrait of those who will be exalted in the celestial kingdom. This remarkable description was included in Section 76 of the Doctrine and Covenants, a vision given through the Prophet Joseph Smith and Sidney Rigdon at Hiram, Ohio, on February 16, 1832, concerning the future kingdoms to which the resurrected souls would be assigned according to their degree of obedience and faithfulness. The celestial soul has various dimensions:

- **The foundation of exaltation**: "They are they who received the testimony of Jesus, and believed on his name and were baptized after the manner of his burial, being buried in the water in his name, and this according to the commandment which he has given— That by keeping the commandments they might be washed and cleansed from all their sins, and receive the Holy Spirit by the laying on of the hands of him who is ordained and sealed unto this power; And who overcome by faith, and are sealed by the Holy Spirit of promise, which the Father sheds forth upon all those who are just and true" (D&C 76:51–53).

  All who enter the celestial realm began the journey of exaltation through the gateway of baptism by water and by fire. Then, by enduring to the end, they were blessed with an assurance that their faithfulness would yield a harvest of celestial glory. One of the key functions of the Holy Ghost, as the Holy Spirit of Promise, is to place a seal of divine approval on all ordinances leading to salvation and exaltation (see D&C 132:7, 18, 19, 26). The highest blessing of the Holy Spirit of Promise is to have one's calling and election made sure (see 2 Pet. 1:10) through the "more sure word of prophecy" (see D&C 131:5).

- **The calling and stewardship of exaltation**: "They are they who are the church of the Firstborn. They are they into whose hands the Father has given all things—They are they who are priests and kings, who have received of his fulness, and of his glory; And are priests of the Most High, after the order of Melchizedek, which was after the order of Enoch, which was after the order of the Only Begotten Son" (D&C 76:54–57).

  The meaning of "the church of the Firstborn" is explained further as follows: "For if you keep my commandments you shall receive of his fulness, and be glorified in me as I am in the Father; therefore, I say unto you, you shall receive grace for grace. And now, verily I say unto you, I was in the beginning with the Father, and am the Firstborn; And all those who are begotten through me are partakers of the glory of the same, and are the church of the Firstborn" (D&C 93:20–22). Members of the church of the Firstborn are "heirs of God, and joint-heirs with Christ; if so be that we suffer with him, that we may be also glorified together" (Rom. 8:17). As such, members of the church of the Firstborn are adopted children of Jehovah, priests and kings (and priestesses and queens) of the Most High, having inherited salvation and exaltation through His atoning sacrifice, being elevated through the new and everlasting covenant of marriage (see D&C 132:19), being "his seed, or they are the heirs of the kingdom of God. For these are they whose sins he has borne; these are they for whom he has died, to redeem them from their transgressions. And now, are they not his seed?" (Mosiah 15:11–12).

- **The divinity of exaltation**: "Wherefore, as it is written, they are gods, even the sons of God—Wherefore, all things are theirs, whether life or death, or things present, or things to come, all are theirs and they are Christ's, and Christ is God's. And they shall overcome all things. Wherefore, let no man glory in man, but rather let him glory in God, who shall subdue all enemies under his feet. These shall dwell in the presence of God and his Christ forever and ever" (D&C 76:58–62).

In this is fulfilled the promise of the Eternal Father to His sons and daughters, that through the plan of salvation and the consummate atoning sacrifice of the Son, they can become as the Father and the Son, taking on the divine nature and rising to their destiny of being gods, with the power and blessing of eternal lives (see D&C 132:24).

- **The society and communion of exaltation**: "These are they whom he shall bring with him, when he shall come in the clouds of heaven to reign on the earth over his people. These are they who shall have part in the first resurrection. These are they who shall come forth in the resurrection of the just. These are they who are come unto Mount Zion, and unto the city of the living God, the heavenly place, the holiest of all. These are they who have come to an innumerable company of angels, to the general assembly and church of Enoch, and of the Firstborn. These are they whose names are written in heaven, where God and Christ are the judge of all" (D&C 76:63–68).

The celestial hosts will take part in acts of the final days when the earth is celestialized to receive forever those who are written in the book of heaven as eternal inhabitants of the divine home of glory and rest.

- **The perfection of exaltation**: "These are they who are just men made perfect

through Jesus the mediator of the new covenant, who wrought out this perfect atonement through the shedding of his own blood. These are they whose bodies are celestial, whose glory is that of the sun, even the glory of God, the highest of all, whose glory the sun of the firmament is written of as being typical" (D&C 76:69–70).

We learn that those who inherit the celestial kingdom are "just men made perfect" through the "perfect atonement" of Jesus. Men and women are saved and exalted by living a perfectly just and righteous life (see Hab. 2:4; Rom. 1:17; Gal. 3:11; Heb. 10:38)—but only on the basis of "the merits, and mercy, and grace of the Holy Messiah, who layeth down his life according to the flesh, and taketh it again by the power of the Spirit" (2 Ne. 2:8). Achieving celestial glory is possible only through the infinite and eternal Atonement of our Savior.

The language of celestial glory in Section 76 begins to lift the veil of the mysteries of God and grant a view of the most transcending of all scenes—the exaltation reserved for those who are perfected in Christ (see Moro. 10:32–33) and are, as exalted beings, admitted into the presence of the Father and the Son, worlds without end. How can you remember to govern your life according to covenant faithfulness and diligently seek to acquire the divine nature of Jesus Christ (see D&C 4:6; 2 Pet. 1:3–8)—thereby being worthy of an inheritance in the celestial kingdom of glory? How does the knowledge of inheriting such a glory through covenant obedience fill you with gratitude and a commitment to live the gospel with even greater commitment to become "just" and valiant in all dimensions of your mortal life? How can you inspire your loved ones to remember this vision of exaltation and make it their governing quest in life?

What Is the Vision of the Glorious Resurrection?

No doctrine in the sacred canon of eternal principles captures the imagination with more compelling urgency than the resurrection. This word derives from the Latin term *resurgere,* meaning "to rise again." Mortals, without exception, understand the process through which the miraculous human frame is gradually transformed over time into an increasingly frail and weathered state, tempered by the elements and reduced to a fraction of its original vitality. Some, either from birth or through trauma, go through this process much more quickly. We know the process all too intimately: strength is diminished, wrinkles abound, infirmities arise.

Is it any wonder that the hope of the glorious resurrection—overcoming the withering and aging process and even triumphing over death—should give us an attitude of peaceful anticipation and the vision of a glorious future? Faith in the truth of the resurrection brings a transformed view of things as they are and as they will be. Those who hope for the fruits of Christ's atoning sacrifice, including its promise of the resurrection, can see things in a different light. In the place of challenging handicaps they see wholeness and liberation; in the place of degenerative illness they see relief and vitality; in the place of separation from loved ones they see everlasting togetherness of the eternal family.

Where can you find the vision of the glorious resurrection at work in your daily life? Consider this: Why is it that when you see an older couple walking together with hands clasped, both are invariably *smiling?* That is the vision of the resurrection and the coming state of exaltation and forever families. These two, perhaps wrinkled and shuffling a bit, look at each other with refreshing love. The wrinkles, so visible to others, are invisible to them. Each sees the other as the fair and attractive person he or she first knew—and as the glorious and restored person he or she will accompany on celestial walks in the resurrected state, just as always.

Why is it when a parent of a child with disabilities and special needs encounters another parent with a child in the same situation—a stranger with the same task in life, to rear and nurture a child of God with physical or mental challenges—there is understanding and compassion and an exchange of admiring encouragement? That is the vision of the resurrection. That is the view of confidence that one day these children of God will walk and talk and socialize with glorious health and a fullness of joy in the celestial realm.

Why is it when a group of widows takes a newly widowed sister into their circle of friendship

they look on her with eyes of understanding and nurture? Having been schooled in the academy of loneliness, they have each learned how to apply the antidote of sociality and service as they await a reunion with loved ones in the future. That is the vision of the resurrection. That is the higher perspective of life that instills hope and generates momentum toward a future sociality coupled with eternal glory (see D&C 130:2).

Why is it that the temples of the Lord are havens of peace and security in a world of turmoil and fleeting pleasures? Because the perspective taught in the house of the Lord transcends the earthly vale of tears and lifts one's spirit to a state of wholeness and completion, a state of bringing all the elements together in an ultimate and permanent bonding through which complete joy and happiness are possible. "The elements are eternal," says the scripture, "and spirit and element, inseparably connected, receive a fulness of joy" (D&C 93:33). That is the vision of the resurrection and the coming state of celestial glory, made possible through the Atonement of the Savior.

In your own situation, what is it about the miracle of the resurrection, and especially the glorious resurrection into the celestial realm, that gives you special joy and hope, that causes feelings of deep love for the Savior, the Author of eternal salvation and exaltation?

Seeing into the Future

Because all things are "present" before the Lord (see D&C 38:1–2), He was able to inspire His prophets to peer into the future and envision His condescension and atoning sacrifice with unmistakable clarity. To Isaiah He gave these immortal words: "For unto us a child is born, unto us a son is given: and the government shall be upon his shoulder: and his name shall be called Wonderful, Counsellor, The mighty God, The everlasting Father, The Prince of Peace" (Isa. 9:6). Countless pronouncements of the Savior's mission in mortality were spoken under inspiration by all the prophets of God prior to His coming. Similarly, He has enabled His servants throughout time to foretell in meticulous detail, as He did, the circumstances of His Second Coming, which is "nigh, even at the doors" (Mark 13:29). As we consider the miraculous sequence of prophecies leading up to the coming of our Lord and Savior in the meridian of time, we are strengthened in our conviction that the word of the Lord "shall all be fulfilled" (D&C 1:38). He has blessed us through scripture with great knowledge concerning the principles and details of His plan for the immortality and eternal life of man. All of this will transpire in the due time of the Lord.

To personalize this insight into the inevitable fulfillment of God's word, we need only consider that the Lord, in His mercy and kindness, has granted to us a direct and personal revelation to bless our lives and illuminate the pathway that lies ahead. That revelation comes through the whisperings of the Spirit from time to time, giving guidance on how to proceed toward the promise of exaltation and eternal lives. That revelation also comes in our own patriarchal blessings—given through the inspiration of a worthy servant of God as a blessed look into the future of our own possibilities. What the prophets said of the coming Christ has already been verified, and will be verified as well in regard to the Second Coming. Likewise, what the Lord has said of our own specific mission and purpose, as pronounced through the Comforter and in our patriarchal blessing, will be verified and confirmed on the basis of our obedience and righteousness. How grateful we should be to the Lord that He has told us what the future holds for all mankind and for us individually, as sons and daughters of the Most High.

How has the Lord blessed you with the ability to envision your destiny in the celestial world? How can you help others to listen to the Spirit and follow the counsel given through personal revelation, such as in patriarchal blessings and other priesthood blessings that make future things seem truly "present" to you here and now?

Real-life Stories for Heart and Mind

The Photograph. A priesthood holder visited a nursing home some years ago to give charitable service to the elderly patients there. One woman, unable to speak, was clutching a small photograph in her hands. She beckoned the visitor to look at it, and he saw there a mother and daughter in close and affectionate embrace. Clearly this frail woman was reliving with joy her youthful memories at the side of a loving mother. Perhaps

her smile confirmed that she was also peering into the future and beholding the time when these two would once more be together in a sphere of peace and rest. That is the vision of the celestial resurrection and glory. And so it is that we go through life one day at a time—remembering the blessed promise of the resurrection, hoping in faith for a time when we, as whole and reclaimed beings, will rise again and enter the rest of God at last, "which rest is the fulness of his glory" (D&C 84:24).

How has the assurance of a future reunion in the celestial hallways of eternity been a comfort and a strength to you and to your family members?

The Joy of Adversity. Adversity is the dark frame around testimony that makes it shine with the brilliance of heavenly light. When Job said, "For I know that my redeemer liveth, and that he shall stand at the latter day upon the earth" (Job 19:25), we are conscious of the excruciating suffering he was enduring, and his testimony of joy and courage is all the more potent and illuminating as a result. One priesthood brother remembers an occasion where adversity served as a reminder of the promise of the Lord to provide a future place of happiness and joy where the tears of mortality would end:

My brother-in-law was a brilliant attorney with a successful practice and a wonderful young family. I recall distinctly hearing him say many years ago, in humble thankfulness to God, that things seemed almost too easy—that his success was almost too effortless. Not long after that he was unexpectedly called home. His family was devastated. We all reeled at the sudden loss. At the funeral, an Apostle of the Lord, beholding the inconsolable sorrow of the wife and children, counseled them to withhold their tears, to see from a higher perspective the plan of life, and to take comfort and joy in the gospel of Jesus Christ that would eventually unite the family once again. Through that valley of adversity passed the route of courage and faith that my sister traveled as she led her little family of survivors forward in the steady knowledge of higher principle, and in the conviction anchored in the words,

"For I know that my redeemer liveth." Were it not for that adversity, she and her little family could not have known the joy of personal triumph over suffering, the bliss of transcendence over sorrow, the peace of victory over life's shadows. I love and admire them for their example and positive attitude.

How has your own life been blessed through the hope of a future realm of celestial glory where families can be together in peace and glory forever? John the Revelator, seeing in vision the coming of the New Jerusalem in the last days, was inspired to write the encouraging words: "And I heard a great voice out of heaven saying, Behold, the tabernacle of God is with men, and he will dwell with them, and they shall be his people, and God himself shall be with them, and be their God. And God shall wipe away all tears from their eyes; and there shall be no more death, neither sorrow, nor crying, neither shall there be any more pain: for the former things are passed away" (Rev. 21:3–4).

Last words. For all of us, there are times of last words. The following story was shared by a priesthood brother who recalls the last time he was able to visit with his father, an elderly widower who had served faithfully for years as a temple worker:

I can recall the last words said to me by my father. He had been experiencing a condition of increasing feebleness, so to assist him in his personal care, I had given him a new electric razor. He looked at it, smiled gratefully, and then, much to my surprise, returned it to me, saying in a weak voice, "Do this for me." He was asking that I demonstrate how to use it, since he was too weak to do it on his own. I bent over and carefully shaved away his whiskers—a kind of father-son sacrament of personal celebration of a long and productive life. That was the last sentence I remember him expressing to me. He passed away not long after. "Do this for me." The symbolic meaning of that phrase echoes still in my mind, for it also implies the exhortation to do those things of righteousness and follow those principles of obedience that he had exemplified throughout his life. What better way for children to honor the name of their parents than to follow their example and emulate the obedient and loyal service they had cultivated as a legacy of faith and courage.

According to the gospels, the Savior's last words included the following: "It is finished" (John 19:30); "My God, my God, why hast thou forsaken me!" (Matt. 27:46); and "Father, into thy hands I commend my spirit" (Luke 23:46). His entire life can be summarized in the phrase "come, follow me" (Luke 18:22)—a glorious variant of the humble words, said in so many ways and under so many circumstances by parents everywhere as a last request to their children: "Do this for me." What are your thoughts about the simple formula for returning to the presence of your Heavenly Father and His Son: "Come, follow me" and "Do this for me"?

Pondering Prayerfully

Additional scriptures to consider and ponder:
- Prov. 29:18
- Matt. 24:13
- John 14:27
- 1 Cor. 15:22–23
- Rev. 2:7
- 2 Ne. 25:23
- 2 Ne. 31:16
- Alma 7:11–12
- 3 Ne. 15:9
- D&C 19:23
- D&C 68:3–6
- D&C 75:16
- D&C 76:40–42
- D&C 109:77
- D&C 121:7–8
- D&C 127:4
- D&C 131:5–6
- D&C 138:17

The following hymns might inspire us about the celestial world that lies ahead:
- "Come, Ye Children of the Lord" (*Hymns,* 58)

- "God Speed the Right" (*Hymns,* 106)
- "O My Father" (*Hymns,* 292)
- "We'll Sing All Hail to Jesus' Name" (*Hymns,* 182)
- "While of These Emblems We Partake" (*Hymns,* 173)

Remember and Be Sure

The vision of the kingdoms of glory, viewed within the framework of the testimony of the Savior and Redeemer, is one of the most compelling and moving scenes we have been given. The rising hierarchy of kingdoms shown in Section 76 of the Doctrine and Covenants—beginning with the utter bleakness and spiritual vacuum of outer darkness (realm of the sons of perdition), continuing upward with the star-like glory of the telestial and the moon-like glory of the terrestrial, and culminating with the pinnacle of the iridescent sun-like glory of the celestial—is indelibly impressed upon all who hope to attain the highest degree of the celestial kingdom.

The Lord wants us to be with Him in the mansions of everlasting glory: "For thus saith the Lord—I, the Lord, am merciful and gracious unto those who fear me, and delight to honor those who serve me in righteousness and in truth unto the end" (D&C 76:5). He wants us to be sanctified and edified to the full extent, even that we become as He is: "Wherefore, as it is written, they are gods, even the sons of God—Wherefore, all things are theirs, whether life or death, or things present, or things to come, all are theirs and they are Christ's, and Christ is God's. And they shall overcome all things" (D&C 76:58–60).

We live in the dispensation of the fulness of times. The purpose of this last dispensation is to restore the fulness of the gospel—including all the priesthood power, authority, and keys pertaining to the salvation, exaltation, and perfection of mankind—so that, "he [God] might gather together in one all things in Christ, both which are in heaven, and which are on earth; even in him" (Eph. 1:10). This is indeed that "restitution of all things" spoken of by Peter (Acts 3:21). All things pertaining to the plan of salvation and happiness have been brought together in and through the Lord Jesus Christ—everything that has been revealed and will yet be revealed between earth and heaven will become one under the direction and power of the Lord Jesus

Christ as the "chief corner stone" (Eph. 2:20). He is the rock upon which we build both individually and as a Church (see 2 Sam. 22:47; Ps. 18:46; 1 Ne. 13:36; 2 Ne. 4:30; Jacob 7:25). He is our foundation (see Hel. 5:12). He is "the life and the light of the world" (D&C 10:70). Through His holy prophets He has restored His Church and kingdom with power and authority to preserve the most sacred unit of the Church, even the eternal family.

The reward for enduring to the end is eternal life—the greatest gift of God (see D&C 14:7). Recognizing the blessings of eternal life will increase our desire and motivation to persevere with all diligence. Enduring requires steadfastness rooted in Christ and a willingness to sacrifice all for the gospel cause. It is not an easy road, and it wasn't intended to be easy; but the result is a state of never-ending happiness (see Mosiah 2:41). Our goal is set: *endure to the end.*

Eternal perspective gives credence to mortality as part of an eternal landscape. Life can be wonderful as we seek eternal truths and then choose to keep the Lord's commandments. When we become humble and devout players on this grand stage of life, we become authentic seekers of happiness rather than simply participants in the mortal experience. Joy and happiness flow from seeking the will of the Father and following in the footsteps of the Son. We are saved and exalted by the grace of God after we have done all in our power to demonstrate our faithful obedience to His commandments and our enduring commitment to live as He would have us live.

When the work of the Millennium has been accomplished, when the earth has been celestialized as the eternal home for the church of the Firstborn, when all the sons and daughters have been assigned residence in the mansions of heaven "to enjoy that which they are willing to receive" (D&C 88:32), when the process of internal increase on the part of earth's harvest of newly exalted sons and daughters of God begins, when the glory of the throne of the Father and the Son is celebrated by the endless praises and worship of the newly inducted faithful and devout—when all of this is accomplished, then the work of the Lord to bring about the immortality and eternal life of the souls assigned to this world will be done. Until then, the winding-up process continues "Until all shall know me, who remain, even from the least unto the greatest, and shall be filled with the knowledge of the Lord, and shall see eye to eye, and shall lift up their voice, and with the voice together sing this new song, saying:

The Lord hath brought again Zion;
The Lord hath redeemed his people, Israel,
According to the election of grace,
Which was brought to pass by the faith
And covenant of their fathers.
The Lord hath redeemed his people;
And Satan is bound and time is no longer.
The Lord hath gathered all things in one.
The Lord hath brought down Zion from above.
The Lord hath brought up Zion from beneath.
The earth hath travailed and brought forth her strength;
And truth is established in her bowels;
And the heavens have smiled upon her;
And she is clothed with the glory of her God;
For he stands in the midst of his people.
Glory, and honor, and power, and might,
Be ascribed to our God; for he is full of mercy,
Justice, grace and truth, and peace,
Forever and ever, Amen." (D&C 84:99–102)

SOURCES

Benson, Ezra Taft, *Come, Listen to a Prophet's Voice* (Salt Lake City: Deseret Book, 1990).

Benson, Ezra Taft, *Come unto Christ* (Salt Lake City: Deseret Book, 1983).

Benson, Ezra Taft, *Ezra Taft Benson Remembers the Joy of Christmas* (Salt Lake City: Deseret Book, 1988).

Benson, Ezra Taft, *God, Family, Country: Our Three Great Loyalties* (Salt Lake City: Deseret Book, 1974).

Benson, Ezra Taft, *The Teachings of Ezra Taft Benson* (Salt Lake City: Bookcraft, 1988).

Benson, Ezra Taft, *This Nation Shall Endure* (Salt Lake City: Deseret Book, 1977).

Brown, Hugh B., *Continuing the Quest* (Salt Lake City: Deseret Book, 1961).

Brown, Hugh B., *The Abundant Life* (Salt Lake City: Bookcraft, 1965).

Cannon, George Q., *Gospel Truth: Discourses and Writings of President George Q. Cannon,* selected, arranged, and edited by Jerreld L. Newquist (Salt Lake City: Deseret Book, 1987).

Church History in the Fulness of Times, rev. ed. (Salt Lake City: Corporation of the President of The Church of Jesus Christ of Latter-day Saints, 1993).

Clark, J. Reuben, Jr., *Behold the Lamb of God* (Salt Lake City: Deseret Book, 1991).

CR, Conference Report

Grant, Heber J., *Gospel Standards: Selections from the Sermons and Writings of Heber J. Grant,* G. Homer Durham, comp. (Salt Lake City: Improvement Era, 1981).

HC, History of the Church of Jesus Christ of Latter-day Saints, 7 vols.

Hunter, Howard W., *The Teachings of Howard W. Hunter,* Clyde J. Williams, ed. (Salt Lake City: Bookcraft, 1997).

JD, Journal of Discourses, 26 vols.

Kimball, Spencer W., *Faith Precedes the Miracle* (Salt Lake City: Deseret Book, 1972).

Kimball, Spencer W., *My Beloved Sisters* (Salt Lake City: Deseret Book, 1979).

Kimball, Spencer W., *President Kimball Speaks Out* (Salt Lake City: Deseret Book, 1981).

Kimball, Spencer W., *The Miracle of Forgiveness* (Salt Lake City: Bookcraft, 1969).

Kimball, Spencer W., *The Teachings of Spencer W. Kimball,* Edward L. Kimball, ed. (Salt Lake City: Bookcraft, 1982).

Lee, Harold B., *Decisions for Successful Living* (Salt Lake City: Deseret Book, 1973).

Lee, Harold B., *Stand Ye in Holy Places* (Salt Lake City: Deseret Book, 1974).

Lee, Harold B., *The Teachings of Harold B. Lee,* Clyde J. Williams, ed. (Salt Lake City: Bookcraft, 1996).

Lee, Harold B., *Ye Are the Light of the World: Selected Sermons and Writings of Harold B. Lee* (Salt Lake City: Deseret Book, 1974).

McConkie, Bruce R., *A New Witness for the Articles of Faith* (Salt Lake City: Deseret Book, 1985).

McConkie, Bruce R., *Doctrinal New Testament Commentary*, 3 vols. (Salt Lake City, Utah: Bookcraft, 1965–1973).

McConkie, Bruce R., *Mormon Doctrine*, 2nd ed. (Salt Lake City: Bookcraft, 1966).

McConkie, Bruce R., *Sermons and Writings of Bruce R. McConkie* (Salt Lake City: Bookcraft, 1998).

McConkie, Bruce R., *The Millennial Messiah: The Second Coming of the Son of Man* (Salt Lake City: Deseret Book, 1982).

McConkie, Bruce R., *The Mortal Messiah: From Bethlehem to Calvary* (Salt Lake City: Deseret Book, 1979–1981).

McConkie, Bruce R., *The Promised Messiah: The First Coming of Christ* (Salt Lake City: Deseret Book, 1978).

McKay, David O., *Gospel Ideals: Selections from the Discourses of David O. McKay* (Salt Lake City: Improvement Era, 1953).

McKay, David O., *Man May Know for Himself: Teachings of President David O. McKay*, Clare Middlemiss, comp. (Salt Lake City: Deseret Book, 1967).

McKay, David O., *Pathways to Happiness* (Salt Lake City: Bookcraft, 1957).

Petersen, Mark E., *The Way to Peace* (Salt Lake City: Bookcraft, 1969).

Pratt, Parley P., *Autobiography of Parley P. Pratt*, Parley P. Pratt, ed. (Salt Lake City: Deseret Book, 1874).

Richards, Stephen L, *Where Is Wisdom?* (Salt Lake City: Deseret Book, 1955).

Romney, Marion G., *Learning for the Eternities* (Salt Lake City: Deseret Book, 1977).

Romney, Marion G., *Look to God and Live* (Salt Lake City: Deseret Book, 1971).

Smith, George Albert, *Sharing the Gospel with Others*, Preston Nibley, comp. (Salt Lake City: Deseret Book, 1948).

Smith, George Albert, *The Teachings of George Albert Smith*, Robert McIntosh and Susan McIntosh, eds. (Salt Lake City: Bookcraft, 1996).

Smith, Joseph, *Lectures on Faith* (Salt Lake City: Deseret Book, 1985).

Smith, Joseph, *Teachings of the Prophet Joseph Smith*, selected and arranged by Joseph Fielding Smith (Salt Lake City: Deseret Book, 1976).

Smith, Joseph, *The Personal Writings of Joseph Smith*, Dean C. Jessee, ed. (Salt Lake City: Deseret Book, 1984).

Snow, Lorenzo, *The Teachings of Lorenzo Snow* (Salt Lake City: Deseret Book, 1984).

Joseph F. Smith, *From Prophet to Son: Advice of Joseph F. Smith to His Missionary Sons*, Hyrum M. Smith III and Scott G. Kenney, comps. (Salt Lake City: Deseret Book, 1981).

Smith, Joseph F., *Gospel Doctrine: Selections from the Sermons and Writings of Joseph F. Smith*, John A. Widtsoe, comp. (Salt Lake City: Deseret Book, 1939).

Smith, Joseph Fielding, *Answers to Gospel Questions*, 5 vols. (Salt Lake City: Deseret Book Co., 1957–1966).

Smith, Joseph Fielding, *Church History and Modern Revelation*, 4 vols. (Salt Lake City: Deseret Book, 1947–1950).

Smith, Joseph Fielding, *Doctrines of Salvation*, 3 vols., Bruce R. McConkie, ed. (Salt Lake City: Bookcraft, 1954–1956).

Smith, Joseph Fielding, *The Restoration of All Things* (Salt Lake City: Deseret News Press, 1945).

Smith, Joseph Fielding, *The Way to Perfection* (Salt Lake City: Deseret Book, 1949).

Snow, Lorenzo, *The Teachings of Lorenzo Snow*, Clyde J. Williams, ed. (Salt Lake City: Deseret Book, 1984).

Talmage, James E., *Jesus the Christ* (Salt Lake City: Deseret Book Co., 1983).

Talmage, James E., *The Great Apostasy* (Salt Lake City: Deseret Book, 1958).

Taylor, John, *The Gospel Kingdom: Selections from the Writings and Discourses of John Taylor*, selected, arranged, and edited, with an introduction by G. Homer Durham (Salt Lake City: Improvement Era, 1941).

Taylor, John, *The Mediation and Atonement* (Salt Lake City: Deseret News Company, 1882).

Teachings of the Presidents of the Church: Joseph Smith (Salt Lake City: The Church of Jesus Christ of Latter-day Saints, 2007).

Widtsoe, John A., *A Rational Theology* (Salt Lake City: Deseret Book, 1937).

Widtsoe, John A., *Evidences and Reconciliations* (Salt Lake City: Deseret Book, 1943).

Widtsoe, John A., *Priesthood and Church Government* (Salt Lake City: Deseret Book, 1939).

Young, Brigham, *Discourses of Brigham Young,* selected and arranged by John A. Widtsoe (Salt Lake City: Deseret Book, 1954).

Young, Brigham, *Letters of Brigham Young to His Sons,* Dean C. Jessee, ed. (Salt Lake City: Deseret Book, 1974).

INDEX

SCRIPTURE INDEX

Following are the scriptural passages discussed in the "Truths to Liken" sections, listed in the order in which they appear in the quadruple combination of LDS scriptures: